Preceding page overleaf: Detail from a map showing a mid-sixteenth century merchantman in the Strait of Magellan. *Bibliothèque, Ministère de la Guerre, Paris. Photographie Giraudon, Paris.*

Opposite: Bronze head of Sir Winston Churchill (1874-1965), by Sir Jacob Epstein (1880-1959). Photograph: *Hamlyn Group Picture Library.*

LAROUSSE ENCYCLOPEDIA OF
MODERN HISTORY

LAROUSSE ENCYCLOPEDIA OF

MODERN HISTORY

FROM 1500 TO THE PRESENT DAY

GENERAL EDITOR: MARCEL DUNAN
Honorary professor at the Sorbonne

ENGLISH ADVISORY EDITORS: JOHN ROBERTS
BERNARD WASSERSTEIN

Foreword by Hugh Trevor-Roper

EXCALIBUR BOOKS
NEW YORK

Contributors to this volume:
Louis Mazoyer and François Souchal: 'Modern Times'
Maurice Baumont, Marcel Dunan and René Ristelheuber: 'The Present
Age'
Additional material for this edition written by:
J. M. Roberts of Merton College, Oxford
Bernard Wasserstein of Brandeis University, Massachusetts

Larousse Encyclopedia of Modern History translated by Delano Ames
from *Histoire Universelle Larousse*. First published in France
by Augé, Gillon, Hollier-Larousse, Moreau et Cie,
Librairie Larousse, Paris

First published in USA 1981 by
Excalibur Books
Excalibur is a trademark of Simon & Schuster

Distributed by Bookthrift
New York, New York

New revised edition 1981

ISBN 0-89673-084-0
Printed in Singapore

MODERN TIMES

THE SIXTEENTH CENTURY

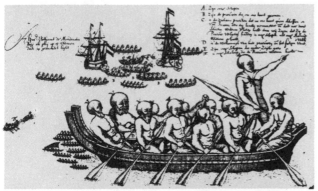

THE SEVENTEENTH CENTURY

THE EIGHTEENTH CENTURY

THE PRESENT AGE

THE ERA
OF THE FRENCH REVOLUTION

THE NINETEENTH CENTURY

THE TWENTIETH CENTURY

COLOUR PLATES

FOREWORD By HUGH TREVOR-ROPER

To a 'universal historian', surveying 'the vast backward and abysm of time', the last five hundred years, as they are nearest to him, must always seem the most important. But our last five hundred years have more than this purely relative importance. The history of the world before A.D. 1500 has a certain pattern. It shows civilisations succeeding each other, repeating each other, perhaps improving upon each other. But the basic character of these civilisations remains comparable. Moreover, the world has room for all of them. But from about A.D. 1500 we can trace a profound change in world history. From that date we find one civilisation, European civilisation, developing and displaying a new and unique character, and, thanks to that character, imposing itself on the whole world. Whatever the future may hold, this change is permanent. The world is now united as never before; and it is united, even after the European empires have passed away, by irreversible European ideas and techniques.

When did this process begin? Such a question always perplexes historians. But the year 1500 is as likely a beginning as any. It was then that Europe, after a period of apparent stagnation, put forth new energies. That was the time of the high Renaissance in Italy, with its lavish, brilliant culture and new forms of military and political power. It was also the time when that culture and those forms were being carried from Italy to the rest of Europe, there to be applied not in petty principalities but in great national states whose energies were already overflowing their old bounds in the discovery and conquest of new worlds. We naturally think of this as a great turning-point in our history. The Europe of Charles V, of Leo X, of Francis I and Henry VIII is unquestionably more vivid, more exciting, more 'modern' than the Europe of the fifteenth century in which an old world seems to be waning and a new is not yet born.

So it may seem to us. We are Europeans. But seen from outside Europe all this, at that time, seemed much less spectacular. At that time Europe still occupied a very small place on the globe. Sulaiman the Magnificent of Turkey overshadowed the Emperor Charles V, and if Sulaiman had any fears, it was not from Europe but from Persia that they came. In India the new Mogul empire of Babar was more splendid than anything which Spain or Portugal had conquered in America or Africa. And in China the Ming dynasty, as 'national' as the Tudors or the Valois, could still look down, with infinite disdain, on the 'barbarians' of the far West. In 1500 Europe, for all its genius and energy, was still but one civilisation among many. There was nothing to suggest that it held any private key to future domination.

Four centuries later it is very different. Since 1500, in spite of crises, revolutions and wars — perhaps even because of such crises — Europe has moved steadily forward and all other civilisations are demoralised before it. The heir of Sulaiman has become 'the sick man' of the West. Persia is divided into European 'spheres of influence'. The English have replaced the Moguls in India. The last Chinese dynasty is in dissolution. Everywhere European arms, European methods of government, European capital, European technology, have transformed the non-European societies. The exceptions only prove the rule. Abyssinia, Persia, Afghanistan, Siam may seem to be independent; but their independence is artificial, not natural: a European device to preserve the delicate European balance in the world. The one great non-European power, Japan, the herald of non-European revival, is great only by adopting and adapting European methods. There is, by now, no other means of being 'great'.

Such is the great change in 'universal history' which took place between 1500 and 1900. Its causes and stages are still something of a mystery. Some historians see the process already determined in the sixteenth century when the Portuguese empire stretched from Macao to Brazil and the Spaniards dominated half Europe and most of America. But were those empires different in kind from the commercial empire of Carthage or the military empire of Rome? Others have discovered the European breakthrough in the Reformation, or even in the English 'bourgeois' revolution of the seventeenth century. But both these movements have medieval precedents. from which no one has yet ventured to deduce the uniqueness of Europe. Still others have looked for answers to much later European revolutions: the 'industrial revolution' of eighteenth-century England, or the 'bourgeois' revolution — perhaps we should say the series of 'bourgeois' revolutions — which began in 1789 in France.

These great questions of historical causation admit no simple and perhaps no single solution. Historical change is indivisible, and its processes cannot usefully be studied in isolation from each other. All we can do is to study the facts in relation to each other, keeping a sense of proportion by making comparisons as we go along. Universal history obliges us to omit much. It can never give a complete picture. It squeezes out some of the drama, some of the richness of national history. It forces us to compress, sometimes to desiccate. On the other hand it enables us to keep this sense of proportion and to make these comparisons, both in time and in space. And if it is skilfully presented, we need not lose the drama, the richness, after all. Illustrations, maps, diagrams can restore to history that colour, that sense of pace, that extra dimension of social life, which mere narrative, if it is to cover the ground and keep the time, can hardly convey.

This, I believe, is the great merit of this second volume of M. Marcel Dunan's *Histoire Universelle*. In a remarkably brief space, but with a remarkable range, it takes us over those five centuries in which Europe came to dominate the world. At the beginning we see the various civilisations of the sixteenth century, equally placed, as it seems, for the race that was to come. All are monarchical; all rest on a rural base; most of them have a military character, with priests, financiers, merchants, philosophers ranged hierarchically around the throne. So far there is no fundamental difference between East and West, Asia and Europe. But gradually the change asserts itself. In the seventeenth century, while the Asiatic empires merely change their rulers, the European monarchies change their character. It is a qualitative, almost a chemical change, and the sooner it is undergone, the sooner the various states of Europe find themselves equipped for the opportunities

that lie ahead. By the nineteenth century Western Europe has been transformed; by the early twentieth century Russia too; by the later twentieth century, perhaps, the rest of the world.

Different times require different means. A revolution that is ' puritan ' in England in the seventeenth century, may be secular in France in the eighteenth. Nationalism which wears one colour in nineteenth-century Europe will look very different in twentieth-century Asia or Africa. The founding of a new colony or settlement in seventeenth-century New England will differ from a similar settlement in twentieth-century Palestine. Anti-capitalist revolution will be different in ' independent ' Eastern Europe and in ' colonial ' Asia. History itself conditions its own course: memories of national greatness colour and form the Italian *Risorgimento* of the nineteenth century. They may do the same to Chinese communism in the twentieth.

A well-presented ' universal history ' enables us to see these differences, to trace these influences, to make these comparisons. It also enables us, behind the differences, to see the resemblances and deduce the constant forces. It will not, of course, replace national history; but it will put it in a new perspective: a perspective which more detailed national history may test and at times correct. In this dialogue between universal and national study, between philosophy and history, M. Dunan's *Histoire Universelle* will, for many readers, play an important part.

It provides an introduction, and a framework to a study which, in itself, has no limits. It suggests fascinating problems and opens tempting vistas. And it does so with all the assistance which modern methods of presentation can provide. This second volume, which brings us up to our own times, can be equally a study in itself or the beginning of a study which will never end.

MODERN TIMES

THE SIXTEENTH CENTURY

The sixteenth century has often been too sharply distinguished from its predecessor, but it is impossible not to see in it the novelty and creativity of a new civilisation. It is only in Europe that the change is obvious, but it marked an epoch in world history because of the part Europe was to play in the next four centuries. Her new world role was announced in the great discoveries and the foundation of the first maritime empires. Meanwhile, the great states of the West were taking shape as national monarchies, two and a half centuries of struggle between the rulers of France and the Habsburgs were beginning, and the Reformation was adding new causes of conflict to those which already existed. Culturally, the unity of Christendom was shattered and the conflict of traditional authority and individual belief accelerated the tendency towards independence of thought which was already to be seen in the humanism of the Renaissance. Asia and Africa were little affected by these forces, though eventually their history was changed by them.

CHAPTER ONE

EUROPE AND THE RENAISSANCE IN THE FIRST HALF OF THE SIXTEENTH CENTURY

POLITICAL REVIVAL

WESTERN EUROPE AND ABSOLUTE MONARCHY

The sixteenth century, no longer much beguiled by the dreams of the Middle Ages, abandoned the idea of a great Christian republic, and began to replace weak feudal kingship with States jealous of their independence and ruled over by monarchs striving to bring about their unity. New influences played upon the political structure of Western Europe. The Renaissance and a fashion for anything pertaining to antiquity re-established the dignity of a Roman Law which tended to identify the will of the monarch and the laws of the land, and re-asserted the pagan notion of a ' hero ', the glamorous leader, the honest tyrant. New social forces sought order; only a strong monarchy, simple, coherent and centralised, seemed potentially capable of taming the feudal world and of asserting a national interest dimly discerned by an emergent middle class.

Each country now developed a passion for greatness, with its king as incarnation of the national ideal; the spirit of loyalty to the Crown was magnified beyond measure. In France, England and Spain, absolutism seemed triumphant. Even the ' mother of Parliaments ' survived

Francis I of France (1515–47). Sometimes considered frivolous, he was rather unpractical in his attempts to contain the ambitions of Charles V, his successful rival for the Imperial throne. *Giraudon*

only as an instrument of royal government. Though States differed in rhythm and certain characteristics, absolutism was established everywhere under a cloak of misunderstanding which was not to be shaken off for more than a century. Nations looked upon it as a necessity, an instrument of liberation and revival; sovereigns saw in it simply a means of exercising dominion, a right acquired for all time, the sole legitimate form of government.

The French monarchy

The French monarchs set the pattern for absolutism. Louis XII (1498–1515) was a mild and sickly king. Francis I (1515–47), an ostentatious nobleman of charming manner and attractive appearance, was as spirited in battle as in his pleasures; he was fickle in decision, selfish, temperamental, and cynically dictatorial. Henry II (1547–59), a huge man, passionately fond of exercise, eventually met death in a tournament; he concealed his love of power beneath mannerisms that suggested the hero wrapt in gloom.

The French kings were symbols of majesty, whom artists portrayed as Roman emperors; they were the ' personification of law ', according to legal theorists. ' Kings by the grace of God, **not** by election or by force ', they governed according to their ' good pleasure ', with the assistance of two councils and, later (1547), four Secretaries of State. The high officers of the Crown helped them in their routine tasks. Some of these were men of strong personality — the Chancellor Duprat, for instance, or the arrogant High Constable, Anne de Montmorency, who forced the inhabitants of Bordeaux to dig up with their finger-nails the body of a governor killed during an uprising. Men like these might occasionally usurp the role of first minister, but most royal servants owed their successes much less to their administrative competence than to the king's favour. Grasping, absorbed in the pursuit of office, jealous of each other, they were held in check by the intensity of competition. Their pursuit of self-interest itself contributed to the development of royal absolutism.

These monarchs gradually ceased to convene the States General, the historical representatives of the nation. The Paris *Parlement* became a simple court of law. Orders were carried out by military governors, local commissioners, and 12,000 officials — the largest administrative body in Europe. Their powers came from royal warrants and they used them to strike mercilessly at disorder and insubordination.

The ruling classes gradually became dependent upon the monarchy. The concordat of 1516 reduced the clergy to submission. Under pain of death the nobles were forbidden

13

to possess cannon or raise troops on their estates. Ruined by economic conditions, they patched matters up with the king so as to secure pensions, and gathered at the Court, where they led a life of pleasure, pomp and gilded dependence. The monarchy, involved in heavy expenditure, openly sold a vast number of public offices. As these invested the holders with privileges, and often led to nobility, men who had money hastened to secure them. Against a loan, which they never expected to be repaid, they could obtain a magistracy; they were proud to represent their sovereign and, because their prestige and power increased with that of the monarch, these officials proved themselves zealous in his cause.

To sustain and show off the lustre of their reigns, Francis I and Henry II proposed to surround the monarchy with all the majesty of the great Roman Empires and all the splendour of the Renaissance. Shunning the gloomy atmosphere of the Louvre of Charles V, the Court, passing beneath triumphal arches, made endless journeys up and down the Loire, visiting castle after castle, going from one sumptuous entertainment to another.

Spain: The Catholic Kings and Charles V

By their marriage in 1489 Isabella Queen of Castile (1451–1504) and Ferdinand King of Aragon (1452–1516) — the Catholic Kings — prepared the way for the unification of Spain. With the aid of inexorable discipline and carnage they put an end to civil war and maintained order with the 'Holy Brotherhood' (the *Hermandad*), founded in 1476. Established first in Castile, it provided a rural police for the suppression of crimes of violence and did its job so well that it soon became unnecessary. Its summary jurisdiction had made important inroads on the nobility's rights of justice. The towns also lost some of their former independence under the so-called protection of the king's agents (*corregidors*); the *Cortes* were restricted to the mere statement of grievances; and the grandees were deprived of lands they had wrested from the Crown in earlier reigns. The religious unity of the kingdom was consolidated: the Moors lost the guarantees granted to them after the capitulation of Granada; the Jews were compelled to choose between baptism and exile. Heretics, dressed in a sulphur-coloured gown, and with their heads covered with a cowl on which devils were portrayed, were led to the stake under the Inquisition. Executioners cut the skin from the hands and skulls of condemned priests with a piece of glass, and removed the flesh from their lips in order to wipe out the imprint of the Holy Oils and of their ordination.

The future Charles V was the grandson of the Catholic Kings on his mother's side: his mother was Joanna the Mad and his paternal grandfather the Archduke Maximilian of Austria. Charles succeeded Ferdinand of Aragon in 1516; looked on as a foreigner in Spain, he delivered its rule over to his Flemish advisers. The death of Maximilian, in January 1519, gave him possession of the Austrian states of the Habsburgs and six months later the Diet of Frankfurt elected him Emperor of Germany. During his absence, the towns of Castile and some of the nobles rebelled in defence of their medieval rights (the *Junta* of Avila, July 1520). This revolt of the *Comuneros* was directed against the royal officials rather than against the King. It was crushed at Villalar, in April 1521. When

A sixteenth-century ivory powder-horn. Gunpowder, playing a growing role in warfare, determined the French victory at Marignano. *Giraudon*

The arms of France and Brittany, united in 1491 when Charles VIII of France married Anne of Brittany, heiress to the last independent duke, thus enabling the monarchy to lay the foundations for absolutism. *Giraudon*

An interrogation by the Holy Office. The Inquisition was established in the thirteenth century to suppress heresy, but its most active period came with the Reformation. *Giraudon*

Charles returned to Spain in July 1522, he could afford to be merciful and was. His power grew to such an extent that, despite his long absences in Italy, Flanders and Germany, Spain now embarked on a period of what was almost complete tranquillity.

The English monarchy: the early Tudors

After the long drawn out Wars of the Roses the country was exhausted. This was a help to Henry VII (1485–1509) and his servants as they sought to rebuild the power once enjoyed by England's medieval kings. Under Henry VIII (1509–47) a difference of atmosphere can be felt. Not only were the royal finances in healthier condition, but the monarchy was more spectacular. Henry VIII was temperamental, violent, proud and avid for fame; beneath a charming exterior he was little more than a ruthless despot. He divorced two of his six wives and beheaded two others; his Chancellor, Thomas Cromwell, perished on the scaffold. The adulation which surrounded him did much to make the English monarchy look more powerful than it really was; yet, however great their power, the Tudors cannot be described as truly absolute sovereigns. Certain basic principles which had evolved over a long period remained alive in the national conscience. For instance, the laws of the land had always stood beyond the reach of the king's authority: imprisonment not backed by a warrant and immediately followed by trial was considered despotic. Parliament, however subservient to royal policy, was not inclined to abandon its prerogatives; it made law and its consent was needed for extraordinary taxation. Its use by the Crown to give statutory enactment to the English Reformation kept alive the principle that the king could not make new laws without the consent of the two Houses.

Henry VII and Henry VIII were anxious not to give the ruling classes the impression that monarchial power threatened the traditional rights of the nation. They pretended to respect the ancient English freedoms, and continued to keep Parliament alive. Cardinal Wolsey, enamoured of grandeur, urged Henry VIII towards a more rigid type of absolutism, but he fell into disgrace in 1530 and it was only his sickness and death in that year which saved him from the scaffold.

Of all the Western nations, England possessed by the middle of the sixteenth century the most brutal despot and the weakest form of despotism. The absolutism of the Tudors was one of simple fact, and not a combination of fact and law — like that of Henry II or Charles V. The forces capable of keeping it within bounds or of destroying it remained intact. It was of little importance that these forces were more or less dormant; it needed only a hardening of the national consciousness to bring them to life.

The three great States of Western Europe differed in their attitudes towards this irresistible rise in royal power. The French nation seemed at one with its kings; it extolled their wonderful achievements, their resplendent victories, their 'unforgettable days'. In abandoning themselves to the 'good pleasure' of their kings, the French abandoned themselves entirely. Spain, too, followed its monarchy loyally, whether through conviction, self-interest or religious duty, for monarchy alone could bring about the unity and greatness of the country. The Emperor himself,

Emperor Maximilian I (1493–1519), the first of the Habsburg family to receive the Imperial crown by succession. Strengthened by possession of the Burgundian inheritance through his marriage to the daughter of Charles the Bold, he set out to re-organise the medieval Empire. *Giraudon*

The City of London at the time of Henry VIII, dominated by the thirteenth-century cathedral of St Paul's.

Henry VIII, King of England, during whose reign (1509–47) the monarchy gained in brilliance and in its absolute power. *Radio Times Hulton Picture Library*

15

Cardinal Wolsey (c. 1475–1530) was both Privy Counsellor and Papal Legate and virtually ruled England in the early years of Henry VIII's reign; but his expensive foreign policy, curtailment of feudalism and arrogance antagonised the nobility and caused his downfall. *National Portrait Gallery*

Cardinal Pole (1500–58) opposed Henry VIII's divorce and took refuge in Italy while his mother and brother were beheaded. A reforming Catholic he took part in the Council of Trent and became Archbishop of Canterbury under Queen Mary. *National Portrait Gallery*

'Peasants Dancing', an engraving by Albrecht Dürer (1471–1528). Dürer was honoured throughout Europe for his unsurpassed mastery of wood-cuts and engravings and expressed the spirit of the German Renaissance in a series of profound religious works.

Opposite: The Black Sea and Asia Minor. Detail from Le Testu's *Cosmographie Universelle,* 1559. *Giraudon.*
Opposite overleaf: Christ in majesty. Sixteenth century Russian icon. Paris. *Giraudon.*

Charles V, was rarely seen by his Spanish subjects; though respectful, Spain remained proud and distant. England gave in passively to the will of its brutal sovereign, who was nevertheless always careful to wear a protective coat of mail. But England did not forget its ' ancient freedoms ' and gave in without surrendering.

Whatever the quality of their absolutism, the great monarchies continued to gather strength. They encouraged order within States, which experienced a rebirth.

THE RISE OF IMPERIALISM: THE ITALIAN WARS

In sixteenth-century Europe the rebirth of States was accompanied by the awakening of imperialism. More powerfully organised, more solidly grouped around their sovereigns, nations became self-conscious; the peoples of Europe were quite ready to agree that warlike aggression beyond the limits of their own frontiers was essential to the defence of their interests and of their so-called rights. They viewed the ambitions of princes as nothing more than the legitimate manifestation of their own national pride. Henceforth rivals, states kept an eye on each other and, following the changing play of circumstances, strove either to impose their own imperialism, or to sustain or restore a balance of power.

In this entirely new situation a nod from Charles VIII, King of France, was enough to make of Italy a battleground where the leading powers fought each other for sixty years. When, as a result of the 1519 Imperial election, Spain and Germany came under the rule of one master, Charles V, rivalry between France and Austria dominated the struggle. It ended in exhaustion: the principle of the balance of power gained a painful victory over dreams of domination.

The Italian campaigns of Charles VIII and Louis XII

As heir to the house of Anjou, Charles VIII (1483–98) decided at the age of twenty-four to take possession of the Kingdom of Naples. To this voracious reader of romance and chivalry, a dreamer with vacant expression and bovine eyes, Italy seemed a stepping-stone on the route to Constantinople; Charles had already begun to picture himself being proclaimed emperor in that city. The nobles, no longer able to expend their energies in feudal wars, strongly supported his plans. Charles relinquished the most valuable spoils of Louis XI for an uncertain promise of neutrality, ceding Roussillon to Spain and both Franche-Comté and Artois to Austria. In September 1494, with ensigns flying and drums beating, he crossed the Alps with his engraved cannon, some of them weighing more than three tons. Throughout the whole march ' the leaves and the stones seemed to cry " France! " '. The people of Milan and Florence welcomed him with peals of bells and wild cheering. During the night a blaze of torches lighted his way into Rome. In February 1495, he entered Naples on a chariot drawn by four white horses, holding in one hand a golden sphere and in the other the rod of empire. But the awakening was brutal. In the following month, after an appeal from Venice and Pope Alexander VI, England, Spain and the Empire united against France. Attacked on all sides, Charles was compelled to retreat; of this first campaign in Italy

Jane Seymour, by Hans Holbein. Third wife of Henry VIII and mother of Edward VI of England. *Marburg*

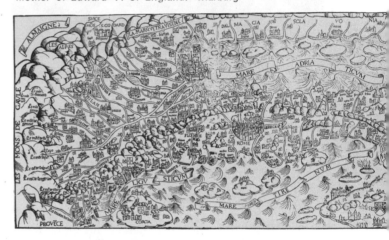

A contemporary map of Italy at the time of the Italian wars, showing the access routes from France and from Germany. Italy became the battleground in a struggle for European hegemony that lasted sixty years. *Giraudon*

Charles V, Emperor and King of Spain, who ruled the Habsburg dominions at their widest extent and whose dream of restoring a universal empire was doomed to failure.

Henry VIII setting out to meet Francis I at the Field of the Cloth of Gold (1520). Francis hoped by providing this sumptuous entertainment for Henry to enlist his support against Charles V. But Henry made terms with Charles V instead.

nothing remained but the smoke of battle.

Louis XII (1498–1515) was the grandson of a Visconti, and has been described as gentle, gracious and kindly. He determined to press a claim to Milan and in two months had conquered it. Eager to avenge the defeat of his cousin Charles VIII, in 1501 he went so far as to seize Naples, with the help of the King of Aragon. But the Spanish soon drove him out, despite the prowess of Bayard at the River Garigliano. Pope Julius II, whose dream it was to dominate the peninsula, dragged Louis into a war against Venice, and then, uneasy about Louis's victories, set Spain, England, Venice and the Swiss against him (the Holy League, 1511). Within two months Gaston de Foix seized two towns, won three battles and proved himself at twenty-two years of age the finest commander of his time. He fell, however, at Ravenna, at the height of victory, on Easter Sunday 1512. The French army was demoralised and again retreated across the Alps. France was invaded, and the English reached the Somme; only a sum of gold persuaded the Swiss to pause at Dijon. Taking advantage of the conciliatory disposition of the new Pope, Leo X, Louis hastened to sign a peace treaty.

Francis I. Marignano and Pavia

Shortly after his accession Francis I (1515–47) raised an army of 30,000 men and in his turn crossed the Alps in order to reconquer Milan. The Swiss were waiting for him along a narrow causeway on the marshy plateau of Marignano. Their square formations bristling with pikes were scarcely affected by the furious charges of the French cavalry but in September 1515, after two days of fighting,

they collapsed under the fire of the French artillery. Francis I knelt on the field of battle to be dubbed a knight by Bayard. The belligerents were exhausted, and when Pope Leo X suggested that they should unite in a crusade against the Turks they gladly seized this pretext to abandon the struggle. Under the terms of the treaties of Noyon and Cambrai (1615–17) the French kept Milan and Spain kept Naples. The Swiss and Francis I signed a peace for all time (November 1516). But an unforeseen event was soon again to threaten the peace of Europe.

After the death of Maximilian of Austria, Charles V, already King of Spain, was elected Emperor of Germany in preference to Francis I (June 1519). Courage and shrewdness combined with cold obstinacy made this nineteen-year-old prince a formidable adversary to France and her frivolous sovereign. Although Charles was born with the sixteenth century, his dream was to restore an anachronistic universal empire in the very teeth of nationalist revival — an empire which, combining the two imperialisms of faith and the sword, would allow him to impose his supremacy on the whole of Europe. Taking as his motto *toujours plus oultre* ('still further'), he decided to make vassals of those states previously incorporated in the Empire, and to win back the former possessions of his ancestors, Burgundy and Picardy.

Alive to this threat, Francis I looked around for allies. The King of England, Henry VIII, met him at the Field of the Cloth of Gold in June 1520; but Henry did not allow himself to be dazzled by twenty-five days of sumptuous festivities: he went away and made terms with Charles V. When hostilities began, only a small number of Swiss mercenaries joined the French forces. Out of personal spite the unbending and taciturn High Constable of Bourbon went over to the enemy. The Germans overran Champagne; the Swiss invaded Picardy, and the Spanish the Basque country. Abandoned by the French after the battle of La Bicoque, Milan was captured and lost again. Bayard died at Romagnano in 1524, symbolically of a gunshot. The Imperial troops crossed the Var, but failed to take Marseilles (August–September 1524). Francis I thought the time was ripe to pounce on Milan, and took it without a blow being struck. He pitched his camp before Pavia and, convinced that his adversaries had no desire to give battle, took scarcely any precautions against the relief troops charged to rescue the town. In February 1525, the Imperial forces burst into his camp at night. Though the French guns were already inflicting heavy casualties on the attacking forces, Francis made them cease fire and himself led his knights in a disorderly charge, without waiting for his infantry. The result was a shocking disaster — another Agincourt. Forced to fight on foot, the King of France lost everything except honour, and surrendered, his face covered in blood; he was taken to Madrid and imprisoned in the gloomy Alcazar, where he wrangled over abdication. He became ill and signed a treaty in which he relinquished Burgundy. But on his return to France he did not consider himself bound by this; in May 1527, the sack of Rome by a band of Germans gave him a pretext to take up arms again. Charles V, engrossed in the Turkish threat and the Reformation, renounced Burgundy at the Peace of Cambrai in 1529.

Now wiser, Francis I rebuilt his forces patiently. The growing strength of Austria, which made Europe uneasy, enabled him to reach a settlement with Venice, the Pope and the Swiss Cantons, while he continued to draw closer to England. Using every means to attain his ends, he came to terms with the heretical German princes in 1532, and even concluded an alliance with the Turks in 1535 — an act which could still shock the Christian world. War broke out again with increased violence and Italy became an unimportant battleground. To halt the Imperial troops the French armies had to turn Champagne into a scorched-earth zone. Henry VIII, who in 1543 had again allied himself with the Empire, took Boulogne. These successes were useless. The Turkish thrust into Hungary, the activities of the Lutheran princes and the indiscipline of his own forces obliged Charles V to sign a peace treaty at Crépy-en-Laonnois in September 1544. England in turn abandoned the war in June 1546. Francis I died heavy-hearted in March 1547, three months after the death of Henry VIII. Having overcome the Protestant princes (April 1547), the Emperor contented himself with striving for the mastery of Germany. Though his power remained more or less intact, he was no longer strong enough to realise his dream of world domination.

Henry II. The abdication of Charles V

Henry II (1547–59) lacked the chivalrous nature of his predecessors; he was a large, muscular man, reserved, awkward and simple-minded. Like all the Valois he allowed himself to be carried away by the dream of Italian conquest. While helping the Berbers against Genoa he sent the Duke of Guise to Rome and planned an expedition against Naples. Since a diversion would assist his activities in the Spanish peninsula, he made a secret alliance with the

German soldier and a camp-follower of the Reformation era. Imperialistic wars and the religious struggles of the period made war a permanent feature of life in Germany. *Marburg*

The development of printing-presses in the sixteenth century had an important bearing on the Reformation, with its emphasis on closer study of the Scriptures. *Giraudon*

German Protestants, which permitted him to occupy Metz, Toul and Verdun. Charles V considered this a threat to his power and proceeded to lay siege to Metz in bitter wintry weather; though heavily bombarded, the position held firm. Harassed by sorties and lacking provisions, the Imperial forces began to grumble; the Emperor was sick, racked with gout, and could move about only on a litter. The order to retreat was given in January 1553. The war dragged on, undecided in Italy and unnecessarily ferocious in Picardy. The Emperor became despondent, and began to regard his setbacks as a punishment. Conscious of the weakness of his excessively widespread empire, he decided not to try to force the hand of God any further in the face of his present adverse fortunes, and in October 1555, at Brussels, announced his decision to relinquish power. In his act of abdication, published in the following January, he gave Spain and its dependencies to his son Philip, and Germany and the Imperial crown to his brother Ferdinand. He retired into a monastery in the wildest part of Estremadura, where he died in 1558.

The Treaty of Cateau-Cambrésis

Charles's abdication did not put an end to the war. The Spaniards, victorious at St Quentin (August 1557), plundered Picardy; panic was already spreading in Paris. Then, in the middle of winter, the Duke of Guise seized Calais; bonfires were lit throughout the kingdom. At grips with formidable financial problems, the exhausted belligerents no longer thought of anything but negotiations. Through sheer war-weariness peace was signed at Cateau-Cambrésis in April 1559.

France kept Calais and saw the last reminders of the Hundred Years' War fade away. Her frontier was strengthened in the east, but she had to abandon most of her conquests, such as Corsica, Savoy and Luxemburg, and renounce her claims in Italy. The treaty of 1559 did not exactly create that kind of 'unjust peace' which Erasmus preferred to 'the most just of wars', but it rankled in the souls of patriots; the loss of Milan and the Two Sicilies to Philip II encouraged the growth of a Spanish imperialism quite as dangerous as the French and Austrian imperialisms had been. Competition for power, closely linked with the awakening of nationalist sentiments, had asserted itself and developed during the wars in Italy. This rivalry and competition, though temporarily allayed, had not been destroyed; it would in the succeeding century once more disturb the peace of Europe.

THE RELIGIOUS REVOLUTION

THE REFORMATION

In the sixteenth century the Reformation shattered Christendom. The Church had need of rejuvenation; the Papacy's prestige was low. Alexander VI — a Borgia — had a Venus inlaid in his emerald cross; Julius II (1503–12) and Leo X (1513–21) were simply spectacular Roman princes; the abuses of the pontifical financial system, the plurality of benefices, the depravity of prelates, the ignorance and coarseness of the clergy were subjects of endless protests from the faithful. In a century as vigorous as the sixteenth, religious fervour, despite the shortcomings of the Church, was becoming more restless and demanding. In a world ravaged by war and epidemics, death became a perpetual obsession. Haunted by the problem of salvation, terrified by the idea of hell, those who believed manifested a desire for a more personal and reassuring religion, a God with compassion for their miseries and whom they could feel in their hearts. The Church seemed unable to satisfy these aspirations. Its interpretations of the Bible obscured its meaning as the living word of God. The Church merely gave the faithful a false security and no consolation. Its piety was wasted; it expended its energies in ostentation and the strict observance of all sorts of puerile devotions.

Heresies were not new; but underground existence had impoverished and stultified those of the Middle Ages. Sorcery, black magic and Satanism, however alluring, led only to a dead end. To souls who, in their thirst for truth, dreamed of a purified Church, the humanists offered only a naïvely optimistic philosophy without warmth and sinew. Such vague solutions only increased the general uneasiness. The spiritual crisis of individuals gave this collective crisis a direction and an outcome that were quite unexpected. A handful of young theologians who had no intention originally of beginning the reform of Christianity found a personal solution to the problem of their salvation; their spiritual debate led them to reject traditions and to break with the Papacy. A large number of the faithful, perturbed by the disorders within the Church, followed their example. Thus the Reformation, beginning as a revival, became a revolution.

Martin Luther

Martin Luther, the son of pious parents, was born at Eisleben in 1483. As a student he narrowly escaped being killed by lightning, and a few days later he lost a friend in a duel. Obsessed with a dread of divine justice, he entered the Augustinian monastery at Erfurt, and became professor of theology at the University of Wittenberg. Mortification and prayer did not succeed in dispelling his agony of mind; but the study of St Paul finally revealed to him in the winter of 1511–12 'the golden key which opens the whole of the Scriptures', providing him with an exciting and reassuring formula of salvation: 'Man is justified, not by works, but by faith.' In October 1517 he posted up on the door of Wittenberg Cathedral ninety-five theses in which, among other things, he criticised the principle underlying the recent sale of indulgences authorised to raise money for the rebuilding of St Peter's in Rome. Luther described himself as 'a blind nag which sets out without knowing where it is going', and declared that all he wanted was to set his conscience free. His visit to Rome eight years before, where he climbed the Scala Santa on his knees, had not awakened in him the least sign of rebellion. His 'theses' created a tremendous stir in Germany. The interest of a few humanists hostile to the Papacy, together with Luther's innate ardour, led him, little by little, towards intransigence. He gradually became more venturesome in his thought. When, in June 1520, the Pope threatened him with excommunication, Luther burned the Bull of Antichrist in a square at Wittenberg (Christmas 1520). Charles V then summoned him to appear before the Diet of Worms. Luther decided to attend 'were there as many devils present as there are tiles on the roofs'. He made a triumphal journey and

The Cathedral at Speyer, where in 1526 one Imperial Diet supported Lutheran reforms and another, in 1529, condemned them. Their 'protests' against the resolutions of the second Diet gave the Protestants their name. *Marburg*

Pope Alexander VI depicted as a devil, or Antichrist, in a broadside of about 1501. The text speaks of his dabbling in black magic. The depravity and corruption of the clergy gave rise to protests among the lay community long before the doctrinal criticism of the Reformation. *Marburg*

An *auto-da-fé*, or public burning of heretics by the Inquisition. The punishments imposed on those who confessed (wearing tall caps) included flogging, fines and penances. The obdurate were condemned to prison or the stake. *Giraudon*

delivered a firm reply to the final demands of the Church. ' My conscience, ' he said, ' a prisoner of the Divine Word, cannot, and will not, retract '. He ran the risk of being arrested and burned alive, but the Diet banished him from the Empire. The Elector of Saxony, who supported him, had him carried off by armed horsemen and conducted to the castle of Artburg in April 1521. But in the solitude of this eagle's nest, his qualms of conscience returned and his nights were filled with dreadful visions; in March the following year, when he had finished defining his doctrine and had translated the Bible into German, he returned to Wittenberg and began to preach again in his monk's robe.

The rebellion of knights and peasants. The Anabaptists

Assisted by the crisis of religious discontent, violent disorders broke out in Germany. Impoverished and jealous of the wealth of the clergy, the unruly knights in the south attacked Church property, and invaded the archbishopric of Trier and the towns of Württemberg. With the help of the princes, the citizens repelled the invaders and razed their castles to the ground (1523). Peasants now began to revolt, often under the leadership of religious reformers, demanding in the name of the Gospel the free use of forests, the suppression of serfdom and the sharing out of communal property. A general uprising followed and in the summer of 1524 castles were ablaze from Austria

21

Martin Luther (1483–1546). A twentieth-century conception by Louis Corinth. Luther's religious notions had immediate and long-term political implications unforeseen by Luther. *Marburg*

Philip Melancthon (1497–1560) painted by Cranach the Younger. Admired as a young humanist by Erasmus. In 1530 he presented the Reformers' case at the Diet of Augsburg. *Marburg*

to the Black Forest. The revolt was fiercely repudiated by Luther, and was crushed in a bloodbath. Another alarming movement was that of the Anabaptists, who preached equality in Christ and the necessity for a second baptism. They eventually organised a government of 'saints' at Münster which became notorious for its establishment of polygamy and communism when the city was besieged. Münster was recaptured in June 1535, the leaders of the movement were suspended in iron cages from the top of the cathedral before being executed, and in the next ten years Anabaptism was ruthlessly harried in Germany.

The progress of Lutheranism

Despite the alarm caused by such early social repercussions of the Reformation, Lutheranism gained strength in Germany. In conflict with their bishops, the Imperial towns in the south eagerly embraced it; the princes of the Palatinate, Hesse, Saxony, Brandenburg and Prussia were won over through German nationalism and by conviction. Charles V was busy with his wars against France, and it

was already too late when he attempted to check the progress of Lutheranism. In March 1529, the Lutheran princes 'protested' — hence their name — against the decision of the Catholic majority of the Diet of Speyer to forbid the further spread of innovation or the further secularisation of Church lands by over-enthusiastic princes. At a new Diet, where Melancthon set forth their doctrine in the moderate terms of the Confession of Augsburg (December 1530), compromise in any form was seen to be impossible. In 1531 the Protestants formed a defensive league and concluded an alliance with Francis I. War did not break out until the year of Luther's death. After first winning a battle at Mühlberg in April 1547, Charles V lost possession of the Tyrol in 1552, and had to escape across the Alps during a heavy snowfall. Completely absorbed in his struggle with Henry II, he entrusted his brother Ferdinand with negotiations. The Peace of Augsburg, signed in 1555, confirmed the division of Germany into Protestant and Catholic states. The Lutheran princes secured religious freedom for their Lutheran subjects and the possession of whatever Church property had already been secularised.

Zwingli. John Calvin and Geneva

While Lutheranism was spreading into the Netherlands, Denmark and Sweden, new reformers were preaching a more radical doctrine elsewhere. Ulrich Zwingli, rector of Zürich Cathedral, had already in 1522 rejected the Mass. His reform was adopted by the Council of Zürich in 1524 and won over a large part of Switzerland. He was killed in 1531, in a war against the 'old Cantons', which had remained faithful to the Papacy.

John Calvin was born at Noyon in Picardy in 1509, and was the son of a Church official. During his studies he became acquainted with the doctrine of Luther, abandoned his intention of becoming a priest and took refuge in Switzerland. His *Institutes of the Christian Religion* was published at Basle in 1536, the year in which Erasmus died. In this work Calvin not only stressed, as Luther had done, the vanity of works and the sole authority of the Scriptures, but rejected the entire ecclesiastical hierarchy and the ceremonial aspects of worship; he upheld the separation of Church and State, denied the Real Presence of Christ in the Holy Eucharist, and considered that Christ's act of redemption worked to the advantage of only the ' elect '.

In 1536, Guillaume Farel, a pious nobleman, full of enthusiasm, engaged Calvin as a professor in Geneva. This town was given over to trade and pleasure; but Calvin strove to make it a 'City of God'. He was frail and of weak constitution, and constantly tempted to return to a life of study. His preaching, his iron will and his boundless energy helped him to overcome the hostility of the old Genevese without having to assume any special status or impose himself upon them as a real leader. The Church Session, of which he was the real inspiration, watched over the faithful, refined their morals, forbade luxury, dances, the theatre, games and festivities. The custom of wearing two rings on one finger, excessively long banquets, lack of perseverance in worship, an ill-considered promise of marriage — any of these exposed the culprit to ecclesiastical penalties ranging from reprimand to excommunication. Wrong-thinkers were dealt with more severely than wrong-doers. ' God ', declared Calvin, ' requires that we forget all humanity when it is a question of fighting for His Glory '. A Genevese who was merely dissolute was made to tour the town in his shirt, carrying a torch in his hand, and to cry for mercy on bended knee. Jacques Gruet was beheaded for having written the words ' complete folly ' on one of the reformer's books; and Michel Servet was burned alive for having denied the Trinity.

Italian and French refugees flocked to Geneva which, under strict control, became the stronghold of the Reformation, the Rome of Protestantism. Thousands of foreign students frequented its Academy which ' receiving wood, sent forth arrows ', storming all Europe with its ardent evangelists. Calvin conducted a world-wide correspondence and behaved as the head of a great Church. Work and sickness finally sapped his strength. ' Lord ', he murmured on his deathbed in 1564, ' you crush me, but I am satisfied that it is your hand that crushes me. '

From Geneva Calvinism spread throughout France (Synod of Paris, 1559), the Netherlands (Synod of Dordrecht, 1578), and Germany (the Palatinate, Hesse, Brandenburg). In Scotland, as a result of civil war, Parliament adopted Calvinism, and John Knox established the Presbyterian Church.

Perhaps England's unhappiest queen. Mary Tudor (1553–58), wife of Philip II of Spain and notorious in Protestant tradition as 'Bloody Mary', for she resorted to persecution to re-establish the Roman Church. Her severity stiffened resistance and the Reformation flourished under her successor Elizabeth. *British Museum*

The title page from the *Grammatica Nova* by Nicolaus Perrottus. c. 1491. *British Museum*

THE INTELLECTUAL AND ARTISTIC REBIRTH

The Reformation in England

The Reformation was brought about in England by the will of the sovereign operating in the context of a popular anti-Papal mood. Henry VIII, a man of cultivated mind and well versed in theology, at first declared against Lutheranism. In his eagerness to marry one of the queen's ladies of honour he decided that he had violated the laws of the Church eighteen years earlier in marrying his sister-in-law, Catherine of Aragon. When Pope Clement VII refused him a divorce, Henry did not hesitate to break with Rome and proclaim himself supreme head of the English Church. He confiscated Church property, hanged 'papists' as rebels, and beheaded Protestants as heretics. He beheaded his Chancellor, Sir Thomas More, and exhibited his head on London Bridge. The 'Anglican Church', born of schism and not of heresy (1539), retained most of the Roman rites and dogmas. With the aid of Archbishop Cranmer, the solemn and sickly Edward VI (1547–53) steered his father's reform towards Calvinism and died at the age of sixteen mumbling a prayer which he had composed himself. His half-sister, Mary Tudor (1553–8), daughter of Catherine of Aragon and wife of

Philip II of Spain, resorted to persecution to re-establish the Roman Church. Cranmer recanted in writing, then retracted; he was condemned to be burnt at the stake; to punish the hand that had yielded he thrust it first into the fire. The reformed religion gained strength through the courage of its martyrs. By the end of the reign of 'Bloody Mary' the Catholic cause already seemed lost. Emboldened and purified by its trials, the Reformation was to triumph finally in England during the reign of Elizabeth. It owed as much to political circumstance as to theological dissidence.

Western Europe, following two centuries of Italian example, renewed its contact with antiquity; a surge of youthfulness turned it away from the Middle Ages. Europe acclaimed the bounty of nature, the grandeur of man, an intoxicating passion for knowledge and the delights of speculative thought. In the favourable setting of the growing towns, patronised by burgher patricians, Renaissance artists responded to the aspirations of the century with an extraordinary vigour. Their creative activity gave them confidence in the future; the Renaissance set up at

A study in chalk by Michelangelo Buonarroti (1475–1564). The Renaissance artists turned from the religious art of the Middle Ages to rediscover the forms and subjects of antiquity. In painting and sculpture the nude regained importance.

Holbein's drawing of Sir Thomas More (1478–1535).

The Pietà Rondanini. Michelangelo was as concerned in his sculpture to convey spiritual meaning — a revival of interest in true religious values — as to achieve perfection of artistic form. He worked on this unfinished sculpture for ten years. *Marburg*

the approach to modern times a kind of triumphal arch commemorating hopes as much as achievements.

Art in the Renaissance

Renaissance art implied the resurgence of the art of antiquity; it gave Christian symbolism a pagan content. It strove for the expression of physical perfection, rediscovering the nude in sculpture and painting. A love of logic also drew it nearer to science. It was an art governed by rules, careful of perspective, proportion and symmetry, conscious of the harmony of parts and deriving its authority from orderliness. While drawing their inspiration from ancient models, artists tried to seal their creative achievements with the stamp of individuality. They signed their works of art; they made names for themselves, pursuing fame, and were honoured in a manner unknown to predecessors who had been regarded only as skilled craftsmen.

The golden age of Italian art

The sixteenth century saw the climax of Italian art. Three great masters, of differing temperament, dominated the age. With a touch of arrogance, Leonardo da Vinci (1452–1519) referred to art as an ' unrivalled opportunity given to man to continue what God has begun '. His quest for perfection is expressed in a mass of unfinished sketches and models and in some superb achievements of sheer painting technique. He was a master both of classical composition and of an almost romantic skill in evoking atmosphere.

In contrast, Michelangelo (1475–1564), a stern dreamer with a turbulent soul, rediscovered the restlessness of medieval Christianity; he foreshadows the art of the Counter-Reformation though he, too, was a careful student of antiquity. He was greatest as a sculptor; a single one of his statues, *Moses* or *Lorenzo de' Medici*, for instance, would have made him immortal. He said he was no painter, but decorated the ceiling of the Sistine Chapel without any assistance — alone with his vision for more than twenty months. The gigantic dome of St Peter's testifies to the boldness of his architectural genius. When he was nearly ninety he would carve earnestly through the long nights, wearing a cardboard cap to which he attached a candle. He was then more than ever despondent at not being able to attain the superhuman, the elusive goal of his soaring imagination.

The ' divine ' Raphael (1483–1520) could draw before he could write. In the sunny district of Umbria, the land of St Francis, and in the dreamy softness of Perugia he became imbued with mysticism. Through his contact with Leonardo da Vinci in Florence he developed complete freedom of style. In the year 1508 he was invited to Rome by Pope Julius II, and there quickly showed what he was capable of achieving. He died at the age of thirty-seven after a brilliant life, rich in opportunity. Infused with idealism, his work is a harmonious synthesis of all the trends of the Renaissance, although it shows neither the richness of Leonardo's imagination nor the power and grandeur of Michelangelo.

The French Renaissance

The Italian Renaissance was accompanied by a revival of

25

The dome of St Peter's, Rome, the greatest of the Renaissance churches. The rebuilding of the church was begun by Bramante (1444–1514) in 1509 under Pope Julius II; Michelangelo planned its completion and designed the dome, which was finished in 1588–90. *Marburg*

Leonardo da Vinci's *Mona Lisa*, a supreme example of his skill in evoking atmosphere and in hinting at mystery. *Bulloz*

art throughout the whole of Europe. In France, the masterpieces of a Gothic tradition helped to produce a composite style of which the Loire *châteaux* are the finest examples. New artistic ideas made their way into Spain through Berruguete, and into the Netherlands through Van Orley. In Germany, they had no effect on the national genius. Though the inspired Albrecht Dürer (1471–1528) came under the spell of the Renaissance, he remained profoundly Germanic both in his woodcuts and in his paintings. The portraits of Hans Holbein (1498–1554) are not unlike Italian art in their restraint, but they show the attention to detail which had characterised the work of Flemish painters of the fifteenth century.

Erasmus and the humanists

The humanists — the word dates from 1539 — turned to ancient literature not only for the eternal truths, but for academic disciplines designed to mould orderly minds.

Erasmus, who was born in Rotterdam about 1466, was the acknowledged leader of the humanists; after abandoning the cloister at the age of twenty-six he led a wandering life across Europe. By the time he had settled in Basle in 1521, he had already won a world-wide reputation through his scholarly works and his correspondence, written entirely in Latin. Holbein portrayed him as a conqueror; Charles V, Francis I and Henry VIII were his patrons; Pope Paul III wanted to make him a Cardinal. Though he criticised the corrupt practices of the clergy and dreamed of adapting ancient culture to Christian institutions, this ailing little man, who could no more endure the smell of fish than the turmoil of inns or the cold weather, was a mystic who loved peace and comfort, and was always disposed toward compromise. He distrusted ' seditious truths ', but his mischievous features, his alertness and brilliance of intellect remind one of Voltaire.

The Italian humanists strove to write the Latin of Cicero. Their revivalist enthusiasm could at times lead to a chilling antiquarianism. But it had also meant a rediscovery of Greek, and through Greek of the Plato who lay behind Aristotle, the idol of the medieval schools. In this way, even before the sixteenth century, the rediscovery of classical letters meant far more than stylistic purification; it implied criticism of the present in the light of ideas and ideals derived from the ancients. In France, thanks to the efforts of the printer Robert Estienne, texts of the ancient writers were becoming more common. Reference to original sources of information and a full examination of them began to be preferred to the debates of the Sorbonne. That body protested when Francis I established the Collège de France, later the centre of the higher sciences. Rhetoric followed in the footsteps of logic and theology. The international character of university life spread the new learning. Brilliantly represented in England by Colet and the scholars of Oxford and Cambridge, it made its way also to the Netherlands, Spain and Germany.

Literature in Italy and France

The rediscovery of classical style brought a new sensitivity, expressiveness, lucidity and a sense of proportion into literature. The other achievement of the age was the appearance of more and more great works in the vernacular; the printing-press was creating the lay reading

Wood-carving of a bookbinder at work, 1555. *Marburg*

Desiderius Erasmus, the most famous of the humanists, by Dürer. *Marburg*

public. In fine, powerful prose, Machiavelli (1469–1527) analysed human actions dispassionately and objectively (*The Prince*). Ariosto (1474–1533), in his epic poem *Orlando Furioso*, invented a whole world of fantasy which reflected the taste for action, chivalrous aspirations and burning sensuality characteristic of the Renaissance. In France the most outstanding writer of the early sixteenth century was François Rabelais (1495–1533). His story of the 'dreadful deeds of valour' of Gargantua combined an inventiveness of mind and a richness of language almost unequalled. Rabelais's aim was to frolic and to amuse. He painted a gaily satirical picture of the society of the period and, rejecting the Christian spirit of the Middle Ages, glorified a yielding to the laws of nature.

The scientific revival

'In half a century', wrote a theologian about the year 1560, 'we have seen more progress among men of science than our ancestors saw in the preceding fourteen centuries.' Expeditions beyond the seas, and the dissemination of Greek and Latin writings through the spread of printing added to knowledge and excited curiosity. From now on experience was to be the source of certainty, and observation the interpreter of nature.

The natural sciences became organised. Gesner, the Pliny of Germany, wrote a *History of Animals*; the science of ichthyology was developed at Montpellier by Roudelet; mineralogy was studied in Bohemia by Bauer, and arsenic, zinc and bismuth were added to the seven metals known to antiquity. Vesalius of Brussels produced the first exact description of the human body; Fracaster, an Italian, developed a theory of organisms rather like microbes (1546); Ambroise Paré, a Frenchman, made use of ligatures to stop haemorrhage, and the mercurial Paracelsus gave a new impetus to therapy. While in Germany Stifel was popularising the plus and minus signs, in Italy Tartaglia was discovering the solution of cubic equations and Cardan the seminal notion of imaginary quantities. In opposition to Ptolemy, and despite the commonly accepted evidence, the Polish monk Copernicus was able to prove in his *De Revolutionibus* (1543) that the earth turned about the sun, and not the sun about the earth.

In his manuscripts, written backwards and with the left hand, Leonardo da Vinci, for whom perfect science and perfect love were one, outlined theories of the

Drawing of a rhinoceros by Albrecht Dürer. The Renaissance was an age of enquiry, of scientific observation as much as of artistic experimentation. In a world full of strange new ideas the artists of the period responded to the grotesque and the exotic. *Mansell*

Sixteenth-century technology: woodcut showing beer-brewing in 1568. *Archiv für Kunst und Geschichte*

A diplomatic document of the Renaissance: the ratification of a treaty concerning ecclesiastical affairs by the King of France in 1527. *Public Record Office*

A page from an Italian manual of the liberal arts. This opens the section on geometry, which like arithmetic and algebra was greatly developed during the Renaissance. The first half of the sixteenth century saw rapid progress in the sciences.

movement of the earth, the tides and the circulation of the blood. Drawn by the practical applications of science, he was not satisfied with constructing elaborate toys like a lion which, when standing on its hind legs, opened its chest and let fall a shower of lilies at the feet of Francis I. He took an interest in submarine navigation and the use of steam; he forecast a ' flying machine ' which he imagined would one day enable man to travel to the Alps ' as on the back of a great swan ' in search of snow to be showered over towns scorched by the sun.

The age of Leonardo da Vinci was also the age of the predictions of Nostradamus, of magic squares, of panaceas and drinkable gold. Even the most broadminded hesitated to throw off the yoke of tradition and to repudiate once and for all their medieval heritage. Copernicus, appalled by the revolutionary character of his theory of the motion of the earth round the sun, refrained from publishing it until thirty-seven years after he had discovered it. Paracelsus looked for the origin of sickness in the ' physiology of the stars '. The inspired Cardan was convinced that the ram's horn changed into asparagus; Christopher Columbus thought the earth possessed a navel shaped like a pear, and Nettesheim that a storm could be produced by burning the liver of a chameleon.

EASTERN EUROPE, TURKEY, THE MEDITERRANEAN

While Western Europe, revitalised by the Renaissance in its various aspects, marched ahead of its time Eastern Europe, where Asia and the Middle Ages still lived side by side, comprised at the beginning of the sixteenth century a vast area of mystery, empty spaces without well-defined boundaries. Practically unknown to other nations, the Scandinavian countries, Muscovy and Poland were still badly organised. Their history, one of blood and darkness, was dominated by incursions of wandering tribes, pirates and wreckers of ships, obscure quarrels between noble families and feudal revolts. But Sweden became a nation during the first half of the sixteenth century, thanks to Gustavus Vasa; Poland experienced a brilliant literary renaissance; Muscovy grew stronger in the iron grip of Ivan IV, though still inferior to the Western nations.

Since the capture of Constantinople, Turkish pressure remained a formidable menace to the frail outposts of Christianity. Swept onwards by the all-conquering fanaticism of their religion, the Turks ruled the Balkans and pressed on the frontiers of Austria, Poland and Muscovy. Once established on the Adriatic and the Aegean, they were drawn towards the Mediterranean. When Europeans were crossing the Atlantic to conquer new worlds, Italy, the most illustrious centre of the Renaissance, was less than fifty miles from the Turkish vanguard across the Strait of Otranto; and beyond Vienna, the proudest capital of Europe, lay the open plains of unruly Hungary.

Gustavus Vasa and the independence of Sweden

In 1502 Sweden cut itself off from Denmark, of which it had never been more than a lawless fief; but in 1520 Christian II re-established Danish rule. A period of cruel repression followed, and encouraged a national rebellion a few months later. The son of one of the victims of the

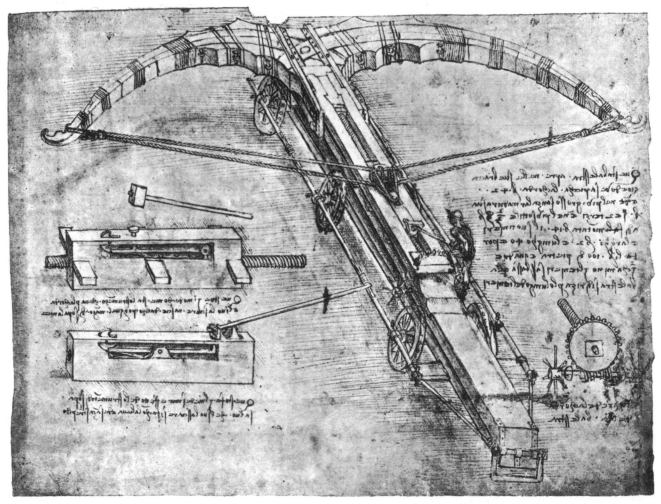

A siege-weapon designed by Leonardo on the principle of the crossbow but never made. Perfection of knowledge in any sphere was to Leonardo a worthy object. *British Museum*

bloodbath, Gustavus Vasa (1490–1560), led the rebellion and forced Calmar, the last Danish garrison, to surrender in 1523. He was proclaimed King of Sweden by the Diet of Strängnäs in June 1523.

As he was unable to extract from the clergy the money necessary for the rebuilding of his ravaged kingdom, he asked the Diet of Västeräs to establish Lutheranism, thus using the Reformation as a political device for the benefit of monarchy and nobility, bribed with monastic property. In 1529 Sweden obtained a Protestant confession of faith. Regarded as a national hero, Gustavus disciplined the nobility and the Diet, which made the crown hereditary in his family. He also did what he could to encourage Sweden's economic activities, by introducing foreign miners and beginning to put to use the vast territory in the north. At his death Sweden was already a strong and solidly established state.

Poland and its golden century

Bordering Lithuania, Poland stretched from the Black Sea to the Baltic, though its actual power bore no relation to its size. Its three kings, Alexander I (1501–6), Sigismund I (1506–48) and Sigismund II (1548–72), who belonged to the Jagiellon dynasty, were forbidden to pass any new laws without the consent of the Diet. They were forced to pay State expenses out of their own revenue and had no regular army, no treasury and no administration. The nobility, unruly, critical and devoid of political acumen, kept their kings conscious of the fact that they were elected sovereigns, and strove to diminish their authority still further. Summoned together in 1535 because of a war against a Moldavian prince, the nobles refused to fight, and mockingly took to massacring poultry in the farmyards. They agreed to lay down their arms only when they had obtained from Sigismund I a promise to remove certain taxes. The poet Krzycki, referring to these deadly maladies of his country, spoke of 'quarrels between brothers, chaos in government, contempt of law, and licence rather than liberty'.

Yet despite its political decay Poland had entered its golden century. Through its relations with the Mediterranean countries which bought its corn in exchange for silk, it felt the Western influence of the Renaissance. Its young noblemen went to Bologna and Padua to study: The Italians who were drawn to the Polish court as a result of the marriage of Sigismund I to a Sforza princess created a taste for elegance, refinement and culture. Artists and humanists found a home there and even the Reformation found its way into Poland; Canon Ilza was condemned as a heretic as early as 1535.

Muscovy and its first Tsar: Ivan IV

The decline of the Mongolian empire encouraged the growth of the principality of Muscovy. From this small

The birth of the Virgin. Sixteenth-century icon. Pskov. *Marburg*

patrimonial estate deprived of an outlet to the open sea, Ivan III (1462–1505) and Vasily III (1505–33) tried to create a state. Freeing it from Tatar sovereignty, they expanded to the west at the expense of Lithuania, and to the north as far as the Arctic Ocean. Ivan III, with his wife, the niece of the last Emperor of Constantinople, took over the emblem of the double-headed eagle and, considering themselves to be of divine origin, held aloof from their subjects. Under their reign Moscow remained almost untouched by the influences of the Renaissance, although foreign architects rebuilt the palaces and the churches of the Kremlin.

Ivan IV (1533–84) was only three years old at the death of Vasily, his father. The nobles took advantage of the minority to plunder the treasury and to dispute among themselves for power. The young prince, supported by the Metropolitan Bishop Macarius, and the Glinskys, his mother's relatives, eventually freed himself from their humiliating tutelage, and had the most insolent of their leaders executed during the Christmas festivities of 1543. An excessive acquaintance with violence and vice from his youth made him an inhuman despot. A fire ravaged Moscow the very year (1547) he had himself crowned, not as a great prince, but as Tsar (Caesar). When bloody riots broke out, Ivan saw in them a divine warning, and announced from a rostrum in Red Square his determination to care henceforth for 'God's people whom God had entrusted to him'. He re-organised the army, the judiciary and the Church. The authority and scope of his government were increased by creating specialised ministries.

Ivan IV extended his kingdom as far as the Ural Mountains by the conquest of Kazan (1552) and to the Caspian Sea by the occupation of Astrakhan (1556). He was convinced that Russia could succeed in political expansion only if it showed itself to be the patron of Orthodoxy among the Eastern Christians, and he was careful during his campaigns to see that his first-line troops carried icons; he had a miraculous cross brought from Moscow to overcome the magic of the Infidel, and he replaced the mosques by churches. As the Cross prevailed over the Crescent, so did the cannon over the bow; for the first time in their history, the nomadic tribes, now faced with Russian artillery, lost their military superiority.

Appreciating the advantages of Western techniques, Ivan IV turned boldly to Europe, whence he procured medical supplies, skilled men and material. He signed a treaty with Sweden which opened up trade routes to the west. With the arrival of the explorer Chancellor in the White Sea, Ivan opened trade relations with England. The first Russian printing-press was set up in 1552.

In remaining aloof from the great drama of the Reformation, Muscovy showed that it had not yet become quite European. The Westerners, who discovered Muscovy at the same time as they were discovering America, deplored the barbarous customs of the Russians, but they nevertheless regarded them as susceptible to profound and decisive changes under the influence of Ivan IV.

The Ottoman Empire: Selim I and Sulaiman the Magnificent

The Ottoman Empire, partly in Asia and partly in Europe, stretched from the Euphrates to the Carpathian Mountains and along half the length of the Danube. Its Sultans were military leaders chosen by the army: they were the successors of Mahomet, the Emirs of the faithful, heirs of the Byzantine emperors; all power was in their hands. Selim the Grim (1512–20) was a tireless warrior and an admirer of Alexander the Great. Sulaiman (1520–66) was surnamed 'the Magnificent' by the Western nations because of his love of display, and 'the Lawmaker' by the Turks, who had a great respect for his remarkable qualities as a statesman. Both were men of culture and refinement, though they were capable of inhuman acts. Selim poisoned his father, Bayazid II, and had no qualms about delivering his vizirs over to the executioners. Sulaiman sacrificed the lives of his son, Mustafa, and his Grand Vizir, Ibrahim, to the gay but ruthless Roxolana, his blue-eyed Russian mistress.

The Ottoman Empire was administered and defended by slaves or renegades, and subject to a hierarchy of military officials, priests and scribes. Three powerful expansionist forces lay at the heart of its existence: its proselytising religion; its people, still essentially nomads on the march; and its army, maintained in a perpetual state of readiness. Along the borders the Turks continually strove to press forward; they had no definite plan, but merely followed the tradition of savage Asia, slaughtering the 'infidels', and winning for themselves a share of the slaves and booty that fell to the victors.

From the moment Sulaiman succeeded to power, the Turkish drive towards the heart of Europe was intensified. In 1521, with the collusion of Serbia, the Turks seized Belgrade, which was considered impregnable, and crossed the Danube. In August 1526, after two hours' fighting, they wiped out the Hungarian cavalry on the marshy plains of Mohács, where King Louis, the last of the Jagiellons, was killed. In 1528, Sulaiman entered Buda, and with his own hands placed St Stephen's crown on the head of his vassal, John Zápolyai. The following year he camped before Vienna, inspiring fear throughout the Christian world. After enduring a month of siege and more than twenty assaults, the town let loose all its bells in jubilation when Sulaiman retreated. But in 1532 the Turks took their revenge; they stormed Köszeg and devastated Upper Austria. After the death of Zápolyai (1540) central Hungary was incorporated in the Ottoman Empire. In 1555 the Turks took Temesvár, but failed to capture Erlau. Forced to undertake a fresh campaign at seventy-one years of age, Sulaiman the Magnificent died beneath the walls of Szigetvar in September 1566. The town fell two days later, and Maximilian of Austria signed an eight years' treaty with Turkey.

Not only did the Turks threaten the continental bastions of the Christian world, but in less than half a century they put an end to European supremacy in the Mediterranean. With the defeat of the Mamelukes (1516–17) Selim occupied Egypt, where he immediately built a fleet. Despite a magnificent defence by the Order of St John, Selim took possession of the great naval base at Rhodes. The Venetians were compelled to evacuate all their positions in Morea and the islands with the exception of Naxos and Andros. The barriers which they had set up in the eastern Mediterranean were definitively breached in 1540.

It was by a fortunate coincidence that the Turks gained access to the western Mediterranean. The pirate Aroudj Barbarossa took possession of Algiers in 1516, and the Spaniards eventually captured and beheaded him (1518). In order to be in a better position to avenge him, his brother Khair ad-Din had himself proclaimed vassal of the Porte.

Backed by the Ottomans, Khair ad-Din then fortified Algiers and began to devastate the Italian coastline. Charles V's counter-measures were of no avail. After the defeat of the expedition which he himself led against Algiers in October 1541, he barely succeeded in keeping Melilla, Oran and Mers-el-Kebir in North Africa. The Turks, who had made an alliance with Francis I, took advantage of Charles's losses and intercepted shipping between Italy and Spain. The Berbers became more and more daring, raiding the European coasts and carrying off with them prisoners into slavery.

In the fourteenth century Othman — the ' Leg Breaker ' — was converted to Islam as the result of a dream in which he saw growing from his loins an immense tree, from which the Tigris, the Euphrates, the Nile and the Danube flowed. By the middle of the sixteenth century his empire extended from the Tigris to Gibraltar and from the cataracts of the Nile to the Danube. All the historic and holy cities of Islam were under its sway. While retaining its influence in Asia his empire had reduced part of North Africa to vassalage and was treated in Europe as a great nation. Its attraction was so strong that every year thousands of fugitives left Christian states to enter its service. The Western nations no longer regarded the Sultans as leaders of rabbles. The painter Veronese, in his *Marriage at Cana*, which portrays the most famous people of his day, included Sulaiman the Magnificent — ' the shadow of God on earth ', ' the Happy Padishah '.

Sulaiman I the Magnificent (1520–66), the greatest of the Ottoman rulers, called the Lawmaker by his Turkish subjects. The ally of France, Sulaiman captured Belgrade, beseiged Vienna and gained control of the Mediterranean. *Giraudon*

CHAPTER TWO

THE FIRST HALF OF THE SIXTEENTH CENTURY OUTSIDE EUROPE

CONQUEST BEYOND THE SEAS

In 1514, the envoys of King Manuel of Portugal, after marching through Rome at the head of a train of three hundred mules carrying treasure from India, presented Leo X with an elephant from Goa. Some years earlier gold bar brought from a far-off New World had been used in the decoration of the church of Saint Mary Major. Little by little Europe became conscious of the opportunities for increased wealth that overseas discovery offered. Up to then Europe had been confined within its continental boundaries; but now it launched boldly across the ocean routes. This expansion was the outcome of the revolutions which marked the beginning of modern times.

Europe began to seek out new ways to obtain more tropical products, not only to remedy a scarcity of precious metals which threatened to paralyse its trade, but also to appease its dominating passion for gold. The religious revival which sparked off the Reformation also disposed Europeans to regard the task of opening sea routes to the pagans of distant countries as a duty, in order to show them the way to heaven. The intellectual Renaissance quickened the desire for more knowledge of the world at a time when astronomy and map-making made navigation easier. Alive to their own interests and to the future, the peoples of Europe regarded conquest beyond the seas as a necessary condition and a legitimate manifestation of power. In a warm-blooded century, when individuals tended to assert themselves, many adventurers dreamed of performing feats of valour, of becoming knights of the ocean, and of seeing new and uncharted stars each night.

Though the upheavals which brought about these great discoveries affected most of Europe, the discoveries themselves were the achievements of two countries: Spain and Portugal. They were well placed for departure on exploratory travel and they had already been drawn into naval expeditions along the African shores. Their religious traditions also allowed them to see their overseas enterprises as a continuation of their crusades.

Vasco da Gama and the route to India

The Portuguese perfected nautical science, and undertook the first great exploratory voyages. Triumphant after their struggles with the Infidel, they endeavoured to take the Moslems in the rear by reaching the mysterious kingdom of Prester John which, according to remote tradition, was situated south of Egypt. Commercial acumen drove them to look for a new route to India so as to obtain spices directly and not through Arab middlemen. Stage by stage they moved southwards along the western coast of Africa. In 1487, Diaz reached the Cape of Good Hope. During these expeditions the sailors expected daily to arrive at the

Vasco da Gama (1469–1524), the Portuguese explorer, who rounded the Cape of Good Hope and reached India in 1498. Like Columbus, but successful, his aim was primarily commercial. *British Museum*

gates of hell, and to see the sinister ocean turn into a salty paste or vast areas of boiling water. When Vasco da Gama (1469–1524) undertook to round the Cape he had difficulty in recruiting his crews. After spending the night in a church in prayer, he left Lisbon in July 1497, with four small ships, 160 men and 12 men condemned to death who were to be used for dangerous reconnaissance work. Making his way round Africa, he celebrated Christmas in the port of Natal, and made a difficult journey up the coast to Mozambique, north to Zanzibar, and from there, driven by the monsoon, he reached Calicut in twenty-three days, despite mutinies, storms and the hostility of petty Arab kings. The following year, his vessels laden with spices and rubies, he regained Lisbon after a difficult return journey (September 1499).

The eastern route to India was no longer a dream. Once again European ships had entered the Indian Ocean, where they had not been seen for more than ten centuries. The enormous wealth they brought back encouraged explorers to try to reach Asia by other routes.

Christopher Columbus and the discovery of America

Imago Mundi, a book published by the French writer Pierre D'Ailly in 1483, had convinced the experienced Genoese sailor Christopher Columbus that the earth was round. He decided to reach India from the west, sailing as far as the Atlantic would take him. The King of Portugal declined to back the expedition; but Ferdinand and Isabella, the Spanish monarchs, granted him, under charter, the viceroyalty of any lands he might discover, together with the title of Admiral of the Ocean (April 1492). With three ships, the largest of only 140 tons, he set sail from Palos on August 3. For thirty-three days he sailed without sight of anything but sea and sky. To learn his speed he would spit into the sea and watch the spittle glide away; or he would walk on the bridge in the same direction as the wave, studying the displacement of the foam along the length of the hull. On October 12 he landed near the Strait of Florida on the island of Guanahani, where he threw himself on the ground to thank God for having guided him to the portals of the Far East. After landing on Cuba and taking possession of Santo Domingo (Hispaniola) he returned to Spain, where he was received in triumph (15 March 1493). A second expedition completed the discovery of the West Indies (1493–6) and a third (1498–1500) took Columbus to the South American mainland. It seemed to him that the Orinoco River, of which he caught a glimpse, must have dropped from heaven. His intractable disposition, however, provoked disorderly outbreaks among his soldiers of fortune at Santo Domingo, where he set himself up as governor. Appointed judge and governor in Columbus's place, Bobadilla seized him and sent him back to Europe in chains. The Spanish sovereigns made up for this insult to some extent by authorising Columbus to make a fourth voyage (1502–4) which gave him the opportunity to sail up the Central American coast. Two years after his final return to Spain he died, discouraged, unappreciated and almost forgotten. He never knew that he had discovered a new world.

The truth, however, began to come out. Following in the wake of Columbus new explorers spread themselves from Venezuela (Little Venice), to the mouth of the Amazon and as far as Rio de la Plata. These lands gradually became recognised as an area distinct from Asia. In 1507, the name America appeared on the map in honour of the Florentine Amerigo Vespucci who, after a voyage to Brazil, was the first to regard the new discoveries as a separate continent. All that now remained was to find out how far away was the real India. In 1513 a Spanish officer named Balboa crossed the isthmus of Panama and discovered on the horizon a limitless ocean. The great adventure of westward discovery thus ended in a double disappointment.

America, which stood as an unexpected obstacle between Europe and Asia, was itself separated by an immense distance from the Far East. The voyage of Magellan proved the world to be infinitely vaster than anyone had imagined up to that time.

Magellan's voyage round the world

Ferdinand Magellan (1480–1521), a Portuguese gentlemen who had been crippled by a wound received in India, accused his country of ingratitude and, when he was about forty years of age, placed himself at the service of

The caravel in which Columbus sailed to the New World on his first voyage in 1492. Basing his belief that the world was round on the book *Imago Mundi*, Columbus set sail westwards in this small vessel still close to medieval design, hoping to reach the East Indies. *Historisches Bildarchiv*

Woodcut showing American Indians making fire and smoking tobacco. Basle, 1494. *Archiv für Kunst und Geschichte*

Natives extracting gold in Hispaniola under the surveillance of *conquistadores*. Despite the official policy, the use of forced native labour in the mines began soon after the establishment of Spanish rule in the Americas. *Larousse*

c

A ceremonial stool similar to one on which Christopher Columbus was carried in Santo Domingo, where he set himself up as governor. His soldiers of fortune soon rebelled against his authoritarian rule and he was humiliatingly ousted by Bobadilla. *British Museum*

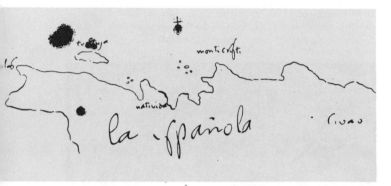

Sketch-map of Hispaniola (Haiti), showing on the left the harbour of St Nicholas, where Columbus lay at anchor on his second expedition to the West Indies (1493–96), during the course of which he completed his exploration and charted the Caribbean islands. *Archiv für Kunst und Geschichte*

A mid-sixteenth-century ship in the East Indies, when direct trade with that region was beginning to establish itself. It carries far more sail than Columbus's caravel of fifty years earlier (*see* page 33). *Giraudon*

Spain. His love of adventure and an intense scientific curiosity urged him to seek out a passage to the west which would lead around the New World to India, the land of spices, without his having to touch Portuguese territory. Charles V put 241 sailors at his disposal, with five ships of a hundred tons. His countrymen resolved to assassinate him on learning of his plans, so he left Seville hurriedly in 1519. Having reached South America, he sailed along the coast; but bad weather held him up for five months at a bay in Patagonia, where he suppressed a mutiny before beginning in August 1520 to make his way through a maze of channels north of Tierra del Fuego. After feeling his way along for thirty-eight days, he discovered the passage which bears his name. On November 21 he reached the edge of a great ocean. Undeterred by the desertion of one of his ships, he crept northwards along the coast of Chile. In an ocean which he was able to describe as ' pacific ' the trade winds pushed him gently to the north-west for four months. By the time he had crossed the Equator his sailors, weakened by scurvy and short of fresh water, had scarcely anything to eat but sawdust, mice and the leather of the mainyard. He was prepared to face fresh mutinous outbreaks when, in March 1521, he reached the Marianas Islands. A month later he was murdered by islanders in the Philippines. Only one of his ships, the *Victory*, managed to return to Seville by way of the Cape of Good Hope (September 1522).

This was the first voyage round the world. Devoid of all commercial importance, it proved that the earth was round, and that a continent independent of Asia existed between the Atlantic and the Pacific. The mystery of the West Indies had been solved, and the period of discovery was over. But by that time the Portuguese and Spanish had already embarked upon their great colonial conquests.

The creation of the Portuguese colonial empire

After a second voyage by Vasco da Gama during 1502 and 1503, the Portuguese had firmly established themselves at Cochin, on the Malabar coast, and from there harried the Arab traders over the whole of the Indian Ocean. Their appalling terror tactics brought them quick success. Egypt, Venice, Gujrat and Calicut united against them. After three years of successful fighting, the Portuguese ended by closing the Hindu ports to all their rivals (1509). The high-spirited Admiral Albuquerque (1443–1515) laid the foundations of the Portuguese colonial empire. He took Goa after a bloody battle and made it his capital. His soldiers set fire to the mosques after crowding the townspeople into them. The capture of the island of Socotra and Hormuz, on the Persian mainland, gave him control of the two routes joining the Indian Ocean and the Mediterranean. In the east he gained possession of Malacca, and died at the moment when, almost in disgrace, he was about to be recalled to Portugal (1515). His lieutenants landed on the Sunda Islands, reached China and pushed towards Japan. It was impossible to sail the oceans without a Portuguese safe-conduct.

The Portuguese also established posts in Guinea, the Congo and in Angola as well as in Asia. Their colonial empire was the first of modern Europe; it stretched along 12,500 miles of coastline from Cape Bogador in the Atlantic to the Moluccas Islands in the Pacific and in 1500 Cabral disembarked in Brazil, near the present-day town of Salvador.

The conquistadores and the Aztecs of Mexico

Unlike the Portuguese, the Spaniards were not satisfied with a few coastal ports. Disappointed in the West Indies, where they found the resources inadequate, they turned to the conquest of the American mainland. There their *conquistadores* came across two civilised nations: the Aztecs and the Quechuas.

By the end of the Middle Ages the Aztecs had built a vast empire on the high plateaus of Anahuac. The absolute authority of their supreme chief, the *tlacatacutli* was second only to that of the high priests. In their caste society the nobles, the soldiers and the magistrates were privileged. Owned by the gods and the State, the land was periodically divided among families. Tilled with wooden implements and skilfully irrigated, the soil bore

maize, tomatoes, potatoes and tobacco — products so far unknown in Europe. Draught animals were not used, and no livestock was raised. The Aztecs lived on pancakes, vegetable foods, pumpkins, chocolate, fattened dogs, flies and flies' eggs. For money they used cocoa beans; they knew nothing of the uses of iron and made wheels merely as toys for children. They were expert in the art of dyeing, and produced fine, brilliantly coloured fabrics woven from cotton, sisal, rabbit hair and, above all, feathers. They were skilled in gold and copper work and, without lathes, produced pottery of vigorous form. Their numerous towns, laid out in wide straight streets, had markets surrounded by porticos, eating-houses, hairdressers and chemist shops. Their 18,000 temples were built in the shape of pyramids; there they worshipped cruel gods like their god of Spring, and Huitzilopochili, the god of war. They regarded human

Above: The Strait of Magellan, discovered by Magellan in 1520 during the first circumnavigation of the globe. In 1614–15 passage through the strait was still an adventure as here, during circumnavigation by Spilbergen's squadron. *Giraudon*

Below: Map of the Gulf of China from an atlas of 1519 dedicated to the King of Portugal. The Portuguese reached China and Japan as early as 1515–16. By bold maritime control they laid the foundations of their colonial empire. *Larousse*

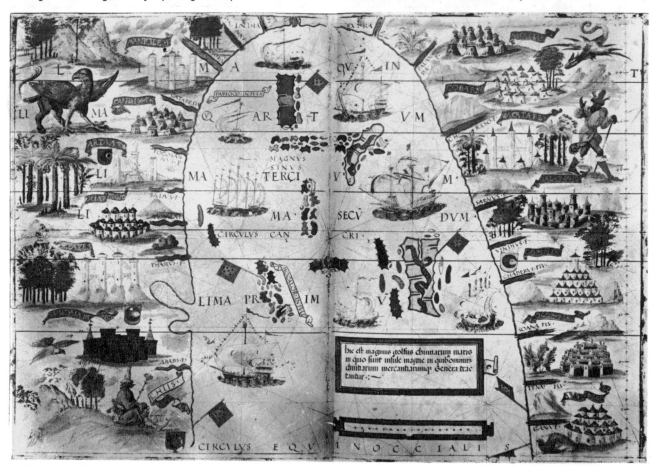

The *conquistadores'* hopes of riches were more than fulfilled by the bullion they found in the New World, much of it made into objects such as this Mexican god, in silver. *Marburg*

An illustration from an Aztec history of 1576. It shows the arrival of the Spaniard in his armour at the Great Temple. The centre figure stands before the great ceremonial drum used at all sacrifices. *British Museum*

sacrifices as necessary to induce agricultural fertility, and to bring back the sun after its daily setting. Victims were stretched on stone tables, before corpulent statues surrounded by demons; with a single stroke of a flint knife, a priest opened them as he would a pomegranate, tore out the heart and threw it bleeding at the face of the idols. The Aztec ritual games were just as barbarous: one of them took the form of a combat between teams for the possession of a solid rubber ball; the losers could be put to death after the match. Even children were plagued to the point of tears, to induce a rainfall corresponding to the abundance of their tears. Sacrificial victims or slaves were obtained during excursions in the country round about. The Aztecs went forth on these excursions to the sound of flute and drum and adorned with feathers; they were protected by thick layers of cotton and armed with maces bristling with sharp stones. Their capital had two names: Tenochtitlán, the ' cactus on the rock ', and Mexico, the ' house of the war god '. The tribes whom they subdued or terrorised looked forward to the coming of a bearded god with golden hair who, rising out of the sea to the east, would come to liberate them.

The Mexican epic of Hernán Cortés

The conquest of Mexico was the work of Hernán Cortés (1484–1547). Sensual and sanctimonius, as avid for adventure as he was for gain, this gentleman from Estremadura set off from the University of Salamanca at the age of nineteen to seek his fortune in the New World. His striking eyes, sometimes flashing, sometimes wistful, distracted attention from his gaunt frame, his projecting ears, and large nose over a full mouth. Velásquez, the Governor of Cuba, entrusted him with an expedition to the North American mainland; but Cortés was of too independent a nature to accept patronage and he failed to get on with his protector. After living some time as a privateer, he left the West Indies abruptly in February 1519, with 660 men, 18 horses and 10 cannon, and founded a little city in the Castilian style at Vera Cruz, on the mainland, whence, five months later, he turned towards Mexico. The tribes along the coast welcomed him as a liberator, and provided him with bearers and soldiers. His horses, regarded as strange monsters, and his warriors, clad in shining armour and carrying ' thunder ', terrified the Aztecs. Their emperor, Montezuma, sent him presents and allowed him to enter Mexico. But the *conquistador* seized Montezuma in his palace and held him hostage; he confiscated his treasure and, meeting no opposition, established a kind of protectorate over Mexico.

Less than a year later, during a religious festival and in the absence of Cortés, his officers massacred and robbed several hundred people of standing. The population of Mexico rose in revolt. Cortes managed to restore order, but burning arrows hurled against the thatched roofs of the Spanish military posts were the signal for a new Mexican uprising. Montezuma intervened, and the Mexicans strangled him. After street fighting lasting several days, the Spaniards were compelled to flee in torrential rain across a narrow causeway between lagoons. Wounded, and forced to abandon his treasure, his cannon and his records, Cortés lost half his effective troops. His Indian mistress, Marina, tended him and gave him excellent advice. He strengthened his alliance with the coastal tribes, re-organised his forces, and led a horrifying punitive expedition against the Aztecs. Thirteen brigantines which he had had conveyed piece by piece from the port of Tlaxcala were launched on the lagoons, and he was thus enabled gradually to tighten his hold over the capital, Mexico. The starving town held out until August 1521. Guatemoc, Montezuma's successor, refused to give up his treasures and was immediately burned alive; the whole country then surrendered. In October 1522, Cortés became Captain-General of ' New Spain '. At first he was showered with honours by Charles V and given the title of Marquis of the Valley of Oaxaca; but he had to give up the direction of affairs in 1526, and ruined himself in expeditions carried out at his own expense in the north of Mexico (1530–36). He took part in the attack on Algiers in 1541, and spent the last years of his life in vain entreaties. Like Christopher Columbus and Vasco da Gama, he died in disgrace (September 1547).

From Mexico the Spaniards extended their sovereignty over Central America. It took them two years to gain control of Guatemala, Nicaragua and Honduras (1524–6). Less fortunate to the north of New Spain, they failed to establish themselves in the areas which today constitute California, Georgia, North and South Carolina. On their return to Mexico, a number of soldiers spoke of an Eldorado which, they said, was to be found in the country of the ' Redskins ', where they had managed to survive by passing themselves off as sorcerers. Impressed by their stories, an expedition led by De Soto set out from Florida in 1539 and, after incredible efforts and privations, reached the Mississippi, where De Soto died heartbroken at not having found the fabulous Seven Cities of Cibola (1542). A year later De Soto's followers returned to Tampico looking like ghosts. The Spaniards were so horrified by this setback that for the next twenty years they abandoned all thought of any new expedition to North America.

The empire of the Incas and the Quechuas of Peru

In the Andean highlands of South America the *conquistadores* came upon a highly organised empire, as they had in Mexico. The Quechuas, who occupied the territory now constituting Bolivia, Peru and Ecuador, lived under the absolute rule of a powerful dynasty known as the ' Children

A sixteenth-century Mexican wood sculpture. The Aztecs lived in an intensely religious society based on the fertility cycle and much of their art was devoted to representing the gods in highly stylised wood and stone figures. *Marburg*

Aztec gods were cruel, even those associated with nature, and this reflected the structure of the Aztec empire, based on conquest and a painstaking agriculture with crude implements. Human sacrifices were made to these gods. *Marburg*

The enormous wealth from the new colonies in America began to produce a characteristically ornate art. Churches were to benefit both in the mother countries and in the colonies, from which comes this Portuguese Virgin. *Bulloz* 37

An illustration from an Aztec history showing the four houses which made up the Aztec nation when it migrated from Aztlan in 1168. A chief is standing on an island in the middle of a lake. *British Museum*

Cortés engages the Aztecs in Mexico. After the Aztec drawings of Lienzo of Tlaxcala.

The Inca Atahualpa being stripped of his riches before Pizarro (1532). *Larousse*

of the Sun ' — the Incas. They were ignorant of the art of writing and used knotted string to count, yet they were learned in mathematics and astronomy; they did not use iron, wheels or arches. They fertilized their fields of maize and potatoes with guano, and terraced and irrigated them. Their taste in pottery was discerning, and as weavers they were ingenious. They built gigantic palaces and temples without using cement, covering the interior walls with gold plaques and brightly coloured fabrics. Their long paved roads linked the principal towns with their capital city, Cuzco.

The Quechuas lived under a totalitarian regime. The people, carefully counted each year and arranged in groups of a hundred, were supervised by a host of officials. They were forbidden to lock their doors, to hunt and fish where they liked, to move about without permission, or to marry outside their district. Clothes, meals, songs, work or pleasure — everything in their lives, even to the style of their hair — were subject to precise regulations. The State, which fed them in time of famine and during their journeys, distributed provisions, grain for sowing, material woven in their factories, and llamas from the stocks reared under State control. The State owned most of the land, and every year it undertook to distribute it among families.

Although the Quechuas indulged in continual war to spread the worship of the sun, they were not as cruel as the Aztecs. Dancing played the most prominent part in their ceremonies, and they sacrificed nothing but llamas, dogs and birds to their solar deities. Judging from some of their religious observances, such as the seclusion of consecrated virgins, the practice of penances and the public confession of sins, their religion was much more advanced than that of other American peoples.

Francisco Pizarro and the conquest of Peru

About ten years after the capture of Mexico, the empire of the Incas was destroyed by the Spaniards. During one of their enterprising excursions in the southern seas (1524 – 6) a certain Francisco Pizarro, a coarse adventurer from Estremadura, was struck by the use of gold on the walls of the temples of Túmbez, on the arms of women, and even in the meanest household implements. In association with a soldier of fortune like himself, one Diego de Almagro, he decided to secure possession of Peru. Charles V, encouraged by previous Mexican successes, finally bestowed on him the title of Captain-General, together with a charter to conquer 200 leagues of land (July 1529). Leaving Panama in February 1532, Pizarro established his base to the north of Guayaquil; on learning that the two sons of the Inca chief were quarrelling over power, he crossed the Andes with 168 men and 67 horses; the Quechuas, impressed by his firearms and surprised in the middle of a civil war, dared not resist him. The Inca Atahualpa, who succeeded in overcoming his brother, was caught in an ambush; the Spaniards killed his escort, took him prisoner and demanded a ransom of as much gold as could be contained in a vast room (November 1532). As Atahualpa agreed to be baptised, they were merciful enough to strangle him a few months later before delivering him up to the flames. Finding themselves in possession of a booty which exceeded all their expectations, the invaders were tempted to gamble, and set about fighting and killing each other. To get his army back into shape, Pizarro led it towards Cuzco, and

Cuzco, capital of the Peruvian Incas, the Children of the Sun. The Spaniards found in the Inca empire a civilised people skilled in feats of engineering and architecture. *Giraudon*

A map of South America commissioned by Henry IV. It clearly shows the state of geographical knowledge at the end of the sixteenth century. Success in exploration and colonial conquest during the early part of the century was largely confined to the coasts; the interior is conjectural. *Giraudon*

The ruins of Machu Picchu, a fortress-town of the Incas not far from Cuzco, built of massive rocks without cement. Such terrain hampered the *conquistadores*. *Rapho*

after hard fighting he took the town in November 1533. While he himself subdued the north, Almagro conquered the southern parts. In 1534, the cruelty of the *conquistadores* provoked a general uprising. Pizarro's brother, besieged in Cuzco for nearly two years, was relieved by reinforcements sent out from Mexico. In the course of reprisals the Spaniards butchered the whole male population of Quito, burned the town, and then massacred the women and children who returned to the ruins. Peru, which became known as New Castile, was henceforth regarded as subdued. The future Lima, founded along the coast as the 'City of Kings', became the new capital (1535).

Soon after the *conquistadores* became masters of Peru, they began to fight among themselves, and they all ended tragically. Hernando Pizarro had Almagro strangled in 1538, and his brother Francisco was assassinated by Almagro's veteran soldiers in 1541. Gonzales Pizarro, their brother, who for a while became absolute master of New Castile, was beheaded on the order of an envoy of Charles V (1548).

Having settled down in Peru, the Spaniards were able to occupy a large part of South America. Despite the resistance of some tribes who preferred collective suicide to submission, they seized the whole of Colombia, the future Nova Granada, where in 1539 they founded Santa Fe de Bogotá. Held in check by the formidable Araucanians, they barely managed to retain the northern coast of Chile. Beyond the Andes they reached Rio de la Plata. By 1534 Mendoza had established himself at Buenos Aires. The Indians of Patagonia and La Pampa, known as Braves, remained unsubdued.

The French expeditions

The Spaniards and the Portuguese met with no rivals. The English carried on piracy in European waters only. France had very little interest in colonial competition. French corsairs called at Brazil, the Cape, Madagascar and Sumatra; Fleury de Honfleur captured the caravels which were carrying the treasure of Cortés back to Spain. Jacques Cartier reached Labrador in 1534, and sailed up the St Lawrence River as far as Montreal (1535). The natives would hold up their children so that he might touch them, and would spend the night dancing in his honour around huge fires beside the river. During a third voyage he took possession of Canada (1541) and, believing it to be near the Far East, was astonished to find neither gold nor precious stones; insufficient backing for his enterprise led to its failure. By 1545 there were no Frenchmen left in North America.

The consequences of the great discoveries

Overseas discovery was one of the fundamental facts of the sixteenth century, in both the extent and the variety of its consequences. The flood of colonial wealth increased the scope of European economy. There took place a great shift in the pattern of trade routes; states bordering the Atlantic intensified their activities, while those which were exclusively Mediterranean lost power. Men began to size up the world; they were enriched by their knowledge, and their outlook was broadened. In the face of animals, plants, races, and even stars whose existence no one had so far suspected, science made bolder, more vigorous progress and scientific curiosity was rewarded by the practical uses to which discoveries were put.

Countries separated by thousands of miles of ocean were ruled by the same sovereign. Mere kingdoms like Spain and Portugal became empires. Their sovereigns were enabled to extend their authority infinitely farther than the world's greatest monarchs had ever been able to do, from the time of Alexander to Charlemagne. The sun never set on the empire of Charles V.

During a century of revival and awakening, Europe had drawn out of obscurity a vast territory where men seemed to be doomed by their isolation to slow evolution. Rudely snatched from the prehistoric, a new continent entered history. From now onwards every occurrence which affected it was a historical starting point; out of these beginnings great states and civilisations were to arise.

Freed now from the mythical forms which had concealed it, the world grew at once larger and smaller. Two absolutely new notions, the immensity and the unity of the world, asserted themselves simultaneously; the immensity of the world was, however, by far the most striking idea. The dramatic blood transfusion of the slave trade between Africa and the New World and the prolific mercantile traffic between Europe and Asia and between Europe and America were the first great links uniting the world.

THE ASIAN WORLDS

Asia itself was too huge, too divided for its history to form a coherent whole. Its principal divisions — Central Asia, Persia, India, China and Japan — were neither nations nor states, but complex civilisations, each with its own distinctive features, its own life, atmosphere and character.

Across the fertile areas of Western Asia, India and China, peasant masses, growing ever more numerous, dwelt under the sway either of tyrannical military feudal systems or of ancient and exhausted dynasties. On the boundless steppes and the mountains of Central Asia roamed ferocious nomadic empires, ever watchful, eager for battle and plunder, waiting only for an opportunity to pounce upon neighbouring peoples.

Early in the sixteenth century, without any concerted plan, some of these tribes returned to the kind of raid carried out by Jenghis Khan and Tamerlane. The red-headed dervishes of Ismail (Kizil-bashes) came to Persia and founded the Safavid Empire, destined to last until 1732. In India the Turks and the Afghans under Babar built up the Mogul Empire, which survived until 1837.

India and Persia remained weak powers under their new masters, who ruled from horseback what they had conquered on horseback. While the monarchies of Europe organised themselves on a national basis, Asia was still in the throes of military, religious and racial domination. Far from giving any precise character to its concepts of law and authority, these despotic regimes clung to obscure mystical notions of power which prevented them from creating modern states. The courts, harems, the cabals of eunuchs, the feudal gangs, the clans and the monasteries, more powerful and influential than institutions, played a complex and original part in Asia's history while continuing to cloud it over.

'A Dervish dansinge'. Turkish drawing from a book of miniatures representing the Habits of the Grand Signor's Court. c. 1620. *British Museum*

Pages relating to surgery from a Turkish medical treatise of the sixteenth century. Though still pre-occupied with holy wars in Persia and in Eastern Europe, the Turks did not neglect the sciences and the arts. *Giraudon*

Within their paralysing grip Asia remained bound to its barbaric and anarchic past. For Asia the sixteenth century was a continuation, not only of the fifteenth, but of all past medieval centuries. It experienced one or two bursts of energy, as in Japan, and an occasional assertion of vigour and individuality, as in Persia, but it knew nothing of the Renaissance.

Persia and the Safavid Empire

To ensure the triumph of the Shiite heretics, who regarded the descendants of Ali, son-in-law of the Prophet, as the sole masters of Islam, a small Turkish and Moslem sect from Azerbaijan — known as the Sufis — had striven since the middle of the fifteenth century to snatch Persia from Turco-Mongolian dominion. Ismail, the grandson of one of its first leaders, took over in due course the leadership of the independence movement. Along the southern frontiers of the Caucasus he imposed his authority on nomadic tribes of primitive and fanatic warriors, and by 1500 he had exterminated the hordes known as the White Sheep, who still held the west of Persia. The following year he entered Tabriz, had himself proclaimed Shah, and thus founded, as the heir of the Sufis, the Safavid dynasty. A daring raid from the mountains took him into the plains, where he seized Mosul, occupied Baghdad, one of the holy cities of Islam, and soon conquered the whole of rich Mesopotamia. Having established his capital at Ispahan, he took possession of Khorassan in 1510, and pushed the Uzbek tribes back towards Transoxiana. Persian unity was henceforth established from Afghanistan to Mesopotamia, and from the Caspian Sea to the Persian Gulf.

The two first Safavids, Ismail I (1501–29) and Tahmasp I (1529–76) were despotic masters of the life and property of their subjects. No one dared flout their orders, even when they became drunk or insane. Remaining true to the traditions of savage Asia, they made no attempt to strengthen the machinery of empire, whose soldiers and officials were recruited only from the seven Kizil-bash tribes. They retained their nomadic customs and character, and left the upbringing of their sons to the mountain people of Azerbaijan. Accompanied by thousands of camels carrying their carpets, chattels and treasures, as well as their harem

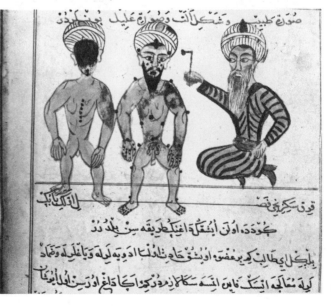

41

Persian miniature (c. 1600) showing worshippers at a fire-altar and before the shrine of an idol. Though officially and militantly adhering to the Sufi sect of Islam, other cultural influences were felt in Persia under the Safavids, and Zoroastrianism had survived since the ninth century.

A painting by Nigari of the sixteenth-century Turkish admiral Barbaros Hayrattiri. *Giraudon*

and their courtiers, they were constantly on the move across Persia to the rhythm of the seasons.

The Safavids were religious even more than military leaders; they were holy figures, attributed with supernatural powers. A bowl of water was immediately sanctified when they dipped their hands into it. As Shiites, they no more recognised the legitimacy of the Caliphs than they believed in the death of the last descendant of Ali. They were convinced that the twelfth Imam was hidden in some mysterious grotto; and that, reappearing like the morning sun, he would emerge at the end of time to ensure the triumph of justice. The Safavids considered themselves the trustees of his power, and they never failed to keep a horse saddled and harnessed in the stables against the day of his return. By virtue of the divine right with which they considered themselves invested, they controlled the powerful theocracy of their faith, and, by merciless persecutions, strove to banish Sunnism from their empire.

While in Europe the Protestants and the Catholics were parting company, the Shiites of Persia and the Ottomans of Asia Minor were already fighting each other in religious wars, despite the fact that they were brothers by race. The Turks treated the sovereigns of Ispahan as 'red-headed rabble', and had them condemned to death by the Ulemas (Moslem theologians). To provoke them into war, they sent them insulting despatches and women's clothes. They also sent the Safavids a chalice, a stick, a monk's cowl, and a toothpick, as a bitter reminder of their priestly origin. Since, according to the Turks, the death of one Shiite was more pleasing to Allah than that of seventy Christians, they waged a war of extermination. Attacked in the east by the fanatical Uzbeks of Transoxiana, the Persians were obliged to fight on two fronts and frequently had to resort to scorched-earth tactics. Their cavalrymen were protected by shining steel helmets adorned with feathers; they were armed with bows and lances, and mounted on horses caparisoned in coats of mail. They therefore found it difficult, despite their courage, to withstand the accurate fire of the Turkish cannon.

Attacked by the Sultan Selim in 1513, Ismail was heavily defeated at the battle of Chaldiran, in which he lost his throne adorned with pearls, his elephants and his harem (1514). Compelled successively to abandon Tabriz, Azerbaijan and Mosul, his position became so desperate that he turned for help to Charles V — one of the most implacable enemies of the Moslem faith. The death of Selim in 1519 gave Ismail a little respite. Shah Tahmasp, Ismail's son, was less fortunate: he lost Baghdad in 1535 and, twenty years later, under the treaty of Amasya, had to yield Mesopotamia to Sulaiman the Magnificent. The Shiites obtained only paltry compensation — access to the holy cities of Islam. Peace still hung in the balance.

The long wars which Persia was compelled to wage did not impede her economic development. Freed from the paralysing supremacy of Turcoman feudalism, the country became one of the most lively commercial crossroads of Asia. Herat took advantage of the reopening of caravan traffic. Ispahan, whose inhabitants already numbered nearly 500,000, recreated the former magnificence of Persepolis. Never before had Persian art attained such splendour. Wide open to the most diverse foreign influences — Venetian, Arab, Hindu and Chinese — it responded to the demands of a cultured court, a society taken up with the sensuous pleasures of living. Its love of the concrete lured it further and further away from the rigid and abstract, which characterised traditional Moslem art. The skill of Persian artists was especially emphasised in small-scale work and illuminated design, even more than in architecture, though in this sphere they produced slender and graceful masterpieces. Bihzad and all the artists of the Tabriz school, careful as they were of elegance and precision, produced work of delicate colouring in which they depicted scenes of chivalry, love and court life.

While Urfi and Moktachan rediscovered the lyrical inspiration of the great Hafiz, numerous epic poets extolled the sufferings of Ali or celebrated the victories of the Shiites over the Sunnites. Under the domination of the Turco-Mongols, Persia managed to preserve its culture, language and religion. Proud of traditions which went back to the time of the Achaemenidae, it became the only Asian country which developed, if not a thorough-going patriotism on the European pattern, at least a vigorous national pride. While constantly evolving a distinct person-ality, it still remained a weak power, harassed along all its frontiers by ruthless enemies. Its delicate and lavish civil-isation was always in danger of the fate which dramatically overtook the great American civilisations after the arrival of the *conquistadores*.

India, Babar the Tiger and the Mogul Empire

India, half the size of Europe and possessing perhaps 100 million inhabitants, was not a true empire at the beginning of the sixteenth century. Ruled for the most part by Moslem military feudal overlords who oppressed the passive Hindu masses, it was divided into several inefficiently organised states, hostile to each other and all equally incapable of achieving unity. Between the inde-pendent kingdoms,of Gujrat to the west and Bengal to the east, the Sultanate of Delhi occupied almost the whole of the Indo-Gangetic plain. Its Afghan sovereigns, the Lodi, were committed to a ceaseless struggle with a trouble-some nobility. Five small Moslem principalities shared the centre of the Deccan. The wealth and increasing weakness of India roused the cupidity of its neighbours. The fierce wandering tribes of Asia, recalling the Turco-Mongolian excursion of 1398, waited for an opportunity to invade.

Babar the Tiger became Sultan of Ferghana in 1494, at eleven years of age, and was driven from his kingdom in 1501. A true descendant of Tamerlane through his father, he dreamed only of aggression. His first troops were a handful of men, whom he led from adventure to adventure, disciplining them and teaching them military tactics. His qualities as a strategist, to say nothing of his energy and cruelty, enabled him to invade Afghanistan and establish himself in Kabul (1504) and in Kandahar (1507).

Although he humoured his disorderly bands, and had only to follow the instincts of his race to conduct himself as a leader of his troops, Babar had not the unpolished, rough temperament of the nomad tribes. He was a gay companion, loving wine and exotic fruit, banquets and feasting. With great curiosity and a keen intellect, he took an interest in everything — the ways of animals, the countryside, irrigation processes, or the method of counting the hours. He loved music, was a witty conver-sationalist, and a studious prince who patronised the arts; he himself wrote poetry. His *Memoirs* were written in a precise and vigorous style, marked by sincerity and vitality.

Babar the Tiger (1483-1530) receiving a state visitor. Though a skilled military leader, Babar was not really interested in the Mogul Empire which he had founded, for he was spirit-ually attached to Persia and had a passion for Persian cultural tradition.

Chinese embroidery showing donors before a shrine of Buddha on the Vulture Peak. Alone in the sixteenth-century world, the Ming Empire practised religious toleration: Buddhists, Taoists and Neo-Confucians lived side by side. This age of tranquillity also produced great work in the graphic arts. *British Museum*

Babar regarded Persia as a kind of spiritual fatherland; imbued with its culture, he was attracted by the high degree of civilisation, its beautiful landscapes and its way of life. The decline of the Turcoman feudal system stimulated his ambition to conquer the country; but the success of the Uzbeks of Transoxiana, and still more the arrival of the Safavids, obliged him to give up his plans. His conquest of the Afghan passes had long before opened up the route to the Indus, and he now reluctantly decided to seize Hindustan which, as a descendent of Tamerlane, he could regard as an inheritance. The fabulous Koh-i-noor diamond, ' the Mountain of Light ' — symbol of the wealth of the Hindu palaces — exercised over the minds of his soldiers a great fascination, just as at the same period the treasure of the Incas enthralled the minds of Pizarro's companions. Babar tried to forget his beguiling Iranian dream, and on two occasions invaded the Panjab in answer to an appeal from his uncle, who had rebelled against Ibrahim, Sultan of Delhi. In 1526 he crossed the Indus with an army that, including servants and merchants, was only 12,000 strong. He came upon his enemies in the plain of Panipat, on the road from Khyber to Delhi, and immediately disposed his forces behind a long line of waggons firmly joined together. As soon as the Sultan's elephants and cavalry had hurled themselves against this obstruction, the fire from his cannon cut them to pieces and a hail of arrows struck them on both wings. He closed in on them and finally routed them by a decisive flank charge. Ibrahim and 15,000 of his men were killed. Three days later Babar entered Delhi, received the Koh-i-noor, and was proclaimed Padishah of India.

At once the Afghan emirs and the Rajput princes buried their quarrels and united against him. Commanded by the veteran Rana Sanga, 100,000 men, recruited on the spot, prepared to repel him. His allies were on the point of betraying him; even his soldiers, wearied after their long excursions, thought only of retreating to the mountains. Against the advice of his officers he decided to proceed with the battle, and sent to Ferghana for 3,000 archers. He harangued his troops and revived their courage; then, with his hand on the Koran, he swore before them never to drink wine again if he vanquished the enemy. His fortune and the fate of India were decided on that day, 16 March 1527, at Khanua, near Agra. First, his ' Lions of the Forest of Valour ' stood firm against the disorderly mass attack of the Hindus; then, passing over to the offensive, they scattered them far and wide. Enemy corpses lay in heaps — there were pyramids of severed heads. It took fierce siege warfare, however, to break the Rajput confederacy. Wherever the Rajputs considered themselves beaten, they burned their women and children alive in the underground passages of their citadels and then went to die on their battlements. In May 1529, when the Bengal chiefs in their turn were overcome, the rule of Babar extended from the Oxus to Bengal, and from the northern Deccan to the Himalayas.

The Great Mogul had no love for his empire. He was a Turk by nationality, a Moslem by religion, a Persian by culture and a nomad at heart. Since he despised the Hindus he cared little if they remained defenceless against poverty, famine and devastation by outlaws. He regarded himself as the leader of an army of occupation, and ruled rather than governed; despite his statesmanlike qualities, his supple intellect and his keen sense of reality, he made no attempt to profit from his conquest or to organise the country. Worn out by his excesses, or perhaps poisoned, he died on 25 December 1530, at the age of forty-seven.

His son Humayun, who succeeded him, was less gifted than his father, but none the less cultivated. Yet he would climb from rock to rock while assaulting fortresses and was even known to gouge out the eyes of the conquered with his own hands. For all that he was not another ' Tiger '; through over-indulgence in opium he continually passed from a state of rapture to torpor. Although his name meant ' the Happy One ', his reign was simply a gloomy succession of disasters. His great vassals rebelled and his brothers snatched valuable territory from him. In 1540 a Bengal sultan, Sher Khan, who had remained faithful to the cause of Lodi, drove him from India; for ten years he wandered across the wastes of Rajputana. Seeking refuge in Persia, he managed to obtain from Tahmasp a small army by promising to embrace the Shiite faith, and taking advantage of the state of anarchy in India when Sher Khan died in 1554 he recaptured Delhi and re-established his empire (June 1555). As a fitting end to an unhappy life, he killed himself falling down the stairs of his library in January of the following year. The tomb which he had built during his lifetime constitutes the only successful achievement of his reign, since it is considered to be one of the marvels of Moslem architecture.

During Humayun's long absence India had benefited from the wise administration of Sher Khan. Land had been re-distributed and the burden of taxation more evenly shared. A 1,500-mile road, dotted with caravanserai, linked the Panjab and Bengal. Nevertheless, the Mogul Empire was still unhappy, unstable and poorly organised, and the conquering nomads were precariously superimposed on the hostile Hindu masses. When Akbar, the fourteen-year-old son of Humayun, took over control of the Empire, it had still not emerged from its age of conquest to become a unified political whole.

The Middle Empire and the Ming Dynasty

While new suzerainties were taking root in Persia and India, the old Ming Dynasty succeeded in maintaining its position in China despite the inefficiency of its emperors. Ching-Ti (1506–22), who came to power at fifteen years of age, and Kea-Tsing (1522–66) soon lost all their vigour under the influence of the harem. They were bound by the most rigid traditions and incapable of putting an end to the everlasting rivalry of their wives and concubines; defenceless against a court which had grown more and more overcrowded, unruly and spendthrift, they led a very secluded life in their palaces at Peking in the very centre of the ' Purple Forbidden City '. They usually chose eunuchs as their ministers and counsellors, and allowed them to gorge themselves with wealth. The sovereigns' exercise of authority over their extensive fiefs was merely theoretical: the princes of the imperial family dispensed justice and gathered round them a train of dependants.

Though their title of ' Sons of Heaven ' gave them omnipotence and the right to deal severely with all who might dispute their supremacy, their well-defined concept of government precluded their acting as real despots. Since their social laws were reputed to emanate solely from universal and harmonious order, they depended entirely on their indefinable, mystic prestige to ensure obedience from

Galloping horses. Persian. The cultural influence of Persia in the early sixteenth-century extended over much of Asia. *British Museum*

A Japanese holy man contemplating the exhalation of his spirit. Religion became a potent force in sixteenth-century Japan, for not only were the Mikados considered great priests, but the monasteries monopolised education, inculcating in the nobility a spirit of endurance. *British Museum*

the Chinese people. Their edicts were exhortations rather than commands. The very idea of monarchical power in the European manner, based on a solid foundation and supported by sound institutions, was absolutely foreign to their minds. Their empire had no State police, no independent tribunals or municipal services. Both its financial system and its army were rudimentary. Officials were too few, and they spent more time supervising the moral life of the people than they did in administration.

Loosely governed, China retired more and more within itself. The Mings had attempted during the fourteenth century to take possession of Indochina and to send fleets towards Java, Calicut, Ceylon and Hormuz. Through lack of interest or helplessness rather than wisdom they threw up all idea of conquest, abandoned naval expeditions, gave up insisting on the payment of tribute by Ceylon, and allowed Tibet to break away gradually from their empire. The elusive Japanese pirates could haunt the Chinese shores with impunity; Mongolian bands, re-organised by Dayan, a descendant of Jenghis Khan, were able to camp on the Ordos plateau, harassing the north-west frontiers, and waiting for an opportunity to penetrate in force into the plains of Hopeh. Ching-Ti undertook to fight them merely as a distraction for a few months from his dull and lonely debauchery. Kea-Tsing at first hoped to hold them by strengthening the Great Wall, and then opened up two markets to them. He was, however, eventually compelled to sever all relations with them because of their bad faith; by 1543 he was ignoring their threats altogether, and declined to take action even when they invaded Shansi or burned the outskirts of Peking (1544).

The Ming Empire was not troubled by religious wars any more than it was interested in wars of conquest. While in India the Moslems were fighting the Hindus, Islam was concerned with the rivalries of the Shiites and the Sunnites, and the Christians of Europe were conducting distant crusades, driving back the Infidel or destroying their own unity, China was the only great nation in the world where the existence of different creeds involved no conflict. Orderly, peaceful, eclectic in their spiritual life, and unequivocal in mental outlook, the Chinese people were more concerned about rites than about dogma, and always well disposed towards varying forms of worship. They left fanaticism to the uncivilised, and were unable to see the merits of intolerance.

China enjoyed a tranquillity that Persia, India and Japan never knew; it was only superficially disturbed by the revolts of its great lords. Despite the burden of taxation, especially that on salt, the peasants were resigned to their poverty. Their patient efforts were sometimes rendered vain by a growing birthrate — so rapid, in fact, that foreigners thought that Chinese women had children every month, or that they always gave birth to quintuplets. Unable to support its 53 million inhabitants, China was as powerless against famine as against the floods of the Yangtze-kiang or Hwang-ho.

However great the weakness of the Ming Empire might have been, there was no question of its decadence. Its thousand-year-old civilisation retained all its lustre; it had no need of a Renaissance to help it to blossom out. The novel assumed its classical form; dramatic art developed. Rejecting the dry materialism of the Neo-Confucians, Wan Yang denied that reason was capable of attaining truth; men, according to him, would not return to the

45

pure inner light without developing their moral intuition through a never-ending spiritual struggle. Taoists wrote of their search after the absolute in terms resembling those of Pascal. Other Chinese turned to Buddhism under the influence of the Buddhist school of Makayana. In the pictorial arts, incomparable paintings of scenes of everyday life were closely linked with the spiritual life — funerary portraits, scenes of the women's apartments, silhouettes of women, landscapes and birds. Though Chinese potters never forsook the use of the camel-hair brush, partridge feathers and luminous celadons, since 1521 they had been using a blue imported from Moslem Persia, and from then on they were to produce pieces in three or five colours, in which their technical virtuosity reached its perfection.

Feudal Japan under the Ashikagas

Isolated in its archipelago, sixteenth-century Japan was a feudal state which had gradually become a jumble of minor principalities, where poverty and anarchy reigned as a result of unending warfare. A series of lazy emperors was followed by a series of phantom emperors. The Mikados, or Children of the Sun, were looked upon as great priests, religious leaders, whose functions as rulers were merely honorary. To support themselves they were obliged to sell the prayers which they wrote in their own ornamental handwriting, and from 1521 onwards they ceased to appear in public at all; so that when they were not taking refuge in monasteries, they lived more or less unknown in the Gosho of Kyoto, surrounded exclusively by women. When their palace was burnt down, it was rebuilt without exterior walls, and stood behind a ridiculous symbolical bamboo fence.

The mayors of the palace, called shoguns and belonging to the Ashikaga family, kept a tight hold on the Mikados, and were regarded as the real masters of Japan; but even their authority was purely nominal. The great lords never succeeded in making their vassals obey them. The feudal hierarchy was in decay at the top. Authority was transferred from the central government to the barons; some of these *daimyos* were of noble descent, others were parvenus or land thieves. While they were for ever rebelling against their overlords or the shoguns, they managed to secure from their own vassals fanatical devotion; and they were continually leading into battle their *samurai* — those faithful two-sabre followers with their fierce faces who were ever in search of quarry. The *daimyos* never failed to support disorder, but they maintained a ruthless discipline on their own estates; they even had a code of honour and, like chivalrous highwaymen, righted other people's wrongs in the intervals between raids.

The Buddhist monks, whose hundred thousand monasteries were like little feudal states, monopolised education and played an important part in the evolution of Japanese thought. They taught the sons of the *daimyos* the religion practised by the sect known as Zen. Under the influence of this rigid contemplative doctrine the Japanese arrived at a complete suppression of his ego and, believing himself capable of overcoming imponderable forces and probing the schemes of his enemies, he loved violence, despised death, and thought only of mastering himself or enjoying a destiny of never-ending victories. The lesser nobility thus acquired an unrivalled morale. Though the kind of life led by the *daimyos* was foreign to that of the great feudal chiefs whose sons did not frequent the monasteries, its influence spread over the whole Japanese people. The Empire of the Rising Sun, despite the formidable forces which threatened it with disintegration, managed in this way to preserve an enormous amount of nervous energy. Feudal anarchy gave it a character quite different from that of Europe in the twelfth century. The slow crumbling of authority did not diminish its political healthiness; nor did it induce the surrender of its will or the weakness characteristic of the Ming Empire during the same period.

Further, the Japanese civilisation showed no sign of decadence. The *No* lyric drama was given new life by the addition of dialogue to the sacred dances which recalled in mime old legends. Painting encountered Chinese influences without sacrificing its own character. The aristocratic school of Tosa provided brilliant painters, who handled with extraordinary precision themes borrowed from romances based on chivalry. The sons and disciples of Kano Massanobu derived their inspiration from nature itself; their bold realism did not preclude serenity.

AFRICA IN THE EARLY SIXTEENTH CENTURY

Europeans of the Renaissance period regarded Africa as a closed, hostile and mysterious world, peopled with bird-men, beings who were half-monkey and half-man, monsters of every description — a world which had stood still since the early days of man. The events which took place in Africa were of limited importance in the general upheaval

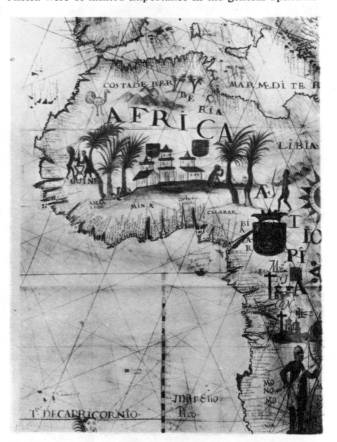

Fragment of a mid-sixteenth-century map of Africa by the famous cartographer Guillaume le Testu. The age of discovery was also an age of spectacular progress in the geographical and cartographical sciences. *Larousse*

which marked the advent of modern times. They included the rise of the Songhoi Empire, the pagan resistance to Islam, the Abyssinian wars, the rise and fall of subordinate kingdoms, and the tentative efforts of Europeans to penetrate into dark Africa.

The empires of Negro Islam

A conquering religion, Islam discovered a vast field for expansion in the open savanna lands south of the Sahara; it encouraged the formation of great Nigerian empires by imparting to the Negroes of the Sudan a taste for power and adventure.

In the western Sudan the Mali emperors were not as influential as might have been supposed from their impressive retinue of eunuchs, musicians, executioners and court fools. Their empire, which in the fourteenth century stretched from the Sahara to the equatorial forest-belt, gradually receded before the attacks of its neighbours. In 1534 it barely escaped collapse. In 1546 the Songhoi sacked the imperial palace before leaving the capital.

In the area around the middle Niger, Mohammed Turre, who founded the Askia dynasty at Gao in 1492, swelled the power of the Songhoi. This splendid prince required seventy leopard-skin bags to hold his robes; during the pilgrimage he made to Mecca from 1495 to 1497, he gave away in alms 300,000 pieces of gold. A remarkable organiser, he created four viceroys, and established administrative offices in the larger centres, a police force, a regular system of taxation, and standard weights and measures. Under his initiative the middle course of the Niger was canalised, agriculture was safeguarded, the Jews who had been driven from Tuat were provided with land, and trade was developed with visiting merchants from Tripolitania. He established a standing army, and added a flotilla. He was of a warlike and temperamental disposition, and embarked on a great number of wars according to his whim. His title of 'Representative of the Prince of the Faithful', bestowed on him by the Caliph of Egypt, did not prevent him from sometimes attacking Moslem principalities. Though unsuccessful in his war with the Mossi (1497–8), he conquered Zaherma, Bagana and Dandi (1500), and invaded the Mali Empire (1505). As the result of a daring raid against the Tuaregs, Agadès was ceded to him. His lengthy old age was disturbed by domestic intrigue; stricken with blindness, he abdicated in 1528 and died a year later. Ishak I (1539–49) failed to re-establish order. The Songhoi Empire did not regain its splendour until the accession of Askia David, who reigned from 1549 to 1582.

Since the fourteenth century the country's reputation for wealth had constantly grown. A saying of the time ran: 'Against prickly heat, use tar; against poverty, take a journey to the Sudan'. Caravans from the Maghrib frequented its markets. Gold from Bambouk was brought to Gao in the form of powder. The Negro gold-washers, who were anxious to keep their secret, declared that it came from a plant uprooted in the month of August, or from the droppings of a large cat which had lived on blood. The salt-pans of Taghezza and Taoudenni were extremely valuable since the scarcity of salt obliged the natives to extract a substitute for it from cow-dung. Moreover, the Songhoi towns were centres of Islamic culture. The Maghrib civilisation took root at Gao,

An ivory mask, probably representing a king in Benin, southern Nigeria. Benin and other coastal states retained their independence despite the establishment of Portuguese trading stations. *British Museum*

Oualata and Djenne. Timbuktu was proud of its university and its long line of jurists, the Ben Baba. The Mauritanian and Sudanese Marabout priests, to whom were attributed a remarkable life-giving force which they communicated through their spittle, soon became legendary characters. It was said, for instance, that when Sidi Ahmed commanded the lions to go away, they all left the Oualata region. He became known as 'the Weeper' as the result of one of his prayers being left unanswered; according to legend, when he was exhumed eight years after his death, tears were still flowing down his beard.

Central Sudan

Despite the zeal of proselytisers, Islam made little progress in central Sudan. In the Hausa Confederation only the merchants and the princes were Moslems. To the east of Chad, the Darfur and Wadai regions remained pagan, as did Bagirmi, which was founded about the year 1500 by an adventurer and organised by the *mbang* Mal (1546–61).

The spread of Islam, a religion of wide scope and doctrine, came to a temporary halt as it neared the Atlantic. It had reached the edge of the savanna, where tropical forests constituted a dividing wall. Since the caravan from the Maghrib had no need to pass beyond the Sudanese markets which were largely supplied from the south, they could no longer contribute towards the growth of Islam. Pagan populations stood in the way of its progress. The two Mossi states of the Upper Volta clung to their traditions and their deep-rooted feudal system. In their struggles

47

against the Songhoi, the Baribas of Borgou had acquired a reputation as excellent fighters. The Peuls (Fulani), wandering stock-breeders, had emigrated from Mauretania towards the Senegal and Niger Rivers. These easy-going and shrewd half-breeds still resisted all Moslem influence.

The failure of Islam in Abyssinia

While pagan resistance in the western regions of Africa remained firm, the old Christian kingdom of Abyssinia, a mighty mountain bulwark between Egypt and the Red Sea, was on the point of being submerged beneath the waves of Islam, which beat against it from all sides. In 1517, the Turkish occupation of Egypt made its position precarious. Fanatical Moslems from the Red Sea coast acquired firearms before Abyssinia. Led by the cruel Mohammed Granye (the 'Left-handed'), they invaded and sacked the central and southern provinces. In 1538, the holy town of Axum was burned down. The Negus of Abyssinia, Lebna Dangheb ('The Perfume of the Holy Virgin') fled to Gondar, and the kingdom seemed lost. For the great Christian communities, however, Abyssinia had ceased to be a myth. The Portuguese, in an attempt to realise their century-old dream of tracing the legendary 'Prester John', sent their first ambassadors to the Negus Eskander (1478–95). Lebna Dangheb made Bermudez, a Portuguese Catholic, the Primate of his Church and sent to Europe in search of aid. In Lisbon, John III agreed to send him 450 musketeers; these troops passed through Massawa, on the Red Sea, where the Portuguese had a settlement, and reached Abyssinia in 1541, a year after the Negus's death. With their assistance Glaodios (1540–60) was able to defeat Mohammed Granye, who was killed in 1543. The Moslem drive was decisively halted for the first time in two hundred years and was destined never to regain its impetus. Abyssinia remained 'the land of Christ', but its Monophysite Christianity, influenced by Jewish beliefs, kept it tied to the Coptic Church. It remained to be seen whether, under pressure from its liberators, it would return to the authority of Rome.

The Nile regions and the Gulf of Guinea

The history of the rest of Africa was still little known. The area around the Nile was disturbed. In Nubia pagans destroyed the Coptic kingdom of Merowe (1504). Between the White Nile and the Blue Nile the King of Sennar subdued the Fung. To the south of Abyssinia the idolaters of Kaffa repelled the Somali Moslems during the reign of Modi Gafa who, like all the kings of his dynasty, remained in the background. The Shilluk from Lake Rudolf founded along the White Nile the first kingdom to be set up by Nilotic peoples. From the Upper Nile the Hima stock-breeders moved down towards the Great Lakes. The most wealthy of these peoples — the Nkole — used to offer a child in sacrifice at the start of a new reign, and also renewed their drum-heads — to them symbols of royal power. The formidable Masai owed their power to a semi-military organisation in which youth played the dominant part.

Around the Gulf of Guinea very few communities spread beyond the stage of family groups. The Temnes moved out from the interior about the year 1500, and founded a kingdom in Sierra Leone. They maintained their traditions, one of which was the practice of killing their king as soon as he became ill; they would then place on his headless body the mummified head of his predecessor. In Dahomey a dissident group around Abomey and Porto Novo succeeded in cutting themselves off from the rest of the Adja, who remained within the Ardre kingdom. In Nigeria the Yoruba strengthened their system of urban life, and a remarkable civilising impulse which had started in Ife reached the principality of Benin in the south.

The Bantu country

Across the Benue River, in the Bantu country, which comprised a third of Africa, dwelt a number of tribes, organised on a federal basis and possessing the rough framework of a political system. They were Loango, between Ogooue and the Congo; the Congo farther south; the N'dongo in Angola; the ancient kingdom of Monomotapa in Southern Rhodesia and Mozambique. All these states had become relatively powerful by the time the Portuguese arrived, but slowly drifted towards disintegration because of the shortcomings of their sovereigns. New kingdoms appeared and two among the great number of tribes grew in importance. These tribes were the Babuka, among whom a man would carry the king on his back so that the king's feet might not scorch the earth; and the giant Bateke, who with their long canoes made ceaseless raids which terrorised the coastal areas. Across the Zambezi River the Bantu of the south-east drove the Hottentots and Bushmen towards the south.

The Portuguese in Negro Africa

From the end of the fifteenth century contact had been established between Europe and the dark-skinned races of Africa. The Portuguese built up trading stations in the Congo along the Gold Coast and the Zambezi River, and their missionaries preached the Gospel to the Bantu. Afonso (1507–46), the Christian king of the Congo, maintained a correspondence in Latin with Rome, made his son the first Negro bishop (1520), and filled his capital — which he renamed San Salvador — with stone churches. Europeans met innumerable obstacles to their efforts to penetrate into the dark heart of Africa. They had to contend with a treacherous coastline, immense forests, malaria, and the poverty of these areas. On other continents they had met and overcome similar difficulties, possibly because of their impatience to reach Asia, or to exploit the fabulous wealth of the New World. They displayed little interest, however, in their African enterprises; it was perhaps to justify their reluctance and their lackadaisical approach to the problems that they treated them as formidable. The reaction of the natives was evident in the fact that they adhered all the more firmly to their primitive ideas. The pressure exercised by Europe on the Negro world, like the drive against the Moslems, served only to harden Africa in its determination to remain isolated at the very moment when the strongest ties were uniting other parts of the globe, and when the vast expanse of America was opening to Europeans.

CHAPTER THREE

EUROPE FROM 1559 TO 1600

In Europe the second half of the sixteenth century had not the splendour and richness of the first; it was a time of continuations — a period of consolidation which held no further great surprises. The instinctive vigour and youthfulness which marked the appearance of modern times lost their initial momentum, as the new movements lost their impetus or met with revitalised opposition.

Having modified the structure and political face of Western Europe, creating modern nations out of certain states, the spirit of revival failed to spread across the whole of Europe. Germany remained in chaos; the 'Germanic' Holy Roman Empire was an archaic feudal structure. The proud House of Austria abandoned its pretensions to supremacy after the death of Charles V, and failed to take up again the task of uniting its ill-assorted domains begun by Maximilian I at the start of the century. Venice alone kept up an appearance of semi-independence in a disintegrated Italy, which was now half-Spanish and impoverished.

Absolutism declined in the country in which it had been most firmly established: France was ravaged by thirty years of civil war, known as the Wars of Religion, which imperilled royal power and the Valois dynasty. In two other Western countries, however, the monarchies gathered strength because they were able to maintain unity of faith. Catholic Spain under Philip II and Protestant England under Elizabeth became the leaders in the game of European politics; the rivalry between these two dominated the history of this period. Spanish preponderance was achieved only with great efforts, and showed signs of being unable to last very long. Elizabeth's England began to pursue a destiny apart: as a maritime power, she remained outside Europe; with the beginnings of an industrial structure, she was already ahead of the century.

The Council of Trent recognised the rupture of Christian unity, thus opposing the Catholic south of Europe to the Protestant north. While the Lutheran movement consolidated itself in Germany, and the separated Churches took on a national character in the Scandinavian countries and in England, the Roman Church managed to pull itself together: it disciplined itself before returning to the attack in the Counter-Reformation.

Humanism and the Renaissance movement began to lose their vigour. Italian art declined. The flowering of Shakespearian England and the 'Golden Age' of Spain were belated revivals. Finally, although the progress of science during the sixteenth century was such that the period might be described as 'modern', its vacillations suggest that the Europe of Copernicus and Nostradamus was closer to the Middle Ages than to the Age of Enlightenment.

Frederick II of Denmark maintained Danish supremacy in the north by defeating Sweden in 1570 after seven years of war. He suppressed piracy in the Baltic Sea, fostered order and industry at home and was immensely popular. *Wallace Collection*

D

German halberds of the sixteenth century. *Victoria & Albert Museum*

FRANCE AND THE WARS OF RELIGION: 1562-98

After the death of Henry II (1559), the important question was no longer whether the new sovereigns of France — who were mere children — would carry on the work of organisation begun by their predecessors, but whether they could maintain the Catholic faith in a country where, from its very beginning, Protestantism had been so vigorous.

Continually reinvigorated by the blood of its martyrs, the Reformation had established itself over a third of France. Despite the Sorbonne and the *Parlement*, 2,500 churches were already holding synods. Protestantism had become firmly established in Picardy, Normandy, Poitou, Dauphiné and Languedoc, at first among the working and middle classes, then among the high nobility. This changed its nature. The nobles who followed the new religion were born soldiers, sometimes ambitious but more often inclined to be critical of the authorities, and they organised Calvinism in a party spirit. Eager for battle, they could count on two resolute leaders of noble lineage: Admiral Gaspard de Coligny and Prince Louis of Condé. The powerful Guise family, who were fiercely devoted to the Catholic faith, were afraid that Coligny and Condé would use the religious conflict in order to gain power; around the Guises, therefore, a determined Catholic party was set up. Religious hatred was inflamed by family rivalries. Francis, Duke of Guise, and his brother Charles, the richest prelate in the kingdom, profited by the weakness of their nephew, Francis II, to apply the edicts against the Protestants with extreme severity. A rash conspiracy by Condé at Amboise led to his arrest. At this moment Francis II died.

Catherine de' Medici, Charles IX, and the massacre of St Bartholomew

Catherine de' Medici, who became regent when Francis II died in December 1560, was anxious to shake off Guise control. An ungainly Italian woman, with large protruding eyes and an easy laugh, Catherine was rather a sceptic in religious matters; superficially she was engrossed in entertaining, hunting and astrology, but she had a taste for intrigue, a passion for power and the keenest ambition for her young son Charles IX. To avoid a war in which the victor would most certainly be in a position to impose his will on the sovereign, she sought a compromise by meetings at Poissy between representatives of both religions. Her Chancellor, Michel de l'Hôpital, whose sole concern was to defend the legal rights of the Crown, launched moving appeals for unity. An edict gave Huguenots limited rights of worship and enraged Catholics. On 1 March 1562, the soldiers of the Duke of Guise massacred a number of Protestants gathered at their place of worship near Vassy. Condé at once called the Protestants to arms in self-defence.

A confused and bitter war, interrupted by brief respites, lacerated France for eight years. Francis of Guise was assassinated by a Protestant in 1563; the Prince of Condé by a Catholic in 1569. The nobility rediscovered its feudal tastes, and the common townspeople their revolutionary instincts; both usually lost sight of the religious character of the conflict. Catherine pursued a policy of opportunism, but became convinced that France was Catholic at heart. The Protestants were encouraged by the peace of St Germain (August 1570) which allowed substantial concessions to the Huguenot nobles. Their new leader, Henry of Navarre, married Margaret of Valois, sister of Charles IX. Coligny was reinstated with all his hereditary dignities. This fine, handsome veteran was an honourable nobleman and prudent politician; a dreamer as well as a man of action, he hoped to push France into a new war against Spain to enable Frenchmen to forget their own quarrels. The contemptible Charles listened to him and waxed enthusiastic about his plans. Catherine, for her part, fearing the complications that war might entail and the loss of influence over her son, drew close to the Guise faction, who decided to assassinate Admiral Coligny.

On 22 August 1572 Coligny was wounded by a shot as he was leaving the Louvre. Charles IX visited him at once and determined to avenge him. The Queen Regent, threatened with discovery, tried to save herself by convincing the king of the existence of a Calvinist plot; she begged him to authorise a massacre of the Huguenot leaders by the Guise. Finally, after hours of discussion, she dragged from him his consent: 'Yes, kill them; but kill them all. Do not leave anyone to reproach me.'

Just before dawn on Sunday, August 24, the Feast of St Bartholomew, a band of ruffians attacked the Admiral in his house; they disembowelled him with their swords and threw him out of the window, naked and still alive. The

The massacre of St Bartholomew, August 1572, a three-day massacre of French Protestants sanctioned by Charles IX. In spite of this slaughter, only a year later the Protestants were granted liberty of conscience. *Mansell*

tocsin was rung and a savage manhunt began. Protestants were shot on the roof-tops; they were butchered in their beds, run to earth in the Louvre, and even in the bedroom of Margaret of Navarre. For three days they were stabbed, drowned, hanged, and their bodies dragged along the streets. The massacre was soon followed by looting. Similar scenes took place at Orleans, Lyon, Rouen, Bordeaux and Toulouse. But the massacre was as useless as it was tragic. The Protestants took up the fight again. The Peace of La Rochelle of July 1573 conceded them full liberty of conscience and moderates had joined their cause.

Henry III, Henry of Guise and the League

Charles IX died in May 1574. Henry III was more intelligent, more cultured, but just as unprepossessing as his brother. He was easy-going, affable and eccentric; he surrounded himself with effeminate favourites and attended balls disguised as a woman. At other times he would think of nothing but death, and take part in processions with his head covered with a penitent's hood. He lost what little prestige the monarchy retained. Henry of Navarre reconstituted the Protestant party under the name of the Calvinist Union. Catholics united in the Catholic League, whose violence and support from the common people soon made it very powerful: its leader, Henry of Guise, revealed himself as the true master of the kingdom.

In June 1584, the death of the last of the king's brothers revived the civil war. As Henry III was childless, Henry of Navarre, the Protestant, became heir to the throne. The League, desperate at the prospect of a Huguenot king, allied with Philip II of Spain and established a troublesome administration in Paris. To Henry of Guise the lack of direction in Henry III's policy was intolerable, and he entered Paris in May 1588, receiving an enthusiastic welcome from the inhabitants, amounting to a riot. The King's soldiers gave way before it. Henry III, who managed to escape to Chartres, was soon compelled through lack of troops and money to submit to the demands of the League.

The States General, summoned together at Blois in October 1588, tried to limit the King's powers. The Guises purged his Council, threatened, and heaped insults upon him. Henry III regarded his position as hopeless and decided to act. The Duke of Guise, when warned of this, dismissed the danger. Summoned to Blois on December 23, he was stabbed by the gentlemen of the Royal Guard. He clung to his assailants until they reached the bed-chamber, where he died at the feet of Henry III. The King, white with fear, had the body covered with an oriental rug. A general uprising followed in Paris. Catherine died in January 1589 and the monarchy at last turned for support to the Protestants. With Henry of Navarre, the King besieged Paris, but on 1 August 1589 he was stabbed to death in his camp by a Dominican monk.

Henry IV and the Edict of Nantes

The Catholic League had lost popularity by allying with Spain. But Henry of Navarre, who now became king as Henry IV, still had to conquer his kingdom. This devil-may-care Gascon had been toughened by his experiences; apparently easy-going he had in fact the strongest of wills. Under his courageous leadership his troops won the day

Henry IV, who restored peace after thirty-six years of civil war in France. He abjured his faith on becoming King for the sake of national unity and introduced a regime of tolerance. *Mansell*

against the League at Arques (September 1589), and at Ivry (March 1590). Failing to take Rouen, he besieged Paris. The starving Parisians made an appalling flour from ground bones, ate raw dog-flesh and held out until the arrival of Philip II's forces. The war dragged on, but the country was becoming more and more disturbed by the prolonged chaos and foreign intervention. The more moderate politicians regrouped and gained ground; the time for negotiation had come. Only one obstacle remained: the King was a Calvinist.

For the sake of France's unity, Henry IV stilled the voice of his Huguenot conscience and on 24 July 1593 took the risky step of abjuration. In March of the following year Paris welcomed him amid great rejoicings. Henry drove the Spaniards from Burgundy and Picardy; the treaty of Vervins of May 1598 ended the war. Henry's patient negotiations, his shrewdness, subtlety and good humour achieved more than force of arms in enabling him to gather together the shattered fragments of his kingdom.

After reducing Brittany and Poitou, the last bastions of the League, Henry now had to re-establish religious peace. On 13 March 1598, the Edict of Nantes secured for the Calvinists political and military guarantees, some freedom of worship and complete liberty of conscience. This regime of tolerance established in France after thirty-six years of civil war was, of course, incomplete and precarious; but it was the only one that Europe knew. In every other country religious unity was being imposed by force. This act alone would make Henry IV a great ruler. But, although under him the monarchy at last emerged from its long crisis, he was unable to repair the economic damage done to France by thirty years of futile warfare.

Philip II of Spain, the most powerful sovereign of his day. Lacking tact and intuition, he ruled his empire through a vast intelligence network and was a slave to paper-work.

A Spanish courtier at the time of Philip II. By centralising the royal power, Philip deprived the nobles of all real political power, gathering them round him at his court. *Marburg*

TWO GREAT REIGNS

Philip II

Master of Spain, part of Italy, Franche-Comté, the Netherlands and a vast empire in America, Philip II was, when he ascended the throne in 1556, the most powerful sovereign in Europe. Brought up without love, he was orphaned at twelve years of age and a widower at nineteen. He spoke in a low voice, never laughed and, such was his taste for solitude, he found happiness only in the gloomy atmosphere of the Escorial, which was at the same time a palace, a monastery and a tomb. Despite his arrogance and pride, he could show humanity providing his authority was not questioned. It was for reasons of State that he felt compelled to imprison his half-insane son Don Carlos. Beneath his icy manner he concealed a sensitive disposition; he loved roses, the oil paintings of Titian and old palaces with their golden hues. He left his desk rarely; all day long he would draft orders, instructions and questionnaires, slowly and scrupulously. If he was heavy and cumbersome in his methods, he still managed to keep control over everything; by making use of underhand methods he sought with dogged resolution to realise projects which were as grandiose as those of his father, the Emperor Charles V.

'Yo, el Rey' (I, the King)

Philip II believed sincerely in the divine right of kings. It seemed to him natural that everyone should address

him on bended knee, and he governed Spain as a despot, relying upon spies and informers. The *Cortes* were deprived of all authority; from Madrid, which had been the capital since 1560, the authority of the State reached out to all the 'kingdoms' and the exercise of local powers was closely scrutinised. Aragon, which remained medieval in character, and whose nobles were as unpolished as brigands, lost some of its privileges after an unsuccessful revolt in 1591. The political role of the nobles was increasingly restricted — to the benefit of the middle class.

Religious unity. The Moorish population

Philip II managed eventually to bring about religious unity in his kingdom by a combined use of the sword and the green cross of the Inquisition. He himself presided at the *autos-da-fé* ('acts of faith') — executions which within ten years rid Spain of Protestants. The Moors of Andalusia were only nominally Christians. They were forbidden to speak Arabic, to possess arms, or to lock their doors. They had to renounce their national costume; women were forbidden to wear the veil; Turkish baths were abolished. They had to give up their marriage ceremonies and even the custom of decorating tombs with branches. At Christmas 1568 Moorish insurrection broke out; it was soon put down in Granada, but held out for two years in the mountains, where, among other things, the Moors gouged out the eyes of priests. Order was eventually restored by wholesale exterminations; the

53

Above: The execution of Count Egmont and Count Hornes in Brussels, 5 June 1568. This and other acts of fierce repression under Alva fired Dutch nationalism and heralded the period of insurrection that lead to Dutch independence.

Larousse

Below: The defeat of Philip II's 'Invincible Armada' by English fire-ships as it lay off the coast of Belgium (1588). Under Philip II Spain suffered her first major disasters — against the English, in the Low Countries and in France. *Radio Times Hulton Picture Library*

survivors were put in chains, even if they had not taken part in the rebellion, and were forced to undertake a slow march towards the north through snow during the winter of 1570; they were dispersed in small groups in the north so that they might no longer prove a menace to the ' true faith '. In October of the following year (1571), the Crusaders of the Escorial destroyed the Turkish fleet at Lepanto, winning a glorious victory over the Infidel.

The revolt of the Low Countries

As champion of the Roman Church, Philip II determined to build up a vigorous Castilian empire to serve the Faith. King Sebastian of Portugal was killed in Morocco, and the extinction of the national dynasty enabled Philip to occupy Portugal, extend his authority over the whole of the Iberian peninsula, and enlarge his colonial empire (1580). But he met with resistance in the Low Countries and from England and France, and this caused his ambitious plans to miscarry.

Philip offended all classes by attempting to continue his father's policy of centralisation in the Low Countries. The nobility succeeded in bringing about the recall of one of his unpopular ministers but then heard, to their alarm, of Philip's intention of enforcing the decrees of the Council of Trent throughout his dominions. Alarmed at the prospect of a popular outbreak by Protestants, a group of noblemen petitioned for a reversal of this policy in the Compromise of Breda (1566); but they were ignored in Madrid. In August a popular attack on Catholic churches convulsed many of the larger towns. Philip responded by sending the Duke of Alva with a new army to subdue his subjects. Fire, rope and the axe restored order temporarily, but what had been discontent now became a revolt. It was saved by the leadership of William the Silent, Prince of Orange, and by the action of a group of semi-pirates, the ' sea-beggars ', who seized Brill and provided the rebels with a base. Alva's harshness kept alive popular hatred of Spain. Despite his recall in 1573, the ten Catholic provinces of the south also rose against the Spanish and united with the others under William's leadership; this lasted until 1579, when a new Spanish general, the Duke of Parma, by exploiting the religious and economic rivalries between the provinces reconciled the south to Spain. Under the leadership of William the Silent and, after his assassination in 1584, under that of his son Maurice of Nassau, the northern provinces carried on the struggle. By the time Philip II died, they were on the threshold of independence.

The Invincible Armada

From 1585 onwards Queen Elizabeth gave her support to the insurgents of the Low Countries, sending an army which checked Parma at a crucial moment. When she beheaded Mary Stuart in 1587, Philip II hurled against her the largest expedition that had been seen since the Crusades. The 130 ships of the Invincible Armada left Lisbon on 30 May 1588, to be attacked by a storm almost at once. Harassed in the English Channel by the English fleet and by fire-ships as they lay off the Belgian coast, they failed to embark Parma's army, and were compelled to try to sail home round the British Isles without maps or pilots. Only about sixty of them escaped the rocks and the violence of the winds and managed to return to Spain.

Unperturbed by this disaster, Philip II hoped to make up for his loss by arranging for the French crown to be given to his daughter Isabel. The energy of Henry IV and three years of unsuccessful war (1595–8) disposed of Philip's aspirations.

Spain at the end of the sixteenth century

Shortly before he died in September 1598, Philip II had a skull wearing a golden crown placed in his room — perhaps an admission of the futility of his schemes and the failure of his forty-two years' reign. His kingdom was ravaged by mysterious epidemics and the influx of American gold had played havoc with the economy. The administration was bankrupt, the country impoverished and depopulated. The exiling of desperadoes to India and Africa was not sufficient to keep down vagrancy. Malcontents appeared among the middle class and the nobility, and mysterious threatening notices were sometimes posted up on the doors of churches.

Despite these ominous signs, Spain remained powerful. The Church and the monarchy, closely linked, had never been stronger. The country had played a leading role in Europe during the last half-century, and God had preserved it from the onslaught of Islam and guided it towards the wealth of the New World. The Spaniards continued, therefore, despite failures, to conduct themselves as a chosen people, and to consider themselves marked out for a great destiny.

Elizabeth I of England

Queen Elizabeth I succeeded her half-sister Mary Tudor in 1558, at the age of twenty-five. She was tall, red-haired, thin and bony; as passionately fond of physical exercise as her father Henry VIII had been; as proud of her dancing as she was of her knowledge of Greek. She loved entertainment and pleasure. Jealous of her freedom and aware of its diplomatic value, she remained a ' Virgin Queen ', but she was not without male favourites. After the execution of her mother, Anne Boleyn, she had always been surrounded by spies, and feared for her life. These experiences developed in her the habit of dissimulation, and left her prudent, suspicious, stubborn and practical, attempting only what she considered possible, preferring to wait upon events, so as to get the best advantage out of them. Her skilful diplomacy, her often-expressed determination to subordinate everything to the national interest, made her in the eyes of her people a truly national queen — the very personification of England.

The ' absolutism ' of Elizabeth

Proud, like all the Tudors, this fierce, hard-eyed queen could spit at a courtier and bully her maids of honour. Her ministers, Walsingham, Francis Bacon or William Cecil, were remarkable statesmen; but she did not heap favours upon them, did not consider herself bound by their counsel, and always knew how to hold them in check by setting them against one another. She executed a thousand people to put an end to a feudal uprising north of the Humber in 1569. Norfolk, the premier duke of England, was beheaded in 1572, and in 1601 the same punishment was meted out to her former favourite, the

55

Seal showing Elizabeth I on horseback and carrying orb and sceptre. Though more subtle in her methods than her father Henry VIII, Elizabeth was like him an absolute monarch without legal props — indeed her Catholic subjects disputed even the legitimacy of her claim to the throne. *Larousse*

Elizabeth on horseback encouraging her troops as they wait for a possible invasion by the Spaniards (*top*). Elizabeth giving thanks in St Paul's Cathedral for deliverance from the Armada (*below*). *Mansell*

Earl of Essex, who had tried to rouse the people of London. She found it less and less easy to control Parliament, which reminded her bitterly of the rights of the nation. Although she treated it with great respect, she summoned it only thirteen times in forty-five years.

In the matter of religious belief Elizabeth was indifferent, but she was conservative in practice; she disliked married bishops. She disapproved of the democratic character of Calvinism and opposed the restoration of pontifical authority in order to safeguard her own. She compromised by establishing a new Church, reminiscent of Calvinism in dogma, of Rome in hierarchy, liturgy and ceremonial (Act of Uniformity, 1564). She showed little consideration in her dealings with the clergy; she would interrupt a preacher in the middle of his sermon and order him to leave the pulpit. Her tolerance towards Nonconformists continued so long as it was consistent with political safety; when Catholicism became identified with disloyalty the celebration of Mass became treasonable and priests were hunted down and hanged.

Mary Stuart

The Catholics, who regarded the daughter of Anne Boleyn as illegitimate, set their hopes on Mary Stuart, the great-grand-daughter of Henry VII. She left France reluctantly in 1560 at eighteen years of age, after the death of her husband Francis, to return to Scotland, of which she was queen. Mary was intelligent, energetic and jealous of her rights and Elizabeth regarded her as a possibly dangerous rival. Mary's Catholic beliefs and her sincere but foolish love affairs scandalised her semi-civilised people, who had only recently been won over to Calvinism by the most severe of reformers, John Knox. Her marriage to the presumed murderer of her second husband let loose a rebellion against her; forced to abdicate (1567), she took refuge in England (1568) where both the Catholics and Spain hastened to involve her in their plots. Before long Elizabeth treated her as a prisoner. Although Elizabeth hesitated to act against a crowned head, and sought to avoid recognising the fact that Mary was bound to represent an alternative to herself in the eyes of disloyal Catholics, Mary was in the end executed (1587).

The rise of England

While Elizabeth defended her throne, England's prosperity increased. Imports, prices, earnings, apprenticeships were regulated and the first known system of public assistance was set up under the Poor Law in 1601. Elizabeth did not hesitate to include in her economic system the imposition of a three days' fast, even though her subjects were Protestants, for the purpose of increasing the consumption of fish. The English fleet was re-organised, and companies were founded to exploit distant markets. With the help of Flemish refugees England supplanted the Low Countries as the main centre for the manufacture and sale of wool. The country's industries, encouraged by capital realised through trade, were modernised; they tended to lose their domestic character and became more centralised. Despite the poverty of agricultural labourers and the increasing number of vagrants, economic progress resulted in a better standard of living and a new taste for luxury. The nobles gave up their castellated manors for luxurious, beautiful houses surrounded by gardens in the Italian style. The middle class furnished their houses with carpets, cushions and feather beds. Yet the century ended with the monarchy heavily in debt after the wars of the reign.

THE COUNTER-REFORMATION

The Inquisition

The Roman Church continued to practise some of the abuses which left it defenceless against its adversaries, but it proclaimed its adherence to tradition; it maintained its dogma, structure and principles of authority. Henceforth it planned to adopt a fighting policy, and called on the Holy Office of the Inquisition for more deadly weapons against heresy; from the Jesuits it insisted upon a new *modus operandi*; through the Council of Trent it demanded a regrouping of forces. A belated revival of the spirit of Catholicism provided the most important force behind it. Originally established to combat the Albigensian heresy, the Inquisition had survived only in Spain. Pope Paul III set it up again in Italy in 1542. Directed from Rome by a congregation of six Cardinals, the Holy Office became a permanent tribunal against which there was no appeal. Its Inquisitors could be sent into every Catholic country, and had the right to confiscate property, to use torture and to hand over heretics and even apparent heretics, without regard to rank, to punishment by the secular authorities. But its standards of justice did not compare unfavourably with the secular courts of the day. When religion was so important in men's lives, it was natural to keep a watch on writers, artists and printers. An ' Index ' kept up to date by the Vatican specified any works which should be burnt.

Ignatius Loyola and the Society of Jesus

Ignatius Loyola was born about the year 1491; his father was a gentleman in rather poor circumstances. Ignatius was seriously wounded in 1521 while defending Pampeluna, and the bones of his leg had to be broken and reset twice. Suffering and spiritual reading led him to the thought of hell. His great love of chivalry led him to the resolve to ensure the salvation of his soul by achieving great exploits in the service of Christianity. When he was better, though still a cripple, he became a hermit after a vigil of arms in the sanctuary of Montserrat. He remained a while with the Dominicans and then, after an arduous pilgrimage to the Holy Land, preached in the streets dressed in a coarse woollen garment. He began his theological studies at the age of thirty-three. Both at Avila and at Salamanca the Inquisition regarded him with suspicion — which he looked upon as a temptation of the devil — because of his scruples, and his zeal and strict penances. He went to Paris to study in 1528. Forced at times to beg in order to live, he continued his proselytism, exercising both his chivalry and his incomparable gifts as a spiritual director. In August 1534, accompanied by a small but enthusiastic group of followers, he made a vow to dedicate himself to the salvation of souls and to set out for the Holy Land. Thus the Society of Jesus was born. The renewal of hostilities with the Turks prevented him from entering Palestine and, in 1537, he placed himself at the disposal of Pope Paul III, who approved of the Society in 1540. Though

deprived of the use of the sword, Ignatius did not regard himself as having left military service when he came under the orders of God. Like a real army on the battlefield, his band of followers obeyed its general and its hierarchy of officers. His ' soldiers ', who were carefully recruited from among healthy young men, took their vows only after ten years' probation. At the call of their superiors they would stop what they were doing — even to the point of leaving a word incomplete if they happened to be writing. Organised and disciplined, the spirit of the Society of Jesus was not to be compared with the violent militarism of the monks of the League. The Jesuits wore no special uniform; their method combined infiltration, envelopment, forbearance and diplomacy. Theirs was a polished fanaticism that was far more effective than the rough methods of the Dominicans. They participated in the life of the world around them and were dispensed from observances which restricted the activities of other monks; the Jesuits had the ability to become ' all things to all men in order to win souls '. As preachers, their language was familiar and they adapted it to appeal to all classes. As propagandists, they appreciated the value of elaborate stagecraft in moving the crowds. In matters of education, they toned down discipline, allowed more room for active methods, competition, open-air exercise, and due preparation for life in the world. As confessors, they were well versed in sophistry; as missionaries, they studied the interests of native populations and adapted Christianity to the religious customs of pagan peoples.

They played a considerable role in the history of Europe and proved to be the most efficient instruments of Papal absolutism. All-powerful at the courts of Vienna and Portugal, they supported Philip II in 'the Low Countries, turned Bavaria into a gloomy replica of Genevese theocracy, uprooted Protestantism from Poland, controlled it in the south of Germany, intervened in France on the side of the Guises, and joined in the plots against Elizabeth in England. In Rome, the vast, stately Gesù Church, which now houses the tomb of St Ignatius Loyola, was the symbol of the sway the Jesuits exercised over the whole Italian peninsula. Through their bold enterprises beyond the seas, Catholicism was able to repair in some measure the losses it had sustained in Europe. They spread the Gospel in Canada; through St Francis Xavier they made their way into Japan; they appeared at the Chinese court in Mandarin robes; they founded a diocese in Brazil and a theocratic government in Paraguay. Over a hundred tailors were employed making shirts for the converts in their Hindu college in Goa.

The Council of Trent

Luther had appealed for a general council at the beginning of the Reformation and Charles V appealed for one after the Diet of Worms. It was now belatedly called together at Trent, in the Italian Tyrol, where it was to contribute towards the restoration of Roman authority. The Protestants refused to participate. Its deliberations, begun in December 1545, were interrupted several times and not completed until 1563. Its decrees curbed the excesses of the pontifical financial system, forbade the plurality of livings, made residence obligatory for prelates, condemned simony and charged the diocesan seminaries with the training of the clergy. The marriage of priests, though viewed favourably by French bishops, remained forbidden. A firm line of demarcation divided Protestantism from Catholicism. The Council rejected all forms of compromise and ambiguity. It reaffirmed the Real Presence of Christ in the Holy Eucharist, pronounced against predestination, accepted the principle of justification by works, and upheld the honouring of saints and the tradition of the seven sacraments. The Pope was acknowledged to rank above all councils, and to be ' the one and only head of the Church '.

The revival of Catholic spirituality

While Catholicism was being re-organised, it acquired a new soul. The Papacy recovered its balance; the indolent Julius III (1550–55) and the forcible Paul IV (1555–9) were still politicians, but they also took an active part in the Counter-Reformation. Pius V (1565–72) lived the life of an ascetic and walked barefoot in processions. Sixtus V (1585–90), formerly a swineherd, kept a strict watch over faith and discipline. The faithful received Holy Communion more often, and returned to the practice of mental prayer. The Breviary, the Missal, the Vulgate version of the Bible and catechisms stabilised and guided their faith from now on. Mysticism was intensified: St John of the Cross rose to the highest summits of contemplation; St Teresa of Avila, forever on the threshold of death and athirst for the love of God, was a visionary and a clear-headed organiser; the holy Cardinal Charles Borromeo, the smiling, simple Florentine Philip Neri, and Germaine Cousin de Pibrac, the most charming of the French saints, were all animated by a serene fervour.

Thanks to the Counter-Reformation, the Catholic Church succeeded in stemming the advance of Protestantism or driving it back altogether. The Church emerged from its trials purer and stronger; it was more assured in its doctrine, more conscious of its duties, more firmly under the control of a single head whose prestige had been enhanced. Though two-thirds of Europe had broken loose from its authority, the Catholic Church yet remained a great force.

THE END OF THE RENAISSANCE

Art

Although Italian art continued to reign in splendour over Europe, in its own country it no longer reached the same heights. The Counter-Reformation paralysed it by attempting to place it at the service of theology. Under the influence of ' academies ' which reduced the methods of the great masters to formulae, art became more and more conventional. This decline, however, was not universal. The works of Caravaggio (1569–1609), the violent painter of ruins and rags, suggested the future Rembrandt. In the republic of the Doges, which escaped both the Holy Office and invasion, two great masters and their disciples upheld the glory of Venetian painting. Paul Veronese (1528–88) revelled in the spectacular; his sensuous nonchalance breathed a new life into the pomp of Renaissance art. Tintoretto (1512–94), caring less about colour harmony and correct design, worked feverishly, decorating many churches with lively murals. In architecture the baroque style began to appear in 1568 with the Gesù Church in

Rome; characteristic were its distinctive treatment of mass, its illusionist perspectives and violent contrasts of light and shade.

Under the twofold influence of Flanders and Italy, Spanish art continued to grow richer. Titian, who died of the plague at the age of ninety-nine, worked under the patronage of Philip II. To the end he preserved the power and splendour of his imagination. Theotocopoulos, ' El Greco ', of Toledo (1540–1614) was indebted to Venice for the magic of his colours, to Spanish Catholicism for his dramatic restlessness; his extraordinary realism and daring were products of his madness.

Confusion and scarcity of money brought about by the Wars of Religion did not weaken the artistic movement in France under the last Valois monarchs. Though no artists of international repute emerged, painters, sculptors and architects produced many fine works during this period.

Literary development

In France there was no more sign of a decline in literature than in art, and two great authors tower above their contemporaries. Ronsard (1524–85) lifted poetry out of its medieval mould; he gave flexibility to the Alexandrine, and to French verse its rhythm and resonance. The school of poets which he formed, known as the *Pléiade*, dominated the poetry of his day. Montaigne (1533–92) retired at thirty-eight years of age to the seclusion of his castle library in Perigord to read and meditate. In his *Essays* (1580) he showed himself to be imbued with the culture

The interior of the Old Swan Theatre, from the Commonplace Book of Arend von Buchell. In France, Spain, Italy and England drama grew to the stature of an art, and plays became popular forms of entertainment.

of antiquity, yet a man of his own day; without recourse to rhetoric or dogmatism he strove to define the art of living naturally in a century still dominated by fanaticism and danger. Criticisms can be made of his philosophy of life; but he remains the supreme expression of the Renaissance mind in France.

In Italy, the brisk surge of youth and spirit of the Renaissance was quelled by the domination of Spain and the effects of the Counter-Reformation. Universities lost their brilliance; humanism gradually abandoned learning and fell into elegant rhetoric. Pastoral poems became little more than insipid idylls, despite their ambiguous voluptuousness. The First Crusade provided Tasso (1544–95) with the theme of an epic poem, *La Gerusalemme Liberata*, which was gaudy, majestic, but obscure. The theatre alone gave evidence of independence and imagination. The *Commedia dell'Arte*, established in 1567, created real-life characters such as Harlequin, Pantaloon and Pulcinella, which immediately captured the French imagination. Portugal participated in the spring-tide of the Renaissance with Camoëns (1525–80), who in his epic *Lusiads* celebrated the voyage of Vasco da Gama.

Spain, which had remained almost untouched by the intellectual revival at the beginning of the century, now began to emerge from its seclusion. Great mystics enriched its religious literature (St Teresa and St John of the Cross). Spanish pastoral romances and picaresque novels delighted Europe. The theatre saw an astonishing development. The Spanish golden age was not to end with the sixteenth century. In 1600, Cervantes, the renowned one-armed veteran of Lepanto, conceived the idea of his *Don Quixote* whilst serving a prison sentence. That same year Lope de Vega (1563–1635), who was already considered the greatest poet in Spain, decided to devote his life to the stage, on which his genius asserted itself in 1,500 plays.

Under Elizabeth, English writing came within the compass of European literature. A large number of translations enabled it to enrich itself from ancient sources and to experience the influence of the Latin countries. Spenser (1552–99), the creator of modern English poetry, showed his great imaginativeness in his allegorical epic *The Faerie Queen*. The clever works of the novelist Lyly (e.g. *Euphues*) and the chivalrous Sir Philip Sidney (*Arcadia*) made linguistic preciosity fashionable. In 1580 the fashion for popular drama began to develop. In the courtyards of inns and colleges beggarly comedians gave before a noisy public plays which were a mixture of suspense, vulgarity, violence and poetry. By the age of twenty-nine, when he was killed in a brawl, the playwright Marlowe had produced two unquestionable masterpieces, *Tamburlaine* and *Doctor Faustus*.

Born in 1564, in the heart of England, Shakespeare became an actor when his father, a butcher, was ruined at Stratford-upon-Avon. So little is known of Shakespeare's life that it has been suspected that the author of the works attributed to Shakespeare was really some famous person of the day who used Shakespeare's name. From 1588 to 1614 Shakespeare produced one or two plays a year. Those of his tragedies which he based on English history, such as *Richard II* and *Henry IV*, reflect the patriotic fervour of England at a time when Spain was threatening the country. But because of his wide experience of life, his powerful style and the timelessness of the characters he portrays, Shakespeare stands above nations and centuries.

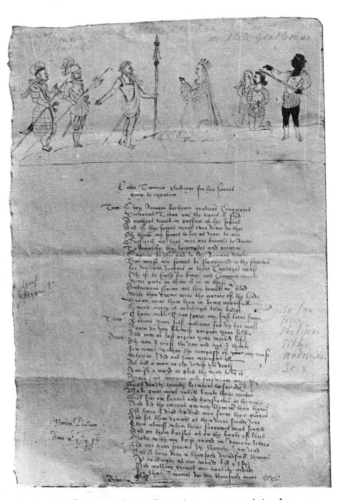

Illustration from a sixteenth-century manuscript of a performance of Shakespeare's *Titus Andronicus*. Shakespeare has survived in critical estimation while most of his contemporaries are now little read, but the Elizabethan age was one in which every man of culture wrote, sang and composed. *Courtauld Institute*

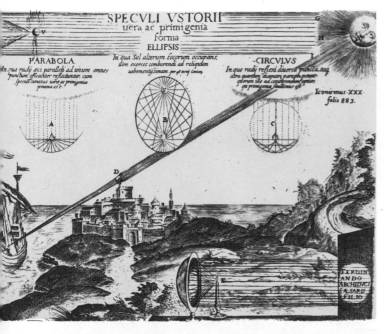

A sixteenth-century diagram illustrating the principle of different burning glasses. It suggests in a practical fashion that the right sort of glass directed from the top of a tower could set fire to a ship at sea. *Radio Times Hulton Picture Library*

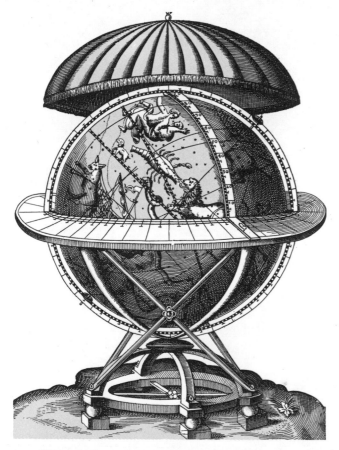

A celestial globe, five feet in diameter, illustrating a treatise by Tycho Brahe. The great progress made by astronomy in the sixteenth century benefited navigation in the years of discovery. *Radio Times Hulton Picture Library*

Scientific development

The progress of science continued throughout the second half of the sixteenth century. Relying upon positive facts furnished by experience, those sciences which depend especially on observation sought to lay down a scientific method, and so turned towards territory as yet unexplored. In 1580 Bernard Palissy put forward the idea that mountains were created by enormous geological upheavals. An Englishman, William Gilbert (1540–1603), published *De magnate* in which he described his research into forces in equilibrium, and distinguished for the first time between magnetism and electricity. The Italian Aldrovandi wrote his *Natural History* and botanists strove to classify plant life more systematically. Plants from America and Asia appeared in European gardens. Progress was made in anatomical studies. When decimal fractions were being brought into use by the Belgian Stevin (1585), a judge at Poitou named Viète (1504–1603) was inventing modern algebra and using letters to indicate coefficients and unknown quantities. Geometry was reconstructed in the hands of Commandino (1509–75).

A Dane, Tycho Brahe (1546–1601), completed a plot of 777 stars in his observatory at Uraniborg. A former Dominican friar named Giordano Bruno foresaw the possibility of introducing the notion of relativity of space and time into the system of the universe. The revision of dates recognised by the Church allowed scholars to contrive a new calendar. On the initiative of Pope Gregory XIII, the date of the equinox was changed to March 21: ten days were eliminated from the current year (5 to 15 October 1582) and thus lost to history. In the sphere of social sciences, Jean Bodin of Angers expounded his theory of sovereignty which attacked the Divine Right of Kings, and established the basis of a systematic political economy (*De la république*, 1576).

In the middle of the Counter-Reformation the Church was more and more firmly resolved to defend tradition against progress. It looked with suspicion upon intellectual, and especially scientific, enthusiasm. Vesalius was accused of having opened the heart of a living man; his condemnation to death was commuted to a pilgrimage to the Holy Land, but during his return journey he was drowned at sea. Bruno was imprisoned for seven years and then burned alive by the Holy Office in 1600.

It was not only religious fanaticism which hampered the development of science; not even the most powerful minds managed to free themselves completely from the burdensome heritage of superstition, error and prejudice. Tycho Brahe remained convinced, despite Copernicus, that whatever happened in the universe was the result of the Earth's being at its centre. The philosopher Campanella, who displayed such daring rationalism in his *Prodomos*, expected a revolution in the last year of the century. Bodin, who attributed magic power to the number seven, nevertheless regarded sorcery as a crime.

Livonian peasant. Conquered by Ivan the Terrible in his push westwards of 1563–70, Livonia was almost immediately wrested back by the Poles and was destined to be incorporated in the Swedish empire in 1660–61. *Giraudon*

CHAPTER FOUR

THE SECOND HALF OF THE SIXTEENTH CENTURY ON THE FRINGE OF EUROPE

EASTERN EUROPE, TURKEY AND THE MEDITERRANEAN

In Eastern Europe the second half of the sixteenth century brought forth a profusion of notable persons, but few important events. The tendencies of the first half of the century slowed down, and often seemed to dry up altogether in agrarian societies which lacked the thriving urban life of the West. Politically the new unity of Sweden dissolved in religious quarrels. Poland was weakened by her abuse of liberty and Muscovy was disorganised by the excesses of despotism. Eastern Europe was linked weakly to the rest of the continent, and its future was uncertain. Only the

A public execution outside the Kremlin, in sixteenth-century Moscow, a frequent scene. Ivan attempted to create a strong state by terror. Confusion and fear were the real effects of his policy, and Muscovy remained weak internally and was considered barbarous abroad. *Marburg*

Ivan IV, the Terrible, the first Tsar (Caesar) of Muscovy. Determined to create a modern state out of his principality, Ivan extended its borders as far as the Urals and the Caspian. He then forced many of the nobles to move into these far-flung domains, but his brutal methods in curbing the power of the nobility could lead only to instability. *Radio Times Hulton Picture Library*

Ottoman Empire, despite the mediocrity of its sovereigns, preserved its stamina and powers of expansion. The Mediterranean, where Moslems practised piracy as a holy war, gradually slipped away from European influence and in all the countries on its shores there was an extraordinary rise in brigandage. By the seventeenth century, Mediterranean conditions were again comparable with those of the fifteenth.

The crises in Sweden

In the young kingdom of Sweden the successors of Gustavus Vasa — Eric XIV (1560–68), John III (1568–91) and Sigismund (1591–9) — put the authority of the monarchy in jeopardy.

Eric XIV loved action and was also a man of intellect. Periodical fits of madness, however, soon changed him into a cruel despot. The failure of his expeditions against Denmark (1563–8), his marriage with a woman of his harem, and the wickedness of a favourite, all made him unpopular. He was deposed and may have been poisoned. His brother John III married the daughter of the King of Poland, a Jagiellon and a Catholic. He made great efforts to reconcile Lutheran Sweden to Rome but succeeded only in offending both sides. Faced with the violent opposition of his subjects, who identified Protestantism with national independence, he was forced to return to the Reformed Church. Laborious campaigns against the Danes and the Russians did nothing to restore his reputation.

His son Sigismund, a Catholic, who became King of Poland in 1587, wished also to reign over Sweden, and had himself crowned at Uppsala in 1592. The Swedes disliked his ardent Catholicism, and for a few years his uncle Charles, a fervent Protestant, exercised a regency. When Sigismund attempted to assert his rights in 1598 his army was beaten and forced to recross the sea. The *Riksdag* announced his deposition in 1599. Only in 1604 with the proclamation of Sigismund's uncle as Charles IX did Lutheran Sweden regain its religious unity. There was still no sign that within a few decades it was to become the leading Baltic power.

The confusion in Poland

Under the reigns of Sigismund Augustus (1548–72), the last of the Jagiellons, Henry of Anjou (1573–4), who was to reign in France as Henry III, Stephen Bathory (1576–86) and the first of the Vasa dynasty, Sigismund III (1587–1632), Poland made some progress, but still remained weak. Three important changes took place, nevertheless, in these years.

Poland grew much larger when, in 1569, its attachment to Lithuania was changed from a merely legal union to a union of fact; the transfer of the capital from Cracow to Warsaw completed the movement of its centre of gravity to the north, and, with the aid of the Cossacks, it began to colonise its Ukrainian territory.

For a long time Poland's religious future remained in doubt, but the Jesuits made it the Catholic country *par excellence* and created the intimate connection of faith and nationality which has lasted to this day. Protestants were excluded from holding public office, but nevertheless enjoyed a large measure of tolerance. With the Counter-Reformation in full swing, Poland would have experienced

Elevation and ground plan of St Basil's Cathedral, Moscow. Under Ivan III many of the palaces and churches of the Kremlin were rebuilt by foreign architects. Their Byzantine character was, however, preserved. Beyond this, Western influence was confined to technical innovations such as cannon. *Marburg*

A Russian icon of the sixteenth century. Convinced that Russia's expansion would depend on her identification with the cause of Eastern Orthodoxy, Ivan made his troops carry icons in their campaigns against the Infidel. Muscovy was unaffected by the Reformation. *Giraudon*

no religious troubles at all if its Orthodox Church, by its recognition of the authority of the Holy See, had not set the adherents to the Greek Church against those who had broken away. The Cossacks, who were faithful to the Patriarchate of Moscow, were savagely persecuted.

Under the Jagiellons royalty had in practice been hereditary; but after the death of Sigismund Augustus, Poland became an aristocratic republic with elected kings. Not only was it weakened by occasional stormy interregna; its sovereigns, all of foreign extraction, were crowned only on condition that they swore to recognise the rights of the nobles (*Pacta Conventa*, 1573). The most energetic of these kings, Bathory, heightened the prestige of the crown by his victories and executed a few nobles; but even he in the end had to resign himself to being king in name only. The nobles, on their side, though they insisted on royal authority remaining an illusion, were more anxious to monopolise power than to exercise it; they did not want firm government even if it was aristocratic. The Diet which represented them assembled every two years and remained in session for only six weeks; its decisions had to be unanimous and a single dissenting voice would paralyse not only the Diet but the whole State (*liberum veto*).

Despite political decline, Polish culture flourished in the afterglow of the Renaissance. Sigismund Augustus welcomed bold thinkers like Sozzini (Socinius), who were driven from Italy. Bathory took as his secretary the humanist Nidek. Although neo-Latin poetry became fashionable, Polish developed into a literary language used by historians and theologians.

Russia under Ivan the Terrible

In the second half of the reign of Ivan IV massacres and military reverses followed conquests. When his young wife died and he was deserted by one of his supporters, Prince Kurbsky (1564), the Tsar gave way to the most violent lust for power. He redoubled the executions, wiping out whole noble families; he massacred the inhabitants of Vali-Novgorod, so that the accumulation of corpses caused the river to overflow; surnamed 'the Terrible', he spread such panic wherever he went that bells were tolled to warn the people of his approach.

His murderous outbursts did not destroy his political acumen. At one time he had thought of abdicating, but he placed a body of reliable men (*oprichnina*) in provinces specially selected as his personal domain, and moved the dispossessed local lords to the outlying parts of his kingdom. This ruthless uprooting of the old aristocracy damaged the prospects for stable government. Although the *oprichniki* were prepared to fight their master's enemies and wipe out treachery, they continually awoke opposition by their excesses. Ivan had longed to create a real nation out of Muscovy, but he succeeded only in organising a Terror. By 1572 he could foresee the possibility of the boyars revolting. Moreover, his foreign policy was a complete failure. Despite a seven years' war (1563–70), he failed to establish a foothold on the Baltic. The Swedes drove him from Esthonia, Ingria and Narva (thus sowing the seed of their future empire), and the Poles expelled him from Livonia and Pskov. Queen Elizabeth of England refused to make an alliance with him. When he died in 1584 he had increased the size of Muscovy by a quarter, but he left the country as weak as it had been on his accession.

63

Ivan's eldest son, Feodor I (1584–98), was a weak ruler. His reign, during which his younger brother Dmitri was murdered (1591), began a time of troubles. Russia was breaking up, though it managed to maintain its vitality on its eastern boundaries. The Stroganoffs, powerful merchants from Novgorod, extended their prospecting beyond the Ural Mountains. The Cossack Yermark, with a handful of irregulars and peasants fleeing slavery, conquered the region between the Rivers Irtysh and Ob. Weighed down by the gold cuirass presented to him by the Tsar, Yermark died attempting to swim across a river (1584). His successors founded Tobol'sk in 1587. The Russians annexed western Siberia and saw a vast field of expansion open up before them. Muscovy had begun by extending Asia into Europe, but by an unforeseen turn of events came to extend Europe into Asia. It failed nevertheless to become a truly European power. Its towns were merely large villages. In culture the Russians were vastly different from Western Europeans; they shut up their womenfolk, smashed their early printing-presses, refused to make use of Arabic numerals, and were unable to do multiplication and division sums.

The Ottoman Empire

After the death of Sulaiman the Magnificent the Ottoman Empire had no great rulers. Selim the Sot (1566–74) was a coward; the epileptic Murad III (1574–95) fathered a hundred and two children; the half-Venetian Mehmed IV (1595–1603) was ruled by the woman who managed his harem. These idle Sultans were, nevertheless, eager to maintain the unity of their empire and merciless in eliminating all possible pretenders to the throne. On his accession Murad III ordered the execution of his brothers. In the interest of his eldest son when he himself was dying, Murad had nineteen of his other sons strangled; his concubines looked on, and sang a hymn on the sadness of destiny.

The main props of the empire were the army and an ancestral tradition of discipline; these remained intact. Christian renegades and slaves, who composed the government staff, always regarded themselves as the personal servants of the Padishah, and were the most useful instruments of his despotism. If the Grand Vizirs took any advantage at all of the indifferent quality of their sovereigns, it was to give proof of an entirely new spirit of resolution and initiative. The Bosnian Sokolli had a finer political sense, broader and more vigorous views than even Sulaiman the Magnificent.

The pressure of the Turks on Eastern Europe continued. Masters of central Hungary, they considered Poland a dependency; they intervened in the election of its kings and imposed heavy taxes on the country. Nothing could equal their contemptuousness towards the Christian nations. Although they were not at war with the Habsburgs, they never ceased to harass the Empire, where it became customary to ring church bells three times a day to call the Moslem faithful to prayer. The victims of the Turkish

The battle of Lepanto, October 1571, in which the Christians, united by Pope Pius V, defeated the Turks. *National Maritime Museum.*

Cochineal cultivation in post-Conquest Mexico. From *Historia Mexicana.* British Museum

tas puestas delas
que se chapodaró
an se de poner pordi
ciembre y Hene
ro para que
Con la prima
Vera Reto
nescan

pone la Cochinilla en las
nueuas plantas passados
seis meses y mas que se
plantaron. la sem
lla se pone por marco ya
bril a los arboles biejos
que a los nueuos es bien
no ponersela hasta q
tengan mas hedad
de seis meses O
VN
AÑO

raids were forced to appear at public victory parades and at the gladiatorial games held in Constantinople. In 1575, setting out from Bosnia, the Turks invaded Austria, taking possession of Raab in 1594. The Prince of Wallachia, Michael the Brave, pushed them beyond the Danube in 1595, but they advanced again the following year. To the north-east their threat to Muscovy was intensified and in Asia the Turks laid siege to Astrakhan (1569) and made a vigorous push towards the Don. In 1571, under the Khan of Crimea, their ships crossed the River Oka, set fire to Moscow and brought back from the expedition over 100,000 captives for their slave markets.

The Turks also strengthened their hold on the eastern Mediterranean. Chios fell into their hands in 1566, Naxos in 1567. In 1570 they captured Cyprus and burned its governor alive. As their raids increased, Pope Pius V united against them in a new Holy League Spain, Venice and Genoa. The struggle threatened to be ruthless. Don John of Austria defeated the Turkish fleet at the Battle of Lepanto, at the entrance to the Gulf of Corinth, in October 1571. The Infidels lost 30,000 men, 117 ships, 650 cannon and 39 standards. It was a short-lived victory. ' A clipped beard ', remarked Sokolli, ' grows stronger '; he re-organised the fleet and exploited rivalries between his enemies. Venice, disillusioned with its allies, signed a defeatist peace, and abandoned Cyprus. The Spaniards then decided to protect the western Mediterranean by making a barrier, of which Tunisia, Malta and Sicily were to be the bastions. In 1573 they took Tunis; less than a year later they were driven out of it with a speed that impressed Europe. Giving up the idea of trying to retaliate in Africa, Philip II signed a truce with the Sultan in 1581; Spanish Barbary ceased to be of any importance. The Turks, not content with the help that the Berber pirates continued to give them, extended their protection over Morocco, and incorporated within their empire the three ' Regencies ' of Tripolitania, Tunisia and Algeria.

Towards the end of the sixteenth century the Mediterranean had ceased to be overrun by galleys eager for battle, but it was infested with corsairs and remained unsafe. It had been a battleground so long, and its economic position had declined so rapidly that social repercussions among the people along its shores were inevitable. Renewed outbreaks of vagrancy and a general increase in lawlessness were reasons for their restlessness, despair and chaotic uprising.

The Turkish Empire consisted of countries of nomads or former nomads, who could withstand banditry much better than the Christian states. The revolts in Syria, the Crimea and Moldavia at that time had no very pronounced effect on the Empire, and Western travellers continued to regard it as well consolidated. It possessed three-fifths of the Mediterranean coastline and stretched to within a hundred miles of Vienna. The Empire seemed to have reached the limits of its expansion, for its armies could not control a greater area; but there was no sign of a decline. The vices that were consequences of a characteristically oriental despotism were to be threats to the regime only when Europe became clearly superior to Islam.

Peruvian kero showing, from left to right, an Indian in Inca costume, a Spaniard and a Negro. Wood decorated with mastic. Mid-seventeenth century. British Museum

EUROPEAN EXPANSION: DOMAINS BEYOND THE SEAS

The ardour of the heroic age had passed. The Portuguese and Spaniards no longer behaved as temporary occupants hastening to exploit conquered countries. They regarded themselves as permanent masters, and systematically opened up the territory to trade with the mother country; or, in an effort to establish the prosperity of the colonies, they attempted to create new resources and to populate them. In America, where the blending of blood and civilisations was making its first effects felt, contacts with the natives tended to become less brutal. In 1580 Spain and Portugal were united under a single rule; their size and wealth made the colonial dominions of Philip II the greatest empire that the world had ever known. Its future nevertheless became uncertain from the moment Elizabethan England, France and the growing Dutch nation began to take an interest in overseas expeditions.

The Portuguese in Brazil

There was nothing accidental about the founding of the Portuguese colony of Brazil, but it lacked determination and enthusiasm. The colony developed more rapidly than could have been expected from its confused beginnings. Its European immigrants were made of much better stuff than those who had discovered it; they came to establish permanent settlements, which by the end of the century had roughly 70,000 inhabitants. Sao Paulo was founded in 1554; Rio de Janeiro in 1557; Natal on Christmas Day 1597.

The first generation of half-breeds began immediately to play an important role. These *mamelucos* were less indolent than the Indians, and more active and pugnacious than the Portuguese. They penetrated into the forests to secure slaves; they travelled up the great rivers, and reached the headwaters of the River Paraguay; they extended the frontiers of Brazil and, in a violent expansionist drive, became founders of sub-colonies.

The quick establishment of sugar as an essential commodity on the European markets assured Brazil of a long period of prosperity. On lands conquered in bitter fighting sugar-cane plantations and sugar mills sprang up everywhere. As the new plantations needed a large and healthy labour force, each large owner was allowed by a statute of 1559 to import 120 African slaves. The ' lords of the mills ' now had the opportunity to grow rich. Golden locks, upholstered beds, silken doublets, never-ending banquets to the sound of bugles and the music of violins — their pretentious opulence was displayed everywhere. They appropriated from the Indies all the accessories of a sensual and easy-going life: sandalwood caskets, the parasol, the fan and the palanquin. From their native mistresses they learned to bath daily; but in the land of their birth it was still considered ' decent ' — to use the word of Erasmus — to wipe one's nose on one's hand.

Though their economic strength developed, their political influence was on the wane. The Captaincy-General at San Salvador and the new captaincies, set up in 1552 and 1556, were given more extensive powers. In their spiritual conquest of Brazil the Jesuits had to face the hostility of both the great landowners and the *mamelucos*. 65

E

It was clear to them that the conversion of the Indians was almost impossible in an anarchic society dominated by violence and money, so they were disposed to support the officers of the Crown. Under skilful guidance from their Provincial, Manuel de Nobrega, the eventual achievement of centralisation was assured.

The Portuguese in the East Indies

The Portuguese succeeded in holding on to the long chain of little islands and small forts which made up their East Indian empire. All native uprisings were ruthlessly suppressed; when the subject races united they were subdued; and the outbreaks of 100,000 Hindus were put down thanks to the energetic efforts of Ataíde, the last of the great viceroys (1568–71).

Although the trade in spices still remained important, trading posts fell far below their earlier levels of prosperity. The increase of Crown taxation combined with the greed of the tax collectors gradually turned away international trade. The Portuguese had allowed their merchant navy to deteriorate, and since they did not handle the distribution in Europe of their East Indian produce, but allowed the Dutch to act as commission agents, they deprived themselves of a considerable source of revenue, and thus assisted their most determined rivals.

The defects of their colonial system soon became clear. Every three years their viceroys were changed, so that most of them sought only to enrich themselves as quickly as possible. Their subordinates copied them, and were encouraged in their malpractices by being authorised to trade on their own behalf. Port officials acted like oriental potentates; the soldiers were never paid punctually and were frequently undisciplined; the settlers were often too few in number (in Goa there were only five hundred). Weakened by the easy-going life of a hot climate, they developed habits of luxury and freedom from worry. The absence of white women brought about a constant cross-breeding, from which emerged a degenerate race much inferior to the Brazilian *mamelucos*. The natives, exasperated by harsh treatment, heavy taxes and the brutal proselytism of the missionaries, deserted the trading posts.

At the very time when Camoens was praising the epic of Vasco da Gama in his *Lusiads* (1579) and honouring 'the all-powerful little Lusitanian nation in Asia', the decline of the Portuguese Indies was about to be quickened by Philip II's annexation of Portugal.

The Spanish Empire

The Spaniards were more intent on consolidating their colonial empire than on extending it. In 1565, however, they gained a foothold in the Philippines. In North America they penetrated into the Colorado basin and founded Santa Fé, the capital of New Mexico (1581). In Chile, despite the resistance of the Araucanians, Spanish rule was eventually extended along the coast from the Atacama desert to Chiloe Island. A number of soldiers who had become unwelcome in Peru colonised the region of Tucuman in Argentina (1550–60), and a handful of daring men established themselves along the banks of the Rio de la Plata, where Buenos Aires, abandoned in 1541 after a brief occupation, was reborn in 1580. In this empire, where the spirit of adventure survived only along the frontiers, the plenipotentiaries of the mother country were able to relax some of their authority without running the risk of separatism. Philip II was tackling serious financial difficulties at home, and he left the men of standing in his overseas provinces to finance colonisation at their own expense. The occasional hereditary rights which he granted them in exchange played a considerable part in strengthening the authority of both the landed aristocracy and the municipal corporations.

Madrid was especially interested in precious metals from the New World. They were transported to Seville every year in two convoys of galleons, and a fifth of the treasure went to the royal coffers. Thanks to the introduction of amalgams in Mexico (1554) and in Peru (1563), low grade ores could be used and this considerably increased activity in the mines. In the frozen wilderness of the Andes, over 12,000 feet above sea level, the city of Potosi with its silver mines had 100,000 inhabitants — the same number as Mexico City — and had become the most important city in South America.

The search for precious metals brought many disappointments and enriched only a few immigrants. When the gold fever eventually died down, the colonists, like the Portuguese in Brazil, turned towards agriculture. Through a new kind of conquest they acquired vast estates. On land patiently reclaimed — 'ennobled' was the word used by Cortés — they sowed wheat, maize, barley, cotton and sometimes rice. The proceeds of large-scale trade and export were a great attraction. Chocolate was becoming the favourite drink of Spain, Europe suddenly began to consume enormous quantities of sweet things, and the immigrants doubled their plantations of sugar-cane and cocoa-trees, as well as continuing to grow tobacco and indigo. The new plantations produced excellent yields and required an ever-increasing labour force. The Spaniards combined greed with an unwillingness to work themselves; they had, therefore, to renounce the policy of exterminating the native population, which most of the *conquistadores* had advocated. Supported by the Church, Philip II protected the natives and reminded the Spaniards on several occasions that they were not to be treated as slaves. His representatives sought to improve the system of forced labour. Puebla, the future granary of Mexico, even became a kind of model town where the colonists had to live off the land without using forced labour. By the royal statutes of 1576–89, those Indians who had been allocated to landowners had to be given two days a week to work on their own holdings. At dawn they would assemble at the cross and recite four prayers before setting out for the fields; they were given one hour's rest during the day, and stopped work at sunset.

Though Don Paniagaca ordered a Spaniard's hand to be cut off for striking an Indian chief, and the old *conquistador* Alonso de Ercilla praised the bravery of the Indians in his poetry, most of the colonists continued to show violent racial prejudice against the subject peoples, and scarcely troubled to improve their lot. Though the natives lost the capacity to develop independently, they failed to adapt themselves to the new life which conquest had imposed on them, and their numbers diminished. In Mexico alone, from 1519 to 1597, their numbers fell from ten to three millions.

Although the various countries which made up the Spanish

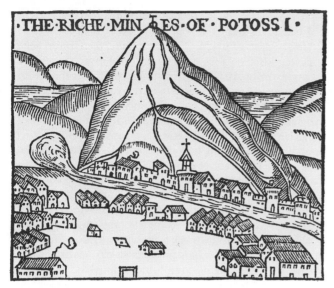

The silver mines of Potosi. New metallurgical techniques brought increased prosperity to the mines of Peru. With 100,000 inhabitants, Potosi now became the most important city of South America. The conquest of Peru, undertaken for gain, trebled the flow of bullion from America to Spain. *Radio Times Hulton Picture Library*

Mexico City, as seen by a sixteenth-century European artist. Built on a lagoon, it was the capital of the Aztecs and the seat of their war god. It was taken over as capital by the *conquistadores*, who dispossessed the natives both physically and by imposing on them stultifying forced labour. *Larousse*

metals and made up of vast empty spaces. Their progress was negligible, and they were regarded as poor relations. There were only 3,000 settlers in Chile. Argentina's only communication with the mother country was by way of Peru. Three enemies — thirst, swamps and Indian looters — lay in wait for the convoys of waggons with their enormous solid wheels drawn by oxen, which ventured along the interminable road to Lima. Far to the south, Buenos Aires, with its three hundred souls, was continually being attacked by Indians who slipped away in their canoes before the alarm could be given. The colonists had to be their own agricultural labourers; they complained of having neither shirts nor shoes, and of the lack of wine to celebrate Mass and wax to make candles.

Not all the 150,000 Spaniards in the overseas provinces resembled these pioneers and the cultural standard of the colonies did tend to rise little by little. Distinguished intellectuals gathered round the Viceroy Toledo, the Erasmian Bishop Zumarraga, and the explorer Gamboa. The sons of Indian chiefs learned to read. The Spanish Indies, where there was no tax on Spanish books, possessed busy printing-presses and classical colleges; a newspaper was published in Peru from 1594; and there were three great universities — at Santo Domingo, Lima and Mexico.

The French expeditions

So far France had no colonial policy. Her special interest lay in the Mediterranean but Gaspard de Coligny, who took his appointment as Admiral seriously, wished to found a colony in Florida for his persecuted co-religionists. Led by Jean de Ribaut, some French Protestants disembarked there in 1562. To the singing of psalms they built a stronghold which they called Charlesfort, and christened three rivers the Seine, the Loire and the Charente. Their fortress fell into the hands of the Spaniards in October 1567; as they refused to recant, they, their wives and their children were savagely put to death.

Despite a Portuguese ban, French ships came to Brazil to trade. With the support of Coligny, Frenchmen settled in the bay of Rio de Janeiro in 1555. But the colony grew weak as a result of religious quarrels, and soon drifted towards anarchy; by 1567 the last of the French had disappeared from Brazilian soil. In 1588 Henry III granted the three nephews of Jacques Cartier a concession in Canada which was intended to be the beginning of a more extensive colonisation of North America.

The French had but a vague notion of peoples and countries beyond the seas. Accounts of travels were full of stories of horned donkeys, animals with human faces, giants fifteen feet tall, monsters who lived on air and flew from tree to tree. Some Brazilian Indians had been brought to France, and appeared at important entertainments before being allotted to a few nobles. Their faces were adorned with emeralds, they danced naked and fought with their shadows. Montaigne, who conversed with them through an interpreter, regarded them as representatives of a happy society, innocent and free, living according to nature. On that account he considered theirs to be superior to European societies. Paradoxically Europe was virtually incapable of self-criticism before it came into contact with a few tribes of 'noble savages', who had hardly emerged from a prehistoric era.

Empire were now under the rule of one master, they still differed as much as they had done before the conquest. New Spain (Mexico) was generally well ahead of New Castile (Peru). The territories recently annexed from Portugal were distant sub-colonies lacking in precious

67

The first English colonies

England was a country of stock-breeders and craftsmen which played only a small part in the great voyages of discovery. Under the reign of Elizabeth, however, it was drawn towards a policy of energetic expansion.

It was the turn of English sailors to be fascinated by the magic of India, and they set out to reach the land of spices by way of northern Europe or America. To the north-east Willoughby foundered within sight of Novaya Zemlya in 1553, and Chancellor failed to get beyond Kara (1556); to the north-west Frobisher explored Greenland (1576) and Davis named the Davis Strait (1588).

After operating for a long time in European waters, the English corsairs under Hawkins appeared in the Gulf of Guinea, where they joined in the slave trade. They sailed swiftly across the Atlantic, skimmed the seas around the West Indies in company with French buccaneers, and ended by attacking the American mainland. These fierce sea-dogs were as cruel as the companions of Pizarro had been, but their goal was profit rather than adventure.

The boldest of them, Francis Drake, had once been a slave-trader; he first commanded a ship at the age of twenty-two. In 1572 an expedition to the isthmus of Panama gave him an opportunity to plunder a convoy of treasure-ships. Leaving Plymouth in November 1577 with five small men-of-war, he reached Peru by the Straits of Magellan; but he lost all his ships except the *Golden Hind* in a storm. He spread terror in Lima, sailed towards the north, made a reconnaisance of California, crossed the Pacific and founded Ternate, the first English colony, in the Moluccas. He then returned to Europe in triumph by way of the Indian Ocean and southern Africa, having accomplished the second complete voyage round the world. On his return he made a present to Queen Elizabeth of the most beautiful of his precious stones, and she came aboard the *Golden Hind* to dub him a knight. The Queen received back seven times the value of her investment in the expedition.

Piracy, which brought much more wealth to England than the conquest of the New World had brought to the Iberian countries, remained a dangerous threat to communications in the Spanish Empire. In the long run it failed to satisfy the aspirations of a people conscious of its power and concerned about its future. For long England had feared poverty and unemployment because of its rapidly rising population. Humphrey Gilbert considered the possibility of creating a completely new kind of colony into which the mother country would be able to pour its surplus population. He believed that, after the elimination of the native peoples, Europeans would form homogeneous self-governing groups. In 1583 he annexed a part of Newfoundland in the name of Queen Elizabeth, intending to people it with English and Irish immigrants. He was, however, drowned in a storm as he approached Europe, and his colony did not survive him. A settlement called 'Virginia' in honour of the 'Virgin Queen' was established a few years later in Florida by Humphrey's half-brother, the brilliant poet-adventurer Sir Walter Ralegh, but its existence was short-lived (1587–90).

When Portugal came under Spanish rule, the English had no wish to depend upon their enemy Philip II for their supply of tropical produce. Like the Dutch, they aimed at a direct trade link with the Indies, where their merchant adventurers had been operating since 1584. In 1600 Queen Elizabeth signed the charter of the first English East India Company. Despite stubborn efforts, England had not become a colonial power by the end of the sixteenth century; but it was none the less well aware of the opportunities for expansion which its fleet and geographical position offered. English overseas ventures were more intricate than the escapades of the *conquistadores*, and they reflected a new tendency in European economics. These ventures, like England's first attempts to settle people in North America, were already a sign of, and a preparation for, the future.

The Dutch entry into the colonial field

The Dutch had rebelled against Philip II, and were therefore no longer able to act as middlemen between the Baltic and Spain, or to obtain spices in the Portuguese ports. Since the downfall of Antwerp had favoured their rise as

Map of India and part of the Persian Gulf by Guillaume le Testu, 1555. Until the 1580s the Indies had been colonised only by the Portuguese, but thereafter they had to face Dutch and English competition. *Giraudon* a naval power, they attempted in an all-out war of independence to enter into direct relations with the spice-producing countries. Their sailors undertook a series of bold voyages. Barents, hoping to reach Asia by sailing to the north of the Old World, got as far as Novaya Zemlya and landed at Spitzbergen; he was the first to winter in the polar regions and died when he was about to be rescued. Houtman, after sailing round Africa, reached Malacca and the Sunda Islands in 1597. Following Magellan, Van Noort accomplished an extremely dangerous journey round the world from 1598 to 1600. The Dutch had fast ships well protected against strong winds, and they were backed by wealthy companies formed for the purpose of overseas trade; they had trading posts in Ceylon, Malacca and the Moluccas; they became firmly established in Sumatra, and even set foot in Japan in 1600. Combining trade with piracy, they did not hesitate to attack Portuguese ships. With their ten thousand sailors, the 'sea-beggars', as they were called, became the 'sea-kings'. Amsterdam, in the tradition of old Venice, now began to replace Lisbon and Seville as the great centre of world trade.

It is hard to appreciate fully what overseas explorations and conquests meant at the end of the sixteenth century. They were not merely an opportunity for a handful of brave men to spead Christianity, to procure gold or to buy spices at better prices. A whole continent awoke to new life in the vacuum left by the collapse of empires, and a civilisation with undreamed of possibilities slowly emerged from the ruins. Europe had become firmly rooted in America. From the Philippines to Panama it girdled the globe, asserting its vitality and considerably increasing its prestige and authority. Although this gave new life to the economy, Europe ended by suffering much more from the abundance of its wealth than it had previously from its poverty. The influx of precious metals from America brought with it a general rise in prices and alarming social upheavals. In countries which were badly equipped technically, like Spain and Portugal, the imports were not used for industrial development, but merely created the illusion of prosperity. Elsewhere, the concentration of capital resulting from increased turnover brought into being new forces throughout Europe; these forces were destined to exercise great influence on politics and society. In England and Holland the role of merchants and bankers in European expansion proved to be as significant as that of explorers, colonists and armies. Maritime and colonial power and wealth were increasingly felt to be inseparable.

THE ASIAN WORLD

The *Singoku*, or 'Age of War', seemed never to come to an end in feudal Japan under the Ashikagas. After splendid beginnings, both the Persian Empire of the Safavids and the Mogul Empire declined. Under the direction of Akbar the Great, one of the most remarkable personalities of modern times, India was the first to recover. Two usurpers, Nobunaga and Hideyoshi, restored central power in Japan. Shah Abbas laid the foundations of Persia's recovery. China alone, under the Ming Dynasty, continued to grow weaker.

Akbar the Great

Akbar, who succeeded his father Humayun in 1542, at thirteen years of age, may be considered the true founder of the Mogul Empire. The beginning of his reign was hard. He had to shake off his mother's tutelage, rid himself of his guardian, conquer a number of unruly provinces and overcome his Hindu opponent Hamu. It was only in 1562 that Akbar really gained control. This bandy-legged, red-faced, thickset prince was brought up in a hard school. Like his grandfather Babar he remained true to the violent traditions of the Timurids. He had been known to knock his minister down with his fist; he would tame elephants or kill tigers himself; he prided himself on his skill as a marksman, piled up pyramids of heads after a battle, and wandered ceaselessly on horseback from one end of the peninsula to the other in search of new adventures. His army eventually numbered 200,000 men and 5,000 war elephants; keeping it firmly under his control, he used it to build the largest empire that India had known since the second century B.C.

Chimerical divinity of the Ming Dynasty. Though the Ming Dynasty was becoming increasingly weak politically and attempted to preserve itself by a rigid policy of isolation, this did not affect the vigour of Chinese artists, who were still producing fine works. *Larousse*

Shoeing a horse. Mogul School, about 1600. Akbar the Great introduced Persian style and culture into the Mogul Empire. *British Museum*

To the west the conquest of Gujrat gave Akbar access to the sea and control of Surat, where Moslem pilgrims took ship for Arabia; to the east he defeated Prince Daud in 1574, and gained possession of Bengal; to the north he occupied Baluchistan and Kandahar, the gateway to Persia (1594); to the south he advanced as far as Krishna in order to stay the advance of the Portuguese. He succeeded in annexing Berar and Khandash after having the heroic queen of Ahmadnagar assassinated. Master of Kabul and Kashmir, and having succeeded in holding off the Afghan tribes, he soon decided to turn rather to India. The Rajputs, chivalrous champions of Hinduism, resisted him fiercely. It was only when the defenders of Chitor and Radhanpur committed mass suicide that he succeeded in taking these two fortresses; hundreds of women, among whom were nine queens and thirteen princesses, cast themselves into a fire rather than accept defeat. In the mountains of Aravalli the Rana Partab remained unconquered.

Akbar was a primitive warrior of despotic character.

His unlimited power was founded on his claim to infallibility; whoever inconvenienced him, or even displeased him, met with instant death. If he wanted gold he squeezed it out of the rich, or confiscated the inheritance of his vassals. His desires and whims had to be satisfied immediately; every day special couriers brought him fruit from Turkestan and ice from the Himalayas. He combined a deep sense of his responsibilities with an earnest desire to go down in history as a great emperor, and he took his role as leader very seriously. In an effort to overcome his violent disposition he smoked opium; his priestly calm, his self-control and majestic bearing made a deep impression on his subjects. He gave public audiences twice a day, worked constantly, received reports personally, and had an army of scribes, inspectors and messengers, which he controlled by devious methods.

The Mogul Empire at first meant nothing more than the establishment of savage Asia into the fertile heart of the Hindu world; it was Akbar who organised it into a state. Orderly administration of the Persian type replaced the Turkish system; central government began to take shape; by keeping the nobles at Court Akbar did away with the old Afghan feudalism. He made numerous reforms — for which he was given the sobriquet 'Law-maker' — and sought to make his empire Indo-Mogul rather than Mogul, so as to broaden its foundations. He tried to conciliate the Hindus by exempting them from the taxes imposed on the Moslems; he allowed them to take up public appointments, even choosing some of them for higher posts; and he encouraged the spread of Hindustani.

His unreasonable financial demands and his avarice to some extent destroyed the good effects of his adminis-tration. To pay for his extravagant mode of life and to swell his exchequer, he increased taxes; as taxation was controlled by eminent but greedy officials, it ended by absorbing half the income from the land. India was over-populated and remained defenceless against famine; the women sold either themselves or their children into slavery, and human flesh was on sale in the market-places.

To conceal the poverty of his empire, Akbar decked his cities with unprecedented magnificence. First he built Allahabad, and then another spacious town near Agra, Fatehpur Sikri, through which the wealthy would ride in waggons adorned with silk and drawn by large dogs; they would attend circus games, or admire the emperor's tigers and his 30,000 palace horses. Like Babar and Humayun, Akbar was a prince of refined tastes, and could live only in sumptuous surroundings. His portraits show him with one hand resting on the hilt of his sabre, while with the other he holds a flower to his nose. He was an enthusiastic student of Moslem drawing and fond of music; he encouraged artists and, though he himself could neither read nor write, built up a vast library. Unlike his predecessors, he did not confine his interests to Moslem civilisation; there was a great revival of Hindu literature and art during his reign. Poems were written in Urdu for the first time. The *Mahabharata* epic was translated into Persian. The seven books of poetry called the *Ramayana*, written between 1574 and 1584 by the Brahmin Tulsi Das, were described by the faithful as purifying, like a bath in the sacred waters. A new style also appeared in architecture combining the subtlety of the Hindu tradition with the austere majesty of Moslem art. Akbar was attracted by anything new, and by all that was good in other forms of civilisation; he was the first Indian prince to smoke a pipe of tobacco. An epileptic, subject to strange visions, he was obsessed by problems concerning the life to come, and was interested in all religions. He gathered together representatives of different religions in a specially built house, so that they might compare their doctrines in his presence. His researches led him to eclecticism: he worshipped before the sun, believed in the transmigration of souls, gave protection to the most progressive among the Shiites, married several Hindu women, allowed Vedic rites to be practised in his harem, and, though he did not recognise the divinity of Christ, entrusted the education of one of his sons to Christian tutors. He found the formalism and sectarianism of the orthodox Moslem faith intolerable, looking upon the Koran as a merely human work. 'How,' he would ask, 'was the Prophet able to ascend to heaven, hold a conversation with Allah which amounted to ninety thousand words, and return to find his bed still warm?'

He made fun of the Ulemas (Moslem theologians), and put them to flight by releasing the palace pigs; he gradually deprived them of all influence, and eventually had them hunted down and put to death. His subjects looked upon him as a prophet. He preached in the Mosque at Fatehpur Sikri, gained recognition of his claim to doctrinal infalli-bility in 1579, and three years later founded a new religion. This new 'Divine Faith' — *Din Ilahi* — allowed the worship of fire and the adoration of the sun, but it was an attempt to compromise between the pantheism of the Hindu and the monotheism of the Moslem. Although he wished it to be a universal religion, Akbar did not seek to impose it by force; he emphasised that one could adopt it without ceasing to belong to any other religion. In 1593, he authorised all those who had accepted Islam under duress to return, if they wished, to their former religion. Thanks to this remarkable emperor-philosopher, the principle of tolerance triumphed in a country where it had so far been unknown.

Akbar died in 1606. Within half a century he had created one of the most powerful states in the world. The history of the great Moguls was now to enter upon a completely new era: the heroic age was at an end.

Japan under Nobunaga and Hideyoshi

Japan emerged suddenly from its feudal anarchy. Oda Nobunaga (1533–82), the descendant of an ancient noble family, firmly established his authority over the province of Owari with the aid of a small army of adventurers and *samurais*. The Ashikaga Yoshitesu, driven from Kyoto in 1565, after his brother's assassination, was supported by Oda, who helped him to regain power, and had himself proclaimed vice-shogun. From that moment Oda's power continued to increase. When Yoshitesu tried to shake himself free of his tutelage, Oda deposed him; he announced the downfall of the Ashikagas and became the virtual dictator of the empire (1575). This unexpected revolution did nothing to alter the position of the Mikados, who continued to lead the life of high priests in their palaces at Kyoto; but it provoked a violent reaction in Japan, accustomed as it was to anarchy and feudalism. The princely cliques and the monasteries forgot their quarrels, and joined forces against the usurper. Oda crushed the rebels, executed their leaders, and distributed among his soldiers the estates of a number of leading vassals. One after another the fortress-monasteries were taken by assault and razed to the ground. Oda Nobunaga was killed at Kyoto in 1582 during a military revolt. His lieutenant Hideyoshi, once a peasant, now a military leader, had the murderer crucified and eliminated all his rivals; the emperor granted him the title of High Coun-cillor, and he eventually became dictator.

This rough but shrewd man of the people was devoid of all caste prejudice. Bent on achieving Japanese unity, he set about creating a centralised state. One after another, Sikok, Kyushu, Tsatsuma, Yedo and Sendai were com-pelled to recognise the authority of the government of Kyoto. Impressed and won over by the energy of the new shogun, the *daimyos* served him loyally and gave up their ceaseless quarrels. Once peace was established there was a rapid movement towards national development. The quickly spreading Zen cult had created among the Japanese a love of action and danger, and they plunged

71

boldly into a policy of expansion which foreshadowed the imperialism of the twentieth-century Black Dragon. They settled in Formosa, attacked the Spaniards in the Philippines, and appeared in Cochin-China and Annam. The *samurai* guards who were supplied to the kings of Siam took the law into their own hands. Supported by the princes of the island of Kyushu, their elusive pirates ravaged the coasts of central China, devastated Fukien, and harried Kwang Shun. They sailed up the Blue River and held Nanking to ransom though it was fiercely defended by the fearsome wolf-soldiers of Princess Wache. Hideyoshi, informed by his pirates of the weakness of the Ming Empire, planned to conquer it. To secure an operational base on the continent he invaded Korea, entering Seoul in June 1592, and advanced as far as Pyongyang. He was impatient to conquer ' the four hundred provinces ' and aimed first to reach the Yalu River and then march down to Peking through Manchuria. Three centuries later Japanese generals were to follow his bold plan. The reaction of the Koreans was unexpected; reinforced by the Chinese, they compelled the invaders to fall back along the southern coast. In 1597 the Japanese again took up the offensive without, however, succeeding in reaching Seoul. The death of Hideyoshi in September 1598 brought the expedition to a sudden end.

To further their ambitious policy the Japanese strove to modernise their country. They entered into trade relations with the Portuguese and allowed the Jesuits to become established at Nagasaki. These European settlers built up a trade in arms, revived the art of printing, introduced clocks, and spread the use of tobacco. Hideyoshi found fault with them for not wishing to teach his subjects the art of building ships. In 1587 he banished missionaries because he disapproved of their excessive zeal and ten years later crucified twenty-four priests. Thus Japan had hardly opened its arms to Europe when it retreated once more within itself.

Japanese art

European penetration exercised scarcely any influence on the development of Japanese art. The treatment of pictures and engravings remained dispassionate, in the Chinese manner. Japanese artists retained their mastery in the decoration of sword hilts, in which inlaying became fashionable, with background lines in relief and damascening in brass. In the sphere of painting subjects began to be taken from everyday life.

Shah Abbas and the Safavid Empire

Until the accession of Abbas in 1587 the history of Persia had been a long series of civil wars and court revolutions. The Safavid emperors, besotted by harem, drink and opium, soon lost their vitality. Shah Tahmasp I (1524–76) was poisoned. Ismail II (1576–7) who had most of his brothers murdered, was strangled during a night of debauchery by twelve assassins disguised as women. Mohammed Khudabanda (1577–85), half-blind, had to dismiss his finest minister under pressure from the army. Hamza died violently in 1587. The Khans of the Caucasus fought an endless struggle with those of Georgia. Devastated by disease and famine, the country became disorganised. Its Sunnite neighbours, taking advantage of its weakness,

attempted to conquer it. In the west, the Turks took up the fight again in 1578 and invaded Georgia; they won a battle at Samra after bitter fighting by the light of torches (May 1583), seized Azerbaijan, and entered Tabriz, the Safavid capital (September 1585). In the east, the fanatical Uzbeks, who were gradually becoming established in what later became Russian Central Asia, reached the Caspian, occupied Herat, and devastated Khorassan. Under its first Safavid monarch Persia had experienced a glorious national rebirth. Now, although its brilliant civilisation still exercised a profound influence over a great part of Asia, it gradually lost its national identity, overwhelmed as it was by the horrors of civil war and invasion.

Abbas I (1587–1629), supported by the Emirs of Khorassan, who had set themselves up as his guardians, seized power at the age of twenty-two after the assassination of his brother Hamza. Brought up in the mountains, he possessed the primitive characteristics of his ancestor Ismail I. His decisiveness, tenacity and courage enabled him to overcome the unruly vassals and re-establish order. This powerful warrior with his big moustache and brisk bearing, who never hesitated to gouge out the eyes of his enemies himself, was able to see things realistically when necessary, and to grasp an opportunity. After a temporary setback, the Turks were reoccupying Mesopotamia; at the same time, in the east, the Holy City of Meshed fell into the hands of the Uzbeks. Abbas determined to give up waging an exhausting war on two fronts; in 1590, therefore, he signed a humiliating treaty with the Turks at Constantinople, under which he recognised most of the Ottoman conquests (Tabriz, Azerbaijan, Georgia). The Iranians promised ' not to revile any of the companions of the prophet, or the Caliphs, or Aïsha the Chaste, the mother of all the faithful '. This apparent renunciation of Shiism did not weaken the emperor's prestige; he no longer had to hold off the Turks, and soon gave proof of his true qualities by a resolute attack on the eastern Sunnites. The Uzbeks were beaten in the vicinity of Herat in 1597, driven from Khorassan, and thrown beyond the Amu-Darya.

For the first time for many years Persia was at peace. Abbas took advantage of this to complete the pacification of his provinces; but, like his contemporary Akbar, he did not hesitate to show his independence in his relations with the nomad tribes who had been responsible for the amazing good fortune of his ancestors. Up to that time the highland Kizil-bashes had provided all the contingents of the Persian army, and had been granted small fiefs in exchange for their service; they maintained that they obeyed none but their feudal chiefs and, jealous of their privileges, were happy to regard themselves as the protectors of the Safavids. Abbas was anxious to be independent of them, and in future he asked them for only a part of his cavalry. With slaves whom he had captured or purchased in the Caucasian countries he built a new army and selected its officers himself. Although this army had not yet acquired national status, it was henceforth permanent; it ceased to bear the stamp of feudalism and could really be called

Early seventeenth-century miniature of Humayun's accession durbar at Agra in 1530. He inherited from Babar an unstable, unhappy empire and was exiled for ten years. He demonstrated a refinement new to the Moguls however which his son Akbar continued. *Victoria & Albert Museum*

A Turkish Sultan of the early seventeenth century. The Ottoman Empire threatened Asia as much as Europe. Holy wars between Shiites and Sunnites were even more bitterly fought than against the Christians. *Marburg*

China and the Ming Dynasty

While Persia and India were being reconstituted, the Chinese Ming Dynasty was proceeding slowly towards its fall. Only the general inertia of the country permitted the Mings to survive. Despite mild bursts of energy, Lung-King (1567–72) achieved little during the course of his reign beyond bringing a few tribes back into his sphere of control. Wan-Li (1573–1620), who became emperor at ten years of age, was a lover of ostentation. He spent the first year of his personal rule draining his treasury and the remainder vainly endeavouring to replenish it by imposing new taxes. The Court was getting more and more overcrowded, and was the centre of intrigues and plots. The women of the harem schemed to get their own sons proclaimed the emperor's successor, and the eunuchs, who disposed of fiefs and government appointments, assisted the most easy-going of the young princes to power. The feudal lords, while extending their influence by thrusting the scholars whom they patronised into public appointments, had just enough energy to foment minor disturbances in the provinces. The badly paid officials plundered the treasury and squandered the country's resources. Although China was now growing maize, which pilgrims had introduced from Mecca, the birthrate was high and the country was no longer able to feed its sixty million inhabitants. A considerable reduction in the amount of land under cultivation followed a renewal of internal disturbance, and many peasants deserted the land to become pirates or bandits.

The Middle Empire succeeded in establishing a protectorate over Korea, yet it became less and less capable of defending its own frontiers. The Tatar Khan, bought over by Lung-King, secured from Wan-Li a part of Shansi province; the Manchus penetrated into Liaotung and founded a capital city at Hingcheng; Burmese forces invaded Yunnan. China, offering feeble opposition to the Malay and Japanese pirates, abandoned overseas expeditions and kept to the mainland. The Ming rulers forbade their subjects to undertake ocean voyages. By 1573 a barrier existed between the interior of the country and the Portuguese trading post at Macao.

The weakening of the Empire was not accompanied by a decline of Chinese culture. The hostility of the imperial eunuchs did not succeed in slowing down the spread of the doctrine of Wang-Tang, whose complete works were published in 1572. Of the literary output under the Ming the novel proved to be the most noteworthy.

Asia at the end of the sixteenth century

By the end of the sixteenth century Asia was still the most densely populated and richest continent in the world. To Western travellers it continued to give the impression of extraordinary vitality, but it failed to play the part in the general development of the world which might have been expected of it, considering its resources and the antiquity of its civilisation. Despite their importance, size, and the prowess of a few conquerors, these vast empires were much more weakly organised than European states.

Though the notion of the world's unity was spreading, the various 'worlds' of which Asia was composed were more separated than they had been at the beginning of

the king's army. He equipped it with five hundred bronze cannon, cast for the first time in his own country, and employed two English soldiers of fortune, Anthony and Robert Shirley, to train his troops in European methods of warfare.

Abbas's sole object in re-organising his empire was to be strong enough to continue his struggle against the Turks. Although it was only during the second half of his reign that he showed his true calibre, he was already worthy of the title 'Abbas the Great'. His ambassadors at Constantinople took precedence over the envoys of the King of France and the Holy Roman Emperor, and surpassed them in magnificence; a hundred cannon shots hailed their arrival, and 19,000 beasts of burden would bear their sumptuous presents for the Padishah.

A sixteenth-century Chinese ship with sails made of reeds and a wooden anchor. By the second half of the century the weakened Ming Empire was unable to defend its frontiers or combat Malay and Japanese pirates and the Chinese were forbidden to undertake ocean voyages.

the century. The abrupt deterioration of the caravan routes of central Asia underlined their isolation. Between Persia and India and the countries of the Far East there was less intercourse than between Spain and the New World. At the moment when control of the seas emerged as an indispensable condition of power, Asia became essentially continental.

In brushing aside the advances of Europe, which offered trading relations from the Red Sea to Japan, Asia safeguarded a mode of life in conformity with her own conception of happiness. She declined to progress, rejecting the means of liberation and advancement which she would have gained through technological advance. Asia was a prisoner of its past; it was more concerned with surviving than with living; it experienced no burst of energy, no creative urge during the turbulent but fruitful period which the Renaissance meant to humanity.

AFRICA IN THE SECOND HALF OF THE SIXTEENTH CENTURY

No single episode in the history of Africa produced lasting progress. The conquest of the Songhoi by Morocco ruined the Sudan. The rise of Bornu had no repercussions beyond the region surrounding Lake Chad. The advance of the Gallas weakened Abyssinia without destroying it, and without their succeeding in forming a new state. Migrations and the slave trade underlined the disintegration of Negro Africa, where early attempts to spread the Gospel failed.

The last days of the Songhoi Empire

It looked at first as though the Songhoi Empire, along the Niger, had a great future. The Askia David (1549–82) pacified the area, re-organised it and administered it wisely; he submitted the country more and more to the influence of Maghrib civilisation. His three sons, however, put his work in jeopardy: Mohammed el-Hadji was dethroned in 1586; Mohammed Bani (1586–8) died just when mutineers were preparing to assassinate him; Ishak II had to face a Moroccan invasion.

Unlike the rest of the Maghrib, Morocco escaped conquest by Turkey. A national and religious revival resulted in its Wattasi dynasty being replaced in 1553 by that of the sherifs of the south, the Beni-Sads: as independent sovereigns of the Sous from 1509 the Beni-Sads had relentlessly taken over the conduct of the holy war against the infidels. Ahmed El-Mansur — the 'Victorious' — (1578–1603) was proclaimed Sultan on the field of battle at Kasr-al-Kabir, where he destroyed an expedition under Sebastian, King of Portugal. His love of power, gold and adventure led him to conquer the Sudan against the advice of his counsellors. He made Marrakesh his capital, and on two occasions raided the salt mines of Taghezza; when Ishak refused to pay him tribute he sent in an army under the command of the renegade Spaniard Djouder. This army, composed of Negroes, Andalusian mercenaries and Turkish deserters, contained 2,500 harquebusiers, 1,500 cavalry armed with lances, 8,000 camels and 1,000 pack-horses. During the

75

four months the army took to cross the desert it lost three-quarters of its effective strength. In March 1591 at Tondibi its firearms threw into panic the herds of cattle which the Sudanese were using as a barricade. Armed only with lances, cudgels and javelins, Ishak's troops were slaughtered despite their numerical superiority, and the survivors fled in disorder. In April 1591, Timbuktu was captured and brutally sacked. Hunted down by men on fast dromedaries, the Askia eventually took refuge in Gourmanche territory, where he was assassinated in April 1592. His death brought about the submission of the whole of the Sudan. Enriched by booty, Ahmed was able to adorn Marrakesh with marble brought from Carrara, where it had been bought against its weight in sugar. Day and night in his workshops 1,400 workmen struck pieces of gold. His victory was, however, a bitter disappointment. The Sudan was a country of barter: it was not productive, and the southern merchants deserted it because of its poverty. The Pashas who henceforward governed the country exhausted it by their extortions, and let it drift slowly towards anarchy. The vacuum left by the disappearance of the Songhoi Empire was destined to throw the whole of western Africa out of balance for a long time to come.

The Mali Empire tried in vain to profit from the defeat of its eastern neighbours. Mamudu III, whose troops were now using firearms for the first time, failed to get possession of Djenne. Discredited by his failure, he had to recognise the independence of his outer provinces. The period of Sudanese supremacy was over. The only region of Negro Africa in which great empires had succeeded in taking root was once more destined to pass through long centuries of obliteration.

Islam and central Sudan. The zenith of the Bornu Empire

Islam grew weaker when Koli-Tenguella (1559–86), leader of the Peuls (Fulani) of Futa Jalon, founded the kingdom of Denianke; but it penetrated into the district around Lake Chad, advanced as far as the Hausa country, took root in Bagirmi after the conversion of Abdullah (1561–1602), and triumphed in Darfur, where the pagan dynasty was overthrown by the Arab Solum Sulaiman in 1596. Following a period of confusion the Moslem state of Bornu once more became strong. Idris III (1571–1603) had at his disposal an army of 25,000 men, armed with firearms brought from Tripoli. He repelled the Tuaregs, strengthened his dominion from Kano to Boulala, and kept the various races of his vast empire fighting against each other, the more easily to rule them. The Arab chroniclers placed him on a level with the sultans of Baghdad and Cairo.

Abyssinia and the growth of the Gallas

Despite the Turkish occupation of Massawa in 1557 and the death of the Negus Glaodios, who died fighting the Somalis in 1559, Abyssinia managed to withstand the Moslem threat. Its resistance discouraged the Danakils, whose attacks ceased in 1578. The Gallas, who had remained pagans, had so far infiltrated very slowly into the south of the kingdom, but in a sudden frenzy of conquest they flung fresh troops against the Abyssinian plateaus. In successive waves they overflowed into the interior of the country, the whole of Choa and most of the western provinces. Instead of co-ordinating their drives, they split up into independent tribes, allowing considerable areas of native population to remain in existence and failing to organise the conquered territory. Sagad II (1559–63) and Sarsa Dangheb (1563–97), without entirely holding off the invasion, succeeded in saving the vital centres of the kingdom. Abyssinia was wearing itself out trying to preserve its independence, and internal strife weakened it further. The Portuguese Jesuits, who had been welcomed by Glaodios, persecuted by Sagad II, and strongly supported by Za-Dangheb (1597–1607), strove to win the country over to the Roman Church. Their activities were thwarted by the local priests and provoked a violent reaction. Religion, after having been for centuries the anchor, the very soul of Abyssinian unity, became a source of discord.

Over the remainder of Africa history throws only occasional flashes of light. All the great kingdoms disintegrated — the Loango, Congo, Ardre, Monomotapa. The revolt of the Keri weakened Sennar. With the exception of Benin, where the art of working in bronze reached its greatest heights, the areas under district officers, which up to then had made some progress, either deteriorated or remained at a standstill. Ardansi (Ghana) tended to dominate the Akan people, and the 'second kingdom' of Louba (Upper Congo) was founded by Hung Mbili in 1585. A number of Peuls (Fulani) established themselves in the Cameroons (Adamawa); some Himas occupied the region of the Great Lakes, and the Zimbas moved into Mozambique. The Bantu of the south-east intensified their pressure on the Bushmen and the Hottentots. As in the case of so many other migrations obliterated by forest and savanna, these were accompanied by so much devastation and slaughter that new civilisations did not arise from them.

The failure of Portuguese colonisation and evangelism

To consolidate their position, the Portuguese in 1574 settled down near Luanda (Angola) and in 1592 took possession of Mombasa (Mozambique) after repelling a Turco-Arab offensive (1585–9). Their attempts to colonise and spread the Gospel were none the less disappointing. In the Congo, the converted Negroes numbered under five thousand. Soon the pagans reacted violently. In 1561, the first Catholic martyr was strangled in the *kraal* of Monomotapa. The Portuguese failed to reach the gold mines in the interior. Faced with the bankruptcy of their large estates, they henceforth confined their interests to the slave trade. Their mulatto descendants (*pombeiros*) proved to be just as savage as the Arab traders. The slave-raids and the resulting disorders brought ruin, a fall in population and disorganisation over extensive areas, even to the very heart of the continent.

Africa in the sixteenth century

During the course of the sixteenth century Africa did not experience any movement similar to the European Renaissance; indeed, it became more than ever backward by comparison with Europe. Nor did Africa experience brutal but fruitful upheavals such as those that occurred in the New World. Deep down its life was in no way affected by the movement of populations and the perpetual instability of states. Africa's political complexion, its customs and beliefs underwent no change. Although its geographical situation did not exactly condemn it to isolation, and although the continent had maintained numerous relations with Asian and Mediterranean countries before the coming of modern times, it had voluntarily remained aloof from external influences. Africa's pagan communities, in which the dead were considered to be as important as the living, and in which individuals played no part, remained too passionately religious to allow them to reject tradition. To Africa progress could mean only sacrilege or treason. Unlike Asia during the golden age of its civilisations — and yet like Asia unchangeable — Africa's inheritance did not include the ingredients of power and splendour which might have disguised the uncertainties of its future.

Bronze head from Benin. Alone among the states of West Africa, Benin neither fell under the Turkish yoke nor succumbed as the result of tribal warfare. During the second half of the sixteenth century the art of working in bronze reached its greatest heights. *Marburg*

THE SEVENTEENTH CENTURY

CHAPTER FIVE

THE OPENING YEARS: 1598-1620

Whereas the sixteenth century opened in discovery and intellectual ferment, the seventeenth century began in relative quiet. Europe, like the other continents, underwent no further essential changes and, except in Russia, enjoyed comparative calm until 1618. The death of Philip II and Queen Elizabeth brought an easing of tension between Catholic and Protestant powers. Spain and England, both weakened by the struggle, abandoned their leadership of the opposing forces, and no other nations were strong enough to assume their roles. In France the royal authority, restored by Henry IV, again became enfeebled after that strong monarch's tragic end. In Germany, where feudal chaos persisted, the religious truce established by the Peace of Augsburg slowly deteriorated into an uneasy armed neutrality. While the Reformation, losing its fire, relied increasingly on the power of the State, the Renaissance survived in the realm of learning. Modern liberalism made its appearance in Protestant countries and baroque civilisation flowered in Catholic Europe. In the East, the Orthodox civilisation of Russia endured a 'time of troubles' which disorganised Muscovy until the accession of the Romanoffs in 1613.

FRANCE'S TEMPORARY RECOVERY

Henry IV (1598-1610)

Henry IV, a Gascon of strong and spirited stock, loved power, but shrewdness, bonhomie and a talent for compromise saved him from being a despot. An attractive personality made him popular with men and successful with women, but he was also a good judge of humanity. 'Many have betrayed me,' he said. 'Few have deceived me.' He was a man of action, and to keep in touch with the mood of his people he made constant journeys on horseback throughout the kingdom. He was indifferent to the reproach that his government 'smelled not of the study but of the stable'. His ambition was to combine two titles to fame: Liberator and Restorer of the State.

The monarchy, degraded by forty years of civil war, regained its authority. 'You are my right arm,' said Henry to his officers of the law, 'but if the right arm becomes gangrened the left arm must cut if off.' Royal agents were sent through the provinces on special missions, and the liberties of the towns were curtailed. The haughty and recalcitrant Marshal Biron, thirty-two times wounded, still believed a great nobleman could conspire against the King

Side by side with the splendours of baroque art the seventeenth century also illustrated scenes of everday life, especially in the north. These homely pictures were usually painted by local artists such as this by Flemish artist David Teniers.

with impunity, but he was brought to the block in 1602.

France was re-organised. Sully managed the finances with the zeal of an accountant, and was able to accumulate reserves of gold in the vaults of the Bastille. He introduced mulberry cultivation, brought experts from Holland to drain swamps, encouraged and protected the peasants. Sully, who worked beneath a portrait of Calvin, also sought to suppress luxury. The King, however, also listened to the advice of his Controller General, Laffemas, a strange, self-taught individual, who developed commerce, forbade the importation of foreign products under penalty of hanging, encouraged the silk industry of Lyon and Tours and founded workshops in the Louvre for the production of tapestry. French exports to Spain drew in American gold from her neighbour. Some of it went into the embellishment of Paris.

France was, however, less happy than these brilliant appearances seemed to indicate. The economy was over-regulated and enterprise was discouraged. The 'chicken in the pot on Sundays' remained a rare luxury, and taxes weighed heavily on the peasants. Efforts to reduce municipal independence produced rebellion. The old feudal spirit was still alive. The former Leaguers had not laid down their arms. The royal mistresses and the intrigues of love

The seventeenth century was a period of turbulence in Europe, an age of civil strife. Events in England, though of great political significance for the future, did little to change the everyday life of the common people, as seen in this late seventeenth-century tapestry. *Victoria & Albert Museum*

Henry IV and his wife Marie de' Medici. Though Henry IV had seemingly been successful in strengthening the economy of France and in building up a cohesive state, disruptive forces still lay beneath the surface and were to come into the open after his assassination. *Wallace Collection*

Marie de' Medici, Regent of France from 1610 to 1617. During these seven years of incompetent rule she undid much of the good work of Henry IV. Exiled by her son Louis XIII in 1617, Marie returned in 1621 and in 1624 persuaded Louis to appoint her protégé Richelieu Prime Minister. *Popper*

affairs cast a cloud over the King: age and the pursuit of pleasure had taken their toll. By his achievements Henry IV prepared the way for absolute monarchy; but he left two grave problems for his successors. The Protestants, to whom the Edict of Nantes of 1598 had granted important privileges, threatened to become an *imperium in imperio*. And a new bureaucratic class was arising — the *noblesse de la robe*, created in 1604 when, by the payment of a new tax, members of the *parlements* could make their offices hereditary and thus gain security of tenure; this might in the future paralyse the monarchy. In spite of the awakening of national sentiment the old disruptive religious ideals had not disappeared; and the Jesuits, triumphant over their opponents in France, renewed there the dream of a vast unified Catholic empire.

In 1610 Henry IV judged that his kingdom had recovered sufficiently to resist the claim of the Habsburg Emperor upon the Rhenish Duchy of Cleves, gateway from Germany into Holland. Making an alliance with the Protestant princes, he gathered an army and decided to march against the Emperor. His intervention threatened to ruin the Counter-Reformation. It was even rumoured that he planned to attack the Pope. At this moment Henry was assassinated by a fanatic. No king of France was ever more deeply mourned.

France from 1610 to 1621

Since Louis XIII was only nine years old in 1610 his mother, Marie de' Medici, a dull and incompetent Italian, was proclaimed regent by the *Parlement* of Paris. Marie, whose political acumen was non-existent, entrusted her power to a compatriot, Concini, whose sole ambition was to enrich himself. The nobles and the Protestants became restive. The States General were convoked in 1614, argued, and achieved nothing. Meanwhile the King, a timid youth, was kept in the background. His friends urged him to action. In 1617 Concini was assassinated, and the Queen Mother ordered to leave Paris. The young King now decided to govern for himself, but in fact left all power in the hands of his Chief Falconer, an obscure gentleman from Provence whom he created Marquis d'Albert, Duc de Luynes and finally Constable of France. The situation worsened, and the great nobles again took up arms. In December 1621 Luynes, the favourite, died of fever during a campaign against a Protestant revolt. France found itself in the same state of weakness, confusion and misery that it had known at the end of the Wars of Religion.

THE HOPES AND FEARS OF CATHOLIC EUROPE

Catholic Europe, under the aegis of Rome and the Habsburgs, still seemed to be a community with pretensions to universality, while Pope Paul V (1605–21) strove, with the aid of the Jesuits, to enforce Ultramontane doctrines.

The Battle between Carnival and Lent. A satirical comment on the Reformation and Counter-Reformation by Bruegel the Elder. 1559. *Kunsthistorisches Museum, Vienna*

Spain under Philip III

Spain, since the abdication of the Emperor Charles V, had been ruled by the senior branch of the Habsburg family; and law, monarchy and faith continued to be closely associated. Mistress of so great an empire that ships could sail round the world without leaving Spanish waters, Spain was still prouder of her ardent mysticism, and the richness of a culture which seemed to prolong her golden age. Languid, wan and indolent, Philip III (1598–1621) was brought up not as a king but as a monk, and his virtues were largely negative.

Incapable of protecting the treasure fleet from the depredations of privateers, he was forced to wind up the war his father, Philip II, had bequeathed to him and sign a peace treaty with England in 1604. In 1609 a twelve-year truce was arranged with the United Provinces. Philip did not abandon the ambitions of the Habsburgs, but aspired to no more than becoming the patriarchal head of Europe and peacefully marrying off the Infantas to the great Catholic sovereigns. Thus his eldest daughter was married to Louis XIII. The prudence of his policy was, however, compromised by his religious intolerance. Moriscos — or Moslems — whose conversion to Christianity was dubious, and whom Cervantes had called ' the leprosy and weasels of the kingdom ', were accused of collusion with the pirates and expelled, taking with them only what they could carry. They perished for the most part of exposure and hunger on the coasts of Africa. Spain thus lost irreplaceable artisans and her most highly skilled farmers; but her economic decline cannot be attributed solely to this. At the same time her national industry was withering away, and the King's favourites, by providing the Court with lavish tournaments, bullfights and extravagant festivals, emptied the royal treasury. As early as 1619 the *Cortes*, noting the depopulation and impoverishment of the country, prophesied its decadence:' Another century and Spain will be extinguished. ... There will not then remain even pilots enough to sail off in search of refuge elsewhere! '

Italy and Belgium

With the exception of the vigorous little Duchy of Savoy and the proud Republic of Venice Italy was dominated, either directly or indirectly, by Spain. The poverty and disorder of the country were ill concealed by the religious pageantry of the Counter-Reformation, the gorgeous carnivals at Venice and survivals of the Renaissance. The decline of the great continental roads strangled its commerce. The Spanish viceroys were harsh administrators and southern Italy, ravaged by pestilence and banditry, seemed to be on the verge of revolt.

Belgium, on the other hand, was independent for the first time and enjoyed a period of brilliant prosperity. As a safeguard against the Dutch contagion the Habsburgs had in 1598 set up Belgium as an autonomous state, governed by the daughter of Philip II, Isabella, and her husband the Archduke Albert, son of the Emperor

The Adoration of the Name of Jesus or, more popularly, *The Dream of Philip II*, by El Greco. 1578–9. The three kneeling figures represent the King, Pope and Doge. El Escorial, Madrid. *Holford*

Philip III of Spain (1598–1621). During his reign Spain lived on her past achievements, unable to control the activities of the Barbary pirates and privateers on the high seas, forced to make peace with the Netherlands and England and paradoxically weakened by the influx of American gold. *Marburg*

Strolling musicians, by Rembrandt. Independence, maritime success and the prosperity this brought encouraged a lively development of the arts in the United Provinces and in Belgium. Scenes from everyday life were often the subjects favoured by burgher patrons. *British Museum*

F

Printing-works at Nuremberg in the seventeenth century, from a contemporary woodcut. Hans Sachs and Albrecht Dürer were sons of Nuremberg, an important cultural centre of Bavaria, bastion of the Catholic south of Germany. Technological progress was to be arrested by the religious wars. *Giraudon*

James I of England (1603–25). A flattering portrait of a physically ill-favoured king. He cared little for the welfare of his subjects and less for the prerogatives of Parliament. *Radio Times Hulton Picture Library*

The baroque style was not confined to spectacular architecture: the taste for the elaborate pervaded literature, music, painting and even the crafts, as is seen in this seventeenth-century German tray. The beaten metal has an ivory centre and is enriched with enamel-work. *Marburg*

82

Maximilian. Brussels became its capital. Antwerp, home of Rubens, thrived with the restoration of peace and as the commercial metropolis of Europe soon rivalled Amsterdam. But these sovereigns left no direct descendants to inherit the throne and in 1621 the country reverted to Spain, which at once sacrificed it to its own interests.

The Habsburgs of Austria and Germany

In Austria the junior branch of the Habsburgs no longer formed a united family. The head of the house, Rudolf II (1576–1612), was a misanthropist who went slightly mad. He shut himself up in his palace at Prague with his alchemists and, retaining possession only of Bohemia, finally left the remainder of his vast patrimony to his brother or his nephews. The Austrian sovereigns were by custom rather than law also hereditary Emperors of Germany; their election had become automatic. But the advantages they gained from their position were derisory. The German Diets met irregularly and had lost all influence. The federal army was little more than a myth. The princes and the cities of the Empire distrusted Vienna. During the reign of Matthias (1612–19), however, the growing strength of the Counter-Reformation put new life into the ancient Imperial dream. In 1609, under the leadership of the Duke of Bavaria, the Catholics formed a Holy League to combat the Evangelical Union composed of Calvinists and Lutherans. Such a league, if victorious, could have given Germany a centralised monarchy. It was this dream which Ferdinand, Matthias's nephew and successor as Emperor, attempted to realise. Ferdinand was kindly by nature and without great intelligence, but from his deep piety he derived a burning will for action and even a kind of heroism. In his youth he had already extirpated heresy in his Alpine duchies in three brief years. Age and accession to power fanned his religious zeal. The Thirty Years' War would soon be the fruit of his fanaticism.

Baroque civilisation

The baroque movement was closely associated with the Europe of the Counter-Reformation and arose in the Mediterranean world. It then developed further in Belgium, spread through the Danubian dominions of the Habsburgs, and reached Poland. Its emphasis on apologetics, Thomist philosophy and the drama of the liturgy, together with its aesthetic flamboyance and chivalrous idealism made the baroque spirit seem at first a reversion to medievalism. In fact, it represented the flowering of a new sensibility, delighting in pomp, movement, dramatic emphasis, and fascinated by mystery and artifice. Its frenzied restlessness and love of theatrical effect are as evident in the paintings of Rubens (1577–1640) with their exuberant expanse of flesh, as in the polyphony of Monteverdi and the first operas (*Orfeo*, 1607; *Arianna*, 1608), the vehement sculpture and the magnificent gilded churches of Bernini (1598–1680), the flowery poetical conceits of Marino, or the prolix and high-flown novels of Madeleine de Scudéry. Baroque, too, was the sumptuous decor of everyday life: the elaborately inlaid furniture, the Venetian mirrors, the corkscrew pillars, the illusionist effects and enchanted gardens. Yet although it contributed to the success of the Counter-Reformation, the movement in the end betrayed its mission. The thirst for the infinite culminated in absurdity. A desire to glorify the mystery of God merely created sanctuaries without mystery, and was dissipated in festivals whose appeal was not to the soul but to the senses. Enamoured of the absolute, the baroque found the visible world intolerable. As the title of Calderón's best-known play suggested, life became a dream. The very people who accepted this austere view could be distracted by mere whimsicality. Baroque civilisation was to be the victim of its own contradictions, and the tragic sense of its own futility drove it to further folly and exaggeration. The inevitable reaction was the desire for a new attitude towards life.

THE DEVELOPMENT OF THE PROTESTANT COUNTRIES

England under James I (1603-25)

The Tudor line ended with Elizabeth and the King of Scotland succeeded her as James I (1603–25). He was thirty-seven years old, physically cowardly and ill-groomed. With his enormous head, bandy legs, stutter and dribbling mouth from which his tongue half protruded, he cut

Guy Fawkes and the conspirators of 1605. The Gunpowder Plot failed, the conspirators were executed and all Catholics suffered. The Plot and its aftermath pointed up the growing problem of conscientious opposition to the Anglican monarchy from Catholics and Puritans. *British Museum*

Contemporary illustration of the truce between Spain and the United Provinces of 1609. Forced to concede this truce by her own weakness and the growing strength of the United Provinces as a maritime and commercial power, Spain kept a hopeful eye on the internal political difficulties of the young nation. *Giraudon*

an unkingly figure. His conception of the royal power was none the less elevated. Highly educated, learned to the point of pedantry, and possessed of great intellectual subtlety, he considered himself the philosopher or, more accurately, the theologian of absolute monarchy. Since James protected Anglicanism, which enjoined submission to the king's will, Catholic conspirators placed barrels of gunpowder in the cellars of Westminster. Discovered in time, the Gunpowder Plot (1605) enflamed public opinion against Rome and was followed by severe anti-Catholic measures. More dangerous than the Catholics, however, was the opposition of extreme Protestants.

Although many of the early Puritans, as they came to be called, remained inside the Anglican Church, distinguished only by their piety and simplicity of life, others had already begun to show extremes of sectarian fanaticism. Some were recognisable by the scriptural flavour of their speech, others by their cropped hair and contempt for luxury. The most determined among them asserted that nobody and nothing should stand between God and the individual man. Bishops (and even the King) might therefore be ministers of the devil. James, remembering his unhappy childhood among the Presbyterians of Scotland, harried these fanatics, driving many of them to emigrate to the New World. But their influence did not decrease.

While Puritanism gave its blessing to individual enterprise the King sold monopolies to raise money. He was, however, a poor housekeeper and was continually in debt. Money had to be obtained by every possible means. Titles of nobility were sold. Arbitrary taxes were put on wood, wine, leather and even currants. He was at loggerheads with each of his Parliaments, and their remonstrances were frequent. His unpopularity was increased by the arrogance of his favourites. When in 1625 the King died, the state of the kingdom was unsettled and the future of its new ruling house, the Stuarts, uncertain.

The United Provinces of Holland

Liberalism had not yet entirely triumphed in the young republic of the United Provinces. Each of the seven provinces maintained its own particular institutions, and its Estates — or local parliament — promulgated the laws which its Stadtholder executed. Permanent liaison between them was provided by the States General in the Hague, which was a Diet, not a Parliament. The Stadtholder of most of the provinces was the head of the house of Orange, Maurice of Nassau, who had succeeded his father, William the Silent, as commander-in-chief of the armies. Maurice, a soldier and man of action, had won great popularity during the war with Spain; on the strength of this he ordered the beheading on the pretext of heresy of his rival, the virtuous Jan van Olden Barneveldt, Advocate General and Grand Pensionary of the powerful province of Holland. Maurice's partisans, nobles and peasants alike, were uncompromising Calvinists and desired a single, central and almost monarchical authority. The burghers of Holland, on the other hand, were in favour of a liberal and peaceful republic which would welcome all comers. The former were for the most part countrymen; the latter were townsmen who had been enriched by the spice trade. They had returned from Indonesia bearing strange idols, escaped the proselytising fury of Puritanism and discovered the virtue of tolerance. The United Provinces, whose ships

The Seven Provinces, flagship of the Dutch Admiral Ruyter (1607–76). The Dutch war fleet powerfully backed the Dutch merchant adventurers, who became well established in Indonesia and were beginning to gain ground at the expense of other colonial powers. *Rijksmuseum*

sailed the seven seas, could not, in fact, form a closed and static society. Faced by a Spain which had not abandoned all hope of revenge, the young nation remained uneasy and still too divided to participate actively in the affairs of Europe.

MUSCOVY FROM BORIS GODUNOFF TO MICHAEL ROMANOFF

The 'Time of Troubles'

Cut off from the open seas, Muscovy played a role in international politics as unimportant as that of the United Provinces. But while Holland was of all European nations perhaps the most open to the currents of contemporary thought, Muscovy was the most closed. Its insignificance was doubly assured by menaces from Poland and Sweden and by problems arising from a long and troubled period of internal strife which endangered its very existence as a nation. After the reign of the incompetent Feodor (1584–98) the energetic Boris Godunoff seized the crown. He met the intrigues of the boyars with a policy of terror and fought a pretender to the throne, the impostor Dmitri who claimed to be the late Tsar's brother and was supported by Poland. But in 1605 Boris died when his partisans were about to desert him, leaving a demoralised and devastated kingdom. For eight years usurpers and adventurers fought for the vacant throne. The peasants and the Cossacks rose, while roving bands of military freebooters sacked the starving towns; everywhere villages were in flames; in the north Swedes occupied Novgorod. In 1611 the disheartened boyars elected as Tsar the son of the King of Poland, whose troops had just occupied Moscow.

The first Romanoff

There arose in Russia a burning desire for liberation from these misfortunes. The Orthodox Church led a desperate crusade against the invaders, Lutheran and Catholic alike. The Troitsa Monastery, which was besieged in vain for more than a year, became the rallying point of national resistance. Before being thrown into prison, where he died under torture, the Patriarch Hermogenes roused the towns of the north. The hopes of the patriots were dashed when a mass uprising was crushed, but a new voluntary army was raised and marched slowly towards Moscow, preceded by church banners and miracle-working icons; night and day public prayers besought the aid of God. In October 1612 the army of liberation entered the Kremlin. An assembly of deputies drawn from all classes — the *Zemski Sobor* — inaugurated its work by a three days' fast and on 21 February 1613 proclaimed as Tsar Michael Romanoff, a boy of sixteen. The Romanoffs were a noble family who had given many proofs of their patriotism. The rhythm of events in Russia again followed a different pattern from that of the rest of Europe. The calm opening years of the seventeenth century began — and ended — fifteen years later in Russia than in the West. The new Tsar Michael (1613–45) appeased Poland by giving up Smolensk, drove out the Swedes and dispersed the roving bands of freebooters. From 1619 he governed in collaboration with his father, the Patriarch Philaret, and, with the support of the *Zemski Sobor*, which sat almost permanently until 1622, he pacified and rebuilt the Muscovite empire. At this moment the Thirty Years' War was already convulsing Germany.

ASIA

In Asia the first third of the seventeenth century, far from marking the opening of a new age, appeared to be a prolongation of the preceding epoch. In India the Grand Mogul Jehan Gir ruled like his father Akbar the Great. In China the decline of the Ming Dynasty continued. In Japan the energetic Shogun Iyeyasu resumed the policy of his predecessor. In Siberia the Russians continued their slow and mysterious progress towards the east. These years without striking or decisive events would be a period of little interest in the history of Asia had not Shah Abbas of Persia carried the power of the Safavid dynasty to its zenith and won a world-wide fame.

The climax of Abbas the Great's reign

Abbas was first and foremost a religious leader ardently faithful to the Shiite traditions of his dynasty. The entire Court was obliged to accompany him on his numerous pilgrimages. Since the Treaty of Constantinople in 1590 his sole ambition had been to wreak vengeance on the Sunnites. As soon as he could muster cannon and musketeers

Polish soldier of the early seventeenth century. The occupation of Moscow by Polish troops and the accession of a Polish Roman Catholic Tsar in 1611 brought Muscovy's 'Time of Troubles' to a head. A strong nationalist reaction under the Orthodox banner achieved liberation under the first Romanoff Tsar. *British Museum*

Turkish decorative script. As the Ottoman Empire lost ground in the east many craftsmen fled from the Ottoman Empire to the more encouraging atmosphere of Ispahan. *Giraudon*

trained in the European manner, he renewed the holy war against the Ottoman Turks. In 1602 he reconquered Tabriz and Kars; in 1604, Georgia and Basrah. In 1623 his troops entered Baghdad by night. Turkish counter-offensives in 1625 and in 1630 resulted for them in humiliating defeats. Abbas completed his conquests by occupying the port of Bender and taking Hormuz from the Portuguese in 1622. His acquisitions doubled the population of his dominions and he restored Persian unity from the Caspian to the Caucasus, from the Tigris to the Indus.

A savage and fanatical warrior, Abbas was, like all the Safavids, cruel and despotic. He had his oldest son murdered; then, in a fit of remorse, insisted that the assassin should bring him the head of his own son. Two of Abbas's other sons were blinded at his orders. Under a sovereign so jealous of his powers, order was brutally maintained. Reforms gave both the army and the State a more rigid structure. The turbulent mountain tribes were forced to renounce their demands; the roads were guarded by police; the spectacle of thieves buried alive, studded with burning candles or dragged with trailing entrails through the streets by horses contributed as much as the vigilance of the archers to a respect for the laws and to the disappearance of brigandage. Special judges were appointed to protect the people from the extortions of provincial governors.

Persian trade developed in the peace these methods provided. The international routes to Europe and to India were made safe and along them travelled glassware, lace and silks, carpets, spices, porcelain and precious stones. European merchants were given privileges. The port of Bender-Abbas was opened to English commerce. Thousands of Armenian craftsmen, fleeing from the Turks, settled in the new town of Mazanderan and in Julfa at the gates of Ispahan, where they resumed their industries. Rest-houses were established at points along the roads for the convenience of travellers. In the capital of the empire, Ispahan, arose buildings and monuments noteworthy for their elegance, easy grace and perfection of detail. The square towers of Ispahan, the bridges over the Zayendeh River, the royal square and the mosques with their monumental porches, were the wonder and admiration of Western travellers. Lovelier still were the running waters of the great gardens of Char Bagh and the delicate blue tiles, touched with gold and exquisitely glazed, which gave a fairy-like impression of lightness and transparency to the walls of the Hall of Forty Pillars.

The Grand Mogul Jehan Gir

Nevertheless, in brilliance, if not in actual power, the empire of the Grand Moguls of India still excelled the Persia of the Safavids. Jehan Gir (1605–28) — ' Conqueror of the World ' — pursued the generous policy of Akbar the Great. Jehan Gir had no racial or religious prejudice, and opened the highest offices in his Court to the Hindu nobility. He authorised free controversy between Sunnites and Shiites, sealed his letters with an image of Christ, allowed the Jesuits to build a church, and at the gates of his palace placed a bell which those with grievances had only to ring to be instantly received. Only his private weaknesses and self-indulgence prevented him from becoming a second Akbar. Opium no longer satisfying him, he took to drink; the Grand Mogul's hands would become so unsteady from alcohol that his officers had to hold his cup while he drank.

In 1611, with great solemnity, he married Nurmahal, a beautiful and intelligent Persian whose husband he had had killed. Nurmahal, who hunted tigers and rode war elephants, was ambitious and, supported by her circle of foreigners, soon imposed her will on Jehan Gir. She lavished favours on her family, signed imperial decrees, minted her own coins and finally replaced the Mogul at the palace window where, according to custom, he showed himself every morning to his people. Having allowed the Persians to recapture Kandahar, Jehan Gir suppressed a revolt by the governor of Ahmadnagar and waged several wars against the Rajputs, though without glory. The end of his reign was marked by a humiliating episode: made prisoner near Lahore in the midst of the imperial camp by one of his own generals, he was conducted to Kabul guarded by an escort of Rajputs; Nurmahal arrived to set him free, but shortly afterwards, in October 1627, he died in Kashmir.

The Ming Dynasty in China and the Manchu peril

The Ming emperors were as weak as the Grand Mogul. In his harem Wan-Li (1573–1620) led an empty and luxurious existence. The child-emperor Hi-Chong (1621–7) entrusted the imperial power to his nurse. Affairs of State he found much less absorbing than the ingenious toys

The Grand Mogul Jehan Gir (1605–28), by a European artist. The obvious wealth of the Moguls made a great impression in Europe, but little was known about the people: these followers are more like American Indians. *Larousse*

A wall-hanging of painted cotton made in Golconda for a European patron c. 1640. The top panel shows two native potentates, the bottom one a group of European traders waited on by Eurasian servants. *Victoria & Albert Museum*

An example of decorative calligraphy: the character of a tiger as represented by a Manchu. Although the Manchus entered China as nomadic invaders they willingly absorbed the Chinese civilisation and studied its rich tradition of art. *British Museum*

Christians being thrown into boiling volcanic water in Japan. Persecution of Christians was begun by the Shogun Hitodata (1616–22) who, unlike his father who had welcomed them, discounted the benefits of Western science and feared political interference by missionaries. *Larousse*

and fascinating mechanical devices which the Jesuits made for him. Meanwhile the empire, torn by strife among the eunuchs and bloodshed among the feudal nobility, lay at the mercy of corrupt functionaries. Over-populated, China was ravaged by famine and slipped into anarchy.

At the end of the sixteenth century, in spite of its weakness, the empire had kept the Mongols at bay and resisted the Japanese. A new danger now threatened. The Manchus, related to the Kin who invaded China in the twelfth century, had peopled the vast forest of the Sungari valley, where they had begun to settle in villages. China began to attract them. A chieftain, Nurhatche (1559–1626), gave them military organisation and grouped them into a single horde. In 1616, these bold hunters, who through the centuries had preserved the energy, violence and adventurous spirit of their Tungus ancestors, invaded the province of Liaotung. In 1621 they made Mukden their capital. The resistance with which the Chinese met the invader was unexpected. The Jesuits had forged for the Chinese cannon capable of hurling a forty-pound shot and culverins light enough to be mounted on camels. When the Manchus attempted to force the Great Wall they were driven back by the fire of Chinese artillery. Firmly established in southern Manchuria, however, they did not abandon their ambitions.

The founding of the Tokugawa Dynasty

Japan, where the dynamic spirit of Zen was still very much alive, presented an increasingly sharp contrast with Ming China. There was a temporary return to the period of civil anarchy in 1598 before Iyeyasu, a warrior of tough and ancient stock, subdued the barons and routed the generals who disputed his power. In 1603 he entered Yedo (Tokyo) in triumph and assumed the title of Shogun. He left the phantom-emperor, the Mikado, undisturbed, and founded the Tokugawa Dynasty, which was to retain power for two and a half centuries. A son of the previous shogun rose against Iyeyasu with an army of nearly 200,000 men, but vanished in the flames of Osaka when it was stormed and all his brothers were massacred. Iyeyasu then pursued and developed the policy of national unity initiated by the 'usurpers' of the sixteenth century. A rigid hierarchy of the feudal nobility was established. The nobles, abandoning their castles, came to live at a court where the personal entourage of the new shogun comprised more than three hundred women and four court jesters. The State offices were shared by the loyal *daimyos*, or feudal barons. A central government was set up in Yedo (Tokyo), which replaced Kyoto as the capital of the archipelago with its twenty million inhabitants; this central administration was represented by commissioners in the chief cities and supported by a ruthlessly efficient police force. The Shogun Hitodata (1616–22) carried on the work of his father Iyeyasu. Japan, which for centuries had been the archetype of the anarchical feudal state, became politically the most highly organised country in all Asia.

Russian expansion in Siberia

In the northern expanses of Asia a boundless world gradually emerged from chaos. The Russians were already masters of western Siberia, where in 1604 they founded Tomsk and in 1618 Yeniseisk. Installed in the most easily cultivated clearings and along the banks of those rivers where fish was most abundant, in territory not unlike that of Eastern Europe, they were pioneers and settlers rather than conquerors. Since the defeat and death in 1600 of Kuchum, the last chief of the hordes, the thinly scattered indigenous population had offered no further resistance. Far to the east, beyond the area which was already colonised, lay the land of adventure. Drawn by the promise of free land, the lure of the unknown and the intoxication of galloping unimpeded towards the rising sun, a mere handful of men, Cossacks and immigrants, repeated in reverse the fabulous journey of Jenghis Khan. A screen of nomad tribes and immense stretches of hostile lands still separated them from the world of China.

EUROPEAN POSSESSIONS BEYOND THE SEAS

In the European domains beyond the seas the opening of the seventeenth century was a period of marking time. The day had passed when, spurred by gold, adventure and missionary zeal, the Western nations had flocked across the ocean to found vast new empires.

The Spanish Indies

The Spanish Indies had passed beyond the phases of conquest and organisation. Communications with Spain were threatened and the colonies were inadequately defended against pirates. Their internal peace, however, was assured by the elimination of the few Indians still unsubdued and by the balance of power which had been reached between the local authorities and the Crown. Spain prided itself on the effects of a century of colonial occupation. Hispano-American civilisation lacked neither richness nor brilliance. Poets celebrated the ' grandeur of Mexico ' which the Regent, Velasco, had made an important cultural centre. In these new domains of Christianity the power of the Catholic Church continued to increase. In Lima convents occupied more space than the rest of the town. Religious processions abounded, with Mystery Plays and *tableaux vivants* in which images of Christ were hoisted heavenwards by ropes and pulleys while bladders of coloured water gave the illusion of blood splashing the Cross. The Inquisition did not, however, succeed in maintaining the purity of the faith, or even the appearance of it. Though certain prelates, like Nogravajio, remained worthy examples of their calling, monks clad in lace spent their days at the gaming table, and the Bishop of Tucuman held audience surrounded by Chinese vases, flowers and incense burners. The native Indians, although Crown, Church and the law attempted to protect them, had little defence against the exactions of the great landowners. The burden of forced labour, the *encomienda*, was crushing even when, as in Peru, the natives who were conscripted to serve in the mines could attend a Requiem Mass for the repose of their own souls before they left.

In Paraguay, on the other hand, the Jesuit missionaries created settlements — known as *reducciones* — in which Indians were gathered into large villages where they gave up polygamy, replaced alcohol by tea, wore long shirts and went to work in groups, singing hymns and preceded by holy images. The priests imposed only the mildest

Persian painting developed initially as illustrations to a text. Chinese influences, however, led to more subtle colours and a wider range of subjects being employed until paintings like this came to be enjoyed in their own right. *British Museum*

A view of Quebec in 1613, five years after its foundation. Though Champlain, its founder (whose house is marked 'H'), secured the nominal allegiance of the Hurons to Henry IV, Sully refused support and Quebec remained a precarious stronghold. *Mansell*

punishments for misdemeanours — twenty-five strokes of the whip was the maximum — and for their entertainment arranged horse races and football games. In these settlements where equality was aimed at and all property was communally shared, even to the table knife which every couple was given as a wedding present, the natives tended to lose their self-reliance. Cut off from their own culture, they were unable to assimilate that of the newcomers.

The French in Canada

The idea of founding miniature European states beyond the seas by means of emigration dawned on the Western powers only gradually. France now resumed the attempts to expand which had failed in the sixteenth century for lack of sufficient economic backing. Samuel Champlain, a gentleman of obscure origins, proposed to create an agricultural and Catholic ' New France ' in North America. On behalf of a company in Rouen, he established in 1605 a base in Acadia (Nova Scotia), and pushed up the St Lawrence River to found the city of Quebec in 1608. Supporting the Hurons against the Iroquois, he persuaded them to recognise the authority of King Henry IV. With his peasant distrust of novelty, Henry's minister Sully refused to see the importance of these distant lands in which no gold was to be found, while the Rouen company was interested exclusively in the fur trade, which it entrusted to agents who were none too scrupulous. In 1620 Quebec had only about sixty residents and showed little promise.

The English settlements

Farther to the south, the English colonial settlements had also begun unpromisingly. English settlers established themselves in Virginia in 1607, and in the following year John Smith founded Jamestown. Although only twenty-seven years of age, Smith had been a pirate in the Mediterranean, a soldier in the Hungarian army, and a prisoner of the Turks; his energies were now entirely devoted to the London Company. But in 1609 he was wounded by the explosion of a barrel of gunpowder and had to return to England; a year later Virginia contained no more than some sixty half-starved colonists. Lord de la Warr, however, came to its relief and Virginia revived. A few years later Negro slaves were brought from Africa and the colony began to grow rich by the cultivation of tobacco. In 1619 there appeared the House of Burgesses, the first representative assembly in North America. In September 1620 a group of English Puritans, who had first taken refuge in Holland from religious persecution, sailed for Virginia on board the *Mayflower*. Storms drove the ship north of its destination and they landed on the rock-bound coast of Cape Cod. The settlers, giving thanks to God, built rough huts and called their village New Plymouth. During their first winter famine and disease almost wiped them out, but with courage, austerity and discipline the little community survived every trial. The colonist solemnly undertook in writing to obey all decisions which were commonly agreed upon. The principles and legend of of these Pilgrim Fathers of New England were to play an important role in the history of the United States.

Dutch activity

The Dutch, though more and more interested in colonial affairs, were still in no position to plant more than the smallest settlements and to establish a few naval posts along the route of their spice trade. In 1617 in North America they founded trading posts for furs at the mouth of the Hudson, on Manhattan Island. In the Far East they reached Annam and Japan. Created in 1602, the Dutch East India Company, supported by the Dutch war fleet, backed by the home Government and well provided with capital, was particularly active in Indonesia. In 1604 the Dutch took Amboina from the Portuguese. In 1617 they landed at Mataram on the pretext of taking sick members of the crew ashore. Concealing small cannon in innocent-looking bundles, they massacred the English garrison which was attending church. Since its foundation in Java in 1619, Batavia had been the base for Dutch operations in these seas. The English were expelled from Java by its governor, Coen. Farther south, Jansoon set sail to find the fabled continent of the Antipodes, reached western Australia and thus discovered another new world.

The adventures of Captain John Smith in Virginia. illustrations taken from his own *General Historie of Virginia*, 1624. On an expedition in search of food for the starving settlers of Jamestown Smith was captured by the Indians, condemned to death and, he claimed, saved by the Indian princess Pocahontas. *Larousse*

C.Smith taketh the King of Pamavnkee prisoner 1608

John Smith taking an Indian chief prisoner. It was through his imposition of discipline on the Jamestown settlers that they survived and in 1608 he became virtual dictator. *Mansell*

CHAPTER SIX

A PERIOD OF CRISES: 1620-60

The period between 1620 and 1660 was one of violence. In Europe, during the Thirty Years' War newly won liberties of worship and thought, championing the rights of the individual, confronted the old dream of a vast and unified Christian empire. In every country the stagnation of the countryside and the anarchy of the feudal nobility opposed the growing force of the centralised State. Though in France the monarchy succeeded in re-establishing its authority, and in Russia under the early Romanoffs in maintaining its position, it fell in England, though its successor was the dictatorship of Cromwell. Against this political background, a new spirit of enquiry shook traditional certainties without supplying others to take their place. Dazzled, and at the same time disconcerted by their new discoveries, men everywhere went through a painful mental and moral reappraisement. Modern science and modern anxiety were born twins.

THE THIRTY YEARS' WAR

Origins of the war

Towards 1620 the Counter-Reformation seemed to be sweeping all before it. Mingling humanism with devotion, the Jesuits strove to reconcile Christianity with the beauties of antiquity and the virtues of stoicism. The golden age of Spanish art owed its brilliance to the inspiration of Catholicism. In Italy, in Austria, in Belgium, the Church came to terms with the popular spirit and turned its religious processions into immense popular festivals. In France the growth of religious societies, the increasing influence of the clergy, the controversy aroused by Jansenism, the popularity of the gentle and trusting St Francis of Sales, the heroic achievements of St Vincent de Paul, all bear witness to Catholic vitality. For such a Church, conscious of its powers of self-renovation, the temptation to provide a political structure was great. The Habsburgs sought to satisfy it by unifying first Germany and then Europe under the banner of the Counter-Reformation. It was this that was at stake during the Thirty Years' War (1618–48), which began as a local German conflict and inevitably turned into a European war.

The Czech drama

The war began when an internal quarrel in part of the Habsburg lands, the Kingdom of Bohemia, turned into one involving other German princes. The Bohemian nobility resisted the Catholicising policies of Vienna and took to arms after hurling three Imperial officials out of a window in the Hradshin Castle overlooking Prague (the 'defenestration of Prague', 23 May 1618). The Czech rebellion turned into a German war when, at the death of the Emperor Matthias in 1619, the Czechs refused to pass their elective crown to his successor, Ferdinand II, and instead gave it to the Protestant Elector Palatine. In 1620 the Elector was banished from the Empire; in November his army was routed by that of the Catholic

Full armour was beginning to disappear from the battlefield at the end of the sixteenth century, when this suit was made. The decoration and flexibility of armour of this quality marks the peak of the craft of armour-making. *Wallace Collection*

League at the Battle of the White Mountain near Prague. The Elector fled, Imperial government was restored, Czech liberties were abolished and the crown of Bohemia declared hereditary in the Habsburg family. The Czech people disappeared from history for two hundred and fifty years. Meanwhile, fighting in the Palatinate had brought the Dutch to the support of the Protestant Union, and when in 1621 Spain again attacked the United Provinces, the two branches of the House of Habsburg were joined in what seemed to be a huge attempt to dominate Europe.

The intervention of Denmark and Sweden and the victory of the Empire (1625-9)

Denmark and Sweden, both Lutheran powers, now joined the resistance to Imperial ambitions, moved not only by feelings of Protestant solidarity, but by the threat constituted by Ferdinand II's maritime projects to the tolls which Denmark exacted from ships passing through the Sound and by Sweden's dreams of Baltic hegemony.

Denmark was the first to attack, but her king, Christian IV, an ambitious prince of the Empire, was caught between the army of the Holy League and the army of the Emperor, the former commanded by the elderly and pious Tilly, who served the Blessed Virgin, and the latter by Wallenstein, an adventurer who served only himself and believed in nothing but the stars. After several defeats he sued for peace, and in the Treaty of Lübeck (June 1629) renounced further intervention in Germany. In March of the same year Ferdinand II had issued the Edict of Restitution, by which all secularisation of Church property that had taken place since 1552 was annulled. This enormous benefit to Catholicism marked the height of Imperial successes. Ferdinand talked of making the Imperial crown hereditary in his family.

At this moment, subsidised by Richelieu, the Swedes disembarked in Germany (June 1630). At their head rode the 'Lion of the North', Gustavus Adolphus (1611-32). A tireless warrior, his colossal Nordic frame would shake with laughter or alternatively with rage; his sudden fits of repentance would be followed by the earnest prayers of a Puritan. He confronted the motley bands of mercenary soldiers who roved and raided Germany with a highly trained national army, recruited by a kind of conscription, disciplined, well organised, swift in manoeuvre, and with greater fire-power than its opponents. This army advanced as in a holy war chanting its faith in the awe-inspiring God of the Old Testament. The Swedes avenged the brutal sacking of the lovely Lutheran free city of Magdeburg in the spirit of Protestant crusaders. In September 1631 they struck like lightning at Breitenfeld and, cutting through Catholic territory between the Rhine and the Danube, seized Mainz and afterwards Munich. Gustavus Adolphus then marched on Vienna. For four months Wallenstein and he manoeuvred against one another. They met at Lützen on 6 November 1632. The battle took place in fog, and this hampered the Swedish army, already weaker than Gustavus would have wished. During the course of the engagement the King, charging with reckless fury, advanced beyond his own lines, was encircled and fell from his horse wounded. A German cavalryman finished him off with a pistol shot in the nape of the neck. Though Wallenstein retreated, losing all his guns, Gustavus's death was a disaster. With him died the last idealism left in the war, which was to continue for sixteen more

terrible years. His army withdrew to the Baltic and the majority of the Lutheran princes negotiated peace. The ambitions and fantasies of Wallenstein had, in the meantime, become a danger to the Emperor himself, who had him murdered in 1634, just before Richelieu threw his 100,000 men into the war.

The intervention of France (1635-48)

From 1635 to 1648 France, led by a Cardinal of the Church, with the aid of Protestant Holland and Sweden, slowly turned the tables on the Catholic powers. The opening phase of the French intervention was unfortunate. In 1636 Spanish forces from the Netherlands crossed the frontier

At the beginning of the Thirty Years' War the Elector of Saxony sided with the Emperor against the Elector Palatine. Saxony was rewarded by the acquisition of Lusatia, where the Elector besieged and took Bautzen in September 1620.

During 1627 and 1628 the Huguenot stronghold of La Rochelle was besieged by the armies of the French king. Siege-towers such as this protected the dykes built by the besiegers to cut La Rochelle off from relief by sea. *Sauvanaud*

93

Seventeenth-century silversmiths made elaborate book-bindings such as this one with clasps. It was made in Germany in typical late Renaissance style and has inscriptions in both German and Hebrew. *Marburg*

Louis XIII, with his minister Richelieu behind him, during the advance on La Rochelle. He entered the city in November 1628. The Huguenots' existence as a nation within the nation came to an end, but they retained freedom to worship as they pleased. *Mansell*

A copper money-box of the seventeenth century, with hasp and staple for a padlock. It may have been used for alms-collecting. *Marburg*

of the Somme, overran Corbie and threatened Paris. Gradually, the tide turned. In 1639 the French occupied Alsace. At sea, the Dutch interfered with Spanish communications with the gold mines of America. The empire of Philip III was ruined by war and the blockade and disintegrated. The revolt of Portugal and of Catalonia enabled the French in 1642 to occupy all Roussillon. From 1643 they struck more frequently and more decisively. In May 1643, five days after the death of Louis XIII, the dashing young Duc d'Enghien, charging sword in hand and hair flying in the wind crushed the 'invincible' Spanish infantry at Rocroi, in the north. Peace negotiations had already begun, but for five more years the armies marched and counter-marched across a ravaged Germany until 1648 brought to France the outbreak of the Fronde, to Spain a second Rocroi at Lens, and to Germany the Peace of Westphalia.

The Peace of Westphalia (1648)

The Treaties of Münster and Osnabrück, signed in October 1648, put an end to the Habsburgs' Imperial dream. The three hundred and fifty heterogeneous states of the Empire were given complete territorial sovereignty, under the nominal authority of the Emperor, who was himself dependent on the Diet. In the religious domain the same lack of unity prevailed: the Edict of Restitution was abrogated, the reformed churches became free throughout the Empire, while Calvinism as well as Lutheranism was officially recognised. Sweden now had a voice in the Imperial councils with votes in the Diet, and the expansion of Brandenburg further curbed the influence of the House of Austria. Above all, France emerged as the leading power in Europe. Her strength was founded less on great territorial expansion (she was satisfied to advance her frontier for the first time to the Rhine and to annex part of Alsace) than to the collapse of Habsburg Spain and the disintegration of Imperial unity. These facts assured her of the power of arbitration.

Germany in the mid-seventeenth century

Behind the diplomacy lay the realities of a great disaster: Germany had reached the limits of her endurance. Cut into fragments, ruled by powerless princelings, she had no means of mitigating the ravages of thirty years of warfare. Commerce and industry were non-existent: once prosperous towns were charred collections of roofless houses where wolves roamed and pestilence raged. Fields lay fallow and peasants were driven to cut down the bodies of the hanged to avoid starvation. Some estimates of population put the losses of the Empire as high as fifty per cent. Even more heart-rending, perhaps, was the moral breakdown, bringing in its train hopelessness and cynicism, an outcrop of fanatical sects and crazed visionaries. Everywhere brigandage and destitution were rampant. In the chaos perished the great Germanic achievement of the civilisation of the free towns.

Spain under Philip IV

Spain, too, had suffered. Portugal had not been reconquered and it took twelve years, from 1640 to 1652, to subdue the rebellion in Catalonia. The war with France continued until the Peace of the Pyrenees (1659) by which Spain ceded Artois and Roussillon to France. The Spanish Infanta was married to the young Louis XIV. Spain, meanwhile, decayed economically and lost population. A land of shepherds, monks and unemployed soldiers, she proudly disdained the realities of the seventeenth century and continued in her quest for the absolute. While fashion among her neighbours decreed clothes of brilliant colour, Spain stubbornly remained in black. She was already the Don Quixote of Europe, desperately seeking to apply medieval solutions to the problems of the modern world.

Sweden

Confused and sporadic warfare in the Baltic since 1617 concluded with the triumph of Sweden. In 1660 and 1661 she signed treaties with Poland, Denmark and Russia which gave her all the shores of the Baltic, now a Swedish lake. Gustavus Adolphus — and even more his remarkable Chancellor Oxenstierna — had turned a poor and backward country largely of forest land supporting no more than a million inhabitants into a first-class power. Excellent administrators were supplied by a cultivated aristocracy whose independence the Crown curtailed in 1655 by limiting the extent of their estates. The Government increased the number of schools and encouraged the university at Uppsala. This cultural effervescence was especially striking during the astonishing reign of Queen Christina, who occupied the throne between the reigns of the warrior kings Gustavus Adolphus (1611 – 32) and Charles Gustavus (1654 – 60). Christina, a young woman of headstrong and enigmatic character, was an enthusiastic patron of literature and philosophy. An ardent admirer of Descartes, whom she summoned to Stockholm, she was capricious, reckless and extravagant. At the age of twenty-seven she abdicated, retiring from Sweden disguised as a man to adopt the Catholic faith and die in Rome thirty-five years later after a career of adventure, scholarly pursuits and scandal.

Much of the visual world of the seventeenth century was still medieval. Here are buildings shown in the background of a picture of Queen Christina of Sweden (1632–54). The cross on the roof bears the three crowns of Sweden. *Marburg*

INTERNAL CRISES

The Thirty Years' War destroyed the lingering nostalgia for a return to the Middle Ages and pointed to the shape of things to come, while at the same time internal crises convulsed the great Western powers. From these crises emerged the modern State — either, as in the case of France, with a strengthened absolute monarchy which would be the bulwark of the traditional order, or, as in the case of England and the United Provinces, with systems of government from which later evolved the forms of liberalism.

Louis XIII and Richelieu

From the beginning of the reign of Louis XIII until the year 1624 France had continued to be weak and divided. The great nobles took up arms. The Protestants formed a state within the state. The *noblesse de la robe*, the hereditary legal class created by Henry IV, hampered the king's freedom to dispense justice. But other tendencies made for unity. In the eyes of the poor the sovereign remained the image of God, their common father, and their sole protection against arbitrary abuse. The middle classes, pious and hardworking, longed for order. As for the nobility, their still feudal passions were tamed in the salons of the *Précieuses*, such as Madame de Rambouillet, where honour became politeness and decorum. The man who succeeded in employing these forces of order to bring about the triumph of the State was Armand du Plessis de Richelieu.

Richelieu was a soldier who belonged to the lesser nobility and had taken up a career in the Church for family reasons. Though in 1622 he became a Cardinal, he was primarily a politician. His intelligence was extraordinary, his pride boundless and his stoicism such that few were aware of the physical disabilities which tortured him. He devoted his life to the service of the monarchy and to the aggrandisement of France. Pity and mercy were unknown to him, but his ignorance of them served France. He became Minister in 1624 and until his death was loyally supported by Louis XIII. His achievements were remarkable. Protestant power was broken when the Huguenots' most powerful redoubt, La Rochelle, succumbed in 1628 after heroic resistance. Peace was made in 1629 and although the Huguenots had their civil equality and freedom of worship confirmed, they lost their fortified strongholds. The nobility was also brought to heel: duelling was forbidden, fortified castles were dismantled and plots and seditions were summarily put down. The executioner dealt with resistance and after 1631 Richelieu faced no serious threat at Court. Louis XIII at last took his kingdom in hand; his commissioners travelled everywhere and his Intendants supervised all departments of State. In the end even the courts of justice were bridled; on one occasion, seizing the president of the *Parlement* of Bordeaux by the robe, Louis was heard to cry: 'On your knees, little man, on your knees before your master.'

Though France escaped reversion to feudal anarchy and being merged in a Catholic empire such as some devout Frenchmen desired, the price she paid was high. The absolute monarchy imposed its own heavy burdens. It did not hesitate to employ propaganda, arbitrary arrest and exceptional judicial procedures. Money was needed and taxes tripled. The poverty of the people was appalling. The demands of the modern State were ill received by the old peasant society. There were uprisings in country districts where Collectors of the Royal Revenue were crushed beneath cartwheels, nailed to barn doors or torn to pieces. Convinced that in dealing with insurrection 'it was better to do too much than too little', Richelieu brutally crushed these angry and confused protests, although in fact they had not seriously endangered royal power.

Mazarin and the Fronde

After the death of Richelieu in December 1642 and the death of Louis XIII in May 1643, the minority of Louis XIV brought a fresh crisis. Mazarin, the Prime Minister, a Cardinal who had not taken priest's orders, and favourite of the regent, Anne of Austria, was unable to impose his authority. His diplomatic skill and address availed him little. His rapid rise to fortune caused scandal and roused resentment. When in July 1648 Mazarin was forced to levy new taxes to meet the cost of the Spanish war, the *Parlement* of Paris, attempting to play the role of Roman Senate and limit the power of the monarchy, drew up a plan of reform. Paris rose in protest against the 'Sicilian scoundrel'. Barricades were erected. The Queen fled to St Germain, where the little Louis XIV slept in the straw. This civil war took its name from the children's slings — or *frondes* — which were used by the mob to stone the windows of Mazarin's followers. Besieged by the royal army, the forces of the Fronde, composed mainly of the Parisian bourgeoisie, lampooned Mazarin, improvised regiments — and got entangled in their long rapiers. But when the mob showed signs of getting out of hand they grew uneasy; nor did they enjoy being deprived by the blockade of Paris of the country delicacies to which they were accustomed. The war ended in March 1649 with a general amnesty.

A year later the Second — or aristocratic — Fronde broke out. It was led by the great Prince of Condé, who rallied the old feudal nobility against Mazarin and the enfeebled Government. The *parlementaire* Fronde at once sprang up again and joined forces with the aristocratic rebels. This time the war was longer and more confused.

Giulio Mazarin, a Sicilian, rose through the Papal diplomatic service before entering the service of Richelieu. Regarded at first as a stop-gap after Richelieu's death he remained in power, with interruptions, for eighteen years until the maturity of Louis XIV. *Wallace Collection*

Jacques Callot, a great engraver, depicted many of the horrors and brutalities of seventeenth-century life in his series 'The Miseries of War'. The punishment of breaking on the wheel by repeated blows with a crowbar was a familiar spectacle. *British Museum*

Albrecht of Austria. Painting by Rubens. *Archiv für Kunst und Geschichte*

For nearly five years France was rent by riots and rival factions, while a revolt in Aquitaine and Spanish invasions attracted an influx of unemployed mercenaries from a devastated Central Europe. From starvation and anarchy a longing for order arose, a longing which was to assure the ultimate triumph of absolute monarchy.

In July 1652 Condé succeeded in taking Paris, although his violence and insolence soon made him loathed. By October he was forced to flee to the Netherlands, where he joined the Spanish forces. The young King shortly afterwards returned to his capital and a few months later Mazarin was again recalled, to remain until his death in 1661 ' as powerful as God the Father at the beginning of the world '. Law and order were restored. In August 1660 the Parisians prepared an enthusiastic welcome for Louis XIV and his young bride Maria Theresa. Flanked by his hundred Swiss guards, the great officers of the Crown and the Marshals of France, the twenty-two-year-old sovereign, wildly acclaimed, revelled in the plaudits of the crowd. France fell in love with its king; the King already loved glory. The age of absolute monarchy had arrived.

THE ENGLISH REVOLUTION

The sides in the English constitutional struggles of the seventeenth century seem, at first sight, more simply defined than the factions which struggled in France. Puritan England, the enemy of priesthood and monarchy, devoted to work and liberty, seems to confront an older England, loyal to Church, King and a traditional social order. The reality was much more complicated than this antithesis of Roundhead and Cavalier. Englishmen of all classes long sought to reconcile their duties under the law with the promptings of conscience and self-interest. They were swayed by the groundswell of economic movements whose nature they could only dimly sense. In the end, the restoration of the Monarchy and Parliament in 1660 showed the eagerness of the vast majority of Englishmen to return to familiar paths as soon as they felt able to do so with safety.

Charles I

Handsome and aloof, Charles I was so deeply imbued with the spirit of monarchy that Parliament, in the Petition of Rights of 1628, found it necessary to remind him of what it asserted to be traditional English liberties. He promptly dissolved Parliament, and for eleven ' years of tyranny ' governed without its aid. His chief minister, Thomas Wentworth, Earl of Strafford, a hard and taciturn man of lucid mind, seemed to be about to apply in England those methods which Richelieu found successful in France. Old taxes were revived, new expedients invented. At the same time the Archbishop of Canterbury, William Laud, reformed the Anglican liturgy. His enemies said it was a copy of the Roman Mass. Voices rose in protest when

Detail from a Japanese screen showing the arrival of St Francis Xavier in Japan. *Musée Guimet, Paris*

G

The reverse side of ' The Great Seal of England 1651 ' shows the republican House of Commons in session. *British Museum*

Van Dyck painted this triptych of Charles I of England to serve as a guide to the sculptor Bernini. The painting survives in the great royal collection at Windsor, but the whereabouts of Bernini's bust is unknown.

A cosmic furnace of the seventeenth century, a period of imaginative research in all branches of science. *Mansell*

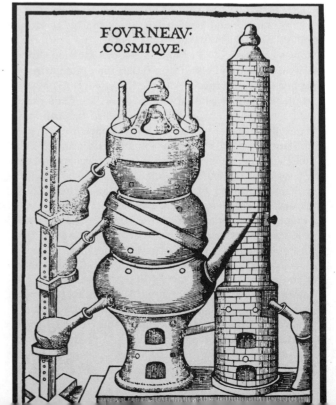

FOVRNEAV. COSMIQVE.

97

The execution of a king — the Anointed of the Lord — horrified the religious and social conscience of the seventeenth century. Charles I died on 30 January 1649 on a scaffold outside Inigo Jones's great banqueting hall at Whitehall.

the Dean began to read from the new prayer book in St Giles' Edinburgh, 23 July 1637; the Bishop ordered silence and had a stool flung at his head by a vigorous female hand for his pains. Presbyterian Scotland erupted. Under the shadow of Edinburgh Castle a huge crowd thronged to sign, some with their own blood, the National Covenant; this declared their faith in and obedience to the reformed religion of Scotland. The Scots war forced the King to summon Parliament; first the Short Parliament of 1640, and then the Long Parliament (1640–53), whose stormy sessions were so fraught with consequence. This time, as was remarked by John Pym, the most spirited of the anti-Government spokesmen, it was a question not of sweeping the floor, but of removing the cobwebs from the ceiling. Charles gave way and assented to an Act of Attainder under which Strafford was executed. In January 1642 he decided to resist and attempted to arrest the Parliamentary leaders. He failed, the City of London gave refuge to the Parliamentarians and Charles left his capital to raise the royal standard in Nottingham in August.

It was civil war, but Parliament, anxious for moderation and sympathetic to Presbyterian rather than more extreme religious views, still treated with the King. Oliver Cromwell, a gentleman farmer who sat in Parliament for Cambridge, raised a regiment at his own expense; called the Ironsides, Cromwell's troops soon served as a model in discipline and Puritan zeal for the new Parliamentary army. This brought a new vigour into the war, expressing as it did the fervour of the extreme Puritan sects, to whom it was the merciless sword of the Avenger, the instrument of the Lord God of Hosts. In a new holy war Puritanism was to scourge the heathen. Beaten at Naseby in June 1645, the King took refuge among the Scots, who turned him over to his enemies. In September 1648 the army ' purged ' Parliament, and what was left of it — a bewildered ' Rump Parliament ' — set up a special court which condemned Charles I to death. In February 1649 Charles died with perfect serenity and dignity before the Palace of Whitehall; as the executioner showed them their King's severed head, a shocked populace groaned aloud.

Cromwell and the Commonwealth

In the new Republic, Parliament was uneasily dependent on the army and Cromwell. Before restoring order in Scotland, Cromwell struck in Catholic Ireland. The fighting was savage. At Drogheda a church full of women and children was burned to the ground. The conquered Irish were bound over to service with the new English proprietors. Thus the Irish problem was created.

At home, though it sought the aggrandisement of England, Parliament lacked energy. In 1651 it passed the Navigation Act which forbade the shipping of English colonial products in any but English vessels; but the Dutch Admiral van Tromp, with a large broom fixed derisively to his masthead, braved the fleet of the Commonwealth with impunity. Meanwhile the Royalists plotted their revenge, and fanatics clamoured for the introduction of divorce, nudism, or communism. Parliament strove to perpetuate its power and in April 1653 Cromwell himself strode into the House of Commons and, addressing the Members with contempt, bade them to go in the name of God. His musketeers then drove them out, and the chamber was firmly locked. A wit wrote over the door: ' This House is to let '. The military dictatorship had begun.

Cromwell's ' Protectorate ' made England an international power again. The United Provinces was defeated in 1655, the Mediterranean was opened to the English fleet and Tunis was bombarded. At the mere demand of England the Duke of Savoy ceased to persecute the Vaudois. Cromwell boasted that he would make the Englishman's name as respected as ever the Roman's had been. In alliance with France he took Dunkirk and in 1655 seized Jamaica.

The reawakening of Royalist sentiment, however, rendered the future of this regime uncertain, and Cromwell was well aware of the fact. Its Puritan austerities made it unpopular. For fear of angering the army he refused to assume the crown. Though he dressed in purple and ermine, received the title of Lord Protector of England and the right to name his successor, he was more and more isolated. He died suddenly in September 1658 in the prime

Judge Jeffreys has been, deservedly, a legendary monster since the 'Bloody Assize' in the West of England in 1685. He tried to escape in disguise after the Glorious Revolution but was caught. *Mansell*

When Cromwell turned out the 'Rump' of the Long Parliament in April 1653, the last link with the constitutional past was dissolved. There followed anxious experiments as he strove to reconcile parliamentary government with the fact that power lay with the army.

of life, unjustly hated for his attempts to find in the exercise of force a new basis for the English State. Men had forgotten what they owed to his earlier services to English liberties.

The Restoration

Cromwell's son Richard succeeded him, but almost immediately abdicated. Military anarchy followed. The people of England longed only for peace and a chance to enjoy life. General Monck occupied London and summoned a Parliament which restored the monarchy. In May 1660, Charles II, son of the executed King, entered London; he was received with such joy and enthusiasm that he was prompted to ask where his enemies were. It was true that the country was thoroughly sick of republican experiments, military tyranny and Puritanism; but it was equally true that the attachment of most Englishmen of the political class to their liberties had greatly increased, and that ideas whose fruits still influence the modern world — tolerance, anti-slavery, feminism and pacifism — had for the first time won a hearing.

THE UNITED PROVINCES OF HOLLAND

The Dutch, too, were grappling with the problem of how to govern themselves, though in very different circumstances. The Dutch Republic had no royal Court or prelates, and few great nobles. It was a country of city-dwellers, merchants and sea-rovers who had grown rich on colonial trade, but one which none the less remained faithful to old and deep-rooted traditions. It tended to evolve institutions halfway between those of modern liberal States and those of the medieval city. From 1621 to 1648, while the renewed war with Spain lasted, the princes of the House of Orange, who were Stadtholders-General and commanders of the army, maintained themselves in power with the support of the common people, who desired strong government and a continuation of the war. Though Maurice of Nassau (1589–1623), Frederick Henry (1625–47) and William II of Orange (1647–50) were obliged to leave the direction of foreign policy to the Grand Pensionary of the province of Holland, they were in reality kings without title. But prosperity and the return of peace brought about the victory of the republican aristocracy, who in 1650 frustrated William II's attempted coup d'état and were not long in suppressing the office of Stadtholder itself (1654). The United Provinces was then governed by peaceful and tolerant burghers of whom the most famous was the incorruptible Grand Pensionary John de Witt.

The fabulous profits of the East India Company had made Amsterdam the financial capital of the world. Freedom of religion and of thought stimulated intellectual activity and the little republic became a centre of the arts, of science and of philosophy. Here Descartes came to meditate; here Leuwenhoek invented the microscope and opened up a whole new world to the eyes of Western man. Nurtured by prosperity, a new civilisation emerged, devoted to calm, beauty and comfort. The towns, girdled by canals, were well ordered and opulent. Public buildings and town halls, erected no longer for princes or for the Church, but for corporations or private families, were embellished by the works of such incomparable portrait and landscape painters as Frans Hals, Ruysdael and Vermeer van Delft. 99

Galileo's condemnation by the Inquisition (1633) and enforced recantation of the heliocentric theory gives him a place in the martyrology of science. He died in 1642, the year of the birth of Newton, who owed to him the foundations of his laws of motion. *Popper*

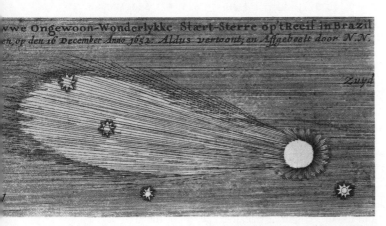

Astronomy made a great popular impression in the seventeenth century. This print shows a comet observed off Recife (Brazil). The invention of the telescope and advances in physical and mathematical theory made this the great age of astronomical discovery. *British Museum*

GALILEO, DESCARTES, PASCAL

The Dutch were not alone in probing the mysteries of life. Western man, having explored the planet he lived on, set about exploring nature itself. Francis Bacon (1561–1626) was the founder of modern scientific method, and the frontispiece to his great work, the *Novum Organum*, was, symbolically, a ship of discovery in full sail. Experimental methods were employed in zoology, botany and anatomy. Mouffet studied insect life. Harvey (1578–1657) demonstrated the circulation of blood. Mathematics, the language of the new science, and a means of describing and interpreting the external world, was often the province of cultured amateurs whose incessant quarrels stimulated its progress. Galileo (1564–1642), who was born at Pisa on the day of Michelangelo's death, evolved a theory relating time and space, reduced space to numeric laws and submitted nature to the laws of geometry. Constructing a powerful telescope, he followed up the discoveries of Copernicus, which had recently been described by Kepler (1561–1630). In 1610 Galileo's startling conclusions were made public: not only did the earth revolve about the sun, but there were thousands of suns and the Milky Way was composed of countless stars. The enclosed world of the Middle Ages was shattered at a blow. Galileo was forced by the Inquisition to abjure such heresies, but the old conceptions of the universe were for ever doomed. The revolution which Galileo caused in physics was caused in philosophy by Descartes (1596–1650). Doubting all accepted knowledge, the only proposition which seemed to him unquestionable was his own existence: he thought, therefore he existed ('*Cogito ergo sum*'). Descartes also argued that a Perfect Being (God) existed. But the material world obeyed purely mechanical laws and Descartes showed how to analyse them in his *Discours de la méthode*, which appeared in 1637. The ground was prepared for science by this.

But in spite of all this, seventeenth-century man often felt lost and deserted. Mathematics and scientific experiments might reveal to him the laws of the universe, but they said nothing of his own individual destiny. If he could not accept the void of his own existence, if the 'silences of infinite space' filled him with terror, his anguish was as limitless as the new heavens which Galileo had revealed. Blaise Pascal (1623–62) was at the age of twenty one of the greatest mathematicians of the century. After a mystical experience, 'the night of fire', he felt illuminated by grace, and 'beyond reason', by the intuition of love alone, strove to attain the living God, the revelation of Whom 'inundated the heart with tears of joy'. He joined the celebrated convent of Port Royal near Versailles.

THE EVOLUTION OF HOLY RUSSIA

In spite of the signs of change which marked the reigns of Michael (1613–45) and of Alexis Romanoff (1645–76) neither modern science nor modern scepticism penetrated the Muscovite Empire. Deeply religious, the Russian people were not disturbed by the doubts and uncertainties that assailed their Western contemporaries. They prayed for the damned and even for the demons; they sometimes displayed true evangelical humility; but their ritual, almost magical in its complexity, led them to cling to ancient customs, to superstitions, to the most minor details of traditional usage. The Tsar Alexis wore long, priest-like robes, chanted with the choir, and when the candles in the cathedral burned low snuffed them with his own fingers. His palace was open to beggars and pilgrims alike, and his chief counsellor was Vasily, the barefooted 'innocent', the 'fool of Christ'. Alexis mastered the violence of his instincts by a profound piety, and deserved his surname 'Very Peaceful'. With his support an élite of laymen and clergy, who called themselves the 'friends of God', strove to reform morals and spread learning. Nikon, an ardent and uncompromising priest of peasant origin, was made Patriarch in 1652 and with the aid of prelates from Constantinople re-organised the Church. The Russia of the Romanoffs not only demonstrated an innovating spirit in religious matters, but also opened itself to Western influences. Foreign technicians arrived to train the army and to found Russia's first factories. In even greater numbers Dutch, German and English merchants set up business in the port of Arkhangelsk and Moscow. Alexis himself exchanged diplomatic correspondence with the King of England. In 1654 Russian ambassadors were received in Paris, where with their long beards and outlandish robes they were taken for Turks.

Muscovite Russia, which had not taken part in the Thirty Years' War, seemed to be about to emerge from her isolation. But she was still too absorbed by internal problems and the threats of her neighbours to involve herself in Europe. From 1632 to 1643 she lost ground in her exhausting struggle with Poland, but in 1654 she was able to recapture Smolensk. Six years earlier the Ukrainian Cossacks had risen against the Poles, and in 1653 had asked for Russian protection; the Ukraine east of the Dnieper thus became part of Russia. Although, as disturbances showed, effective government was slow to establish itself in Russia, Alexis Romanoff continued the wise policy of his father Michael and during the first half of his reign, until 1655, was able to maintain his authority.

ASIA

In Asia, as in Europe, the second third of the seventeenth century was a period of crises, and the rhythm of events quickened. China was convulsed by the Manchu invasion, which swept away the ancient Ming Dynasty. In India the Grand Mogul Jehan was driven from the throne by his fanatical son Aurangzeb, who thus assured the triumph of proselytising Islam. Persia lost its vigour after the death of Abbas. Japan abruptly severed relations with the rest of the world and withdrew into her own shell. The Russians, in the course of their march towards the rising sun, reached the borders of the Far East and clashed with Chinese troops.

The Manchu invasion and the fall of the Ming Dynasty

Chung-Cheng (1627–44), the last of the Mings, was gentle, scholarly and retiring — and quite unable to prevent the disintegration of his empire, ravaged as it was by famine, crushed by taxes, and plagued by incessant rebellions. Li-Tzu, a peasant who had become the chief of several rebel bands, enforced his authority over all the central provinces. Rather than pay their soldiers, Chinese generals often encouraged them to live by loot and plunder

The founder of the Romanoff dynasty which ruled Russia until 1917: Michael Feodorovich (1613–1645). Feeble and irresolute, he conceded much to Russia's enemies in the West. But during his reign pioneers crossed Siberia and reached the Pacific. *Marburg*

Gilded and bejewelled statuette showing the birth of Buddha. This seventeenth-century Tibetan work illustrates the persistence of Hindu influence in Buddhist art and belief since the Gupta period of the fifth century. *Marburg*

Seventeenth-century Hindu painting moved away from simple imitation of Persian styles to reach a new level of sophistication and observation. This miniature shows a camel with a curtained litter, of the sort in which ladies travelled.

off the land. Their ritualistic conception of warfare prevented them from defending the empire with efficiency: they were less interested in fighting than in negotiation. They would attack an enemy stronghold on three sides only, leaving the besieged to escape by the fourth; they regulated the movements of their troops according to the position of the heavenly bodies, and marched from a town by the west gate in summer and by the east gate in winter. Such defenders could not keep the Dutch from occupying Formosa or the Manchus from becoming a threat north of the Great Wall. By 1627 their barbarous and ambitious chief Tai-Tsong had led the Manchus into the province of Chih-li. In 1629 he appeared before the gates of Peking, and retired only after offering sacrifices on the tombs of the twelfth-century Golden Kings and proclaiming his own rights over China. When he died in 1643 his soldiers chose as their chief his seven-year-old nephew Shun-chi, and marched towards the passes of Chai-Kai-Kur.

Commanded by General Wuen-Sen Kwai, the pick of the Imperial troops were able to keep the invaders at bay. But the robber warlord Li-Tzu, seizing the opportunity offered by the absence of the Imperial army, marched on Peking, which was delivered into his hands through the treachery of a eunuch. In April 1644 the Emperor Chung-Cheng stabbed his daughter and in despair hanged himself. General Wuen-Sen Kwai, impatient to avenge the Emperor, signed an armistice with the Manchus. The General's own parents had been massacred by the usurper and, throwing caution to the winds, he appealed to his former enemies for help. Together Imperial and Manchu troops descended on the capital. Li-Tzu left the city in flames and fled. Once they had entered Peking, the Manchus refused to leave. They proclaimed the downfall of the

Ming Dynasty and placed their own chief, Shun-chi, on the Imperial throne. General Wuen-Sen Kwai, duped by his allies, now perforce became their accomplice. Made viceroy, he turned his fury against Li-Tzu, whom he pursued from province to province and eventually slew at Nanking. At almost the same time northern China submitted to the Manchus; but southern China remained to be conquered. A Ming prince, who had been hastily proclaimed Emperor, was defeated at Nanking and was drowned. His partisans committed suicide in thousands. Supported by the Portuguese of Macao, the provinces of Kwangsi and Kwang-ti were more difficult to reduce. Kiu-Che-Tzu, a Chinese converted to Christianity, defended Kweilin so heroically that when the Manchus eventually took the city they honoured him with a magnificent funeral, having first beheaded him. The resistance of mainland China came to an end in 1651 with the occupation of Canton.

The pirates of Fukien long remained loyal to the Mings. One of them, named Koxinga, whose career was brief but astonishing, made his headquarters in the island of Amoy, where he equipped a fleet and harried the Chinese coast. Such was his audacity that in 1657 he sailed up the Yang-tze and laid siege to Nanking. When the Manchus destroyed his bases one after the other Koxinga set sail for Formosa, drove out the Dutch and in 1661 proclaimed himself king. The son of a Japanese woman and a pirate who had been brought up by the Spanish, his dream was to found an immense maritime empire in the Orient which would be open to European influences. In 1662, aged thirty-nine, he was preparing an expedition against the Philippines when he died.

The Manchus were little concerned with the sea. To protect the conquests they had made they reinforced their army, entrenched themselves firmly in all strategic positions and, although they became settlers and cultivators of the soil, remained soldiers. Affirming their rights as conquerors, they exempted themselves from taxation. They also assumed the right to enter official careers without sitting those examinations which the Chinese, failing time and time again, often reached old age — sometimes the age of a hundred — before passing. Yet to modify the time-honoured institutions of the ancient Middle Empire seemed to the newcomers almost a sacrilege. They therefore retained the former administrative staff, merely teaming each important official with a Manchu inspector. The Chinese who co-operated with the conquerors were heaped with favours. Almost the only obligation imposed upon them was to wear pigtails as did the Manchus themselves. The new Dynasty of Purity, or Tsing, which replaced the Dynasty of Light, or Ming, dealt severely with the indolence, confusion and corruption of the civil service and gave the Empire new life, and the health and vigour of its nomad conquerors.

During the childhood of Shun-chi the actual direction of affairs had been in the hands of regents; but in 1651, at the age of fifteen, Shun-chi decided to rule for himself. The Emperor was deeply imbued with the doctrines of Confucius and he governed with wisdom, but he became unbalanced at the death of the young Empress Tong-Sao-Wan, who had perhaps been poisoned, and immolated thirty people on her tomb before trying to cut his own throat. His friends frustrated his attempted suicide, but he pined away and died in 1661. He was twenty-five years old.

The Great Mogul Shah Jehan (1627–66) deposed by his son Aurangzeb in 1658. One of his monuments is the exquisite Taj Mahal, built as a tomb for his beloved wife, Mumtay-i-Mahal. *Mansell*

A seventeenth-century lattice window in the South Kanara district showing an interlacing cobra pattern. The Mogul emperors fostered Indian artists in this period by providing an outside stimulus to their imaginations and a rich patronage.

The Grand Mogul Shah Jehan and his son Aurangzeb

India at this time was as rich in episodes of violence and events of importance as China. Shah Jehan (1627–58), though he refused to allow his subjects to fall flat on their faces in his presence, was nevertheless determined to reverse the weak policy of Jehan Gir, his father. He put an end to palace intrigues, eliminated his rivals, suppressed the revolts of his provincial governors, recaptured Kandahar from the Persians and Hongai from the Portuguese. In the Deccan he extended his domination from the Arabian Sea to the Bay of Bengal. But the death of his favourite wife demoralised him and he lost his grip at a time when his sons, the Mogul princes, were at loggerheads. Dara, his eldest son, was a scholarly man interested in all forms of religion, friendly towards the Hindus; he dreamed, like Akbar the Great, of giving the Mogul Empire a broader basis and a more up-to-date organisation. His brother Aurangzeb, austere, fanatical and impetuous, did not share his tolerance or his ideals. In mountain retreats, where from time to time he would retire to lead the life of a dervish, and in the heat of battle, when at the appointed hour he would dismount from his horse to say his prayers, Aurangzeb showed himself to be a fanatic. He thought only of ways and means to make a Hindu revenge on the Moslems impossible. To Aurangzeb a policy of force and terror seemed indispensable.

Appointed viceroy of the Deccan, he invaded the Shiite sultanates of Golconda and Bijapur. His father and his older brother, who were as worried by his fanaticism as by his ambition, disowned him, and he was twice forced to interrupt his conquests. In September 1657 Shah Jehan fell ill. Aurangzeb formed an alliance against Dara with his two other brothers, the vacillating Shudja, and Murad,

a rough cavalry officer. In April and May 1658 victories at Dhermat and Samurghat enabled him to enter Agra. Shah Jehan was besieged in a fortress. The water supply soon failed and his officers deserted, leaving the Grand Mogul to be defended only by a battalion of fat Manchu women. He capitulated and was kept in captivity until his death eight years later. As soon as he was proclaimed Emperor at Delhi in July 1658 Aurangzeb disposed of his brothers. Murad he encouraged to drink and then, accusing him of drunkenness, threw him into prison; three years later he had him put to death. Dara, before being decapitated in his prison cell, was displayed in rags and carried through the streets of Delhi on an old and mud-bespattered elephant. Shudja was defeated near Allahabad and took refuge in the Arakan, where he was devoured by wild animals. The triumph of Aurangzeb decisively affected the future of India. Whereas the great and generous Akbar had dreamed of transforming the Mogul Empire into an Indo-Mogul Empire, Aurangzeb reverted to the bigoted sectarianism of the Mongol Babar, and to the traditions of a fiercer and more warlike Asia.

During this period of civil war India was scourged by plague, cholera, famine and the ruin of her industries. Never had destitution and misery been screened behind a more sumptuous façade. Shah Jehan was a great builder who covered the Empire with monuments in which Persian traditions blended harmoniously with Hindu elements. Agra, even more than the new city of Delhi, was now full of wonders. Few buildings in the world rivalled the exquisite mausoleum of the Taj Mahal, or matched the elegant majesty of the mosque of Jama Masjid, the splendour of the Peacock Throne, with its twelve emerald pillars with feet of gold, its trees sown with pearls and its great facing pairs of birds, scintillating with precious stones.

The decline of the Safavid dynasty

After an era of great splendour the new Persian emperors presented a sorry spectacle of degeneration. Shah Abbas had made the decline of his dynasty likely by decimating the imperial princes and by having his successors brought up by women and eunuchs. His grandson, Shah Safi (1629–42), was less of a king than a public hangman. But in spite of his pitiless executions, he allowed palace quarrels, revolts in the provinces, sedition in the army and treason among his governors to develop. Under Murad IV, the Turks took Azerbaijan and Mesopotamia from him. Abbas II (1642–67), who became King at the age of ten, was tolerant to Christians and his troops regained Kandahar; but he was little more than a sadistic drunkard.

Iyemitsu and Japanese isolation

In Japan the new Tokugawa Dynasty did not lack vigour. The Shogun Iyemitsu (1623–51) consolidated the regime of order and authority which had been created by his grandfather, Iyeyasu. In order to keep the feudal lords — or *daimyos* — under strict control he obliged their families to reside in Yedo, while they themselves had to spend six months of the year in the capital. If one of them died without an heir or committed a crime the Shogun at once confiscated his property. The policy he adopted towards foreigners was of graver consequence. At the end of the sixteenth century Japan had welcomed European influences enthusiastically and been tempted by the prospect of playing her part in world affairs. Iyeyasu had grasped the importance of the Pacific. His relations with the West were both cordial and profitable. His son, Hitodata, suspecting that Western missionaries might be the forerunners of Western political and military penetration, as indeed they had sometimes been in the New World, persecuted Christians as a matter of elementary precaution. But Iyemitsu's xenophobia was without basis: there was no danger of foreign intervention. Without warning he simply closed his empire to the outside world. All Westerners were forced to leave the archipelago with the exception of a few Dutch, who were authorised to reside under humiliating conditions on a prison-island near Nagasaki. Half-breed Spaniards and Portuguese were also expelled. The Japanese themselves were forbidden to build ocean-going ships, to sail the high seas or to live abroad. If they returned to their native land after residence in a foreign country, they were immediately put to death. The Empire of the Rising Sun thus cut itself off from foreign influence, and until 1854 evolved without attending to the outside world.

The Russians in contact with the Chinese world

Just when Europeans were being expelled from Japan, other Europeans had for the first time penetrated to the Far East overland. In 1638 the Russians, who were not yet installed on the Baltic or the North Sea, reached the Pacific (the Sea of Okhotsk) having crossed one by one all the great rivers of Siberia. Their march towards the rising sun had carried them as far from Moscow as the sixteenth-century expeditions had taken the *conquistadores* from Madrid. Turning southwards, they crossed the Stanovoy Mountains, and invaded the Amur basin, where in 1651 they founded the fortified town of Albazin. Sailing up the River Sungari in 1655 they attempted to penetrate the Manchurian forests, which were rich in furs. Ten thousand Chinese troops, supported by a few cannon, succeeded in stopping them. In 1658, while the Voivode Pachkof established himself on the shores of Lake Chilka, the audacious Stepanoff and two hundred Cossacks were slaughtered north of Fuchin. The world's two most extensive empires, Russia and China, were engaged in their first battles for the domination of Eurasia. The struggle was to continue.

EUROPEAN POSSESSIONS BEYOND THE SEAS

The gold crisis

The former colonial power of Portugal had collapsed in spite of independence and the restoration in 1640 of the Portuguese royal house. Meanwhile, from 1630, trade in the Spanish Indies had abruptly declined. Though it was the great period of buccaneers, piracy was only partly to blame. Actually the mines were nearly worked out, while gold and silver were being retained by the colonies themselves or shipped to the Far East via the port of Acapulco. During the second half of the sixteenth century Europe had been flooded with gold from the New World. It no longer arrived, and the Old World was entering a period of monetary shortage, of economic difficulties and depression.

The heroic days of New France

In North America colonisation was proceeding in a dramatic atmosphere. In 1627 Richelieu had obtained an undertaking from the *Compagnie de la Nouvelle-France* to install at least three thousand Catholic colonists in Canada within fifteen years. Though he lost Quebec to the English during the Anglo-French rupture of 1629 to 1632, Champlain continued until his death in 1635 his remarkable efforts to develop the valley of the St Lawrence. Paddling upstream in birch-bark canoes, the missionary fathers persisted despite the hostility of Indians who scalped them, scalded them with boiling water in mockery of baptism and flayed them alive. Richelieu died in the same year, 1642, that Montreal was founded, as the future of New France darkened. Adventurers now mingled with the respectable peasants from Normandy and Poitou. The authority of colonial governors, too frequently replaced, and often in disagreement with the Church, became tenuous. The Iroquois appeared under the very walls of Quebec and paralysed the entire colony. The Company was deeply in debt and renounced its monopoly. The abandonment of the colony was considered. Meanwhile the colonists were exposed to starvation at the least delay in ships from France. In 1663 the colony was placed under the direct authority of the Crown.

The English colonies in America

The English colonies in the New World reaped the benefit of the upheavals which were taking place at home. They received not only those fleeing from religious persecution but also bankrupt tradesmen and unemployed labourers. Maryland, which was founded by Lord Baltimore in 1632, became a refuge for Catholics, though it was in fact open to Christians of all denominations. Liberally supplied, the new colony made as much progress in six months as Virginia had in six years. To the north, from Massachusetts, founded by Puritans, groups overflowed into Connecticut, where New Haven was built in 1638. Roger Williams, driven out by intolerant Nonconformists, set up a true democracy in Rhode Island, in which State and Church were separate and total liberty of conscience was guaranteed. His benevolence towards the native Indians was exceptional. In other colonies they were frequently whipped for not respecting the Sabbath, sentenced to twelve days' hard labour in the service of the white man who caught them drunk, and treated in general like ' contemptible offspring of the Devil '. Indian reaction was, not unnaturally, violent. In 1622, in Virginia, the Indians cut the throats of several hundred settlers, and were driven back into the mountains only after twenty years of fighting (1622–44). In Connecticut the destruction in 1638 of the redoubtable Pequod tribe anticipated a general uprising. For forty years New England had continuous Indian warfare. Although they remained united against the natives, the English colonies already displayed marked individual differences, and in 1643 refused to be grouped together under a single governing body. The southern colonies espoused the cause of the Stuarts, while in the north Cromwell and the Commonwealth were popular. All, however, aspired to administer themselves, to elect assemblies and, except in Virginia, to choose their own governors. After a period of hardship, trial and uncertainty, it became evident that the hostility of nature, far from condemning the colonists to extinction, had stimulated their energy and given them the strength required for further development. They formed more than a lively England in miniature across the seas, in which English institutions and political quarrels were reproduced: they had already outdistanced the Old World on the road to liberty.

The West Indies

The Spanish had not taken full advantage of the West Indies. The English occupied Barbados in 1627, St Kitts in 1623 and Jamaica in 1655. Meanwhile the French appeared in Martinique, Guadeloupe and Santo Domingo, where the results of their colonial efforts were happier than in Canada. In 1644 the introduction of sugar-cane into the islands and the profitable trade with Europe and North America which resulted made the West Indies one of the most valuable of colonial possessions.

Dutch colonial expansion

Though at war with Spain from 1621 to 1628, the United Provinces pursued an increasingly vigorous colonial policy. The West Indies Company, which was formed in 1621, established trading posts in North America along the Hudson River; these survived with difficulty ten troubled years between 1637 and 1647. Even in 1650 New Amsterdam — the future New York, whose population was destined to exceed that of all Holland — counted no more than 1,500 inhabitants. In the Atlantic, Dutch privateers waged ferocious war against rival shipping, took Curaçao, penetrated Guiana and between 1624 and 1630 seized several Brazilian ports. In 1634–44 Maurice of Nassau-Siezen, with the aid of a group of artists, town-planners and men of learning, founded a liberal and humane Dutch Brazil which welcomed Jews from Spain and Portugal. After his departure, however, the policy of exploitation pursued by the West Indies Company brought about a general uprising, and the Dutch were driven from Brazil. In this part of the world they retained only Curaçao and part of Guiana. The achievements of the Dutch East India Company were more lasting. In South Africa it founded the Cape Colony (1652). In the Indian Ocean it drove the Portuguese from Ceylon. It consolidated its positions in Indonesia, where Batavia became the largest commercial centre in the Far East. Tasman discovered Tasmania in 1642 and then New Zealand, thus putting an end to the dreams of a vast southern continent. Although the Gulf of Carpentaria was explored, Australia itself for long remained practically unknown. As late as 1726, Swift could place the kingdom of Lilliput in the very spot occupied by Lake Torrens, without violating his readers' sense of credulity.

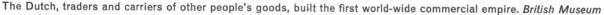

The Dutch, traders and carriers of other people's goods, built the first world-wide commercial empire. *British Museum*

The ceiling of Louis XIII's throne-room at Fontainebleau. *Marburg*

CHAPTER SEVEN

THE ZENITH OF ROYAL POWER
EUROPE AND THE TRIUMPH OF ORDER

The period of confusion had ended: between 1660 and 1680 European history revolved around France and Louis XIV. Catholic Europe, shaken by the Thirty Years' War, weakened by the decadence of Spain and the new Turkish assaults on Austria, abandoned all hopes of establishing a new Holy Roman Empire. Protestant Europe was paralysed by Swedish anarchy, Dutch improvidence and the conflict in England between Parliament and Charles II. Romanoff Muscovy was rent by schism and frightful peasant risings. In these circumstances Louis XIV was able to defy rival powers. Versailles symbolised the splendour and majesty of the new classicism, and was a fit setting for the triumph of monarchy by Divine Right — a triumph more complete than the West had ever known. Under its *Roi Soleil* France reached the height of her prestige and intellectual and cultural brilliance.

THE SITUATION IN EUROPE

The decadence of Spain

The Kings of Spain retained their pomp, solemnity and pride, but continued to lose their authority. Mariana of Austria (1665–79) ruled as Regent in the name of her son Charles II, a deformed weakling with a passion for ceremonial. Fond of good living, Mariana attempted only one reform — to put the kitchens of the royal palace in order. Even in this she failed. The real power was wielded by her favourite, an Austrian Jesuit of little talent who was at the same time Minister and Inquisitor-General. His task was in any case difficult. American gold passed through Spanish hands only to enrich England, France and the United Provinces. Agriculture declined. Nomad shepherds who had displaced settled farmers transformed the plateaus of Castile into sheep runs. Through pride of caste the nobles refused to work in any way or take part in trade. The Church, the sea, service at court — or haughty destitution: for the Spanish *hidalgo* there was no other choice and some staved off hunger by selling the contents of their castles at bargain prices. The country's finances were chaotic; the treasury was empty. Merchants and tradesmen refused to give credit, even to the King's household. Religious faith, the traditional mainspring of the nation's vitality, lost its vigour. Nor was there any force to check the intellectual decline of a country which had owed the triumphs of its Golden Age to its burning convictions.

English unrest and Dutch improvidence

Unrest in England also contributed to the successes of Louis XIV. Charles II was thirty years old at the time of his triumphal entry into London in May 1660. Elegant and sceptical, witty and selfish, he might well have been a man of the eighteenth century. A refined sensualist — Louis XIV bought him with women and gold — he held himself and everybody else in mild contempt. Perhaps he shared the convictions of his friend, the philosopher Thomas Hobbes, that the corruption of men and their eagerness to tear each other limb from limb rendered order essential. His temperament inclined him towards Catholicism, which seemed to support the authority of kings; but, far too intelligent to clash openly with his subjects, he maintained his position by deft changes of policy.

In the eyes of the English his youth and love of pleasure at first symbolised a violent anti-Puritan reaction; Cromwell's body was dug up and hanged. In this favourable climate Charles re-established much of the royal prerogative. The privileges of the Anglican Church were restored. With the French alliance and the conversion of his brother and successor, James, Duke of York, to Catholicism, a pro-Catholic policy seemed a possibility. Then in 1665 plague ravaged the country, and in the following year fire swept London and burned 13,000 houses to the ground. A year later a Dutch naval squadron sailed unchallenged up the Medway. In the face of these signs of Divine Wrath there were mutterings about the licentiousness of a court where idolatry had taken root.

Charles was still anxious to improve the lot of Roman Catholics. In 1670 he concluded a secret treaty with Louis XIV which promised both Charles's adherence to Catholicism and help for France against the Dutch. In return, Charles received subsidies. After this, he issued a declaration freeing both Protestant dissenters and Roman Catholics from some of their disabilities. But Parliament forced the withdrawal of these concessions and passed the Test Act of 1673, which obliged all civil or military servants

Military firearms in the early seventeenth century were hard to load, liable to misfire, and very inaccurate. This made the protection of musketeers by pikemen essential. *Mansell*

The ballad-singer kept popular tradition alive, commented on passing events, and transmitted political and religious propaganda. *Mansell*

Plague made its last great appearance in England in 1665. It terrified contemporaries, many of whom regarded it as a divine judgment. Within a century, better quarantine arrangements had virtually eliminated the threat in Western Europe.

The Great Fire of London struck doubly hard in following so soon upon the Plague. Yet it made possible Wren's churches and the planned rebuilding of the city during the expansion of the second half of the seventeenth century.

of the Crown to repudiate on oath the 'Real Presence' in the Eucharist, and thus excluded sincere Catholics from public office. In 1674 Parliament also reversed Charles's foreign policy by breaking off relations with Catholic France and making peace with the Protestant United Provinces. Later, it attempted to exclude the Catholic Duke of York from the succession. Charles, defending the rights of the royal succession, survived the crisis with the help of the House of Lords. (He had been forced, nevertheless, to concede in 1679 a Habeas Corpus Amendment Act which formed a landmark in the protection of individual rights.) In this crisis, too, the names of Whig and Tory appeared; though their meaning was soon to be confused, the Tories, broadly speaking, were for the monarch's lawful prerogatives and the Whigs for the liberty of the subject and the independence of Parliament. Although Charles called no parliament after 1681 and maintained the political stability of the country until his death in 1685, England, deeply divided and uncertain of the future, remained incapable of playing the important part in European affairs which she had played under Cromwell. The Dutch Republic, though it had twice held its own against the English at sea, had also grown weaker. Its rich republican merchants, more interested in prosperity than in glory, pared down State expenses and were distrustful of the army, which they suspected, and not without reason, of planning a dictatorship. In spite of John de Witt, they refused to vote money for the army and left their fortifications unrepaired. Their improvidence was such that they even sold munitions to France and replaced trained Orangist officers by their own sons, who had no taste for fighting.

Germany and the Great Elector

Germany, which John de Witt compared to a skeleton held together not by nerves but wires, whose individual members were incapable of making the least movement, was a nullity. The German princes led more or less independent existences of petty intrigues and efforts to ape the court-life of Versailles. Only one of them, the Elector of Brandenburg, looked towards the future. Frederick William, the Great Elector (1640–88), was a man of extra-

ordinary appearance with a minute head, but combined patient self-control with burning ambition. The obstacles which faced him were formidable. The scattered Hohenzollern possessions were riddled with autonomous rights inherited from the Middle Ages. Brandenburg itself, the centre of his power, was a poor land of marsh and sandy soil. He overcame these handicaps by centralisation and internal colonisation. Imbued with a sense of duty and proud to serve the State, his counsellors stripped the local Diets of their prerogatives and, riding roughshod over all opposition, founded the Prussian bureaucracy. Dutch families were encouraged to assist in draining swamps, while French, German and Swiss refugees from religious persecution poured into Brandenburg. With State aid the newcomers cleared wastelands, built dykes to control the Spree, replaced the pig-sties of the Dorothea district of Berlin with houses, and introduced industries which until then had been unknown. The Elector, who controlled the economic life of the State, himself built factories, established a postal system, and prohibited peasants from marrying until they had either planted six oaks or grafted six fruit trees. Nobles and commoners alike paid an excise on food which supported a small but well trained and equipped army. While in Sweden the nobles were quarrelling during the minority of Charles XI (1660–79), plundering the treasury and encroaching on the royal domains, the Great Elector met and crushed the Swedish army at Fehrbellin (1675) and conquered western Pomerania. The conquest was premature, and in August 1678 Sweden's ally, Louis XIV, obliged Frederick William with a brief stroke of the pen to restore what had cost him so many years to gain.

Austria and the revival of Turkey

In spite of the Emperor Leopold (1657–1705), who was sickly, thick-lipped, gloomy and vacillating, a 'clock that constantly needed rewinding', Austria was the only Germanic power capable of obstructing Louis XIV's ambitions. But her freedom of action depended on the Ottoman threat. Austria alone stood in the way of Turkey's dangerous advance into Central Europe.

Since the opening of the seventeenth century the Ottoman Empire had been in decline. The renegades who had so often revitalised Turkey had become harder to find. Her best soldiers, the Janissaries, no longer formed an élite and had become little more than a seditious and plundering rabble. The 'four ministers of the Devil', wine, coffee, tobacco and opium, demoralised Turkish society. The sultans, dominated by eunuchs and favourites, withdrew into their harems. Turbulent nobles seized the provinces, while in Constantinople the army disputed power with doctors of Islamic law, the Ulemas. Osman II was dethroned and executed in 1622. Though Murad IV (1623–40) temporarily set the empire on its feet again, the sex-mad Ibrahim I (1640–48) went insane and was strangled with a bowstring. Mehmed IV (1648–87), a child of seven, learned at the start of his reign to write the words: 'Obey me, or I shall have your head cut off.' Yet rioters were able to invade his palace, strangle his grandmother and remain unpunished.

In 1656, after eight years of anarchy, another Mehmed, a Grand Vizir of Albanian origin, inaugurated a brilliant line of rulers: the Köprülü. By energy alone — plus a bloodbath of assassinations — he restored order. More scholarly, honest and above all more humane, his son Fazil Ahmed (1661–76) pacified the empire and restored its prosperity, modernising the country without violating Ottoman traditions. Turkey, re-organised and rejuvenated, could at last resume the offensive against the infidel. From 1661 to 1664 assaults on Austria confirmed Turkish suzerainty over Transylvania. In 1669 Crete was wrested from the Venetians. In 1681 the grasping and ostentatious

A German ecclesiastical box of the seventeenth century, elaborately ornamented with enamel and silver work. Despite the economic ruin which followed the Thirty Years' War German princelings and the Catholic Church commissioned many costly works of art in imitation of richer neighbours.

The baroque style at its most elaborate and beautiful risked transforming the church from a temple to a theatre. This example was built at Wies, Bavaria, between 1746 and 1754.

Kara Mustafa (1676–89), who had succeeded his brother-in-law as Grand Vizir, planned to take advantage of a Hungarian revolt against the Habsburgs. In 1684 he assembled a powerful army and marched on Vienna, which was already devastated by plague. Austria, with all its forces mobilised in the defence of Christianity, was in no position to thwart the ambitions of France.

THE ASCENDANCY OF FRANCE

Monarchy by Divine Right

On the death of Mazarin in March 1661 Louis XIV, who was twenty-two, decided to be his own prime minister. The humiliations of the Fronde were still vivid in his memory, and since childhood he had hated disorder. Mazarin had not only taught him to enjoy work, but had trained him in the profession of kingship. In a society still humanist in tone, Louis's intention was to be something more than a mere hero modelled on the great examples of classical antiquity. His rule, responding to the widely felt need for authority engendered by a long period of disorder, was inspired by absolutism and the notion of Divine Right as Bossuet later defined it: 'The royal authority is sacred. God appointed kings as his ministers on earth and through them reigns over His people. Majesty in a prince is the image of the grandeur of God. And what grandeur for a single man to possess! He is himself the State. From him flow the orders which co-ordinate and direct the actions of magistrates and captains, citizens and soldiers, the provinces, the armies on land, the ships at sea. He is the image of God Himself, who, seated on His throne above, directs all things.'

The King

A passionate huntsman who loved outdoor life, merry-making and festivities, Louis XIV might have become a second Henry IV. But, conscious of his dignity and of his mission, he very soon set about masking the man behind the sovereign. Made taller by his high periwig and high-heeled shoes, with carriage and features always composed as though he were about to appear on the stage, he learned his role so well and played it with such authority that all Europe soon referred to him as *the* King.

The ideal of perfect and flawless monarchy, of which Louis XIV became the supreme embodiment, demanded the maintenance of a perfect, flawless and unchanging order. This implied the danger of rigidity. The King, too sure of his doctrine, read little, travelled little, and never left France or escaped from himself. He began to behave as though time itself had stopped on the day of his coronation. All change seemed to him corruption; all novelty decadence. He was unable to grasp that the kingdom would evolve apart from the throne and, in time, turn against it. Occupying the centre of a system by definition perfect, a system of which he was the soul and *raison d'être*, the temptation of pride became irresistible. In the beginning of his reign he demanded veneration less for his person than for the idea which he embodied. He was full of youthful romanticism and capable of genuine tenderness. Later, in his thirties, his victories, the gross flattery of his courtiers and the adoration of all France led him to think of himself as the 'beginning and end of all things';

As a young man, Louis XIV was devoted to amateur theatricals. Here he is shown in costume for a ballet in the congenial role of the Sun. He was later to exploit the theatrical and spectacular possibilities of monarchy as no ruler before him.

he drew aloof in solitary grandeur. He abandoned his early mistress, the shy and not very beautiful La Vallière, whom he had naïvely but truly loved, and took instead the beautiful and insolent de Montespan. His conception of monarchy became more pagan than Christian. Like the Roman Emperors of the third century he identified himself with the sun and, according to Saint-Simon, would have had himself similarly worshipped had it not been for fear of the Devil. The hall of mirrors at Versailles still reflects his narcissism.

Though every hour of the sovereign's existence was marked by ritual, the culminating ceremonies of the day corresponded to solar events: like the sun the *Roi Soleil* rose and set in public. At night, the King would glance around the assembly to give someone the honour of carrying his candlestick. Gentlemen of the bedchamber on one side and gentlemen of the wardrobe on the other then removed his shoes, stockings and breeches. The royal breeches were at once wrapped in red taffeta, while the prince of highest rank produced the royal nightshirt. The first gentleman of the bedchamber assisted the king into the right sleeve, the first gentleman of the wardrobe into the left. If anyone raised his voice the ushers silenced him. At their signal, all except a few favoured persons then withdrew. The King then wiped his face with a napkin

In the later seventeenth century, the wearing of wigs became general in good society. This wig belonged to Louis XIV and has been mounted on a wax effigy of his face as it appeared in middle life. *Giraudon*

which a prince of the blood presented to him between two silver-gilt dishes and retired to his bed, which was protected by a gilded balustrade guarded by an officer. Before it men removed their hats and women genuflected as though in church before the high altar.

The fairy-like festivals and fêtes of Versailles constantly celebrated the glory and almost supernatural power of this sovereign. The flower-beds were renewed twice a day by means of interchangeable pots. Hundreds of wax torches, supported by masked figures, turned night into

In October 1652 the young Louis XIV entered Paris and royal government was established on the ruins of the Fronde. This contemporary print shows the Louvre and the Pont Neuf of that epoch. *Mansell*

day, illuminating the foliage as brilliantly as the sun. Tropical plants bloomed in the depths of winter. Invisible musicians lured the wanderer towards labyrinths or fountains. At nightfall, on some enchanted isle, theatrical spectacles and ballets would take place under a shimmering canopy of fireworks. In these spectacles the King himself would play the leading role: the simple shepherd, the conquering hero or, perhaps, Jupiter among the gods.

The triumph of the State

The reign of Louis XIV saw the triumph of the State. Society was still patriarchal and the King was the supreme patriarch. If he sent men to prison or into exile, he usually did so at the request of their own families. But in Paris, already a large city, a political police was being formed. Louis, faithfully served by commoners who owed everything to him, held the reins of government firmly in hand. The *Parlement*, theoretically the kingdom's highest legal body, was silenced. In the provinces the King's Intendants, henceforth 'provincial kings', kept tight control over local magistrates. They usurped the traditional functions of the rural nobility, checked the independence of the provincial representative bodies, intervened in the financial affairs of the municipalities, and in the teeth of localism patiently built up a central administration. At the end of the reign they were no longer simple commissioners, but bureaucrats in the modern sense of the word, the forerunners of the Napoleonic prefects.

Colbert

In the economic field an outstanding minister strove to protect and increase the nation's prosperity. Colbert (1649–83), the son of a merchant draper from Rheims, brought to the service of the monarchy the sober virtues of his class. He was a hard and methodical worker who, like all his contemporaries, measured the riches of a nation by the quantity of gold and silver in its treasury. He therefore encouraged the founding of numerous industries even by bribing qualified foreigners and bringing them secretly into France. He imposed rigid State control, and manufacturers who received subsidies had, at the risk of the pillory, to observe minutely detailed regulations. The State itself set the example in the workshops which produced the famous Gobelin tapestries.

Efforts to restore religious unity

To perfect the unity of the kingdom, the subordination of the Church and eradication of heresy had to be achieved. In 1682 the General Assembly of the clergy of France recorded the victory of Gallicanism in Four Propositions asserting that the Gallican Church was, and would continue to be, governed by its own laws. Gallicanism was the name given to the tendencies in the French Church which emphasised independence of Rome and the local authority of the Crown in matters of Church government, while claiming to remain completely orthodox in doctrine. A quarrel with Rome followed. Meanwhile, Louis XIV forced the Jansenists to submit and worked for a reconciliation with the Protestants. A peaceful compromise between Christians of diverse sects did not seem an impossibility. This was the opinion and hope of the great German philosopher Leibniz, remembered for his optimistic belief that ' all was for the best in the best of all possible worlds '. The Catholics, on their side, were in favour of creating an Academy of Biblical Studies and stated that what they desired was religious unity, not uniformity.

The King's army

The same moderation was observed in the field of international affairs. Louis XIV had not yet sacrificed French interests to Catholic and dynastic imperialism, but continued the policy of Richelieu and Mazarin. His chief objective was to push back and fortify the exposed northern and eastern frontiers. Louvois, his Secretary of State for War, was an arrogant upstart, flattering and obsequious towards the King, enflaming his master's love of glory. But his energy and will-power, his intelligence and constant care to leave nothing to chance were remarkable; and the army he forged became the first French standing army. All its officers were appointed by the King. Commoners and gentlemen of limited means could obtain commissions without having to purchase them. Rank depended no longer on patronage alone, but on length of service. Little by little a uniform in the royal colours

Babar and his army saluting the standards by throwing kumis on them (an old Mongol custom). c. 1595. British Museum

ایستاده کرده یک یک مغول به یک دست کاو یک دست کرما س

سفید دراز نمی لبسته در دست خود گرفته ایستاده اس

دیکری سه پارچه سفید دراز اپایان تر از قطاپس نوغ

بسنه و از نیزجوب توع کذرانده واورده یک کیار

became general, discipline was tightened and military training improved. Also the troops were paid more regularly. Fire-power was increased by the recently invented grenade and, even more, by the flintlock musket.

Classical warfare

The classical order which the army adopted appeared even in warfare itself. Undoubtedly the greatest service which Louis XIV rendered Europe was that he curbed the murderous instincts of men at war by imposing rules which were as strict as those which the literary critics of the period affirmed to be necessary in art. Something analogous to the spirit of chivalry was created in spite of the developments of military technique. Few battles were fought — one or two during a campaign — and armies retired into winter-quarters during inclement weather. Looting was forbidden and extreme courtesy was observed between rival commanders. Defeat was measured not by the number of dead, but by the number of regimental colours lost to the enemy. The most technical of all military actions — the siege of a fortress — was carried out with great formality and even elegance. Vauban (1633–1707) greatest of military engineers, turned the art of the siege with its calculated moves into an almost intellectual pastime; and the court in its finery would attend the capture of a stronghold as though taking part in a royal fête.

The War of Devolution and the war with the Dutch

Classical warfare was justified by sound legal pretexts. In 1665 Philip IV of Spain died and Louis XIV, who was married to Philip's oldest daughter, at once claimed the Spanish Netherlands in her name, invoking the Belgian custom of ' devolution ' by which she was, he claimed, entitled to inherit her father's possessions. He invaded Belgium and Franche-Comté (1666–7). Deeply disturbed by French aggression, the United Provinces, England and Sweden joined to impose their arbitration in 1668.

Louis did not forgive the Dutch for having checked him in the midst of victory. In 1672 he crossed the Rhine, determined to annihilate the home of heresy and republican tradesmen, which Colbert and French commercial interest longed to ruin. In a triumphal sweep he occupied nearly all the interior of the country. The Dutch, destroying in a few brief days the work of centuries, cut their dykes, flooding the polders and, in face of the harsh peace terms that France offered, recovered the heroic patriotism they had displayed in the days of the sea-beggars. John de Witt was held responsible for the disaster and murdered; the office of Stadtholder was revived and William III of Orange given almost dictatorial powers. He was twenty-two, a strict and fanatical Calvinist, and detested Louis XIV not only as the invader of his country but as an idolater. He reversed the diplomatic situation by obtaining the alliance of the Emperor, Spain and several German princes. But although the French at first gave ground, they soon

A camp scene (signed Paras). Mogul School c. 1600. British Museum

H

counter-attacked. Between 1675 and 1678 town after town in Franche-Comté and Belgium fell. In the Mediterranean, Admiral Duquesne destroyed the Dutch fleet. In the Treaties of Nymegen (August and September 1678, and February 1679) Louis XIV, magnanimous in his glory, dictated the peace terms. Though the United Provinces remained intact, France took Hainaut from Spain, a further portion of Flanders and all of Franche-Comté. Louis XIV was the arbiter of Europe. Paris, intoxicated with pride, called him Louis the Great. The court moved permanently to Versailles. Classical France was at her zenith.

FRENCH CLASSICISM

The reign of Louis XIV owed its grandeur more to the extraordinary creativity of French classicism than to military glory.

Literature

Authority and discipline had also invaded French intellectual life without, however, dampening baroque exuberance. The Académie Francaise, made a national institution by Colbert and housed in the Louvre, formulated the strict rules of classical literature modelled on the ancients. Rarely in the history of literature were so many masterpieces produced in such a brief span. Bossuet was in the first rank of religious orators; La Fontaine published his famous *Fables* between 1668 and 1679. But the works of two men of genius were outstanding: the tragedies of Racine (1639–99) and the comedies of Molière (1622–73). Keeping within the classical mould and in flawless verse, Racine's tragedies hinged upon destructive passions and displayed astonishing psychological insight. Molière was equally successful in exploiting and transcending the limitations of classical drama, satirising the foibles of human society with great comic gusto and lucidity. His lampooning of religious hypocrisy and social and intellectual snobbery is still vivid today, and his reputation remains intact and unrivalled after three centuries.

Classical art and Versailles

Artists were grouped in academies, strictly supervised by the King's official painter Lebrun. After studying in Rome they would return to collaborate in the creation of those vast architectural projects which, as it was said, ' in default of striking victories on the battlefield arrested the attention of all eyes and bore witness to the grandeur of the prince '. In the marshlands of Versailles, far from the noise and bustle of the capital, was built the most glorious residence that the world had ever seen. Raised on an artificial terrace, the palace faced the setting sun; its majestic west façade, austere yet harmonious, commanded an immense park skilfully ordered to produce a landscape of great beauty and almost architectural formality. Carpets of grass and flower-beds looking like embroidery bordered tall clipped hedges. Ornamental waters sparkled in marble basins, flowed down cascades and spread in sheets over stepped marble tiers where hundreds of statues gleamed and scintillated. The gardens descended gently through terraces to the sides of the Grand Canal which ran to the horizon. The elaborate formality of the gardens was repeated

within the palace itself. The setting was made for pomp and ceremonial. The walls were of multi-coloured marble, the galleries adorned with trophies and victories, scrolls and garlands of laurel and palm. On the ceiling planets and divinities escorted the Sun's chariot. Numerous paintings depicted the exploits of Louis XIV: with golden breastplate and brow haloed with glory, grasping a thunderbolt, he could be seen entering Dunkirk, laying siege to Douai, crossing the Rhine, or majestically giving laws to the Empire surrounded by the pleasures of peace.

OTHER CULTURAL INFLUENCES

From Leibniz to Spinoza

As depicted in the allegorical paintings at Versailles, Louis XIV appeared to be the unique centre of the universe. Elsewhere, however, other movements were taking place which pointed towards a different future. At a time when Louis XIV, occupied with personal glory, was employing the physicist Huygens to canalise the waters of Marly, the German Leibniz devised a new form of differential and integral calculus, while the Dutch Swammerdam's microscopic studies of the insect world revealed the immense complexity of the minute. In England Newton was preparing to reduce the physical world itself to a set of equations. In Germany the Romantic Age which would displace the Age of Enlightenment was already foreshadowed in mystical poetry and Lutheran pietism. In Amsterdam a gentle grinder of optical lenses, Spinoza (1632–77), a non-orthodox Jew, was identifying divinity

The wife of a seventeenth-century townsman, going shopping. Ladies of high fashion would have worn skirts to the ground. Practical considerations required the housewife to have shorter ones.

Versailles. By creating out of nothing this elaborately formal palace and its gardens Louis XIV displayed his political acumen: by gathering the nobility at Versailles to lead a parasitic court life he divested them of power. *Larousse*

Moscow, where Peter the Great grew up, was beginning to be a little better known in the West at the end of the seventeenth century. But it remained a barbarous medieval jumble, more of the Orient than of Europe. *Mission Weiss*

with nature and knowledge, criticising holy writ and monarchy, substituting the social contract for divine right, and quietly propounding ideas which would send Louis XIV's second successor to the guillotine.

Muscovy

When unity, authority and reason were triumphant in France distant Muscovy was in tumult. The second half (1655–76) of the great reign of Alexis Romanoff was convulsed by revolts which threatened to overthrow both religious discipline and the social order. The ambitious Patriarch Nikon, whom the Tsar considered too powerful, was dismissed in disgrace in 1658, though the Council of Moscow (1661–7) upheld his reforms. Partisans of the Old Faith refused to accept this return to Greek usages and withdrew from the official Church, which adhered more and more closely to the monarchy. To safeguard Orthodox unity the Tsar had recourse to the gallows and the stake. His soldiers besieged the Solovki Monastery for ten years and when it fell the monks were put to the sword. The schism — or *raskol* — rent the entire empire. Convinced that the Antichrist had arrived to announce the end of the world, thousands of men lighted piles of faggots and, invoking the name of Jesus, threw themselves into the flames. Priestless fugitives fled to the forests or to the steppes where they formed visionary communities

of saints. Strange sects arose: flagellants, self-mutilated eunuchs, dancers, leapers, whirlers. Religious chaos was matched by social anarchy. The nobles took measures to ensure that their serfs did not escape. In 1667 an adventurer, Stepan Razin, a *raskolnik* — or dissenter from the established Church — roused the Don Cossacks. Three years later, welcomed everywhere as a liberator, he seized Astrakhan and marched on Moscow. He had become a legendary figure. It was believed that he was invulnerable and could turn his enemies to stone with a glance. Peasants and deserters swelled the ranks of his army, and at his call the serfs revolted against the nobles. There were peasant risings as far away as the White Sea. Equipped in the Western fashion, the Tsar's armies eventually put down the insurrection in 1671. Stepan Razin was wounded, taken prisoner, and quartered in Red Square.

Muscovy seemed to have reverted to the Middle Ages, and her *raskolniks* strove to fan the people's hatred of foreigners. Nevertheless commerce was developing and the country was not entirely closed to foreign influences. For two centuries the Tsars, having chosen a wife from among the daughters of the nobility, would have her submitted to inspection by matrons. When in 1669 Alexis became a widower he continued this odd custom for the sake of form; but the girl he married was a person of advanced manners whom he had admired in the salons of his boyars for the grace with which she danced the   115 polonaise and the courante. The new Tsaritsa had little respect for tradition and would appear in an open carriage wearing neither veil nor rouge; she brought up her children in the Western manner. Feodor, the oldest, reigned obscurely during the troubled years between 1676 and 1682. Her youngest son became Peter the Great.

ASIA

In world history the second half of the seventeenth century was as much the age of the Grand Mogul Aurangzeb (1658–1708) 'Dominator of the World', or of the Chinese Emperor K'ang-hsi (1662–1722) 'Unfailing Prosperity' as it was that of Louis XIV. The zenith of their long reigns coincided with the years of Louis XIV's triumph. Their talents were very different from his and they owed their success to themselves alone. Their reigns were not the happy culmination of a long historical evolution, nor did they command wide national support. Each represented only a conquering minority. In the case of India this minority had been established for more than a century, but was almost entirely isolated from the non-Moslem masses. In China, though their behaviour towards the vanquished was more conciliatory, the conquerors had been installed for only eighteen years. In both countries the powerful personality of the sovereigns enabled them to raise their vast empires to the pinnacle of their prestige. Thus Asia, a continent of teeming masses where the individual counts for little, furnished in these two remarkable men an outstanding example of the role which the individual can play in history.

The zenith of the reign of Aurangzeb (1658–89)

Aurangzeb, the last Grand Mogul worthy of that name, dreamed only of warfare, the prestige of his empire and the glory of God. He had little ambition to be a lawgiver like his ancestor Akbar, or a builder like his grandfather Jehan Gir. He no longer listened to the complaints of his subjects, nor supervised his civil servants. Opposed to reform of any kind, he seemed unaware of the increasing poverty of his domains. As chief of an invading minority whose rights to the throne were questionable, he decided to withdraw from his sumptuous court and live with the army. His troops — more than 200,000 men — were so well paid that even the ordinary soldiers all wore jewellery. Guns carried by camels, light cannon called stirrup-guns, which never left the Emperor's side, enormous bronze cannon mounted on huge carts drawn by as many as five hundred oxen — such was the powerful artillery which supported his musketeers, his herds of fighting elephants, and the confused swarm of his cavalry.

A series of energetically waged wars gave Aurangzeb's empire its greatest territorial expansion. In 1661, after hard fighting through the jungle, he imposed vassalage and a tribute on the King of Assam, and seized Chittagong. From 1667 to 1672 he subdued the Afghan tribes in the north-west. In the Deccan peninsula he occupied the small feudal states which had replaced the Vijayana Empire, and annexed the rich sultanates of Golconda and Bijapur.

By his fire and passion, his violence and horsemanship, Aurangzeb recalled memories of Babar; but he was the only Grand Mogul who was at once a swordsman and a 'saint'. Emaciated and as taciturn as a dervish, he retained the asceticism of his youth even after he ascended the throne. He ate plain millet bread and drank only water. He slept on the bare ground, despised luxury, and fled all pleasures. In his Puritanism he banned music, birthday celebrations, blasphemy and foul language. Tobacco filled him with even greater horror than alcohol and opium. An ardent partisan of Sunnite orthodoxy, he knew the Koran by heart, twice copied it out in its entirety, embroidered verses from it on his standards and, to conform with tradition, worked with his own hands. He manufactured tarbooshes, observed all the fasts, built mosques and alms houses, gave lavishly to charity and in 1665 led 400,000 of his followers to Kashmir on a pilgrimage which lasted more than eighteen months.

His strong religious convictions drove him to extremes. The grim and inflexible fanaticism which he displayed throughout his reign led to greater acts of violence than even the impulsive sectarianism of Babar. He imposed on non-Moslems a humiliating poll-tax, the *jizya*, put a certain number of infidels to death, defiled the temple of Allahabad by cutting the throat of a sacred cow within its precincts, destroyed the temple of Vishnu at Benares and placed Hindu 'idols' under the steps of the great mosque at Agra so that the Faithful should have the pleasure of trampling them underfoot.

Since its conquest by the Turco-Iranian invaders from Afghanistan in the beginning of the sixteenth century, Brahmanic India had never thought of insurrection. Now, for the first time, Aurangzeb's intolerance aroused the Brahmans. Immense crowds gathered in Delhi to protest against the *jizya*. For three days they allowed themselves to be crushed beneath the feet of charging elephants. From 1659 the region of Bundelkhand became a permanent hotbed of rebellion. Inflamed with the 'Divine Name' by the fakirs, peasants surged on Delhi; the revolt was stamped out in blood. In 1669 a dangerous uprising of the Jats, provoked by the destruction of a temple, was checked; but it continued to simmer until in 1686 it boiled up again. In the hope of wiping out the Hindu kingdom of Marwar, Aurangzeb attempted to dethrone its boy-king Ajit Singh, whose father had died heroically in the Mogul's own service. Such treachery wounded the Rajputs' sense of honour and, already resentful of the *jizya*, in 1678 they flung their superb bearded and turbanned cavalry against the troops of the Grand Mogul. The Rajputs, proud sons of the Sun and the Moon, were fearless fighters, for they believed that death on the field of battle took them straight to Indra's heaven. Akbar, Aurangzeb's son, was charged with the task of confronting them, an undertaking he disapproved of and very quickly abandoned. He took refuge in the Deccan with the Mahrattas; but Rajputana was none the less invaded and pillaged by the Moslems.

The Sikhs and the Mahrattas

The religious aspirations of the Sikhs and the Mahrattas were mingled with equally passionate nationalistic aspirations. With them, a new India stirred, inflammable and tragic, and in which nothing remained of that sixteenth-century India which had so easily been conquered by the Turco-Iranians. Since the days of the teacher Nanak

Alexis Mihailovich, father of three Tsars, among them Peter the Great. He recovered Smolensk and Kiev from the Poles, imposed a code of law, and rescued Russia from the troubles which had threatened it in the early seventeenth century.

Krishna being rowed across a river to keep a tryst with Radha. This mid-seventeenth-century miniature from Udaipur is an example of the school of Hindu painting which flourished in Rajputana from the sixteenth to the nineteenth century.
Radio Times Hulton Picture Library

(1469–1539) the Sikhs had practised in their Himalayan fastnesses a reformed Hinduism freed from caste and certain observances. From this sect the Guru — or teacher — Arjun (1581–1606) had forged a nation. When he was put to death by the Moslems his son Hargovind (1606–45) engaged in a war with the Moguls which continued after the accession of Aurangzeb. When in 1675 a new Guru, Teg Bahadur, was captured he chose to be executed rather than renounce his faith. Under his successor Govind Singh (1675–1708) the Sikhs achieved a heightened form of mysticism. Devoting several hours a day to meditation, to hymn-singing and to repeating the name of God, they carried their heads erect, were trained to look straight ahead and henceforth could be distinguished from other Hindus as much by their bearing as by their long hair and steel bracelets. When baptised in water which had been stirred with a two-edged sword they became 'singhs' or lions. In order to be as strong as the Moslems they made it their duty to eat meat, and their endurance disconcerted the troops of the Grand Mogul, who believed that heathens — *kafir* — must of necessity be degenerate. Without entirely subduing the Sikhs, Aurangzeb succeeded at least in keeping them away from the Indo-Gangetic plain.

In the north-west of the Deccan, in the highlands of the Ghats, Sivaji-Bhonsle (1627–80) 'son of the devil and father of trickery' rebelled against his overlord, the ruler of Bijapur. Granted an interview with the general sent against him, he pretended to embrace him, but strangled him with his steel-tipped fingers. The Mahrattas supplied him with diminutive but agile horsemen who were highly skilled in guerilla fighting. In the fervour of his Hinduism Sivaji wished not only to destroy Moslem domination, but the social system imposed by Brahmanism, which seemed to him intolerable. In this system the Sudras of his caste, which was the most despised, were constantly reminded of their inferiority. If a Sudra was found reading the Vedas his tongue was cut out; if he so much as listened to the Vedas being read, molten lead was poured into his ears. Sivaji dreamed of delivering the Hindus from such injustice, of breaking down the walls which separated them and uniting them into a single nation. His army was swelled by numerous bands of peasants who considered him a protector and a hero. He became more and more daring and, penetrating the interior of the Mogul Empire, attacked convoys, held Moslems to ransom, and in 1664 surprised and sacked Surat. In 1665, through the mediation of the Rajah of Marwar, he came to an agreement with Aurangzeb. He was invited to Delhi, where he scandalised the court by upbraiding the Grand Mogul for not having received him with more honours. He escaped, hidden in a basket, regained his mountain stronghold and renewed the struggle. On his death in 1680 Mahratta power was firmly established in the peninsula, from the Gulf of Bengal to the Arabian Sea. Sivaji's son, Sambaji, though courageous, was less capable and did not take advantage of the strife between Prince Akbar and his father the Grand Mogul, nor of the disaster which befell the imperial army, decimated by famine, in the pass of Ramghat. In 1689 he was captured by Moslem horsemen and brought before Aurangzeb, who immediately had him quartered.

At the cost of incessant warfare, usually on more than one front, the Grand Mogul succeeded in maintaining the unity of his empire and in keeping the Hindus under control. Islam had not enjoyed such power or been so

Krishna and Rukmini's wedding. Miniature from Malwa, 1688. Reformed Hinduism under nationalist banners was born of Mogul harshness in Bundelkhand, Rajputana and the Himalayas.

aggressive even in the days of Babar. Aurangzeb's army was the largest in the world and his wealth incalculable. At the age of seventy-one, after thirty years of rule, he remained both physically and mentally young. Master of an empire in which the Moslems were outnumbered by two hundred to one, he was sufficiently energetic to oppose numbers by force, and sufficiently fanatical to deny an awakening subcontinent all hope of ever being understood by its conquerors.

China under the Emperor K'ang-hsi (from 1667 to 1697)

Under the Emperor K'ang-hsi China achieved a splendour and prestige which had every appearance of being lasting. Since the death in 1661 of K'ang-hsi's father, Shun-chi, the country had been ruled by four regents. But on the death of his uncle Soei in 1667 K'ang-hsi decided, at the age of thirteen, to govern for himself. The portrait which the Jesuits have left of him is reminiscent of the classical descriptions of Louis XIV: ' A well-proportioned figure, an air of majesty which made it easy to distinguish him in the midst of a thronged court, a nobility of soul which gave him absolute mastery over his own passions, a sensible and sound judgment . . . ' Violence horrified him; though he condemned one of the regents to the block, he at once commuted the sentence to life imprisonment. During his campaigns he shared the life and hardships of his soldiers, and retired to his own tent only when he had made sure that they were comfortably encamped. While Louis XIV disliked the battlefield and Aurangzeb liked nothing better, K'ang-hsi made war from a sense of duty, and was as unmoved by the intoxication of victory as he was by the seductions of glory. His activities embraced all fields — administration, diplomacy, religious affairs, cultural life. Willing to work long hours, gifted with a lively intelligence and more than common powers of observation, he easily surmounted all the difficulties which the new Manchu dynasty encountered.

His ancestors had been Tatar nomads and nothing gave him more delight than to abandon the pomp of the court and hunt antelope on the steppes of Mongolia. As an emperor, however, he in no way resembled those chieftains of hordes, his forebears. He upheld the traditions of the Mings and his deportment was that of a true Son of Heaven. Before a military campaign he would himself fill the ' stirrup cup ' of the departing general, and in spring plough the first furrow of the year. In philosophy he was a disciple of Confucius. Since his mandate was of celestial origin, it was his duty to see that peace reigned in his empire, and to maintain between the social order and the ' universal order ' the most perfect harmony. While he was rebuilding Peking, which had been burned to the ground in 1644, his chief preoccupation — in every way symbolic — was to remain faithful to the aesthetic and religious principles of the Ming architects who had constructed the inner city in the fifteenth century. While the Grand Mogul was ruthlessly bent on destroying survivals from the Hindu past, the Emperor K'ang-hsi was behaving as though the Tatars had conquered China only in order to preserve its ancient civilisation.

Though he maintained an efficient military organisation which was capable of preventing attempts to avenge the conquest, he treated the conquered Chinese with unswerving moderation. He respected their ancient traditions and returned to them some of the land which the Manchus had unjustly seized. From their numbers he recruited fifty thousand soldiers, or a fifth of his army, and allowed them to fill high positions in the government. On his orders the policy of invigorating and cleaning up the administration which his father had initiated was energetically pursued. Only three hundred girls remained in the Imperial Palace. The stewardship of the regents was strictly examined and breaches of trust were severely punished. If a master killed a slave he had previously gone unpunished; now he was condemned to one hundred strokes of the rod. The small proprietor was favoured at the expense of the great domains which the Mings had allowed dangerously to expand. Thus K'ang-hsi consolidated Chinese unity.

In recompense for the services he had rendered to the invaders in 1644 General Wuen-Sen Kwai had been entrusted with the distant mountainous provinces of the south-west, where he became more and more independent of Peking. He appealed in 1674 for a national uprising against the Manchus but was answered only in Fukien and the Canton region. The Jesuits in China cast three hundred and twenty cannon which they named after all the saints in the calendar to put down the revolt. Wuen-Sen Kwai was deserted by a part of his troops and died in 1678; four years later, when Yunnan was retaken, the Sino-Manchus slaughtered his family.

The frontiers of the Chinese Empire

In 1683 K'ang-hsi easily took possession of Formosa, where the son of Koxinga, betrayed by his own men, submitted. But in central Asia, where the Mongols had again taken the offensive, the task was more difficult. The Chakhars of Outer Mongolia were defeated in 1676 and forced to recognise Manchu suzerainty. In Upper Mongolia the cunning and energetic Galdan, whose ambition was to re-establish the empire of Jenghiz Khan, united the Dzungar tribes and was soon master of all eastern Turkestan (1680–85). Two years of warfare (1688–90) delivered Mongolia into his hands, and, hot

The Indian Bodhisattva Avalokitesvara became a favourite in China as the feminine Kuanyin. This banner, painted on linen, shows the typical long garments and draperies, and the left hand in the position of *vitarka mudra*. *British Museum*

The war with the Dzungars enabled K'ang-hsi to extend his authority over all the Mongol territories. In 1691 the Khalkas accorded in sign of homage 'three genuflections and nine prostrations'. He outlawed inter-tribal war, made them his vassals, put them on his pay-roll and, coming occasionally to pass a few days with them, quickly won their friendship. Since the beginning of time, the fierce tribes of Asia had menaced, pillaged or conquered their settled neighbours. Now for the first time they recognised a master who, although of the same race, had renounced nomadic ways. Contact with the Sino-Manchus soon turned hunters and shepherds into farmers, and Chinese peasants could live in security throughout the land. The victory of gunpowder over the bow and arrow was the victory of the cultivator over the nomad. Forests and steppes receded before the axe and the plough. In central Asia the conditions of life abruptly altered and a new age dawned.

To the north of Manchuria K'ang-hsi was obliged to check Russian expansion. The Muscovites were established in the valley of the Amur and in 1682 had appointed a governor who resided in Albazin. Native hunters and Chinese fur traders found the Russians dangerous competitors. In 1685 the fortress of Albazin was attacked and set aflame by 15,000 Sino-Manchu troops with two hundred cannon. But the Cossacks reoccupied the position, and a long siege ensued. The fortress finally fell to the Chinese two years later. The Russians, always patient and tenacious in their policy of expansion, preferred to negotiate rather than continue an unequal struggle. By the Treaty of Nerchinsk in 1689 they agreed to remain on the far side of the Stanovoy Mountains and to destroy the fortress of Albazin. K'ang-hsi was the first to sign a treaty between China and a European nation. More important, by fending off the peril which threatened his native land he demonstrated that the Middle Empire possessed in its new masters formidable and efficient defenders.

Chinese civilisation

K'ang-hsi was unwilling to see a European power established on his frontiers, but he had no personal prejudice against Europeans themselves. Christian missionaries were welcomed; the Jesuits were received at court in Peking and given positions of trust. The Emperor was interested not only in the progress of Western science which the missionaries revealed to him, but in literature too, which he considered important as a means of spiritual revival and as an instrument of instruction. He protected writers, had the classics of Confucianism translated into Manchu, and ordered the publication of a dictionary. Being highly cultivated himself, he too wrote works destined for the edification of his people.

Chinese art contributed to the grandeur of K'ang-hsi's reign as much as French art had contributed to the glory of Louis XIV. From the imperial ceramic factories emerged masterpieces of dazzling beauty: glazed or flambé vases, crackle-ware china of the 'green' and 'black' traditions, monochrome porcelains in ox-blood, peach-skin, sapphire blue. K'ang-hsi also built his Versailles: the Summer Palace, north-west of Peking, with its enormous flights of marble steps guarded by grimacing monsters, triumphal arches in green, red and violet lacquer, wooded groves from which rose the bright shaft of a pagoda, calm,

in pursuit of the princes of Khalka, he reached the Great Wall of China, where K'ang-hsi sent an army with artillery against him. Entrenched behind a swamp, the Dzungar tribesmen beat off the imperial troops but, impressed by the cannon, retired towards Turkestan (September 1690). Five years later a new raid brought them as far as the banks of the Kerulen. To put an end to the menace K'ang-hsi advanced through hostile territory to meet them. His cannon forced Galdan to flee towards Kobdo (June 1696) and less than a year later he poisoned himself to avoid being taken alive by his victorious adversaries.

winding rivers in which were reflected hump-backed bridges, vast floral masses and dream palaces with golden roofs bristling with fabulous beasts. Above all the Garden of Prolonged Spring revealed the refinement of Chinese art, its grace and its sense of richness and mystery.

Japan under the Tokugawas

The triumph of autocracy in Japan had preceded the reigns of Louis XIV, Aurangzeb and K'ang-hsi. But, though the authority of the Tokugawas was well established, it did not approach that of the two other great Asian monarchs. In the course of this brilliant period in the history of Asia only the flowering of Japanese art prevented the empire of the shoguns from being entirely eclipsed by India and China. In painting, in sculpture, in wood and ivory carving, and in the superb damascening of sabre hilts Japanese artists revealed an inimitable sense of vitality, subtlety of observation and sureness of hand.

Persia and the Safavids

During this period Persia possessed only the shadow of a king. The drunkard Sulaiman (1666–94), besotted by his minions, auctioned off public offices, abandoned the Bahrein Islands to the Arabs without a struggle, and Kazan to the Uzbeks. Because the moon was in the sign of Scorpio he refused to allow his fleet to sail against the Russians, who were devastating the shores of the Caspian. Though in part due to the vigour of the Persian minister Sheikh Ali, the tranquillity which reigned within the kingdom reflected not so much the loyalty of Sulaiman's subjects as their lassitude.

The empire of the Safavids, which the great lyric poet Sa Ib praised so artlessly, had little to be proud of except the past brilliance of its culture. Caravan drivers still recited the poems of Hafiz and Saadi as they crossed the deserts. Persian literature and humanism had spread throughout Asia. The Iranian language was spoken at the court of the Grand Mogul and at the court of the Grand Turk. In the romantic eyes of Western travellers Ispahan still symbolised the poetry, the mystery and the fabled splendours of the Orient.

EUROPEAN POSSESSIONS BEYOND THE SEAS

During the zenith of Louis XIV's reign French colonial expansion continued, especially in North America, where the seeds of Anglo-French rivalry were being sown. At the same time the West Indies were feeling the effects of Spanish decadence, while the Dutch, less audacious than at the beginning of the century, fell back on their spice route and concentrated on trade with the Far East.

Colbert and French expansion

Although he dreamed of a France which would extend from Spitzbergen to Madagascar, Colbert was a businessman, who viewed colonisation as a 'book-keeping operation'. He thought of New France in terms of spice and sugar. His relations with the colonies were purely financial, and the system he applied was that of reserving colonial

To Europeans Persia was the mysteriously beautiful land of elegance and *douceur de vie* represented in its poetry and painting. Here Persian ladies and gentlemen picnic in a mood and setting reminiscent of Watteau. *British Museum*

commerce and its profits exclusively to the mother country. If he had recourse to joint-stock companies — which incidentally were poorly financed by a public uninterested in overseas ventures — he gave them a much less free hand than that enjoyed by similar companies in England and the United Provinces. On the whole, his spice policy in the Indian Ocean was a failure; the French were unable to gain permanent foothold in either Ceylon, Madagascar or Persia. The trading post at Pondicherry in India, founded in 1673, was an exception and turned a village of straw huts into a town of 60,000 inhabitants. Colbert's policy in the West Indies was on the other hand very successful. French possessions there doubled in size. The slave trade, entrusted to the Senegal Company in 1673, was encouraged by bounties. Sugar-cane was more widely cultivated and methods were improved. In 1681 two hundred French ships called at the islands, which had 47,000 inhabitants of whom 29,000 were slaves, while only about thirty vessels visited Canada. The comparison shows the important part which the West Indies played in the French economy. Yet the great strides made in the West Indies were largely spontaneous, and, paradoxically, it was in Canada that Colbert's organising genius was to bear the greatest fruits.

New France had in 1663 become a Crown colony administered from Versailles. The Iroquois were repulsed and the French soldiers settled in the territory. Between

The Dutch settlers on Java found an advanced civilisation revealed especially in its many temples. These were lavishly embellished with sculptures in the Hindu fashion but declined with the arrival of Islam. *Marburg*

1663 and 1681 peasant families sent from the west of France increased the number of colonists from 2,500 to 10,000. They were, however, still few, and perforce learned to co-operate with the Indians. An adventurous race of half-castes — the offspring from the union of French trappers and native women — they were, like the French peasant immigrants themselves, rootless and footloose. The wide spaces of America fascinated and lured them on. By 1690, while 300,000 English settlers clung firmly to the coastal rim of the continent, a handful of French had already taken possession of the immense interior. Unknown to Versailles, traders and trappers, still dreaming of the North-West Passage, set forth on bold expeditions, accompanied by equally daring missionaries. In 1673 Louis Jolliet and Father Marquette descended the Mississippi as far as Arkansas. Between 1678 and 1682 La Salle explored the whole of the Mississippi and in the name of the King, for whom he named it, took possession of 'Louisiana', at the mouth of the river. The French empire in America was, however, too destitute of men to remain more than the dream of trappers clad in buckskin.

English expansion during the Restoration

Charles II married Catherine of Braganza in 1661. As her marriage portion Catherine brought him Bombay, and in 1666 he encouraged the East India Company to found

in Bengal a trading post which was later to become Calcutta. The British West Indies, of which Jamaica was the most valuable, were increased by the acquisition of the Bahamas, and in 1670 had more than 100,000 inhabitants. But the vital step was the occupation by the English of an uninterrupted Atlantic coast between French Canada and Spanish Florida. In 1667 New Holland had been ceded to England by the Treaty of Breda, and Nieuwe Amsterdam had become New York; in Delaware the Swedes were ousted by the foundation of Pennsylvania, which in 1675 William Penn had made a refuge for Quakers where brotherhood reigned and every colonist could vote. Philadelphia, founded in 1682, would soon become the greatest port in the New World. A little before this, a group of Charles II's courtiers founded a colony south of Virginia and called it Carolina. Here large plantations were formed and worked by Negro slaves. Thus a conflict of attitude was already foreshadowed: between the north, which had cradled liberal democracy, and the south, which preserved the aristocratic sentiments of Restoration England.

None the less the political organisation of the colonies became more and more uniform. Charles II, with an overseas empire in mind, turned chartered colonies into Crown colonies, in which governors replaced proprietors and managers. With the Restoration, not only defeated Puritans but bankrupt Cavaliers poured into America. Persecuted French Protestants, who were refused refuge in Canada by Versailles, were welcomed in Charleston, capital of Carolina. Feeling on the Indian frontier was embittered by this influx of newcomers. The Indians, incapable of understanding European notions of property, would sell the land on which they hunted and then refuse to leave it. In 1675 the revolt of the great Indian chieftain ' King Philip ' merely led to harsher repression. Everywhere the advance of the pioneers brought the disappearance of the Indians.

The Spanish Indies and Brazil

Thanks to the Anglo-Spanish Treaty of Madrid in 1670 and the Franco-Spanish Treaty of Ratisbon in 1684, the West Indies ceased to be scourged by buccaneers. The result was a renewed era of cultural and material prosperity. Universities sprang up and printing-presses multiplied. An audacious grafting of baroque on to native art produced buildings of dazzling originality. In Mexico a nun and poetess, Ines de la Cruz (1657–91) whose achievements also embraced science and music, graced the Viceroy's court. Nevertheless the slackening of that religious zeal which had always inspired the Spanish genius became marked after 1660. Concubinage became more common among the clergy, and local authorities shirked civic duties which formerly their faith had made obligatory. The Indians were protected by the Crown and by the Church, but the law became inoperative by the failure of magistrates to enforce it. Natives who fell into debt were obliged to work on the great estates or *haciendas*, and from this semi-serfdom arose the miserable class known as peons. The mercantile demands of the Portuguese government, enflamed by the sugar fever, caused an even more rapid fall in the native population. The Jesuits had to defend their missions and villages against colonists and half-caste *mamelucos* in search of slaves. In 1661 their colleges were taken by assault, and in 1684, they were forced to provide forced labour to planters and gold prospectors.

121

CHAPTER EIGHT

THE END OF THE GREAT REIGNS

Between 1680 and 1715 Europe united to resist the arrogant pretensions of Louis XIV in a series of wars which were for long indecisive. When they were over no single state was strong enough to dominate the continent, and Europe regained the political equilibrium lost after the Treaty of Westphalia. France, at the cost of an exhausting effort, managed to remain a great power, but serious internal crises damaged the prestige of her monarchy. In England another revolution took place; the Stuarts were evicted and a constitutional monarchy firmly established. Great Britain was about to enter on a period of world-wide maritime and commercial supremacy. The decline of Poland and Sweden, the growth of Prussia and the ebbing of the Turkish tide changed the shape of Eastern Europe. The first victories of Peter the Great were a brutal announcement that Russian power must henceforth be reckoned with. In an intellectual atmosphere less strict and becoming

more 'enlightened', Europe strove to digest and come to terms with these new factors, and with others, cultural and scientific, which were to accelerate her progress and increase her influence over all the other continents.

THE INORDINATE AMBITIONS OF LOUIS XIV

After the Treaty of Nymegen Louis XIV, intoxicated by victory, dreamed only of extending his hegemony. In 1683 he was secretly married to Madame de Maintenon, a pious Catholic, who doubtless urged him to become what the Habsburg family had once been: champion of Catholic imperialism. If so, she preached to the converted. As Louis himself confessed, 'conqueror' seemed to him the most noble of titles and self-aggrandisement a sovereign's most worthy and agreeable occupation. Invoking obscure

The coronation procession of James II. The former Lord Admiral (when Duke of York) had as one of his canopy-bearers the diarist Samuel Pepys, loyal servant of the Stuarts and the Royal Navy. *Mansell*

rights, he began to nibble and encroach upon his neighbours. From 1685 coalitions against him were continually formed.

The revocation of the Edict of Nantes

At the same time Louis decided to realise his 'grand design' of destroying heresy. Bribery had proved fruitless as a method of conversion. Only a handful of vagabonds had accepted the bonus offered for conversion: six livres per soul — the price of a pig! Louvois tried billeting his dragoons on Protestant families. The soldiers co-operated with enthusiasm, forcing cupboards and smashing furniture for the joy of destruction to the night-long roll of drums. Obstinate Calvinists were strung up by the feet; their wives were whipped, inflated with bellows and tossed into the street in their shifts. As Saint-Simon said 'from torture to taking Communion rarely takes more than twenty-four

A broadside against Louis XIV. The religious policy of the 'Sun-king' inspired distrust and alarm among his neighbours both on religious and political grounds. Protestant propaganda made good use of these fears. *Mansell*

The Revocation of the Edict of Nantes may have driven as many as 200,000 Huguenots from France. Louis XIV did not reap advantage from his policy. His enemies and potential enemies were strengthened economically and morally by the persecution. *Radio Times Hulton Picture Library*

hours', and entire towns, like Montauban, renounced Calvinism rather than become hosts to missionaries in jackboots. Louis XIV was convinced that all the Protestants were converted, and on 17 October 1685 revoked the Edict of Nantes. Protestant pastors were given fifteen days to leave France, their churches were destroyed and, except in Alsace, the reformed cult was everywhere outlawed.

In the Cévennes a few indomitable souls attempted an uprising. But possibly as many as 200,000 of the Protestant élite gave up everything for their faith and at the risk of their lives left their native land. This mass emigration, which weakened France, enriched England, the United Provinces and Brandenburg, which received the refugees. Everywhere they inflamed hatred of the 'popish tyranny' and hastened the growth of new and revolutionary ideas. Men already spoke of the right of the people to rise against their governments. Protestant states, with which Louis XIV had until then often been allied, now saw in him a threat to European liberties.

THE CHANGING PATTERN OF EUROPEAN POWER

Three new factors also helped to turn the balance of power against France: in the east, the Turkish withdrawal and the resurgence of Austria; in the west, the revolution of 1688 which brought Louis XIV's greatest enemy, William of Orange, to the English throne; in the north, the adherence to the Protestant bloc of Brandenburg and Sweden.

The Ottoman withdrawal and the revival of Austria

In 1683 the Grand Vizir Kara Mustafa besieged Vienna with 300,000 men. The Viennese, abandoned by their gloomy emperor Leopold, each night strove to repair the breaches in their ramparts, until, on September 12, John Sobieski, King of Poland, swept down from the heights of Kahlenberg and, like a crusader of old, cut the Turkish army in pieces. All Christendom rejoiced, and Venice, the Emperor, Poland and soon Russia joined in a crusade

against the Turk. In 1686 Buda fell, and, in the following year, Athens (where Venetian artillery blew up the Parthenon, which the Turks had turned into a powder magazine). In this crisis, Hungary made her crown hereditary in the Habsburg family, while everywhere the Christian populations rose against Islam. Köprülü III saved the situation momentarily, but was killed in 1691. In Prince Eugene of Savoy the Imperial armies had found a great commander at thirty-four. In 1699 he forced on the Turks the Peace of Carlowitz which gave the Emperor Transylvania and all the Hungarian plain. The Ottoman Empire for the first time had to give up European territory. Internal dissension further weakened the Turks. With the disappearance of the Köprülü line of Grand Vizirs in 1710 there was nothing to halt Turkish decadence. A power vacuum began to appear in the south-east of Europe, and with it the 'Eastern Question'.

Austria was now able to turn against France. In spite of the mediocrity of her sovereigns — Leopold I (1658–1705) and Joseph I (1705–11) — her prestige had never been greater. The monarchy was strengthened and modernised by legal reforms, the creation of a standing army, and the transformation of the great nobles into loyal servants of the Crown. Vienna became a gay and lavish capital, 'a Paris on the Danube', the crossroads of Germany, Italy and the Near East. A rich theatrical tradition began which would bear fruits in the Opera, and baroque architecture achieved new splendours; never had the Germanic imagination been expressed in stone with such fantasy and exuberance as by artists such as Fischer von Erlach and Hildebrand.

The revolution of 1688 in England

The resurgence of England was not, like that of Austria, due to success in war but to a successful revolution, which was to have great international repercussions. James II (1685–8), though an excellent sailor, was totally lacking in political sense. Ignoring the Pope's advice, he flaunted his Catholicism at the very moment when the revocation of the Edict of Nantes had exasperated the entire Protestant world. Jesuits reappeared and Mass was openly celebrated at Whitehall. In Scotland, things were worse still; dragoons hunted down the Puritans, who were punished by torture and execution. Judge Jeffreys and his Bloody Assizes punished an attempted uprising in the south-west by the Duke of Monmouth, a natural son of Charles II. Then in April 1687 the King issued a Declaration of Indulgence, which granted both Catholics and Dissenters entire freedom of worship, thus hoping to divide Dissenters from Anglican churchmen. English Protestants comforted themselves with the thought that James II's successor would be his daughter Mary, an Anglican married to William of Orange, champion of the Protestant cause on the continent; but in June 1688 the King's second wife gave birth to a Prince of Wales who was at once baptised a Catholic. The rumour spread that the child was not in fact the Queen's son. Londoners showed their feelings by celebrating the acquittal of 'the Seven Bishops', who had been prosecuted for having criticised the Declaration of Indulgence, and William III was invited to come to England 'to defend Protestantism and liberty'. The revolution of 1688 was brief. When William of Orange landed at Torbay on November 3, the future Duke of Marlborough, John

Louis XIV backed the wrong horse in supporting James II and his son, the Old Pretender. At the reception of James after his escape from England, it may be noted, muffs were *de rigeur* — it was, after all, early January.

Churchill, marched against the invader and then coolly turned his army over to him. Abandoned by everyone, James II fled from London and took refuge in France.

Parliament was less trusting than it had been in 1660 and the new sovereigns, William and Mary, were obliged to accept a Bill of Rights. Henceforth Parliament's share in power was undisputed. The powers of the monarch were derived no longer from hereditary Divine Right but from the will of the nation, as the change of rulers clearly showed.

The Toleration Act of 1689 assured freedom of worship for Dissenters, but not for Catholics. In this fashion England's fifty-year-old crisis was resolved. Mary, who had played a minor part in affairs, died in 1695, leaving William alone on the throne. He was first and foremost a Dutchman, mainly interested in his new kingdom as a means of resisting Louis XIV, and spent much of his time on the continent. England thus began her experience of constitutional monarchy. The House of Commons, after 1718 re-elected every seven years, represented the landed interest which provided the ruling class. Anne, Mary's sister, succeeded to the throne in 1702 and at her death in 1714 the crown reverted to the nearest Protestant heir, the son of the Electress of Hanover. He ascended the throne as George I, King of the United Kingdom of Great Britain, two islands under one government since the Union of England and Scotland in 1707.

William and Mary, accepted as joint sovereigns in order to preserve the Stuart descent (she was the daughter of James II). Though seventeenth-century *décolletage* sometimes went to spectacular extremes, it seems unlikely that Mary would have made quite so complete a concession to fashion as this plate implies.

125

A wedding party of members of a German upper-class family at Riga. *Marburg*

Britain now entered an age of great commercial and maritime activity. Her merchants profited from the sufferings of the United Provinces. A huge trade in the import and re-export of colonial produce began to provide the profits which would later finance agricultural and industrial advance. The first steps were taken in the technological innovations on which the industrial revolution was later to be based. The Bank of England, founded in 1694, stabilised public credit and created a vested interest in the Revolution settlement. London, rebuilt in stone after the Great Fire of 1666, had 750,000 inhabitants, and was twice as big as Paris. Over it rose the great dome of St Paul's, Wren's masterpiece, the symbol of the city's new wealth and pride.

North-eastern Europe

In north-eastern Europe Sweden and Brandenburg broke their traditional alliance with France.

The disastrous defeat at Fehrbellin (1675) had roused popular indignation against the Swedish nobility. Charles XI took advantage of this to persuade the Diet to give him autocratic powers in 1680. He ruled his kingdom with skill, restored the royal domains at the expense of the aristocracy, re-organised the army and the fleet, and developed trade in the Baltic. The new Sweden was resolutely hostile both to French mercantilism and to persecuting Gallicanism. In 1697 Charles XII, a boy of fifteen, came to the throne. The Swedes were disconcerted by the odd appearance and even odder behaviour of their new sovereign, with his narrow head, his elongated brow, his thin, frail and lanky figure and loutish manners. His true nature, however, soon appeared.

He abruptly declared himself to be of age and, on the day of his coronation at Uppsala, wrenched the crown from the hands of the Archbishop. Brandenburg, Denmark, Poland and Russia formed a coalition to take advantage of the youthful king. They had reckoned without Charles, whose greatest desire was to emulate the heroes of antiquity. In the wars which followed, his audacity and military genius became clear. In him, the Swedish meteor reached its zenith. Striking swiftly, Charles landed in Copenhagen

and forced Denmark to accept a humiliating peace. Shortly afterwards, in November 1700, in a blinding snowstorm, he charged impetuously across the swamps of Narva, losing a boot, his hat and his horse, but not resting until the Russian army had capitulated. Fresh victories delivered all Poland into his hands and in July 1704 his protégé, Stanislas Leszcynski, was in July proclaimed King of Poland. Two years later Charles invaded Saxony. But his adventures consumed Sweden's last resources: all depended on the genius of one man. Charles had already once defeated Peter the Great but at Poltava in July 1709 the Russians triumphed, and Charles took refuge with the remnant of his army in Turkey, where he stirred up the Turks to make war on Russia. Meanwhile the Swedish empire, too vast and too ill-assorted, crumbled. Its days of grandeur were over.

Frederick I of Prussia

The patience of Brandenburg was finally rewarded. The Great Elector was succeeded by the Elector Frederick III (1688–1713) who by loyalty and flattery at last managed to obtain from the Emperor the cherished title of King of Prussia. Thirty thousand horses transported the court to Königsberg where on 18 January 1701, dressed in a vast purple mantle with diamond buttons, this sickly, almost hunchbacked little man, ridiculously enamoured of etiquette, became Frederick I, first ' King in Prussia '. In the course of the banquet which followed he flew into a rage with the Queen because she had perpetrated the sacrilege of taking snuff during the service. Whenever the new king drank, nine cannon salutes celebrated the act. Kingship had merely accentuated his whims and vanity. He arranged in advance the minutest details of his own funeral so that nothing should be lacking on such a solemn occasion. Yet though he was ' great in little things ' he was not, in spite of Frederick II's remark, ' little in great things '. He was a Hohenzollern and knew how to manage his revenues. He inspected schools, welcomed the persecuted and naturalised his Huguenot immigrants. After him, the future of Germany lay no longer with Austria, but with Prussia.

Polish anarchy

Louis XIV's Polish friends were no compensation for the loss of his Protestant allies. Poland had joined in the crusade against the Turks from 1683 to 1689, and the enterprise was both exhausting and unpopular among her Orthodox subjects in the east. The Cossacks of the Ukraine revolted. Polish peasants increasingly resented serfdom and treatment as an inferior race. By refusing to accept the discipline essential to a modern state, the nobility added to the traditional anarchy. In the Polish Diet a single dissenting voice was sufficient to paralyse the assembly. The poet Kochowsky bitterly wrote: ' With a single word, *Fiat*, God created the world. With the single word, *Veto*, we destroy Poland.' The heroic John III Sobieski (1674–94) was overwhelmed with political humiliations and died in despair. The crown was put up for auction. A Saxon succeeded him who was an admirer of Louis XIV, and made himself unpopular from the moment of his accession in 1696 as Augustus II. From 1701 to 1705 the Swedish invasion plunged the country into further chaos.

THE DECLINE OF LOUIS XIV

The War of the League of Augsburg

To put an end to the encroachments of France, the Emperor, Spain and a few German princes united in 1686 to form a defensive alliance: the League of Augsburg. Louis XIV replied by laying waste the Palatinate. Louvois's scorched-earth instructions to his officers were brutal: towns, villages and crops were to be destroyed, so that the enemy could not subsist. The Habsburgs mobilised German indignation. William III led the Protestant bloc into the struggle which lasted nine years. In the Netherlands the Duke of Luxemburg won so many victories and captured so many regimental colours that he was known as the 'tapestry-maker of Notre Dame', but he made no attempt to annihilate his enemies. Luxembourg's preoccupation was with style, with stately and majestic manoeuvre, and he treated battle as an intellectual and chivalrous pastime. At sea the English and Dutch fleets were defeated in 1690 off Beachy Head, but two years later in the battle of La Hogue the result was reversed. Neither episode was of great importance, but an invasion to restore James II to the English throne was made impossible.

Peace was brought about by general exhaustion. In the Treaty of Ryswick (1697) France was obliged to recognise William III as King of England, and of the conquests she had made since 1679 only Strasbourg and Sarre-Louis were retained. The Dutch were permitted to place garrisons in certain fortresses on the border of the Spanish Netherlands, thus foreshadowing the future neutrality of Belgium. French expansion had at last discovered its limits.

The War of the Spanish Succession

Louis XIV was now sixty years old. Rich living had made him fatter, his features had become lined, his teeth were falling out and his hands were emaciated. But with age and illness and with the devout habits he had acquired under the influence of Madame de Maintenon, he had gained wisdom. Working nine hours a day, weighing the advice of his counsellors, and sincerely concerned with the welfare of his people, he displayed the greatest moderation in attempting to solve the problem which absorbed the attention of all Europe: that of the Spanish succession.

Charles II of Spain had no children. His death had been long expected and the question of who would inherit his immense possessions was pressing. With great restraint Louis XIV at first negotiated a partition with the Emperor. The grandees of Spain, indignant at seeing Europe play dice with the patrimony of their dying sovereign, made him name as his heir a Bourbon, Philip Duke of Anjou, the second grandson of Louis XIV, so that the Spanish inheritance should not be divided. Then, on 1 November 1700, Charles died. Sixteen days later, after much soul-searching, Louis XIV accepted the will and abandoned the partition scheme. Since Austria claimed the throne of Spain for the son of the Emperor, the Archduke Charles, war was inevitable. Louis believed that the combined forces of Spain and France would be invincible. In practice Spain was less of an asset than a liability.

Louis XIV, acting with less than his usual acumen, alienated the Dutch by occupying in the Spanish Netherlands the frontier towns which were garrisoned by Dutch troops under the peace terms of Ryswick and the English by recognising the Old Pretender. In September 1701 a Grand Alliance was formed by England, the Dutch Republic, the Empire, Denmark and most of the German princes. It was the last achievement of William III, who died in March 1702.

France still had the largest armies in Europe, but had to fight on several fronts: in Germany, in the Netherlands, in Italy and in Spain itself, where the Austrian claimant to the throne had landed. Moreover, the Grand Alliance was directed by two leaders of outstanding skill: Prince Eugene, who had defeated the Turks, and the Duke of Marlborough, a strategist of genius. They were backed by the iron will of the man to whom William III had bequeathed his loathing of France: the Grand Pensionary Heinsius.

The French advance on Vienna in 1704 was cut short in Bavaria by the crushing defeat of Blenheim. No one in Versailles dared to report the disaster to the King, and it was left to Madame de Maintenon to tell him that he was no longer invincible. Eugene then drove the French from Italy and Marlborough drove them from the Netherlands. In 1706 the Archduke Charles, supported by the English, the Portuguese and the Catalans, was installed in Madrid. Lille fell in December 1708 and in the winter which followed France was ravaged by famine and invasion. Chastened, Louis XIV swallowed his pride and sued for peace. He renounced all claims to the Spanish throne, and to Lille and Strasbourg; but his opponents demanded that he should make war on his own grandson Philip. This was too much, and Louis XIV appealed directly to his own people. Priests read from the pulpit a message in which the King explained his desire for peace, denounced the bad faith of the enemy, and begged for a final effort. In September 1709, in the mists of Malplaquet, a French army inflicted terrible slaughter before retiring to leave the allies only a Pyrrhic victory. In Spain, too, French fortunes revived.

In 1711 the Archduke Charles became Emperor on the death of his brother Joseph I. The British were no more willing to see Spain reunited to Austria, as in the days of

In the seventeenth century, chemistry began to emerge from alchemy, although it made nothing like the strides of physics. Here is an engraving of distillation. Four alembics rest on the large brick stove which heats them. *Giraudon*

For military purposes, flint-lock muskets began to replace match locks in the early seventeenth century and had done so completely by 1700. These highly decorated examples are hunting-pieces made for wealthy sportsmen. *Victoria and Albert Museum*

the Emperor Charles V, than they had been to see it united to France. They therefore withdrew from the coalition. Enraged by this, the allies threw 130,000 troops against France; but at Denain in July 1712 Villars's forces pierced the· Imperial lines, and the offensive which Prince Eugene was preparing against Paris was broken. This unexpected French victory hastened the conclusion of peace. In 1713 and 1714 the Treaties of Utrecht and Rastadt put an end to thirteen years of conflict.

The peace of Utrecht

By the Treaty of Utrecht Philip V retained the major part of the Spanish heritage, but renounced all rights to the crown of France. The Spanish Netherlands, Milan and Naples passed to the Austrian Habsburgs. The Duke of Savoy received Sicily and the title of king. The Dutch again garrisoned their frontier fortresses, but constant war had left the republic exhausted and it now became a power of secondary importance. Britain benefited most: from Spain she took Gibraltar and Minorca; from France she obtained Nova Scotia, the gateway to Canada, and important commercial privileges in French overseas possessions. Since a Bourbon reigned in Madrid Louis XIV's honour remained intact, and France retained her strategic frontiers with Lille, Dijon and Strasbourg. Though the Grand Alliance had not succeeded in destroying French power, French will to dominate had been broken and France was obliged to relinquish the ascendancy she had enjoyed in Europe since the Peace of Westphalia.

THE END OF THE REIGN OF LOUIS XIV

Poverty and popular discontent

The reign of the Grand Monarch, which had begun so gloriously, ended sadly. Since 1688 warfare had been almost continuous; industry was at a standstill and foreign trade ruined. The privileged classes escaped the payment of taxes and the immense cost of the wars had to be met by other means. Louis XIV was obliged, as Saint-Simon puts it, to search for money in ' the very bones of his subjects '. He humiliated himself in vain before the tax farmers; the national debt continued to increase and bankruptcy appeared inevitable. Among the demoralised peasantry the mortality rate was appalling. Driven to keep alive by eating acorns, or bread made of couch-grass and ferns, they broke out in uprisings which were repressed only with difficulty. During the winter of 1709 France, as Fénelon said, ' lived only by a miracle '. The cold was so bitter that in Paris priests found the Communion wine turned to ice. Fields which had been sown were frozen hard; the country-folk had no money to buy anything, and artisans and tradesmen in towns felt the pinch in their turn. By August insurrection growled in the capital. At Versailles, where lackeys from the palace had been seen begging, a hungry mob shouted insults and curses even under the King's windows. Lyon revolted. Thirty thousand peasants besieged Cahors. In Dijon the crowd chanted: ' Let us do what the English did to their king'.

The revolt of the Camisards

Checks to Louis XIV's religious policy accentuated the difficulties and confusion which marred the end of his reign. Though the Jansenist convent at Port Royal was destroyed and even the bones in the cemetery dispersed, the Jansenists themselves, formally condemned in 1713 by the Papal Bull *Unigenitus*, made an alliance with the *parlementaire* Gallicans and refused to accept defeat. Protestantism revived in the face of persecution. Visionaries, children — ' little prophets ' — reawakened the biblical fervour of Languedoc. In July 1702 in the solitary valleys of the Cévennes passive resistance gave way to open revolt. Undaunted by deportations and the burning of their villages in October 1703, the Camisards — so called from the white shirt or *camise* which formed their uniform — held out for three years against the royal armies. Villars was sent against them and in 1704 obliged Jean Cavalier, the most important of their leaders, to surrender. Languedoc, broken and exhausted by the horrors of persecution, was still unpacified. There in 1705 the ' Children of God ' provided new Huguenot martyrs for the scaffold. Only in 1709 was the revolt suppressed. In 1710 the head of the last rebel, Abraham Mazel, was impaled on a stake for three days and then publicly burned. But Protestantism nursed its wounds in secret and survived in ' synods of the wilderness '.

Seventeenth-century stained glass window: Noah (top register) and a mystic vessel. St-Etienne du Mont, France. *Giraudon*

The new spirit

The spectacle of such public disaster gave birth to a new spirit of criticism. Vauban, the great military engineer, demanded justice for the poor in a book recommending tax-reform, and thereby lost the favour of the King. Fénelon condemned the egoism of the monarch in the name of feudal and Christian virtues. The Intendant Boisguillebert deplored State control of the economy. Everyone was heartily sick of wars, which had gone on too long. The younger generation thought of nothing but a life of ease. Faith in the monarchy had not disappeared, but, indifferent to memories of past glory, it owed its fervour to the hopes it entertained of a new reign.

The death of the King

In the sombre atmosphere of Versailles, which took its tone from the deep piety of Madame de Maintenon, Louis XIV, who had lost his son and his grandsons, wondered if he himself had not been responsible for the unhappiness of his kingdom. At the end of August 1715 he knew that he was dying. Preserving to the end his admirable self-control, he gave orders for his funeral and advice to his heir, the future Louis XV, then a child of five. On September 1, in the royal bedchamber hung with red brocade embroidered in gold with fleurs de lys, the King, alone, breathed his last. Lampoons and laughter followed his funeral cortège. His overlong reign, which ended to the accompaniment of derision and sarcasm had marked, none the less, one of the great eras of history. The French monarchy was never again to achieve the power and brilliance it had known under Louis XIV.

THE DEVELOPMENT OF WESTERN THOUGHT

The new ideas and sentiments which appeared in France, even before the death of Louis XIV, arose not only out of the dilemmas which marked the end of the reign, but also out of a wider intellectual movement which affected all Western Europe. The view that the universe was a mechanism had begun to spread and to become common property. Mathematics had been immensely strengthened by the development of differential and integral calculus, and its application to physics permitted accurate experimental methods which were rich in results. Philosophy became utilitarian, technical advance drove out metaphysics and science invaded the workshop. An automatic loom and the first steam engines made their appearance. The advance of science encouraged the idea of progress and the superiority of the Moderns over the Ancients. There were no longer any accepted truths which could not be challenged and, if found wanting, corrected. Even in the realm of religion, arguments based on authority were no longer sufficient. The reports of travellers, together with references in the works of pre-Christian authors, revealed the great diversity of human beliefs. So much wisdom in

At the age of five, Louis XV presided over his first *lit de justice*, a special royal session of the Parlement of Paris at which royal decrees were registered. It derives its odd name from the cushion on which the royal law-giver sat.

pre-Christian days, or in lands where Christ was unknown, made men sceptical about the necessity of Grace. Monarchy, in the past closely allied to the Church, was vigorously attacked. John Locke (1632–1704), the philosopher of the English Revolution, asserted the natural and inalienable rights of the individual. He denied Divine Right and demonstrated that society arose from a social contract freely entered into, from which it followed that the people were sovereign though not, presumably, to the point of overriding the rights of individuals. The audacity of such new ideas and reforms which were everywhere put forward and discussed was perhaps less disconcerting than their abundance and confusion. Adjustment was not easy. Intellectual Europe was not only in revolt against the past, but was examining itself and questioning its future. Though the classical traditions had been abandoned, the new attitude towards life was still undefined. The masses, in any case, remained untouched by these innovations. It was among a small cultural élite that reason and the critical spirit slowly ushered in the Age of Enlightenment.

PETER THE GREAT AND THE TRANSFORMATION OF RUSSIA

At this time unexpected events were taking place in Russia which abruptly changed the direction and rhythm of her historical development. After the death of Feodor in 1682, Sophia, a daughter of Alexis Romanoff, acted as regent in the name of her brother Ivan, and of her half-brother Peter. Concealed behind the twin throne of the two child-sovereigns, Sophia could observe through a peephole everything that took place in the council chamber. Young Peter, left to his own devices, roamed through the German quarters of Moscow and got drunk with the grooms. His favourite game was playing at war, though the cannon with which his battalion of small boys was armed fired only wooden balls. He was a precocious giant, violent and temperamental, who was restive under the tutelage of his half-sister. When in 1689 Sophia had the effrontery to welcome her favourite, who had been beaten by the Turks, under triumphal arches Peter gathered together a few regiments and shut her up in a convent. On the death of his mother Natalia, to whom he had left the business of

The surrender of Breda in 1625. Painting by Velasquez. Prado, Madrid. *Holford*

I

government, Peter was seized by a desire to try his strength and to astonish Europe by an expedition against the Turks. During the course of his first campaign on the shores of the Black Sea in 1695 his artillery fired all day long without once hitting the target. He was repulsed, but in 1696 he defeated the Turks and finally captured Azov at the mouth of the Don.

In the following year, he scandalised the Russian people by going abroad incognito, accompanied by a few intimate friends and his clowns. His fits of rage and drunkenness, his extravagance and personal slovenliness made a poor impression in Holland, England, Austria and Poland, where he was considered a semi-barbarian with no future. Terrified by his thundering voice, his wild gestures and grimaces, people in the street fled at his approach. But wherever he went a burning curiosity consumed him. He was determined to find out all there was to learn about Western technical achievements. He studied astronomy, geography, even anatomy and surgery, and worked as a common shipwright in naval docks. He was still amassing information when news of an insurrection of the *strel'tsy* — or guards — recalled him to Moscow. He returned in time to preside at the execution of the rebels and to observe their bodies adorning the battlements of the Kremlin. His determination to modernise Russia was ruthlessly enforced. He summoned the boyars to his palace and himself cut off their beards and shortened the long skirts of their greatcoats. Foreigners and Russians devoted like himself to contemporary ideas formed his circle of friends and advisers. He was twenty-seven and impatient to bring his empire up to date, to make successful war, 'to open a window' on to the sea, on to the West. While in Western Europe public opinion was slowly beginning to count, in Russia, still dominated by its past, a single revolutionary was preparing a revolution.

A modern impression of the vigour of Peter the Great, depicted on an inspection of the building of St Petersburg (now Leningrad). This 'window on the West' became the capital of Russia until after the Bolshevik revolution in 1917. *Viollet*

Peter the Great's plans for westernising Russia extended to the cutting of the traditional long beards of the boyars. An attempt to clip them forcibly caused such an outcry that in 1698 it was abandoned and a graduated tax was put on beards. *Radio Times Hulton Picture Library*

ASIA

The 'years of triumph' of the two great Asian emperors were — like those of Louis XIV — cut short before the close of the seventeenth century. In India during his 'years of ruin' the Grand Mogul Aurangzeb was engaged in exhausting and unremitting struggle with the Mahrattas, a struggle which he did not live to finish. In China, the longer K'ang-hsi's reign lasted, the more apparent became its faults and failures.

Aurangzeb's 'years of ruin' (1689–1707)

When in 1689 Aurangzeb had the Mahratta chief Sambaji quartered before his eyes he believed he had put an end to the Hindu uprisings. The illusion was soon dispelled: the 'mountain rats' renewed the guerrilla war. Swiftly dispersing and as swiftly regrouping, they struck continually, ambushing the Mogul's forces and often in the space of a few hours reconquering by surprise fortresses which the imperial armies had taken months to reduce. As they withdrew, the Mahratta guerrillas would cut the grain and burn the fields so that the Mogul's cavalry sent in their pursuit were forced to halt for lack of fodder for their horses. Ultimately the entire Deccan fell into Mahratta hands. Like the roving bands of armed men during the

Hundred Years' War in Europe, numerous brigand groups pillaged the country, sowing panic everywhere.

Aurangzeb's army was no longer as good as it had been at the beginning of his reign. Its best elements, the Shiite Persians and the Rajput cavalry, had been driven away by the Grand Mogul's own bigotry. With its hundreds of thousands of non-combatant camp-followers, tradesmen, beggars, valets and women, the imperial army rapidly deteriorated into an unwieldy mob. In wild and mountainous terrain the Mogul's elephants, heavy bronze cannon and musketeers (who before firing had first to fix their forked gun-rests) were of little use. The imperial soldiers, richly arrayed, effeminate, covered with diamonds, and commanded by officers who were carried in palanquins, bore little resemblance to the companions of Babar the Tiger. Aurangzeb's Turco-Iranians had now been installed for more than a century in the fertile plains they had conquered; luxury and a tropical climate had softened them and, though they shared the racial prejudice and bigotry of their Emperor, they were no longer capable of the sustained effort and crusading zeal which an interminable struggle with a subject people demanded. Aurangzeb, however, refused to be discouraged. He continued the war with energy, as unsparing of himself as he was indulgent of his unruly officers. He appeared personally on the field of battle, and at the age of more than eighty led his own company of warriors. But he wasted his strength in operations of little strategic value which he pursued stubbornly to the end, and did not win any really decisive engagement.

Absorbed by these campaigns, Aurangzeb neglected the Empire. The seeds of treason and revolt which his own fanaticism had sown sprang up on all sides. Ajit Singh, the Rajah of Marwar, personally directed the resistance of the Rajputs. In their Himalayan mountain fastnesses

Aurangzeb, Grand Mogul (1658–1707). He was a religious fanatic and a fine soldier. The hatreds and rivalries he left behind helped to bring about the disintegration of his empire at his death. India was thus left open to European intervention. *Radio Times Hulton Picture Library*

The mice bury the dead cat. A Russian cartoon on Peter the Great's death. He changed Russia too radically for any complete return to the past, but conservative forces reasserted themselves when he died and prevented further innovation. *Radio Times Hulton Picture Library*

Under the Mogul Empire, and especially under Shah Jehan, Indian art responded to western and realist influences while preserving the delicacy of execution and subtlety of observation inherited from the Persian schools. *British Museum*

the Sikhs remained unconquered. India was no longer governed. The roads and even the towns had become increasingly unsafe. Government functionaries, left unpaid and unsupervised, pillaged the country. The starvation which raged through the countryside invaded the great cities. Behind the splendid facade of its marble palaces Delhi was a vast dung-heap, where hundreds of thousands of half-naked living skeletons, crouching in their mud huts or bamboo shelters, struggled to exist on handfuls of rice.

Aurangzeb was aware that his empire was tottering. The knowledge embittered him and he grew suspicious of

everyone. Doctors who prescribed medicine for him were obliged to take it themselves. He retained the families of his subject princes as hostages. He decided that he loathed his five sons and for seven years he allowed the gentle Shah Alan to languish in prison while Mohammed was left to die in the dungeons of Gwalior. His general head-quarters at Ahmadnagar was even gloomier than Versailles during the last days of Louis XIV. In this improvised city of nearly five million men Aurangzeb felt more than ever deserted and alone. Wherever his eyes came to rest he saw only God, that ruthless God whom he had served so ruthlessly. His soul was filled with a terror which his own piety exacerbated. On the threshold of the next world, ' followed by a prodigious caravan of sins ', he dreamed only of damnation and eternal punishment. Death delivered him from this earthly anguish in March 1707. His fanaticism forever destroyed the great dream of Akbar the Great: a reconciled India. His violence and the reactions it provoked had made even Babar's ambition impossible to realise: an India permanently dominated by Islam. It would not be long before the Empire of the Grand Moguls, exhausted by half a century of futile warfare, was dismembered.

The final years of K'ang-hsi

Until his death in 1722 the Emperor K'ang-hsi retained all his great prestige. Nevertheless shadows clouded the last years of his reign. It saddened the Emperor to see his court in Peking become the scene of intrigues, and because of the unpopularity of Prince Yung Cheng, heir to the throne, he feared that his own death would be followed by prolonged dynastic struggles. The period of his great victories had passed. Central Asia, which he had every right to believe pacified, was again in movement. The Dzungar leader, Tsewang Rabdan (1697–1727), was quite as ambitious as his uncle Galdan had been, and was regrouping the Mongol tribes. In 1717 he invaded Tibet and took possession of Lhasa, where partisans of the Manchus were immediately slaughtered. The Emperor did not react vigorously. His first expedition against Tsewang Rabdan was checked, and he waited until the autumn of 1720 before liberating Tibet and installing in Lhasa a pro-Manchu Dalai Lama. In the north of the Empire the Russian threat still existed. The Russians now pushed towards the north-east, taking possession of the Kamchatka peninsula (1696–1701). Far from renouncing their policy of expansion towards the south, however, they sent ' missions ' to Peking, at the same time organising a network of caravan routes across Mongolia. Though their infiltration remained pacific, the Chinese suspected that these traders were merely preparing the way for the more warlike Cossacks. Peter the Great's conquest in 1722 of the western regions of the Caspian did nothing to reassure them.

K'ang-hsi was, however, less worried by Europe than disillusioned. Religious questions interested him immensely and he was pleased when his Jesuit protégés saw in ancestor worship an act of filial piety, in ceremonies in honour of Confucius a homage to virtue, and in the doctrine of *T'ien* — the heavens — an equivalent to the Christian notion of God. But when in 1715, after much argument and wrangling, Pope Clement XI formally condemned the Chinese rites as idolatrous, the Emperor found the decision not only absurd but wounding to his pride and two years later he prohibited the preaching of Christianity. Hence-

forth, foreigners could enter and reside in China only with special permission.

The Emperor's attempts to invigorate the intellectual life of China, though remarkable, were disappointing. Literature and philosophy, directed rather than protected, declined in quality. Painting was clumsily guided and tended to degenerate into academic banality. Nor, though the Emperor did something to raise the standard of public morality, did he succeed in eradicating deep-rooted Chinese customs. In a land where triumphal arches were erected to State functionaries who had *refrained* from extortion, he had to be satisfied with a reasonable modicum of virtue. Moreover, he could not feed his growing number of subjects. Between the end of the sixteenth century and the middle of the seventeenth the population of China probably rose to 60 millions. Agricultural development did not keep pace with this increase and, despite a cuisine which included such delicacies as caterpillar jelly, spider jam and birds' nests seasoned with ginseng root, the inevitable consequences of over-population ensued: under-nourishment and famine.

The Chinese bore with hunger more cheerfully than with the presence of the Manchus. Listless, delicate, hairless, almost feminine in temperament, they reacted strangely to the presence of their rough, bearded conquerors. They were humiliated that such barbarians had so easily subdued their empire. They were disconcerted when the barbarians adopted their own ancient traditions. In order to forget intruders who had come to disturb their vision of the world they embraced a new master more tyrannical than the Tatars. Opium, which they formed the habit of smoking, brought peace. They had always lacked an interest in politics. Their indifference to the problems of government, their dislike of militarism, their refusal to see beyond the immediate circle of the family and the workshop had never before taken on such proportions. Powerful though it might be, the China of K'ang-hsi was no more unified a nation than the China of the Mings had been.

Asia at the end of the seventeenth century

In power and in riches Asia at the end of the seventeenth century was greater than all the rest of the globe put together. The great reigns of Abbas, of Aurangzeb and of K'ang-hsi had considerably heightened its prestige. Though Asian customs amazed Western visitors, who were astonished to see white instead of black worn for mourning and the roofs of houses built before their foundations, Europeans were wonder-struck by Asia's enormous treasures. Above all, they were impressed by Asian despotism. The least of Asia's sovereigns wielded more power than the most absolute monarch in Europe. The courts of the ' Kings at the end of the world ' — such as the Nguyen Emperors at Hué and the Trinh at Hanoi — surpassed even Versailles in magnificence. No one in Siam dared even to pronounce the name of the King, Phra-Naraï, who in 1685 treated Louis XIV as an equal. His white elephant was fed from a golden vessel. To approach him his ministers had to crawl. When, to the sound of trumpets, he descended the River Menam in his gilded junk hundreds of thousands of his subjects, with folded hands and faces pressed to the ground, lined the river banks to render him divine honours. When the princess of Siam sallied forth she insisted that everyone should hide. When her ladies-in-waiting talked too much she would have their mouths sewn up; if they talked too little, they were slit open to the ears.

In the extravagance of its splendour seventeenth-century Asia was a prolongation of the preceding centuries, while Europe in the age of Louis XIV had left behind the Europe of Charles V. The progress of Asia was imperceptible in spite of a few uncertain ' awakenings ' such as that of Hindu nationalism. With Lao-Tsze, Asia remained convinced that ' one can see one's way without looking out of the window ', that ' one can know the entire world without leaving the house '. Asia refused to be influenced by the outside world, tended to rebuff Christianity and derived the minimum profit from her dwindling contacts with foreigners. Her desire to follow her own way of life and pattern of development deprived her of the material advance achieved by the West, which continued to outdistance her in technical progress. Would she have escaped stagnation had she been less isolated? The example of Japan suggests that the answer is no. Japan was, of all Asian nations, the most strictly guarded from the rest of the world. And yet profound changes took place in Japan during the second half of the seventeenth century. While the strong political structure which the Tokugawa Dynasty had given the country remained, the emergence of new classes upset the social equilibrium. Merchants carried swords, political opportunists wormed their way into the nobility, and the *daimyos* themselves speculated in rice. A monied aristocracy replaced the old fighting feudal nobility.

It was the final defeat of the nomads rather than isolation that doomed Asia to immobility. The empires which the nomads had founded at the beginning of the sixteenth century were everywhere in decline. Aurangzeb was one of the last of the Grand Moguls, and in Persia the gentle and pious Husain (1694–1722), who was dethroned after his capital was taken by the Afghans, was one of the last Safavids.

Far from recalling the sweeping campaigns of Tamerlane and Jenghis Khan, the Manchu occupation of China in 1644 had been effected with the minimum of bloodshed and almost by trickery. Once established in the Middle Empire, the Tatars assimilated and defended the settled civilisation they found there. The wild nomadic raids of Galdan had ended in failure as the tide ebbed. In Muscovite Siberia as in Mongolia, subdued by K'ang-hsi, the nomads had withdrawn or, pacified, had settled in villages, and with backs patiently bent were now working the soil which once had known the reckless beat of their horses' hooves.

A period of history had come to a close. The days of the great invasions were past. Savage Asia had sheathed her claws and fertile Asia had prevailed, prolific Asia with her immobility, her wisdom, her amorphous populations, indifferent to the passage of time, resistant to progress, easy-going, passive — an immense stagnant pool where no currents stirred, in which every flame was extinguished. India was a congeries of religious sects, China a collection of families. Japan was a feudal society, and Persia a culture rather than a state. None of these empires was in any individual sense a nation. If Europe had more life than power, Asia had more power than life; but her power lay dormant and in chains. Her history was disturbed only by a few despots of outstanding cruelty and by occasional natural calamities.

A Japanese rendering in wood of a European. The model for this trumpeter was probably a Dutchman, since only the Dutch were allowed to trade with Japan, whose self-imposed isolation was to last until the nineteenth century. *British Museum*

Kitagama Utamaro (1754–1806) was one of the greatest designers of Japanese colour prints. His work was imported into Europe before the end of the eighteenth century and was especially esteemed by the Dutch. *Rijksmuseum*

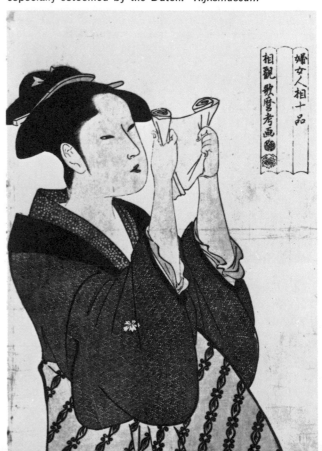

The illustrations of Theodorus de Bry (1528–1598) to Hariot's *Briefe and True Report of the New found land of Virginia* (1595) gave Europe its first visual images of the North American Indians. This is a stockaded village in Virginia.   *Mansell*

EUROPEAN POSSESSIONS BEYOND THE SEAS

Anglo-French rivalry

The Dutch Republic, while retaining her Indonesian conquests and important posts along the spice route, was no longer a significant rival for England. On the other hand, the English and French competed keenly in the North Atlantic from Canada to the West Indies. The first phase of the struggle was indecisive. The warships of New England failed to capture Quebec and the Treaty of Ryswick restored the *status quo*. But when the Franco-Spanish Bourbon bloc gave France a monopoly of the slave trade with the Spanish Indies, England was the danger which threatened her American colonies. The maritime and colonial clauses of the Treaty of Utrecht registered an important, though not a final, British victory in the colonial contest. The acquisition of trading posts in Hudson Bay was commercially advantageous, and the annexation of Newfoundland and Nova Scotia gave Britain command of the gateway to New France.

In the Spanish Indies, which for the most part fell under British economic control, Britain received not only the slave trade monopoly for thirty years, but the right to send one trading vessel to Porto Bello and to Vera Cruz — a right which soon proved to cause far more trouble than its exercise was worth. At the same time the war had linked Britain to Portugal by the Methuen Treaty of 1703. Nine-tenths of the manufactured products which Brazil was obliged to purchase exclusively from the homeland came in fact from British trading stations in Lisbon and Englishmen became a nation of port-drinkers.

Europe did not yet wish to subject Asia to her political control. The English, French and Dutch East India Companies aimed at commerce only, while in China the Jesuits were attempting not domination of but integration with the local civilisation. In America, on the other hand, a new cutting of the white race and of Western civilisation was taking root.

The English colonies in North America

Most of the 350,000 inhabitants of the English colonies in the New World were English, though there was a sprinkling of French Huguenots and German Pietists. The southern colonies remained aristocratic and slave-owning, the northern still Puritan, but tending to become less dominated by their pastors. Religious fanaticism was discredited by the witch hunts of 1690–92, hysterical outbursts of superstitious horror in which hundreds of unfortunate women were hunted down and twenty hanged or pressed to death. A reaction set in after these dreadful episodes and tolerance won the day. Education flourished in the public schools and the colleges of Harvard and Yale. The America of the 'Witches of Salem' was beginning to give way to the America of Benjamin Franklin.

During the Restoration the Stuarts had attempted to control more closely the government of the colonies, and their policy was continued after the revolution of 1688. In this way, the English colonies, like French Canada, underwent increasing subordination to the mother country. English mercantile interests welcomed the use of royal authority to consolidate the commercial privileges of the mother country. By 1715 all the colonies except Rhode Island, Connecticut, Pennsylvania and Maryland were royal provinces under governors named by the King, though usually there was also an assembly, elected by the local notabilities, which ratified the laws and passed the budget. The colonists resented the governor's power of veto and Britain's exclusive right to colonial trade. Harrington's Utopian *Oceana*, published in 1658, had already predicted that the colonies would, when adult, proclaim their independence. For the moment they were grateful that the representatives from London behaved like reasonable men and closed their eyes to smuggling. The French danger, and commercial interest as well as genuine loyalty, still united them to the mother country.

Spanish and Portuguese America

The accession to the throne of Spain of the French House of Bourbon brought changes to the Spanish colonies. The old monarchy, which had been the titular head of a federation in which the Spanish colonies were almost on an equal footing with Spain itself, was succeeded by a centralised imperial government. This modernisation after a long period of decadence at first increased the prosperity of the Spanish American colonies. Their population now exceeded that of Spain itself. Mexico City, with its 150,000 inhabitants, was thirty times as populous as New York, and possessed a school of mines, a botanical garden and an academy of sciences and art. But uniform administration robbed the Spanish American colonies of individuality and reduced them to the rank of ordinary colonies. In the long run it made easier a break with Spain.

Portuguese Brazil, on the contrary, enjoyed a much more supple organisation which enabled her to preserve her unity. Brazil was a true federal state in which each province had its own captain-general, government and treasury. Brazilian society continued to be dominated by the proprietors of vast plantations devoted to the cultivation of sugar-cane. They formed the ' old Brazil ' of the north-east; but in the region of São Paulo a young and more adventurous Brazil was taking shape. Here in 1694 the goldfields of Minas Gerais were discovered and the wealth which flowed from them revivified the economy of Western Europe and contributed to the eighteenth century's atmosphere of optimism.

AFRICA IN THE SEVENTEENTH CENTURY

Africa continued in her own manner. The essential elements in African history at this period were the closing of Abyssinia to Europe, the zeal of Islam in North Africa, and in Negro Africa the great renaissance of old traditions.

The Maghrib: piracy and holy war

Though the regencies in Algiers and in Tunis remained in the hands of a Turkish military oligarchy, both cities had, to all intents and purposes, become independent of Constantinople. Algiers was ruled by a Dey, chosen by the corsair captains. Tunis was ruled by a Bey who was originally elected by the Spahis. In 1705, however, the Bey Hussein ben Ali made the title hereditary in his family and founded a dynasty which endured until the twentieth century. Both regencies had seized the opportunity to live by privateering offered by the conflicts in Europe. The Algerians added ocean-going vessels to their fleet of galleys and in 1616 spread terror as far as Iceland. Algiers grew richer and bigger. From 1550 to 1650 the city's population doubled, till it was over 100,000 without including 35,000 captives. Clustering around its steep-hilled bay, the city overflowed with the corsairs' heterogeneous booty: porcelain from Utrecht, Venetian glass, English clocks. Though St Vincent de Paul's Lazarists were freely permitted to give consolation to Christian slaves, captives were at once set free if they embraced Islam. The ardent piety of the Moslem people was expressed by the erection of mosques with great cupolas inspired by those in Constantinople.

In Morocco, the death of the great Sultan El-Mansur in 1603 was the prelude to a long and confused struggle for the succession. Mystic brotherhoods roused the people against the corruption of the sherifs and the towns. An independent corsair republic was set up at Salé which waged a relentless holy war against the Portuguese and the Spanish still occupying a few *presidios* — or fortresses — along the coast. In 1654 the new dynasty of the Alawites was raised to power by the traditional defenders of the faith, the desert nomads. The most remarkable member of the new ruling house was Mulay Ismail, who from 1672 revived Moroccan power. Mulay Ismail, who fathered at least seven hundred sons and an unknown number of daughters, was a despot of fiery temperament who liked to cut his enemies' throats with his own hand. Not only in his ardent passion but also in his simplicity, religious zeal and strict devotion he resembled that other champion of warlike Islam, his contemporary the Grand Mogul Aurangzeb, and extended his rule throughout all Morocco.

In the mysterious and almost inaccessible highlands of Abyssinia a Christian culture survived in the middle of pagan Africa. This fragment of a seventeenth-century fresco shows saints of characteristically semitic and non-negroid features.

The privateers of Salé, whom he welded into a military organisation called the 'Volunteers of the Faith', took El-Mamora from the Spaniards in 1681, Larache in 1689 and Arcila in 1691. The English, who had received Tangier as part of Catherine of Braganza's dowry, were forced in 1684 to evacuate it. The Sultan even dreamed of an alliance with Louis XIV against Spain, and proposed to marry a daughter of France, the beautiful Princess of Conti. The project fell through with the dynastic union of France and Spain, and Mulay Ismail had to be satisfied with building himself a Versailles at Meknès. Eager to leave an enduring monument to his greatness, he personally directed the work of construction, cracking the skulls of careless workmen and not hesitating to give the others an example by handling a pick himself.

The closing of Abyssinia

Abyssinia, an island of Christians in the midst of Islam, had triumphed over the Somalis only to suffer the attacks of the nomad Gallas, who had also adopted Islam. This new danger brought the Negus Socinios (1607–32) closer to the Jesuits, who promised him the aid of the King of Spain. In 1622 the celebrated Portuguese Father Paez obtained the public conversion of the Negus. Three years later another Jesuit, Alfonso Mendez, became the *abuna*, or Patriarch, of the Abyssinian Church. But the prohibition of the Jewish Sabbath and certain Latin ritual reforms resulted in a resistance movement of 'Old Believers' led by Fasiladas, the King's own son. In 1632 Socinios was overthrown by a popular uprising. Fasiladas (1632–67) was proclaimed King and at once drove out all the foreign missionaries, beginning with the *abuna* Alfonso. Establishing his capital at Gondar — which remained the capital of Abyssinia until 1839 — he devoted himself to the restoration of the Monophysite Church and the revival of its Judaeo-Christian traditions. Abyssinia cut herself off from Europe at the same time as Japan. The Abyssinians, like the Asians, rejected Western cultural influence as soon as they realised the blow it would deal to their own ritualistic conceptions of the universe.

Internal religious wrangling and the cessation of European aid would have injured Abyssinian efforts to withstand the pressure of Islam had not Iyasu I, one of the greatest sovereigns in Abyssinian history, come to the throne in 1682. He repulsed the Gallas, mastered the feudal chieftains, codified the law and disciplined the judges. He abdicated in favour of his son, who nevertheless assassinated him in 1698. Ten years later, at the demand of all his people, Iyasu the Great was canonised. Faithful to the tenets of her national church, which reconciled Christianity and Judaism, Abyssinia remained the holy guardian of the Ark of the Covenant before which her priests danced.

The vicissitudes of Islam in Negro Africa

Islam, supported by the Arabian fleets which commanded the African shores of the Indian Ocean, crept down East Africa from the land of the Gallas and the Somalis to Zanzibar. In 1698 warships from Muscat seized the Portuguese trading posts to the north of Cape Delgado and thus for two centuries European penetration of these regions was held back and Moslem influence prevailed.

From Lake Chad to the Nile, in direct communication with the holy cities of Arabia via Egypt and Tripolitania, Islam preserved a puritanical rigidity which refused all compromise with the Negro world's philosophy and way of life. The advance of Islam was the advance of a warrior aristocracy which had come from the north-east to impose its dominion over the natives. In this manner Bagirmi and Darfur were conquered towards 1600. Between 1610 and 1635 a descendant of the Caliphs of Baghdad implanted the faith solidly in Wadai. Except in Darfur, where a curious synthesis of Koranic law and old African myths existed — the king had a ritual 'twin' and a sister-wife — this enforced Islamisation was little more than a thin veneer over Negro beliefs and produced no cultural fruits.

In the regions of the Niger River, on the other hand, Berber Islam had fascinated the Negroes with its technique of inducing ecstasy and its brotherhoods which altered without suppressing the ancient African secret societies. In the seventeenth century this phase of genuinely Negro Islamisation came to an end with the downfall of the two Moslem empires of Songhoi and Mali. Songhoi had been invaded in 1591 by Spanish renegades in the service of Morocco. The Sultan El-Mansur had hoped to find an Eldorado there. Disappointed by the poverty of the country, he lost interest in his conquest. From 1612 his successors did not trouble even to send Pashas to the Songhoi city of Timbuktu. Elected by acclamation of the army, the Spanish 'Pashas' and afterwards their half-breed descendants, the *Arma*, thought only of exploiting the country. The peasants were ruined by taxes and requisitions. They died of famine while the Islamic élite of Timbuktu were outlawed or murdered. Isolated in their strongholds, attacked by their neighbours on the north and south alike, the *Arma* were finally conquered by the Tuaregs. The Mali Empire did not survive the secession of the non-Islamised Bambara, a tribe of the Mandingo peoples, and during warfare which lasted between 1666 and 1670 was finally destroyed. The Mali Emperor retired to the village which had seen the rise to power of his dynasty, and his descendants live there today as district chieftains.

The last flowering of Negro civilisations

Despite their apparent political fragmentation, the Negro peoples were bound together over vast stretches of territory by the ancient traditions of Africa and the activities of their secret societies. They flourished more powerfully than ever on the ruins of the great Moslem states. The Dogon and the Mossi consolidated their positions. Between the Niger and Lake Chad, in a region of large towns, the Hausa principalities settled their differences and freed themselves from Bornu domination. Henceforth independent, they repulsed every attack of Islam for two centuries. Other Negro peoples went further than simple federation and formed powerful kingdoms. The warrior states of the Dahomey and the Ashanti spread to the edges of the tropical forest lands. Around Segu, between the River Niger and the River Bani, a great sovereign, Biton Koulibali (1660–1710), organised the kingdom of the Bambara. His armies, supported by a flotilla and a corps of engineers, completed the unification of the territory and delivered the final blow to the Mandingo Empire. Then, after repulsing the Moroccans, Biton Koulibali conquered the Macina and penetrated as far as Timbuktu. The Bambara, who used hieroglyphic script, conceived of a strange animistic universe in which water and light were the expressions of the Divine Word, and in which everything was ordered and regulated from the celestial powers to earthly rubbish. The subtlety of their behaviour and their observance of minute ritualistic details reminded one observer of the great civilisations of the Far East. Between Dahomey and the Lower Niger, the kingdom of the Yoruba impressed European travellers by the richness of its plantations, the size of its towns — some of more than 100,000 inhabitants — and the strange splendour of Ife, its 'city of the gods' where, near the enormous palace of the Grand Pontiff, rose the 'hill of three palms' which symbolised the axis of the world. From about 1575 to 1650 Yoruba culture flourished at Benin. Its art, whether in terracotta or cast in bronze by a complex method of covering the clay original model with melted wax, obtaining a mould and refilling it with molten bronze, had nothing in common with primitive art; it had achieved true classical perfection. The human face, neither mask nor double, was reproduced with the accuracy of a portrait, but transfigured by an exceptional sweetness, serenity and harmony. There exists a terracotta torso of a girl treated with a delicate tenderness which rivals the finest work of the Greeks.

Though Europeans established on the coasts of Africa were astonished by such remarkable civilisations, they did nothing to preserve them. On the contrary the Europeans themselves contributed to the slow but inexorable disappearance of African culture. The plantations of America and the West Indies demanded an ever-increasing quantity of Negro labour and the slave trade, which Europeans pursued with the help of African kings, stripped and devastated the continent hundreds of miles inland. Even

the most humane white men made no effort to understand the natives, and saw in them only their shortcomings. The Dutch, settled on the Cape of Good Hope in their neat, clean, thatched and whitewashed houses, proud of their lovely gardens full of Mediterranean plants, described their Hottentot neighbours as 'dirty, stinking animals' and could see in the men with their greasy hair nothing but thieves who would steal even the buttons off your clothes, and in the women only their legs bound in sheepgut. The Negroes, feeling despised, drew in upon themselves and, refusing to accept any influence of European origin, thought only of preserving the purity of their own traditions. The old and the new cultures which had come into contact since the sixteenth century clashed rather than mingled and seemed conscious only of their differences and incompatibility. For the next two centuries the contrast between the increasingly revolutionary attitude of Europe and the immobility of Asia and Africa became even more striking.

Until the end of the eighteenth century, little was known by Europeans of the interior of Africa. Only the coastal and river peoples came into direct contact with Europe, often through the slave-trade. From one of these peoples, the Yoruba, came this drummer. *Marburg*

Cockfighting. An engraving by Hogarth.

THE EIGHTEENTH CENTURY

CHAPTER NINE

THE FAILURE OF THE ENGLISH PEACE

THE EUROPEAN STATES

Great Britain

After first directing and then deserting the European coalition against Louis XIV, Great Britain emerged from the war strengthened with new possessions, vigorous in commerce and with a new security since the removal of the land frontier with Scotland in 1707. The restrictions imposed on her monarchs and the legal safeguards which buttressed the rights of individuals and their property made her an object of admiration to critics of absolutism in other countries, like Voltaire and Montesquieu. Such observers often misunderstood English institutions, but the achievements of English culture in the Age of Enlightenment were less open to misinterpretation; Newton and Locke were followed by Berkeley and Hume. The wealth and progressiveness of this society were directed by a

ruling class which grasped, though sometimes with difficulty, the principle that Great Britain's major international interest was to preserve the peace, whose rupture could endanger the growth of trade.

It was not only the fact that war was expensive and hampered commerce which made peace desirable. There was also a new royal house on the throne whose position had to be consolidated against the threat of a Stuart restoration such as was attempted in 1715 and 1745. At the death of Queen Anne in August 1714 the prearranged succession of the Elector of Hanover had met with little resistance. Only a few Tories disliked it, and the landing in Scotland of James Stuart — the Old Pretender — came to nothing. The Whigs had a majority in the new House of Commons, and the Whigs were in favour of the new king. The first two Georges of Hanover were unattractive men whose interest lay in Hanover, where they preferred to pass their time. George I, a dissipated drunkard, spoke no English but had at least the merit in the eyes of his English subjects of not tampering with their liberties. Under him, the Whig leaders completed the exclusion from office of their rivals, the Tories (who were suspected of Jacobite leanings). The Whigs represented a wide coalition of interest, often of opposing interests; hence their tendency to split into rival factions. Party names meant less and less as the century wore on.

The first two Georges were obliged to rely on Whig support although the Whigs had been traditionally in favour of reducing the prerogatives of the Crown and the Tories in favour of preserving them. The Crown had still considerable powers and could give vital support to a minister who, like the great Sir Robert Walpole, could control the House of Commons. The House of Commons reflected the dominant society of the day — a society of landed aristocrats and gentry who increasingly improved their estates by enclosing commons and bringing new land under cultivation. The rising industrial middle class was later to complain that it was too often excluded from Parliament by the landed proprietors and electoral reform became by 1800 one of the major issues of British politics. But all through the century there were spokesmen for commercial interests to be found in the House of Commons; and the ruling class was never closed to new blood, which sought admission to it with wealth or talent.

Shortly after the end of the war Britain and France encountered curiously similar difficulties. The long conflict had left the public finances of both countries in a deplorable state. The return of peace brought with it a relaxation of morals, an appetite for pleasure, and also a wild search for financial expedients. Law's system in France was contemporary with the British South Sea Bubble. The British Government had accepted the South Sea Company's scheme to take over the whole national debt not held by the Bank of England and the East India Company. There was a rush for South Sea shares, which sent their price from one hundred to one thousand pounds. Then came the crash, and the subsequent scandal touched Members of Parliament and even the Government. Stanhope, who had not taken part in the speculation, died suddenly in 1721, bringing Walpole to power. Walpole skilfully wound up the South Sea Company, restored national credit and remained in power for the next twenty-one years.

Sir Robert Walpole personified the English governing classes of the day. He was a member of the gentry, a great landowner, cynical and jovial, a believer in the policy of 'wait and see', with a shrewd sense of what was practicable. He controlled the House of Commons by sheer ability, concessions of policy and by the means of patronage and favour which all Governments employed in the eighteenth century to build up majorities. When George II came to the throne (1727) Walpole used his friendship with Queen Caroline to consolidate his influence on the King. In foreign affairs he was helped by the French Prime Minister, Fleury, in this struggle to keep the peace. As the years went by, growing prosperity seemed to make his domination even more secure. But he antagonised a small but growing group of Whig politicians, who resented exclusion from the sweets of office. They taunted him especially with the neglect of British interests and honour abroad. The outbreak of colonial war with Spain in 1739

A French cartoon satirising Britain's weakness during the Austrian Succession War. France (on the right) failed to exploit this weakness however, and Pitt (on the left) was able to revive the patriotic enthusiasm of his country. *Larousse*

In the sense that his power rested on control of the House of Commons, Sir Robert Walpole was England's first Prime Minister. Appropriately, he is depicted in the House, in conversation with its presiding officer, the Speaker.

(and its merging in a European struggle in 1740) gave them their chance. When Walpole could no longer control the House of Commons, George II could not keep him in office. In 1742 Walpole resigned; his successor, Carteret, pleased the King by pursuing a policy of safeguarding Hanoverian interests; but in 1744 he was forced out by another group of politicians from the Whig oligarchy.

The Jacobite rising in Scotland in 1745, although it gave a bad fright to the Government, in fact ended the danger of Scottish separatism. After the defeat of 'Bonny Prince Charlie' at Culloden the Highlands were ruthlessly harried and subjugated. Ireland was quieter, but was in the long run to prove the most intractable problem in British political life. The crux of the problem was that the vast majority of the population were Catholic and, 139

Eighteentn-century military discipline. At the shooting of three Scottish highlanders, a hundred others are put on parade as witnesses. Their guards stand with reversed arms, a sergeant with a halberd standing behind them. *British Museum*

because of this, subjected to harsh restrictions, with no political rights. They had not even the right to own property or sign a long lease. In consequence they became tenants at the mercy of landlords, in conditions of the greatest economic insecurity. The professions were closed to them, and Irish industry sacrificed to the interests of the growing manufacturing districts of England. Even the Parliament in Dublin, although it was composed only of Protestant landlords, complained vigorously of the arbitrariness of the Government in London. From mid-century agrarian disorders were endemic. Those who could do so began to emigrate to America.

England's social life at this time provided another contrast with her constitutional and economic success. The towns were dirty and unsafe, inhabited by mobs brutalised by gin and the spectacle of public executions. The rural gentry lived coarse, isolated lives on their estates. ' Society ' — in the narrow sense — was dissolute, drunken and debauched. Even the clergy of early Hanoverian England did not always lead edifying lives. But at Oxford a small group of earnest men had gathered around the Wesley brothers. These men, nicknamed Methodists, by the passion of their teaching, first from the pulpits of the established Church, and then outside it, strove to awaken a new

A British infantryman, about the middle of the eighteenth century. He wears the tall cap of a grenadier. Such men were chosen for their stature and imposing appearance. Frederick William I of Prussia recruited giants for his grenadiers from all over Europe. *Mansell*

spirit of Christianity in peoples' hearts, and, without embroiling themselves in theological controversy, to revive the evangelical virtues. The Methodist revival led to an important philanthropic movement and a great revival of enthusiasm in all denominations. Literature began to show a new sensibility, too. The first true novels were the immensely successful satire *Gulliver's Travels* by Swift, and Defoe's *Robinson Crusoe*, an implicit panegyric of the capacities of the individual to overcome difficulties. This optimism was repeated in Fielding's splendidly robust *Tom Jones*, a brilliant picture of English life. With Richardson's *Pamela* and *Clarissa Harlowe* sentiment and high moral tone came in, and came in at great length, for these

Town and country life blended in the eighteenth century. Hogarth's engraving of Southwark fair, a gathering-place for charlatans, traders, hucksters, players and clowns, portrays this blend. *British Museum*

bestsellers were long books. They quickly achieved widespread renown in Europe and began the diffusion of a pre-Romantic sensibility.

The United Provinces

On the continent Britain could count on the support of two allies who had once been her rivals at sea and in the colonies but were now in decline: the United Provinces and Portugal.

Yet at the beginning of the eighteenth century the Dutch Republic appeared to be at the pinnacle of its prosperity. The barrier fortresses which it garrisoned permitted encroachments in the new Austrian Netherlands, while advantageous customs tariffs guaranteed the wealth of Dutch traders. The Dutch East India Company and the West Indies Company distributed regular and handsome dividends. Finally, the republican regime had been restored, and the Grand Pensionary Heinsius governed until his death in 1720. Only in the province of Friesland was the Stadtholder a member of the House of Orange. But something seemed to have gone wrong: Dutch products sold less well, Dutch textiles met serious competition from those of France. The cities had declined, except for

Amsterdam, which was the centre of international banking and for this very reason liable to be shaken by British and French financial crises. Dissensions arose between the provinces. In 1722–3 the northern provinces clamoured for reforms to which the southern provinces refused to agree. The Prince of Orange, William IV, was too young to exert authority. After his marriage in 1734 to the daughter of George II British influence in the United Provinces grew with the fortunes of the House of Orange. But the governing burgher oligarchy hesitated to follow Great Britain on a path which led to war. A French invasion, however, at last roused the country. Then, following the traditional pattern, the people demanded that William IV of Orange be made Stadtholder-General. William, however, could do nothing to right the situation, or even carry out the reforms which had been undertaken. He died in 1751, leaving a child of three to succeed him.

Portugal

Owing to its geographical situation Portugal, even more than the United Provinces, remained outside the mainstream of European politics. Like the United Provinces, Portugal possessed a vast colonial empire from which she derived sufficient wealth to doze in comfort, lulled by a false sense of prosperity. In reality, after the Methuen Treaty Britain had practically taken over the foreign trade of Portugal and Brazil and local industry was condemned to virtual stagnation.

John V, who had reigned since 1706, devoted himself to pious exercises and to the founding of convents. Two years before his death in 1748 he received his reward from the Pope: the title of ' Very Faithful '. Since John V desired peace, and threats to peace came chiefly from Spain, he married his son José to a daughter of Philip V. Portugal settled back in her torpor, her despotism, the pomp of her sumptuous court and her awe of religious order.

France and the Regency

Bourbon Europe — France and Spain — faced Britain and challenged her commercial, maritime and colonial ambitions, though in fact France alone offered serious competition and, even then, was not prepared to fight. All France, and particularly the court of Versailles, had welcomed the death of Louis XIV with a sigh of relief. His heir and great-grandson, Louis XV, was five years old at the time, and the old King had provided in his will for a regency during the child's minority which would entrust the young heir's education to the clan of ' legitimised princes ' — the Duke of Maine and the Count of Toulouse — royal bastards who had been recognised almost as 'princes of the blood'. Louis's nephew Philip of Orleans had the will annulled by the *Parlement*, in return granting that legal body the full right to present remonstrances or public protests — a measure of great future significance.

The Duke of Orleans was refined and intelligent but also lazy and dissipated. His circle of friends — the *roués* — turned the seven years of his regency into a disorderly reaction against the preceding reign. Aristocratic amateurs proved they could not govern. Philip suppressed the Secretaries of State, who had been agents of absolutism, and replaced them by councils composed of noblemen. Though this collective administration was not entirely unsuccessful, 141

The stage-setting and theatre of the eighteenth century were often elaborately baroque. This painting by Pannini shows a concert given in honour of the birth of the Dauphin. *Larousse*

John Law as Don Quixote. But this hostile cartoon was after the failure of his scheme and the discrediting of paper money. *Larousse*

the council dealing with religious matters again brought the Jansenist controversy to the boil, while the financial council, in spite of certain energetic measures against the tax farmers, was unable to remove the deficits problem bequeathed by Louis XIV.

At this moment a Scot, John Law, appeared on the scene. He had given much thought to the problems of credit and the circulation of paper money. His ideas clashed with the accepted theories of economics and were in advance of their time. But Law won the confidence of the Regent and was given free rein to try out his theories. His career was spectacular but brief: in 1716 he founded, with capital composed largely of the national debt, a private bank issuing paper money which was honoured by the royal treasury. In 1717 he created the *Compagnie d'Occident* with shares payable in bank notes and put on the open market. In 1718 Law's private bank became the Royal

Bank. He supervised the monopolies and the farming of taxes, issued more paper money and raised a loan. His success was so prodigious that by 1720 he had become Controller General or finance minister. Crowds of speculators besieged his bank, trampling each other underfoot in their eagerness to buy shares, which rose to giddy heights. More paper was issued — too much. Suddenly the shares toppled and the system collapsed. Law fled. Though the crash discredited the idea of paper currency and delayed for many years the proper organisation of credit, Law had stimulated the French economy and, moreover, lightened the public debt. But the crisis and the spectacle it afforded of fortunes made and lost by gambling on the stock exchange deeply affected public feeling about investment and paper money.

After Law came a return to traditional financial expedients. The last years of the Regency were dominated by the ministry of Dubois, who has perhaps too often been judged by Saint-Simon's remark that 'all vices fought within him for leadership'. He was also remarkably clear-sighted and surprisingly efficient. He put an end to the unwieldy aristocratic councils and, reverting to Louis XIV's methods, reinstalled the Secretaries of State. He imposed Ultramontane orthodoxy as laid down in the Papal Bull *Unigenitus*, and as a reward received in 1721 a Cardinal's hat. Two years later he died.

In 1723 the Regent also died, and was replaced by the Duke of Bourbon, another prince of the blood. The health of the young Louis XV was causing uneasiness. The demands of foreign policy had provided him with a fiancée, a Spanish Infanta, still a child, who was brought to Versailles to be educated. Bourbon decided to abandon this engagement in order to ensure that the young king had a direct heir who would frustrate the hopes of the Orleanist line. He chose as a bride for Louis the daughter of Stanislas, the dethroned King of Poland, Marie Leszcyńska. The Infanta was packed off to Spain again. The Polish marriage was celebrated in 1725; Louis XV gained a fruitful spouse who later brought France Lorraine. But the immediate result was the disgrace of the Duke of Bourbon, who was sacrificed to the outraged fury of Spain.

Fleury

The reign of the young king's tutor, Fleury, now began. Fleury, who had been Bishop of Fréjus, was seventy-three when he became a Cardinal and Prime Minister of France. He was gentle, wise and patient, an incomparable diplomat who had great influence over his royal pupil. He loved peace and under him France's prosperity revived. Unlike Walpole, however, Fleury followed Colbert's policy; industry was strictly controlled by the State and royal workshops were given preferential treatment. Nevertheless internal and external trade grew. As Controller General, Orry, a former Intendant, introduced the most rigid economies.

But the *Parlement* and the Jansenists remained problems. The *Parlement* of Paris protested angrily at Fleury's confirmation of the Bull *Unigenitus* as the law of the Church and the State. A drama which was often repeated during the course of the century ensued: remonstrances by the *Parlement*, royal sessions to bring them to heel (*lits de justice*); the exile of councillors, their recall. Against this background, real administrative reforms went unnoticed.

Louis XV during the Regency. His youth gave an opportunity for centrifugal forces repressed by Louis XIV to appear again. The Regent, the Duke of Orleans, was the centre of a brilliant society. *Marburg*

Philip V, first Bourbon king of Spain. Uxorious and irresolute, he allowed his wife, Elisabeth Farnese, too great a freedom to shape Spanish policy in the interests of her sons. But, during his reign, Spain began to recover from her decline under the Habsburgs. *Deutsche Fotothek Dresden*

Fleury died in 1743 at the age of ninety. In spite of the unpopularity of his minister's peace policy, the King remained loyal to him until the end. Then, echoing his great-grandfather's words, Louis XV announced that he would govern for himself. With his youth and great charm Louis became the 'well-beloved' king, intelligent but impenetrable. He quickly became bored with his job as king and, allowing his favourites to play a part in public affairs, he preferred private policies known as 'secrets'. From 1745 to her death in 1764 his mistress the Marquise de Pompadour exercised great influence. The war which began in 1740 sent prices up. In 1747 and 1748 famine was rife. The Government seemed to drift aimlessly. Louis XV began to disappoint his subjects.

In the world of art and literature, however, France set the tone. French was spoken universally among the educated, and French authors therefore enjoyed a wide public. Yet they often turned for inspiration to England. One of the most successful books of the century, *L'esprit des lois*, which Montesquieu published in 1748, owed much to John Locke. Voltaire's *Lettres Philosophiques* were inspired by his sojourn in England. From England too the Abbé Prévost, author of *Manon Lescaut*, borrowed the formula of the sentimental yet realistic novel. Elsewhere in Europe, French art was triumphant. French architects were imitated or brought to work abroad. Painting had revived with the poetic or langorous canvases of Watteau, Lancret, Natoire and above all Boucher; portraiture, too, became more supple. In 1737 the opening of a *salon* of painting gave a wider audience to such artists. All these works reveal the society which gathered in the refined atmosphere of the *salons* to play music, to discuss matters of interest and simply to exchange bantering conversation. It was this society which first stressed the possibility that man might attain happiness here and now, without waiting for the hereafter.

Spain under the first Bourbons

Of the possessions of Charles V, Bourbon Spain still retained the immense overseas empire. Spain was traditionally a maritime nation, but in the eighteenth century her strength was at first dissipated in struggles for dynastic ends. Philip V was undoubtedly full of good intentions; but he was subject to fits of discouragement and abdicated in 1724 in favour of his son, only to return to the throne seven months later on his son's death. He was dominated by his second wife, the scheming and ambitious Elisabeth Farnese, niece of the Duke of Parma, whose sole preoccupation was to obtain the Duchies of Parma and Tuscany for her sons. Philip V allowed her to advance the fortunes of such adventurers as Alberoni, the clever son of an Italian vine dresser, who, like Dubois, became a Cardinal, and the Dutchman Ripperda, the one as disastrous to Spain as the other. Finally Philip chose and supported a Spanish minister, Don Jose Patiño. Patiño, a man of the middle classes, carried out far-sighted plans which were of benefit to the country. In many ways he was similar to Colbert, even to sharing Colbert's unpleasant character. Patiño's work was continued by another Spanish minister, Enseñada.

By birth a Frenchman, Philip V remained a Frenchman at heart. Spain at the beginning of the eighteenth century was still far from enjoying national unity. Philip struggled against Spanish routine and local particularism, reduced the number of councils, created Intendants whom he sent to the provinces, and founded royal workshops. Patiño was particularly interested in maritime trade. He developed the port of Cadiz with its superb situation at the expense of Seville. He made shipping more flexible by permitting vessels to be chartered by private owners under royal licence, and he himself founded two trading companies. Finally he rebuilt the Spanish fleet and assigned to it as its first mission the suppression of smuggling.

When Philip V died in 1746 he had at last, by remaining firmly independent of his native France, reconciled his subjects to the Bourbon dynasty. That he had occasionally felt homesick was apparent from the solitary palace he built at la Granja, a typically French building set in the midst of gardens designed in imitation of the gardens of Versailles. His son, Ferdinand VI, who reigned until 1758, resembled him in more than one way (among others in also being governed by his wife, Barbara of Portugal). His health and his reason rapidly deteriorated. During his reign, in 1753, a Concordat was signed with the Holy See which granted broad powers in ecclesiastical matters to the temporal sovereign — a remarkable step forward in a country where the Church was so powerful and owned so much land. With Philip V a certain spirit of independence of Rome had been introduced in Spain, together with a tendency towards moderation and tolerance, unfamiliar in the land of the Inquisition.

The Swiss Cantons

The thirteen Cantons of Switzerland led an existence unaffected by international politics, except for the demand which existed for the Swiss mercenary soldiers, who were hired by all countries. The Treaty of Aarau in 1712 had put an end to the civil war between Catholic and Protestant Cantons. Berne and Zürich had been victorious over the five Catholic Cantons, which in 1715 signed an alliance with the King of France. The other cause of internal dissension was social. The humbler classes, especially the peasants, were harshly exploited by a patrician oligarchy and on several occasions revolted, as for example in 1734 and 1738 at Geneva. A new commercial middle class, imbued with liberal ideas, was rising. The textile industry, both cotton and silk, made great strides, especially in Zürich; by the middle of the century the Swiss Confederation was one of the chief textile producers of Europe. Situated at the crossroads of western and central Europe, Switzerland played a significant part in the propagation of contemporary ideas.

The Holy Roman Empire

In the eighteenth century the Holy Roman Empire consisted of over three hundred principalities and cities. The power which the Imperial dignity conferred on the Austrian sovereign over this heterogeneous collection was theoretically important and practically small. The political influence of the Holy Roman Empire as an organisation was negligible. Inevitably, it was weakened by the fact that some of its princes, including the Habsburg Emperor himself, also ruled over lands outside the Empire. The Elector of Brandenburg was King of Prussia, the Elector of Hanover was King of Great Britain, the Elector of Saxony was King of Poland. On the other hand, the

In 1661 Louis XIV renewed the alliance with the Swiss cantons first made in 1516. Down to the end of the *Ancien Régime*, Swiss Guards recruited under the terms of this alliance served as personal guards of the Kings of France. *Larousse*

King of Denmark possessed the Duchies of Oldenburg and Holstein which belonged to the Empire, while the King of Sweden held part of Imperial Pomerania. Such confusions encouraged their owners to pursue personal and independent policies. The Empire itself no longer had a common policy, and if it had had one, the means to implement it were lacking. Increasingly the Emperor could count on his own inherited dynastic resources alone to enforce the decisions of the Diet, and though during the War of the Austrian Succession an Imperial army was raised it was raised only with the aid of British subsidies. The rivalry between Austria and Prussia drained away most of the strength the Empire possessed. Princes who feared Austrian ambitions and encroachments believed Prussia to be the champion of Germanic liberties. In practice their interests were purely selfish. Their desire was to be left in peace to fatten in mediocrity. The chief ambition of the average German princeling was to keep a sufficiently brilliant court and to build a palace sufficiently handsome to enable him, even at the risk of financial ruin, to maintain his rank and follow French fashions. Only the more enlightened gave pensions to writers, or patronised learning and the arts.

The drill sergeant of Prussia

Since the accession of Frederick William I, Prussia had undergone a profound internal transformation. In his own day Frederick William, who was said to have the mentality of a drill sergeant, was detested for his fits of violence and cruelty. With his gross and boorish manners, his pride in displaying contempt for philosophy and his conscientious psalm-singing, few took him seriously. ' I am,' he would say, ' Chief of the General Staff and Minister of Finance to the King of Prussia ', thus defining the

Warrior on horseback wiping his sword. Japanese painting. British Museum

土佐左近光章

programme of his reign. His accomplishments were as austere as the sacrifices he demanded of his subjects. Under him the Prussian State acquired a cohesion and a discipline which existed nowhere else, founded not on nationalism — a concept which still belonged to the future — but on absolute despotism. All his subjects participated in an enterprise which turned Prussia into a vast military barracks. The army was the King's passion; he held that it was the best means of forming the citizen. In 1733 he established conscription: the country was divided into cantons, each of which was obliged to furnish and maintain a military contingent. In addition to their regular training, drilling and reviews, these soldiers were sent when necessary to work in the fields as labour units, for the King was careful to see that agriculture was not neglected. Great tracts of land were reclaimed for cultivation and livestock increased in number — all with the object of supplying more food for more soldiers. The nobility, too, was associated with the King's overriding military policy; in 1722 he founded the Cadet School in Berlin which was to form a professional officer class, perfectly trained in the art of war. The administration was centralised and the former military councils fused into the *Generaldirektorium*. Frederick William created State factories to produce army supplies. So that his people should not be softened, he banned the importation of foreign products — which were also a drain on the currency. Thanks to his system of excise duties on consumer articles money poured into the royal coffers and accumulated there. In this Spartan atmosphere the inhabitants of Prussia learned what it was to live under an autocratic regime.

Frederick William bequeathed his cherished and magnificent army to a son whose behaviour as a youth had caused him much concern. The young Frederick showed as little taste for the paternal routine as for the paternal thrashings he was given. When he planned to run away and was stopped, Frederick was forced by his father to witness the execution of the friend 'who had abetted him. He was then put through a rigorous apprenticeship which left such a deep mark upon him that he came to render homage to the work his father had done. On the death of his father in 1740 the new King, Frederick II, seemed in every way a contrast to the old. Slim and graceful, witty yet given to meditation, Frederick II wrote and composed music. As King, one of his first acts was to found an Opera in Berlin. He was sceptical if not impious. The exalted idea he had of his position, however, was quite as great as that of his predecessor. But Frederick William merely practised autocracy, while his son made a theory of *raison d'Etat*, or State morality, which had no connection with private rules of right and wrong. Another aspect of Frederick II's character helps us to understand him: he was a fatalist, ready to stake everything on a throw. This was very different from the cautious realism of his father. In brief, Frederick added his own qualities to the forcefulness and originality of his father. The two great Hohenzollerns of the eighteenth century were to leave a deep imprint, material and moral, on European civilisation.

FRIDERICUS WILHELMUS
Rex Borussiæ Elector Brandenburg &c etc.

Frederick William I, King of Prussia (1713–40), father of Frederick the Great. Inflexible and brutal even to his family, he drilled his subjects like a crowned sergeant-major to leave behind an army, an administrative machine and a war-chest second to none.

Austria under Charles VI

To the south of Germany along the banks of the Danube the Habsburgs reigned over an immense state which contained as many people as France. But its mixed population made its power more apparent than real. Charles VI, who came to the throne of Austria in 1711, was aware of these failings and of possible remedies, but could not overcome his irresolution. Throughout his reign he was obsessed with the idea of assuring the transmission of his entire domain to his daughter and only child, Maria Theresa. With this aim he obtained the formal adherence of most European states to Maria Theresa's cause, by making them sign a document recognising his daughter's rights, which was called the Pragmatic Sanction. Charles VI also proclaimed the indivisibility of Austrian territories.

Yet, hedged in by the austere protocol of the court of Vienna, he was unable to make those administrative reforms which could have been the basis of such unity. On the contrary, the concessions he made to other states in the Empire in order to persuade them to accept the

Chapel of the Rosary, Church of Santo Domingo (1596–1659) in Puebla. Built by Mexican Indians. *S. Harrison*

Vienna, still a fortified city in this eighteenth-century print, withstood its last siege by the Turks in 1683, when Austria stood for the last time in its historic role as bastion of Europe against Islam. *Larousse*

Maria Theresa, Empress 1740–80, left a legend of warm-hearted piety and love for her subjects behind her. Devoted to her House, she struggled to maintain intact the Habsburg domains. *British Museum*

Pragmatic Sanction only increased their privileges and independence and further weakened the Emperor's authority. In vain efforts to obtain greater cohesion he also persecuted his Protestant subjects. Austria suffered from a chronic complaint, lack of money. This obliged her to borrow and to accept subsidies. Thus, when it was most necessary to raise and maintain an army, Austrian foreign policy was most at the mercy of foreign creditors. Taxation, hampered by a complex and decrepit system, did not produce enough money to cover expenses, and Charles VI's great idea was to bring prosperity to his new acquisitions by expanding foreign trade. The speculative fever which had struck London and Paris now reached Central Europe. Charles instituted a Superior Council for Commerce, equipped the port of Trieste, created a Far Eastern Company and encouraged an Ostend Company, which was quickly sacrificed to threatened British interests.

In 1740, while still young, Charles VI died of a sudden illness, leaving the task of defending the unity of the Austrian dominion to his daughter. It was a responsibility which Maria Theresa, pious, a good wife and a good mother, faced with courage and tenacity. In founding his hopes on his beloved daughter Charles VI had for once not been deceived.

The Netherlands

Within the Habsburg dominions the affairs of the Austrian possessions in Italy and the Netherlands were directed in Vienna by the so-called Council of Spain (so named to make it plain that the Emperor considered the Bourbon Philip V a usurper). The Austrian Netherlands were cut off from other Habsburg territories and were encumbered by the Dutch-held barrier fortresses and by the closing of the River Scheldt, which artificially stifled their economic life. They were ruled by a governor, a prince of high rank like Eugene of Savoy or, from 1741, the Emperor's brother, Charles of Lorraine, who was an enlightened and generous administrator and soon became popular. The eleven provinces' traditional prerogatives included the right to

Canaletto's picture of St Mark's square, Venice. By his day the Most Serene republic was the decayed preserve of a narrow, hereditary oligarchy. The city was also the centre of European pleasure and distraction. *Mansell*

146

elect councils and to authorise taxation, which limited the central power. Nevertheless, the Austrian desire to impose centralisation made itself felt, sometimes harshly, although it never made the Belgians regret the passing of the previous Spanish occupation. A revival of industry and craftsmanship was fostered by the fleeting renewal of foreign trade carried on by the short-lived Ostend Company, by the internal trade to which the construction of new highways gave impetus, and finally by a long peace.

Italy

In the Italian peninsula the Habsburgs had been awarded the former Spanish possessions, but Elisabeth Farnese's attempts to gain Italian territory were not altogether unsuccessful. Italian principalities were used simply as small change in ephemeral bargains, and were sold, exchanged and passed from hand to hand without the slightest consideration for the wishes or interests of their inhabitants. In Tuscany and in Milan, which remained in their possession, the Habsburgs began to introduce a few modest reforms. After a period of Austrian domination, Parma and the Two Sicilies fell to the Bourbons.

Italy remained, as it was said, ' a geographical expression ': Austria, Spain and France strove for influence in a peninsula comprising many tiny states, of which the most important from the international point of view was the Kingdom of Sardinia. The House of Savoy, 'in the person of Victor Amadeus II, reigned on both sides of the Alps, in Savoy and in Piedmont. Since the Treaty of Utrecht Victor Amadeus also reigned over Sicily, which entitled him to be called King even though in 1720 he exchanged Sicily for Sardinia. In 1748 Novara was added to the King of Sardinia's holdings on the mainland. Thus in the eighteenth century the House of Savoy had already begun a gradual unification of Italy, ultimately achieved through sound financial organisation and a superb army. They were the same instruments which Prussia was employing, and, similarly, led in the long run to hegemony.

In the north the maritime republics of Genoa and Venice were also independent. In the past, they owed their wealth to Mediterranean trade, but their economic importance had declined (to the benefit of Leghorn and Trieste). Genoa turned for aid sometimes to France, sometimes to Great Britain. Venice was an artistic centre of the first importance, both for painting and for the theatre. Canaletto and especially Tiepolo carried baroque art to its greatest heights and worked as far afield as Warsaw, London, Würzburg and Madrid. The renown of the playwright Goldoni had spread to France, where he was invited by Louis XV.

In the centre of the peninsula the Papal States, the temporal domain of the Holy See, might have been expected to remain aloof from the stresses of international politics. In practice, they could do so less and less as the century went on.

The fragmentation of Italy hampered its economic development; but thanks to the persistence of its artistic and humanist traditions the peninsula remained a cultural centre where palaces of great beauty could be admired, skilful painters commissioned and where music was still a flourishing art. Scarlatti and Vivaldi were followed by Sammartini, who gave the sonata its classical form, while Pergolesi rendered similar service to *Opera Buffa*.

Denmark

Denmark, of which Norway still formed a part, derived its importance from its key position between the Baltic and the North Sea. Its ships undertook long voyages not only to Africa and in the Indian Ocean, but to Greenland and Iceland, which were possessions of the Danish Crown. Trading companies were founded on the model of the British and French companies, but lack of capital made their success short-lived. Unable to compete with Britain, Denmark preferred to court a British alliance and accept British subsidies. Like the United Provinces and Portugal, Denmark was more or less a British client. The Danish sovereigns Frederick IV (1699–1730), Christian VI (1730–46) and Frederick V all sought peace and fostered economic expansion. But this benefited Denmark and not Norway, which seethed with discontent.

Sweden

The power of Sweden had been dissipated by the ambitions of Charles XII, whose far-ranging military campaigns had decimated the male population and irreparably damaged the kingdom's treasury. Charles's victories over Danes, Russians and Poles were blotted out when his disastrous defeat at Poltava forced him to withdraw to Turkey, where he passed five years under the protection of the Sultan. In 1711 he persuaded the Turks to attack Russia, but, learning that Peter the Great was preparing an offensive against Swedish Pomerania, he returned to hurl himself vainly into the fray at Stralsund. Finally, in 1718, while disputing possession of Norway with the Danes, he was shot in the trenches before Fredriksten.

The crown of Sweden was elective, and this was a cause of weakness and disorder. Charles XII's sister, Ulrica Leonora, ascended the throne only after having agreed to the conditions laid down by the Diet. When she decided to resign her authority to her husband, Frederick of Hesse, further concessions had to be made. Rival factions openly accepted bribes from foreign agents: the ' Caps ' were paid by Russia and England, while the ' Hats ' received money from France. In 1738 the French Ambassador helped the ' Hats ' to overthrow Arvid Horn, who since 1720 had governed with the support of the ' Caps ' and had undertaken to restore the country's prosperity. Industry was developed as well as large-scale commerce; joint-stock companies were founded. Sweden not only exported the high-grade iron ore for which she was famous, but also began to process it herself. In spite of a deplorable political system the country slowly recovered from the ruin Charles XII had left behind. But on the death of Ulrica Leonora in 1744 civil war broke out and in 1751 Russia imposed on Sweden her own candidate for the throne, Adolphus Frederick of Holstein.

Poland before the partition

The Polish crown, like the Swedish, was elective. In Poland, too, there was a Diet, a senate, an oligarchy of nobles — the magnates — and factions who relied on foreign aid. Owing to the right of the ' free veto ' the country was even harder to govern than Sweden. In addition Poland was a mosaic not only of different peoples — Poles, Lithuanians, Russians, Germans — but also of conflicting religions. The Catholic majority was violently opposed to the Protestant and Orthodox minorities, to say nothing of the Jews, who monopolised trade. Finally the Saxon kings were foreigners who did not even live in Poland, and were more concerned with their German duchy than with their huge and anarchic kingdom.

By its geographical position, in contact with the great powers of Nordic, Eastern and Central Europe, Poland was bound to be a frequent bone of contention. Thus the victories of Charles XII provisionally gave the throne to Stanislas Leszcyński, a young noble who symbolised the spirit of patriotism and national resurgence until in 1707 Peter the Great reinstalled the Saxon Augustus III on the throne. Augustus attempted to establish a hereditary and absolute monarchy, but the magnates had recourse to their traditional procedure: they united against the King in the Confederation of Tarnograd. With Russian arbitration anarchy was successfully restored. Polish decadence grew more apparent while the country stagnated as a semi-protectorate of Russia. France, her traditional ally, by striving to defend Polish 'liberties' merely gave rise to further confusion.

Russia under Peter the Great

At the beginning of his reign Peter I, violating Russia's traditional isolationism, had undertaken an extended tour of Europe. With his brutality and astounding vitality, Peter made light of the prejudices of old Russia. His greatest stroke was to build himself a new capital, St Petersburg, at the entrance to the Baltic, the sea to which he himself had won access. Then he applied himself to a series of drastic reforms, more as circumstances suggested than according to a systematic plan; for his driving ambition was to enlarge his empire, and it was in seeking ways to achieve this that he upset and profoundly altered the institutions, social structure and economy of Russia. He was a close student of the Western world and he profited by what he learned there. The old and outworn *duma*, or council of boyars, was replaced in 1711 by a Senate whose members were appointed by Peter. It was entrusted with virtually full governmental powers during his frequent absences and controlled the administration of finance, the judiciary and the provincial governors. The eight new 'colleges' which he created transformed the old haphazard Muscovite bureaucracy. They were intended to simplify the administration and supersede the maze of departments, thirty or forty in number, which were hidebound, enmeshed in formulae and corrupt. Though these sweeping reforms did not always much disturb the local authorities, they nevertheless shook the traditions of Russia.

Then, since his policy of imperialism was costly, Peter proceeded to renovate the tax system. The yield was improved, but after his second trip abroad, during which he spent a month in Paris in 1717, he grasped the further necessity of developing trade and industry. He stimulated private enterprise and founded factories; but Tsarist autocracy did not mix well with capitalism, and the results were disappointing. Peter succeeded, however, in enlarging the army and building a fleet. In order to associate the nobility with his work he forced them into military service and in 1722 created the 'table of ranks', by which a man's status was determined by the position he occupied on the ladder of State service, military or civilian. Birth, money

Catherine I, Tsaritsa 1725–27, was put on the throne by the royal guards at the death of her husband Peter the Great. She was intelligent and vigorous, but unable to use the royal power effectively because of the circumstances of her accession. *Giraudon*

Once a great commercial city, Novgorod kept in the eighteenth century little except the monuments of its past importance in its wealth of churches and belfries. The building of St Petersburg completed its eclipse.

and favouritism did not thereby cease to count, but a door had been opened to men of lower rank to enter the officer, and hence, the serf-owning, hereditary class. This class in fact was Peter's chief concern; the serfs remained beasts of burden to be exploited. Towards the clergy he was hostile. He refused to appoint a new Patriarch on the death of the old one and, to manage Church affairs, instituted a Synod, which he kept firmly under his thumb.

The reforms of Peter the Great, often harshly enforced, further strengthened the Tsarist autocracy. Throughout his reign insurrections and rebellions continued. In 1707 and 1708 he was obliged to crush Cossack revolts. The Old Believers, or *raskolniks*, had not admitted defeat; the nobles themselves — at least those of the ancient nobility — formed plots and placed hope in Peter's son and heir the Tsarevich Alexis. In 1718 Peter replied by torturing Alexis and putting him to death. In order to avoid a

Riga was founded in the middle ages as a centre for German missionary activity in the East and remained a German cultural outpost. This limewood statue of an eighteenth-century bishop comes from the city. *Marburg*

Riga in Livonia (Latvia) was an important port in the eighteenth century. Russia acquired it in 1721, after the Great Northern War, along with Livonia, Estonia and other territories. Its German aristocracy and merchant class were favoured by the Tsar.

scramble for the throne, he announced that he would himself appoint his successor. In 1725 he died without having done so, and a period of more than fifteen troubled years ensued — though the imprint which Peter the Great had left on Russia was not effaced.

The boyars attempted to regain their influence and the Tsaritsas who occupied the throne often left royal power to their favourites. In 1727 after the brief reign of Catherine I, Peter the Great's widow, his grandson Peter II came to the throne at the age of twelve. Peter II's death three years later was the signal for dynastic strife, which ended on the victory of Anna Ivanovna, a niece of Peter the Great. Anna was a cruel and strange woman during whose reign three Germans exercised a virtual dictatorship: Biron, her favourite; Ostermann, who directed foreign policy; and Münnich, who commanded the army. Before she died in 1740 Anna had designated as her

successor her grand-nephew Ivan VI. But German domination of the Government exasperated public opinion. Elizabeth, Peter the Great's daughter, posing as champion of Russian traditions, seized the throne. She revived certain of her father's reforms — the Senate and the Colleges, which had been abolished — but she was indolent and left the affairs of State to the care of favourites. She was not hostile to French influence, especially cultural influence, and Russia was thus a little less shut off from Western enlightenment. The work of Peter the Great was safeguarded and that of Catherine the Great prepared.

With her eyes on the West, Russia had little time to spare for the distant East, where the immensities of Siberia remained almost completely unpeopled save for a few indigenous tribes. None the less Russian sovereigns began to show some interest in the long neglected Asian annex. They organised expeditions to make surveys and scientific observations. At sea, Bering showed in 1728 that Asia was not connected with North America and made a report on the eastern Asian coast. From 1733 to 1743 Anna Ivanovna had the coastal regions of the Arctic explored. These voyages of reconnaissance were the preliminaries to the colonisation of Siberia.

ALLIANCES, WARS AND PEACE

The northern peace

During the first years of the eighteenth century, while the West was engaged in the war of the Spanish Succession, Charles XII had, as we have seen, attempted to establish Swedish hegemony on the plains of northern and eastern Europe. The victory of the Russians renewed the coalition of Russia, Saxony and Denmark against Charles. Peter the Great pursued his advantage by pushing forward along the Baltic coast, and was even preparing to invade Sweden itself when Britain, alarmed by this threat to the balance of European power and more especially to her own Baltic trade, intervened to shatter the ambitions of the Russian conqueror. During a visit to Paris Peter tried in vain to rally the French Regent to his cause. France 149 remained loyal to the British alliance.

The death of Charles XII did not immediately restore general peace in the north. In 1720 Sweden came to terms first with Russia's allies and by the agreements of Stockholm almost completely withdrew from Germany. Hanover received Bremen and Verden, purchased from Denmark as early as 1715, while Prussia obtained Stettin and the greater part of western Pomerania, thus acquiring new ports on the Baltic. But the principal heir to the former Swedish provinces was Peter the Great himself who, having first consolidated his conquests, was in 1721 the last to make peace. By the Treaty of Nystadt he retained possession of Livonia, Esthonia and Ingria. Only Finland escaped his grasp. The empire of the Tsars had drawn nearer to the West. It gained a wider seaboard and hence greater access to trade with the outside world. Its contact with Western methods and diplomacy became closer. Russia was from this time to play an increasingly important part in international affairs.

After the brief Russo-Turkish hostilities of 1711 had been terminated by the Peace of Adrianople (1713), Turkey again went to war, this time against Venice, whose Mediterranean trade conflicted with the interests of the Greek subjects of the Sultan. The victorious Turks occupied Morea, which was Venetian territory, and at the beginning of 1716 laid siege to Corfu. At this moment the Emperor intervened, offering his alliance to Venice. Prince Eugene defeated the Ottoman army and in 1717 captured Belgrade; his great victory over the Infidel was celebrated by the entire Christian world. Though by the Treaty of Passarowitz in 1718 Turkey retained Morea, Austria made extensive territorial gains: a slice of Wallachia and part of Serbia, including Belgrade and the Banat of Temeşvár. Prince Eugene's success had opened for Austria the prospect of a policy of Danubian expansion; but Italy still exercised a more powerful attraction over Charles VI.

The Anglo-French alliance

By the settlement of 1713–15 Britain took part in continental struggles in order to preserve the peace, even if she often did this by subsidising continental allies. She was also especially involved in the affairs of Hanover. The peace treaties had not settled every problem: the Bourbons of France and Spain renounced the ultimate union of the respective crowns with reluctance, but neither Philip V nor Charles VI was resigned to the partition of the Emperor Charles V's vast domains. The issues were confused and complicated by countless intrigues. The eighteenth century was above all the epoch of secret diplomacy whose hidden manoeuvres, contradictory policies, and sudden and surprising reversals did not often achieve very much. Such techniques were less and less suited to negotiations which had to deal not only with the classic disputes of dynastic ambitions — wars of succession flourished in the eighteenth century — but also with the economic rivalry born of maritime and colonial trade.

In 1715 the newly established House of Hanover in Great Britain and the Regency in France both needed peace to consolidate their precarious tenure of power. Dubois and Stanhope co-operated to defeat the intrigues of the Spanish Queen, Elisabeth Farnese, Philip V's second wife, which were already threatening to upset the arrangements made at Utrecht. Alberoni, her minister, planned a war in Italy with the object of gaining principalities for Elisabeth's two sons. Stanhope and Dubois joined with the United Provinces in the Triple Alliance (1717) to meet this threat. The basis of the alliance was the mutual interest of the British and French Governments in their own dynastic stability and certain commercial agreements which were favourable to Britain and the United Provinces.

The Triple Alliance was seriously tested almost at once, in May 1717, when the Emperor Charles VI ordered the arrest in Milan of the Spanish Inquisitor-General, an insult to Spain which led to a declaration of war by Philip V. Alberoni sent a force to seize Sardinia and intrigued with Charles XII of Sweden (whom he urged to invade Norway), with the Stuarts, and with Turkey. In France Spanish agents hatched a plot against the House of Orleans, which was soon discovered. Britain now intervened and Charles VI, fully occupied with the Turkish war, and realising that his interests lay with the maritime powers and France, himself joined the Triple Alliance, which thus became Quadruple by the treaty of August 1718. He renounced his claim to the Spanish throne and agreed to exchange Sardinia for Sicily, where he dreamed of establishing a Habsburg kingdom in the south of Italy. Philip V stubbornly continued the struggle. Though the two states were not at war, a British fleet in the Mediterranean under Admiral Byng destroyed the Spanish fleet off Cape Passaro. This left the Spanish army in Sicily isolated. Then in 1718 Great Britain and France declared war on Spain and Philip V had soon to sue for peace. At the end of 1719 he dismissed Alberoni and in January 1720 by the Treaty of London agreed to join the Quadruple Alliance. The war was over. It was the time of the South Sea Bubble and, in France, of Law's financial experiments: speculation was vastly more interesting than warfare. Dubois, depending less on British support, considered the possibility of reviving Franco-Spanish friendship and in March 1721 the Bourbons of France and Spain were reconciled by the betrothal of the Spanish Infanta (then five years old) to Louis XV.

But soon afterwards a new threat to peace arose. In 1722 the Emperor Charles VI, deciding that the Austrian Netherlands should share in the profits of international trade, gave his blessing to an Ostend Company, modelled upon the great colonial Companies. London and Amsterdam bitterly resented such competition. At the same time the Emperor was eagerly engaged in seeking recognition for his Pragmatic Sanction (*see* p. 145) even at the price of broad concessions. In France the Duke of Bourbon had arranged Louis XV's marriage to Marie Leszcynska and sent the Spanish Infanta back to Madrid. Philip V, embittered by the affront, lent an ear to the projects of a new adventurer, Ripperda, a Dutchman at the Spanish court, who had conceived the highly original idea of an alliance between Spain and Austria. Charles VI, for his part, was irked by the opposition to the Ostend Company. The astonishing reconciliation between him and Philip V took place in April 1725: it was agreed that Spain should recognise the Pragmatic Sanction and the Ostend Company, while Don Carlos — son of Philip V and Elisabeth Farnese — was promised Parma. In September Britain retorted by signing a treaty with France and Prussia. War seemed imminent after this new Triple Alliance had been formed, although no one really wanted to fight. Walpole in England and Fleury in France were able to control the belligerence of their ministers Townsend and

Chauvelin. Fleury persuaded the Spanish not to attack Gibraltar and arranged a congress at Soissons with the object of reaching a general settlement. Charles VI, tempted by a guarantee that the Pragmatic Sanction would be respected, agreed to suspend the activities of the Ostend Company. Philip V, though at first unwilling to commit himself, ended by agreeing to negotiate with Britain, France and the United Provinces; in 1729 at Seville he granted them commercial privileges in the Spanish colonies in exchange for the promise that his son Don Carlos would receive Parma, Piacenza and Tuscany. Finally all the signatories agreed to suppress the Ostend Company. The Austro-Spanish alliance had proved harmless and Britain had got what she wanted. Only France had cause to be disappointed, because Charles VI had been offended by her refusal to recognise the Pragmatic Sanction. In March 1731 the Emperor concluded a treaty with Britain which ratified the decisions reached in Seville. A little later Spain, too, accepted the settlement and before the end of the year Don Carlos was Duke of Parma.

The Polish succession

Various plans had been made for the Polish succession even before the King of Poland's death — one of which, made by Augustus II himself, consisted of a division of the kingdom among the neighbours. When he died (1 February 1733), Austria and Russia agreed to support Augustus's son. France and the Polish nationalists, on the other hand, still supported Stanislas Leszcynski, who in exile had become Louis XV's father-in-law. Stanislas was elected King by a large majority, whereupon the Austrians and the Russians invaded the country to install Augustus III on the throne. This was the war which Fleury had feared and for which Chauvelin, violently anti-Austrian, had clamoured. Louis XV had, in all decency, to defend his father-in-law, and the struggle with Austria broke out again. Fleury had made certain that France was not without allies: there was Spain, still on the alert in Italy; there was Sardinia, very eager to acquire the Duchy of Milan; and there was Bavaria. The aged minister nevertheless temporised as long as he could and military operations were accompanied by active diplomacy.

In distant Poland the principal object was to save face, and honour was satisfied by the heroic death of the Count of Plelo at the head of a small French contingent; Augustus III then took possession of the country. But in the west Austria was attacked on several fronts in 1734. Her ally Lorraine, whose Duke, Francis, had recently married the Emperor's daughter Maria Theresa, was occupied without difficulty, and French troops took the offensive on the Rhine. In Italy the Austrians were defeated and Milan conquered; but instead of marching on Vienna the victorious armies marked time. In 1735 Fleury began negotiations. By October France and Austria had concluded the preliminaries of the so-called Third Treaty of Vienna, which was later accepted by the remaining belligerents. Negotiations for peace were dragged out because Charles VI, who was in the meantime waging war on the Turks, hoped in this way to make better terms. When, in 1738, the Treaty of Vienna was finally ratified it made notable alterations in the map of Italy. Francis, Duke of Lorraine, had been given Tuscany, Parma and Piacenza. The Duchy of Lorraine was awarded to Stanislas Leszcynski, who retained

his title of King, but renounced the throne of Poland. Since Stanislas's heirs were the children of his daughter, the French Queen, this meant that at his death Lorraine would revert to the French royal house. Don Carlos received the Two Sicilies, while the House of Savoy was given Novara and Montferrat. Finally, France recognised the Pragmatic Sanction. The crisis which in origin had been Polish thus ended in an exchange of crowns and territories which chiefly affected Italy.

The Turkish war

After the acceptance of the Pragmatic Sanction by almost all Europe Charles VI would willingly have remained at peace. Since 1726, however, he had been allied to Russia. In 1735, while the West had been at war, the Tsaritsa Elizabeth had ordered the capture of Azov, a Turkish town. Charles VI, in his turn, invaded Wallachia and Serbia. The Turks, though taken by surprise, recovered swiftly. Mehmet Pasha re-organised the army; Villeneuve, the French Ambassador, and the Comte de Bonneval, a French adventurer who had embraced Islam, advised the Sultan. The Austro-Russian offensive was halted and the Turks, counter-attacking, laid siege to Belgrade. Negotiations took place under the mediation of Villeneuve and in 1739, by the Treaty of Belgrade, the Habsburgs relinquished Belgrade itself together with most of the territory acquired at Passarowitz. The Russians retained Azov only on condition that its fortifications were destroyed, and Russian troops were to withdraw from the Crimea and Moldavia. The French were rewarded for the part they had played

Frederick II (1712–86) just after his accession to the throne. Frederick the Great's system of absolutism, in which the king was the first servant of the state, laid the foundation for Prussia's greatness and was imitated all over Europe.

Anna Amalia, widow of Ernest Augustus II of Saxe-Weimar, acted as regent for her son until he assumed the government in 1775. Under him, Saxe-Weimar was the first German State to be granted a liberal constitution. *Marburg*

Drying and salting cod from the Newfoundland banks. Dried fish sustained one of the great trades of the eighteenth century, and disputes over the fisheries caused quarrels between France and England well into the nineteenth century.

in the Turkish victory by the grant of commercial privileges in the Levant. In 1740 French influence in the Near East was further strengthened by the *Capitulations* which the Sultan signed in favour of Louis XV and his Christian subjects. Thus at Belgrade and at Vienna Fleury had obtained two striking diplomatic triumphs.

The Austrian succession

France had played the role of arbitrator on the continent, and in 1740 she desired peace. Hostilities, however, broke out again both in Europe and in the colonies. In the West Indies Britain and Spain had already come to blows towards the end of 1739. In May 1740 Frederick William of Prussia died, and five months later, in October, his death was followed by that of the Emperor, Charles VI. The accession of a young woman of twenty-three to the throne of the Habsburgs unleashed a host of claimants who, furnished with the flimsiest of pretexts, illustrated the bad faith and insincerity of those who had agreed to that Pragmatic Sanction which had been the prime object of Charles VI's policy and the obsession of his reign. The husbands of Maria Theresa's two cousins, the Electors of Bavaria and Saxony, the King of Sardinia, the King of Prussia — all scrambled greedily to seize what they could of her rich inheritance. The most cynical and able of them made his entry into history by an act of blatant aggression: Frederick II, coveting Silesia, threw himself on it without warning and, profiting by this surprise attack, beat the Austrians at Mollwitz. The audacity of his blow shook all Europe. Meanwhile Charles Albert of Bavaria offered himself as a candidate for the Imperial throne. Fleury would have preferred to remain neutral, but, over-ridden by the anti-Austrian party, he declared himself for Charles Albert and reluctantly decided to intervene in German affairs. By the Treaty of Nymphenburg in 1741 he ensured the alliance of Spain, Prussia, Sardinia, Saxony and Bavaria. French armies invaded Germany. Maria Theresa, assailed on all sides, faced her enemies. She rallied her subjects at the cost of granting certain political concessions and, on British advice, bought off her most dangerous adversary by signing an armistice with Frederick II in which she yielded Lower Silesia. But Prague, besieged by the French, capitulated in November 1741, and in January 1742 the Bavarian candidate was elected Emperor as Charles VII.

Britain entered the fray after the fall of the peace-loving Walpole. King George II himself took the field in command of the armies which fought to defend the Pragmatic Sanction. Frederick broke the armistice he had signed and demanded the whole of Silesia, which with a bitter heart Maria Theresa abandoned to him in the Treaty of Breslau in July 1742. Thanks to British subsidies, however, the position of Austria had improved by the end of the year. Prague was retaken and the French forced to retreat. In 1743 George II, the last British monarch to command his army in the field, defeated the French at Dettingen. The Emperor Charles VII now declared himself neutral, while in September Walpole's successor, Carteret, formed a powerful anti-French coalition at Worms. In this position, France had no resource but Spain. The two countries signed the so-called Bourbon 'Family Compact' and Spain officially declared war on Britain and Austria. Louis XV in person led an offensive against the Netherlands but it was the generalship of Marshal Saxe which stabilised the situation by the end of 1744. In Britain the warlike Carteret had been excluded from power. Charles VII died in January 1745 and his son hastened to make terms with Maria Theresa at Füssen, while Maria Theresa's husband, Francis of Lorraine, received the Imperial crown. France continued to fight without particularly knowing why, and by the following year, 1746, everyone was heartily sick of the war. Great Britain regretted the subsidies she paid in Germany, and the Scottish rising of 1745 in support of the Young Pretender had alarmed the entire island. Though a French attack on Piedmont failed to detach Sardinia from the British alliance, Marshal Saxe continued to be successful in the Netherlands and occupied Brussels. Negotiations were opened at Breda,

Both France and England sought Indian allies in their North American struggles. The Cherokee, two of whom are shown, lived in the southern Alleghenies until they removed in 1838 to Oklahoma.

upset by further French victories, and then resumed in haste at Aix-la-Chapelle in 1747. Louis XV said he would be satisfied with the reciprocal restitution of all colonial conquests. It was again in Italy that the changes in the map took place; the House of Savoy acquired part of the Milanese and Don Philip, the second son of Elisabeth Farnese and son-in-law of Louis XV, became Duke of Parma and Piacenza. Many campaigns had been fought for these meagre results. Nor, although Italy had been stabilised at last for fifty years, had the Peace of Aix-la-Chapelle eradicated the causes of future conflict: Maria Theresa was not resigned to the loss of Silesia.

THE EUROPEAN COLONIES

Canada and Louisiana

Portugal, Spain and the United Provinces were still maritime powers of consequence, but colonial rivalry was more and more confined to Britain and France. Throughout the world, in the West Indies as in the East Indies, the British and the French were neighbours. In North America the British colonies on the Atlantic coast were hemmed in by Louisiana to the west and by Canada to the north. The huge area of French Canada had already been eaten into by the Treaty of Utrecht and almost the entire population of New France — in 1717, about 19,000 — was concentrated in the St Lawrence valley. Canada lived in isolation, selling little to the motherland and, thanks to the activity of smugglers, buying even less. New France was left to defend itself against the British and against the Indians, some of whom, like the Iroquois, were British allies. To the south of the Great Lakes the vast Illinois territory contained only a few trading posts and missionary settlements. As for Louisiana, it remained almost unpeopled: in the middle of the century it contained, at the most, some 2,500 French inhabitants. At the mouth of the Mississippi, New Orleans — so named in honour of Philip of Orleans, the Regent — was founded in 1718.

The thirteen British colonies

With the creation of a North and a South Carolina and the foundation of Georgia in 1732 the British colonies had become thirteen in number. In contrast with Canada they continued throughout the eighteenth century to be swelled by European immigrants. Despite the efforts of London they were not all Crown colonies. In the middle of the century three of them still had proprietors and two had charters; but almost everywhere an assembly represented the interests of the colonists and such assemblies, by their right to approve the budget, were able to exert pressure on the governors representing the royal authority. In spite of differences of origin and religious faith, and economic and social divergencies between the southern colonies, with their great plantations worked by Negroes, and the Puritan northern colonies, all the British settlers felt an increasing sense of solidarity in face of the French, their common enemy, and also before the problems posed by their trade relations with Great Britain. Agriculture and trade were officially the only means of livelihood permitted, and the colonies were obliged to buy from and to sell to the mother country only. New England in fact carried on a thriving trade with the West Indies; when, in 1733, Parliament passed a law placing a prohibitive tariff on the import of molasses, only non-enforcement made it tolerable. In 1750 another law was passed forbidding the colonies to smelt or work iron. The colonists felt irritated, but for many years such grievances were suppressed by the struggle with Canada. Causes for this struggle were not lacking: the frontiers in the region of the Great Lakes and Nova Scotia were ill-defined, and bitter rivalry existed among trappers and fur traders. British and French settlers alike had clients among the various Indian tribes, and under cover of Indian warfare the two nations were often at grips even when their Governments were officially allied.

In 1744 war broke out again. Louisbourg, which the French had fortified on the rocky island of Cape Breton at the entrance to the Gulf of St Lawrence, was captured by New Englanders but, in spite of their protests, was restored to France by the Treaty of Aix-la-Chapelle. The same treaty set up a mixed commission to delineate the frontiers in Nova Scotia and in the Ohio valley, but its work settled nothing. Meanwhile French and British vied with each other in building forts on the shifting frontier.

The West Indies

The West Indies provided the classic example of colonial exploitation. Their soil was rich and yielded the colonial goods which were most prized in Europe: sugar, rum, tobacco and coffee. West Indian traffic was highly organised and complex. Slave-traders unloaded the Negro labour needed in the colonies and sailed off again with the cargoes of tropical produce that made the fortunes of merchants in such European ports as Liverpool, London, Amsterdam, Nantes and Bordeaux. In addition, illegal traffic with the Spanish colonies drained into the West Indies Spanish gold, which thus returned to northern Europe. The governors who represented the sovereign clashed with the local assemblies of the planters, who were becoming increasingly rich and powerful. In such cases the royal authority normally chose compromise. 153

Caribbean Indians make overtures to French settlers. Two of their heavy canoes are depicted, probably inaccurately, since such *piraguas* were usually dug-outs and of narrow beam.

The population balance was altering and the Creole peasantry was progressively swamped by the mass of imported Negroes. Immense plantations were formed in which local food crops were abandoned in favour of intensive cultivation of export crops.

The continual expansion of production and trade in export crops — especially sugar — exacerbated Anglo-French rivalry. France seemed to possess an initial advantage: British West Indian sugar was more costly to produce than that grown on the French islands, where the land was better cultivated and had not been exploited for as many years. British planters took alarm at the French trade in molasses with Boston. On several occasions the British tried to occupy certain islands which still remained in the hands of neutral buccaneers — Tobago, St Vincent, St Lucia, Santo Domingo — but the French succeeded in frustrating their attempts although they could not prevent losses of ships and cargoes.

The Anglo-Spanish war

The British West Indies were a centre of contraband trade and a great slave market which furnished Negro labour for all America. Spain, meanwhile, was incapable of supplying her vast dominions with the products they required, or even of assuring the transport of such products. In 1713 the *asiento* had given to Great Britain the right to furnish African slaves to the Spanish dominions and the exclusive privilege of sending a single merchantman once a year to a Spanish colonial port. But smuggling had gone far beyond this to become a national industry, which was encouraged by British authorities. In France smuggling was officially forbidden, but in practice the merchants of both countries competed for the prizes of illicit trade. The international exchange of goods increased during the eighteenth century and a large part of it was illegal.

To parry the danger of British commercial encroachment, Spain resorted to acts of repression and attempted to enlarge her fleet. She was, however, unable to shake British naval supremacy. Clashes between Spaniards and Englishmen became more frequent on the ill-defined frontier between Florida and Georgia and on the coast of Honduras, where the British exploited the rare woods supplied by the tropical forests. The Spanish excise officials became increasingly troublesome while the British seized Spanish galleons laden with gold. Madrid insisted on the right to search British ships sailing the Spanish Main. In March 1738 a certain Captain Jenkins denounced before the House of Commons the indignity he had suffered at Spanish hands and brandished a casket which was alleged to contain his own ear, lopped off by a Spaniard. An attempt to negotiate differences failed: in May 1739 Spain denounced the *asiento*. Bowing to the wave of public indignation, Walpole reluctantly declared war. Admiral Vernon sacked Porto Bello, an important trading post which the Spanish had fortified in the Panama isthmus, while Admiral Anson, dispatched to the Pacific, pillaged ports and captured the 'Manila galleon' which traded between Acapulco and the Philippines. The marine and colonial struggle which was thus launched was to last for twenty-four years.

An indigo factory in the French West Indies. Until the discovery in the nineteenth century of fast synthetic dyes, vegetables dyes were used in enormous quantities. Indigo was one of the most important colonial products.

Spanish America

Rigidly controlled from Spain, the colonies of Latin America would have been stifled but for the activities of the smugglers. Madrid maintained a heavy and autocratic hand on colonial affairs, and as late as 1778 it was their policy to reserve colonial traffic not even for Spaniards alone, but solely for Castilians. Fortunately the Spanish Crown lacked the machinery to enforce its policy. Thanks to contraband trade the economy of the colonies, based on agriculture, stock-rearing and mining, progressed constantly during the course of the century. From Mexico, or New Spain, missionaries explored Arizona and Texas, which were then settled by Spaniards. Many thousands of colonists from Spain itself and from the Canary Islands occupied the new territories. In New Mexico maize, wheat and vines were planted, and livestock was raised in the neighbourhood of the mines, which required beasts of burden. Mexico City was linked to the sea by newly constructed roads, along which towns like Telapa and Durango sprang up. In South America the Viceroyalty of New Granada was created, corresponding roughly to modern Venezuela, Colombia and Ecuador. This new province flourished, and its mines, developed later, increased its importance. Farther south, from Uruguay to the Andes, Jesuit missionaries in the Chaco had established a genuinely theocratic state in which their object was to protect the natives from the corrupting influence of European colonists. Their situation was not without difficulties, particularly since the British had established inter-continental routes for their contraband trade and wished to revive the route which passed through the Chaco. The alternative road, farther south, was still largely under Spanish control, although it passed through the territory of Sacramento on the Rio de la Plata, which was occupied by Portugal. Hostilities between Spain and Portugal were thus added to the Anglo-Spanish conflict.

The Spanish Crown, hoping to give fresh life to its American possessions, encouraged the creation of the Guipuzcoa Company and re-organised the Council of the Indies. Yet the living standards of the majority of the colonial population remained extremely low. Little by little there emerged a class of mixed blood which longed for more liberty and resented the contempt in which they were held by the colonist of pure European stock. It was these people who, in Peru in 1741 and in Mexico in 1742, first attempted to revolt against the authorities: the attempts were, however, rapidly suppressed.

Brazil

In Brazil the vast Amazon basin remained impenetrable and unexplored. But, at the beginning of the eighteenth century, important gold and diamond deposits were discovered in the Brazilian province which, for this reason, took the name Minas Gerais, or general mines. Agriculture and cattle-raising developed around the mines and spread to the interior. African slaves were introduced in great numbers to work the land. Unlike Spain, Portugal gave every facility to British merchants and slave-traders. The south of Brazil slowly became of greater importance than the north, and in 1763 Rio de Janeiro replaced Bahia as capital of the country.

In 1720 a Viceroy was appointed, but the important

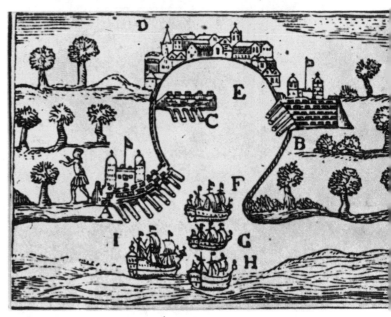

In 1739 Admiral Vernon sacked Porto Bello and destroyed its fortifications. This was a spectacular opening to a dull war.
Radio Times Hulton Picture Library

administrators remained the Captains-General, named by the King. In theory Brazil existed purely for the benefit of Portugal, but in practice the application of this principle was much less rigidly enforced than in the Spanish colonies. The colonial councils of Lisbon had less authority than those of Madrid, and more power was given to local municipal assemblies. The spirit of revolt was lacking because Brazil had in reality already a certain autonomy. Furthermore, white settlers, half-breeds and Negroes mingled more freely. The chief obstacle to the development of Brazil seemed to be less a restrictive colonial policy than the indolence and scarcity of the population.

The slave trade

Western Africa, the great reservoir of slaves, became more and more stripped of population as the prosperity of the American colonies increased and the demand for labour grew. The Arabs, too, were active slavers and in Marrakesh, Tripoli and Zanzibar their traffic in Negroes continued. But the ravages caused by the European powers were much more systematic. European trading posts were spread along more than two thousand miles of the West African coast. In these posts Companies with monopolies erected forts, especially on the Gold Coast, which furnished slaves of the highest quality. Those of the Benin coast were considered to be of lower grade. The major part of the trade was carried on by the British and the French, who in this, too, were competitors. Agents of the Companies parleyed with tribal chiefs or kings who, enticed by worthless trinkets and the novel European products they were offered, would drive the prisoners they had captured to the coast for sale. To pay for further imports more exports were required, and the tribes rivalled each other in providing prisoners. In the process they decimated each other. The consequences for Africa were disastrous: the slave trade impoverished the continent and destroyed the natural evolution of Negro African civilisation. For the New

The East India Company's 'factory' at Fort St George, Madras. Captured by the French in 1746, it was restored to the Company in 1748. Although besieged again (1788–9) it thereafter remained in British hands while the Peace of Paris (1763) assured British domination of India.

World it was to pose a grave social problem, that of integration and the absorption by other races of a mass of coloured workers, quickly acclimatised and rapidly growing. Towards the end of the century the intensification of the slave trade and its barbarity ultimately moved the public conscience. In England Wilberforce became the champion of the anti-slavery movement while in France a Society of the Friends of the Blacks was formed. Later Freetown, in Sierra Leone, was to become a refuge for former slaves.

The African ports of call

Along the sea route to the East Indies stretches of the African coast had already been occupied by the pioneers of the spice trade, the Portuguese having settled in Angola and Mozambique and the Dutch at the Cape of Good Hope. In the Portuguese colonies relations between the missionaries and the natives were sorely aggravated by the slave trade. The expulsion of the Jesuits in 1758 virtually put an end to their experiment in humane colonisation. The Portuguese had also been forced to abandon the coast of Zanzibar. At the southern extremity of Africa the Dutch, who had been joined by a certain number of French Huguenots, trekked inland from the Cape, and cleared the land, armed with a strict Puritanical faith and a firm contempt for the native Hottentots and Bushmen whom they drove before them. Towards the end of the century, however, the Dutch encountered a more dangerous and highly developed Negro race, the Kaffirs, who came from the north. Off the eastern coast of Africa the large island of Madagascar had especially attracted the French. An attempt at conquest by an adventurer named Beniovski was supported for a while by the French Government, but ended in failure. On the other hand the Mascarene Islands in the Indian Ocean — comprising Mauritius (then the Ile de France) and Réunion (then the Ile Bourbon) were to become, under the governorship of La Bourdonnais, a base for supplies and attack on the British. In 1764 the islands became French Crown possessions and were peopled and cultivated by white colonists.

The rival Companies in India

In the beginning the European trading posts on the Indian coast were primarily ports of call and warehouses for trade with the Far East. They had been founded because of the difficulty of entering and setting up establishments in China itself. A lively trade had always taken place in spices, but monetary transactions were equally profitable: in the Far East silver was rarer than in America and hence more precious. In Europe gold was fifteen times as valuable as silver, while in China it was only ten times as valuable. In consequence American silver was attracted to the Far East where it was traded for gold at an advantageous rate of exchange.

While the Dutch and Portuguese possessions scraped along as well as they could — the Portuguese were especially dedicated to missionary work — the trading posts of the British and French Companies were hives of activity. The British Company had its headquarters in London but was administered by its representatives in Bombay, Madras and Calcutta. The French Company, which had suffered certain ups and downs at the time of Law's financial experiments, was now supervised by royal commissioners and hence enjoyed less freedom of action than its rival. From 1730 its shareholders received fixed sums of interest instead of dividends, and this tended to sap the Company's initiative. Under the governorship of Lenoir in 1723–5 the concessions of Yanaon in Madras and of Mahé on the Malabar coast were added to the principal holdings of the French Company at Chandernagore and Pondicherry. Dumas, who was the real founder of French India, became Governor in 1735 and inaugurated a new form of colonisation; Dupleix, his successor from 1741 to 1754, adopted and developed it. Dumas conceived the idea of raising, arming and training a small force of natives, the Sepoys, and of interfering in the internal affairs of the Hindu states by offering them the services of these soldiers. He received in exchange various concessions advantageous to the Company, and even obtained from the Grand Mogul the title of 'Nabob' which gave him a position in the administrative hierarchy of the Mogul Empire. During this time the British Company pursued a prudent and purely commerical policy from which it derived sufficient profit to lend more money to the Government, and to increase its dividends.

The appointment of Dupleix to the post of governor occurred at the time when peaceful rivalry between France and Britain came to an end. Dupleix was enterprising and experienced in Indian affairs, but was a man of difficult temperament. At first he attempted to maintain the Company's neutrality in spite of the declaration of war; but in December 1744 the capture of a French ship unleashed hostilities. A call for help was made to La Bourdonnais in the Mascarene Islands. La Bourdonnais was a seaman and a remarkable warrior, though as difficult a character as Dupleix. With the aid of his squadron Madras fell in 1746. Dupleix, who wanted to tear down the town, and La Bourdonnais, who preferred to exact a stiff ransom for its restoration, wrangled acrimoniously. La Bourdonnais sailed back in a rage to the Ile de France (Mauritius). Dupleix remained in Madras, but without La Bourdonnais was unable to consider further conquests. Madras was restored to Britain in 1748 by the Treaty of Aix-la-Chapelle; but Dupleix's prestige in France remained immense.

CHAPTER TEN

ASIA AND AFRICA

THE DECLINE OF THE MOSLEM EMPIRES

The Ottoman Empire

By the eighteenth century, the Ottoman Empire, still sprawling over eastern Europe, Asia Minor and North Africa, no longer offered a serious threat to its neighbours. A small minority of Turks, appointed by the Sultan, occupied the chief administrative positions, commanded the troops and controlled finances. Strict centralisation was needed if these scattered officers were to be kept in hand. No such centralisation existed. In Constantinople the Sultan's idleness, palace intrigues, plots hatched in the harem, the meddling interference of the privileged military corps of Janissaries, even riots among the populace, hampered every attempt at reform; Grand Vizirs succeeded each other with bewildering rapidity, and removal from office frequently meant decapitation. Terror was still the rule at the Sublime Porte and it was by cruelty that officials, small and great, maintained a semblance of discipline.

The finances of the Empire were chaotic. Taxes were farmed out and a swarm of middlemen pocketed the greater part of what they collected. To outwit the corrupt Turkish officials the Sultans relied more on the Greeks, a minority race who played an increasing part in Ottoman affairs. Seamen and merchants by tradition, the Greeks, though Christians, had obtained a practical monopoly of the Empire's internal and external trade, thus making themselves indispensable. They adapted themselves so well to the situation that the Sultan chose Greeks rather than Turks to govern his Slav principalities where, invested with the title of *hospodar* — lord or master —they often behaved with more arrogance than the Turks themselves. Thanks to the Greeks the Ottoman Empire still had a share of international trade. At the beginning of the century the English of the Turkey Company were the main foreign influence, but after 1730 the French predominated, helped both by diplomacy and by the quality of their products.

The Sultan Mustafa II had been deposed in 1703; his successor and brother, Ahmad III, lasted until 1730, when he was replaced by Mahmud I (1730–57). Under these Sultans the Turks nursed their desire to efface the humiliation of the Treaty of Carlowitz. In pursuit of this aim, Turkey was more or less at war for forty years. The Turkish revenge came finally because of the force and energy of the Grand Vizir Mehmet Pasha, who obtained the Treaty of Belgrade of 1739. Internal disintegration, however, continued and the empire was little by little reduced to the defensive. Mustafa III, who came to the throne in 1757 (after Osman III's brief reign) doubtless intended well: he founded an academy on Western lines and had a few European books translated, but such whims were the extent of his reforms. Once again French advisers succeeded temporarily in instilling a little energy into the government at Constantinople by supporting the efforts of reforming Grand Vizirs. Mustafa III succeeded

Early eighteenth-century Turkish portrait of a young European gentleman. Though hostilities continued in Eastern Europe, French and English merchants were welcomed in the Ottoman Empire and had a growing political influence. *British Museum*

in putting down dangerous insurrections in Morea and in the Ionian Islands, but the spirit of revolt rapidly gained ground among the subject Christian populations. Mustafa's brother, Abdul Hamid I, succeeded him in 1773. He proved equally irresolute and another procession of short-lived Grand Vizirs began. Every attempt to reform the outworn system seemed doomed to failure. The conservatism of Islam remained obdurately opposed to Western methods and technical innovations. In spite of its rapidly evolving European neighbours, the Ottoman Empire stagnated and withdrew into its past.

Throughout the empire high officials, amassing enormous fortunes by corruption, played the part of feudal lords. In Kurdistan and in Syria the Pashas behaved like independent local sovereigns. In Syria independence even took on a religious aspect when a heretical Shiite sect challenged the Sultan's spiritual supremacy and won

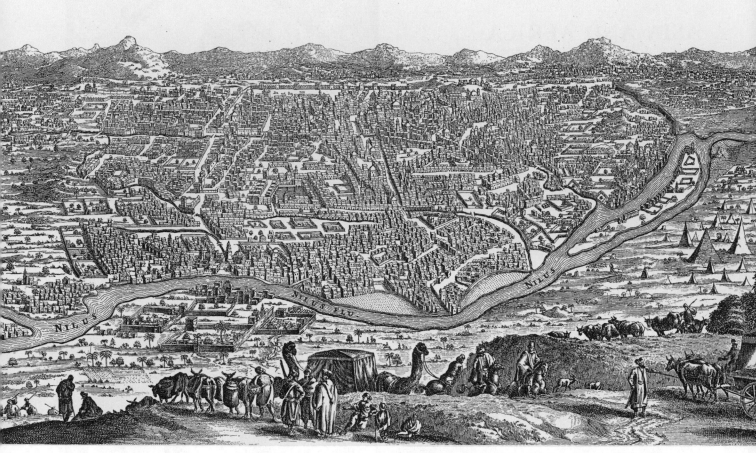

Despite the revival of the Ottoman Empire during the second half of the seventeenth century under the Köprülü, the provinces maintained their virtual independence. Cairo, shown here in a contemporary engraving of about 1670, was to stagnate economically in the next century of anarchy. *Mansell*

much of the country to their belief. In Arabia, a land of nomads, Mehmet ibn Abdul Wahab was the founder of a reformed sect, the Wahabis, which gradually detached Arabia from its religious obedience to Constantinople. Finally, in the Mediterranean, important provinces like Egypt and the regencies of Algiers and Tunis were even more successful in ignoring the Sultan's authority.

Egypt

The real power in the empire had fallen into the hands of the Beys, who commanded the militia. Two of them especially had out-distanced the others in importance: the Emir al-Hadjdj, who was in charge of the organisation of the pilgrimage to Mecca, and, still more important, the Sheikh el-Beled Ali Bey, Governor of Cairo. These two posts were the exclusive preserve of the Mamelukes, former slaves from Georgia and Turkestan. The Mamelukes had penetrated all positions of importance, taken charge of provincial administration and the farming of taxes. Their ascendancy had not been achieved without violent personal quarrels, generally resolved by poison or dagger. Such quarrels kept Egypt in a state of anarchy which helped neither its prosperity nor its security.

The rich Nile valley remained inadequately cultivated. Commerce languished. Though there was a little traffic between Alexandria and the West, the Red Sea was closed to European shipping, and the important East India trade, which had once brought prosperity to Egypt, now followed the route around the Cape of Good Hope.

In Cairo, the chief urban centre and political capital, dictators came and went. In 1720 Cherkes Mehemet Bey, a Mameluke and chief of the Janissaries, slew all his rivals and even deposed the Pasha before being murdered himself four years later. In the midst of the ensuing anarchy the Sublime Porte attempted vainly to intervene. In 1744, another commander of the Janissaries, Ibrahim, became all powerful and remained so until his death ten years later. Then, from 1757 to 1772, the country was tyrannically governed by Sheikh el-Beled Ali Bey. Ali Bey had the instincts of a conqueror and, having made himself master of Upper Egypt, turned his attention to the Hejaz. His generals seized Mecca, invaded Syria and occupied Damascus. One of them thereupon wrested the power from Ali Bey and shortly afterwards was killed in the course of a fresh campaign in Syria. Anarchy again ensued. Two Beys, Murad and Ibrahim, eventually imposed their authority. At this moment Constantinople finally decided on armed intervention. In 1786 the Turkish commander marched on Cairo, but quickly abandoned the task of pacifying the country.

The victims of the arbitrary rule of the Egyptian Beys

were not only the Egyptians themselves but also many foreigners who, in defiance of risk to life and limb, took their chances on the banks of the Nile. In Cairo and Alexandria the French colony was the most numerous and French products were much in demand. But, towards the end of the century, after their success in India, the British gained in influence. Nevertheless, in the eventuality of a partition of the Ottoman Empire, France was in a strong position to lay claim to Egypt.

Tunisia

In Tunisia, too, the Pasha, representing the Sultan, was forced to yield his authority to the local high officials — Beys and Deys — who were in command of the troops or entrusted with the collection of the taxes. In this way the Beys of the Murad dynasty rose to power in the seventeenth century. At the beginning of the eighteenth century they were replaced by a dynasty founded by Hussein ben Ali, a Spahi officer who assumed the title of Bey. The title became hereditary in his family, which from the eighteenth century onwards gave a certain unity to the history of Tunisia. Rather than living by preying on European shipping in the Mediterranean, the Beys chose normal trade methods which they could more easily control for their own profit. From 1710 they signed numerous treaties with foreign powers — Great Britain, France, Spain, the United Provinces and even Austria. The European population of Tunis and other Tunisian towns increased. In 1710 Hussein's nephew, Ali Pasha, rebelled and had Hussein beheaded. Modifying his predecessor's policy, Ali treated foreigners if not with open hostility at least with less cordiality. In 1756 his own son rebelled and disorder reigned in Tunisia. The Algerians profited by the confusion to intervene. Ali was beheaded in his turn and his rebellious son Mehemet was proclaimed Bey, but obliged to recognise the overlordship of the Dey of Algiers. Order was restored and the dynasty was consolidated during the reign of Ali Bey (1756–82) who granted France commercial facilities at Bizerta and Cape Bon. Xenophobia reappeared with Ali's son, who made war on Venice and Spain and in 1790 succeeded in throwing off the Algerian protectorate.

A Saharan caravan, as drawn by an eighteenth-century French artist. Despite growing commercial relations, the French knew little of North Africa, as witness the long-haired Asian camels, the oxen and the turbans, against a green landscape with the odd exotic palm tree. *Bibliothèque Nationale*

Algiers in the eighteenth century. Successful like their neighbours in Tunisia and Morocco in gaining practical independence of Constantinople, the Deys of Algiers differed from them in that they were forced to make trade concessions to Europeans through their own weakness. *Radio Times Hulton Picture Library*

Algiers

In Algiers the Deys succeeded in acquiring power by the seventeenth century, but the office was elective and frequently led to assassination. Moreover the authority of the Dey extended over a much smaller area than present-day Algeria. The Beys of the three provinces, Mascara, Medea and Constantine, enjoyed a large degree of autonomy and the nomad mountain tribes evaded all control. The fleet fell into decay; European action at sea threatened the corsairs and the trade in Christian slaves. The Deys were obliged to make terms with foreign merchants: the French African Company obtained three establishments on the coast, at La Calle, Bône and Collo. Spain, which had lost Oran in 1708, recaptured it in 1732. Mehemet ben Oman, the most remarkable of the Deys, held power between 1766 and 1791. He encountered and overcame two dangerous crises: an insurrection of the Kabyles, which he put down with difficulty, and in 1775 a Spanish invasion by sea. By the end of the century of all foreign merchants the French were in the strongest position in Algiers as well as in Tunisia and in Egypt.

Morocco

The sovereign of Morocco was able to treat the Sultan of Turkey on a footing of equality; his Empire extended over an immense territory and laid claim to authority as far as the Sudan. Between 1672 and 1727 the throne was occupied by the redoubtable Sultan Mulay Ismail, who subjugated the country and threw out the Europeans on the coast. During the first quarter of the eighteenth century Morocco enjoyed relative peace. Trade was reasonably active in the Mediterranean port of Tetuan and in Salé on the Atlantic, in the great inland commercial centre of Marrakesh, Meknès and above all Fez. Caravans arrived regularly from the Sudan. The resultant prosperity allowed Mulay Ismail to build his imposing palace at Meknès. After his death the *Abib*, a privileged military élite, made and unmade Sultans, plunging the country into a state of anarchy. Finally Mulay Mehemet (1757–90) imposed his authority and restored order; he drove the Portuguese from Mazagan, but failed to reduce Melilla. Then cupidity led him to make terms with the Europeans. The Danes obtained a monopoly of trade on the Atlantic coast, while the Dutch predominated on the Mediterranean coast. France also obtained advantages and a Frenchman was commissioned to construct the port of Mogador.

By and large piracy on the Barbary coast diminished during the eighteenth century but Europeans were only moderately interested in the possibilities of trade with North Africa. Exports of value — wheat, leather and tropical fruit — were few in quantity and in any case the Berbers and Arabs showed little eagerness to engage in trade relations. They relied on the commercial activities of the Jews who had settled in their towns. Little progress was made in the Maghrib and, on the fringe of the Western world, Tunisia, Algeria and Morocco maintained brutal customs in a daily life that remained medieval.

Negro Africa

During the eighteenth century the political structure of Negro Africa changed continually in the constant warfare which was in large measure due to the slave trade and the religious fanaticism of the Moslems. In the enormous Sudanese region the progressive dissolution of the Songhoi Empire brought about the formation of ephemeral kingdoms, the union of tribes under a single chieftain or around urban centres. Such towns retained a certain degree of Islamic civilisation, though the Negro peasantry often remained unshaken in their animistic beliefs. Even the semblance of Moroccan authority, which had maintained relative peace in the Sudan, vanished on the death of the Sultan Mulay Ismail in 1727. From that time the raids of the Tuareg nomads caused havoc in the settlements of the Sudan.

Some kingdoms managed to survive. In the west the Toucouleurs, who were fanatical Moslems, conquered the Fulbe people and in 1720 set up a theocratic kingdom in Futa Jalon. Fifty years later the Fulbe who had adopted Islam founded another kingdom in Futa Toro, which also was ruled by an elected High Priest. Eastwards and farther inland, the powerful kingdom of Bornu, founded in the sixteenth century, was in decline. Ruled by a despot who lived in the midst of a brilliant court, Bornu was unable to maintain its suzerainty over the area to the east of Lake Chad, where two independent kingdoms emerged: Wadai and Bagirmi. Still farther to the east Darfur developed its Islamic culture; here, too, the sovereign was surrounded by an elaborate court with complicated etiquette. In all these states Islam gained adherents during the course of the century. Farther south, however, the teachings of the Prophet met greater resistance from native animism.

Abyssinia

In the rest of Africa only one country had achieved a fairly advanced form of civilisation. The mysterious kingdom of Abyssinia was of ancient origin and by tradition Christian, though non-orthodox; it stubbornly resisted Islam, which surrounded it on all sides. At the beginning of the eighteenth century the ancient dynasty, which claimed unbroken descent from Solomon, still occupied the throne in the person of the Negus Jesus, who governed a country with some degree of centralisation from his capital, Gondar. In 1708 he was assassinated by one of his sons, and an anarchic period of palace revolutions ensued which hastened decadence and revived feudalism. In 1719 another son of the Negus Jesus seized the throne and massacred the Catholic missionaries. After his death in 1729 his son Jesus II displayed little energy; his sole ambition was to have a palace built for himself at vast expense, for which purpose he imported artists from Smyrna. Meanwhile, in the provinces, the Governors became more and more independent. During the years 1767 to 1772 a Scot, James Bruce of Kinnaird, travelled through Abyssinia, and on his return gave a very pessimistic account of the country which caused great interest in Britain; but, engulfed in civil wars and bloodshed, Abyssinia remained virtually closed to the outside world.

The birth of the Virgin. Bulgarian icon of the late seventeenth century. Sofia. *Giraudon*

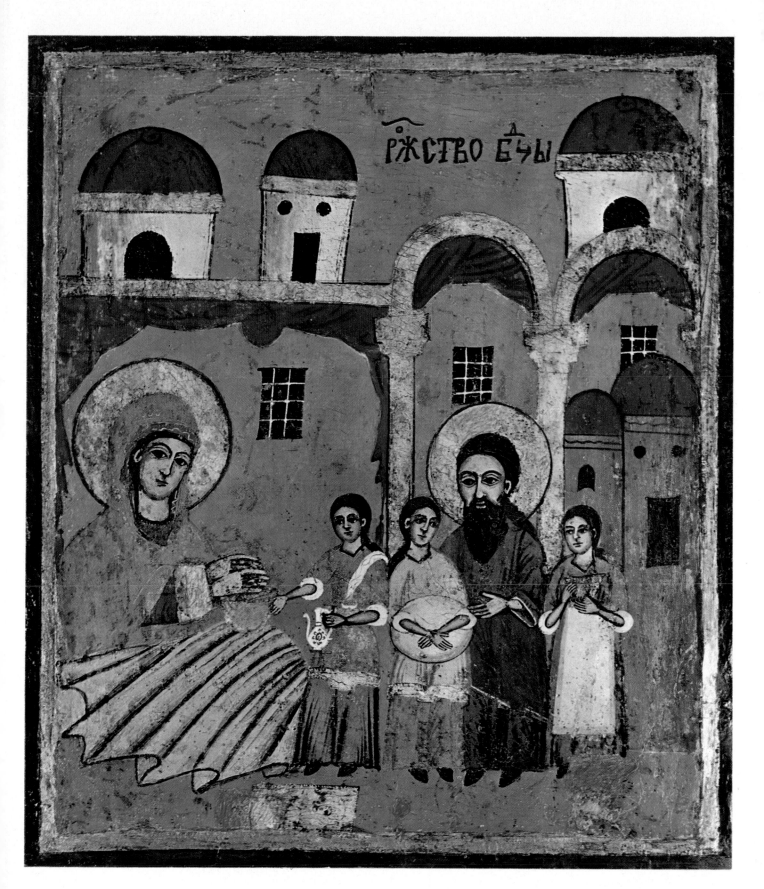

Persia

After a brilliant renaissance in the seventeenth century Persia again lived under the menace of the neighbouring nomads; above all, the country was threatened from the north and from the east by savage bands of Turcomans and Afghans. Softened by a life of luxury, the Safavid sovereigns were incapable of resisting their assaults. In 1710 the Afghan tribe of the Ghilzais invaded the Empire, led by their Emir Mir-Mahmud who in 1722 drove Tahmasp II, the last of the Safavids, from Ispahan. Mir-Mahmud then proclaimed himself king. The usurper's success was a signal for all the neighbours to share in the spoils. The Turcomans seized Khorassan while the Russians took Derbent and Baku, important posts on the trade route to India which they proposed to develop. In the west, the Turks reconquered Armenia, Azerbaijan and Iraq, which they had lost in the seventeenth century. Religion provided a link of sympathy between the Turks and Mir-Mahmud's successor, Aschraf, since the Afghans and the Ottomans professed Sunnite orthodoxy while the Safavids had been Shiites. The Treaty of Hamadan confirmed Turkey in the possession of the reconquered provinces and stipulated the spiritual authority of the Sultan over Persia.

This settlement was rudely disturbed by the arrival on the scene of a new conqueror, Nadir Shah, a Turcoman from the Khorassan frontier. Nadir Shah had the wit to present himself as the champion of Tahmasp II and of the Persians against the Afghans. In 1730 he defeated the Afghans and reinstalled the Safavid sovereign in Ispahan. Then he turned against the Turks, who at the time were threatened by Austria and Russia. Nadir Shah's victories were followed by a new Treaty of Hamadan (1732) which restored the former frontier. In 1735 the Russians were so impressed by his military prowess that they returned Derbent and Baku. War broke out again with Turkey. Then, at the pinnacle of his glory, Nadir deposed the incompetent Tahmasp II and himself accepted the imperial tiara.

Driving beyond the frontiers of the Empire, he attacked Afghanistan, took Kandahar and then invaded India. He defeated the Grand Mogul and sacked Delhi. The new Persian power, founded on force of arms, was at its zenith. Nadir, the last great King of Kings, who was himself not even an Iranian, devoted himself to maintaining the grandeur of his adopted country. Inspired by Western examples, he planned reforms, but did not live long enough to realise them. In spite of its privileged position at the crossroad of Europe, Asia Minor and central Asia, Persia did not benefit from a pattern of international trade which in the eighteenth century was dominated by maritime traffic. Incessant warfare impoverished the country. The success of Nadir Shah was a brilliant but brief interlude in the story of Persian decline. In 1747, when the Turks had finally resigned themselves to suing for peace, Nadir died.

After him Persia rapidly disintegrated. Of Nadir's

Benkei Oniwaka and the monstrous fish, an incident from a legend illustrating Oniwaka's fearlessness. Some Japanese painters still used traditional subjects in the eighteenth century, but a new school of art dwelt on the life of courtesans.

Nadir Shah, whose military prowess not only expelled the Afghans, forcing a reversal of the first Treaty of Hamadan, but extended Persian power to India, where he sacked Delhi. *Radio Times Hulton Picture Library*

Seventeenth-century painting of a young man. Persian. *Wm. Swaan*

A Hindu god in handbeaten copper, from Nepal. Since the early seventeenth century the Himalayas had been a redoubt of Hinduism; even Aurangzeb had been unable to crush the militant Sikhs. With the disintegration of the Mogul Empire in the eighteenth century they became leaders of Hindu nationalism. *Coleman & Hayward*

The Muni Shri Sukderti preaching to a concourse of Sadhus on the occasion of Rajah Parekshit renouncing his kingdom, c. 1757. Constant shifts of power in India marked the decline of the Mogul Empire and opened the subcontinent to exploitation by Asian and European intruder alike. *Victoria & Albert Museum*

conquests his heirs preserved only Khorassan. The Afghans regained their independence. In the south and in the west Kerim Khan, chief of the Iranian tribe of Zend, attempted to re-establish national authority over the empire, but was obliged to limit his ambitions to restoring unity to western Persia, establishing his capital at Shiraz. He founded a new dynasty and reigned until 1779. Aga Mohammed, a Kajar Turk, attempted to follow in the footsteps of the great Nadir but though he gained victories over the Zend tribesmen and over Khorassan, he was held in check by Russia. The end of the eighteenth century saw the waning of a great civilisation, refined in its manners, literature and art, but which had, as it were, developed in a vacuum. India excepted, Persia's contact with the outside world had been slight, and no deep or profitable relations had been formed with the West.

India

A patchwork of races and religions, India had known a brief period of unity during the Mogul domination, but Aurangzeb's death in 1707 was followed by rapid disintegration: the native princes regained their independence while the great Moslem officials carved out for themselves kingdoms in which they founded local ruling families. Aurangzeb's successors fought among themselves so bitterly that there were five Grand Moguls within the space of twelve years; even Mohammed Shah, one of the stronger sovereigns, was incapable of stemming the feudal tide, though his reign lasted from 1719 to 1748. The Grand Mogul exercised at least a nominal suzerainty over the empire, and this was recognised by those who divided the real power among themselves. In this way the symbolic unity of India was to be maintained for over a century longer.

Three principal Hindu groups broke free from Moslem domination: the Rajputs, the Mahrattas and the Sikhs. The Rajputs were scattered from the north-west of the Deccan to the banks of the Indus. Their loose confederation of principalities, governed by Ranas and Rajahs, was incapable of the co-operation necessary to form a powerful state. The Mahrattas, whom Aurangzeb had found it so difficult to subdue, were more dynamic. Driven back to the western coast, they recognised in theory the sovereignty of Sahudji, the grandson of Sivaji, and his successors. The real power, however, fell into the hands of the Peshwas, who acted as mayors of the palace and resided at Poona. Under their direction, and especially under the energetic rule of the second Peshwa, Baji-Rao (1720–40) the Mahrattas continued their expansion in every direction, achieving control over the northern Deccan up to the banks of the Ganges by the middle of the century. The Peshwa divided these conquests among the chief Mahratta families, and thus created feudal dynasties which endangered the cohesion of the Mahrattas. The Sikhs formed a group apart: not only was their religion monotheistic, but in their caste-less social system and in their military superiority they were unique. The Sikhs had certain affinities with their neighbours, the Afghans.

While these three Hindu groups asserted their individuality, the Moslems established two principal states: Bengal and Deccan. Deccan was the creation of Nizamul-Muk, one of Aurangzeb's chief officials, who progressively made himself master of almost all southern India

and overlord of such important provincial rulers as the
Nabob of the Carnatic, where the British and the French
had trading posts. For a time Bengal constituted a viceroyalty ruled by a grandson of Aurangzeb; but it soon
disintegrated, Behar, Orissa and Oudh breaking away
from the Mogul's authority.

In all these states rivalry and quarrels for succession
permitted Europeans to interfere and gain a foothold.
From this period the history of India became the story
of the struggle between the French and the British. As
the authority of the Grand Mogul weakened he became
incapable of rousing any movement of resistance and was
forced to submit to the will of his neighbours — first
Nadir Shah of Persia, and then the Afghans, who had
found a leader in Ahmed Shah. Ahmed had united the
nomad tribes under his banner with the prime object of
organised plunder. He seized Kandahar and Kabul, raided
the Panjab and penetrated as far as Delhi, which he pillaged
in 1756. When he reappeared three years later the Grand
Mogul had rallied the Sikhs and the Mahrattas to the
cause of the empire. The Hindus, however, were unable
to co-operate and in 1761 the Mahrattas suffered overwhelming defeat at Panipat. The Afghans, whose aim
was simply loot, failed to exploit their victory, and
Ahmed's son, Timur, did not even return to raid the east.
Furthermore, the Sikhs had taken advantage of the disorder
to seize the Panjab and in 1764 established their capital
at Lahore. The Panjab now played the role of an autonomous buffer state between India and Afghanistan.

The eighteenth century had been disastrous for the great
Moslem empires. One of them, Persia, had broken up
and practically disappeared. India was little more than the
façade of an empire which the British could dismember
as soon as it pleased them to do so. The disintegrating
Ottoman Empire already showed signs of becoming ' the
sick man of Europe '. Islam had little sympathy with, or
taste for, Western ' enlightenment '. Moslem civilisation
lived on its past, had fallen into routine and no longer
produced masterpieces of literature and art. The Islamic
world had nothing to hold it together except its religion
— and even in religion heresies still broke out. Its unity
was at an end.

THE FAR EAST

Though Europeans had taken possession of much of the
Americas without great difficulty, they had made only a
few breaches in the Moslem world, except in India which
was in any case only partially Islamised. Their efforts
were checked, above all in the Far East, where Europe
was opposed not only by an alien religion, but by ancient
cultural and racial forces, effective political organisation
and huge populations.

The Indonesian archipelago

In spite of its proximity to China Indonesia did not belong
to the Chinese world, but was rather a prolongation of
Islam among peoples who were predominantly of Malay
race. Together with the Philippines, a Spanish missionary
outpost, the archipelago was the single important enclave
of white colonisation in the Far East. There the Dutch

The Summer Palace of the Manchu Emperors, built on the
outskirts of Peking in an artificial landscape as part of the
reconstruction of Peking after 1644. Like Versailles, the
Summer Palace symbolised the power of a great empire.

Tibetan scroll showing Lamaist gods. Tibet resisted full
incorporation into the Chinese Empire through the strength
of its religion as much as by its remoteness from Peking.
Marburg

East India Company jealously guarded its monopoly of trade and exploitation. Thanks to the Company's privileged position in the Indian Ocean and the western Pacific it continued to make great profits. From Java it obtained silk and indigo as well as the traditional spices. The Company worked the natives hard, but did not administer many areas directly, usually preferring to work through the small Moslem kingdoms. The decline of the United Provinces and the enfeeblement of the Dutch fleet brought about a gradual decline in the Company's trading stations, while the Company itself was weakened by corruption. Britain gained a foothold. After the Anglo-Dutch War of 1780 the Dutch began to cede certain parts of their huge colonial empire.

Indochina

The diverse peoples of Indochina, constantly at odds with each other, had few traits in common except that in the eighteenth century they were all equally resistant if not downright hostile to European penetration. Christian missionaries were persecuted and driven away. Indochina resisted all outside influence and all civilisation, whether native or imported. Its population in the eighteenth century was much smaller than it is today.

In the west of the peninsula the weakness of the tribes occupying the fertile river valleys attracted conquerors from the north. In this way the warlike Burmese overran the state of Pegu in the middle of the century, and despite resistance restored unity under their own rule. Towards 1760 they invaded Siam, and seven years later Ayuthia, the Siamese capital, fell into their hands. Though their power had declined, the Siamese rallied round an energetic leader, Phaya Tak, who had succeeded in making himself king, and removed the capital from Ayuthia to Bangkok. In 1782 he was assassinated, and one of his generals, Phaya Chakkri, founded a dynasty which was to rule until the end of the nineteenth century. Victims of the continental attacks and encroachments of their neighbours, the Thai principalities of Laos and Cambodia — between Siam (Thailand) and Annam (Vietnam) — were too weak to defend themselves.

The kingdom of Annam, occupying the length of the eastern coast, was the largest state in the peninsula. The Annam royal dynasty, the Le, recognised the suzerainty of the Emperor of China and relinquished actual power to viceregal families who conducted themselves as though they were in fact independent sovereigns. The Nguyen, viceroys in the south, pushed forward to extend their domination over Cochin-China. While in Tongking in the north savage outbreaks against the Jesuits occurred, Jesuit missionaries were being received with honour at the Nguyen court at Hué. Western penetration of the peninsula was at this time limited to missionary work, in spite of the desire of European powers to establish ports of call on the route to China. Towards 1770 the insurrection of the Tay-so'n convulsed the kingdom of the south, and the plight of the young sovereign, Nguyen-Anh, driven back into Cochin-China, appeared to be desperate. The saviour of the dynasty appeared in the person of Pigneau de Behaine, the French Bishop of Adran, who decided to return to Versailles to ask for military support; this would incidentally permit France to become firmly established in the kingdom. During the bishop's voyage the Tay-so'n put an end to the reigns of the Le and the northern viceroys, the Trinh, and shared out the major part of the country. Pigneau won over Louis XVI to his cause and a treaty of alliance was signed in November 1787. But in face of official reluctance to take action, the bishop was himself obliged to prepare the expedition. In 1789 the reconquest began and, thanks to the combined efforts of Pigneau and Nguyen-Anh, concluded with the coronation of the latter as Emperor under the name Gia-Long.

Manchu China

Throughout his long reign the Emperor K'ang-hsi had successfully laboured for the unity and consolidation of his vast empire. His most dangerous adversaries, the Ili tribes of western Mongolia, had been subdued. On his death in 1722 K'ang-hsi was succeeded by his son, Yung Cheng, who, without his father's flair, tried to continue his policies. In 1731 the Chinese occupied Kobdo in western Mongolia, but their army was crushed by the Ili tribesmen. After a fresh expedition in 1734 to drive them beyond the Altai range, a truce was concluded in 1735. The Ili were submitted to Chinese authority, represented by a resident official in command of a garrison at Kulja. The defeated tribesmen quarrelled among themselves and gradually ceased to be a danger.

The Manchu policy of landward expansion entailed the risk of clashes with Russia, whose interest in trade routes across central Asia and access to warm-water ports had increased. The Russians, however, were still not numerous in these deserted regions, and preferred to remain on good terms with their neighbours. In 1727 the Treaty of Kiakhta confirmed the Treaty of Nerchinsk signed some forty years before, and reasserted that Russia had no claims in Manchuria. She was, however, accorded trade facilities and given the right to maintain a kind of embassy composed, like those of other Western powers, of religious missionaries. Diplomatic relations remained uneasy and suspicious.

Distrust largely explains the attitude of the Chinese towards the Western world and their anxiety to secure the frontiers of their empire. In the seventeenth century Europeans had been welcomed, through the offices of missionaries, especially the Jesuits, at the imperial court. But although 300,000 Chinese were said to have been converted to Christianity the mass of the population, and still more the literate classes, remained convinced of the superiority of the Chinese way of life and philosophy. Even K'ang-hsi, who had long shown sympathy for a religion he judged to be not incompatible with Chinese belief, had at last prohibited the preaching of Christianity (*see* p. 132). Yung Cheng, his successor, at once displayed his hostility. In 1724 he ordered the expulsion of the missionaries, except for a handful who were permitted to remain at Court because of their scientific knowledge. By condemning the Jesuits' attempted synthesis of Chinese and Christian belief, Europe had largely condemned its own progress in China.

China now withdrew behind her inhospitable frontiers, warned by the disturbances in India which had invited European intrusion. No new European settlements were founded in China during the eighteenth century. Since they already occupied it, the Portuguese retained Macao,

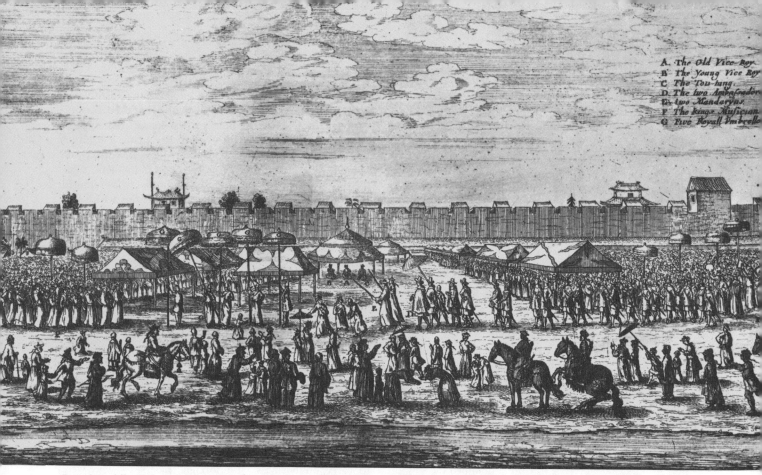

French and English merchants were forced to operate through the Hong at Canton, where heavy taxes made it clear that they were there on sufferance. Nevertheless, friendly relations were formally maintained, as at this entertainment given for ambassadors outside the walls of Canton. *British Museum*

A Chinese mandarin of 1700. Despite widespread corruption, the efficiency of the administrative system which had been built up over the centuries and taken over by the Manchus from the Mings was a key factor in preserving an empire which had lost its impetus. *Radio Times Hulton Picture Library*

which they hoped to make into an international port. On the south coast the Spanish held a few concessions; in 1742 they tried to occupy Formosa, but were soon forced to abandon the attempt. The British and the French, arriving too late, had no choice but to trade through the intermediary of the Hong at Canton; and the Hong — a corporation of merchants authorised by the Emperor to carry on such trade — increased its exactions in order to meet the heavy taxes it was forced to pay.

Yung Cheng died in 1735. The long reign of Kien Lung, his successor, lasted until 1796. The Emperor Kien Lung had little taste for the military life, neither leading his armies nor directing campaigns in person. On the other hand he was an excellent administrator and a man of culture. Though he did not banish the learned Jesuits from his court, they were not replaced when they died, so that the time finally came when the Chinese no longer knew enough about casting iron to manufacture cannon. Kien Lung did not profess quite the same repugnance for Christianity as his predecessor, but by an edict of 1736 he none the less forbade his subjects to be converted. In 1742 the Holy See itself destroyed all hopes of reconciliation by issuing the Bull *Ex quo singulari* which confirmed previous condemnations of Chinese religious practice. A persecution of Christians broke out in 1747. Thereafter missionaries who succeeded in penetrating China did so only clandestinely and lacked the earlier Jesuits' thorough knowledge of the country. Catholic communities dwindled away, and in 1771 Kien Lung condemned Christianity as being contrary to the laws

165

of the empire. In this manner ended a cultural exchange which could have altered the destiny of a large part of the human race.

In the west of the empire trouble broke out almost simultaneously in Tibet and in Mongolia. The two imperial commissioners, together with all resident Chinese, were massacred at Lhasa in 1750; the army which Kien Lung dispatched had, however, no difficulty in restoring order. The Dalai Lama was put under stricter surveillance than previously and made more closely dependent on Peking; but Kien Lung realised that it was in his interest to conciliate the 'Pope' of Buddhism, and heaped the Dalai Lama with honours. The subjugation of Tibet remained personal in that the Dalai Lama acknowledged himself to be the vassal of the Emperor and not of China (so that in 1912, when China was proclaimed a republic, he was able legally to resume his independence). The Chinese overlordship of Tibet offered Kien Lung an excuse to penetrate Hindu territory. In 1791 the Gurkhas, who inhabited Nepal and made frequent raids into Tibet, were driven back by the Chinese army as far as their capital, Katmandu, where they were forced to acknowledge Chinese suzerainty.

The truce in Mongolia was broken in 1754, following yet another squabble among the Ili tribesmen over the question of succession. The pro-Chinese candidate, Amursana, who had taken refuge in China, obtained the support of Kien Lung. But he fell out with his protectors and, suddenly inciting the tribesmen to mutiny, massacred his Chinese supporters. After this, it was decided in 1757 to put an end to the chronic indiscipline of the Ili and they were more or less totally exterminated. A certain number, including Amursana himself, succeeded in escaping across the frontier into Siberia. Others were deported. In their place emigrants from various regions were installed, especially Moslem farmers from Kashgaria. In 1771 thousands of Turgot families, who had formerly migrated to Russian territory, returned to Mongolia, attracted by Kien Lung's generous treatment and the offer of land from which the Ili had been driven. The former domain of the Mongol tribes, Dzungaria, was without pretext simply annexed by the empire. In 1758 the Chinese army proceeded to occupy Kashgaria. The new conquests in eastern Turkestan were formed into the province of Sinkiang, the 'New Border' province. The Manchu Emperors again displayed a supple and tolerant religious policy towards their Moslem subjects in eastern Turkestan.

Kien Lung was equally anxious to strengthen his frontiers in the south and the south-east. In 1767 he sent an expeditionary force against Burma which obliged it to recognise Chinese sovereignty. The Annamites, for their part, never challenged the nominal suzerainty of the Emperor at Peking. The Manchu Emperors' great dream of hegemony and territorial unity could be fully realised only when all of China proper was entirely subjected to Peking. Unfortunately, in the mountains of the south the wild Miaotse tribesmen refused to accept any authority and constituted a permanent threat to the peaceful valley folk who cultivated the soil. In 1775 Kien Lung undertook their systematic pacification.

By the end of the century Chinese power was in appearance formidable; but the Empire's expansion was the result not of exuberant growth and energy but of a desire for security. The Manchu Emperors had not after all injected new vigour into traditional China; it was China that had absorbed them. They adopted the institutions and the administrative system of their Ming predecessors, although they strove to improve the lot of the masses. In their efforts to achieve this aim they made a decision fraught with future consequences: they increased the number of landowners, or at least of landholders, since former proprietors were ground-landlords who retained rights over the land itself. Many huge domains which had been formed by imperial grants of land were now confiscated and shared out. The policy of breaking up the great estates was applied in an authoritarian manner and seems to have produced results. In any case the population rapidly increased: towards 1750 it may have numbered 150 million inhabitants. In other words, China contained by far the greatest mass of people on the surface of the globe. In the realm of technical knowledge, however, China had for long remained stationary, while the nations of the West were furnishing themselves with the physical means to dominate the modern world. Though a few new ideas and scientific discoveries imported from the West served to amuse and rouse the curiosity of the scholars and the learned, they were put to no practical application. As for external trade, it remained insignificant, and in 1771 the Hong was actually abolished, although the merchants who composed it continued individually to carry on business with foreign traders — who were still closely confined in Canton.

In the course of their other preoccupations the Manchu Emperors did not neglect the embellishment of their capital. Peking, the 'Purple' and once forbidden city, had been burned to the ground in 1644. It was sumptuously rebuilt in the same symbolic architecture which demonstrated that the Emperor was the Son of Heaven and the centre of the world. In the outskirts of Peking a Summer Palace was erected. In this Chinese Versailles the influence of the Jesuits was apparent in the harmonious grouping of pavilions and gardens. But in reality, though it dominated an empire so immense and so populous, China was in slow decline.

Viewing foreigners with increased distaste, and more impenetrable than ever, China became fixed in her proud grandeur, isolation and ancestor worship. She had the benefit of long reigns and of great emperors, and the rivalries of European nations had preserved her in large measure from serious outside interference. But she remained at the mercy of circumstances which were susceptible to change, and when the world beyond her borders had undergone an industrial revolution and grown irritated by her exclusiveness, China no longer possessed the means to defend herself.

Japan

In the eighteenth century the empire of the Rising Sun presented a brilliant façade. Peace reigned throughout the archipelago; the system of government seemed to have attained equilibrium; at Kyoto the Emperor's rôle was confined to the performance of his religious functions; surrounded by his court at Yedo (Tokyo) the Shogun, head of the powerful house of Tokugawa, in practice wielded almost complete power, helped by a large following of *daimyos* and *samurai*. Only a few great rival families escaped his authority and ruled semi-independent domains which were often extensive. The country was organised as a feudal hierarchy, basically military, and divided into castes; this system no longer served any social purpose, but the Shogun had preserved its structure. In practice *samurai* and *daimyo* alike lived at the expense of the peasant who, in spite of the great advance in agriculture, was often left with not enough to eat. Famine, when it occurred, was hard to combat because of customs barriers between provinces. Japan's difficulty in feeding its thirty million inhabitants led to abortion and infanticide. In contrast to the rest of the world in the eighteenth century the population of Japan remained stationary. The artisans who worked in the towns gave rise to a middle class, the *chonin*, who, trading in merchandise and money, enriched and greatly influenced the economic life of the country. It was this class which furnished those who were anxious to make profitable contacts with foreign traders.

For the moment such contacts were reduced to the minimum, since only the Dutch were authorised to exchange a limited number of products, from their confines on an island off the coast of Nagasaki. Christianity was prohibited, and the only noteworthy influence from the outside world came from China. Officially the religion of Japan was Buddhism mingled with elements of the national cult. From China Confucianism brought to this slightly arid religion its message of generosity and tolerance. From China, also, came a form of Buddhism with mystical tendencies which contributed to a deepening of spiritual life. Although these religious currents did not succeed in alleviating the wretchedness caused by the vices of the regime, they set in motion a spirit of resistance to the absolute power of the Shogun. Mystics like Mabuchi denounced the scandal of keeping the Mikado isolated and powerless. The movement gained ground not only in religious communities but among the *samurai* themselves, who were often so impoverished that they were forced to renounce their rank and earn their livelihood in the towns. From this period foreign influence tended slowly to increase. European scientific discoveries and technical innovations were not unknown. Certain people, struck by these glimpses of the outside world, realised that change was inevitable.

The despotic shoguns distrusted these symptoms and issued severer edicts. In 1710 Iyenobu legislated against the love of money which degraded the *samurai*, and two years later introduced measures to prevent peasants from leaving their land. During the long reign of the Shogun Yoshimune (1716–45) European ideas were less unfavourably received, but monetary inflation was not checked. Iyeshige (1746–60) and Iyeharu (1760–86) persisted in a policy of ostentation which only emphasised the contrasting misery of the people. In 1787, following a famine which had ravaged the country uninterruptedly since 1783, riots broke out in Yedo, the capital.

In a climate of moral disarray traditional virtues were relaxed, as the art of the period demonstrates. Though certain delicate masterpieces in the traditional manner were still produced, the subject matter of painting and prints increasingly dealt with the life of courtesans, who occupied a special place in Japanese culture.

Few hints of change could be observed in this isolated corner of the globe, hidebound in its strict observance of ancestral traditions and its rigid social and administrative organisation. Change, however, was not far off.

The *Samurai* Kato Yomoschichi Morikane drinking a cup of saki. Under the despotic rule of the shoguns peace and apparent prosperity were maintained only at the cost of the social and economic disruption of Japan. The Shogun's power rested on a feudal military hierarchy of *daimyos* and *samurai*. *British Museum*

167

Frederick the Great, King of Prussia 1740–86, reviews his soldiers.

CHAPTER ELEVEN

THE SEVEN YEARS' WAR
AND BENEVOLENT DESPOTISM

In appearance the Seven Years' War at first seemed to be only a continuation of the War of the Austrian Succession. It proved to be much more, spreading over large portions of the world and bringing to a climax a half-century of Anglo-French colonial rivalry.

The Seven Years' War

The Treaty of Aix-la-Chapelle left behind it rancour and an unsatisfied desire for vengeance. In Vienna Maria Theresa could not bring herself to give up Silesia. Kaunitz, her ambassador to the court of Louis XV from 1750 to 1752, urged an Austro-French alliance; Versailles still preferred to maintain the alliance with Frederick II, who was admired both as a *philosophe* and as a statesman. In London George II feared that his Hanoverian Electorate would be gravely imperilled by another war against France allied to Prussia. Accordingly, he sought to confirm the Austrian and Russian alliances which guaranteed the integrity of Hanover. Maria Theresa, however, was well aware of the aim of British policy and realised that

it could do nothing to further her own designs. In the end an Anglo-Russian treaty alone was concluded, at St Petersburg in 1755. The Anglo-Austrian alliance, because of reciprocal disillusionments, had practically ceased to exist.

In 1756 the Franco-Prussian alliance expired. Frederick II offered to renew it, but Versailles, in a cautious mood, made no haste to reply to the proposal. The King of Prussia began to feel isolated. George II seized the occasion to suggest an agreement and Frederick, who had just learned about the Treaty of St Petersburg, hastened to sign the Convention of Westminster (January 1756). In it Britain and Prussia reciprocally undertook to guarantee the security of Silesia and Hanover. Frederick also sought to preserve the French alliance, but at Versailles the wind had changed. Madame de Pompadour had won the King over to the Austrian cause. The news of the Convention of Westminster was received at Versailles with indignation, and France refused to renew the Prussian alliance. Having thus isolated herself, she was almost forced to come to an agreement with Austria. After forty years, and after the breakdown of the British alliance, France adopted the diplomatic alignment advocated by Louis XIV before his death. Nevertheless this reversal of alliances, marking the end of the ancient enmity between Bourbon France and the Habsburg House of Austria, struck contemporaries with an astonishment bordering on shocked disapproval. The first treaty of Versailles, made in May 1756, contained an undertaking by France and Austria to protect each other, with a promise of military aid in case of aggression. The treaty was especially advantageous to Maria Theresa, who alone feared invasion and could, moreover, remain neutral in the Anglo-French conflict.

That conflict, in fact, had already begun in the colonies. In India the British and the French had scarcely ceased to fight (under the cloak of struggles for succession among the native princes). In North America, each defied the other from the rival forts built along the Ohio frontiers. Frontier incidents increased the solidarity of the Thirteen Colonies, which in 1754 sent delegates to a continental congress at Albany in New York to study a plan for federal union. The delegates appealed for help to London, where the Government realised that war was inevitable and sent reinforcements to the colonists. Nevertheless, things at first went badly for the Anglo-Americans, and the French, with their Red Indian allies, had the better of it in the preliminary skirmishes. Then in the next year hostilities took a grimmer turn: the 17,000 French Acadians who had remained in Nova Scotia after the territory had been assigned to Britain in 1713 were driven out, and their possessions seized without indemnity. At sea, more than three hundred French merchantmen were captured by Admiral Hawke. In May 1756, France officially declared war. Then the French seized Minorca, a sobering blow to a people unaccustomed to naval reverses. Calcutta also fell to the French.

The central theatre of the struggle now suddenly became the continent of Europe, until now at peace. Frederick II had taken alarm at the Franco-Austrian defensive alliance, and in September 1756, again without warning, he struck, this time invading Saxony. Thus began the Seven Years' War. The shock of this fresh aggression produced indignation and counter-measures. It brought the Franco-Austrian alliance into effect, and Russia joined it. Frederick, confronted by a powerful array of enemies, found a single ally in Great Britain, whose policy was now directed by William Pitt. In 1757, however, a Franco-Austrian army occupied Hanover, while in Canada, under the energetic command of Montcalm, the French had captured Fort Oswego and Fort William Henry. Frederick's further invasion of Bohemia had ended in failure and late that summer the net of his enemies — French, Austrian, Russian and Swedish — closed around him. He acted with astonishing rapidity. Driving westwards into Saxony again, he surprised the French army, and in the battle of Rossbach won an overwhelming victory (November 5). A month later at Leuthen he defeated the Austrians. The British revoked the armistice made in Hanover, and Hanoverian troops again took up arms under the command of the Duke of Brunswick, another able soldier. With Brunswick and Frederick, the Anglo-Prussian forces were well served in their commanders.

Though the French and the Austrians had been driven back the Prussian army was imperilled by a Russian

At the battle of the Plains of Abraham (13 Sept. 1759), which decided the fate of Quebec, both opposing commanders were killed. The death of Wolfe, the British commander, a brilliant major-general at thirty-two, is shown in this picture.

Quebec fell in 1759, the *annus mirabilis* of the Seven Years' War. A year later, Montreal surrendered to the British and at the peace all Canada passed to the British crown. Only part of the Antilles remained French in America. *Mansell*

offensive in 1758. The Russians were halted at the battle of Zorndorf, but Frederick suffered heavy losses. Everywhere the conflict had become a war of attrition, the chief result of which was to lay waste the north of Germany. In America, however, British sea power, directed by the genius of Pitt, had begun to tell. Montcalm obtained no reinforcements and Louisbourg — the key to Canada — Fort Frontenac and, on the Ohio, Fort Duquesne — the link between French Canada and French Louisiana — all fell into British hands. In India Robert Clive, who was originally a merchant's clerk working for the East India Company, cleared the French out of Bengal and in 1757 won the decisive victory of Plassey.

169

The year 1759 was disastrous for Frederick. He was beaten by the Russians at Kunersdorf and Prussian territory was invaded. Elsewhere, however, the British continued to supplant their French rivals. On September 13, on the Heights of Abraham, General Wolfe defeated Montcalm. Both perished heroically on the field of battle, but Quebec passed into British control. The loss of Quebec was the death-knell of French Canada: shortly afterwards Montreal in its turn capitulated.

In 1760–61 the war awaited decision only on the continent; in India, the last colonial theatre of war, the struggle ended when the last Governor of French India, Lally-Tollendal, was defeated at Wandewash. After this, French India was lost. In Europe the Russians entered Berlin, but the King of Prussia continued desperately to fight. He defeated the Austrian armies at Liegnitz and at Torgau, but he was at bay when the news broke that Elizabeth, the Empress of Russia, had died. A Prussian collapse was averted, for Elizabeth's successor, Peter III, was a fanatical admirer of Frederick. He made not only peace with Prussia, but an alliance. Peter, however, was overthrown a few weeks later and his wife, who usurped the throne in 1762 as Catherine II, withdrew from the war. In Britain, the fall of Pitt brought the ending of subsidies; but Frederick had recovered possession of Silesia and once more had the upper hand. The war, however, languished. In France, where it was unpopular, Choiseul had come to power in 1758 but had failed to redress the ill-fortune which attended French arms. He had no alternative but to drag Spain into the conflict. In 1761 a new Bourbon Family Pact was signed with Charles III, which provided that Spain should declare war on Great Britain in exchange for Minorca, then occupied by the French. The Pact proved useless: British fleets seized Cuba and the Philippines, and the dispatch of a British force to Lisbon frustrated an attempted Franco-Spanish invasion of Portugal.

France and Spain were now prepared to negotiate and in February 1763 the Treaty of Paris was signed. In America Louis XV ceded New France to Britain, and that part of the Louisiana territory situated west of the Mississippi to Spain, compensation for Florida, which Spain relinquished to the British. Great Britain restored Havana and Manila to Charles III. In India France recovered only Pondicherry and two other trading posts, the remainder of her Indian possessions being ceded to Great Britain. Minorca was restored to Great Britain and certain valuable West Indian islands to France. Both powers withdrew from the continental war. From the British standpoint it was a great peace; for the French, though it did not appear so to contemporaries, it was a disaster. The long Anglo-French colonial duel had ended in the effacement of France.

In Germany, Frederick's success and Austria's lassitude soon led to negotiations, and the Treaty of Hubertsburg was signed five days after the Treaty of Paris. By it the *status quo* was restored, and Maria Theresa finally recognised Frederick's right to Silesia and Flatz. France, it would seem, in the phrase with which the century summed up exhausting labour for small reward, had 'worked for the King of Prussia'. The outcome of the war, however, could be regarded as a personal triumph for Frederick the Great, who in the eyes of Germans remained a national hero and had completed the first phase of the Prussian exclusion of Austria from Germany, which was to be completed only in 1866.

The first partition of Poland

The Seven Years' War had scarcely ended when Europe was threatened by a crisis farther east. In 1763 the death of Augustus III of Saxony again raised the question of the Polish succession. The Polish 'Patriots' were no more

Thomas Augustine Arne (1710–78) a lawyer and musician. One of his most popular airs was *Rule Britannia*, first heard in 1740, which the British people found crystallised their feelings of power, ambition and pride. *National Portrait Gallery*

Stanislas Poniatowski, King of Poland 1764–95, sought in vain to bring Poland the reforms she required. He failed, and presided over his country during its partition between Russia, Prussia and Austria. *Larousse*

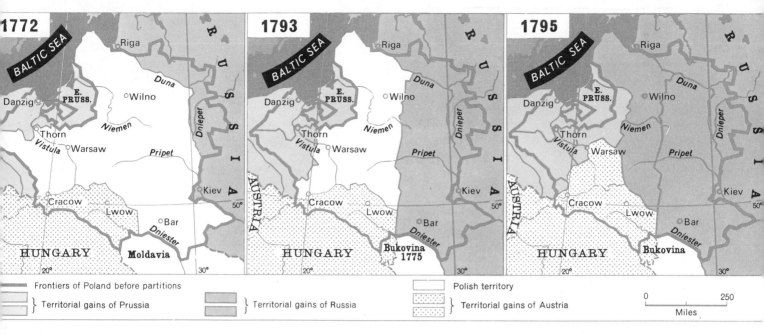

PARTITIONS OF POLAND AT THE END OF THE EIGHTEENTH CENTURY

free from foreign pressure in choosing a sovereign than they had been during the previous election. Austria wanted to ensure the continuity of a large buffer state between herself and Russia and favoured Augustus's son. Catherine II, on the other hand, was eager to strengthen Russia's influence in a disorderly Poland. France, formerly so influential, was divided between the partisans of Saxony and those of a French nobleman. Frederick II wanted to maintain the existing electoral anarchy as a guarantee of Polish weakness and persuaded Catherine to agree with him. Russia and Prussia signed a treaty of alliance in April 1764, and agreed on a candidate, Stanislas Poniatowski, a Polish nobleman and Catherine's lover, who was elected King. He proved to be less manageable than she had anticipated. In 1766 he attempted to introduce certain reforms that clashed with the wishes of the 'Patriots', who were uncompromising defenders of that *liberum veto* which had always hampered efforts to govern Poland effectively. Catherine at once seized on the pretext of posing as the champion of the Dissident Orthodox minority, which was alleged to be oppressed by the Catholic majority. At the Diet of 1767 certain Polish dignitaries were arrested by order of the Russian ambassador; religious equality was proclaimed and guaranteed by the Tsaritsa. Such blatant intervention on the part of a foreign power was indignantly countered by Polish Catholic nobles, who in 1768 formed the Confederation of Bar to rid the country of both Stanislas and the Russian usurpers. Civil war broke out and the Confederation appealed to France. France sent some help and the French ambassador urged the Sultan of Turkey, Mustafa III, to declare war on Russia 'in defence of Polish liberty'. When, in October 1768, Russian troops crossed the Ottoman frontier in pursuit of Polish confederates and set fire to a village, Turkey at once declared war on Russia, and the Polish question became international.

After indecisive operations the Russians succeeded in crossing the Dniester and in 1769 occupied Moldavia

and Wallachia. This alarmed Europe, especially Maria Theresa, who was disturbed by a Russian advance into territories she considered to be her own preserves. As a form of insurance she occupied the small Polish county of Zips, formerly a Hungarian possession. Frederick was delighted: events were moving even more quickly towards partition than he had dared to hope. In 1769 he had a meeting at Neisse with Joseph, Maria Theresa's son and co-regent, and it was resolved that Russia's advance must be checked. But the armies of Catherine II were again victorious in 1770, while her fleet, which had weighed anchor in Kronstad the year before, reached the eastern Mediterranean after sailing round Europe. A Russian landing in Morea, which was intended to support an uprising of the Greeks, hung fire; but Alexis Orloff, commander of the expeditionary force, destroyed the Turkish fleet at Chesme (4 July 1770). This Turkish disaster caused a stir throughout Europe, although the victorious Russian squadron could not force the Straits.

Frederick and Joseph met again at Neustadt in September 1770 to mediate and decide what terms should be offered. Frederick proposed to tempt Russia's appetite with Polish territory — and seize a share of the booty himself. In Poland, meanwhile, anarchy was raging. The French envoy Dumouriez, instead of supporting Poniatowski, was aiding those who intrigued against him, and French influence in Poland had become negligible. To bring round Austria and Russia to his point of view, Frederick played a subtle game. He sent his brother Henry to St Petersburg where the principle of partition was finally accepted. This was hastened by Maria Theresa's own policy, for her hostility to Russia was such that in July 1771 she went so far as to sign a treaty of alliance with Constantinople. In view of the fact that the Habsburgs had for generations been the enemies of the Turks this alliance was a stupefying event; but in eighteenth-century diplomacy such radical re-alignment was no longer unusual. In reward for Maria Theresa's aid the Sultan promised her a part of Wallachia, which had been occupied by the Russians since 1769. The negotiations were of course secret and Catherine was ignorant of this astonishing new political alignment. Frederick, however, gave her an inkling of its possibility and, as he had foreseen, she fell upon Poland and urged its partition among the three. There remained only Maria Theresa to convince. Maria Theresa's conscience protested at such barefaced brigandage, but even more she feared being left out of the bargain.

In July 1772 the Act was signed which carved up a defenceless Poland and it caused much righteous indignation among those who were not signatories. Maria Theresa, for all her tears, received the largest slice — Galicia, with more than two million inhabitants. Catherine gained a million and a half new subjects in White Russia. Frederick's portion had a population of less than a million, but his plan was taking shape: to link East Prussia and Pomerania by the acquisition of Polish West Prussia. In addition he was installed on the lower Vistula, along which travelled wheat from the Polish plains.

The victim was helpless. A carefully picked Polish Diet consented to the partition lest the whole country should be devoured. France, Poland's traditional ally, made no

A German wood panel of the mid-eighteenth century. It shows a huge carved sun in relief surrounded by a decorative trellis work of acanthus leaves. *Marburg*

move. Turkey could not act alone and the Austrian alliance had proved a broken reed. Maria Theresa and Joseph, well satisfied with their share of Poland, hastened to abandon the Sultan, if only to avoid irritating their accomplice, Catherine. Negotiations for peace between Turkey and Russia were opened, but it required two new campaigns before the Sultan's envoys would accept the Treaty of Kutchuk-Kainardji (July 1774). By this treaty Russia obtained not only territory which extended her frontier to the Dniester — with Azov, Kertch and the shores of the Black Sea — but also navigation rights for her fleet in the Black Sea, a commercial advantage long coveted. Finally, the Russian sovereign was recognised as the special protector of his Orthodox co-religionists who were Turkish subjects. This clause was of far-reaching significance, for it supplied later Tsars with a pretext to intervene in Turkish affairs.

The miscalculations of Joseph II

Between the Partition of Poland and the French Revolution the only important international event took place outside Europe: the American War of Independence. Meanwhile the ambitions of the Austrian Emperor, Joseph II, periodically caused tension. In 1775, shortly after the Treaty of Kutchuk-Kainardji, the Emperor demanded, and obtained, from the Sultan Bukovina, which had formerly been attached to Podolia. Later, in 1778, he attempted to seize parts of Bavaria at the death of its Elector Maximilian III without a direct heir. This only enabled Frederick II to pose as the champion of the rights of German princes. Joseph's attempts to obtain French support had already failed and when Frederick invaded Bohemia and opened the so-called 'War of the Bavarian Succession' Joseph found himself alone. As it happened, operations were soon halted. France proposed mediation and Russia joined her. In May 1779 the Congress of Teschen restored peace. Of the Bavarian inheritance Joseph received only a small slice of territory by the River Inn, a poor compensation; but Frederick, as skilful as ever, had derived appreciable benefits: the expectation of inheriting the Margravates of Anspach and Bayreuth, which were enclaves in Bavaria of a collateral branch of the Hohenzollern family, and a blow at Habsburg influence in Germany.

Joseph II then turned his attention to the difficulties which had arisen between Turkey and Russia over the Khan of the Crimea. Eager to exploit the situation, Joseph arranged a meeting with Catherine in 1780 in the hope of sharing the possible Turkish spoils. Maria Theresa, who thoroughly disapproved of these schemes, died at the end of 1780. When trouble in the Crimea began again in 1782 Catherine suggested her 'Greek project' to Vienna. This plan had been inspired by her protégés, the Phanariotes — who derived their name from their origin in the Greek quarter of Phanar in Constantinople — and who, under the distant suzerainty of the Sultan, now governed in Moldavia and in Wallachia. According to the project, these provinces were to form a kingdom of Dacia: a Greek empire would thus be carved out for Catherine's grandson, whose name, symbolically, was Constantine. Russia would be satisfied with a strip of territory bordering the Black Sea, while Austria would gain Serbia, Bosnia, Dalmatia and Istria. Compensation was to be given to Venice, and France would be offered Egypt. This colossal plan of partition did not tempt Vergennes; Joseph, too, hesitated and drew back. Catherine acted alone and sent Potemkin, her successful general and reigning favourite, into the Crimea. By the Convention of Constantinople in January 1784 the Sultan was forced to hand over to the Tsaritsa the Crimea and the province of Kuban. Her ambitions had been furthered, but the Emperor gained nothing.

During the War of American Independence Joseph II was tireless in his efforts to take what advantage he could of the situation. When Britain declared war on the United Provinces he seized the occasion to abolish on his own authority the system of Dutch-held barrier fortresses in the Netherlands. Then, in a further attempt on Bavaria, which he still coveted, he proposed to the Elector of Bavaria an exchange of Bavaria for the Netherlands, which in any case were too far from Vienna to be easily governed. He tried to draw France into the scheme by the offer of Hainaut and Luxemburg. Vergennes once more prudently refused. The heir apparent to Bavaria, Charles August, Duke of Zweibrücken, haughtily protested as he had before. At the same time Joseph, perpetually dissatisfied, decided to reopen the Scheldt to navigation. As in the days of Charles VI's Ostend Company, this attacked the economic privileges of the maritime powers and violated the Treaty of Münster, of which France was the guarantor. In such ways Joseph II succeeded in antagonising everyone. In Germany a 'League of Princes' was formed at the instigation of Frederick II against the Emperor's pretensions. The Elector of Bavaria changed his mind about·exchanging his duchy for the Netherlands. Vergennes then approached Joseph on the sore subject of reopening the Scheldt and in 1785 the Emperor was obliged to give way.

Checked in the west, Joseph once again turned his attention to the east, where Catherine II, more than ever bent on glory, had asked for his co-operation. In 1787 she organised her famous excursion through the Crimea, a propaganda tour with triumphal arches and brilliant retinues, to advertise to the world Russian progress towards the south. She met the Emperor at Kherson on the shores of the Black Sea. But Joseph II was less enthusiastic than he had once been. Furthermore the Turks, at whom the threat was directed, took the initiative by declaring war. Meanwhile in the north Sweden found the moment propitious for action, and Gustavus III crossed the Russian frontier without the formality of declaring war. His was no longer the Sweden of Gustavus Adolphus or of Charles XII, and Catherine staved off her new enemy with the aid of a Swedish-Finnish conspiracy against Gustavus. Although in 1788 Joseph joined Catherine in the war against Turkey, the Turks, contrary to general expectations, were not unsuccessful and ambitious schemes for a partition of the Ottoman Empire had to be postponed. Then, in 1790, the luckless Emperor Joseph II died having achieved none of his diplomatic aims. Events in Western Europe made Catherine anxious to end the Turkish war and a peace treaty was signed in 1792. But the obvious weakness of the Ottoman Empire and the precariousness of Poland meant that Eastern Europe had still not found an equilibrium.

Enlightened despotism

In the second half of the eighteenth century, and especially after the Seven Years' War, some European states appeared to become more sharply aware of their backwardness by comparison with Great Britain and France. This awareness was strengthened and spread by the cosmopolitanism of the governing classes and the enthusiasm of some of them for the new ideas which were abroad. The result was the curious phenomenon of reforms, many of which seemed liberal and progressive at first sight, imposed from above and in an authoritarian manner. In all countries, elements of a common inspiration for these reforms in the ideas of the *philosophes*, and the manner in which they were applied, lent them the appearance of a broad general movement, or even of a systematic doctrine, to which historians in the nineteenth century gave the name 'Enlightened Despotism' or 'Benevolent Despotism'. There was certainly a family resemblance in the trend's manifestations, but there was also great diversity

Hans Joachim von Zieten, most brilliant of Frederick the Great's cavalrymen. Having studied light cavalry tactics under Austrian command he introduced them to the Prussian army with outstanding success. He wears the cap of a Hussar regiment. *Marburg*

from one state to another, and never a general theory of government.

One inspiration can be traced in Louis XIV's autocratic theories of monarchy. Like Louis XIV the 'Enlightened Despots' sought to establish a royal power without limits by means of a centralised administration of which they were the supreme head, by the creation of a bureaucracy entirely devoted to their interests, and by taming the nobility. But such a despotism in the eighteenth century was tempered by the new and enlightened ideas which were in the air, even though some of them remained more theoretical than practical: the abolition of remaining feudal and aristocratic privileges, forced labour, serfdom and torture; a desire to improve the administration of justice, to levy taxes more equitably, to ensure that a greater number could reach a high level of education, and the establishment of religious toleration. Toleration, naturally, led to the acceptance of all forms of belief. It also meant bringing the clergy to heel, and greater freedom from Roman control. The Church was to cease to be a rival authority to the State. In the latter part of this programme — if Enlightened Despotism can be said to have had a programme — the influence of *philosophes* like Voltaire was undeniable. Many of the monarchs or powerful ministers who could claim to call themselves Enlightened Despots were not averse to advertising their familiarity with such advanced views and used them to justify their policies before current opinion.

173

Austria under Maria Theresa and Joseph II

Under Maria Theresa herself the term Enlightened Despotism is perhaps less appropriate than Benevolent Maternalism. Her reforms were real, but also a prelude to the more systematic reforms of her son Joseph, with whom she governed as co-regent for fifteen years. She began tentatively and prudently to try to strengthen the State after the loss of Silesia in 1748. To raise money to ensure safety against another such humiliation administrative and legal reforms were urgently needed. The Empress realised that she could not openly flout the complex and varied traditions of the diverse peoples who formed her empire. To obtain success she must flatter and tread warily. Her first efforts were directed towards the administration and its outdated institutions. In 1749 Haugwitz persuaded her to adopt a first series of reforms which were in principle excellent if in practice too drastic; the various existing councils were to be replaced by centralised and specialised departments — for foreign affairs a State Chancellery, for the administration of justice a Supreme Court of Appeal, for military matters a War Department, and, most important of all, for political and financial questions the *Direktorium*, which in fact deprived the former Chancelleries of State of their functions. Before the end of the Seven Years' War, which revealed the defects of these measures, a new series of reforms was launched at the instigation of Kaunitz. An able diplomat, Kaunitz affected the greatest possible respect for traditional institutions; but in practice he took steps to bring about centralisation, creating, for example, a Council of State which overrode all interdepartmental disputes. In the same year, 1761, the *Direktorium*, which had been much criticised for the excessive centralisation of its powers, was replaced by a chancellery for political affairs and several specialised departments for financial matters. In the administration of the provinces reforms were also introduced. Uniform administrative areas were created — ' governments ' and ' circles ' — whose functionaries were responsible no longer to the individual Estates, but to the Crown. Austria was becoming bureaucratic. Hungary nevertheless retained much of its autonomy, since Maria Theresa hesitated to offend the powerful Hungarian magnates.

Financial reform was more difficult. To apportion taxes more justly an official register of real estate was planned which would include the property of the nobility, until then exempted from taxation. Meanwhile, the Empress was obliged to rely on subsidies from the provincial Estates, who granted them with reluctance. The issuing of notes by the Bank of Vienna, which had become the State Bank, did little to improve the condition of the Treasury. On the whole, Maria Theresa's initiative in economic fields was negligible. Austria remained an essentially agricultural country in which, for lack of good roads, even internal trade was slight. The port facilities at Trieste were developed, but with disappointing results.

The Empress was more interested in the army and in education. It was her desire to make of the army an instrument ever ready to defend the frontiers. In this, no doubt, her Prussian neighbour served both as an example and a stimulus. She founded a school for officers and piously instituted for their benefit a possibly unappreciated ' Tribunal of Chastity '. Her educational policy was guided by the same high moral principles. Her counsellor,

Joseph II, son of Maria Theresa, ruled alone after his mother's death from 1780 to 1790. He attempted revolutionary changes in the structure of the Habsburg Empire and almost caused its disintegration because of the opposition he aroused. *Kester Lichtbild-Archiv*

the Dutch doctor Van Swieten, drew up a strict plan of study which she proposed to apply in the numerous educational establishments then founded. A board of censors kept a severe eye on all foreign books imported; at this time intellectual life in the capital of the Habsburgs was not notable for its brilliance. Maria Theresa's piety was, however, far from ultramontane. She much admired several works inspired by Bishop Febronius, whose doctrines were similar to those of the Gallicans in the French Church.

On the death of the Emperor Francis I in 1765, his son Joseph was elected without difficulty to the Imperial throne. Maria Theresa then began to share the government of Austria with him as co-regent. Joseph's unscrupulous and, worse still, unsuccessful foreign policy discredited him in the eyes of his contemporaries. Cold and secretive, he was intelligent and he had a gift for organisation. Though endowed with a capacity for hard work, he suffered from a lack of realism and seemed to pursue grandiose dreams; he was too systematic and too harsh in applying otherwise excellent ideas. Like many of his contemporaries he was over-influenced by the powerful personality of Frederick the Great. Joseph failed to grasp that what Frederick autocratically, and even brutally, accomplished in the plains of northern Germany could not be repeated in his own Habsburg possessions without encountering opposition from powerful vested interests. He lacked political sense.

Completing the work which his mother had initiated, he merged the ancient historic provinces of his extensive domains into a single state, and divided it into thirteen areas, each under a governor. The servants of the new bureaucracy, dependent on the Crown, were from 1784 permitted to use only the German tongue, which thus became the official language. When Maria Theresa died, Joseph embarked on those reforms which were dearest to his heart, reforms which epitomised the spirit of Benevolent Despotism. In 1781 two edicts were promulgated:

one abolished serfdom, which hampered the improvement of agricultural production; the other proclaimed religious toleration. He furiously attacked ' those parasites ', the religious orders, and closed seven hundred monasteries, confiscating their goods and using their wealth to found schools. Though he disliked monks, the secular clergy were encouraged, educated in State seminaries and nourished on the anti-ultramontane and Jansenist doctrines of Febronius. In 1782 Joseph outlawed pilgrimages and religious processions. The Pope, Pius VI, was alarmed, and came to Vienna in person. Though courteously received he obtained nothing from the stubborn Emperor, after whom this attempt to establish a national, secular Church in Austria was called ' Josephism '.

Joseph II's economic and financial reforms were less systematic. On the one hand he was a protectionist and discouraged the import of foreign luxury articles. On the other hand he removed all restrictions on the internal circulation of grain and in 1782 abolished trade guilds. The great official register of real estate which had been planned was not completed, and the Emperor's dream of a single tax payable on all landed property remained unrealised.

Towards the end of his life protests arose from every quarter of his dominion. The Hungarians objected furiously to being brought into line with the remainder of his subjects and were outraged at the transfer of the crown of St Stephen to Vienna. In the ' circles ' of Transylvania, Hora led a revolt which was ruthlessly crushed in 1784. Even the supine Lombards murmured. Then, on the eve of the French Revolution, the Belgians rebelled. Everywhere the nobles complained that they had been ruined by the liberation of their serfs. Ultramontane churchmen attacked his ecclesiastical reforms. Discouraged but clear-sighted, Joseph II proposed for his tomb the epitaph: ' Here lies a Prince who failed in all he undertook '.

The Austrian Netherlands

Among the scattered possessions of the Habsburgs the Netherlands were unique. Not only were they far from Vienna, but they enjoyed traditions of urban liberty and a brilliant civilisation which brought them nearer in spirit to the Western nations than to the still feudal monarchies of Central Europe. Hence their resistance to Viennese centralism. Under Maria Theresa there was a certain revival of prosperity. Subsidies and the abolition of vexatious guild regulations helped local industry, especially the manufacture of linen for export. Coal-mining also made progress. In 1769 Maria Theresa founded the Academy of Brussels. After the suppression of the Jesuits several royal colleges were opened, but their programmes of study were too advanced to have much appeal to a population still deeply imbued with the spirit of the Counter-Reformation.

Maria Theresa had been too wise to interfere with the traditional political organisation of the eleven provinces, and they had accepted the guardianship of Austria without much resentment. The situation changed for the worse with the accession of Joseph II, who despised the Belgians and had wanted to exchange them for Bavarians. He began by curtailing the financial powers of the provincial councils. Then, by an edict of January 1787, he wiped out the old political and judicial divisions. The eleven provinces were redistributed in nine ' circles ' and lost their former privileges. Resistance was at once organised and took the form of a refusal to pay taxes. Trautmannsdorf, the Austrian Governor, rigorously applied the measures which had been adopted and suppressed the riots which resulted. Brabant and Hainaut, which were hardest hit, led the insurrectionary movement. The Emperor remained firm and refused all compromise. The year was 1789 and in France revolution was in the air. It found

A representation of Venice in 1765. By this date her ancient commercial hegemony was in ruins and other ports were gathering the trade which had once come to the lagoons. Soon, Trieste was to become the major port of the Adriatic. *Radio Times Hulton Picture Library*

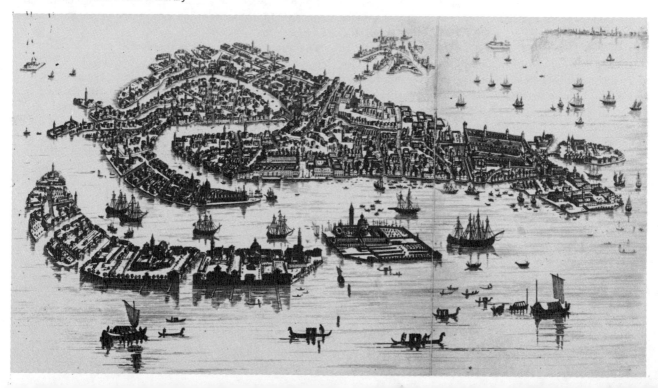

echoes in the neighbouring Netherlands among liberal reformers grouped around Vonck. The common struggle against Austria had drawn Vonck closer to his political opponent, Van der Noot, leader of the other current of opinion, which was aristocratic, traditionalist and Catholic. Armed revolt broke out in Brabant and spread to the rest of the country. Joseph II, who had his hands full in the East, could for the moment do nothing about it, and in December 1789 the Constitution of the United Belgian States was proclaimed in Brussels. The task of crushing the rebellion fell to Joseph's successor, Leopold II, but though unsuccessful, the uprising had revealed the liberal aspirations of the Belgians and the birth of a national sentiment eager to throw off the yoke of a foreign sovereign.

Italy and the Holy See

Italy was more than ever a zone of Austrian influence in the second half of the eighteenth century. The Duchy of Milan was a direct possession of the Crown while Tuscany was ruled by an Austrian archduke. Even in Naples and Parma the Bourbon sovereigns were married to Habsburg archduchesses. All these states shared with the Austria of Joseph II a common trait: namely the attempt to enforce a strict control over the clergy, who were considered to be agents of the Holy See.

In the Milanese Joseph II, like Maria Theresa before him, had the good sense to use officials who belonged to the aristocracy of the country. In spite of the suppression of the Senate, the Habsburgs' Lombard subjects did not suffer from the impression of being persecuted. They made little protest at measures aimed at curbing the Church's power, such as the Concordat of 1746 and the founding of a State seminary at Pavia. Furthermore they took pride in Pavia and Milan, which were outstanding cultural centres and boasted such figures as Volta, the inventor of the electric battery, and Beccaria, a jurist of international renown.

On the death of its Grand Duke Francis of Lorraine — who in 1745 became the Emperor Francis I — Tuscany fell to his second son, Leopold — himself a future Emperor — who reigned in Florence from 1765 to 1792. Leopold introduced humane judicial reforms and attacked feudal rights. In religious matters his hostility towards the Holy See surpassed even that of his older brother Joseph II. He was much influenced in this by Scipio Ricci, Bishop of Pistoia. Gallicanism, transplanted to Tuscany, mingled with certain elements of Jansenism and, greatly affected by the sovereign's desire to enjoy the revenues of vacant ecclesiastical offices, led to Ricci's attempt in 1786 to challenge Papal authority in a synod of his clergy; the majority of the clergy refused to follow him in such extravagance.

In Parma, whose Duke Philip, son of Elisabeth Farnese, had married a daughter of Louis XV, the minister Du Tillot wielded power from 1759 to 1771. Even after Philip's death in 1765 he remained in office during the minority of Philip's oldest son, Ferdinand, and suppressed the financial privileges of the clergy and the Roman Inquisition. Ferdinand, who reigned until 1802, dismissed Du Tillot when, after his marriage to an Austrian archduchess in 1769, French influence in Parma began to decline.

In Naples Don Carlos, who became King of Spain in 1759, initiated drastic reforms with the aid of his anti-clerical minister Tanucci. Legal codification was also begun by Tanucci, who grappled with the administrative tangle caused by the existence of eleven different legislative bodies and, under Don Carlos's successor, Ferdinand IV, continued his work for a further sixteen years. Ferdinand IV — also married to an Austrian archduchess who, incidentally, succeeded in getting rid of Tanucci — refused to acknowledge the theoretical suzerainty of the Pope over his domain. He did everything in his power to have the Jesuit Order suppressed. On the other hand, under Ferdinand IV lack of capital and unwillingness to disturb the powerful landed nobility, who were exempt from taxation, held back economic improvement.

The other states of Italy remained outside the Habsburg-Bourbon influence and were less affected by the breath of reform. Nevertheless in the kingdom of Sardinia, under Charles Emmanuel III and Victor Amadeus III, able sovereigns devoted to their duties, a legal code was published. Turin became an intellectual centre and an academy was founded. The two maritime republics of Genoa and Venice remained under the domination of a conservative aristocracy but they, too, carried out some reforms. Venice was more celebrated, though, as a centre of artists and pleasure-seekers. Its festivals and carnivals, its painters, Guardi and Belloto, its dramatists, Goldoni and Gozzi, drew a golden veil over its period of decadence.

Finally, in the Papal States the burning issue was the fate of the Society of Jesus, which was suppressed by Clement XIV in 1773. The Popes had to defend themselves against attacks from all quarters, but their dominions, while remaining the worst governed in Italy, experienced some economic improvements as a result of the policies of Cardinal Ruffo.

Enlightened Despotism, then, did not produce a national regeneration in Italy. It scarcely shook Italian torpor, the roots of which lay in economic stagnation. Such benefits as limited reforms had brought about were appropriated by an aristocratic minority. Italian princes lacked the means to make their despotism absolute, and for this reason were forced to be satisfied with anti-clerical measures which were relatively easy to enforce and which prepared the ground for the eventual dissolution of the Papal States.

The Prussia of Frederick the Great

War had left Frederick II little time to organise his kingdom before 1763. Until then, he toyed with the two most pressing problems: the simplification of a legal system which was extremely involved, and the development of the army. At the peace, his first task was that of reconstruction of his devastated provinces, which he undertook doggedly though somewhat unsystematically. Frederick made much of his devotion to the *philosophes* but in practice the interests of the State took precedence over all philosophical theories. He was more a political pragmatist than an Enlightened Despot and remained well

The death of St Ephraim Desiro. Cretan icon (thought to be seventeenth century) from the Monastery of Gouverneto, north-west Crete. *John Donat*

within the Hohenzollern tradition, being primarily concerned with the army and the treasury. An efficient army could be produced by maintaining the traditions established by his father, regular exercises and by rebuilding the officer corps. As for finance, Frederick economised at all costs, and increased his revenues by means of heavier indirect taxation and by establishing a system of State control over certain products. The sale of salt, tobacco and coffee was a State monopoly, as was the postal service. To ensure that his functionaries did not abuse their positions to line their own pockets he saw that they were highly paid.

Frederick was aware that the wealth of a nation depends equally on the number of its inhabitants and on the prosperity of its trade and industry and was tireless in his efforts to attract Germans from more densely populated regions like Würtemburg to his own kingdom, and especially to East Prussia. He opened veritable recruiting offices in foreign countries. To peasant pioneers he lent horses and seed-potatoes, which did well in the sandy plains of the north. He liberated the serfs on his own domains. At the end of his reign Prussia numbered six million inhabitants: in other words, the population had doubled in fifty years. After 1763 industry, too, made considerable strides, but the methods Frederick employed were reminiscent of Colbert rather than of the industrial economy which was just beginning to appear in Great Britain. Frederick nurtured the infant industries of Prussia by means of a wall of high tariffs at the frontiers. To stimulate the circulation of capital he created loan and mortgage banks and in 1767 the Bank of Berlin. As production rose, so did exports, especially of cloth and wheat.

In the realm of education Frederick the Great also clearly revealed his sense of the practical, ignoring his own personal tastes for the sake of what he considered expedient. Himself an admirer and speaker of French, he encouraged the teaching of German, which was the language of the administration and therefore more useful. With the aid of his minister Zedlitz he reformed secondary school instruction, with the practical aim of turning out good civil servants. In 1763 he made elementary schooling compulsory in theory (in practice the plan proved too costly). Religious toleration was the rule, and the King himself, a freethinker and given to sarcasm, indulged in witticisms at the expense of the clergy. Yet he was glad to open his frontiers to the secularised Jesuits of all countries, for they were educated men who could be of value to the State.

In other words, Frederick examined all problems, social and human, in the light of the over-riding interest of Prussia, of which he considered himself merely the first servant. The great enterprise of codifying the law, the *Corpus juris fredericianum*, which was enthusiastically begun at the opening of his reign, was not put into force until 1794, in the reign of his successor. Frederick's abolition of torture was a spectacular measure calculated to put him in the front rank of enlightened sovereigns who, it must be admitted, were admired by a public opinion

The Dukes of Savoy came of a dynasty which succeeded in the seventeenth and eighteenth centuries in turning a petty dukedom into the nucleus of a nation state. The foundations were laid by Victor Amadeus I (1630–37). *Larousse*

Victor Amadeus's grandson Victor Amadeus II (1675–1730) became King of Sicily after the Spanish Succession War, but had to exchange it for Sardinia in 1720. Under him the country won a seat at the council of nations. *Larousse*

The ornate interior of a Bavarian rococo church at Amorbach, 1742-47. *Archiv für Kunst und Geschichte*

L

Charles Emmanuel III (1730–73), son of Victor Amadeus II fought with Maria Theresa in the Austrian Succession War. The Treaty of Aix-la-Chapelle brought him part of Lombardy to add to the dominions of the house in North Italy. *Larousse*

Charles Emmanuel's son Victor Amadeus III (1773–96) brought great prosperity to Sardinia but was overtaken by the wars of the French Revolution. By May 1790 Sardinia had been defeated and Nice and Savoy surrendered to France.

formed and often misled by flattering writers. In reality morals and manners gained little from his reign. His pragmatism and his cynicism spread and many contemporaries considered the society of Berlin corrupt. Nevertheless when he died in 1786 Frederick left behind him a renewed and more powerful Prussia, and a reputation which had long since spread throughout Europe. For writers of the German literary renaissance he incarnated the very genius of Germany. One of his manuals had been Voltaire's *The Age of Louis XIV*, and he was eager that his reign should be known as 'The Age of Frederick II'. The rise of Prussia was without doubt one of the most remarkable occurrences of the eighteenth century. Frederick, with his refined Machiavellianism, was one of its most remarkable figures, whatever damage he may have done indirectly by hampering Germany's understanding of political liberalism.

Frederick's death was followed by a sudden and curious religious revival. The new King, Frederick William II, lacking both will and ability, relinquished the government to ministers who were members of the mystic Rosicrucian sect. They at once set in motion what amounted to an inquisition to eradicate free thought. Liberty of expression was almost abolished by the religious edict of 1788, and the philosophy courses of the great Immanuel Kant were suspended. The slackness of the new King was reflected throughout the State and abuses developed. In spite of this, however, the essentials of Frederick's work survived.

The Empire in Germany

In spite of the example given by Austria and Prussia the reform movement made little headway in the remainder of the Empire. Traces of enlightenment were discernible: the development of a cultivated élite, and the awakening, still hesitant, of a common national sentiment throughout Germany. Only the larger principalities made serious attempts at reform. In Saxony Frederick Augustus III (1763–1827) inaugurated his long reign with a policy of planned economy. The administration of justice became more humane, industry progressed, and a real effort was made to improve public instruction; serfdom, however, was not touched. The states in the west were more highly developed. Bavaria owed reforms to a wise sovereign, Maximilian Joseph III (1745–77), and his minister Kreittmayr, who re-organised the legal system. In this traditionally Catholic duchy there was a growth of toleration towards Protestants. During the reign of Charles Frederick (1738–1811) the Margravate of Baden also introduced religious toleration. His neighbour Charles Eugene (1737–93), Duke of Würtemburg, merely dissipated his fortune in debauchery and neglected an administration so deplorable that the country was impoverished and its inhabitants driven to emigrate. Such contrasts illustrated the personal responsibility of the despots for the destiny of the subjects entrusted to their 'enlightenment'.

Russia under Catherine the Great

Peter III of Holstein had succeeded the Tsaritsa Elizabeth in 1762. The new Tsar's German origin, brutal manners and contempt for everything Russian displeased everyone. His wife, Catherine of Anhalt-Zerbst, was a German too, but she was a fervent convert to Russian Orthodoxy.

Catherine II, Tsaritsa 1762–96. Of German extraction, she identified herself completely with Russia, even going as far as to be admitted to the Orthodox church. Under her, Russian expansion to the South and West began in earnest.

A Russian icon, showing the Virgin and child, and, below, the three traditional Russian saints, George, Nicholas and Dimitri. *Marburg*

Immanuel Kant (1724–1805) author of *The Critique of Pure Reason*. The founder of German idealist philosophy, he admitted to philosophical thinking the emphasis on feeling which he found in the writings of Rousseau.

She was also afraid of being supplanted as the Tsar's wife by a favourite. A plot was hatched with a group of army officers, the backing of certain regiments of the Imperial guard, and the support of members of the Holy Synod. Catherine was then acclaimed as Empress by the Senate. Peter III was imprisoned and a few days later was found dead in his prison cell. No one had any illusions about his death: the glorious reign of Catherine II had begun with a crime.

The new Tsaritsa proposed to shake her new subjects out of their traditional apathy. Moved by ambition, a taste for publicity, a desire to astonish the universe and to earn the praise of the *philosophes*, she proposed to do great things. She, too, had read the *philosophes*; but, in the event, she made more use of them than they did of her. Intelligent and a realist, Catherine well knew that a backward if not barbarous country like Russia could not be governed by abstractions, however enlightened. She had no doctrine, and even gave the impression of feeling her way. Basically, like Peter the Great, she made her real ambition the triumph of Russian imperialism, and to realise that ambition it was necessary to secure her own position of absolute authority.

More than the other so-called enlightened sovereigns, Catherine was a despot, and even a cruel one. Nothing was done about liberating the serfs, since the entire regime and the whole Russian economy was founded on the master-serf relationship. Actually Catherine worsened serf conditions by secularising large tracts of land belonging to the Church, a measure which won the applause of the opponents of 'fanaticism' but which had the social consequence of transferring the serfs from Church domains, where they were relatively well treated, to much harsher conditions under the Crown. Their wretchedness was further aggravated by frequent gifts of Crown land to favoured nobles. Among the peasants faint rumblings of confused protest ensued, encouraged not only by ill-treatment and starvation, but by mysticism and super-stition. Discontent overflowed with the harsh measures Catherine took to extend colonisation and land-reclamation towards the south and the east. In 1771 a Cossack visionary named Pugachov claimed to be the late Tsar Peter III, thought to have been murdered but miraculously alive. 179

Cossack skirmishing with Prussian dragoons. The Cossacks, distinct communities, already supplied the Russian army of the eighteenth century with its best light cavalry. *S.C.R.*

At Tsarskoe-Selo Peter the Great built his summer palace to match the great winter palace on the Neva in St. Petersburg. The architect of both was Rastrelli, one of several Italians who embellished Russian building in the eighteenth century. *Larousse*

A Russian embassy is received by the Sultan in 1775. The Treaty of Kutchuk Kainardji of 1774 marked the first great triumph of Russia against the Turk. By it Russia received privileges to intervene for the Sultan's Christian subjects.

He collected a large peasant following, to whom he promised all that their hearts desired, and went to war to drive the usurper from the throne. The Imperial troops were taken aback by this sudden explosion of popular fury and in the region of the Don and the Volga were faced with a dangerous civil war, during which the most brutal atrocities were committed. Catherine, genuinely frightened, had sent her best generals. Pugachov was defeated by Suvorov, hunted down, captured in 1774 and finally executed in Moscow. This spontaneous wave of insurrection among the serfs should have served as a warning to the Tsaritsa. In a way, it did. By a ukase, or edict, of 1785 she reduced the status of the serfs to that of mere chattels, and banishment to Siberia became an everyday occurrence.

Catherine had planned to regularise and codify the entire administration. In 1765 she submitted her plans to a ' Great Commission ' of 564 deputies who represented the free classes of the population and were armed with lists of grievances. The arguments and discord which resulted served chiefly to convince the Empress that she must ignore such advisers and in future act as she herself saw fit. In 1775 she reformed both the administrative areas and the judicial system. The country was divided into fifty provinces which were in turn further subdivided; each province was supplied with its own tribunals of varying importance, nobles, peasants and merchants all having their own. After this attempted reform, which did little to modify the slow-moving immensity of Russia, her efforts — such as the Charter of the Nobility of 1785 — merely reinforced the local power of the nobles and even further widened the gulf between the classes. The right accorded to the nobility to take part in trade and industry further lessened the likelihood of a new middle class emerging in the towns. The organs of government changed little; gradually the Councils turned into Ministries. The Senate was composed of nobles who deferred to the Tsaritsa's lover of the moment: after the reign of the Orloffs, Potemkin was all-powerful from 1774 to 1791.

Catherine's whims and her love of publicity were not, however, the whole story. She was responsible for the creation of cities of future importance: Kherson, Sevastopol, Odessa. Though her efforts to reform taxation were fruitless, the army was kept in good condition. The economic development of the country was such that stifling industrial regulations could progressively be abolished and Russia became a unified customs area. In the Urals metallurgical enterprises were ceded by the State to private owners. New regions were put under cultivation and, when necessary, peopled by attracting foreign settlers. In this way a colony of Germans was established on the banks of the Volga.

As for education, like every eighteenth-century sovereign influenced by the *philosophes*, Catherine had a plan in mind at the beginning of her reign, but she neglected it for lack of money. The sons of the nobility were in practice the sole beneficiaries of foundations like the Smolny Institute, the university of Nijni-Novgorod, and the School of Cadets, institutions disproportionately enlarged by, and for, the benefit of Catherine's friends among the *philosophes* — Diderot, d'Alembert and others.

From the French sculptor Falconet she commissioned the most grandiose equestrian figure of the eighteenth century: Peter the Great on his fiery steed, dominating an enormous rock. It was the symbol of her ambition, for Catherine herself wished to continue the work of the great Peter in first opening this vast Eastern nation to Europe and first revealing its latent power. The happiness of her people, however, meant little to her: under her guidance Russia pursued more firmly than ever a course in which a despot and an aristocratic minority were united in the exploitation of the masses. By the end of her reign the country was feeling the effects. 'Enlightenment' had brought little but corruption to Holy Russia, and Catherine the Great, the 'Semiramis of the North' left behind her a slightly tarnished glory and very few regrets.

Poland after the first partition

Stricken by the rapacity of her neighbours and the partition of 1772, Poland attempted to rise to her feet again during the reign of Stanislas II (Poniatowski). Stanislas was an 'enlightened' sovereign in as much as he corresponded with blue-stockings and patronised physiocrats; but he was very far from being a despot. Indeed, between foreign intrigues and pressure and squabbles among the rival parties of the Polish Diet, the King could scarcely maintain his own authority. If reforms were in fact undertaken this was not on the King's initiative but because a cultivated minority of the nobility were conscious of the dangers which lay in wait for their nation. Nothing, however, was done to rescue the economy of a country in which great landowners willingly left huge estates uncultivated. There was no commercial or industrial middle class, and no money. Only the smallest army could be maintained, and that was too large in the eyes of Catherine II, who had never relinquished her idea of making Poland an annex of Russia. Reforms were limited to the re-organisation of public instruction after the suppression of the Jesuits. The Educational Commission, whose guiding light was Kollontaï, set about its task in a very modern spirit. In 1788, on the eve of the French Revolution, the Great Diet was convoked. Too late it had decided on a vast programme of reforms, which in any case would not have provided Poland with the 'despot' she needed in order to survive.

Denmark and Struensee

In Denmark Frederick V, who reigned from 1746 to 1766, began a few administrative and humanitarian reforms with the aid of his minister, Bernstorff; but they were interrupted by Danish involvement in the Seven Years' War. Christian VII, who succeeded Frederick V as King of Denmark and Norway, was a sovereign of bizarre tastes and little ability. Nevertheless he succeeded in exchanging Oldenburg for Schleswig-Holstein, thus rounding off Danish territory more neatly. True Enlightened Despotism in Denmark began only with a German, Struensee, whom the Queen, who was his mistress, raised to the position of Chief Minister in 1770. In a year and a half of almost absolute power Struensee achieved an impressive number of reforms. He re-organised the country's finances, its economy and its legal system. He centralised the administration, liberated the serfs and imposed religious toleration. He did all this with such ruthless brutality that a plot to remove him led to his arrest in January 1772, and his execution. After his death Andreas Bernstorff,

Christian VII, King of Denmark and Norway from 1766 to 1808, during whose reign two able ministers, Struensee and Bernstorff, brought the radical reforms of Enlightened Despotism to Denmark. *Larousse*

a nephew of the earlier minister, came to power. But Struensee's reforms were not annulled, and by the end of the century Denmark enjoyed great prosperity, based largely on a thriving maritime trade.

Sweden under Gustavus III

The weak Adolphus Frederick, who reigned in Sweden from 1751 to 1771, failed in 1756 in an attempt to strengthen the power of the Crown, but the country continued to remain profitably at peace. In 1771 he was succeeded without difficulties by his nephew, Gustavus III. Gustavus, who was only twenty-five, had received a French education and in France had become personally acquainted not only with statesmen but with intellectuals. Intelligent and ambitious, his immediate aim was to shake off restraints on the Crown's power, and at the same time to free Sweden from foreign interference, especially British and Russian. Actively supported by French money, he achieved what amounted to a coup d'état by persuading the Estates to vote a new constitution giving the King the right to convoke them only when he wished. From then onwards, he was in reality an enlightened despot. With the collaboration of able ministers he abolished torture and improved the administration of justice. Under his reign, the economic life of the country began to suffer when

Russian iron-ore began to compete in the British market. Swedish intellectual life, on the other hand, prospered under his patronage of the arts and of the theatre. In 1786 he founded the Swedish Academy.

After a long period of peace Gustavus's ambitions gradually grew. To put an end to Russian intrigues among members of the Swedish Riksdag he went to war in 1788 with Catherine II. In the following year he successfully quelled a rebellion of nobles in Stockholm and assumed dictatorial power. In 1792 he fell, a victim of another conspiracy among the nobles which revealed the extent of his achievements in undermining the privileges which had helped to preserve the political decadence of Sweden.

Spain under Charles III

On the death of Ferdinand VI in 1759 Don Carlos (1716–88) became King of Spain. He had been king at Naples for twenty years. Less striking than the other great sovereigns of the second half of the eighteenth century, he nevertheless patiently carried out reforms which were frequently excellent. Like his ancestor Louis XIV, Charles III was an absolute monarch and applied himself to centralising the administration, extending the system of Intendants, reducing the powers of the *Cortes*, and attacking the privileges of the nobility. Again like Louis XIV, he preferred to choose his ministers — Florida Blanca, Campománes — from the middle class. Himself a pious man, he nevertheless affirmed the supremacy of the State over the Church, quarrelled with the Holy See, attacked the Inquisition and, above all, the Jesuits. In 1766 riots broke out in several parts of the kingdom. They were provoked by misery and want, and public fury was directed towards the unpopular Italian minister Squillace. Charles III saw the hidden hand of the Jesuits in the revolt, and summarily decreed their expulsion from Spain. In the final condemnation of the Jesuits Charles's action carried weight. The closing of Jesuit colleges furnished an occasion to reform the educational system, but the King had little hold over the universities, and though reforms were made the results were disappointing.

In his plans for reconstruction Charles III was handicapped by lack of money, in spite of the gold which came from the colonies and a fiscal reform which extended the system of State control over the collection of revenue throughout almost the whole of Spain. In 1782 he authorised Cabarrus, a French banker, to set up a bank which issued shares, paper money and functioned like a State Bank. This version of Law's experiment failed. In spite of these difficulties, it was the Government, rather than private enterprise, which achieved important economic progress. Officially, Spain was mercantilist and protectionist. Nevertheless the spirit of the eighteenth century and the theories of the physiocrats penetrated Spain by means of ' Economic Societies ' or ' Societies of Friends of the Country ', which were created on the model of the *Sociedad Vascongada*, founded in the Basque provinces in 1765 by an enlightened nobleman named Peñaflorida. In these societies the provincial intelligentsia would gather to discuss methods of promoting prosperity; they complemented and supported the efforts of the King and his able adviser Campománes. Campománes encouraged an enterprise in the Sierra Morena, where a pioneer, Olavide, built villages, installed irrigation and attracted settlers.

Charles III, son of Elisabeth Farnese, and king of Spain 1759–88. The Spanish crown was his second; since 1735 he had been Charles IV, King of Naples and Sicily. In each kingdom, his reign was a period of reform and improvement.

With the improved exploitation of its natural riches the country not only met its own textile requirements but produced a surplus for export. The Government removed all restrictions on the circulation of grain and also granted freedom to trade with the colonies to several seaports, measures which tempered a strictly authoritarian economic system that could otherwise have strangled the country. All in all the Enlightened Despotism of Charles III distinctly improved conditions. At the end of the century the kingdom contained over ten million inhabitants. Charles III had done much, but he had not deeply altered the country's structure, and at the end of his reign Spain still lagged behind the other Western powers.

Spanish America

In America Spain had enlarged her Empire by further exploration and new settlements. In the extreme south the coast of Patagonia was occupied, but off the coast a dispute arose between Great Britain and Spain over the Falkland Islands in which Charles III was worsted. In North America Spanish Franciscans settled on the Pacific coast and in 1783 founded San Francisco. The Spanish pushed as far north as Vancouver, but there clashed with the British in Nootka Sound and were forced to give up their claim in 1790. The British had already begun to establish themselves in Honduras, where in 1763 Charles III had given them the right to cut tropical woods. On the other hand Spain acquired a part of Louisiana from Louis XV and lost Florida only for twenty years.

Charles III made no essential changes in the administration of his immense empire, though centralisation was increased. In 1788 further Captaincies-General and a new Viceroyalty, La Plata, with a capital at Buenos Aires, were created. Spanish economic policy continued in principle to exclude colonial trade with anyone except the home country. Even the slave trade was now reserved for Spain, which had acquired from Portugal the African islands of Fernando Po and Annobon as bases for slaving.

The Jesuits, after being banished from Portugal and France received their final blow when they were expelled from Spain on 31 March 1767. They were opposed because of their influence at court and through education, and their quarrels with other orders. *British Museum*

During the War of American Independence these restrictions were, none the less, slightly relaxed. Whereas trade had been strictly limited to three or four ports in America and to Cadiz alone in Spain, in 1776 thirteen Spanish ports were authorised to trade with twenty-four American ports, while in certain cases direct traffic between Spanish colonies was permitted. The production of colonial goods increased and European plants such as wheat, barley and flax were also introduced with success. In the new colony of La Plata cattle-raising and the breeding of horses and transport mules flourished. But the chief source of riches was still the gold and silver mines of Peru and Mexico, whose output increased.

This wave of material prosperity did not solve social problems. Though the native Indians were protected against slavery by the laws of Spain, their condition often remained wretched, especially in the mines of Upper Peru; Creoles, or American-born Spaniards, were still deprived of all political rights. In founding the new universities of Santiago and Havana, Charles III's principal motive was to assimilate culturally the inhabitants of the colonies to those of the mother country. Intellectual progress, however, favoured the growth of liberal ideas, especially among the Creoles. As Creole loyalty to the Crown wore gradually thinner, the gulf between the Creoles and coloured races became wider. Insurrectionary movements were born of starvation and racial grievance long before they became struggles by the colonists for independence. The most

important uprising, led by the Inca Tupac Amaru, was a sudden resurgence of Indian protest. Though the powers of repression were ever on the alert, the Spanish colonies were, by the end of the century, simmering with a dangerous discontent which the King, in far distant Spain, failed to take into account.

Portugal and Pombal

Until Joseph I came to the throne in 1750 Portugal had vegetated. Her experience of Enlightened Despotism was to prove much harsher than that of Spain, thanks not to the new King but to his minister, Sebastian de Carvalho, Marquis of Pombal. For a quarter of a century Pombal was an implacable and cruel dictator. Nevertheless he firmly established the absolute power of the monarchy and gave the country the jolt it needed. He was famous both as the energetic rebuilder of Lisbon after the devastation of the terrible earthquake of 1755, and as the savage dispenser of justice who drowned in blood a conspiracy against the King among the upper nobility. He persecuted the Jesuits spectacularly, expelled the Order from Portuguese territory, even executing a few of its members. He pursued his policy of religious toleration by subordinating the Inquisition to the King's authority and by encouraging opponents of the Holy See. In the same secularising spirit he reformed the University of Coimbra in 1772 and began the teaching of science. He re-organised

183

the army and the navy and balanced the budget. He undertook a vast programme of economic reforms which he enforced by measures which were sometimes authoritarian — ordering what crops were to be grown or what factories built — and sometimes liberal — abolishing vexatious commercial regulations and thereby fostering trade with Brazil. He did not overcome all resistance to his will, and after the death of the ineffectual Joseph I in 1777, Joseph's daughter, Maria I, dismissed Pombal and issued a royal decree denouncing him as an 'infamous criminal'. But the reaction which followed did not destroy his achievements.

Brazil

Much of the national wealth of Portugal depended on her possession of Brazil. Pombal's Brazilian policy was as energetic as that which he pursued at home. To settle the outstanding dispute with Spain he suggested as a compromise that the Portuguese colony of Sacramento should be exchanged for Spanish territory situated between Uruguay and Paraguay. The Jesuits of the Chaco were opposed to this, since it would dismember their own semi-autonomous republic. Armed intervention and the expulsion of the Jesuits from Brazil in 1759 finally allowed the matter to be settled by two treaties in 1777 and 1778, under which Portugal gave up Sacramento in return for certain territories to the east of Peru and in Guiana.

Pombal strove ceaselessly to centralise the administration of the colony and to increase the power of the Crown's officers. The last of the semi-independent Captains-General disappeared and municipal councils were obliged to keep strictly within the limits of their powers. Pombal made the mining of diamonds a State monopoly and he also claimed certain rights over the exploitation of the gold mines, which showed some signs of becoming worked out. His efforts to stimulate agricultural production were seconded by commercial companies, in which it was said that Pombal himself had interests: the Para and the Maranhao companies, created in 1765, and the Pernambuco and Parahyba Companies, founded in 1769. The production of cocoa, rice and indigo increased, and so did the population. New towns were founded in the interior. On the whole Brazil benefited from Pombal's despotic measures. The Indians were especially fortunate, for in 1755 he freed them from slavery. On the other hand it was still necessary to import Negroes from Africa. After Pombal's fall Brazil continued to develop at a rapid pace. To its traditional agricultural products a new crop with a rich future was added: coffee. But the very prosperity of the country caused increasing discontent among the Creoles, who became more and more restive under restrictions imposed by the distant and decadent Government of Portugal. With British and French merchants had come fresh ideas and books. The War of American Independence reminded the more educated colonists that they, too, were Americans and that Brazil was a community also capable of self-government.

Countries unaffected by Enlightened Despotism

Despotism and reform, often brutally enforced, were necessary in countries with monarchical institutions and a backward social structure. Such were the nations of Central, Southern and Eastern Europe. Conditions in Western Europe were very different. Great Britain and France had already entered a new age, in which economic factors and the demands of public opinion played a part hitherto unknown. As for the Dutch Republic and Switzerland, they were not monarchies and provided no soil in which Enlightened Despotism could take root.

The Dutch Republic was a nation of free burghers where serfdom had disappeared and feudal rights were weakened. Dutch free enterprise had fostered great commercial expansion, but in spite of — or perhaps because of — British competition the system suffered from hardening of the arteries: Dutch bankers and shipbuilders were too inclined to be satisfied with the comfortable position they had acquired. The House of Orange still provided the Stadtholders, and was still opposed by the anti-British party of the Regents. A third and new party calling itself the Patriots aspired to liberal reforms, turned for inspiration to the French *philosophes*, and burned with ardour for the rebelling American colonists. The difficulties which Great Britain was having with her colonies offered Dutch merchants an opportunity for revenge. They supplied the insurgents with merchandise, capital and even munitions. But by and large the Dutch Republic gained very little from this new outburst of activity. Great Britain declared war on it, and the best it could do against Joseph II's threat to reopen the Scheldt was to sign the Alliance of Fontainebleau with France in 1784. At this moment the two opposition parties, the Patriots and the Regents, joined in an effort to overthrow the Stadtholder William V, a prince of little energy who was married to the sister of Frederick William II, the new King of Prussia. The Orangists appealed to the Prussian army and, by a coup d'état in 1787, the Stadtholder was reinstated with all his prerogatives intact.

The Swiss Cantons, too, continued to be governed by an aristocratic oligarchy. They also grew richer, thanks to peace and the prosperity of agriculture and industry. In Geneva the legal barriers between social classes again provoked troubles in 1766 and 1781. Meanwhile, Joseph II's Bavarian intrigues caused uneasiness in Switzerland, and in 1777 the Cantons renewed their traditional alliance with France for a period of one hundred and fifty years. They revised the federal constitution and, though no real reforms were made, at least the spirit of reform developed among the educated classes. Religious toleration gained ground, a remarkable trend in a land where Catholics and Protestants lived in such close proximity. A National Helvetic Society was formed in which all contemporary opinions were represented. Switzerland thus participated in the intellectual movements which stirred the eighteenth century.

It is not easy to generalise about the effects produced in Europe by changes made during the period of Enlightened Despotism. Too often surface reforms, which were the most spectacular, led to the neglect of deeper reforms more urgently needed, while attempts to solve economic problems were inadequate and unsystematic. Yet bureaucratic machinery was strengthened and the principle of legislative sovereignty made some headway. Some attempts at reform, nevertheless, were so clumsy that they merely accentuated the evils they were intended to cure. At bottom, the system of monarchical absolutism was out of date, and attempts to prop it up were doomed to failure.

Volunteer recruiting in England often drew on dubious resources. Conscription arrived with the French Revolution. *Mansell*

Signing the Declaration of Independence at Philadelphia, 1776. *Mansell*

CHAPTER TWELVE

THE PREFACE TO A NEW AGE

THE AGE OF REASON

The eighteenth century was set on living by the light of reason, and in an effort to do so destroyed as much as it constructed. Although the critical spirit already existed it was perfected in the eighteenth century and came to be accepted almost superstitiously as an infallible method of ascertaining truth. Traditions and religious principles which the previous century had respected were no longer spared. Christianity and the Papacy were favourite targets, attacked at first on behalf of a vague deism and then, more boldly, in the name of a free thought which no longer hesitated to declare its nature: Holbach and Helvetius, for instance, were confessed atheists. The intellectual world rallied to the banner of the new enlightened philosophy and against it the Church seemed powerless. No new Bossuet rose in its defence. The Popes themselves, though often men of great holiness — for the eighteenth century was by no means entirely an age of impiety — lacked the

strength to defend their faith. During the pontificate of Benedict XIV (1740–58) a campaign began against the Jesuits, who with their single-mindedness and discipline were considered the most dangerous enemies of progress. Clement XIII (1758–69) tried with little success to defend the Society. Clement XIV (1769–74) was not well disposed towards the Jesuits, and a year before his death issued the Papal brief *Dominus ac Redemptor* which suppressed the Society. The last Pope of the century, Pius VI (1775–99) was incapable of resisting the tendency of the Church to break up under local leadership into semi-Erastian Churches; he achieved his greatest success in the more secular sphere of patronage of the arts.

Freemasonry, which was outside, if not opposed to the Church, entered the continent from Great Britain; the first lodge was founded in France in 1721. Its lodges, and similar secret societies, were recruited chiefly from the ranks of the well-to-do and the aristocracy, who were still the only classes to be seriously affected by loss of faith in Christianity. But the noisiest adversaries of Christianity were the *philosophes*, of whom Voltaire was the uncrowned king. Brilliant and scathing in all that he wrote — historical essays, tragedies, satirical tales, above all in the innumerable letters and lampoons which circulated throughout all Europe — Voltaire led the battle, armed with his matchless irony. Well-educated (by the Jesuits) and coming from a middle-class family, Voltaire was never a democrat. On the contrary, he was the defender of Enlightened Despotism, although after an unhappy visit to the court of Frederick the Great (1751–3) he was often scathing about individual despots. He was the enemy of injustice and won additional fame by his tireless efforts to awake public opinion over such scandals as the judicial murder of Calas (1762). He died in 1778 at the age of eighty-four, venerated as the patriarch of the Enlightenment. Still more potent in the war against traditional beliefs was the *Encyclopédie*, edited by Diderot and d'Alembert. Though it was officially condemned on the appearance of its first volume in 1751, between then and 1772 sixteen further volumes were published. It was an imposing summary of the knowledge of the time, in which Experience and Reason took the place formerly occupied by Revelation.

The spread of the new ideas

The intellectual and scientific curiosity of the age was unquenchable. The classifications of Linnaeus and Buffon introduced order into natural history. Experiments and discoveries made in physics, chemistry and astronomy were discussed with passionate interest. Curiosity was not confined by frontiers: the indigenous races of distant lands were described and studied; China was the infatuation of the intelligentsia; people became aware that Christendom was not the only great civilisation. The image of a united humanity dazzled the eighteenth century, in spite of its superficial cynicism, and cosmopolitanism led to pacifism. The Abbé de St Pierre founded the *Club de l'Entresol*, where from 1726 to 1731 some of the most original minds in Europe gathered. His *Project for Perpetual Peace* anticipated the League of Nations. This extension of rationalism tended to produce efforts to improve the existing state of society, rather than plans to overturn it. Then, in 1750, appeared the *Discourse on Science and the Arts* by Jean-Jacques Rousseau, the first manifesto to say that society itself was the source of corruption. Followers of Rousseau revered Nature as the only moral guide and, in reaction to the withering blasts of Voltairian irony, put their faith in sensibility. Condillac, on the other hand, whose *Treatise on Sensation* appeared in 1754, reduced all mental processes to sensation and heralded a scientific empiricism which ran counter to spiritualist and rationalist currents of thought. The same tendency, logically pursued, brought David Hume to absolute scepticism and Jeremy Bentham to a utilitarianism based on a calculus of pleasure. At the end of the century Immanuel Kant's reaction against these philosophies was to produce the philosophy of idealism. The anti-rationalist current also gave rise to a school of quasi-enlightened mysticism, illustrated in the esoteric works of Emanuel Swedenborg, magicians like Mesmer, St Martin and Cagliostro, and

An eighteenth-century wood-carving of a fiddler. Germany had a long tradition of wood-carving and most villages, as well as the larger towns, had craftsmen illustrating contemporary life. *Victoria & Albert Museum*

An engraving by Hubert of Voltaire presiding over a dinner party which includes the Abbé Maury, Condorcet and Diderot. This famous group of philosophers was responsible for the ideas which overthrew conventional Christian society and was an important factor in the French Revolution.

Jean-Jacques Rousseau (1712–78), father of romanticism and champion of the heart against the head. With the best of intentions he injected Western culture with a virus one of whose latest manifestations was Nazism.

An eighteenth-century hand-loom. The output of looms was to be transformed by the introduction of steampower, and the first modern industrial economy — that of Great Britain — was built on expansion of textile production.

A design for a balloon, steered by sails. It is a hot-air balloon, basically similar in design to that of the brothers Montgolfier, who made the first ascent in a balloon in 1783. The first hydrogen balloon flew in the same year. *Mansell*

the spread of sects of mysticising initiates such as the Rosicrucians. Social customs, too, underwent a change: feeling became fashionable and tenderness found expression in philanthropy and devotion to humanitarian causes. Rousseau's *Discourse on Inequality* and *Social Contract* contained the germs of future national and democratic movements.

Literary and artistic movements

Classicism lost its appeal and its place was usurped by the literature of sentiment typified by Rousseau and Goldsmith in their novels *La Nouvelle Héloïse* and *The Vicar of Wakefield*. In 1760 the poems of 'Ossian' appeared, which were forerunners of romantic lyricism. The renaissance of German literature followed this new path, already partially explored by Klopstock and Lessing; and with Goethe and Schiller a national poetry and drama emerged. In France, the satirical and picaresque spirit was not yet dead as Laclos and Beaumarchais, the creator of Figaro, demonstrated.

In the fine arts, too, a change appeared towards the middle of the century. The discovery of the ruins of Pompeii in 1748 excited a new interest in the art of antiquity which was reflected in architecture and sculpture. Winckelmann, the German archaeologist, was the leading spirit in this revolution of taste, a salutary reaction to the excesses of rococo which had deformed the earlier beauties of the baroque. In painting Fragonard continued the charming mannerisms of his *fêtes galantes*, but a new school found its interpreter in David, whose *Serment des Horaces* burst on the Salon of 1785 like a challenge. England, too, displayed true originality in the graceful portraiture of Reynolds and Gainsborough, which was rivalled only when Spanish art was awakened by the astonishing genius of Goya. Austria and Germany produced the greatest masters in the field of music: Bach, who died in 1750; Beethoven, who was born in 1770; and Mozart (1756–91).

Technical and economic advances

The Age of Reason was not only a period of intellectual ferment, of challenge to tradition and artistic refinement. It also saw the beginning of an economic and technical advance which affected the future of European society quite as much as the new and revolutionary ideas. The strides made in pure science were rapidly followed by an advance in applied science, and inventions appeared at a bewildering rate, above all in Great Britain. Furthermore, in the eighteenth century a genuine science of economics was developed, again based on a reversal of seventeenth-century orthodoxy. Arguing against the absolute power of the sovereign to regulate the production and distribution of goods — in other words against Colbertism — a group of British and French economists proclaimed the benefits of free trade and untrammelled industry, the source of well-being and prosperity for all. The British, and especially Adam Smith, author of *The Wealth of Nations*, asserted that labour was the source of all wealth, while the French physiocrats — Quesnay, Dupont de Nemours and Mirabeau — held that wealth was produced by agriculture alone. All agreed, however, in defining the laws of '*laissez-faire*' which brought about the extraordinary economic development of the century which followed. As a result of their advocacy customs barriers were lowered, guild regulations were relaxed, and monopolies were broken. Large-scale agriculture and industry, international commerce, the capital market, developed in Great Britain and in France. Economists said that the functions of the State should be limited to ensuring economic freedom. A new order, political as well as economic, was thus appearing from the second half of the eighteenth century. The resulting increase in production and trade, together with an influx of precious metals from the New World, brought about inflation. Prices rose steadily and the poorer classes suffered in consequence. But most people participated to some extent in the general prosperity, and populations grew rapidly throughout Europe and in America. The demographic explosion of the modern era had begun.

French problems at the close of Louis XV's reign

The end of the Old Regime in France is the story of an impossible search for financial stability hampered by the selfish hostility of an élite which utterly failed to face its responsibility. As early as 1745 a courageous finance minister, Machault d'Arnouville, had attempted to bring order into the confused and inadequate fiscal system. He proposed new taxes on the privileged classes, who joined forces to defend themselves, and in 1754, against his better judgment, Louis XV gave way and removed Machault from office.

Meanwhile, the unending struggle of King and *parlements* continued. Further quarrels had arisen between the French episcopate and the *parlements* over the harrying of Jansenists. In 1753 the King banished the *Parlement* of Paris to Pontoise. When it was allowed to return, the quarrels broke out again and soon the *Parlement* of Paris, supported by the provincial *parlements*, was claiming to act as the representative of the nation and to interfere in the working of government. As the *parlements* were judicial bodies in no way similar to the British Parliament, this was

Louis XV, painted as a young man by De la Cour. His reign brought France disasters abroad and the loss of a colonial empire: at home, Louis never overcame the problem of reconciling authority and privilege which was to drag down his successor. *Mansell*

Madame de Pompadour, most famous and able of the mistresses of Louis XV. She was a patron of letters and learning, and led the party at court which advocated an Austrian alliance from 1753 onwards. *Marburg*

unconstitutional, although they profited from the confusion caused by their names. Soon they succeeded in posing as the defenders of the well-being of the whole nation against arbitrary power. This was mere demagogy; in fact they were defending their own privileges and those of the nobility, to which the *parlementaires* belonged, against royal authority. They were to succeed in staving off effective reform until 1789.

In this dispute, Louis's popularity waned. The financial needs of the Seven Years' War (which began in 1756) soon embittered the conflict between Crown and *Parlement* even more. The Duc de Choiseul, who was in charge of foreign affairs, handled them with distinction, but the wisdom of the policy with which he was identified (the alliance with Austria which resulted from the Diplomatic Revolution) was much questioned. Louis himself disliked Choiseul and regarded his presence in the Government as a sop to the *philosophes* and a favour to Madame de Pompadour. When the Seven Years' War went badly, Choiseul attempted to retrieve matters by negotiating a 'Family Compact' with Spain. After the peace (1763) he re-organised the army and navy to prepare for revenge on Britain. In 1768 he purchased Corsica from Genoa. But the financial problems of the monarchy remained unsolved; finance ministers came and went, meeting with resistance from the *Parlement* as soon as they attempted tax reform. Inflation made the fiscal problem insoluble. The public treasury should, in fact, have benefited from the increased return on agricultural land; but any attempt by the Government to share in the profits was constantly frustrated by the *Parlement*.

A diversion was caused by a scandal involving the Jesuits, and here again the magistrates won the day. A certain Père Lavalette, who had founded a trading company in the island of Martinique, had several ships captured by the British and became bankrupt. His creditors, merchants of Marseille, brought an action against the Society of Jesus, to which Lavalette belonged, and won their case in the local court. The Jesuits then made the fatal error of appealing to the *Parlement* of Paris, which ordered an investigation of the constitution of the Society and decided that the absolute power of the General of the Jesuits was incompatible with the authority of the King. Louis XV himself attempted to hush up the affair, but the magistrates pushed it to its logical conclusion in 1763: the Society was suppressed and its property confiscated. As the great majority of the schools in France were run by Jesuits, this meant a crisis in education. *Parlementaires* and the intelligentsia were overjoyed.

Victorious in their contest with the Jesuits, the *parlements* — those of the provinces imitating Paris — returned to the offensive, this time by refusing to register fiscal edicts. The *Parlement* of Rennes, in Brittany, even succeeded in forcing the resignation of the royal governor of that province. Madame de Pompadour had died in 1764 and Choiseul, deprived of her support, fell into disgrace in 1770. His last public act had been to arrange the marriage of the future Louis XVI to an Austrian archduchess, Marie Antoinette.

Towards the end of his reign, Louis XV at last showed some signs of energy. Terray, his finance minister, had by various expedients improved the financial situation. Though his Foreign Minister, the Duc d'Aiguillon, achieved little, his Chancellor Maupeou — the third member of the so-called 'Triumvirate' — scored a triumph for the monarchy. By thwarting the efforts of the *parlements* to unite in their pretensions to represent the will of the nation, he drove them to acts of rebellion. A royal edict of February 1771 sent the recalcitrant magistrates into exile and imposed radical reforms: the abolition of office-buying; the appointment by the King of special magistrates to dispense free justice; and the breaking up of the *Parlement* of Paris into smaller, less unwieldy and less powerful bodies. Despite gibes and protests the 'Maupeou *parlements*' which were thus created gave satisfaction. This was the extent of Louis XV's reform by Benevolent Despotism; but he undertook it too late. He died, discredited, in May 1774.

Great Britain in the reign of George III

Walpole's rule had not long survived the outbreak of the War of the Austrian Succession and he resigned in 1741 when his Parliamentary majority crumbled away. The most brilliant of his critics, William Pitt, was the outstanding figure among those who followed him in ministerial office. He was a great orator and a shrewd interpreter of public opinion, upon whose support he could rely because he expressed its sense better than any of his colleagues; he resigned in 1754, when the King appointed one of his enemies, Henry Fox, to the ministry, but only to be reinstated two years later because public opinion insisted on it. Pitt's attitude epitomised British pride, which the trials of war, far from reducing, had only fortified. It was Pitt who organised the world-wide operation which won for his country a vast empire. But difficulties, beyond those inevitable to a wartime ministry, arose from the moment George III came to the throne in 1760. The young sovereign who had succeeded the second George was no mere Hanoverian, but had been brought up in Great Britain and was proud to be British. He was capable and fully conscious of his royal responsibilities, to the point of wishing to assume all the duties and powers of his exalted office. In this ambition he was opposed by the Whig politicians who had monopolised place and profit since 1714. George at once took the offensive and profited by war-weariness to replace Pitt by the King's Scottish tutor, Lord Bute, who concluded the peace of 1763. But George had acted too hastily; Bute was unpopular with Parliament and people, and he was soon obliged to dismiss him.

One reason had been the excitement of public opinion by John Wilkes, a Member of Parliament who had attacked Bute and the King in his paper, *The North Briton*. When he was arrested for libel a complicated tangle of litigation began involving the privilege of Members and the legality of general warrants. Wilkes, however, also fell out with his fellow-Members and retired to the continent until 1768. He had briefly focused the dislike of some of the Whig politicians who felt alarmed by the King's evident determination to play a more positive part in government than his predecessor had done. This led the King into a series of attempts to find a ministry which, supported by royal patronage, could provide stable government against the background of rising difficulties with the colonies (*see p. 195 ff.*). The elder Pitt (now ennobled as Lord Chatham) was reconciled with the King, but was too ill to be effective. Finally, in 1770, George chose Lord North as his Prime

Lord North (1732–92), unwilling Prime Minister of George III, whose ministry presided over the loss of the American colonies and whose subsequent coalition with his opponent, Fox, was widely regarded as an act of consummate political treachery. *Radio Times Hulton Picture Library*

Hogarth's etching of John Wilkes, friend of liberty, and thorn in the side of the early governments of George III. His career forced decisions on many issues affecting the liberty of the subiect. *British Museum*

Minister. By this time, dissatisfaction was high. A small number of politicians bitterly attacked the use of royal 'influence' to win votes (although the practice was normal in the eighteenth century). At that moment Wilkes again caused a diversion. He was identified with the cause of Parliamentary reform, and when he was elected to the House of Commons the ministerial majority twice voted to expel him. This only dramatised his position. In 1774 Wilkes was elected Lord Mayor of London and 'Wilkes and liberty' became the cry of the reformers and the mob. In the same year he was again elected to Parliament and at last allowed to take his seat.

Important though the constitutional issues raised by Wilkes were, the Government survived. Even the collapse of the hopes of a colonial settlement when war at last broke out with the Americans in 1776 did not shake George's determination to keep North in office. But the disasters of the war damaged the Government's popularity still more and intensified the demand for Parliamentary reform. By 1780 Ireland, too, seemed on the point of rebellion. A new opposition movement based on the country gentry arose in Yorkshire. Finally, George III had to let North resign (1782). At the end of 1783 he found another minister who suited him: William Pitt the Younger, second son of Chatham, a reserved, able and austere young man of twenty-four. He was the King's choice, as North had been, and was to become famous as the refounder of the Tory Party (though he always called himself a Whig). But he was also a reforming minister, anxious to embark upon financial, administrative and Parliamentary reform. Under him the country recovered swiftly from the disaster of the war.

In the middle of the eighteenth century Great Britain was still an agricultural country which exported grain; by the end of the century this was no longer true: industry had become the island's chief activity, and some grain and foodstuffs had to be imported. There were many causes for this economic revolution: the natural wealth of a land rich in coal and iron, the growth of a world-wide market which absorbed the products of the 'workshop of the world', a freedom of enterprise which encouraged private initiative, and a host of technical innovations. The textile industry was transformed by Hargreaves's invention of the spinning-jenny (1764), Arkwright's water-frame and Crompton's 'mule', and finally of Cartwright's power-loom (1785). The use of coke furnaces in smelting iron was improved, while James Watt perfected the steam engine and heralded the age of coal. Coal-mining itself had considerably benefited from the use of water pumps and the employment of tip-trucks running on rails. Large-scale production meant lower prices. Exports, in consequence, soared. Internal trade was also intensified by the construction of better roads and of canals. Banks sprang up everywhere and credit began to be organised much as it is today. In all these fields Britain was considerably in advance of the rest of the world.

But the other side of the picture of technical progress was already becoming visible. In the dreary streets of smoky factory towns a wretched proletariat was beginning to form at the end of the century. To check the excesses of this rudimentary capitalism the workers had already shown tendencies to unite: the first 'trade union' was founded in 1776. Government regulation was almost as early: in 1802 a law was passed to improve the working

191

Pitt the Younger. The Revolutionary and Napoleonic Wars overtook his plans for financial and political reform, but his example as 'the pilot who weathered the storm' made him the true founder of the nineteenth-century Tory party.

This telescope, of four-foot aperture and forty-foot focal length, was the most advanced instrument of its age. It was built at Slough by Sir William Herschel. *British Museum*

conditions of children in cotton mills. By the end of the eighteenth century the public behaviour of the governing class had improved slightly; the appearance of Methodism and the Evangelical movement within the Anglican Church had contributed greatly to this. On the eve of the French Revolution, then, Great Britain had fully regained, improved and assured her economic position. Stronger than ever, she was a united nation and proud of her greatness — a greatness which she had won at sea, and which sea-power maintained.

The birth of British India

After the Treaty of Aix-la-Chapelle (1748) the fairly large forces which both the British and the French had in India suddenly found themselves without employment. At this exact moment struggles for succession broke out simultaneously in the Carnatic and in the Deccan. The rival claimants appealed for help, two to the British, two to the French. Both Companies, expecting to be paid for their help, now engaged in the internal affairs of India, and thus again faced each other on the battlefield. Operations in the Carnatic went badly for the French, but Bussy, whom Dupleix had sent to the Deccan with a small force, successfully entered Hyderabad. His protégé awarded Dupleix a sum of money and the provinces of Arcot, Trichinopoly and Madura. Then Clive, as active and enterprising as ever, appeared on the scene and overwhelmingly defeated the French at Trichinopoly. In Paris the belligerent and costly policy of Dupleix found little favour, and instead of receiving the reinforcements he had asked for, Dupleix was relieved of his office. In December 1754 the British and French alike agreed to renounce further interference in native affairs and to relinquish their protectorates over native territories. The Companies undertook, in short, to limit their activities to their original purpose, namely to carry on trade from their trading posts. The merchants' view thus prevailed over that of Dupleix, an empire builder in advance of his time, and France never recovered the influence she had carried in the Empire of the Grand Mogul.

On the outbreak of the Seven Years' War Louis XV sent Lally-Tollendal to India with a small army. The new — and last — French Governor did not lack military skill, but he despised and quickly alienated the Indians. Since he was scarcely more happy in his military enterprises, being defeated at Madras and finally capitulating at Pondicherry in 1761, the native princes preferred to treat with the British. Bussy was recalled from Hyderabad by Lally-Tollendal and shortly after his departure the Deccan was lost. Everywhere the British patiently replaced the vanquished French. They had, however, suffered certain setbacks in Bengal, where the Nawab Siraj-ud-daulah declared against them and, seizing Calcutta, had allowed some hundred sick and wounded British to perish miserably in the infamous 'Black Hole'. In 1757, Clive avenged the incident by recapturing Calcutta and inflicting a crushing defeat on the Nawab at Plassey, which securely established the British protectorate over Bengal. By the time the Treaty of Paris was signed in 1763 Great Britain had nothing more to fear in India, either from the French or from the native princes. The few remaining French trading posts restricted their activities solely to trade. The French Company rapidly declined in importance and in 1770 was dissolved.

Tippoo Sahib (1750–99) fought the British on several occasions. He made peace in 1784 when he became Sultan of Mysore but after attacking Travancore was forced to cede half his kingdom and was finally killed in the siege of Seringapatam. *Victoria & Albert Museum*

In 1764 the British pensioned off the Nawab of Bengal. Robert Clive (1725–74) is here depicted taking formal control (*diwani*) in Bengal, Behar and Orissa. *Min. of Public Building and Works*

Warren Hastings's vigorous governorship of Bengal and governor-generalship of India (1772–88) led to his impeachment after retirement and a trial lasting seven years which was followed by acquittal. Here Burke and Fox attack him.

The British grip on India tightened. Clive's policy of open intervention was richly rewarded by large sums received in the form of tribute, tax or simply lump payments but it exasperated the native princes who were thus fleeced. Even in Britain the arrogance of those returning, enriched, from India — the 'Nabobs', as they were called — outraged public opinion. Clive himself was attacked for having abused his position, although a Parliamentary inquiry recognised the services he had rendered to the State. He died by his own hand in 1774. In the previous year a Regulating Act had been passed which put the East India Company under Parliamentary control, a belated recognition that Britain could not interfere in Indian affairs solely as a trader with no responsibilities for government. When Warren Hastings, the first Governor under the new Act, arrived in Bengal in 1772 he found that the Mogul Empire had disintegrated into warring fragments. During the American war he had to deal with the Mahrattas and Haider Ali, Sultan of Mysore, who invaded the Carnatic. The French were not slow to take advantage of British difficulties and a French squadron under Admiral Suffren harried the British at sea. The Peace of Versailles (1783) put an end to these skirmishes in India, and the son of Haider Ali, Tipoo Sahib, signed

with Great Britain the Treaty of Mangalore (1784). Warren Hastings had achieved much, in the teeth of opposition from his council. (But he had also made many enemies, and after he returned to Britain an attempt was made to impeach him for cruelty and corruption.) He resigned in 1785, the year after Pitt's Government had passed another India Act which set up a Board of Control for India in London. It was appointed by the Government and represented another step towards bringing India directly under the Crown.

Exploration of the Pacific

Voyages of exploration, which had been rare in the first half of the century, became frequent after the Seven Years' War. Even as early as 1722, Roggeveen, in Dutch service, had ventured into little known Pacific waters and had reached the Samoan Islands. After 1763 peace encouraged disinterested exploration. Certain progress had been made in the technique of navigation, instruments were improved and antiscorbutics made scurvy less of a menace. The educated public was fascinated by accounts of voyages in strange seas. A great question still remained unanswered: was there a continent south of the Pacific

193

Captain Cook was killed by natives in a scuffle over the possession of a boat in the Sandwich Islands, 14 February 1779. In the nineteenth century these islands, better known as Hawaii, came more and more under United States influence, finally transformed into annexation in 1898. *British Museum*

James Cook, 1728–79, greatest explorer of the Pacific, who made three great voyages there. He discovered eastern Australia and Hawaii, and showed that New Zealand was insular. He penetrated the Bering Strait and explored the American and Asian Arctic coasts. *Bavaria Verlag*

which counterbalanced the continental masses of the northern hemisphere? British and French seamen — for once in peaceful competition — set sail in search of it, carrying with them men of learning: geographers, botanists, physicians. In 1763 Bougainville visited the Falkland Islands, and in the following year John Byron, grandfather of the poet, founded a settlement there — an Anglo-French bone of contention — and continued to sail round the world. In 1766 two other English navigators, Wallis and Carteret, took to sea together, but after sailing through the Straits of Magellan, followed different courses. Wallis, to his enchantment, discovered Tahiti and sailed on as far as the Marianas Islands (the Ladrones), while Carteret reached New Ireland and New Britain by way of the Solomon Islands. In 1768 Bougainville again set sail and in his turn explored the tropical Pacific, Tahiti and the New Hebrides. He named the Louisiade archipelago, followed the coast of New Guinea and returned by way of Java. His *Voyage Around the World* was a great literary success.

But the problem of the hypothetical southern continent remained unsolved. In 1768 the Royal Society commissioned James Cook to go to Tahiti to observe from there the transit of the planet Venus. His further instructions were to search for the unknown continent. In 1769, after a sojourn in Tahiti, Cook sailed towards the south, made a survey of the coasts of New Zealand and discovered that it was composed of two islands. Then in 1770 he approached eastern Australia and sighted Botany Bay, narrowly escaping disaster on the Great Barrier Reef, and returned by way of New Guinea and Batavia. Eager to pursue his investigations further, Cook, now Captain Cook, again set sail from Plymouth in 1772 and for many months explored the South Pacific, crossing the Antarctic

Circle and reaching the Great Ice Barrier, this time without finding a trace of the continent. The object of his third voyage in 1776 was to discover the fabled North-West Passage — another great preoccupation of the eighteenth-century mariner — which was supposed to connect the Atlantic and the Pacific north of the American continent. In the course of his voyage Cook discovered the Sandwich Islands (Hawaii), but off the coast of Alaska was prevented from proceeding farther by a wall of ice. He returned to Hawaii, where, in a trivial dispute with the natives about a stolen boat, he was killed. Much remained to be explored in the immensities of the Pacific Ocean. In 1785 Louis XVI sent out another great navigator, La Pérouse, who made many scientific observations in the tropical islands of the Pacific which supplemented the pioneer work of Cook.

In 1788, the year following this sketch, Captain Arthur Philip, whose ship is drawn here, brought the first convict transports to Port Jackson, Sydney Cove. The first free settlers did not arrive until 1793; there were then eleven of them. *Mansell*

In addition he surveyed the north-west coast of the Pacific, the coast of Korea and Chinese Tartary, and discovered the strait between Yezo (Hokkaido) and Sakhalin which is named after him. Sailing southward from Botany Bay, he mysteriously disappeared; over forty years later the wreckage of his ships was found north of the New Hebrides.

Though Europeans in the eighteenth century discovered many new lands in the Pacific and collected much information about their flora, fauna and native inhabitants, they made no effort to settle, being content to give names to their discoveries. They were of the opinion that these islands, inhabited by primitive races, had no real value and were little more than curiosities of nature. But on the eve of the French Revolution the British reconsidered this opinion and the era of Pacific colonisation began. After the loss of the American colonies the British Government looked for somewhere to send deported convicts, and the eastern coast of Australia, where the climate seemed healthy, was decided upon. In 1788 the first contingent of convicts landed at Botany Bay, bringing with them a few specimens of European plants and domestic animals. In this modest way British Australia was founded.

The exploitation of the West Indies

In the West Indies the Anglo-French duel had not concluded with the eviction of France. During the course of the Seven Years' War Pitt had had Guadeloupe, Martinique and the neutral islands occupied, but by the Treaty of Paris in 1763 Great Britain restored her conquests, with the exceptions of St Vincent, Grenada and Tobago. From what remained of her West Indian possessions France continued to derive great profit. An effort to re-organise the islands was made, and a Governor-General appointed to ensure political unity. Garrisons were sent from France to protect the islands from attack. The same social problems which beset all America were not long in arising: the struggle among three classes — coloured, landless whites and rich planters. To maintain their jealously guarded privileges the planters formed their

own Chambers of Agriculture in 1763 which became part and parcel of the administration. The coloured community meanwhile was riddled with secret societies. Both population and production rose. The policy of trading exclusively with France was relaxed from 1767.

The history of the British West Indies was more disturbed. The example of the thirteen rebellious colonies was near at hand, and the white West Indian planter, too, would gladly have broken free from the shackles colonialism imposed on his trade. During the War of American Independence serious trouble occurred. The French seized Santo Domingo and Tobago, and British domination of the West Indies seemed momentarily threatened. The naval victory of the Saints was, however, to restore British authority. In 1787, a number of free ports were set up with limited rights of trade with the colonies of other states. Small United States vessels were allowed to trade with them only in 1794.

The birth of British Canada

After the British victory, sealed by the Treaty of Paris, Canada was placed under the authority of British governors — Murray and after him Carleton — who understood the inhabitants and respected the customs to which they were attached. This intelligent policy bore its fruits and became even more liberal with the example of threatened trouble in the thirteen neighbouring colonies. The Quebec Act of 1774 was a humane and wise measure; it granted freedom of worship to Canadian Catholics and recognised the majority of their French civil rights. In return it required an oath of loyalty to the King, obedience to British laws and the appointment by the King of a governor assisted by a council. Finally it annexed to Canada the territory which lay between Ohio and the Great Lakes. The Canadians demonstrated their gratitude by repulsing both the appeals and the attacks of their 'insurgent' neighbours. Many 'Loyalists' from the rebelling colonies took refuge north of the Great Lakes and in Nova Scotia. There was inevitably a certain friction between British colonists and French Canadians, but no intermingling. This meant that each community could be apportioned its own territory in the country, and such a division was set out in an Act of 1791. It divided the country into the French-speaking province of Lower Canada and the English-speaking province of Upper Canada and established representative assemblies in each, though ultimate responsibility still rested with the London Government. In Acadia — henceforth Nova Scotia and New Brunswick — the English were in the majority, but Acadians who had earlier been expelled were allowed to return. The two neighbouring communities, whose sole bond was the Crown, got along together as well as could be expected. The French Canadians, much influenced by their priests, led patriarchal lives and produced large families. They ran little risk of being numerically submerged by the English, in spite of numerous immigrants from Great Britain.

The War of American Independence

In 1763 her colonists in North America were loyal to Britain, and rejoiced with the mother country over their common triumphs in the Seven Years' War. Yet twelve years later the American subjects of George III took up

George Washington (1732–99), Commander-in-Chief of the American forces in the War of Independence and first President of the United States (1789–97). He declined a third term as President, though he had been accused of scheming to make his office permanent. *Larousse*

prosperous, and both their numbers and their wealth were rapidly increasing. By 1763 their popular assemblies, although checked by royal and proprietary governors and councils, had the dominant voice in determining domestic matters, and the power of these bodies was growing. The colonists were content to let Crown and Parliament manage foreign affairs, nor did they complain bitterly against British regulation, through the Acts of Navigation and Trade, of their maritime commerce and industry. It is easy to see now that the wishes of the colonists would determine the extent of British authority over them in the future, for they were becoming too powerful to be held in subjection against their will by a nation three thousand miles away which had potent enemies on the European continent. Whether the Americans would achieve political freedom within the British Empire or outside it depended upon British policy toward them.

British politicians in office in London in 1763 were not fully aware of the strength and maturity of the colonies; before 1775 relatively few British leaders saw that it was necessary to give the Americans what they wanted, if the colonies were long to remain within the Empire. In 1763 British power and pride were at a peak, and Crown and Parliament, instead of seeking to please the colonists, undertook to assert dominion over them as never before. A Ministry headed by the Earl of Bute (1761–3), and its successor, dominated by George Grenville (1763–5), enlarged the British garrison forces in North America and sought to restrict American westward expansion, reserving a huge area in the Appalachians to the Indians (some of whom had risen in Pontiac's rebellion of 1763). Furthermore, it attempted to limit colonial maritime trade and also to impose taxes for revenue upon the colonists by authority of Parliament. The Sugar Act of 1764, levying a threepence per gallon duty on molasses imported from non-British islands in the West Indies, and especially the Stamp Act of 1765, aroused a storm of protest in America. The Stamp Act required that the colonists purchase stamps for various legal documents, newspapers, and other papers; it met little opposition in Parliament.

The colonists reacted strongly against this attempt to put the clock back, concentrating their resistance against the stamp duties. Such duties had never before been imposed upon them by Parliament, and they claimed that they violated their constitutional rights as Englishmen, since they elected no Members of the House of Commons. ' No taxation without representation ' became the rallying cry. The prevalent sentiments were expressed in passionate oratory by Patrick Henry in the Virginia House of Burgesses in May 1765. Very few inhabitants of the Thirteen Colonies were disposed to bow to British authority. Later that year a Congress held at New York attended by delegates from seven colonies demanded the repeal of the Stamp Act. The law was not enforced in the Thirteen Colonies, except briefly in Georgia. Stamps sent to America were destroyed or sequestered by the colonists, who also forced those appointed as stamp distributors to resign their posts. There was rioting in several American cities, including Boston and New York. To bring pressure on London the Americans also began to limit their orders of British manufactured goods and to postpone payment of their debts to British merchants. The strength of the colonial resistance is in some part to be explained by the fact that Canada and eastern Louisiana had become British

arms against Britain; by 1783 their independence was recognised and the British Empire had been stripped of its most valuable possession. The Bourbon monarchies of France and Spain played an important part in this surprising reversal.

While the inhabitants of the Thirteen Colonies did not desire independence in 1763, it is nevertheless true that the ties between them and the mother country were weakening. Six generations in the American environment had made them less British. The colonists were numerous and

A riot in June 1768 in Boston, Massachusetts, led to the landing of British troops there in October. They were very unpopular and the town refused to provide quarters for them. *Radio Times Hulton Picture Library*

by the Peace of Paris, so that the Americans no longer needed protection against the French.

Surprised by American defiance, Britain chose not to use force. A new Ministry headed by the Marquess of Rockingham repealed the Stamp Act in 1766, although it passed a Declaratory Act which asserted that Parliamentary authority over America was no less complete than it was over England. The colonists were much pleased by the outcome. But the question of the right of Parliament to tax the colonists for revenue was unwisely revived in the following year by Charles Townshend, Chancellor of the Exchequer in the 'Ministry of All the Talents' recently formed by William Pitt and George III. Under Townshend's leadership duties for revenue were placed upon tea, certain kinds of paper, lead, and painters' colours imported into the colonies. It was speciously claimed by Townshend that the constitutional protest by the colonists against taxation without representation was confined to internal levies such as the stamp tax. The proceeds of the Townshend taxes were to be used to pay the salaries of a number of royal officials in America, and to help to defray the cost of maintaining the British military forces in America. The royal officials, hitherto paid by colonial assemblies, were to be freed from influence by the assemblies. The Ministry of All the Talents also made renewed efforts to restrict American westward expansion and maritime trade and moved British regiments nearer to the settled parts of the Thirteen Colonies (1767–8).

A second Anglo-American crisis quickly developed. John Dickinson, in his letters to newspapers of a 'Farmer in Pennsylvania', declared that the Townshend duties constitutionally differed in no way from the stamp tax, and most of the colonists accepted his view. A British attempt to enforce the Acts of Navigation through a new Board of Customs Commissioners located at Boston and new Admiralty Courts placed in several cities likewise roused colonial displeasure. The majority of the colonists demanded repeal of the Townshend levies and gradually organised a boycott of British goods to persuade British merchants

Riots over the Stamp Act (1765) broke out in many American cities. A congress of delegates from nine colonies protested and the Act was repealed in 1766. *Mansell*

The 'Boston Massacre' of 5 March 1770, when the taunts and threats of a crowd led to shooting in which five citizens were killed. *Radio Times Hulton Picture Library.*

197

and manufacturers to support them. Some colonists who were reluctant to join in the boycott were subjected to economic and physical coercion. Again the British Government gave way to the colonists. Under the leadership of Lord North the duties were repealed in 1770, except for the tax on tea, which was maintained more to assert the right of Parliament to tax than to take money from colonial pockets. The second Anglo-American crisis thus came swiftly to an end, with the Americans abandoning their boycott on all goods except taxed tea. But before it was over there were ominous incidents at Boston. In 1768 British troops had been sent there to protect the Customs Commissioners and to maintain order in the city. The Redcoats engaged in skirmishes with civilians. In February 1770 a customs informer defending his home dived into a mob and shot and killed a boy. On March 5 some soldiers badgered by another mob shot at their tormentors, killing five of them and wounding six others. Although the troops were withdrawn from Boston soon after, this ' Boston Massacre ' inflamed colonial sentiment.

There were few serious quarrels between Britain and her American colonies during the three years following the Boston Massacre. Both the colonies and the mother country prospered, and there is reason to believe that some prominent Americans did not scruple to drink British-taxed tea. In Massachusetts Samuel Adams, an extremist who was one of the first Americans to desire independence, sought almost vainly to rekindle the fires of controversy. In 1772 and 1773, however, there began to appear colonial committees of correspondence organised to enable the Americans to resist more strenuously when they were again challenged.

A third Anglo-American crisis which led ultimately to American rebellion and independence began in 1773, the principal immediate cause for it being the Tea Act of that year sponsored by Lord North, who had become Prime Minister and who was the creature of George III. By that law the East India Company was relieved of the burden of a heavy duty imposed upon its tea brought to Britain and was also permitted to sell its tea directly in America. It thus became possible for the Company, even with the payment of the Townshend duty in America, to sell tea cheaper than Dutch tea, which the colonists had been smuggling into their ports. The Tea Act tempted the colonists to buy cheaper British tea — and to pay the Townshend tax upon it. They did not take the bait, recognising that purchase of the East India Company's tea would mean acceptance of Parliamentary power to tax them for revenue. Instead they either destroyed or seques-tered tea sent across the ocean by the Company, so making sure it would not be sold or used in the colonies. The Boston Tea Party of December 1773, in which three shiploads of tea were dumped into Boston harbour, was an especially famous incident.

This response to the challenge carelessly posed by a usually cautious Lord North, because it coupled defiance of Britain with the destruction of valuable private property, aroused keen resentment in London. The North Ministry undertook to punish and make examples of Boston and Massachusetts. Under its leadership Parliament passed four Coercive Acts which closed the port of Boston, until that city repented its behaviour, and remodelled the govern-ment of Massachusetts so as to increase British authority within it. At the same time Parliament gave its approval

to the Quebec Act. The colonists, considering this act to be as coercive as the other four, denounced all of them as the ' Intolerable Acts '. Neither Boston nor Massa-chusetts bent before the will of Britain. Although Redcoats entered Boston to enforce British regulations, the people of Massachusetts set up a Revolutionary Government outside the city in the autumn of 1774 and began to prepare for armed conflict. Governor Thomas Gage, who was also Commander-in-Chief of the British army in America, did not have enough strength to attack them and asked for reinforcements and orders.

Meanwhile most of the people of the Thirteen Colonies rallied to the aid of their Massachusetts brethren. Twelve of the colonies (Georgia did not act) sent delegates to the First Continental Congress, meeting at Philadelphia in September and October 1774. That body contained many eminent Americans, including George Washington, Patrick Henry, and John and Samuel Adams. It promised to help to defend Massachusetts if the British troops marched out from Boston to attack. It demanded of Britain the repeal of the ' Intolerable Acts ' and of several other measures passed by Parliament after 1763, on the grounds that they violated the rights of Englishmen and the natural rights of mankind. To enforce that demand the First Con-tinental Congress organised the Association, a system of committees to prevent the importation and consumption of British goods. If Britain did not yield, the committees were later to prevent the export of everything but rice to Britain and the British West Indies. The boycott of British products thus established was rigidly enforced in

On 19 April 1775 occurred the first battle of the American War of Independence, when British troops clashed with colonials at Lexington (pictured here) and Concord. *Radio Times Hulton Picture Library*

Bunker Hill commanded the harbour of Boston and was soon occupied by American forces. On 17 June 1775 their entrenchments were stormed, at the cost of heavy casualties, by British forces. *Mansell*

the winter of 1774–5, and mob violence silenced those Americans who, preferring to accept British authority, opposed it. American militia drilled everywhere in preparation for fighting, although hope continued that Britain would repent her actions.

In the early months of 1775 the British Government decided to assert its sovereignty by force. In the Conciliatory Resolution passed in February Parliament promised not to levy taxes for revenue in any colony which paid its share of the expense of defending the Empire, a compromise not satisfactory to the colonists. Limits were placed on the sea traffic of New England, and orders were sent to General Gage to make use of his forces to re-establish British authority. In consequence, on 18 April 1775 Gage sent a detachment of troops from Boston to Concord to destroy military supplies collected by the Patriots at Concord. Paul Revere and others rode ahead of the British to warn the countryside. At Lexington the following morning armed hostilities began. The Regulars destroyed part of the stores at Concord, but were assailed by Patriot militia and pursued back to Boston. Thousands of the militia then gathered on the land approaches to the city, investing it. The War of Independence had begun.

Britain was unable to put large forces in the field before July 1776. Meanwhile the Patriots took the offensive. The Continental Congress, which reconvened in May 1775, assumed general direction of the war effort, appointing George Washington Commander-in-Chief of its army. The Patriots invaded Canada but failed to capture Quebec and were finally forced to fall back. However they compelled the British to evacuate Boston in March 1776, and suppressed Loyalists who took up arms for Britain.

The colonists, coming to believe that their political rights could not be safe in the British Empire, resolved to seek independence, and it was asserted by the Continental Congress on 2 July 1776. Two days later that body endorsed the Declaration of Independence, the famous document principally written by Thomas Jefferson, in which the Americans justified their separation from Britain. Invoking the rights of mankind, including that of revolution, against tyranny, the Declaration made many charges against George III and Parliament to prove that it was necessary to seek independence. Not all of the charges were well founded in fact but the attempt to win independence was essentially justified. While the Congress proceeded toward separation from the mother country, the Governments in all the Thirteen Colonies collapsed and the first American states came into being.

Britain, despite dissension at home, where many sympathised, at least to some degree, with the colonists, resolved to employ greater force, and was able to put nearly 45,000 men in the field in North America in 1776. During the second half of that year a British army penetrated New York State from Canada. Another large army led by General William Howe drove Washington from New York City and finally across the Delaware River. However at Trenton, on December 26, Washington routed and captured a large part of a Hessian garrison. The campaign ended on a note of cheer for the Patriots. In 1777 the British again took the offensive. But the Americans had been strengthened with weapons, other military equipment and cash secretly sent to them by France. General Howe captured Philadelphia, but was unable to destroy Washington's forces, which finally went almost intact into winter

'Washington at Princeton' by M.M. Sanford. Washington's success at Trenton in 1776 was followed by victory at Princeton when his army crept round the encamped English and attacked from the rear. *New York State Historical Association*

The surrender of Cornwallis, at Yorktown, Virginia, on 19 October 1781, was the decisive military event of the War of Independence. It was inevitable, once De Grasse's fleet entered Chesapeake Bay. The British government proceeded to ask for peace terms.

quarters at Valley Forge, west of Philadelphia. Meanwhile other Patriots under General Horatio Gates halted a British army advancing from Canada led by General John Burgoyne and forced its capitulation in October 1777.

The defeat of Burgoyne was a great turning-point in the war. Many European officers, including the Marquis de Lafayette, had earlier joined the Patriots. Both France and Spain had surreptitiously helped, France even before the Americans asked for assistance. In Paris and Madrid an opportunity was seen to avenge defeat in the Seven Years' War and even to destroy the British Empire. Both countries, however, hesitated to enter the conflict for many reasons, including a fear that the Patriots were too weak to continue the struggle. The French Foreign Minister, Vergennes, favoured intervention almost from the beginning of the conflict and Benjamin Franklin, sent to Paris as one of three Commissioners by Congress, had won many friends for America there. The news of Saratoga enabled Vergennes to take France into the war. On 6 February 1778 the Government of Louis XVI endorsed two treaties by which France recognised American independence and entered into a military alliance with the United States. The parties agreed they would fight until American independence was achieved, on the assumption that French recognition of the United States would lead to hostilities between Britain and France; and indeed they began the following June. In April 1779, promised Gibraltar and Minorca by Vergennes in return for her help, Spain decided to intervene in the conflict. At the same time, the British blockade of French ports led to friction with other European states. Vergennes astutely fomented feeling against Britain, and the 'League of Armed Neutrality' was formed at the instance of Catherine the Great in 1780 to resist British interference with neutral shipping. Included in the league were the Baltic powers. The Dutch, though neutral, were so anti-British that before the end of 1780 Britain declared war on them. Thus Britain had to face a Europe that was hostile or coldly neutral; her only ally was Portugal. In North America she had the help of the Tories and Indian savages. After 1778 the War of American Independence became a great international struggle, fought in the English Channel, at Gibraltar, in the Mediterranean, on the west coast of Africa, in the Indian Ocean, and in the West Indies, as well as in North America. England had never been more isolated or in greater peril.

The news of Saratoga and the approaching entry of France into the war had led to changes in British policy. The North Ministry, badly shaken, sent the Carlisle Commission to America to offer the Patriots as much as autonomy within the Empire. The offer came too late and Congress did not even consider it. In view of the changed military situation instructions were sent to a new British commander in the Thirteen States, General Sir Henry Clinton, to evacuate Philadelphia and to take the defensive, at least temporarily. Clinton concentrated his army at New York, where it was watched until 1781 by a Patriot army under Washington.

Clinton's fear was that his army might be caught between Washington and a French fleet; he did not undertake a major offensive in the northern states, but embarked there upon a war of waiting and endurance. The American General Benedict Arnold turned traitor, but his defection did not seriously hurt the Patriots. The appearance of a French squadron off Rhode Island and the landing there of a small French army in 1780 convinced Clinton of the value of prudence.

In 1779 Clinton nevertheless felt strong enough to mount offensives in the southern states where the Tories were numerous. Savannah, then Charleston, fell to British arms. By the summer of 1780 Georgia and South Carolina seemed to be firmly in the British grasp. But the Patriots in the south resorted to partisan warfare, and received help from Congress and General Washington. The British commander Lord Cornwallis twice invaded the interior of North Carolina, but was checked, the second time by the redoutable American General Nathanael Greene. Leaving the far south to the care of his subordinates, Cornwallis led part of his forces to Virginia. After his departure, Greene, with the help of the partisans, rapidly pushed back the remaining British contingents into Charleston and Savannah.

In Virginia Cornwallis collected an army of more than seven thousand men and built a base at Yorktown. In 1781 France, making a great effort, sent a powerful fleet under Admiral de Grasse across the Atlantic. In the late summer, acting in concert with Washington, de Grasse sailed from the West Indies to the Chesapeake. Defeating a British fleet sent to rescue Cornwallis off the mouth of the Chesapeake, he penned in Cornwallis from the sea. The French squadron from Newport joined de Grasse. Meanwhile Washington led the bulk of his army southward, together with the French troops from Newport, and attacked Cornwallis from the land. With French soldiers landed by de Grasse and American forces that had earlier taken the field in Virginia, Washington had more than seventeen thousand men. Cornwallis was surrounded, and his only hope was that a British fleet and army would come to his rescue. A relief expedition set out from New York but Cornwallis was forced to surrender while it was en route. He and his army laid down their arms on 19 October 1781.

The British disaster at Yorktown marked the end of major operations in North America, although Britain's red-skinned allies continued the struggle. In consequence of the defeat, Lord North's Ministry fell early in 1782. Britain gradually came to accept the loss of the Thirteen Colonies as final. Entering into negotiations with American Commissioners, including Franklin, at Paris, the British recognised an independent America with territory reaching to the Mississippi in a preliminary peace treaty signed in November 1782.

Meanwhile the war had also gone rather badly for the British elsewhere. French forces captured eight West Indian islands from them, and the Spanish seized Mobile, Pensacola and Minorca. A French squadron under the redoubtable Suffren won control of the Indian Ocean. But in 1782 Admiral George Rodney decisively defeated de Grasse in the West Indies in the Battle of the Saints, and it became evident that a protracted Franco-Spanish investment of Gibraltar could not force its surrender. France and Spain, as well as Britain, were war-weary, and began bargaining with Britain. In a preliminary treaty Spain obtained Minorca and the Floridas, but not Gibraltar; France secured Senegal, and Tobago and St Lucia in the West Indies. In September 1783 a final peace was signed at Versailles embodying the preliminary agreements. Although Spain did not secure Gibraltar and France did not profit much in terms of territory, France had attained

Admiral Rodney, victor in the Battle of the Saints, 1782, the only major naval battle won by Britain during the American War of Independence. Rodney had already made a reputation in the West Indies in the Seven Years' War. *Victoria & Albert Museum*

The Constitution of the United States of America, signed in 1787, gave stability to the badly strained Confederation. Machinery was provided for its amendment, and, with one great exception, Americans have been able to confine their disputes within constitutional bounds ever since. *Radio Times Hulton Picture Library*

her principal object in waging war, American independence.

It is not unlikely that the Patriots would have won their freedom without open French assistance, but they were grateful for French help. Economic factors prevented France from winning as great a share of American overseas trade as she had hoped. The Americans continued to carry on the bulk of their maritime trade with Britain. Those in France who were unhappy with the Old Regime had a special satisfaction. The Bourbon monarchies of France and Spain had assisted in bringing into being the American Republic and had advanced the cause of popular government everywhere. Colonialism had been dealt a heavy blow, and the Declaration of Independence became an inspiration to freedom-seeking peoples around the globe, including the French.

The Constitution of the United States

During the war the Patriots began to reconstruct America, both politically and socially. Each of the Thirteen States acquired a written constitution, and a central government was officially established in 1781, when the Articles of Confederation, the first written constitution for the whole nation, went into effect. Many reforms were made by the new states between 1776 and 1789. Each of them established a Bill of Rights. A two-house legislature was usual, together with a popularly chosen president or governor, who was given little power. The right to vote was widely extended, to include property-holders and taxpayers. Religious discrimination was largely ended, together with primogeniture and entail. Almost all the states stopped the importation of Negro slaves from abroad. Some of them forbade hereditary honours (the Articles of Confederation declared that neither the states nor the central government should issue titles of nobility). The states were truly republican in form, although the suffrage was not extended even to all white males. The way to political democracy was opening.

At the end of the War of Independence the states faced many economic problems. The ravages of war, economic dislocation, inflation and heavy debts placed burdens upon them. They had lost about 50,000 useful citizens, Tories who were banished or who fled to Canada and other British areas. A severe post-war depression in 1785–6 added to their troubles. It was not relieved by quarrels over tariffs, navigation and boundaries. In some states taxes were so heavy that citizens lost their homes because of non-payment. In Massachusetts farmers led by Daniel Shays, a Revolutionary veteran, took up arms in 1786 to save their homes, and Governor James Bowdoin had to call out the state militia to suppress the insurrection. By 1789, however, prosperity had returned, and the difficulties encountered by the states decreased.

The central government had also been plagued by economic distress. The funds for its operation were supposed to be supplied largely through requisitions upon the states. The latter often failed to meet their obligations, and the Government was threatened with bankruptcy. Moreover under the Articles of Confederation Congress had insufficient power to solve the problems of the nation. It was unable to act vigorously to defend American interests against Britain and Spain or to put an end to wars with the Indians beyond the Appalachian Mountains. At times so many delegates were absent that a quorum was lacking to do business. Attempts to give Congress funds and authority through amendment of the Articles failed because that constitution could not be changed without the unanimous consent of the state legislatures. Before it vanished, however, the Government of the Confederation scored one brilliant success. After 1780 the states began to cede to it their claims to lands west of the Appalachians. In 1787 the Congress passed the Northwest Ordinance, which provided for the future of the region between the Great Lakes and the Ohio and Mississippi Rivers. Territorial status and a measure of self-government were to be given to settlers there as soon as their number warranted those steps. Their personal rights were assured; land was set aside to support public education; and slavery was forbidden. Three to five states were to be created within the area, each of them to be politically equal to the thirteen original states. The Ordinance was executed and its basic principles were steadily applied as the nation spread westward to the Pacific. The Americans did not try to hold their own people west of the Appalachians in colonial subjection. Eventually Alaska and Hawaii were to become states.

George Washington and others realised, even before it was established, that the central government under the Articles would be too weak. The embarrassments of the 1780s convinced many that the Government must be strengthened to provide for defence, to deal with the Indians, to protect American maritime commerce, to remove restrictions upon internal trade, and to assert the dignity of the new nation. Conservative-minded men, merchants, lawyers and planters, who felt that political and social change in the states had been excessive, especially advocated the creation of a stronger central government, which they hoped to dominate. In 1786 a gathering held at Annapolis, Maryland, to consider means to prevent interference with inter-state commerce asked the states to send delegates to a convention at Philadelphia that would propose changes to strengthen the federation. The

invitation was endorsed by Congress, and the Convention began sessions in the spring of 1787.

The Convention laboured from May to September. Delegates came to it from all the states except Rhode Island. They formed a body distinguished by some genius and much ability. Among them were Washington, who gave dignity to the body, serving as its president; James Madison and George Mason, also from Virginia; Franklin, James Wilson, Robert Morris, and Gouverneur Morris of Pennsylvania; John Dickinson of Delaware; Alexander Hamilton of New York; Roger Sherman and Oliver Ellsworth of Connecticut; and John Rutledge and Charles Cotesworth Pinckney of South Carolina. Jefferson and John Adams, serving as diplomats in Europe, were not present. The most effective man in the Convention was Madison, who played such a large part in the making of the Constitution which was drawn up by the Convention that he is often called 'Father of the Constitution'.

The Convention early decided that the central government must be so strengthened that it would be able to function adequately for the needs of the American people. Toward that end it chose to make the Constitution, rather than to try to revise the Articles of Confederation. There were serious disputes among its members. Delegates from the smaller states feared that they would be dominated by the larger states. A compromise was reached whereby the smaller states were assured of equality of representation with the larger ones in a second chamber, the Senate. Men from the south quarelled with delegates from the north, but their differences, too, were mediated.

The French commander Rochambeau and Washington prepare the attack on Yorktown. *Radio Times Hulton Picture Library*

There was probably not a man in the Convention who was entirely satisfied with its product. Nevertheless, in September the Convention was able to submit for ratification a superbly drawn instrument of government which, with some changes, has endured for many generations. Altogether fifty-five men attended the Convention; only forty-two were present at its close; and only thirty-nine signed the Constitution. It provided for a strong central government with generous enumerated powers that could be exerted directly upon the citizenry. These powers included authority to levy taxes, regulate inter-state and foreign commerce, issue and regulate currency, and make war. Provision was made for a President, a Vice-President, a two-house Congress, and an independent federal judiciary. Checks and balances were inserted in the executive, legislative and judicial branches toward preventing any one of them from becoming tyrannical. In effect the Constitution apportioned sovereign power, giving a part to the central government, reserving a second part to the states, and saving a third part for the people. The system proposed by the Convention was truly federal, but the central government was given sufficient authority so that the system was actually both federal and national, as Madison judiciously described it. The Convention not only made the Constitution, but declared that it would go into effect as soon as it was approved by nine conventions specially chosen to consider it in the states. The Philadelphia Convention had no legal authority to stipulate this method of ratification, but the arrangement was accepted, despite the fact that it conflicted with the provisions of the Articles of Confederation.

Whether or not to ratify the Constitution was much debated in 1787–8. The document was denounced by many who believed that the Articles of Confederation were satisfactory, or that they could be made so with some amendments, or at least that the central government proposed by the Constitution was too powerful. They were called Anti-Federalists, their principal leaders being Patrick Henry and Richard Henry Lee of Virginia and Governor George Clinton of New York. Conspicuous among the champions of the Constitution, called Federalists, were Washington, Madison and Hamilton. Hamilton, Madison and John Jay, of New York, defended it in the famous *Federalist Papers*, which took the form of letters sent to the newspapers. The Constitution was attacked on almost every conceivable ground. It was vehemently charged that the central government would become tyrannical, and that the northern states would seize control of it and discriminate against the southern ones. Opponents of the Constitution made much of the fact that it did not contain a Bill of Rights (apparently omitted by the Philadelphia Convention as unnecessary) to protect the individual against arbitrary action by the President or the Congress or the federal courts. The Federalists replied that the Constitution, not without fault, was as good as could be devised; that the charges of its enemies were largely unfounded; and that any necessary amendments could be made after it had been adopted. In general, the proponents were more numerous on the seaboard and the Anti-Federalists were stronger in the interior. The bulk of the merchants, lawyers and wealthy planters were Federalist; Anti-Federalism was strongest among the small farmers.

By the summer of 1788 eight state conventions had endorsed the Constitution, some of them unanimously. Then New Hampshire and Virginia, by narrow margins, gave their approval. Without the consent of Virginia, the most populous state, the new union could hardly have been formed. It was the influence of George Washington, quietly exerted, and the expectation that he would be elected as the first President, together with the able leadership of Madison, that carried the day for the Constitution in Virginia against the bitter opposition of Patrick Henry. New York, in which Hamilton had striven mightily for the Federalists, then ratified. Eleven states having ratified the document, the Congress of the Confederation arranged for elections under the new system. A new Congress was elected late in 1788, and Washington was unanimously chosen President early the next year. That spring he took his oath of office in New York. North Carolina and Rhode Island finally endorsed the new system, in 1789 and 1790 respectively. To assure ratification of the Constitution, many of the Federalists had promised to support amendments to protect the individual against federal tyranny. In 1791 the Bill of Rights, contained in ten amendments, was added to the Constitution.

Much has rightly been said about the merits of the Constitution and of the men who made it. Scholars have suggested that it might not have been approved, had it been put to a popular vote. It was, however, sanctioned in republican style. Critics have said that the driving forces behind the Federalists were special economic interests; on the other hand it was apparent that the economic interests of all could be improved by the adoption of the Constitution. Some have said that it was the equivalent of *Thermidor* in the French Revolution, that it marked a conservative reaction; but the provisions of the Constitution were hardly less democratic than those of the average state constitution of the time. Taking a broader, international view, one sees the Constitution to be, like the state constitutions, a truly radical instrument. Perhaps even more remarkable than the great work done by its framers was the way in which the Americans made their decision to ratify it. It was not imposed upon them; they freely debated its merits and its faults; they did not indulge in serious violence (no one was killed) during the contest over it; and the change from the Confederation to the permanent Union was accomplished in an almost ideal republican manner.

With the inauguration of President Washington a great future for the American nation was virtually assured.

The twilight of the Old Regime

On the death of Louis XV in 1774 the hopes of France turned to the new king, who was twenty years old and surrounded with a halo of virtue which contrasted with the debauchery of his predecessor. Louis XVI was steeped in good intentions, but he was more timid and even weaker than his grandfather. Marie Antoinette, the new queen, was gracious, unimaginative, full of zest for life and, in the opinion of the sedate, frivolous. Louis XVI's first task was to find a loyal adviser to act as his chief minister, and until 1781 this office was filled by the Comte de Maurepas, who was responsible for the changes which took place in the Government personnel. Terray and Maupeou were dismissed and Vergennes, a conscientious diplomat, was put in charge of foreign affairs. The navy was given to Turgot, former Intendant of Limousin and a physiocrat

Marie Antoinette, daughter of Maria Theresa and sister of Joseph II, with her husband, Louis XVI, and their three children. Good-natured and warm-hearted, her lack of political understanding and her unpopularity as a foreigner made her the evil genius of her husband. *Victoria & Albert Museum*

who had contributed to the *Encyclopédie*. Turgot was later made finance minister. Then Malesherbes, another friend of the *philosophes*, joined the Council. In enlightened circles these choices were applauded, yet the new Ministry meant the destruction of the work Maupeou had achieved. In 1774 Louis XVI himself reinstated the *Parlement* of Paris to the position it had held before Maupeou's reforms. Turgot, who was a doctrinaire rather than a politician, attempted fundamental reforms. By the abolition of inter-provincial customs duties in 1774 he established free trade in grain; this caused uproar because shortages were blamed on it. A series of riots called the *guerre des farines* showed the popular hostility to this policy in 1775. In 1776 six famous edicts abolished the royal *corvée*, which was replaced by a tax on landed property, noble and non-noble alike, and suppressed the guilds, which still controlled industry and entrance to trade on medieval lines. Turgot also carefully scrutinised the list of royal pensions, reducing many and cutting out others entirely. He contemplated a tax system based on land evaluation, and the establishment of elective municipal councils. But when Turgot's projects became known to those whose entrenched privileges were threatened, hostility, especially from the *Parlement*, was such that Louis XVI was persuaded to dismiss his wisest minister. The next finance minister revived the *corvée* and reinstated a certain number of guilds.

Reforms which modernised the military organisation and the fleet were more successful and more enduring. But the financial situation grew worse, and in 1777 the King in desperation entrusted finance to Necker, a Genevan banker, who, being a Protestant, was legally ineligible for the post of finance minister or a position in the royal Council. Necker, who nevertheless inspired confidence, was at least able to float a loan. He then attempted a few mild reforms, such as the provincial assemblies experimentally established in 1777 in four provinces to collect the revenue. In order to revive the waning credit of France he published in 1781 an over-optimistic *Account Rendered to the King* on the state of the kingdom's finances. In it, to the intense annoyance of the King's courtiers, he revealed the sums they received as pensions. Again in 1781

pressure from the privileged classes compelled the King to dismiss his finance minister. In the same year Maurepas died, and Louis XVI became the dupe of court factions who kept him out of touch with the life and the real problems of the nation. Everywhere the reactionary aristocracy had its way: in the re-registration of property so that tenants were forced to pay more, in a regulation which required officers to prove that all their four grand-parents were of noble birth.

In 1783 Calonne became finance minister and, profiting by the sense of optimism which followed the Peace of Versailles, was able to raise loans. He encouraged extravagance on the grounds that it was good for trade, and in 1786 signed a commercial agreement with Great Britain. William Eden, the astute member of the Board of Trade who negotiated the treaty, was fully aware of the relative economic strength of the two countries and, without granting in return particularly great advantages to French agriculture — with the exception of wine — he obtained customs conditions which sacrificed France's budding industries to their powerful British rivals. Meanwhile prices rose and the people regarded with growing hatred the continual festivities of the court. Not only the sovereign, but the institution of monarchy, was brought into disrepute. In 1787 France was bankrupt and Calonne was at the end of his tether. The *Parlement's* hostility to any attempted reforms could, from long experience, be anticipated; Calonne therefore advised the King to summon an Assembly of Notables — 144 in number — to review the situation and consider the proposals he had to offer. The Notables proved as unwilling as the *parlementaires* to make a sacrifice for the country's welfare. Calonne resigned and the Archbishop of Toulouse, Loménie de Brienne, became chief minister. He dismissed the Notables and simply addressed himself to the *Parlement*, for he, too, had reforms to propose: humanitarian, such as the abolition of torture and the *corvée*, and the admission of Protestants to public office; and institutional, such as the setting up of provincial assemblies to limit the power of the Intendants. The *Parlement* tried its strength against the power of the monarchy, refusing to register any edict which lessened its own privileges; and making an appeal to popular opinion, demanded the convocation of the States General.

Then, on 8 May 1788, the *Parlement* was summoned to Versailles, where reforms more drastic than any Maupeou had imposed were placed before it for immediate registration. By these measures the judical system would have been totally overhauled and the powers of the *Parlement* curtailed. The *parlementaires* took an oath to refuse compliance. It was the signal for an aristocratic revolt: in the provinces the *parlements* protested and riots broke out in Rennes, Dijon, Pau and in Grenoble. Provincial Estates gathered together of their own accord. From all quarters arose the clamour for a meeting of the States General, which had not been summoned since 1614. Louis yielded. Brienne convoked the States General and resigned. Necker was recalled to borrow a few million livres to tide over the bankrupt State until the meeting of the States General, which was arranged for 1 May 1789. Though the *Parlement* had been restored to its former position, public opinion was no longer duped by its pretensions. The public wanted real reforms, and its impatience to have them soon precipitated the events which brought down the curtain on an age.

THE PRESENT AGE

In a political sense it is still proper to date the age in which we live from the French Revolution. The shock carried by that Revolution and the spread of its principles has produced repercussions ever since. They will continue today, whenever people claim the rights of national self-determination and of equality before the law. The social history of France, and Europe too, was permanently changed by the institutions set up when the Third Estate seized power and turned the States General into the National Assembly. But in 1917, with the inauguration of the Communist world and the intervention of the United States in a European struggle, another era began while the one which started in 1789 had still to run its course in Africa and Asia. Technical changes, too, have become more rapid than ever before; trains, cars, aircraft, the telephone, radio, cybernetics and nuclear energy have so transformed the world that we are further removed from the environment of Robespierre than he was from that of Charlemagne.

Man's environment has been totally changed, not geologically or by radical alterations of climate, fauna and vegetation, nor by a redistribution of the earth and the waters, but simply because his powers of invention suddenly increased and did so faster and faster. Yet man himself has changed little, if at all. His brain is not structurally different from that of his prototypes, settled

On 5 May 1789 the States General of France assembled at Versailles for the first time in a century and a half. It was to be their last meeting. Six weeks later they met as the National Assembly and the history of modern France began. *Mansell*

or nomadic, warrior, peasant or priest. So when on 21 September 1792 the members of the Convention believed that they were justified in dating that 'moment' as the Year I, they may be said to have marked, if not the beginning of the contemporary world, at least the opening of a revolutionary phase in history, a point from which continual change became a normal fact of human existence. Because there are no neat dividing lines or clearly defined 'turning-points' in world history, much of the old world still lived on long after 1789. When a king was executed in 1793, there still remained just as many kings in the world in the eyes of most of the globe. The republican ideal, launched by the 'insurgents' of the Thirteen Colonies in America, now embroidered and developed by the theorists of France and tried out by the French nation in arms, would little by little spread all over the world. Yet the twenty years which immediately followed the Revolution, full of astonishing constitutional experiments and essays in social progress, also saw the entire old world close its ranks to resist the threat of revolution. They ended with the apparent victory of reaction. From another point of view, the great struggle which for over twenty years occupied the centre of the historical stage was the last episode in the third Anglo-French Hundred Years' War, in which command of the seas and constitutional monarchy established a century of supremacy for Great Britain.

LES·QVA·TRE·VERITEZ·DV·SIECLE·DAPRESENT·

The priest (who prays for all) the soldier (who fights for all) the peasant (who feeds all) and the lawyer (who feeds off all). A view of the structure of the *Ancien Régime*.   *Coll. L. Ferrand*

THE ERA OF THE FRENCH REVOLUTION

CHAPTER THIRTEEN

THE LAST YEARS OF THE EIGHTEENTH CENTURY

THE EUROPEAN MONARCHICAL CRISIS

The States General

The solemn opening session of the States General, convoked by Louis XVI, took place on 5 May 1789 at Versailles. The States General of France had last met in 1614. The Deputies had then been elected by orders — Nobles, Clergy and the Third Estate — and the precedent was followed, though the Third Estate had been doubled in number, so that it contained half of the eleven hundred Deputies. It represented the interests of the huge majority of the population as against the three or four hundred thousand represented by the other two ' privileged ' orders. On the eve of the occasion a spectacular procession had wound its way towards the church of St Louis to present to the King ' the homage of the Clergy, the respect of the Nobility and the very humble supplications of the Third Estate '. The formula underlined the distinctions expressed in the costumes worn by the three orders taking part in the procession: the sober, untrimmed tricorn hats, plain coats, small cloaks and black stockings of the Third

Estate; the silken stuffs embroidered in gold, the white stockings, swords and plumed hats of the Nobility. Among the Clergy, two hundred-odd parish priests wore simple cassocks, while the hierarchy of France moved resplendent in purple robes, episcopal surplices and capes, or the red hats of Cardinals.

Causes of the Revolution

In each parish of France a *cahier* was drawn up which listed the grievances and desires of the people. On these were based the instructions given to the delegates to the States General; they reveal, as well as anything can, what the French people thought in 1789, even though we must allow, of course, for the preponderant share of the literate and better-off in drafting them. Their tone was not republican; they did not attack the monarchy. The privileged classes resented 'ministerial despotism'; the partisans of the old 'provincial liberties' complained of 'centralisation', personified by the Intendants; admirers of British constitutional monarchy complained of the concept of Divine Right. Others attacked the influence and wealth of the clergy, social inequality, feudalism and the burdens laid on the peasant. The involved and needlessly complex machinery of government, the industrial crisis which had followed the Anglo-French Commercial Treaty of 1786, and the agricultural crisis due to poor harvests in 1787 and 1788, with the consequent scarcity, rise in prices and haunting fear of famine, had made these even heavier than usual in 1789. It was unfortunate that neither Louis XVI, who, though brave, was stupid, nor Marie Antoinette, the proud daughter of Maria Theresa, could sense the opportunity which existed for the monarchy to take the initiative and lead the movement for reform. Disorder began even while the delegates were travelling to Versailles. Insurrection, pillage and street massacres were familiar in France whenever in the past the forces of order were weak or abuses excessive: the turbulent countryside reminded noblemen of earlier *jacqueries*. In Paris, there may even have been some deliberate provocation of disorder, but corruption and foreign propaganda, always blamed, were more often denounced than discovered. Such myths were later important in linking political opposition with treason in the eyes of suspicious patriots. 'English gold' was blamed both by the Convention and the Empire — British revenge, it was supposed, for French aid to the rebelling British colonists. Certainly foreign powers, alarmed by the power and spreading influence of France, gave support in arms and money to her opponents, and thus contributed to the tragic struggles which marked the course of the Revolution.

The Deputies

The people responsible for the great upheaval which makes the year 1789 so memorable in world history were typical of the three classes whom the King, nearly bankrupt and powerless to enforce reform on the privileged orders, had called together for consultation. Among many obscure names were some destined to become famous. Outstanding among the Nobility were the Duke of Orleans, Grand Master of French Freemasonry, and the Marquis de Lafayette, famous since the war in America, who was a personal friend of George Washington. The Clergy

included Cardinal Rohan, who had been involved in the scandal of the Queen's Necklace; Henri Grégoire, Jansenist, fervent democrat and future regicide; and the Bishop of Autun, Charles Maurice de Talleyrand-Périgord, who was to propose the confiscation of the property of his own order. The Third Estate counted many lawyers, among them Robespierre of Arras and intellectuals like Volney and the astronomer Bailly. But the leaders of the Third Estate were two deserters from the privileged classes: the Comte de Mirabeau and the Abbé Sieyès. Mirabeau, whose stormy youth and scandalous love affairs had on occasions led to *lettres de cachet* and his imprisonment, was to finish as the defender of the monarchy he had

Marie Joseph Paul Yves Roch Gilbert Motier, the Marquis de Lafayette, hero of the American War of Independence, Commander of the National Guard of Paris in the early Revolution, and self-appointed conscience of the constitutional monarchy. His bravery was equalled by his vanity. *Neurdein*

N

209

Drinking the health of the *Tiers Etat* — the Commons. The figures are those of a craftsman and a washerwoman. The *Tiers Etat*, however, included everyone who was neither noble nor a cleric — about ninety-five per cent of the nation. *Giraudon*

The first great revolutionary act: when ordered to leave its meeting-place, the National Assembly adjourned to a nearby tennis-court, where its members took an oath not to disperse until they had given France a constitution. *Mansell*

done so much to undermine. The Abbé Sieyès, who had acquired immense popularity by a pamphlet entitled *What is the Third Estate?* (published a few months before the States General assembled), was to be the oracle and inspiration of successive republican constitutions.

The National Assembly

The States General spent nearly two months in arguing whether they were to vote by order (when the two privileged orders would always outvote the third) or by head. Finally, on June 17, estimating that it represented ninety-six per cent of the nation, the Third Estate proclaimed itself the National Assembly; and, asserting its sovereign powers, declared that only taxes to which it would consent were to be legal. Meanwhile among the Clergy resistance had crumbled and the parish priests had come over to the Assembly. The Court was startled. When the King turned them out of their usual meeting-place the Deputies of the Third Estate hastily assembled on a tennis court nearby, where they took an oath not to separate again 'until the constitution of the kingdom was established on solid foundations' (June 20). Three days later they were imperiously reprimanded by the King and required to separate immediately. Whether or not Mirabeau made his legendary reply that they would not budge 'except at the point of the bayonet', the Third Estate did not obey. The more liberal section of the Nobility and the remainder of the Clergy joined them. On June 27 Louis XVI himself yielded and sanctioned the joint meeting of the three Estates.

Intervention of the populace

1789 should be called the Year of Fear. The King was afraid of the Assembly and concentrated troops at Versailles. The privileged classes trembled for their privileges. The Third Estate feared an aristocratic or royal counterattack. Meanwhile in Paris, crowded with refugees from the nearer provinces and unemployed victims of the industrial and agricultural crises, the mob believed the Nobility were plotting against them. In such an atmosphere fear was infectious and it erupted in riots all over France. In the countryside, mysterious rumours of 'brigands' provoked the famous *Grande Peur*, with its accompanying looting and burning of *châteaux*. When Necker, whom the privileged classes distrusted, was dismissed by Louis XVI (July 11), Paris at once began to riot. On July 14 the mob, searching for weapons, tried to enter the prison-fortress of the Bastille. Launay, the Governor, opened fire, but cannon were dragged up and Launay capitulated. As he was being taken to the Hôtel de Ville the mob, unhindered by his escort, slaughtered him — just as, soon afterwards, they slaughtered the Intendant of Paris.

Almost everywhere in the provinces the example of Paris was followed, new municipalities seized power and the townsmen armed themselves. The King in alarm recalled Necker and came to Paris, where he sanctioned the municipal revolution. The utter collapse of authority was by now universal. The reports of the *Grande Peur* led nobles and clergy alike to join in the enthusiastic votes by which the Assembly swept away feudal privileges, serfdom and tax exemptions. But a right-wing 'monarchical' party, anxious to restore the King's executive power in face of the manifest danger of total anarchy, had begun to appear in the Assembly. The extremists decided on forceful tactics. Five or six thousand rioters — mainly women enraged by food shortages — marched on Versailles and took the palace by surprise. In triumphal procession they escorted a reluctant royal family back to the Tuileries: 'the baker, the baker's wife and the little baker's boy' — as guarantees against famine. The Assembly followed and continued their sessions in Paris. The victory of the popular revolution was complete.

The Federation

Amid the collapse of the decrepit Old Regime France itself almost disintegrated. From village to village, from town to town, from province to province, improvised 'Communes' fraternised with each other and formed 'Federations'. One, the Federation of Franche-Comté, Lorraine and Alsace at Strasbourg (Strassburg), ran up over the bridge on the Rhine the tricolour flag and the inscription: 'Here begins the Land of Liberty'. The Assembly gave its blessing to this popular movement by organising in the Champ-de-Mars the festival of 'National Federation' to celebrate the fall of the Bastille on 14 July 1790. From all parts of the kingdom delegates came to demonstrate their support for the constitution which was being forged — a constitution which Louis XVI, too, swore to maintain, after Lafayette, in the name of the National Guard of France, had taken the oath to be 'forever loyal to the Nation, to the Law and to the King'. On this day the heterogeneous patchwork of France, patiently sewn together by a long line of kings, freely consented to its own fusion into a single nation, soon to be proclaimed indivisible. From this day in 1790 — and not from the fall of the Bastille which, however, it also celebrated — dates the French national holiday.

Early difficulties

Unity among the politicians of the Assembly was troubled by ideals, passions and interests sufficiently contradictory to provoke, if not party strife in the modern sense of the words, oratorical duels between the spokesmen of antagonistic and constantly shifting groups. It was the beginning of that conflict between 'Right' and 'Left' which has passed into the world's political vocabulary. The terms derived from the chance seating arrangements of the 'moderates' to the right of the president's chair, and the 'advanced' Deputies to the left of his chair during a debate on whether the King should have a legislative veto. Other discussions, equally virulent, took place in the political 'clubs' — derived, or at least deriving their name 'club', from British examples — which gathered in Paris. The club of the Jacobins — or the 'Society of Friends of the Constitution' — communicated with the whole country by means of its network of hundreds of affiliated provincial clubs. The club of the Feuillants was composed of those moderates like Lafayette and Sieyès who had broken with the Jacobins. The club of the Cordeliers was more democratic, and very influential among the smaller tradesmen of the capital; its orators included the lawyer Danton and Marat, the 'Friend of the People'.

In this polemical uproar, in which the press with its innumerable journals, tracts and pamphlets also joined, the Assembly achieved much of positive value. There were,

On 14 July 1789 a crowd asking for arms was fired upon by the guards of the Bastille. The old prison-fortress was attacked and surrendered after some hours of fighting. The news led the king to recall Necker. *Musée Historique d'Orléans*

Louis XVI, king of France 1774–92. Less able and more conscientious than Louis XV, he suffered from a fatal combination of obstinacy and indecisiveness which made him unable to lead the nation in an attack on privilege. *Mansell*

211

however, consequences of its work which were unfortunate or even disastrous: by leaving the country the King's two brothers had set an example to the *émigrés*; the number of adversaries or victims of the new order was growing; the financial crisis had become worse; and the embers of the religious struggle had been fanned. Finally, on 20 June 1791 Louis XVI and his family fled from Paris. He was stopped at Varennes and brought back to Paris accompanied by the curses or the stony silence of his subjects. He was at first 'suspended' by the Assembly and then 'reinstated' on the fiction that he had not attempted to escape, but had been abducted. The moderates could not envisage orderly government without a king, but the extreme Left demanded his dethronement. A monster petition was carried to the national altar in the Champ-de-Mars where the National Guard fired on the demonstrators (July 17). The blood of fifty people slain cemented the barrier of fear and hatred between the constitutional bourgeoisie and the democrats. But the constitution was at last completed and accepted by the King (14 September 1791).

Political, social and economic measures

When the Constituent Assembly was dissolved two weeks later, the Constitution it had created founded a new world. Yet many of its institutions were to have only ephemeral life; its preamble, on the other hand, remains immortal: the *Declaration of the Rights of Man and of the Citizen*. The declaration was inspired by its American forerunner of 1776 but differed profoundly in the universal nature of the principles it set forth: all are born with equal rights; since social distinctions are founded on usefulness to the community alone and the laws are the same for all, public office should be accessible to all; liberty of the person, freedom of thought, freedom of speech and the press, of work and of ownership are natural and inalienable rights; all sovereignty resides in the nation; the law is an expression of the general will; as the upkeep of the armed forces of the nation and the expenses of its administration demanded a common contribution to be borne equally by every citizen, the total amount and basis of taxation will be determined by the citizens themselves or by their representatives. Finally, it proclaimed the separation of the legislative, executive and judicial powers. The Constitution itself contained articles in which jurists developed the principles laid down in the preamble, distorting some in the interests of stability; they added no Declaration of Duties to balance the Declaration of Rights. British and American parliamentary experience was rejected, and in their reaction against absolute monarchy the authors of the 1791 Constitution deprived the executive of all real power and subordinated it to the Legislative Assembly. The 'King of the French' was then merely 'the first public servant' of the sovereign nation. He did not even have ministers sitting in the legislature. One right over the Assembly the King retained: he could suspend the enactment of its decrees for at least four years by his veto; and it was the exercise of this right which brought about his downfall. The legislative body was composed of representatives elected for two years, whose persons were inviolable.

Local government assumed a new shape; France was divided into a new hierarchy of authorities. The largest were the eighty-three Departments artificially carved from the old provinces and given purely geographical names — from local rivers or mountains — in order to obliterate the memory of earlier historical unities. Other relics of the past abolished by the Constitution were the feudal system, orders of chivalry, the sale and inheritance of office, professional or craft guilds, and the vows laid on monks and nuns. Civil marriage was instituted. In violation of the principles of the Declaration of Rights, it recognised for electoral purposes two classes of citizens — 'active' and 'passive' (who were distinguished by property qualifications). This inconsistency was from the first attacked by Robespierre and Marat, who advocated universal suffrage. Freedom of the press was, in the case of opposition papers, curtailed on the pretext of suppressing 'calumny and abuse'. Freedom of association was hard to reconcile with the closing of religious houses or with the law which prohibited workers from forming trade unions or organising strikes. Economically, the abolition of internal customs barriers, freedom to practise crafts without the restriction of the guilds, and free trade all joined with the liberation of land from the restraints hitherto placed on its free transfer to initiate the era of market-society in France. With it came the free play of supply and demand and the impact of capitalistic competition; inevitably the operation of these forces created new economic problems. They were forerunners of worse trials in the mature capitalist society of the next century.

Financial and religious measures

The majority of the nation had wanted universal liability to taxation and the Constituent Assembly hastened to satisfy it with three new 'contributions': a land tax, a tax on personal property, and licences to exercise a trade or profession. But the public showed no more zeal to 'contribute' than to be taxed. The Government still had no revenue. By the end of 1789 Talleyrand, supported by Mirabeau, proposed and carried the nationalisation of Church property. In exchange the State promised to pay the expenses of public worship, and priests' salaries, and to be responsible for education and public assistance. Against the confiscated landed property the Assembly issued *assignats*, or bonds, representing rights to buy, on presenting them, land assigned to their holders. This was a way of mobilising the new resources at once and the *assignats* soon acquired the value of currency. But more and more were printed and they rapidly depreciated, as the paper money issued by Law had depreciated some seventy years before. This began to cause discontent. The extent to which the property involved changed hands — and later the property of wealthy *émigrés* as well as Crown lands was confiscated — is hard to establish with precision, but certainly much land was bought by the better-off peasants and the middle class.

Though the seizure of the Church's time-honoured possessions had not much moved a still Catholic nation, the Assembly erred in enacting a Civil Constitution of the Clergy to regulate the new Church settlement. Gallican and even Jansenist in spirit, it reduced the number of medieval dioceses to one for each Department, and the number of parishes to one for each Commune. The choice of bishops and parish priests was left to the electorate, and they were paid and lodged by the State. Resistance

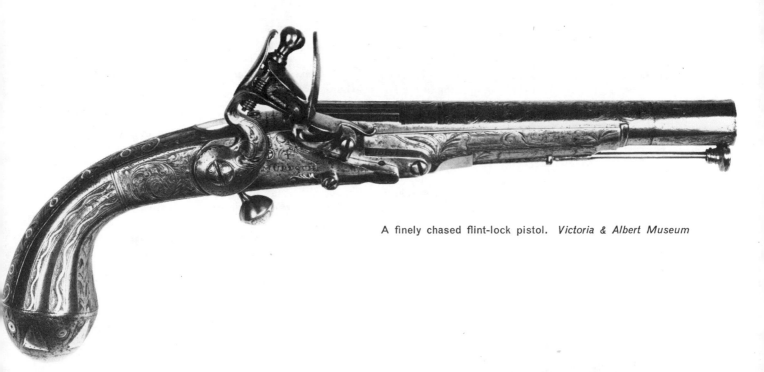

A finely chased flint-lock pistol. *Victoria & Albert Museum*

to the measure was met by the Assembly with a requirement that priests should swear an oath of allegiance to the Civil Constitution or else resign their benefices. When almost all the bishops and half of the parish priests refused, they were at once removed and replaced. In April 1791 Pope Pius VI condemned the Civil Constitution, but too late to prevent a schism which split the Church in France into two camps: the compliant Constitutional clergy and the non-juring priests who refused to take the oath. Much of the bitterness which followed arose from this split.

Europe in 1789

Although 1789 is the most important date in the history of France and one of the turning-points of European and indeed world history, it appeared at the time to be simply one more year characterised by the usual dynastic ambitions, court intrigues, cabinet shuffles and small-scale conflicts. The vast clash of ideas and armies which closed the century was still to come.

Three sovereigns occupied the centre of the European stage: the Emperor at Vienna, the Empress of all the Russias, and the King of Prussia. Joseph II finished his disappointing reign with a war with the Turks in the east, and a Belgian uprising in the west. Catherine II was grappling both with the Swedes and with the Ottoman Empire in her self-appointed role of Christian crusader; the elderly Tsaritsa was even more interested in Poland, the other field of Eastern Europe ripe for harvesting, which had been partially dismembered in 1772. That unhappy kingdom was making an effort to pull itself together in face of the obvious intentions of rapacious neighbours who encouraged and subsidised its internal disunity. King Stanislas Poniatowski had convoked the Diet which was attempting to write a Constitution to regenerate the State.

While Joseph II was anxious to safeguard his independence and the lands he still possessed, Frederick William II of Prussia dreamed of renewing the conquests of his

Honoré Gabriel Riqueti, Marquis de Mirabeau (1749–91), a Provencal nobleman elected to the States General by the Commons and widely regarded as a traitor to his class. A great orator, he used his influence to urge France towards constitutional monarchy. *Larousse*

uncle, Frederick the Great. But uncle and nephew were physical and moral antitheses. Frederick William II was fat, gross and headstrong; whereas his uncle had abhorred women, he was particularly susceptible to them. He was influenced by a series of charlatans culminating in a kind of German Alberoni, a certain Count Herzberg, whose ambition it was to set all Eastern Europe aflame in order that Prussia might impose her armed mediation. Herzberg hoped thus to gain Thorn and Danzig, and to pay off Austria with territory wrenched ultimately from the new Sultan, Selim III. These intrigues came to nothing, but made it doubly important to Vienna and St Petersburg to see that France, traditionally the ally of Poland as well as of Turkey, remained out of the picture. The French Foreign Minister, Montmorin, a childhood companion of Louis XVI and a friend of Necker, was prudent, not to say timorous. France intervened neither in the troubles in Holland in 1787 nor in Belgium where the revolt of Liège and then of Brabant brought about the departure of Austrian troops during the last months of 1789.

The first reactions of Europe

In those European circles in which French literature and philosophy were much admired by a cultured reading public, whether aristocratic or upper middle class, and among those of advanced or progressive opinions, the first news of the events in France was received with sympathy and even enthusiasm. In Britain some of the Whigs — Fox, Sheridan, Erskine and others — showed a lively interest in the first groping attempts of France to attain a parliamentary system, while the Society of the Revolution — that of 1688 — sent an address to the National Assembly. The philosopher Jeremy Bentham supplied Mirabeau with a plan of legal reform. In Germany, a land of visionaries, there were many enthusiasts, Rhinelanders especially. The Prussian Baron von Cloots, who renounced his title, changed his name to Anacharsis and became French, and Georg Forster, who sailed with Captain Cook, came to the festival of National Federation on July 14. Even in Königsberg, Kant, the author of the *Critique of Pure Reason* and the *Metaphysic of Ethics*, interrupted the ritual of his daily stroll at the news that the Bastille had fallen. The news was naturally greeted with approval at Weimar, whose Duke Charles Augustus was a Freemason and whose capital, with Herder and Wieland, Goethe and Schiller, was known as the Athens of the North. Individuals welcomed the news, from Switzerland — Ochs at Basle, Lavater at Zürich — to Russia, where La Harpe, the earnest, lofty-minded Swiss republican, directed the education of the Tsaritsa's grandchildren.

The violence of the Paris mob, however, soon sobered the European audience. Among the German nobility the burning *châteaux* of France were a terrifying reminder that the Anabaptists could reappear, while Russians recalled the bloody peasant uprising under Pugachov. In Great Britain Burke, quarrelling with his friend Fox, published in 1790 his *Reflections on the French Revolution* which saw only evil in the outbreak of the ' swinish multitude ' against the rule of law and order. The monarchs of Europe were not, however, at first disturbed by thoughts that the revolution could be dangerously contagious. Joseph II, especially since his visit to Versailles, strongly disapproved of his sister's and brother-in-law's way of

life, and had absolutely no wish or intention to defend their authority. His chief anxiety was to make certain that the French did not encourage his Belgian subjects, who in January 1790 had proclaimed their independence. He himself died in February to be succeeded by his younger brother Leopold, who as Grand Duke of Tuscany had already presided over enlightened reforms. Meanwhile the Belgian insurrectionists had split into two camps, the Catholic Statists and the left-wing Vonckists; and, abandoned by France, they were easily dealt with by Leopold. Of a conciliatory temperament, Leopold agreed to an Austro-Prussian Treaty which restrained Frederick William, and came to a friendly arrangement with the Hungarians, who had been stirred up by Herzberg. In August Catherine II signed the peace of Verela with Gustavus III of Sweden, but the state of Eastern Europe remained as unsettled as before.

Britain, where Pitt was Prime Minister, considered that all war was harmful to trade and to British financial recovery. Nevertheless an incident in which her old colonial rival Spain was involved nearly precipitated trouble. In the spring of 1789 the seizure by Spanish coastguards of a British ship carrying contraband in Nootka Sound on the west coast of Vancouver Island was followed by demands which, in the beginning of 1790, almost led to a rupture with Madrid. The House of Commons voted a million pounds to rearm the fleet. Charles IV, who had succeeded his father on the Spanish throne in 1788, appealed to France in the name of the Bourbon Family Pact. Montmorin at last judged the moment opportune for a display of national pride; but the Constituent Assembly repudiated the Family Pact and Madrid was obliged to cede Nootka Sound to the British.

The Constituent Assembly against the King

The Nootka Sound incident, in itself of minor interest, gave rise to an important debate in the Assembly on the right of the monarch to make war and peace. Mirabeau, either from conviction or, as his opponents said, from venality, had placed his eloquence at the service of the Crown. The decree of 22 May 1790, by which Montmorin's warlike proposal was defeated, expressed Robespierre's views in words which were to become an integral part of the Constitution of 1791: ' The French nation renounces the undertaking of any war the object of which is conquest, and will never employ its armed forces against the liberty of any people. ' The formula at least deserves an honourable place in the history of human aspirations. The Constituent Assembly had in fact already begun to clash with established European interests. The abolition of feudal rights had included those of certain German princes with estates in Alsace. At the beginning of 1790 they protested to the German Diet and the Emperor. The Constituent Assembly replied by denouncing all contracts made through the errors of kings and therefore all obligations to the Emperor. Thus the new revolutionary law substituted the will of the people for the former international law which had respected treaties signed or engagements undertaken between monarch and monarch.

The renunciation of war for conquest was, in fact, soon followed by a campaign of propaganda: with the firm conviction that revolutionary France was the new incarnation of earthly happiness, it was not long before an

offer of French nationality was extended to all peoples who aspired to be free. To begin with, there was the question of Avignon and the county of Venaissin, which since the Avignon Popes of the fourteenth century had belonged to the Holy See. But in 1789 the Papal Legate had been driven from Avignon by the local democrats. In 1790 blood flowed between partisans and adversaries of the Pope, and the democrats clamoured for union with France. Annexation, advocated by Robespierre, was for several months rejected by the Assembly, but finally decided on in September 1791 in the atmosphere of rupture with Rome.

In the meantime Louis XVI and Marie Antoinette had sent emissary after emissary, official, unofficial and secret, to urge those sovereigns whom they believed to be concerned about their fate — the Emperor Leopold, especially — to intervene, as though spontaneously, in the common cause of all royalty. When their plea was unanswered and they had decided to flee, their arrest at Varennes struck every crowned head in Europe with stupor. The Emperor, signing peace with the Turks in order to leave his hands free, proposed a gathering of European monarchs to consider the situation. The British Cabinet was hostile to the project and convinced that Britain had all to gain by the increasing anarchy in France and by the disorganisation of the French colonies, ripe for the plucking. Neutrality seemed to offer Britain all the advantages of successful war without risks. Charles IV collected a few troops on the Spanish frontier but, lacking money and men, was inclined towards neutrality. In Naples Ferdinand IV, the other Bourbon monarch, ordered subversive literature to be burned, but stopped at that.

The royal family fled from Paris in June 1791, trying to reach loyal troops near the north-eastern frontier. Delayed at the village of Varennes, they were recognised and stopped. The local National Guard prevented their rescue by the soldiers sent to escort them. On his return to Paris, *(below),* Louis was suspended from the kingship, but re-instated later. Neither his prestige nor that of the monarchy ever recovered from the effects of his attempt to escape. *Mansell*

215

The King of Sardinia proposed a military agreement, but instead of furnishing soldiers asked for them; he explained that they were needed to re-establish tranquillity in his own domains which had been disturbed by the revolutionary contagion. Catherine II warmly approved of a monarchical crusade, but insisted that her part in it should be confined to restoring the previous state of affairs in Warsaw, where the Poles had been allowed by their Constitution of May 1791 to abolish the traditional causes of anarchy — and hence their susceptibility to Russian influence. Only Gustavus III of Sweden was really prepared to act, but he was generally considered a Don Quixote.

Finally at Pillnitz in August 1791 Leopold and Frederick William II, urged on by the Count of Artois — Louis XVI's brother and the most militant of the *émigrés* — published a declaration which proclaimed their resolution to act — provided only that all the other sovereigns of Europe would agree to join them. In reality Leopold did not want war and, in spite of British reluctance to participate, was in favour of a European Congress to lecture France and avoid the necessity of armed intervention. When, on September 12, in an effort to repair the unfortunate consequences of his attempted flight, Louis XVI ratified the Constitution, the old Austrian Chancellor Kaunitz remarked that God was to be thanked that the King of France had got them all out of a nasty situation. When Frederick William II heard the news he exclaimed: ' The peace of Europe is at last assured ! '

The Legislative Assembly

The Constitution, too abstract in conception and proving in practice a source of division, did not long survive the Constituent Assembly. Its failure was made certain when, on their separation, its members declared themselves ineligible for re-election to the legislative body which the Constitution provided for. New Deputies, entirely without the experience of their predecessors, would be likely to make things worse. What Robespierre had foreseen occurred: in the new Legislative Assembly the Left of the preceding Assembly became the Right: the Feuillants, Constitutional Royalists, who at first controlled it, split into two rival factions: the ' Triumvirate ' — Lameth, Barnave, Duport — and the friends of Lafayette. In the centre a mass of floating independents little by little withdrew their support from the Right and voted with the Left. The Left, though in a distinct minority, was the vanguard of the Revolution. Its leaders were the Anglophile journalist Brissot, the philosopher-marquis Condorcet, and a group of ambitious and persuasive orators from the south, Isnard, Vergniaud, Guadet, Gensonné — mostly from the region of Bordeaux in the Department of the Gironde, hence their later name *Girondins*. To the extreme Left were the Republicans — republican not from admiration of the institutions of republican antiquity but from dislike of the monarchy — Carnot, a captain in the corps of engineers, and the epicurean magistrate Hérault de Séchelles.

The dominant tone of the new Assembly — in contrast with that of the old — was intolerance and belligerency. When it first met on 1 October 1791 it diverted attention from the rise in prices by attacking the non-juring clergy. A decree threatening them with prison or deportation was too much for Louis XVI's religious scruples and he

vetoed it, as he vetoed measures summoning *emigres* to return to France within two months under pain of loss of citizenship, forfeiture of property and even death. This brought down the fury of the clubs and the popular orators on the King's head. For some time, indeed, they had been attacking the counter-revolutionary activities of the King's two *émigré* brothers, the Counts of Provence and Artois, and the blustering threats of some thousands of *émigrés* who had taken refuge in Coblenz under the wing of the Elector of Treves. ' Let us tell Europe that if the cabinets of foreign courts attempt to stir up a war of kings against France we shall stir up a people's war against the kings ', said one Deputy. Brissot was even more belligerent: ' A people who after twelve centuries of slavery have won liberty require a war to consolidate it. '

The Girondin Left wanted a war in order to defend the Revolution from its enemies and to spread by means more effective than propaganda the gospel of the Rights of Man. The Ministry, it is true, was in favour of peace, but it contained a warmonger in Narbonne, a natural son of Louis XV. Many of the Feuillants thought that war would restore the prestige of constitutional monarchy, while the Queen and the court thought it could be used to overthrow the revolutionary regime. Abroad, the *émigrés* worked hard to make a war inevitable. Only a few Jacobins like Robespierre were worried; they feared that a war would bring just what their opponents hoped from it and they distrusted Lafayette, the man who had shot down the republicans in the Champ-de-Mars, because he was bound to be the French commander in the field.

A demand had been made to the Elector of Treves that he should disperse the *émigrés* he was sheltering by the end of December. The Emperor persuaded him to comply with the French request. But in January the Left demanded not only a simple promise but formal guarantees that the *émigrés* should be dispersed. This done, the Emperor Leopold, in spite of his recent mistrust of Prussia, signed the Treaty of Berlin with Frederick William in February. They agreed to pursue a common policy in the affairs of France and Poland and shortly afterwards Prussia and Russia also made a secret agreement to have a new partition of Poland. At this moment the war party in France was hoping for an alliance with the liberal powers, Great Britain and Prussia, against reactionary Austria, Russia and Spain. Efforts to obtain diplomatic support from London and Berlin were rebuffed. In Britain Talleyrand was received with marked coldness. In Berlin French emissaries, charged with the mission of offering the Prussian Duke of Brunswick supreme command of the French army, were equally unsuccessful. (Brissot, meanwhile, even envisaged this ducal strategist and Freemason of the highest degree as a possible king of France, to be elected in place of Louis XVI!)

The Girondin Ministry

Louis XVI and Marie Antoinette now chose to jump out of the frying-pan into the fire. Staggered by the resignation of their more moderate ministers, they refused Lafayette's offer of help and appealed to the Girondins to designate a new Cabinet. According to the Constitution, the King's ministers could not be chosen from the Assembly, and Claviere thus became Minister of Finance. The Ministry of the Interior was given to the ' virtuous ' Roland and

After the civil war and the panic caused by the invasion of the summer of 1793, the Terror began to turn on the leaders of the Revolution itself. The first batch to go to the guillotine were the followers of Brissot, the so-called ' Gironde '. *British Museum*

The Girondins were not a party, but a group of men identified as a faction by their enemies. They included a group of brilliant orators from Bordeaux (the department of the Gironde) who distrusted both the power of Paris and of the extreme Jacobins in the Convention. *Popper*

Opposite page: an aristocrat. Class-hatred played a big part in the Revolution and as it progressed ' aristocrat ' (or ' *aristo* ') became a generalised term of abuse, applied (like ' *bourgeois* ' or ' *bolshevik* ' in the twentieth century) to anyone politically unsympathetic to the speaker. *Mansell*

Camille Desmoulins, orator and journalist, was a friend of Danton and Robespierre. The latter destroyed him, together with Danton and other popular leaders who wished to relax the Terror. They were guillotined 6 April 1794. *Mansell*

Dumouriez was the new Minister of Foreign Affairs. Small, sturdy, rather ugly, but with agreeable features and — like Robespierre — always neatly dressed and powdered, General Dumouriez was fifty-three. Although an officer of the old royal army he was, through his hatred of Austria, a friend of Brissot, while at the same time remaining on good terms with the court. From his point of view war was desirable whatever its outcome. His role of saviour was assured: in case of reverse he would sweep away the throne and remain dictator; in the event that victory consolidated the monarchy he would become Constable of France.

Dumouriez and the war

Determined to be the first to strike, Dumouriez decided that there was no reason to conciliate Vienna further. Leopold had died on March 1, and Francis II, who in July would be elected the last Emperor of the Holy Roman Empire, was young and less patient and prudent than his father. Francis was not only indignant at the affronts suffered by Marie Antoinette, his aunt, but at the injustice done to the Alsatian princes and to the Pope by the annexation of Avignon. Both Governments sent ultimatums. On 20 April 1792 France declared war ' against the King of Hungary and Bohemia ', a formula optimistically designed to encourage the neutrality of Prussia and the other princes of the Empire. Only seven Deputies voted against it. Louis XVI had, unknowingly, made his own dethronement certain, and initiated twenty years of war. The French campaign began badly. The royal army had deteriorated; undisciplined, it murdered one of its own generals, and made the world believe there was nothing to fear. On the other hand, the allies — Austria and Prussia — were little better prepared. Each distrusted the other and both were distracted by Russian activities in Poland. Polish affairs and the slowness of the Coalition to get under way saved the revolutionary regime in the first year of war.

The Polish question

The Polish patriots had set about regenerating their mutilated country by agreeing on a constitution which made the monarchy hereditary in an elected dynasty, abolished the *liberum veto* and the nobles' right of insurrection, and established religious equality. No one, however, had dared to emancipate the peasants. The Polish Constitution was completed on 3 May 1791, a few months before the French Constitution; the partisans of Russia immediately began to plan an insurrection for the restoration of the ' traditional liberties ', with the promise of armed support by Catherine II. Russia was at that moment at war with Turkey; but after the victories of the Russian General Suvorov, the loss by assault of Ismail and the destruction of his fleet in the Black Sea, the Sultan Selim III sued for peace. The Treaty of Jassy in January 1792, by which Catherine acquired a modest portion of the Ukraine between the Bug and the Dniester (where she founded Odessa), left her hands free in the west. She made doubly certain of quiet on this front by sending General Kutuzov on a special mission to the Sultan in 1793–4 to encourage friendlier relations between the two countries. Her appetite for Poland was whetted by personal considerations.

Marie Antoinette, daughter of Maria Theresa, went to the scaffold in October 1793. She had done great damage to the cause of the monarchy and her husband by her intransigence and lack of judgment, but she died bravely. *Mansell*

On the death of the adventurer Potemkin who, in her own words, was 'almost her idol' she had consoled herself with a young man named Zubov. Though of modest ability Zubov was greedy and in a hurry to win a princely fortune in the neighbouring kingdom of Poland and to assure his future before his sexagenarian protectress died. Catherine, deciding that an Austro-Prussian war with France was now certain, ordered her own troops into Poland.

The Polish Diet met in Warsaw (16 April 1792) and made arrangements for mobilisation — though of the nobles only. Stanislas Poniatowski was voted a loan of thirty million florins: never had a King of Poland had such means put at his disposal. But the anti-Russian party had momentarily forgotten that Stanislas Ponia- towski originally owed his throne to the fact that he had been the Tsaritsa's lover. Meanwhile the confederation of the pro-Russian insurgents, gathering at Targovitsa, at once denounced the 'tyranny which was forging Poland's chains' in a manifesto in which the times of former anarchy were glowingly described as the 'epoch of the reign of law'. The Poles of Warsaw, whose zeal for rebellion had been fanned by Herzberg, counted on Prussia to defend their independence; but Frederick William coolly gave them to understand that circum- stances had changed. In the court at Vienna the Tsaritsa found the atmosphere equally chilly. Since 1781 an Austro- Russian alliance had existed, and in 1789 had been re- affirmed for a further eight years. As Austria had been attacked by France, Russia should have given her ally military support. Catherine forestalled the inevitable Austrian demand for help in two letters, sent in April and May, in which she ironically denounced the 'sub- versive' activities — meaning the Polish Constitution — which endangered her frontiers and compared her own grave problems to those the Emperor would have to face in France. 'The revolutionary elements of Warsaw', she explained, 'are in constant touch with those in Paris', and she reserved for herself the task of dealing exclusively with the former.

Complicated negotiations followed between Russians and Prussians, and Prussians and Austrians, concerning what each could count on gaining from the war. Vienna and Berlin at last agreed that energetic measures were to be taken against France, as a prelude — in the eyes of Frederick William — to a new partition of Poland. The Duke of Brunswick, who commanded the Prussian army, was ordered to march on Paris. The role of the *émigrés* was restricted to secondary operations in Upper Alsace. The allies counted on 42,000 Prussian troops and 100,000 Austrian. But the opening of the campaign was delayed by the election and crowning of the Emperor, and by further discussions.

The fall of the monarchy

This vacillation and delay was both disturbing and incom- prehensible to Louis XVI and Marie Antoinette, by now convinced that their personal safety depended on the arrival of foreign troops. Their emissaries urged the allies to come to their rescue. The danger facing the King deepened rapidly when he refused to sanction a new penal decree against non-juring priests. His constitutional guard was dissolved and the Assembly authorised on

Dr Guillotin's invention. This device made possible the quick and humane despatch of thousands of victims of the Terror. It stood in what is now the Place de la Concorde. It remains the legal method of execution in France today. *Mansell*

June 8 the formation of a camp near Paris for 20,000 armed men who were expected to arrive from the Departments to take part in the celebrations of July 14. Louis XVI agreed to give up his guard, but also vetoed the auth- orisation for so dangerous a force to gather in the capital. On June 13 the King, exasperated by Roland's remons- trance, dismissed him, together with his Girondin friends.

Three days later Dumouriez resigned from the Cabinet and left Paris to assume command of the army in the north. The Left, Girondins and Montagnards, infuriated by the King's two vetoes and his ineffective Feuillant Ministry, organised a popular invasion of the Assembly and the Tuileries. Louis XVI — for a moment crowned with the revolutionary *bonnet rouge* — did not give way and kept his ministers. On July 6 he presented a declaration of war on Prussia to the Assembly and when the Assembly declared the country to be in danger, he renewed his constitutional oath during the festival of national Federation on July 14.

On that day Francis II, who had been elected Emperor about a week before, made his solemn entrance into Frankfurt, and a Holy Roman Emperor was crowned with the pomp and ceremony of centuries — for the last time. The problem of Poland was momentarily solved — by Russian occupation. In spite of the heroism of Kosciuszko the little army of Stanislas Poniatowski had been forced to capitulate; the King himself was obliged to adhere to the Confederation of Targovitsa and to permit the confederates to restore the old Constitution. Catherine II, who planned to keep the whole of Poland for herself, declined for the moment to discuss partition. The Prussians and the Austrians, not unnaturally distrustful of this attitude, kept covetous eyes on Warsaw while pretending to march on Paris.

The *émigrés* were fêted at Mainz and urged that the allies should threaten France with reprisals if the King and Queen were harmed. The Duke of Brunswick's response was a Manifesto (25 July 1792) which threatened all Frenchmen who dared defend themselves with the direst punishment, and Paris with total ruin for the least violence done to the royal family. This provided the revolutionaries with a pretext for decisive action. Danton, supported by his Cordelier colleagues, persuaded the Deputies of Paris to vote for the overthrow of Louis XVI, and left the capital in no doubt that the King was in league with the foreigner who had threatened its destruction. The volunteers who had arrived in Paris from the provinces stormed the King's palace on August 10 and slaughtered the Swiss Guards. Paris rose, an insurrectional Commune was installed in the Hôtel de Ville, and the King and his family circle sought refuge in an Assembly half emptied by fear. Only 284 of the 630 Deputies were present, almost all belonging to the Left. They decided that Louis XVI should be suspended from his functions; they decided further that a National Convention should be convoked by universal suffrage to revise the Constitution.

The First Terror, the invasion and Valmy

A 'provisional executive council' was set up which included the recently dismissed Girondins and, as Minister of Justice, the man of the hour, Danton. But real authority was exercised by the Commune and the city of Paris, which from the start demanded that the royal family should be held in the prison of the Temple. Danton was both the strong man in the executive council and the Prosecutor-General of the Commune. The poor man's Mirabeau, with his pockmarked face and extraordinary eloquence, he remains the most enigmatic and controversial figure of the Revolution. That he was corrupt and mercenary, that secret funds from various sources passed through his hands, there can be no doubt. And yet he became the leading spirit in the national defence and his passionate cry for daring, and yet more daring — '*de l'audace, encore de l'audace*' — became proverbial. He was also the author of the First Terror. 'The tenth of August', he told the Council, 'split France into two parts. One remains attached to the monarchy, the other wants a republic. The latter, which it is impossible to deny is in the extreme minority, is the only one on which

The Temple, one of the medieval prisons of Paris where victims of the Terror were incarcerated. *Mansell*

A caricature of Tom Paine, author of *The Rights of Man*, citizen of France by adoption, but soon in trouble with its revolutionary government. During the American War of Independence he had written with great effect for the rebel cause. *Radio Times Hulton Picture Library*

you can rely to fight. To stop the enemy and frustrate his designs we must, in my opinion, strike terror into the hearts of the Royalists. '

The fathers, mothers, wives and children of all *émigrés* were quickly declared to be hostages of the State. Non-juring priests were imprisoned. Houses were searched for suspects. These measures filled the prisons with those who were more and more widely called and known to the mob as the 'suspects'. In Paris the new Commune raided their dwellings, suppressed 'aristo' newspapers, overturned royal statues, requisitioned and melted down the silverware, chalices, candlesticks and even the bells of churches and convents. In the provinces the munici-palities followed this example, setting up Vigilance Com-mittees which forced their way into private houses and requisitioned food supplies.

Lafayette's reaction to August 10 had been an attempted coup d'état. He ordered Dumouriez to march on Paris, but when the order was ignored he fled to Liège, where he was imprisoned by the Austrians.

With the imprisonment of the King Europe finally broke off diplomatic relations with France. The last two foreign diplomats to leave were the Minister of the United States and the British Ambassador. On the following day, however, the Assembly awarded French citizenship to foreigners who were 'defenders of the cause of liberty', naming the Americans George Washington and Thomas Paine, the Englishmen Bentham, Wilberforce and Priestley, the Germans Klopstock, Schiller, Campe and Cloots, the Italian Gorani, the Swiss Pestalozzi and the Pole Kosciuszko. It was a symbolic gesture of solidarity with all peoples, through those who were best qualified, morally and intellectually, to represent their nations. Danton, who had instructed Talleyrand to prepare a circular letter of explanation and reassurance to all the Chancelleries of Europe, sent Talleyrand himself to England where, though he was scarcely more cordially received than on the first occasion, he at least succeeded in delaying a complete rupture.

Already in August the Prussian army, supported by an Austrian corps, had invaded Lorraine. Longwy fell. On September 2 Paris learned of the capitulation of Verdun, where the loyalists had welcomed the enemy as a liberator. Would Brunswick, who had signed the threatening manifesto, find similar people to welcome him in Paris? Panic swept the capital. The Commune prepared for the massacre of the imprisoned 'suspects' so openly that Desmoulins and Danton arranged for certain of their protégés to be released. From September 2 to 6 the gruesome slaughter went on in the prisons. Similar scenes of carnage took place, as though by contagion, at Versailles, Meaux, Rheims. Meanwhile in the Argonne Dumouriez and Kellerman barred the route to Paris. The cannonade at Valmy cost the Prussians no more than two hundred men and the French some three hundred. It was little more than a skirmish, but the Duke of Bruns-wick's Prussian army, reputedly the best in Europe, retreated. The Prussian retreat was turned, by dysentery, into a rout. Goethe, the greatest German of his age, was present at the battle of Valmy and, asked by his companions what he thought of its outcome, is said to have remarked: ' This field and this day mark the beginning of a new epoch in the history of the world; you will be able to say, " I was there! ".'

EUROPE AND THE FIRST FRENCH REPUBLIC

The birth of the Republic

On 20 September 1792, the day of Valmy, the new Assembly, which had been elected under the shadow of the ' First Terror ', met in the Tuileries. It called itself the Convention — a name borrowed from the American Revolution — and consisted of 749 Deputies who had, for the most part, been elected by a minute portion of the population. As though the exceptional casualties among Deputies had been foreseen, 298 substitutes were also elected who would almost all eventually be required to replace those who were executed, committed suicide, were imprisoned or proscribed. The Girondin Left of the Legislative Assembly now formed the Right. The Centre was even more unstable than it had been. Well to the Left of this moderate ' Plain ', were the extremists, the Montagnards or ' Mountain ', so named because they occupied the highest benches in the Assembly. Among them sat not only Danton, Robespierre and Carnot, but ' the People's Friend ', Marat, with his hideous skin disease, the young and handsome Saint-Just, Barère, soon to be known (from the flowery language and convivial jests used by him towards his victims) as the Anacreon of the Guillotine, the one-time Vicomte de Barras, the unfrocked clerics Fouché, Chabot, Billaud-Barennc, the poet Marie-Joseph Chénier, André's younger brother, the painter David, the actor Collot d'Herbois, and a Deputy from Paris, the Duke of Orleans, henceforth known as Philippe Egalité. On September 21 — its second day of existence — the Convention decreed that the monarchy was abolished. On the following day it decided that all public acts would be dated from the Year I of the Republic. Finally, Robespierre considering this indirect manner of introducing the new regime to be ' furtive ', it grandly proclaimed on September 25 that the ' French Republic was one and indivisible '. It set about making a new constitution for France.

The revolutionary offensive

The birth of the Republic was marked by military success. The occupation of Savoy was followed by the request of a ' National Assembly of the Allobroges ' — a Gallic tribe which had once lived in Savoy and Dauphiné — to be united to France. In November an eighty-fourth Department was added to the Republic and named Mont Blanc. Nice, too, was annexed, while Basle in Switzerland broke away from the Confederation to become first the Republic of Rauracia, and finally in March 1793 the French Department of Mont Terrible. The occupation of the Rhineland was followed in March 1793 by the annexation of the left bank of the Rhine. Meanwhile, after Valmy, Dumouriez had swept the invaded territory free of Prussians, relieved Lille, and invaded Belgium, where at Jemappes, near Mons, he inflicted on the Austrian army a defeat which resounded throughout Europe. After this he was able with ease to occupy all Belgium in a matter of days. The Assembly's ' defensive ' war had, in fact, turned into a war of ' liberation ' and propaganda.

Dumouriez knew the Belgians and was well aware of their longing for independence. But Danton arrived in

On 21 January 1793 Louis XVI was guillotined after a trial before the Convention. 683 deputies out of 721 declared him guilty. Only 361 voted for his death without conditions and 360 voted for lesser punishment. *Larousse*

Belgium as Commissioner on the day after the famous Edict of Fraternity of 19 November 1792, which promised aid to all peoples 'who wished to recover their liberty'. The immense wealth of the Belgian clergy made him favour the annexation of Belgium. The increasing demands on the treasury were changing the nature of the war; it was becoming one of conquest and exploitation. A decree of December 15 proclaimed 'war on the *châteaux*, peace to the cottages', abolished Belgian feudalism and, to the fury of Belgian Catholics, confiscated all seigniorial and ecclesiastical property. By February 1793 Belgium had yielded sixty-four million livres. But the country was by then near revolt, and Danton saw in annexation the only means of preventing a counter-revolution. This he justified with a new doctrine: 'The borders of France are determined by nature; we shall reach our natural frontiers at four points: at the ocean, the banks of the Rhine, the Alps and the Pyrenees; and no power can stop us.' In March the local assemblies both of the Belgian provinces and the Rhenish provinces were forced to ratify their annexation by France. By that time a general European Coalition was in existence against the Republic.

The trial of Louis XVI

At home, the Convention had at once to decide on the fate of the King. The Montagnards and the Commune demanded his head. The Girondins, aware of the sentiments of the great majority in the provinces, hesitated. Paris, as one of them pointed out, was only one of eighty-three Departments and its influence should be valued appropriately. The discovery at the Tuileries of papers in a soon notorious 'iron chest' which gave evidence of the King's correspondence with the *émigrés* and of his counter-revolutionary manoeuvres made a trial inevitable. The Convention decided to try Louis XVI itself. Robespierre told the Assembly: 'Your duty is not to pronounce sentence for or against a man; but to enact a measure of public safety, to protect the nation itself.' The trial lasted from 11 December 1792 to 20 January 1793 and the King denied all the charges. That he was guilty of 'conspiring against the liberty of the subject and criminal action against the safety of the State' was recognised almost unanimously. An appeal to the people was rejected by a large majority, but in a house of 721 Deputies there was only a majority of one for death without qualification. Louis was guillotined on 21 January 1793, admired, at last, for his dignity and courage. A monarchical age heard the news in other countries with horror.

The First Coalition

Pitt, whose chief concern was to restore British prosperity by financial reform, had believed in 1792 that Britain could count on fifteen years of peace. He had, therefore, reduced the armed forces to a few thousand sailors and soldiers. After the outbreak of war on the continent he still pursued a policy of neutrality, though it is true that the Cabinet had begun to feel uneasy about certain signs of internal political and social restiveness, encouraged by events across the Channel. This policy was quickly abandoned when the armies of the Convention invaded Belgium and reopened the Scheldt to navigation in spite of international agreements to which France had been a party. The Dutch Republic, protesting, appealed for help on the strength of the alliance with Great Britain. Towards the end of December, the House of Commons voted to raise 20,000 naval recruits, and passed the Alien Act, submitting foreigners to strict supervision and the possibility of deportation. British opinion had been hardening ever since August 10; with the King's execution rupture became inevitable. The British court went into mourning; Pitt — forgetting Charles I — denounced Louis XVI's execution as the most atrocious crime in history. On February 1 the Convention declared war on both the United Provinces and Britain.

The chief minister of Charles IV of Spain, the Count of Aranda, a Voltairian and a sympathiser with the Revolution, had in his desire to gain time gone so far as to treat refugee priests with hostility. He was soon replaced by the Queen's lover, Godoy, the absurd hero of a royal triangle which was the scandal of Spain and the laughing-stock of all Europe. Godoy, when the result of the trial in Paris became known, broke off negotiations for neutrality and dismissed the French Ambassador. The Convention declared war on Spain on March 7. The break with Rome had already taken place on January 13 when a Secretary of the French Embassy had been killed during a riot — provoked by his tricolour cockade. Naples, Tuscany, Venice Parma and Modena then followed the King of Sardinia into the Coalition. Pitt signed treaties of alliance with seven countries and arranged to subsidise six more. Russia

also came into the Coalition in March. With the exception of Switzerland and the two Scandinavian states — in Sweden Gustavus III had been assassinated by discontented nobles and been succeeded in March 1792 by Gustavus IV — the whole of Europe was now united against the Republic. London armed, equipped and paid the Coalition, while Vienna supplied in the person of the Prince of Coburg a strategist who was initially victorious: two names became the bogies of France — Pitt and Coburg.

Dumouriez invaded the United Provinces and then withdrew, to be defeated at Neerwinden on March 18. Thoroughly exasperated by the manner in which the Convention obstructed his plans, Dumouriez now negotiated a secret armistice which left his army free to march on Paris. Finally, he turned over to the Austrians the envoys the Assembly had sent to arrest him, including the Minister for War, who had come to relieve him of his command, and then deserted, taking with him a thousand men, including eleven generals. One of these was the young Duke of Chartres, son of Philippe Egalité and later to be Louis Philippe.

This disaster and the loss of Belgium were followed by the loss of the left bank of the Rhine. Coburg besieged Valenciennes, while a Spanish army invaded Roussillon. French defeats continued, and the calling-up of an additional 300,000 men in February did not mend matters. Indeed, the attempt to raise further troops drove the peasants of Brittany and the Vendée, traditionally attached to their priests and loyal to the local aristocracy, to rebellion. This spontaneous revolt of countrymen against the Republican townsmen of the west soon became a well organised resistance movement. A ' Catholic and Royal ' army was formed which, sustained by arms and money supplied by the British, held out for months against the troops of the Republic.

The first Committee of Public Safety

The defection of Dumouriez compromised his Girondin supporters. A storm of inter-party strife burst out in recrimination and accusation. Danton kept his head and, thanks less to his gift of persuasive eloquence than to his clear-sightedness, he was able to give some direction to affairs. Never losing sight of the Revolution's ultimate aims, he was always an opportunist in the means by which he achieved them. On August 10, threatened by counter-revolution and invasion, he had co-operated with the Girondins, whom he later helped to destroy. On January 31 he had proclaimed the new doctrine of ' natural frontiers '; but the setback in Belgium and the insurrection of the annexed populations with each withdrawal of their ' liberators ' opened his eyes: on April 13 he apologised for his decree on aid to all oppressed peoples which could, he now recognised, ' engage the nation to come to the aid of a handful of patriots who might wish to start a revolution in China! ' But throughout he sought to preserve the Republic.

Its survival was by no means certain. The lower classes

Revolutionary committees manned by activists sprang up all over France from 1792 onwards. They carried much of the burden of administration and even began to threaten the authority of the Convention itself. *British Museum*

Le moulinet by Lancret (1690–1743). *Archiv für Kunst und Geschichte*

Revolutionary tribunals followed the repression of the civil war in 1793. Lyon stood a two months' siege and a harsh repression followed its collapse in October. *Bibliothèque Nationale*

On 13 July 1793, Charlotte Corday, a girl from Normandy, murdered Marat, the journalist and hero of the populace of Paris. Her act helped to unleash the Terror which led to the execution of the Gironde. *Archiv für Kunst und Geschichte*

in Paris again threatened to revolt. The increasingly rapid depreciation of the *assignats* had sent the cost of living still higher, while Jacques Roux, the 'Red Priest', and the *enragés* fanned the people's fury against the profiteers and 'sharks' who cornered the market in food-stuffs. To deal with the provinces the Convention sent eighty-two representatives 'of the people' — Deputies on Mission — into the Departments in March with full powers. Official status was conferred on the unofficial Vigilance Committees of each Commune, while at Danton's suggestion the revolutionary tribunal of the previous autumn was resurrected. On 6 April 1793 Danton, with his super-human energy, re-organised the committee of general defence which had fulfilled the executive function. It was reduced to nine members and renamed the Committee of Public Safety. Danton at once became its most influential member. His position on it was further strengthened by the election to it of his friends, which was a clear defeat for the Girondins. For the first time, all real power was centralised in the hands of a few resolute and competent Deputies.

Danton also supervised foreign affairs. On April 13 he persuaded the Assembly to declare that it would 'not in any manner intrude in the governmental affairs of other powers'. It was a return to pre-Revolutionary attitudes. Accompanied by secret diplomatic activity, which in fact came to nothing, it was an attempt to ease international tension. Robespierre at once attacked the new policy. The spring of 1793, however, ended in a more

A contemporary portrait of Beethoven by Josef Stieler. *Archiv für Kunst und Geschichte*

savage struggle between the Montagnards and the Girondins. The Girondins had dared — like Brunswick a year before — to threaten the capital. The Montagnards — Danton, Robespierre and Marat — closed their ranks against the common enemy, the 'accomplices of Dumouriez'. On May 31 and June 2 mobs armed by the Commune and led by Hanriot broke into the Assembly and at cannon point dictated the arrest of twenty-nine Girondin leaders. The victory of the Montagnards was complete and its significance was not only political but social. The heroes of the '*sans-culottes*', the mob of small tradesmen, artisans and their employees, had triumphed over those of the bourgeoisie.

The Montagnard Convention and the Terror

The defeat of the Girondins was at first confined to Paris and their supporters added to the confusion in the provinces. By August, while France was invaded by the Coalition, sixty Departments had more or less risen against the Convention. Lyon guillotined its Jacobin mayor, Paoli delivered Corsica to the British, Toulon opened its port to them and proclaimed the Dauphin — imprisoned in the Temple — King Louis XVII. From Caen came the young Charlotte Corday who murdered Marat in his bath. At the same time, the Paris *sans-culottes* were agitated by the economic results of inflation and blockade. The *assignat* stood at a fifth of its nominal value. The popular move-ment pressed for extreme measures; in July hoarding was made punishable by death. A new Constitution, embodying a recognition of the popular right of insurrection, was approved by the Convention and by plebiscite; but as it was plainly impossible to put it into effect in the critical situation of the moment, its application was 'suspended' 225

until peace was restored.

On 10 October 1793 the Convention decreed that 'the provisional government of France would be revolutionary until the restoration of peace'. The country was not to expect constitutional government. The situation all too obviously demanded a regime which was strong, centralised and armed with dictatorial powers. This was partly a concession to popular demand, partly an attempt to regain control of the shivered administrative machine. 'Revolutionary government', said Robespierre, who had replaced Danton on the Committee of Public Safety, 'owes every protection to good citizens; to the enemies of the people it owes only death.' The Law of *Frimaire* in the Year II (4 December 1793) defined the powers of this temporary extra-constitutional regime and centralised in the hands of the Committee of Public Safety the institutions which had appeared in response to revolutionary needs: the Terror had been regularised. The Committee of Public Safety — the 'Great Committee of the Year II' — directed diplomacy and the war, had secret funds and controlled the employment of all officials, civil and military. From September 1793 to July 1794 its membership — which included Jean Bon Saint-André, Carnot, Barère, Couthon, Saint-Just — remained unchanged and 'united in their will to win'. Beside it, the Committee of General Security was the chief organ of the political police. The Revolutionary Tribunal pronounced sentence from which there was no appeal on the indictment of the Public Prosecutor. The 'Deputies on Mission' to the Departments, with their plumed hats and tricoloured sashes, were sometimes bloodthirsty and unjust, but always implacable agents of the Terror, who supervised generals in the field and dealt ruthlessly with those in the provinces suspected of counter-revolutionary tendencies. Hundreds were executed after hurried trials in which there was no possibility of acquittal.

By the decree of 5 September 1793 Terror became the order of the day. A special 'revolutionary army' of 6,000 good revolutionaries helped its enforcement outside Paris. It imprisoned suspects on the denunciation of local revolutionaries. Price controls were introduced. In October

Marie Antoinette was another victim of the familiar disaster of the diplomatic marriage, this time arranged to demonstrate Austro-French solidarity. Her isolation in the French court which disposed her to rely on Austrian advice, and the gay and extravagant life she led in the early years of her dull marriage, left her friendless and unprepared when the French crisis broke out. Despite much vigorous secret diplomacy in the months following the flight to Varennes she was brought to trial on 14 October 1793. The contemporary engraving above shows her facing her accusers who condemned her unanimously. Like her mother, Maria Theresa, she revealed courage in adversity, and David's sketch of her on the way to the scaffold, shown below, captures her pathetic dignity. *Bibliothèque Nationale. Giraudon*

A contemporary engraving of the execution of Marie Antoinette in 1793. Although it seemed that the monarchy was finished, twenty-two years later another Bourbon sat on the throne of France. *Flammarion*

Possibly the most repellent of the revolutionary leaders was the most single-minded and effective among them, Maximilian Robespierre (1758–94). With his colleagues on the Great Committee of Public Safety, he saved France. *Giraudon*

Marie Antoinette, who had suffered every insult and indignity while in prison, was carted to the guillotine. Other victims soon followed her, among them the Girondin leaders and the former Duke of Orleans, Philippe Egalité. Others were hunted down, died of starvation, or committed suicide. Republican fanaticism took myriad forms. The Convention no longer dated events from the birth of Christ, but from the birth of the Republic. A Republican calendar was adopted in which the week consisted of ten days and the *Décadi* replaced Sunday. There were three decades to a month. Months and days were renamed. At Rheims, the Holy Ampulla, which contained the oil with which the kings of France were anointed, was smashed by a member of the Convention. In many places extremists turned violently on the institution of Christianity itself. The Cathedral of Notre Dame was renamed the 'Temple of Reason' where a chorus-girl was enthroned as the Goddess of Reason. Commissioners of the Convention or of local Jacobin clubs altered the names of villages, districts and streets which recalled Christianity, royalty or feudalism.

The excess of this anti-religious frenzy, the sacreligious masquerades in which sacred vessels and ecclesiastical vestments were held up to ridicule, made the problem of order much worse by offending many countrymen. They also shocked Robespierre. This affected struggles of factions within the Convention which contained both moderates and rabid 'de-Christianisers'. The so-called *enragés*, partisans of the atheist Hébert, and spokesmen of the ragged and hungry and of those who automatically loathed the rich, also attacked religion. Danton and his friends, known as the 'Indulgents', opposed Robespierre's severity and narrow middle-class virtues with their — relative — moderation. Both factions, however, perished on the scaffold early in 1794. Some were condemned as atheists and 'agents of Pitt' while others were charged with financial corruption. Hébert was guillotined in April; Danton and Desmoulins in May. This was a lesson both

to the people, whose economic grievances had been expressed by the *enragés*, and to those Deputies who had felt like Danton that the Terror could be relaxed. The Committee of Public Safety introduced new repressive measures with the law of June 10 — 22 *Prairial* — which threatened the life of every member of the Convention, depriving the legislators of their immunity and sweeping away the last safeguards for the protection of persons accused of political offences. This law unleashed the 'Great Terror', a six weeks' orgy of butchery during which more than 1,300 victims, including the great chemist Lavoisier and the poet André Chénier, died on the guillotine.

The fall of Robespierre

This bloodshed was becoming harder to justify because the war was going better and the civil war had been overcome. People began to blame the Terror on Robespierre's 'dictatorship'. This was unfair, but understandable. Though not the dictator he was later made out to be by enemies (and by former supporters who betrayed him) he was much more in the public eye than other members of the Committee of Public Safety. He presented much of its political business in the Convention. Also, it was clear, he was a fanatic. Unfortunately, he was that rare sort of politician who means everything he says. A Rousseaunian, he was not a socialist — the bourgeois Montagnards were no more real socialists than the *sans-culottes* — but he was opposed to the excessive inequality of wealth, which he considered a corrupting influence. His young disciple Saint-Just, to whom 'opulence was an infamy', even had it decreed that the possessions of 'suspects' should be distributed among indigent patriots; but this measure of social democracy remained on paper only, and like two other creations of the Convention, public assistance and free primary schooling, was never put into practice. Robespierre was aware that the sacrifices demanded by the Committee

227

Hostility to Christianity was a constant and sometimes violent element in the French Revolution. Here is one of its frivolous aspects, the adoration of a chorus-girl as Goddess of Reason in Notre Dame. *Bibliothèque Nationale*

Robespierre was finally overthrown by a cabal of politicians at the end of July 1794. Released by friends, he was re-arrested after a scuffle in which he attempted suicide but only succeeded in shooting himself through the jaw.

presupposed a public spirit unmotivated by self-interest which — following the example of Montesquieu and Rousseau — he called 'Virtue'. He thought this Virtue could be stimulated by Terror and a new religion.

To Robespierre the idea of a Supreme Being and the immortality of the soul was a constant and necessary reminder of justice; hence it was social and republican. The Committee decreed that holidays should take place every ten days — on the *Décadi* which replaced the Christian Sunday — and Robespierre dedicated the first festival, which was celebrated on 8 June 1794, to the Supreme Being. He had been elected President of the Convention four days previously and his first public act was to preside over the ceremony. The cult of the Supreme Being offended the atheists, insulted the Catholics and for the first time gave people something to laugh at in Robespierre. Many people were already frightened of him because they had lined their own pockets during the Revolution; others, Deputies in the Convention, felt that they, too, were in danger when Robespierre talked about the need for a new purge. The events of *Thermidor* were precipitated by all these people, effective suddenly because the rank and file of the Convention at last summoned up courage to face a thirty-five-year-old dictator whose contempt for them had been heightened by the intoxication of absolute power. The Committee of Public Safety was itself divided, and the Committee of General Security had begun to plot against Robespierre and his friends. On 9 *Thermidor* (July 28) Robespierre was openly accused by Tallien of despotism, and when he vainly tried to obtain a hearing he was arrested and imprisoned. The Commune briefly set him free and sheltered him in the Hôtel de Ville. He was thereupon declared an outlaw; the *sans-culottes* did not come to his rescue; the Hôtel de Ville was entered by an armed force. Robespierre, found with his jaw shattered by a bullet, was dragged bleeding to the scaffold. There the guillotine, to which he had sent so many before him, had the last word. With Robespierre perished his henchmen in the Assembly, and the militants of the Commune of the Year II. The majority of the Convention had again taken a hand in the Revolution.

Carnot and victory

Victories were being won at last. This had made Robespierre seem more dispensable, so that Carnot, their ultimate author, was doubly an agent of the coup of *Thermidor*, directly as a plotter in the Committee and indirectly as the 'organiser of victory'. While a professional soldier in garrison at Arras, Carnot had become acquainted with Robespierre, but in spite of their affinities — both hated Britain, both were Freemasons, deists and morally austere, the one being quite as incorruptible as the other — the two men, also similar in their love of authority, disliked each other. Carnot was summoned to the Committee of Public Safety in August 1793 because of his outstanding technical abilities. There he took over the direction of military affairs, prepared measures to be taken for the supply and training of the troops, drew up plans of operations and appointed field commanders. When the recruitment of troops proved insufficient he had the Assembly decree a mass levy (August 23) calling to arms all unmarried men between the ages of eighteen and twenty-five. This gave him numerical superiority over the Coalition.

In the course of the winter 1793–4 he organised regiments by amalgamating battalions of untrained volunteers with veteran battalions.

To supply these fresh forces with arms, munitions, uniforms and rations, he was obliged to construct countless new factories and workshops, and to devise — with the aid of scientists like Monge and Berthollet — more rapid methods of manufacture, to invent substitute products, to cast 20,000 cannon in one year, and to requisition horses, waggons, clothes, shoes. Perhaps his main achievement was to create 'Republican spirit', a new morale, a sense of sacrifice and better discipline. This, together with the fact that the higher ranks of the army, purged by the guillotine, were now filled by younger men, permitted new offensive tactics, the hurling at the enemy of masses of men with cold steel; though this was effective, it sometimes cost the Revolutionary armies casualties as high as one in three. In leading such charges Carnot himself gave the example. He was at Jourdan's side in October 1793 during his first victory at Wattignies, which relieved Maubeuge. Two months later Hoche liberated Landau. The frontiers were again secured and on 26 June 1794 Jourdan won the decisive battle of Fleurus, which enabled the Republic to re-annex Belgium and, shortly afterwards, the left bank of the Rhine. In the winter months of November 1794 to January 1795 Pichegru occupied Holland. But Britain retained her supremacy at sea.

The reaction to 'Thermidor'

The 9 *Thermidor* was not a coup d'état of the Moderates against Terrorists. It was, in reality, a settling of accounts between extremist leaders. But Robespierre's execution released a mood of relaxation in the Assembly and the whole country. The change in the political atmosphere was overdue, and the results of *Thermidor* were therefore rapid and irresistible. In the Convention, power shifted from the the Left to the Centre, and from the Centre to the Right. The 'Thermidorian reaction' thus set two currents in motion: one, in the hopes of the Royalists, which accentuated the swing to the Right; the other, based on the fear of this, which made further revolutionary disturbances likely as a means of resisting the swing.

In the Assembly the majority, henceforth the moderates of the Plain, at first supported the 'reformed Terrorists' responsible for Robespierre's death. They had the Jacobin clubs closed in November and brought extremists to trial. There began to appear organised bands of right-wing dandies; their startling costumes were an ostentatious gesture of rejection of the Republican austerity. The law of 22 *Prairial* — which had unleashed the bloodiest phase of the Terror — was annulled, executions became rarer, and the prisons began to empty. Those who had been banished by the Assembly were now recalled and rehabilitated. Though the great Royalist uprising in the Vendée had been crushed, peasant leaders like Stofflet still continued guerrilla warfare. To put an end to it, the Convention restored freedom of worship in February 1795. In Brittany Hoche, the 'peacemaker', came to an agreement with the Chouan Royalist leaders, who were offered an amnesty. In May a general reopening of churches was authorised, with the sole proviso that priests would undertake to obey the laws.

A soldier of the Republic. The object on his bayonet is his bread ration. The republican armies abandoned the parade-ground neatness of the *Ancien Régime*. The powdered pigtail, for example, gave way to undressed hair. *Viollet*

In 1796, the insurrection of peasants in the west of France was at last ended as a serious threat and the civil war which had begun in 1793 came at last to an end. General Hoche was mainly responsible for this success.

Price controls had greatly contributed to the unpopularity of Robespierre, not only among the bourgeoisie but among small shopkeepers. The Assembly abolished them at the end of December 1794 and prices at once soared upwards. In the resulting inflation the *assignat* stood at two per cent of its nominal value. The harvest of the preceding year had been poor and the peasants insisted on being paid not in paper but in coin. High prices were thus aggravated by scarcity. By the end of March there was no bread in Paris. On 1 April 1795 hunger marchers from the suburbs besieged the Assembly, which appealed to General Pichegru for help. The troops quickly restored order. On May 20 the insurrection began again, more violently than ever. The Convention itself was invaded and the severed head of a Deputy was brandished on a pike in front of the president of the session. The surviving Terrorists in the Convention felt that their day had returned and tried to form a provisional government. Their attempt miscarried. The six who made the attempt were condemned to death and committed suicide. The moderates now determined to make sure of Paris and used the army to disarm the Paris *sans-culottes*. The lives of all surviving members of the dreaded Committees who had directed the Terror were now threatened; but Carnot, the organiser of victory, was saved by a Deputy's appeal for gratitude.

The Royalists now suddenly sprang to life again, especially in the southern Departments. From Lyon to Aix, in Tarascon and Marseille, the *Compagnons du Soleil* and the *Compagnons de Géhu* spread counter-revolutionary terror, the White Terror. Plots were formed to rescue the Dauphin — Louis XVII to the Royalists — who was still a prisoner in the Temple. In June 1795, however, the Dauphin mysteriously disappeared, and his uncle, the Count of Provence, proclaimed himself King under the name Louis XVIII. His Declaration of Verona, tainted with extreme reactionary sentiments, divided his partisans, while he sacrificed his most devoted followers in the armed uprising of 15,000 Breton Chouans and in an abortive landing of three *émigré* regiments at Quiberon, which were surrounded and destroyed by Hoche. Though Frenchmen only had been concerned in the episode, the Royalist forces had been financed in Great Britain and supported by British naval units. The French civil war thus formed part of a larger picture, the unending duel between the French Revolution and Europe.

Europe and the Partitions of Poland 1793-5

Europe's attitude towards France had hardened. Lord Auckland, the British representative at a conference of the allies in Antwerp in April 1793, proposed to dismember the new Republic, Dunkirk and the colonies falling to Great Britain, Artois and Flanders to Austria, Alsace and Lorraine to Prussia, Navarre and Roussillon to Spain, while the left bank of the Rhine and the Alps would be restored to their original owners. But unforeseen French successes had made this proposal out-of-date. Some of the Coalition now turned to the easier pickings available in the east.

The retreat of the Prussians from Valmy had already been influenced by second thoughts about Poland. Catherine II urged Frederick William to sign an agreement with her without the Austrians, who were deeply engaged on their own western front. On 23 January 1793, two days after the execution of Louis XVI, arrangements for the Second Partition of Poland were therefore concluded. The Tsaritsa awarded herself the Ukraine and White Russia while the King of Prussia claimed Thorn and Danzig. Although Frederick William promised to continue fighting the contagion beyond the Rhine, Francis II — or rather his new Minister of Foreign Affairs, Thugut — awoke sharply to the realities of the situation. Thugut was as eager for Austria to share in territorial booty as he was indifferent to the fate of the Emperor's aunt Marie Antoinette. When the Russians urged the partition of France as a hotbed of democracy, Thugut made it plain that his master would be better suited with Cracow, comfortably within reach, than with far-off lands yet to be conquered.

Catherine, not satisfied with having restored the old regime in Poland for the benefit of the Confederates of Targovitsa, now insisted — a concession to the spirit of the times — on obtaining the ratification of the Treaty of January by the Poles themselves. This was also Frederick William's wish. To strengthen his position in Poland he deployed half his army as a corps of observation in the east. Finally on June 17 the new Polish Diet met at Grodno. Elections had taken place in the midst of Russian troops and were influenced by fear and bribery. Not unnaturally the immense majority of the delegates were pro-Russian. The most troublesome of those who were not pro-Russian were arrested by order of the Russian Ambassador. When the Diet none the less still resisted he threatened it with cannon. On July 22 a treaty was signed which ceded to Russia exactly what she had demanded in return for her 'protection' against Prussian demands. It was to uphold these that Frederick William decided to turn his back on the war in France.

On the French front in the beginning of August the Coalition still enjoyed a certain numerical superiority, with at least 250,000 Austrian, British, Prussian, Hanoverian, Hessian and Dutch troops. But instead of marching on Paris the Coalition dallied. Instead of invasion they began a siege. The British, who seized Toulon and Corsica and were believed to have inundated France with spies and counterfeit *assignats*, were, in the eyes of the Committee of Public Safety, the most dangerous adversaries. A British blockade intensified French hatred for 'the new Carthage' and also caused difficulties between Britain and the few remaining neutrals. Practically, however, it made colonial trade a virtual British monopoly. When the United States protested at the seizure of three hundred American ships, John Jay, who presented the protest to London, negotiated the Treaty of November 1794 which bears his name. It not only regulated trade between the United States and British North America but cleared up some grievances left over from the War of Independence. Meanwhile in 1793 the colonists of Santo Domingo had called in the British to crush a Negro insurrection under the leadership of Toussaint Louverture. The British occupied the island, as well as Tobago, Saint-Pierre-et-Miquelon and, in India, Pondicherry.

That the blockade had begun to hurt was soon apparent. Pitt was officially declared 'the enemy of the human race'. On September 21 the Convention passed a 'navigation act' modelled on Cromwell's, and on October 9 decreed that no merchandise of British manufacture should enter France, condemned those who co-operated in the importation or sale of British goods to twenty years in irons, and denounced as 'suspect' any person found in

The Prince de Condé led the émigré movement abroad. A contemporary cartoon shows him trying to stir an Ostrich (Autriche = Austria) into carrying him back to France. *Larousse*

possession of such goods. This did not modify the British attitude. Pitt said he would not compromise with a people whose avowed aim it was to extirpate from the face of the earth all honour and all humanity. In Parliament a huge majority voted for redoubled naval and military effort. At home, severe measures were taken against those suspected of sympathy for France. Abroad, British statesmen anxiously strove to hold the Coalition together and poured out money for this purpose.

In Poland, now two-thirds under foreign occupation, secret societies prepared an uprising for which Kosciuszko, a refugee in Leipzig, gave the signal in March 1794. Forming a provisional government in Cracow, he declared war on Russia and Prussia. The Russian commander in Warsaw was forced to evacuate the city after two days of bloody street fighting accompanied by the looting of houses which belonged to pro-Russian magnates. Foolishly, Robespierre saw this simply as an aristocratic revolution, and in July the Committee of Public Safety refused to treat with the envoy Kosciuszko had sent to him. In fact, Poland saved France: every Prussian soldier who could be spared was sent to the east and Thugut was determined to be sure that Austrian interests there did not go by default. A month previously another treaty had been concluded at the Hague

between the Anglo-Dutch and the Prussians, who were to have provided another 60,000 men. The Poles shattered this scheme, and the battle of Fleurus (June 26) followed. Jourdan occupied Liège on July 27, the day of Robespierre's fall. By the end of June the Prussians had seized Cracow and the Austrians had occupied Lublin. Although Frederick William was thrown back from Warsaw, the scattered Polish forces were everywhere swamped by the converging Russian armies. In November the capture of Praga, a suburb of Warsaw, and the massacre of its population, delivered the capital to Suvorov. Early in January 1795 Russia and Austria came to an understanding about a third and final partition of Poland, in which Prussia's share would be pared down. Months of haggling followed until in October Poland disappeared from the map for over a century. Austria obtained Cracow, Prussia received Warsaw, while Russia took Vilna and the rest of Lithuania. The miserable Stanislas Poniatowski abdicated and retired on a pension of 200,000 ducats to Russia, where he died on 12 February 1797.

The negotiation of the Third Partition of Poland had taken more than nine months, and this was the second service which Poland rendered to the French Republic. After *Thermidor* the directors of French policy supported the skilled diplomacy of their agent in Basle, Barthélemy, who grasped that the Prussians would not be averse to the conclusion of a peace which would let Frederick William and the North German states out of the war. Through his Prussian colleague, Baron Hardenberg, he successfully concluded the Treaty of Basle (5 April 1795) which established 'peace, friendship and understanding between the French Republic and the King of Prussia'. Frederick William recognised French occupation of the left bank of the Rhine until the restoration of general peace and, in case French occupation became permanent, the Republic undertook that Prussia would be 'justly' indemnified elsewhere. This could hardly mean anything but at the expense of Austrian influence in Germany. Prussia and Prussia's protégés would, meanwhile, be protected by a neutral line of demarcation north of the Main.

This was the first recognition of the French Republic by a king; previously the Republic had been recognised only by a Grand Duke, when Tuscany resumed her neutrality in February. It was also a diplomatic success which paved the way for others. The satellite Batavian republic which was set up in the Netherlands on the arrival of Pichegru's troops, concluded on May 16 an offensive and defensive alliance with the French Republic; it stipulated a 'rectification' of the Belgian frontier and the payment to France of an indemnity of one hundred million florins. The Stadtholder, who had taken refuge in Britain, called upon the Dutch colonies to welcome the British, who at once became masters of Ceylon and the Cape of Good Hope. On July 22, Barthélemy signed the second Treaty of Basle with the Bourbons of Spain, who obtained the liberation of Louis XVI's daughter by ceding the Spanish part of Santo Domingo. The Anglo-Austro-Russian treaty of alliance signed in September at St Petersburg did little to offset these successes because of Russia's determination to concentrate upon her interests in Eastern Europe. The year 1795 ended bleakly for the Coalition, with the Convention's annexation of Belgium, which was divided into nine new Departments, as almost its last act before it dissolved.

The end of the Convention

Much of the most constructive work of the Convention was done in its last months, and much of it was often initiated by Deputies who had not played important parts in the great political struggles of the previous five years. The special commissions which had been patiently at work on proposals for reform now put forward their plans. One important achievement was the enactment at last of an educational system which provided that one school in every Canton should furnish elementary instruction. Secondary education was entrusted to 'central schools', one for each Department and two for Paris. These had disadvantages and had to be reformed later, but they provided a basic structure of secondary institutions. Higher education had already been partially organised and was supplied by a series of special institutions which the law of October 25 established on a firm basis: the Central School of Public Works, the future Polytechnique, which trained engineers; a teacher training school, which was badly conceived and replaced in 1808 by the École Normale, still in existence. Schools of Law and Medicine were substituted for the earlier faculties which the Revolution had suppressed. The Academy of Music and the Museum of Natural History were established. The cultural work of the Convention was completed by the creation or re-organisation of other important scientific and artistic institutions. To crown their efforts here the Convention included in the same Act the creation of the National Institute of Science and Arts, the successor to the five academies founded by Richelieu and Louis XIV. This Institute performed the invaluable service of unifying weights and measures, and introduced the metric system.

In August 1795 the Convention had voted the so-called Constitution of the Year III which had one striking and novel feature: its preamble was a declaration of the rights *and duties* of man and of the citizen. Its inspiration was bourgeois and, excluding the indigent and the illiterate, it limited active citizenship to those who paid taxes on land or personal property, and to soldiers who had served in the field. In this respect, with its 'active' and 'passive' citizens and voting qualifications dependent on property, it was a return to the Constitution of 1791. But there were essential differences. A single-chamber Assembly had proved to be an instrument of tyranny, and as a safeguard against a repetition of the Terror a bi-cameral system was adopted. The legislature consisted of two bodies: a Council of Five Hundred which initiated and proposed measures to a Council of 250 Ancients, which was to reject or pass them into law. The Five Hundred had to be at least thirty years of age, while the Ancients must be over forty and either married or widowers. The executive was to consist of a Directory of five members, one Director retiring each year. In this way it was hoped to avoid the monarchical spectre of a single executive officer, like the President of the United States. The Directors would nominate ministers, but have no control over the Councils; nor would the Councils have any control over the Directors, once elected. Thus the principle of the separation of powers was respected; unfortunately, cases of disagreement were not provided for. This was an invitation to coups d'état. Nevertheless, the administrative anarchy that had reigned in the Departments and Communes — which during the Terror had become almost autonomous — now began to disappear and a minimum of centralised control was restored.

Haunted by the danger from the Left and from the Right, the Convention, remembering the fate of previous constitutions, trembled for the work it had achieved and took the startling precaution of enacting that two-thirds of its own members must be returned in the elections for the new legislative body. The 'Law of Two-Thirds' was unpopular in Paris. Royalists and reactionaries took the chance to attack the Tuileries, where the Convention was sitting. This time the Convention was prepared; the insurrection of 13 *Vendémiaire* was dispersed with a 'whiff of grapeshot' from the guns of a young Brigadier General who had distinguished himself at the siege of Toulon. His name was Napoleon Bonaparte.

The Directory

The ex-Deputies of the Convention re-elected in accordance with the Law of Two-Thirds formed the majority in the future legislative Council of the Five Hundred. The newly elected remainder tended to the Right; the ex-Convention men accordingly found it easier to remember their Jacobin past than might otherwise have been the case. The first executive Directory consisted entirely of men who had voted for the King's death. Sieyès, one of them, disapproved of the new Constitution, refused the position offered to him and was replaced by Carnot, another regicide. La Revellière-Lépeaux, who had fought the Royalists in the Vendée, was a little hunchback who had founded Theophilanthropy, a secular and republican religion which held services in churches seized from Christians. He had been elected to the Directory by the greatest number of votes.

In contrast Barras had received the fewest, but he was the only one of the five who remained in power throughout the five years of the Directory. He came of aristocratic stock and was a former royal officer, but he had served as a Deputy on Mission and had taken command of the Convention forces during the *Vendémiaire* insurrection. The other two members of the first Directory were the Alsatian Reubell, a lawyer with a sharp tongue, a fighting advocate of the 'natural frontiers' policy, and the Norman Letourneur — like Carnot a captain in the Corps of Engineers.

Seated at first at a rickety table in the dilapidated Luxembourg Palace, the new Directors very quickly surrounded themselves with the handsomest furniture in the once-royal residence. Their costumes were resplendent: orange-red cloaks embroidered in gold, close-fitting tunics and hose of white silk, cross-belted swords and hats crowned with tricoloured plumes. The sumptuous decor and dazzling attire were not simply a manifestation of bourgeois vanity, or an effort to ape the aristocracy of the recent past. Nor was it merely compensation for the humble manner in which the Third Estate had been obliged to dress at the opening of the States General in 1789. Its object was twofold: visibly to break with the tradition of the red bonnets of the Jacobin *sans-culottes* and, by means of outward display, to gain the prestige which the regime sorely needed. The uniform which David designed for the Deputies of the two Councils was no less flamboyant: velvet caps and rich embroidery; a classical toga, white with a scarlet mantle for the Five Hundred; deep purple with a white mantle for the Ancients. As for the

Barras, a nobleman, patronised the young Bonaparte, plotted against Robespierre, became one of the first five Directors and was the only one of them to remain in office during the whole course of the Directory's rule. *Larousse*

programme of the new regime, it was proclaimed to the nation in a resounding series of aims: ' to consolidate the Republic, to extinguish party strife, to restore peace, to revive commerce and industry, to re-establish plenty and public credit, to replace the chaos inseparable from revolutions with social order '. The European war continued, and three domestic dangers still threatened the existence of the republic: financial collapse, Jacobin violence and a Royalist counter-revolution.

The finances of the Directory

The first peril — financial collapse — was the most pressing. The continued devaluation of *assignats* had now left the Government's credit in such a precarious state that it could no longer print a sufficient amount of paper money for its daily needs. The gold louis, worth 2,000 paper francs when the Directory came to power, rose to 3,000 eleven days later, and by the end of December 1795 to 6,500. The Directory urged the vote of a forced loan of 600 millions in coin, and exploited in advance the hypothetical collection of this sum by issuing ' rescriptions ' — a kind of promissory note or warrant — which in their turn quickly depreciated in value by ninety per cent. In February 1796, the minister Ramel finally checked the galloping inflation — the louis then stood at 7,000 paper francs — by destroying the plates from which the *assignats* were printed and by issuing ' territorial bonds ' to be exchanged for *assignats* at the rate of one to thirty-three. They were repayable in State property which, when confidence in the new bonds also failed, was literally thrown away; the scandalous mismanagement benefited speculators only. Finally in September 1797 the desperate expedient of cancelling two-thirds of the public debt was adopted. Bankruptcy was camouflaged by describing the remaining obligation in the Great Book of the Public Debt as the ' consolidated third '. The re-minting of silver and gold currency — in which, since September 1796, taxes had to be paid — the resurrection of indirect taxation and, above all, the establishment of direct taxation, slowly began to rebuild confidence in the credit of the State.

The Second Directory

The political dangers which faced the Directory arose also from its own composition. Its members were regicides, ex-revolutionaries who had, as it were, fallen on their feet. They were a privileged minority caught between two fires. On one side there was the vast Catholic and Royalist population of the provinces whose leaders in Paris were active. On the other side were the Jacobins, humiliated in the reaction which had followed Robespierre's death, but now admired by the poor and hungry, inflamed by the scandalous behaviour of the new rich. Corrupters and corrupted, politicians like Barras and Tallien, bankers like Ouvrard and Récamier, helped to give Paris a bad name for immorality and dissipation. How much of the moral indignation of the critics of the Directory was justified is another matter. They were offended by such spectacles as the ' *Incroyables* ', with their affected voices, rolling ' r's ' and pretentiously extravagant attire, and of their fashionable female counterparts, the ' *Merveilleuses* ', with their daring and diaphanous costume. Hundreds of dance-halls flourished and people flocked to the cafés to forget the gloom of the Terror. In the restaurants — an innovation of the Revolution — caterers and ex-chefs from the Palais Royal — now the Maison Egalité — revealed the secrets of gastronomy to customers who emptied the contents of former royal or aristocratic cellars. In the gaming dens speculators from the stock exchange gambled their winnings with those who had grown rich by supplying the army. In the middle of this frivolity, some two thousand democrats had formed a club — known as the *Panthéon* — which became a centre of militant resistance. In February 1796 this ' hotbed of anarchy ' was closed by the police. Its leaders, among whom was an Italian disciple of Robespierre, Buonarroti, preached the doctrines of Babeuf, the French precursor of communism, who had rebaptised himself Gracchus and edited a paper called *The Tribune of the People*. Babeuf was influenced by the anonymous author of the *Code of Nature* published in 1755, and advocated an egalitarian society for the attainment of universal happiness. In this society no one would inherit wealth, and private property would be abolished. The conspiracy of Babeuf's disciples led in May 1796 to a plan to overthrow the Government by force and establish communism. The plot was, however, betrayed at the last moment. Some thirty of its authors were condemned to death, including Babeuf.

The Directory's action against Babeuf and his followers was easier because a restoration of the monarchy was in the air. It had financial backing from London and had gained the support of French generals, notably of Pichegru. The restoration of the monarchy would simplify arrangements for peace, which the British Cabinet now desired, on condition that the treaty provided for a French withdrawal to the old frontiers. The Chouan Royalists again rebelled, and were crushed, but no sooner was Royalism stamped out in one place than it rose in another. More dangerous than insurrection was the spreading of Royalist sympathies in the country, a movement discreetly conducted by propagandists subsidised by the British diplomat Wickham in Switzerland. A ' Philanthropic Institute ' provided a network of Royalist agencies throughout the provinces, while in Paris a group of reactionaries met in a club in the Rue de Clichy. Elections in March and April 1797 swept away 205 of the 216 members of the old Convention who had stood for re-election, and were a triumph for the Right. Pichegru became president of the Five Hundred, while a member of the club in the Rue de Clichy became president of the Council of the Ancients. Finally, Barthélemy, who had negotiated the Treaties of Basle, had Royalist leanings and was known to favour peace, replaced Letourneur on the executive Directory.

Pichegru continued after Lafayette and Dumouriez the tradition that the Republic could not control its generals. Bonaparte, it is true, dealt a crushing blow to the Royalist cause when he sent his emissary Augereau with troops from Italy to Paris for the coup d'état of *Fructidor* — 4 September 1797. ' I have come here to kill the Royalists ', Augereau stated on the occasion of this, the first coup d'état of the Directory. It was managed by three of the Directors. Barthélemy was deported and Carnot — now a partisan of peace — fled. The new right-wing majority in the Council was dealt with by cancelling the election in forty-nine Departments and shipping off sixty Deputies without trial to Guiana. The Terror was revived against non-juring clergy and returned *émigrés*.

On the Second Directory Barthélemy and Carnot were replaced by two ministers of the Left, Merlin de Douai, who had lately administered the law of ' suspects ', and François de Neufchâteau.

This was not the end of the constitutional troubles of the Directory. After the rout of reaction, Jacobins were returned in the elections of the following year in such force that the Directors again quashed the elections in the coup of *Floréal* (11 May 1798). A year later the opposition of the Legislature forced the resignation of three Directors (the coup of *Prairial*, 18 May 1799) and from this time the swing to the left was irresistible. A new law of hostages was passed and a new forced loan was ordered. The Jacobin club reopened. It was obvious that a new revolutionary crisis was at hand. Sieyès, who now shared with Barras the leadership of the Directory, determined to end the feebleness of the regime by resort to the power of the sword — the recipe of *Fructidor*. He began to look around for a soldier. On 9 October 1799, Bonaparte landed at Fréjus, in the south of France.

Europe from 1795 to 1797

The Law of Two-Thirds had meant the upholding of the policy of the Republican Revolution abroad as well as at home. There were three aspects of this policy: a stubborn defence of French territory, anti-Royalist propaganda, and further conquest to obtain ' natural frontiers ' and the economic benefits of occupation. There had been a slight relaxation of tension between France and Austria in December 1795 when Louis XVI's daughter and a few French Royalist civilians had been exchanged for the members of the Convention whom Dumouriez had delivered to the Austrians and two of Danton's emissaries who had been taken prisoner. But to persuade Austria to make more substantial exchanges — in Belgium and the left bank of the Rhine — threats to Vienna itself were needed. A threefold attack on Austria was planned by Carnot: Jourdan was to invade Austrian territory by the valley of the Main and Moreau by the valley of the Danube, while a diversionary attack on Austrian possessions in northern Italy was entrusted to Barras's protégé, the young General Bonaparte.

Bonaparte's Italian campaign of 1796 at once revealed a master of the art of war. Entering Italy along the coast, he defeated the Sardinians in a swift succession of battles and separated them from their Austrian allies. On April 28 he dictated an armistice to Victor Amadeus, King of Sardinia; Victor Amadeus survived this humiliation for only a few months and his son, Charles Emmanuel, whose continental possessions were wrenched from him in 1798, was to abdicate in 1802 in favour of his brother Victor Emmanuel. Bonaparte, defeating the Austrians again at Lodi in May, entered Milan in triumph. Though the city welcomed him as a deliverer from Austrian tyranny, it was forced to pay a huge indemnity. The French then turned south, systematically plundering as they went. Armistices were successively imposed on the Dukes of Parma and Modena, on the King of Naples and on the Pope himself. Everywhere vast financial contributions were extorted and art treasures, pictures, precious manuscripts, antique sculpture, forcibly exacted. Bonaparte was now master of all northern Italy, and peace treaties, renouncing their adherence to the Coalition, were signed in the autumn

MANIFESTE POUR L'AUGUSTE MAISON AUSTRO-LORAINE.
Sur la signature des préliminaires de paix.

Austria, unable to fight on, had to sign the preliminaries of Leoben in April 1797. The terms were not harsh and by the final Treaty of Campo Formio the following October she gained the lands of the former Republic of Venice. *Larousse*

Charles faced Bonaparte on the River Tagliamento. He was thrown back into the Alps and Bonaparte invaded Carinthia. With Bonaparte's outposts at Semmering only twenty leagues from Vienna, Thugut at last agreed to negotiate.

In the preliminary discussions at Leoben in April 1797 Francis II agreed to relinquish the Austrian Netherlands and to recognise the ' limits of France as decreed by the laws of the Republic ', in return for compensation to be determined later during a Congress at Rastadt, which would arrange the final terms of peace between France and the Holy Roman Empire. In secret clauses the two powers agreed on the dismemberment of the Venetian Republic. Bonaparte had boldly acted on his own authority; the Directory had to accept the terms because it dared not thwart the enthusiasm of France for a peace. On 18 October 1797 Bonaparte signed the Treaty of Campo Formio, which contained a secret clause, agreed to by Austria, which covered French territorial demands on the Rhine. The Treaty of Campo Formio crowned Bonaparte's first Italian campaign and assured his fame in France as conqueror and peacemaker in the tradition of the Revolution. Since the Emperor promised to recognise not only the Rhine frontier, but the satellite republics, Bonaparte had fulfilled the twin objects of revolutionary policy: the acceptance of the ' natural frontiers ' of the Republic and the spread of its revolutionary ideals.

In August 1796, over a year before Campo Formio, France and Spain had signed the defensive and offensive Treaty of San Ildefonso, which reversed the naval situation in the Mediterranean and powerfully contributed to the decision of the Italian states to withdraw from the Coalition. Britain had already made overtures for peace with France in March 1796 and, when Spain declared war on her in October, renewed her offers. At the same time, since the defeated armies of Austria could not be relied on, Britain sought in St Petersburg the support of another great land power with a strong army. Catherine II agreed to send 60,000 men under Suvorov to Italy and even attempted to draw Prussia into a new coalition; but this grave risk to the Directory and to Bonaparte disappeared when, on 6 November 1796, Catherine died. The Directory was less fortunate in its effort to invade Ireland. December storms wrecked Hoche's attempted landing, though the island worried the British until the insurrection of 1798 had been ruthlessly stamped out. Meanwhile Great Britain alone remained at war with France, and France now had allies, two of whom, Spain and the United Provinces, were naval powers of importance. Britain's freedom from invasion depended solely on the superiority of her fleet and the object of her naval strategy was to prevent a concentration of enemy vessels. In February 1797 the Spanish fleet off Cape St Vincent was badly mauled by Admiral Jervis, and later that year, in October, the Dutch were defeated by Admiral Duncan in the battle of Camperdown. Nevertheless, two weeks after the victory of Cape St Vincent the Bank of England was obliged to suspend payments in gold, and throughout that dark spring the fleet upon which everything depended lay paralysed in Portsmouth and in the Thames estuary by mutinies at Spithead and the Nore. Corsica had also been lost; Pitt judged that peace was indispensable. Negotiations were opened at Lille in July by Lord Malmesbury, who was confident of being able to buy the support of Barras

by Parma and Naples. In February 1797 the Pope, Pius VI, was forced to sign the Treaty of Tolentino by which he relinquished all claim to Avignon and the Venaissin in France, and in Italy ceded Bologna, Ferrara and the Romagna to Bonaparte.

Meanwhile in Germany Jourdan had been defeated by the Archduke Charles, brother of Francis II, and forced to retreat; in consequence Moreau, too, had prudently withdrawn. The Austrians were thus free to turn against Bonaparte in Italy. In a series of brilliant engagements he met and vanquished the Austrians at Castiglione, Roveredo, Bassano, Arcole and Rivoli. On 2 February 1797 the Austrians capitulated at Mantua. In the Po valley Bonaparte set up two short-lived republics, the Cispadane and Transpadane Republics, which later — between October 1796 and June 1797 — he formed into the Cisalpine Republic, including Modena — the Duke of Modena being deposed — and the former Papal Legations. In Genoa Bonaparte overthrew the aristocracy, created the Ligurian Republic and allied it with the French Republic. In January 1797 he incited the democrats of Venice to rebel and in May his troops arrived 'to restore order ', having first dealt with Verona, where that Easter the population had demonstrated their loathing of French occupation. The once proud Republic of Venice would soon be extinct and its possessions cynically flung to Austria in compensation for Austrian losses elsewhere. Meanwhile Austria made a final effort, and the Archduke and of his protégé the new French Foreign Minister, Talleyrand. They were abruptly closed by the coup d'état of *Fructidor* and the warlike attitude of Reubell.

Europe from 1798 to 1799

The brief appearance of Bonaparte at the Congress convoked in the little Bavarian town of Rastadt to discuss the compensation for the German princes dispossessed by French annexation of the left bank of the Rhine gave him a glimpse of the diplomatic world of pre-Revolutionary Europe. On the same day that it ratified the Treaty of Campo Formio, the Directory appointed Bonaparte commander-in-chief of the 'Army of England' which was ordered 'to assemble without delay on the Atlantic coast'. A rapid inspection of the Channel ports in February 1798 revealed to Bonaparte the lamentable condition of the French fleet and the present impossibility of challenging the British navy or attempting a serious invasion of the British Isles. He decided to attack Britain at another point — in the East. Vast projects floated through a mind already haunted by the exploits of Alexander the Great, and the idea of an expedition to Egypt attracted him. His new friend Talleyrand agreed with him that a French Eastern Empire would strike a fatal blow at British trade and bring that island of shopkeepers to its knees.

'Europe', Bonaparte had said shortly before this to Desaix, 'is a molehill. There are no great empires and no great revolutions except in the East, where six hundred million people live.' He took with him to Egypt not only the military élite of the Army of Italy, but what amounted to a supplementary general-staff of scholars, engineers, artists and even writers and printers skilled in Greek and Arabic. The mission of attacking Britain by means of cutting her route to India, where he counted on the insurrectionary aid of Tipoo Sahib and the Mahrattas — his orders even included the construction of a Suez Canal — exactly suited his temperament. 'You are', he said to his troops as they embarked in May 1798 from Toulon, 'one of the wings of the Army of England.' After capturing Malta from the Knights of St John, he landed at Alexandria, proclaiming that he had come to re-establish the authority of France's traditional ally, the Sultan, whose sovereignty had been usurped by the Mamelukes. By thus presenting himself as a liberator of the fellaheen from their oppressors, by undertaking to respect the religion and customs of the country and by promising to help to restore the agricultural prosperity which had once made Egypt the granary of ancient Rome, he ensured the benevolent neutrality of the mass of the population. The Turkish Government, however, was not deceived about French intentions.

Bonaparte's most spectacular victory, the Battle of the Pyramids, broke the savage power of the wild Mameluke horsemen, whose picturesque costume became a decorative motif in the scenes of Napoleonic glory. In the meantime Admiral Nelson had been cruising with a small fleet in the Levant in search of the vast French armada which had miraculously escaped him off Toulon. He discovered it anchored in the bay of Aboukir, and on 1 August 1798 attacked. In the ensuing Battle of the Nile the French fleet was utterly destroyed. Bonaparte was now cut off from France. He penetrated Syria and crushed a Turkish army at Mount Tabor, but his advance on Constantinople or perhaps — for no certain knowledge of his ultimate aims exists — towards India, was checked at Acre by the Turks, reinforced by a British naval squadron under Sir Sydney Smith. He withdrew into Egypt. His expedition, though a strategic failure, had brought a long neglected province of European civilisation back into the orbit of the West, and revealed its fabulous archaeological wealth. Modern Egypt, with its veneer of French civilisation, dates from Napoleon's expedition, as modern Egyptology dates from the discovery of the Rosetta Stone by Napoleon's soldiers in 1799.

This Eastern episode, then, had no immediate consequences, though its importance for the future was great. While it was taking place the news of Nelson's great victory of the Nile, the clumsy policy of the Second Directory and Pitt's tenacity had revived the Coalition — the Second Coalition. Bonaparte was recalled, but before his orders arrived he had already abandoned both his enterprise and his army and embarked for France. In the preceding year, before Bonaparte had sailed from Toulon, the Directory had annexed two more states, Mulhouse, an enclave on the upper Rhine which had joined the Republic voluntarily, and Geneva. Meanwhile, the French general Brune had aided the Vaudois democrats to rebel against Berne and set up a republic centred on Lausanne. Then in April, destroying the ancient Swiss Confederation, he formed the Helvetic Republic, soon bound to France by an offensive and defensive alliance. In December 1797 General Duphot was killed during riots in Rome, and the pretext was seized for invading the Papal States, proclaiming a Roman Republic and deporting the octogenarian Pius VI to Valence, where he died some eight months later. The spoils of Rome swelled the loot from Berne to cover the expenses of the Egyptian expedition.

In spite of Bonaparte's proclamation on landing in Alexandria that he had come to restore the Sultan's authority, the Sublime Porte was not reassured, nor did Britain neglect to point out the invader's real aims. On September 9 Turkey declared war on France, under pressure not only from Britain but from Russia. Paul I, who had succeeded Catherine the Great in November 1796, had been systematically kept out of affairs by his mother and had reached the age of forty-two in an atmosphere of contemptuous hostility which had gravely affected the balance of his sombre and unstable mind. He had inherited from Catherine only loathing for the Revolution, which led him to shower favours on the *émigrés*, in whom the rest of Europe had by now more or less lost interest. Louis XVIII was installed near Riga. On the capture of Malta certain of the dispossessed Knights of St John decided to offer Paul I the title of Grand Master of their order, an honour accepted with childish enthusiasm. He then formed an alliance with Britain and Turkey and, when the British occupation of Leghorn encouraged the King of Naples to attack the Roman Republic, joined the Second Coalition. But the French repulsed the Neapolitan attack and in January 1799 seized Naples itself. The monarchy was abolished and in its place the Parthenopean Republic proclaimed. The King of Sardinia had been driven from Piedmont, and Austria declared her intentions in April 1799 by putting an end to the Congress of Rastadt and murdering the French plenipotentiaries. Prussia hesitated. In November 1797 Frederick William II had died, to be succeeded by his twenty-seven-year-old

The mission of Bonaparte to Egypt in the summer of 1798 opened one of the most dramatic episodes of his career. France watched spellbound and his prestige was immeasurably benefited. *Larousse*

son Frederick William III. Shy, suspicious and vacillating, Frederick William III evaded the advances of the Coalition, and also those of Sieyès, the Prussophile Ambassador-Extraordinary of France. He had inherited from his father not only the policy of lucrative neutrality, but Count Haugwitz, a minister who until 1806 would be that policy's chief exponent.

The Directory's maritime diplomacy was scarcely less adroit and nearly led to a dangerous rupture with the United States. Although the United States then had only four million inhabitants and its future greatness was unsuspected, it was a republic and as such a potential ally. George Washington, who had done so much to achieve his country's independence, had in 1789 been elected its first President, and, with the admission of Vermont, Kentucky and Tennessee in 1791, 1792 and 1796, the thirteen original states of the Union had become sixteen. In April 1793 the United States had made a declaration of neutrality, but Washington was leader of the Federalist Party which, after Jay's Treaty with Britain, was inclined to be pro-British. When France protested against the treaty Washington replied by recalling his ambassador, Monroe. After Washington had refused a third term of office John Adams became President in 1797. Adams renewed contact with France by sending a mission of three plenipotentiaries with instructions to settle differences on the exclusion of American goods. Talleyrand's unfortunate attempts to bribe the envoys caused wrath in both countries (the scandal was known as the X.Y.Z. Correspondence because Talleyrand's agents were designated by these letters in reports to Congress). In January 1798 the Directory aggravated the effect of its prohibition on neutral goods by an even stricter decree, which almost precipitated war. George Washington was called from retirement to reassume command of the

American army, while Congress passed two anti-revolutionary laws, the Alien Act of June and the Sedition Act of July 1798. The moderation of President Adams, however, smoothed over the situation until agreement was reached in 1800.

On the continent the Coalition of 1799 had at its command 300,000 troops, a number soon to be doubled, while France could raise only some 200,000. Jourdan's plans for conscription, which in times of war would call up all Frenchmen between the ages of twenty and twenty-five for unlimited military service, had not yet been put into effect. The subject republics — those ' clockwork governments ' as Madame de Staël called them because they had to be wound up from Paris — bullied and exploited, financially bled and politically browbeaten, seethed with unrest. In Belgium there were Royalist uprisings. The Cisalpine Republic was overthrown and the Austrians, reinforced by Russians under Suvorov, overran northern Italy and reoccupied Milan. The French withdrew from Naples and on August 15 Joubert was defeated and killed at Novi. The little Franco-Italian republics fell like ninepins. Anglo-Russian forces landed in Holland. In Switzerland, however, France was saved from total disaster by Masséna's victories at Zürich on September 25 and 26. In Holland Brune restored the situation in October, while the Tsar, Paul I, quarrelled with the allies and withdrew from the Coalition. The Directory, in fact, was already saved, though all of Bonaparte's conquests in Italy, except Genoa, had been lost. This was the situation when Bonaparte himself returned from Egypt. Every faction in France looked to him as a saviour. Those who advocated war to the death and those who wanted peace; moderate Republicans, reanimated Jacobins, even Royalists, seeing in him a new General Monck to usher in the Restoration — all now placed their hopes in Bonaparte.

General Bonaparte, the hero of revolutionary romantics wherever French armies had not been. *Marburg*

CHAPTER FOURTEEN

THE NAPOLEONIC EPOCH

EUROPE AND THE FRENCH CONSULATE

' Brumaire '

The aim of the conspirators who mounted the coup of *Brumaire* was the achievement of constitutional revision by using as an instrument the prestige and popularity of Bonaparte. The essence of what happened was that the instrument took charge.

At first, all went well. The Council of Ancients decreed,

on the morning of 18 *Brumaire* (9 November 1799) that the Legislative Assembly should be transferred to St Cloud. Bonaparte was to superintend its removal and guarantee its safety. He took an oath to preserve the Republic and sent a general to take command of the guard of the Directory, two of whose members, Sieyès and Ducos, were in the plot. Barras resigned; the other two Directors agreed to comply. Proclamations appeared bearing Bonaparte's

The Emperor reviews his troops. Unsparing of his soldiers' blood or effort, Napoleon nevertheless carefully cultivated the legend of their personal attachment to him.

rhetorical question to the regime which was about to be overthrown: 'What have you done with the France I left so brilliant? I left you peace, I find war. I left you victories, I find defeat. I left you the millions of Italy, I find laws of exploitation and misery.'

On the following day, at St Cloud, the plot almost miscarried. The Council of Five Hundred contained many staunch Republicans and Jacobins. Most of them knew nothing of the plot. When Bonaparte appeared before them an uproar broke out. His outlawry was demanded. He was saved only by the quick action of his brother Lucien, President of the Five Hundred, who called the troops waiting outside to clear the hall of the 'hirelings of Pitt' who were destroying the liberties of the Republic. This was quickly done. Later that night a committee of Deputies and Ancients favourable to revision of the constitution decreed a provisional government of Bonaparte, Sieyès and Ducos to exercise power as 'Consuls' until a new constitution should be drawn up. Sixty-one members of the Legislative Assembly were expelled and the Directory came to an end. France did not protest; government bonds rose rapidly on the stock exchange when the news of the coup spread.

The Constitution of the Year VIII

Bonaparte had not yet become the figure of the Napoleonic legend. He was not even the principal personage in the newly improvised Government, whose outstanding member was the ex-Abbé Sieyès. The constitution which Sieyès

helped to draw up, however, in spite of its basis in the popular choice of 'notables' who would take office, was bound to throw effective authority into Bonaparte's hands. The revisionists had no intention of losing control of the new regime to popularly elected bodies and set up this time four assemblies: the Council of State, the Tribunate, the Legislative Body and the Senate. Only the Council of State, chosen from experienced jurists, had any importance. Tribunes, orators and critics whom ten years of political argument had formed debated the proposed laws, but had no power to vote. The Legislators, weighing the arguments of the first two chambers, voted but could not discuss proposed legislation. The Senators, appointed for life, supervised the activities of the other chambers and chose their members. In the Senate the ex-regicides who had survived the Terror, reaction and the Directory survived again through Consulate and Empire.

The Executive consisted of three Consuls — Bonaparte, Cambacérès and Lebrun — who had been named in the Constitution itself, and were appointed for ten years. Unlike the provisional Consuls, they were not of equal rank. The First Consul promulgated the laws, appointed and dismissed ministers, Councillors of State, ambassadors, army and naval officers, and members of provincial and local administrations. He also named the judges of criminal and civil courts, though he could not revoke their appointments. He presided over the Council of State. The function of Cambacérès and Lebrun was formally consultative and practically political; left-wing opinion was reassured by Cambacérès, once a member of the Convention and

239

The *coup d'état* of *Brumaire* (9–10 November 1799). A highly imaginative version of the dismissal of the Council of Five Hundred. In fact, Bonaparte was shouted down and saved only by his brother's presence of mind in summoning the waiting soldiers when Bonaparte hesitated. *Mansell*

Napoleon signing the Concordat with Pius VII in 1801. Their friendship ended in 1809 when the Pope excommunicated the French invaders of the Papal States and was promptly taken prisoner. *Radio Times Hulton Picture Library*

Minister of Justice, while Lebrun, a former secretary of Louis XV's minister Maupeou and a member of the Constituent Assembly of 1789, reassured the Right. Both gave Bonaparte excellent advice, one on legal re-organisation, the other on matters of financial reform. As the text of the new constitution was being solemnly studied at the street corners of the capital the *Gazette de France* reported a conversation overheard between two Parisians: 'What's in the Constitution?' To which the reply was: 'Bonaparte'.

Napoleon Bonaparte

Napoleon Bonaparte was born on 15 August 1769 at Ajaccio in Corsica, which had become French territory the year before his birth. He was thirty when he became First Consul. His family was patrician though poor and Napoleon had been strictly brought up by his mother, Letizia Ramolino, a matron of Roman impressiveness. Through his father's influence Napoleon obtained a King's bursary and at the age of ten was sent to school at Brienne. Five years later he became a cadet at the Military School in Paris, where he zealously pursued the study of mathematics, essential to his career as an artillery officer. Meanwhile he had mastered the subtleties of the French language, although to the end of his life his pronunciation and spelling of French remained poor. His father, a spendthrift lawyer, had been a deputy of the Nobility in the Corsican Estates. When he died Napoleon, who was sixteen, and his brother Joseph, who was one year older, were left to provide for the six younger members of the family: Lucien, Elisa, Louis, Pauline, Caroline and Jérôme. The revolt of Paoli, who led the movement for independence from revolutionary France, and the subsequent occupation of the island by the British, drove the Bonapartes from Corsica. Poverty and austerity had made Napoleon sympathetic towards the new revolutionary ideas, and during the civil strife in Corsica he had been a Lieutenant-Colonel in the National Guard. In 1793, when Toulon was recaptured from the Anglo-Royalists, he so distinguished himself that he was made a Brigadier-General. After the 13 *Vendémiaire* he became a Lieutenant-General. He was commander-in-chief of the Army of the Interior when in March 1796 he married Josephine, widow of General de Beauharnais, who had been guillotined two years previously. To the perspicacity of Carnot he owed his opportunity to reveal his strategical genius in command of the Army of Italy; his call to power he owed to Sieyès.

The privations of his early years and the rigours of his recent campaigns had left their mark and he was worn and thin. Under his tousled hair his sallow features were emaciated. The slight figure and rather puny appearance of the First Consul gave no hint of the future portliness of the Emperor. Consumingly ambitious, he united in politics as in war the contradictory gifts of thoughtfulness and sudden improvisation, of swiftness to sum up a situation and long memory, of unrestrained imagination and geometric precision — all served by a keen sense of his own authority. It was after the battle of Lodi,

The Emperor Napoleon by Jacques-Louis David. *Giraudon*

during his victories in Italy, that he was struck by a sudden revelation of his exceptional future. After that, with a touch of Corsican superstition, he increasingly trusted to his lucky star. The expedition to Egypt developed in him a sense of fatalism and affinity with the Islamic world which he showed during his proconsular period in Cairo. With the revolutionary religion of devotion to the Republic he associated the military cult of honour, and offered it as an ideal to the entire nation when he set about the task of reconciliation and regeneration which, in his view, was entrusted to him when a plebiscite in January and February 1800 gave 3,000,000 votes in favour of the new Constitution and only 1,500 against. Napoleon was to use this device again and became the first modern plebiscitory dictator.

The Pacification

Bonaparte began internal pacification even before the results of the plebiscite were known. In his proclamation of December 15, recommending the adoption of the new Constitution as being ' founded on the true principles of representative government ', he added: ' The powers which it provides will be strong and stable, as they must be to ensure the rights of the citizen and the interests of the State. ' The Revolution had, in fact, accomplished its purpose and the Revolution was over. On Christmas Day 1799 the new institutions came into effect. On that day Lucien Bonaparte replaced the astronomer Laplace as Minister of the Interior and announced that ' the Government no longer recognises the existence of political parties and in France sees only Frenchmen '. Napoleon well knew that the restoration of political peace was the most urgent item on his programme.

His first spectacular gesture was to abolish the *émigré* list. This removed a sword of Damocles which had hung over many Frenchmen, since the denunciation of any kind of absence from normal residence entailed the risk of being put on the *émigré* list, with its consequences: confiscation of property and danger of death. Soon the First Consul extended an amnesty to *émigrés* still living abroad and undertook to restore their estates if not yet sold. On the other hand, possession of ' national property ' by the buyers of Church and *émigré* lands was guaranteed by the Constitution. The vested interest in the Revolution was preserved. Meanwhile political prisoners were released and men of all parties were recalled from banishment. Non-juring priests were set free, and churches restored to Christian worship. Bonaparte also dealt with the Chouan uprisings with a mixture of firmness and conciliation. In this way the basis of the regime in public opinion was made as broad as possible. But the censorship was restored and sixty of the seventy-three political newspapers published in Paris were suppressed. The *Moniteur* became the official journal and chief source of public information.

Gérard's portrait of Napoleon as First Consul. The Consulate was the period of his greatest legislative and diplomatic achievements (and of the record Italian campaign). *Mansell*

Josephine de Beauharnais (1762–1814) married to Bonaparte in 1796 and divorced in 1809 so that he could marry and obtain an heir. In so far as he could love anyone, Napoleon loved her. *Marburg*

The Executions of the Third of May, 1808. French reprisal after the uprising quelled by Murat's mamelukes. Oil on canvas. 1814. Goya. *Prado, Madrid*

Internal re-organisation

To the average Frenchman the most obvious and exasperating effect of the Revolution had been the breakdown of regular administration. To restore it the Consulate had at its disposal a remarkable team of experts, rich in the experience of ten revolutionary years of trial and error. The Council of State, under the direction of the Second Consul and often of the First, worked in specialised groups which in a few years gave France much of its modern administrative structure.

The law of 17 February 1800 organised the regional and local administration of the country on a basis which a century and a half was to leave unaltered. Within the general framework of the Departments (which, including Belgium and Geneva, then numbered ninety-eight and were soon to be joined by the four Rhenish and six Piedmontese Departments) the Communes were grouped in four hundred departmental subdivisions, called 'Arrondissements'. At each of these three administrative levels was an agent of the central authority whose appointment was made or revoked by the Government: for the Departments, a Prefect — the names Prefect, Consul, Tribune and Senate were all derived from Roman history; for the Arrondissements, a Sub-Prefect; for the Communes, a Mayor. Each was assisted by an appropriate locally elected Council. The Prefects were entrusted with the immense labour of setting the country on its feet again. Their responsibilities included not only public order and security but economic rehabilitation and the inauguration of the new institutions. They were chosen, therefore, after very careful deliberation, for ability alone and without regard to previous political affiliations, so that survivors of revolutionary assemblies like Jean Bon Saint-André mingled with men like La Rochefoucauld and representatives of other widely held, but divergent, opinions. To enhance their prestige they were provided with a uniform richly embroidered in silver and a sword like that carried by the old Nobility. On the whole, the Prefects served the regime well. They were the Intendants of the Old Regime all over again.

Like administrators, judges too became appointed functionaries, although the jury system was maintained. The Council of State continued the work of unifying French Law — labours which culminated in the drawing up of the Civil Code which would be Napoleon's proudest achievement. The indispensable financial re-organisation produced another hierarchy of bureaucrats, whose task it was to remedy the abuses inherent in the system of farming taxes and other methods of collecting revenue which had proved so unpopular. Here again the machinery proved its efficiency, for the directors and inspectors who assessed taxes and the collectors who gathered them were, like Prefects and Magistrates, to survive every succeeding regime. Under the Consulate finances were entrusted to Gaudin, an able and honest minister, who startled his contemporaries by producing balanced budgets. French credit, spurred by the vitality and military success of Bonaparte, was restored with a rapidity which astonished the world. Above all a sound banking establishment now existed that issued notes which, unlike the *assignats*, inspired confidence. The Bank of France, created in February 1800 and modelled on the Bank of England, was at first a private bank, but supervised by the State, and it

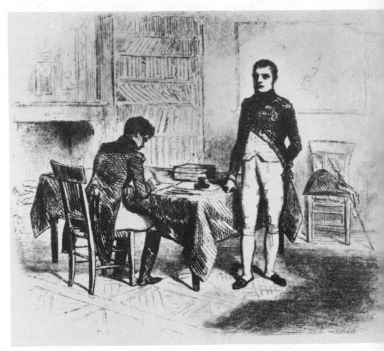

The First Consul dictating to a secretary. Napoleon always gave an intense attention to the punctual fulfilment of administrative business. On occasion he employed as many as four secretaries at once in dictation and administered France from his campaign-tent.

Medal commemorating the battle of the Pyramids, 1798, which decided the fate of Egypt and brought the French Revolution to the Near East. The awakening of extra-European national feeling had begun. *Giraudon*

A British militiaman of 1814. The British army of the Revolutionary and Napoleonic wars did not show itself very able until the Egyptian campaign of 1801. Though committed only in relatively small numbers it thereafter showed high qualities of training and leadership. *Mansell*

was soon authorised to issue paper money honoured at its face value by the State Treasury.

Religious and intellectual policy

The Consulate also sought to solve the religious question which so divided France. The Concordat signed in Paris on 15 July 1801 had been rewritten twenty-one times and on several occasions negotiations had almost been broken off. It was imposed by the Pope on a reluctant Curia and by Bonaparte on an anti-clerical Government: it restored religious peace and brought French Catholics back to the Roman obedience. It gave France an established Church for over a century. Bishops who had served under the monarchy were made to resign (thirty-six refused); the new bishops, who included both non-juring and constitutional clergy, were appointed by the First Consul and canonically instituted by the Pope. The Concordat recognised a reduced number of dioceses — sixty — and made no claim for the restitution of Church property. In exchange, salaries were to be paid to the clergy by the State. The Concordat was solemnly proclaimed in April 1802, but it was supplemented by Articles in which Bonaparte unilaterally completed the submission of the Gallican Church to the State and, re-organising the Calvinist and Lutheran consistories, undertook to pay salaries to Protestant clergy as well. Civil marriage remained. The Church thus gained less than had been hoped from the Concordat, but outweighing all disadvantages was the fact that France, though Republican, was again formally Catholic.

The educational system, too, was reformed. The ' Central Schools ' of the Directory had produced disappointing results and were replaced by *Lycées*. These State-supported secondary schools were primarily intended to prepare the youth of the bourgeoisie — in comfortable circumstances or holding bursaries — for the liberal professions or for careers in the civil services and the armed forces. The State provided the personnel and prescribed curricula which were uniform in all *Lycées*. They combined the sciences, mathematics, physics and chemistry with the classical studies of the colleges of the past. The system was perhaps too rigid, but it created a fine group of institutions. In spite of the publication of Chateaubriand's masterpiece, *Le Génie du Christianisme*, however, the Consulate did not see a revival of the arts. The painter David was at the height of his creative powers, but had already been celebrated before 1799. Scientific France was more impressive; the Institute could boast of such illustrious men as Monge, who led the scientists during Bonaparte's Egyptian campaign, Berthollet, the chemist, and Lamarck, the great botanist and zoologist who was a forerunner of Darwin.

The pacification of the continent

In 1799 France was at war with Europe as well as with herself. Peace abroad was as urgently needed as peace at home. For seven and half years Europe had been at war with the Revolution. Britain had always opposed France and now this great adversary was again joined by Austria and Russia. The disappearance of Poland from the map, the eclipse of Sweden and the rupture with Turkey had deprived the Republic of traditional allies, and the emergence of Russian power had destroyed the

243

Paul I (1796–1801). The Tsar feared the French Revolution and joined the Second Coalition against France. However his loyalty was precarious and he turned against England before being assassinated in March 1801. *Hachette*

reply was more diplomatically phrased, but equally negative. Nevertheless, Francis had recovered from his earlier belligerence. Although he still wore the uniform of a general, he was no soldier and his brother, the Archduke Charles, whom Bonaparte considered a first-class strategist, was doubtful about the Emperor's valour. The Austrian Chancellor Thugut, on the other hand, deserved the epithet ' War Baron ', and his loathing of revolutionary France was equalled only by Pitt's. In his reply to Talleyrand, the French Foreign Minister, Thugut affected to doubt the pacific intentions of the French Government.

Bonaparte thought of meeting Austrian hostility with a revival either of the old Turkish alliance of the days of Francis I, or of Louis XV's alliance with Prussia. The first expedient misfired. At Berlin, although Frederick William shared Bonaparte's hostility to Austria, the Minister Haugwitz remained deaf to all Talleyrand's appeals for action. No matter how profitable actual intervention might be, the best that Prussia could offer was her mediation. In Egypt an agreement which Kléber had made with Sir Sydney Smith at El Arish had not been recognised by the British Government, and Turkish forces moved into Egypt. Kléber defeated them at Heliopolis. To consolidate this success Bonaparte decided to abandon discussion and to impose terms of peace. It was the beginning of the great campaign which culminated at Marengo.

In a bold and spectacular manoeuvre Bonaparte crossed the Alps by the Great St Bernard Pass and outflanked the Austrian army, tied down by Moreau, who had been sent to occupy the south bank of the upper Danube. The day of the battle of Marengo, 14 June 1800, began badly for Bonaparte but ended well, thanks to the timely arrival of General Desaix, who turned the tide and, in the process, was himself fatally wounded. The Austrians, driven from Lombardy, withdrew to the River Mincio. Marengo was decisive for Bonaparte, whose career defeat would have ruined; but it did not mean that the war was yet over. It was not finished until December 3 when Moreau defeated the Austrians at Hohenlinden and imposed peace at the gates of Vienna. Although Austria had guaranteed not to sign any separate peace before February 1801, discussions nevertheless opened at Lunéville as early as October 1800. Cobenzl — who, since September, had succeeded Thugut — came to an agreement with the French in February. The Emperor and the Empire again recognised the extension of French territory to the banks of the Rhine as far as the frontier of Holland — still the Batavian Republic and of necessity a French ally. The Helvetic and Cisalpine Republics reappeared. On the other hand, Austria retained possession of Venetia, Istria and Dalmatia, which Bonaparte had previously offered her in compensation for her losses in Italy. By thus sharing spheres of influence in southern Europe the two rival continental powers seemed, in the Treaty of Lunéville, to have assured the pacification of the continent.

The end of the maritime war

Great Britain — which included Ireland since the Act of Union of 5 February 1800, under which a hundred seats in the House of Commons were accorded to Protestant Irishmen — was as victorious at sea as France was on land. British fleets were everywhere supreme. French and Dutch colonies had been seized and that

old balance of power. The might of Russia, like that of the Emperor Charles V some two centuries earlier, was potentially immeasurably greater than that of any European state, but the Tsar of Russia, Catherine the Great's son Paul I, was unbalanced if not actually insane. He was an unstable and incalculable element in the diplomacy of his day. As a monarch he was a declared enemy of the Republic and, in his rage at Bonaparte's invasion of Egypt and his whimsical ambition to regain Malta as Grand Master of the Knights of St John, allied himself to Austria and Britain, only to quarrel with them soon afterwards.

Before dealing with Paul I, Bonaparte approached Britain and Austria with offers of peace. On Christmas Day 1799 he had appealed to George III, asking: ' How can the two most enlightened nations in Europe, both stronger and more powerful than their security and independence demand, sacrifice their trade, their internal prosperity and the happiness of their people for the vain ambitions of grandeur?' To the Emperor Francis II he wrote: ' During the next campaign vast armies will treble the number of casualties which the renewal of hostilities has already produced. The known character of Your Majesty leaves me in no doubt about the true wishes of your heart.' The response from London was slow in coming and, when it came, insulting; from Vienna the commercial competition eliminated. A very profitable contraband trade had grown up with the Spanish American colonies, Lord Wellesley was making progress in India and the occupation of Egypt was imminent. Nevertheless Britain regarded Europe with misgiving. The French Revolution, stigmatised by Burke's *Reflections*, had instilled in the Tory majority a horror which Bonaparte's rise to power and the success of French arms only deepened. To the vast majority in Britain Bonaparte was simply another and more dangerous revolutionary ogre.

From the moment he became First Consul Bonaparte had given thought to maritime problems, and at Brest particularly stimulated naval preparations. But, like the Convention before him and the Directory, which had invented the Continental 'System' that he would later develop into the 'Continental Blockade', Bonaparte realised that without mastery of the seas he could do little against Britain and began to look for allies. On 1 October 1800 at San Ildefonso he had concluded a secret pact with Spain, by which, in exchange for a promise to provide an Italian kingdom formed of Tuscany and the former Papal States to the cadet branch of the Spanish royal family — represented by the Infante, the Duke of Parma — he had obtained Spanish Louisiana and six Spanish men-of-war. The day before this pact was concluded Joseph Bonaparte had signed the Treaty of Mortefontaine with the envoys of President John Adams, which put an end to the 'quasi-war' between the United States of America and France, and re-established between the two republics a 'firm, inviolable and universal peace'. The agreement not only settled the broad outstanding sources of conflict between the two countries and included favoured nation clauses but, more significantly, cited two fundamental principles of international law: that the flag protects the merchandise, and that neutral merchantmen plying their lawful routes are exempt from search by belligerent navies.

This doctrine of the 'Freedom of the Seas' inspired the Tsar to conclude with Sweden, Denmark and Prussia a League of Armed Neutrality which, in fact, meant a break with Britain (December 1800). The Danes occupied Hamburg and Lübeck, while the Prussians marched into Hanover, thus closing the Baltic, the Hanseatic towns and the German river ports essential to British trade.

Franco-Russian relations were improved by Bonaparte's unprompted gesture of returning Russian prisoners of war freshly equipped, while common hatred of the 'sea tyrants' drew the two nations so close together that in January 1801 Paul I went so far as to expel Louis XVIII from Mitau, sent envoys to Paris to discuss an alliance, and, envisaging a combined expedition to India, ordered a corps of Don Cossacks into Central Asia. On 21 March 1801 the Treaty of Aranjuez reinforced the agreements reached at San Ildefonso about Louisiana and the creation of an Italian 'Kingdom of Etruria' for the benefit no longer of the Duke of Parma, who had abdicated in favour of the French Republic, but of his son. On March 29 the miserable King of Naples was dragooned by the French garrison into ceding the island of Elba, opening his fortresses to French troops and closing his ports to the British. Even Portugal was not spared. Under John of Braganza, who acted as regent for his mother, the insane Maria I, Portugal remained a British client. Lucien Bonaparte, now Ambassador at Madrid, instructed Godoy

General Kléber, left by Bonaparte in command of his forces in Egypt in 1799. In June 1800 he was assassinated. *Archiv für Kunst und Geschichte*

In 1803 Napoleon sold Louisiana (the area between the Mississippi and the Rocky Mountains) to the United States and thus doubled the area of the new republic. It opened the way to the unimpeded westward expansion overland which took up most of the following century. *British Museum*

to invade Portugal, and in the brief 'War of the Oranges' which followed further ports were closed to British shipping, the Spanish royal house made a fortune, the town of Olivenca was retained by Spain and, by the Treaties of Badajoz and Madrid in June and September, Portugal paid a large indemnity. An even more curious treaty was concluded in June 1801 at Tripoli with the Bey Yusuf Pasha, which guaranteed the freedom and security of maritime and commercial relations between Tripoli and France. Its object was not only to curb the activities of the Barbary pirates but to protect 'Capuchin fathers and other religious missionaries' as well as the caravans of pilgrims to Mecca. In the following December and February two similar agreements were reached with the Dey of Algiers and the Bey of Tunis.

The League of Armed Neutrality struck Britain a blow which was all the more severe in that the island's industry was going through a crisis after a bad harvest. But it was a domestic problem — the Irish question, which has been fatal to so many British statesmen — that brought Pitt's famous Ministry to an end. Pitt believed that Catholic emancipation was both wise and just, and when in February 1801 George III stubbornly opposed him Pitt resigned. Addington formed a new Cabinet, in which Hawkesbury took charge of the Foreign Office. He at once began negotiations with France, and immediately encountered stumbling blocks — above all, the question of Egypt. But soon two dramatic events, which could have caused the war to flare up again, actually facilitated peace. On the evening of March 23 Paul I was assassinated by a group of conspirators belonging to the upper nobility, aristocrats who were pro-British both by conviction and, since they exported wood and grain to Britain, by self-interest. Led by Count Pahlen, the Military Governor of the capital, and by Count Panine, the Vice-Chancellor, with accomplices like the brutal General Bennigsen and the Zubov brothers (whose sister had been the intimate friend of Whitworth, the British ambassador recently sent home as the moving spirit of the 'British party') the conspirators had mentioned only the word 'deposition' to Paul's successor, thus securing his tacit assent. The succession of Tsar Alexander I removed Britain's gravest apprehension. Five days later, on 2 April 1801, a British squadron under Admiral Parker and Vice-Admiral Nelson forced the Sound, crippled the Danish fleet, bombarded Copenhagen and obliged Denmark to accept an armistice. The assassination of the Tsar and the battle of Copenhagen broke the Northern League, which had threatened to make the continental blockade complete. Sweden, Denmark and Russia all decided to make peace.

At about the same time the British and the French had finally decided to negotiate. The preliminary discussions at London, foreseeing an uneasy peace, had stipulated the immediate cessation of hostilities and, as soon as the treaty was ratified, the reciprocal return of all conquests which had been made — except Ceylon and Trinidad — and the evacuation of Malta and Egypt, Malta to be restored to the Order of St John of Jerusalem and Egypt to the Turkish Sultan. Meanwhile, in Egypt itself Kléber had been assassinated and his place taken by the erstwhile Marquis de Menou, a convert to Islam who took the name Abdallah. Menou's declaration that Egypt was a French protectorate again convulsed the country. Towards the end of September a British force under Sir Ralph Abercrombie invested Alexandria and forced the French to capitulate. Both sides were by now weary of a war which seemed to offer neither the prospect of decisive victory. Lord Cornwallis went to Amiens to negotiate the definitive treaty. Agreement was delayed by several incidents which took place during the winter of 1801-2, notably the transformation of the Cisalpine Republic into the Italian Republic and the election of Bonaparte himself to its presidency for ten years. At the same time, January 1802, Bonaparte's Lombard friend, Count Melzi d'Eril, was made vice-president and sent to Milan to act in Bonaparte's name. Hawkesbury wrote to Cornwallis to denounce the boundless ambition and contempt for Europe which the occurrence illustrated. But the negotiations proceeded in sessions which were often stormy, especially on the question of Malta, its fortifications and the nature of its future neutral garrison. Finally, on 27 March 1802, the Peace of Amiens was signed.

Consul for Life

Most Frenchmen felt vastly grateful to Bonaparte for having put an end to the sacrifices in blood and money which war had exacted. He had indisputably restored order and internal security, re-established civil and religious peace, and affirmed those 'strong and stable' powers he spoke of when he took office. His achievements had not, however, been unopposed by the two extremes of political opinion, Royalist and Jacobin. On the morrow of *Brumaire* the Royalists hopefully believed that their hour was come: Louis XVIII himself had begged Bonaparte to restore his sceptre and crown and, in return, receive any reward he named. The First Consul's reply had been: 'First you would have to march over the bodies of 100,000 dead.' Jacobin plots, like that of the Corsican Arena and the Italian Ceracchi, led their authors to the guillotine, but a Royalist attempt to assassinate the First Consul — the explosion of an 'infernal machine' in Paris on Christmas Eve 1800 — resulted in eighty killed or wounded in the neighbourhood of his carriage, while Bonaparte himself was saved only by the presence of mind of his coachman. This gave Bonaparte a chance to strike at the opposition on both sides. The Royalist authors of this assault were put to death, but 130 Republicans were deported and others were shot or condemned to police supervision inside France. As if to balance them, some hundred militant Royalists were imprisoned. But it was clear that Bonaparte himself was still in danger of fanatics or of hired assassins acting on behalf of those who were determined to strike down the regime by killing its leader. In view of Bonaparte's popularity after the Concordat and the Peace of Amiens the ex-regicides in 1802 once more displayed their talent for self-preservation by advocating further extension of the Chief Executive's powers.

Already the Senate had 'purified' the Tribunate and the Legislative Assembly when — from January to March — new appointments to those two bodies took place. Opposition in them from enemies of the Concordat and upholders of parliamentary traditions was almost eliminated. On 6 May 1802 a message from the Consuls communicated to the Assemblies news of the Peace of Amiens. An elaborate charade followed in the Assemblies, which eventually accepted the proposal of the Council of State that

Louis XVIII, who returned from exile in 1814 to rule France until 1824. He died while still reigning — an achievement which had escaped his predecessor and the only three French monarchs who followed him. *Victoria & Albert Museum*

Marshal Ney, 'bravest of the brave', led Napoleon's cavalry at Waterloo and was later shot by the restored Bourbon for his adherence to the returned Emperor during the Hundred Days. *Bavaria Verlag*

the people of France should approve that Bonaparte be made Consul for life. In the plebiscite which followed over three and a half million voted in favour of the proposal and a mere eight thousand voted against it. On August 2 the Senate proclaimed Napoleon Bonaparte — his first name had been employed in the wording of the plebiscite and its use now became universal — Consul for Life. Two days later the Constitution of the Year X conferred on Napoleon the royal prerogatives of pardoning the condemned and of naming his own successor. The powers of the Senate were enlarged and *senatus consulta* — or decrees of the Senate — were increasingly to replace the debates of the other assemblies. Other changes further centralised power.

The monarchical tendency which these constitutional changes embodied was reflected in the country itself: nostalgia for the past had replaced earlier revolutionary fervour. The sense that an ' élite ' served a useful purpose — an élite quite different from the former aristocracy of birth or money — suggested to the newly appointed Consul for Life the creation of the Legion of Honour, which at that time was in no way a decoration or the Order — modelled on those of the rest of monarchial Europe — that it was to become under the Empire. Its first members were soldiers of outstanding valour whom the Revolution had already honoured. These, together with civilians who had rendered distinguished service to the nation, were to be organised in salaried cohorts with subalterns, majors — later commanders, from the traditional word — and general officers. The Assemblies criticised the project but a new dominant and cultivated class was emerging. A court circle, still discreet, largely military and predominantly young, formed around the First Consul at the Tuileries or in his private residence at Malmaison. Once more *salons* were held, and in conversation at such gatherings the word ' citizen ' was heard less frequently than the word ' monsieur '. Fostered by agricultural societies, the stock exchange and resuscitated chambers of commerce, agriculture and trade again prospered. Industry benefited both from the high tariffs erected against British goods and from new markets created by French domination of the continent.

Europe and the Consular peace

The Batavian Republic, a co-signatory of the Treaty of Amiens, bewailed the loss of Ceylon, and Sémonville, the French Ambassador, made certain that the end of hostilities did not entail a departure of the French garrisons or a slackening of Dutch naval preparations. No one, in fact, thought that the Peace of Amiens was more than a truce. Peace in the Helvetic Republic — that other ' sister ' republic which France had forced Europe to recognise — was even more precarious. The unity which had been imposed on Switzerland in 1798 by the victory of the local democrats and the French army under Brune over General Aloys von Reding and the patrician Cantons was suited neither to the deep-rooted federalist tradition of the country nor to the mountainous character of its geography. In the Malmaison Act of April 1801 Talleyrand and Stapfer drew up a Swiss Constitution which resembled that of the Consulate, with two Consuls drawn from old local families, a Chamber of Deputies and a Senate. It proved unworkable and after repeated crises Reding, the champion of Swiss independence, was called to the post of First Landamman, or magistrate. Certain pro-French senators, however, forced his resignation and appealed to Bonaparte, who withdrew the French occupying forces — a skilful move which demonstrated to the world both his own moderation and the dangerous consequences of removing the French garrison. As he had foreseen, the aristocracy at once swept away their adversaries, and it was only the hasty return of French troops which saved the democrats from being massacred. Reding sought and found support in London, where the newspapers opened public subscriptions for the cause of Swiss freedom, while Ney was sent to Switzerland in the twin capacity of military Commander-in-Chief and French Minister Plenipotentiary. He dispersed the Federalists, but again Bonaparte displayed his talent for diplomacy. His Act of Mediation of 1803 proclaimed the equality of the nineteen Cantons and the independence of their governments, but imposed a central authority — of annual duration — to maintain inter-Cantonal relations with the Mediator, composed of a Landamman and a Diet. By a complementary arrangement Switzerland guaranteed to provide France with four regiments for a period of twenty-five years.

The new Tsar, Alexander, pursuing Paul I's policy, was in agreement with Bonaparte on the subject of Franco-Russian mediation in Germany, which would favour their respective protégés. Compensations which had been promised to the German princes in the treaties of Basle, Campo Formio and Lunéville for their losses on the left bank of the Rhine were the pretext for, rather than the real object of, the annexations and secularisations which were now decided upon. Talleyrand, the principal negotiator, made a fortune out of the transactions. Territory which amounted in area and population to one-sixth of Germany was allotted to Prussia, Bavaria, Hesse-Cassel, Würtemberg, Baden, Nassau, etc. Austria, gaining scarcely more than two Tyrolean bishoprics, was badly hit by the loss of all those small ecclesiastical states now secularised and of the now mediatised free cities — clients which in the past had assured her preponderance and voting majority in the Imperial Diets. The disappearance of the ecclesiastical Electors of Cologne and Treves — the Elector of Mainz, the Arch-Chancellor Dalberg, alone survived and was transferred to Ratisbon — and the promotion to the electoral college of the princes of Würtemberg, Baden, Salzburg — given in indemnity to the Grand Duke of Tuscany — and Hesse-Cassel meant that there would henceforth be six Protestant Electors to four Catholic Electors, a proportion which excluded the possibility of an heir to the Habsburg Francis II being elected to the Imperial throne. These dispositions were submitted to the Diet of Ratisbon in August 1802 and after long debates accepted almost in their entirety, being registered in the Diet's final ordinance — the *Reichsdeputationshauptschluss* — on 25 February 1803. The mosaic of German states, large, medium and minute, which had existed since the Treaty of Westphalia in 1648 and in 1789 formed the first German Reich, was greatly simplified and the number of Imperial cities reduced from fifty-one to six: Augsburg and Nuremberg — both soon to be Bavarian — Frankfurt and the three Hanseatic towns of Lübeck, Hamburg and Bremen. The Ordinance of 25 February 1803 was the final assault on the Church, which had remained rich in the medieval conditions still existing in Germany. It

prepared the way for the now inevitable and not long delayed end of the Germanic Holy Roman Empire.

In Italy, Piedmont had been governed since the battle of Marengo by Jourdan, who maintained the fiction that he was simply the French Ambassador. When in June 1802 Charles Emmanuel IV abdicated, France held that the country no longer had a legitimate sovereign, and on that slim pretext annexed it, dividing it into six French Departments. The brother of the abdicated king, Victor Emmanuel, who refused to accept this territorial amputation, was not even recognised by the French Government as King of Sardinia. In Milan, Bonaparte, who had been ' elected ' president at Lyon, displayed the liveliest interest in ' his ' Italian Republic, which he organised in the French fashion. Vast public works were launched with an ardour rarely witnessed in Italy. The *Foro Bonaparte* was built and the completion of Milan Cathedral undertaken. Although the country undoubtedly benefited from the material progress made, the Milanese found the burden of paying for it little to their taste. In the middle of the peninsula the Papal States enjoyed relative peace and security, thanks to the Concordats which had been signed: the Concordat of Milan, under discussion since February 1802, was completed on 16 September 1803 and complemented the Concordat signed in Paris the year before. When its Duke died in October 1802 Parma was annexed to France. In Tuscany his son had been created ' King of Etruria ' with the title of Louis I. A degenerate, Louis reigned only long enough to turn over that citadel of Enlightened Despotism to clerical obscurantism and in 1803 died of ' conjugal over-exertion '. The Queen acted as Regent for the child Charles Louis, until their French protector chose to make other arrangements. The Court of Naples intrigued busily: there, too, Bourbons reigned, closely allied by marriage with the Habsburgs, though now the oldest son and the daughter simultaneously married the daughter and the oldest son of the Spanish Bourbons. These marriages began unhappily, as their exuberant mother-in-law the Queen of Naples — who at the time affected a keen admiration for the genius of the First Consul — confessed.

Italy had, in fact, passed more and more under French control, but the small Republic of Genoa — the Ligurian Republic — was still allowed by Bonaparte to remain independent of the Italian Republic to avoid the risk of a too rapid unification turning Italian public opinion against France. Bonaparte gave the Ligurian Republic a constitution modelled on that of Milan, with three electoral colleges — the *possidenti*, *dotti* and *commercianti* — appointing a Legislative Council and an executive Senate with thirty members, presided over by a Doge. These worthies, designated by Bonaparte himself, gratefully placed his statue in front of the national palace together with a statue of Christopher Columbus. A republic was even established at Lucca, complete with a Senate and, instead of a Doge, a Gonfalonier, who was the incarnation of docility.

Friction between Britain and France

Addressing the House of Commons, Sheridan quoted from Burke's scathing remark that where France had once been the map of Europe was a blank. Sheridan urged his listeners to look at that map now. Wherever the eye fell all was French. His words exactly summed up the impression which his compatriots had formed of the seemingly irresistible expansion of the Republic, in which they beheld a series of illegal encroachments and conquests made in the midst of peace. Still worse, Bonaparte, far from limiting his field of action to his continental neighbours, had shown interest in the entire globe and notably in the seas: in the Mediterranean — where Britain had been careful not to evacuate Malta — in the Atlantic and in the Pacific. Such a challenge to British naval supremacy was intolerable, and as Napoleon's ambitious designs became more obvious a renewal of the war became more likely.

In the Mediterranean, after the treaties with Tripoli, Algiers and Tunis, a treaty with Turkey was signed in Paris on 25 June 1802 which renewed the earlier Capitulations, agreements ensuring freedom of navigation for merchantmen of the Republic in the Black Sea. The treaty also granted the right to form French establishments on the shores of the Black Sea and even contained a reciprocal guarantee of the integrity of the other's possessions — not, however, without certain secret reservations. General Brune left France in October to become Ambassador in Constantinople. As the recent victor over Anglo-Russian forces which had landed in Holland he was especially fitted for a post in which he would have to compete with influential representatives of the British and Russian courts. Brune was extremely successful until the dramatic publication in Paris of the ' Sebastiani Report '. Sebastiani, a Corsican Colonel of Dragoons, who in 1801 had been entrusted with the mission of taking to Constantinople the preliminary draft of the treaty, which at that time Selim had not yet ratified, proved such a keen observer of the scene in Eastern Europe and the Levant that he was sent to the East again at the same time as Brune, though his destination was Cairo by way of Tripoli. The official subject of this second mission was to persuade General Stuart to evacuate Egypt, to inform the Egyptian Pashas of the Franco-Turkish peace treaty and to prepare the way for a renewal of friendly relations and trade with the Levantine ports. Sebastiani's journey, from which he returned by way of the Ionian island of Zante, supplied him with material for a detailed report on the military, political and economic situation in the Near East, in which he concluded that ' six thousand French troops would be sufficient to conquer Egypt ', and that the Ionian Islands, if asked, would instantly declare their allegiance to France. On 30 January 1803 this report was published in the official *Moniteur*. Its effect on British opinion may be imagined, and the first reaction of Addington's Cabinet was a decision, in view of the likelihood of war in the East, to retain Malta, with its superb harbour and fortifications, despite the terms of the Treaty of Amiens.

In the West Indies, when bitter strife had broken out between Creole colonists, half-castes and Negro slaves, the British had intervened and occupied Santo Domingo. The British had finally been driven out by the Negro liberator Toussaint Louverture, who brought the entire island under his own rule. Toussaint was vaguely recognised by the Directory, who awarded him the rank of general. In January 1802 Bonaparte sent an army to Santo Domingo under the command of General Leclerc, his brother-in-law. Leclerc captured Toussaint, who died shortly afterwards as a prisoner in Fort Joux. Influenced

A painting by David showing Napoleon crossing the Alps. Napoleon inspired a great deal of adulatory art, and this picture contains delicate references to Hannibal and Charlemagne scattered among the rocks at the horse's feet. *Giraudon*

by Josephine, who had herself been born in the West Indies, and her circle of Creole friends, Bonaparte then reintroduced slavery, which the Convention had abolished. Santo Domingo at once rose against the whites in a wave of violence. Yellow fever, too, decimated the Europeans. Leclerc died in November 1802 and his successor, Rochambeau, was forced to capitulate a year later. Haiti, thenceforward a Negro state, remained French in language only.

In North America Louisiana, ceded by Spain to France, offered a potentially rich colonial empire of immense area, since it then comprised the territory west of the Mississippi from Canada to the Gulf of Mexico, which embraced no fewer than thirteen of the present United States. It also held the key to the inland trade of the Mississippi basin, the rich city of New Orleans. In September 1802 General Victor was apppointed Captain-General of colonial Louisiana. The following April, however, Bonaparte decided to sell the Louisiana territory to the United States, his decision having been prompted by President Jefferson's discreet hint that the United States might otherwise take it by force. In any case Bonaparte was well aware that the inevitable renewal of war at sea would make such distant territory impossible to defend. 249

He looked to the other side of the world for a field which might offer a better chance for successful enterprise. In the East, French trading posts in India had, at least in theory, been restored by the Peace of Amiens, and to reoccupy them Bonaparte appointed Decaen, an extreme Anglophobe, as Captain-General. Secret instructions issued to General Decaen reveal that Napoleon entertained grandiose projects for the conquest of India. Decaen sailed for India, where Anglo-French relations were already so strained that he had no sooner arrived than he had to take refuge in Mauritius — then the Ile de France — where he was forced to remain until 1810. Some years previously, in May 1799, while Bonaparte was invading Syria, the Governor-General Lord Wellesley, older brother of the future Duke of Wellington, had besieged Tipoo Sahib in Seringapatam, his capital. Tipoo Sahib was killed when the town fell and the Empire of Mysore was liquidated. In 1801 followed the 'Second Mahratta War', when Wellesley, receiving reinforcements from British troops in Egypt, broke the power of those Indian princes who were supported by French mercenaries and imposed on the Grand Mogul at Delhi the protectorate of the East India Company, thus paving the way for the final conquest of India.

Bonaparte sent Admiral Baudin beyond Ceylon, which the British now occupied, and the Dutch colonies in the Indonesian archipelago to explore the islands of the South Pacific. In 1801 Baudin reached Australia — then New Holland, so called by the Dutch who first explored it — where the British, naming the east coast New South Wales, had installed a colony of convicts at Botany Bay. Baudin carefully surveyed a large stretch of the southern Australian coast — facing Tasmania — and called it Napoleon Land. The published account of his voyage revealed to Baudin's compatriots a map of a vast *terra incognita*, on which only long stretches of the coast were filled in and provided with place names. Only two of the names given in the French section survive today: those of Baudin's frigates, the *Géographe* and the *Naturaliste*.

The renewal of war

Mercantile circles in London had hoped that the peace treaty of Amiens would contain commercial clauses renewing the Eden Treaty of 1786 with France, which the delegates of the States General had denounced as 'ruinous'. Bonaparte knew French opinion on the subject and opposed the suggestion not only on grounds of French economic interest, but also because he had already acquired a taste for conquest and commercial imperialism. Meanwhile he was angered by the hospitality the Comte d'Artois and the Royalist *émigrés* received in Britain, to say nothing of the slanderous attacks of British pamphleteers and the crude caricatures of him which appeared in the London papers. The British Cabinet, already gravely concerned by Bonaparte's annexation of Belgium and Antwerp — a 'pistol aimed at the heart of England' — became alarmed by the continued growth of Napoleon's power on the continent, while the heated argument over Malta and Egypt added fuel to the fire. The French Ambassador in London was the 'jackbooted' diplomatist, General Andréossi, while in Paris the British Ambassador was that same Lord Whitworth who was widely thought to have been involved in the assassination of Paul I in

St Petersburg. Bonaparte's blustering comments on Whitworth's acrimonious demands went the rounds of Europe: 'The English want war; but if they are the first to draw the sword I shall be the last to sheathe it.' After a verbal ultimatum in April 1803 Bonaparte outlined his renewed plans for a continental blockade. 'We have', he told his Senate, 'acquired a sufficient length of coastline to render us redoubtable. We shall form a coastal system which is impenetrable, and in the end England will bewail with tears of blood the war she means to start.' His Coastal System was to grow until it became the Continental System.

On May 16 Great Britain opened hostilities by placing an embargo on French shipping, and an Admiralty order to seize all French vessels on the high seas, together with their crews and merchandise. Bonaparte replied six days later with an order putting an embargo on all British merchandise and, in reprisal for the seizure of French mariners at sea, he declared that all British subjects travelling or residing in France were prisoners of war. A month later he went to Boulogne to supervise in person preparations for an invasion of Britain which had begun before the truce of Amiens. An enormous number of troops were concentrated in great camps along the North Sea and the Channel coast. To transport them a vast flotilla was assembled, and the coast bristled with forts and batteries. Simultaneously orders were given to attack Hanover, and the Adriatic ports of Ancona, Brindisi and Otranto were occupied, possibly as bases for an attack on Malta or Egypt. Much of Europe was at Napoleon's disposal — Holland, Switzerland, Spain, Portugal — but the question remained: could he rely on the loyalty and total support of such unwilling allies? From June to December he strengthened his position by a series of treaties — with the result that Britain at once broke with those who signed them. The attitude of Prussia, however, remained strictly neutral, while in Austria and in Russia it was felt that the moment to take up arms again was fast approaching.

The establishment of the Empire

Before Pitt had formed the Third Coalition and the war was renewed in earnest, further attempts against the First Consul's life were made. The 'infernal machine' which the Royalists had exploded on Christmas Eve 1800 had failed in its object, but the Royalist plot of 1803 was more carefully prepared, and involved not only such fanatical Royalists as the Breton George Cadoudal but distinguished generals of the Republic like Moreau and Pichegru. Bonaparte himself had recognised Cadoudal's ability and tried without success to win his support. Cadoudal crossed to Britain where the *émigré* Comte d'Artois — Louis XVIII's brother — made him a Lieutenant-General. In August 1803, some three months after war had been declared, Cadoudal landed in Normandy and with the aid of agents who were party to the plot secretly reached Paris. He was liberally supplied with British money, and the object of the plot was to kidnap or assassinate Bonaparte. In Paris he made contact with Moreau and Pichegru with a view to setting up a triumvirate after Bonaparte's removal. But Bonaparte was well served by his police and *agents provocateurs*, and all three were arrested. Pichegru, who had once before betrayed the

A fanciful rendering of a plan for the simultaneous invasion of England by balloon, tunnel and barge. Napoleon's plans were less elaborate and depended upon a brief command of the Channel which he never achieved.

Republic, hanged himself in his cell; Cadoudal and his eleven obscure accomplices were guillotined. Eight others, condemned to death, were saved by Josephine's intervention, while Moreau's sentence of two years' imprisonment was commuted into banishment and he went to America.

From his retreat in Britain the Comte d'Artois had woven other plots, one of the most spectacular of which involved the British Minister in Munich, Drake, who had been manoeuvred by a certain ex-Jacobin *agent provocateur* into supplying sums of money to finance a coup d'état. Details of this plot furnished material for thundering denunciations which were published in the *Moniteur*. Drake and his colleagues in Stuttgart were dismissed from their posts, but they had already confided the Royalist plans

Napoleon had first declared that the invasion of Britain was possible in 1798 and Britain was alarmed by rumours of invasion plans, such as this raft, supposedly designed to transport French troops across the Channel. *British Museum*

Napoleon's dynastic ambitions were fulfilled in 1804 when he and his family were proclaimed hereditary rulers of France. The title of 'king', with its unfortunate associations, was rejected in favour of that of 'emperor'. *Mansell*

to the police spy, supplied details of *émigré* concentrations and information that seemed to connect conspirators in Paris with the expected arrival of a 'Bourbon Prince'. It so happened that a Bourbon prince, the Duc d'Enghien, the last Condé, was living in Baden, close to the French frontier. Bonaparte decided to kill him, and d'Enghien, an innocent young man who had no complicity in the plot, was kidnapped, carried off to Vincennes and at dawn on 21 March 1804 hurriedly and secretly shot. The conscience of the civilised world was shocked by this political crime, and monarchists like Chateaubriand expressed their indignation. But the Jacobins and the regicides welcomed it; the blood of a Bourbon ranged the First Consul clearly with them. In the army, the Senate and other chambers of Government, opinion had been so shaken by the possibility of Bonaparte's removal that a torrent of patriotic speeches ensued, congratulating him on having 'frustrated the schemes of the enemy'. The Civil Code, ironically, became law on the day of the execution.

The relief so widely felt assisted another constitutional change. In the Tribunate it was proposed in April to adopt the principle of heredity, and the idea spread. Only Carnot voted against it as he had voted against the Life-Consulship. On 18 May 1804 a *senatus consultum* 'entrusted the government of the Republic to a hereditary emperor, Napoleon Bonaparte' and to his direct descendants in the male line, in default of whom he was granted the right to adopt his brothers Joseph and Louis, whose heirs 251 would then inherit the imperial dignity. (Lucien and Jérôme, having quarrelled with Napoleon over their choice of wives, were not mentioned.) A plebiscite gave the change the overwhelming majority of three and a half million votes to two thousand five hundred. The plots to assassinate Napoleon were a reminder that, without hereditary succession, one life alone stood between France and anarchy. The new constitution also conferred on the Senate a fictional responsibility for the freedom of the press and the liberty of the individual. A new Imperial entourage had titles — Arch-Chancellors, Arch-Treasurer, High Constable, Grand Admiral — which recalled the days of Charlemagne and the Capetians. The highest honours were awarded to Napoleon's brother, to Murat, Cambacérès and Lebrun, Talleyrand, Berthier and to the most outstanding generals of the Revolution: Masséna, Augereau, Jourdan, Lannes, Lefebvre. The revised Constitution also altered the nature of the Legion of Honour, which by decree became an Order with a decoration like those of the Old Regime. A new hierarchical society was being established.

This return to monarchical ways, or rather this aping of monarchical appearances, far from displeased the courts of Europe. But the kidnapping and execution of the Duc d'Enghien had been sternly condemned by the Tsar of Russia. Napoleon retorted with a cutting allusion to the assassination of Alexander's own father, Paul I. Another monarch displayed his indignation by returning the ribbons of their Orders to all sovereigns who had not, like himself, protested. The youthful King of Sweden, Gustavus IV, though mentally unstable, had the wit to refer to the end of his life to the Emperor Napoleon as ' Monsieur Bonaparte '. (Gustavus was deposed in 1809 by his subjects who were by then weary of his eccentricities.) On the other hand, Dalberg, the Arch-Chancellor of the Holy Roman Empire and Archbishop-Elector of Ratisbon, was among the first to congratulate Napoleon on his new title. Coming from the President of the German Diet itself, this was tantamount to dropping once and for all the matter of the Duc d'Enghien's murder. The Batavian, the Italian and the Helvetic Republics hastened to express their approval of the new Emperor. As soon as the King of Spain heard the news he sent his official compliments. In Vienna, where the Chancellor Cobenzl was sufficiently naïve to interpret the event as a success for the counter-revolutionary cause, the creation of a French Empire seemed chiefly to pose questions of court etiquette. Did not a hereditary emperor, for example, take precedence over an elective emperor? The only solution of this knotty problem seemed to be to create for the Habsburgs an Imperial title which was also hereditary, and it was decided that Francis II, Emperor of Germany by election, was also by dynastic right Francis I, Emperor of Austria: a twin title which he bore until 1806 when the Holy Roman Empire ceased to exit. This matter having been satisfactorily settled, Francis could, on a basis of parity, recognise Napoleon as an emperor whom, in Cobenzl's phrase, ' one could only be honoured to have as a colleague '. Before similar recognition was won from Russia a new war had to be fought. The same was true in the case of Turkey, where Franco-Turkish negotiations were compromised in advance by agreement between the Tsar and the Sultan. Negotiations were, in fact, so sterile that Brune, the French Ambassador, withdrew in disgust.

Francis I, Emperor of Austria (1806–35) and previously the last Holy Roman Emperor. Alarmed by the revolutionary danger, he exercised an inefficient personal despotism, showing wisdom only in leaving foreign affairs to Metternich. *Marburg*

Napoleon took to the role of Emperor with great enthusiasm. The Pope agreed to a coronation in Paris and at the ceremony Napoleon took the crown from him and crowned himself to show his independence of the Church. *Giraudon*

THE WORLD AT THE TIME OF NAPOLEON I

The coronation at Notre Dame

Napoleon's Carolingian, Capetian and Bourbon predecessors had claimed supreme power by ' divine right ' sanctioned by the Church at their coronations. Napoleon was anxious to invest his dynasty with the same charismatic authority. He was both impressed by the practical value of myths over men's minds and himself susceptible to the memories of the Roman Empire, a tradition which the nomenclature and art of his regime were often to recall. The Pope, Pius VII, who hoped that further advantages might be gained from good relations with the new Empire, was persuaded to preside at the coronation. On 2 December 1804, in the cathedral of Notre Dame, the magnificent ceremony, vividly portrayed by the painter David, took place. Napoleon and Josephine, previously united only by civil ceremony, had on the preceding day

A sketch of café life under the Consulate. Such scenes of peace and plenty became increasingly rare as soldiers were called away to more desperate battles and the French economy was drained by the wars. *British Museum*

A cartoon of 1805, the year of Trafalgar and Austerlitz, when England and France divide the world, Pitt taking the ocean, and Napoleon carving off Europe. The cartoon is by Gillray. *Deutsche Fotothek Dresden*

been married according to the rites of the Church. Napoleon, when he had been anointed and had received the pontifical benediction, crowned his wife before the altar, having first taken and placed the two golden laurel wreaths on his own head. Napoleon's act of crowning himself was not, as was frequently averred, a spontaneous gesture of personal independence; it had been pre-arranged after long discussions on the ceremony, which also dispensed with a public Communion and other traditional features of French coronations. But its significance was widely grasped: a Pope, the head of Catholic Christendom, had journeyed from Rome to consecrate a self-made Emperor.

The Third Coalition

After the proclamation of the Empire the State Council in Milan also declared that the government of the Italian Republic was to be entrusted to an irremovable king and offered the crown to the Emperor of the French, with the stipulation that at Napoleon's death the crowns of Italy and France should be separated. In May Napoleon went to Milan and assumed the Iron Crown which Charlemagne had worn a thousand years previously. After appointing his stepson Eugène de Beauharnais Viceroy of Italy, he joined the Ligurian Republic to the Empire, dividing it into three French Departments. The Republic of Lucca was turned into a principality for his sister Elisa. Then Napoleon returned to Fontainebleau to prepare the invasion of Britain.

The expeditionary force concentrated around Boulogne had slowly grown until it now comprised seven army corps, 150,000 men. Two thousand craft had also been assembled; flat-bottomed boats, Dutch barges, pinnaces, gunboats. Napoleon was sure that he needed only twelve

Cossacks, the redoubtable Russian light cavalry. Although at first beaten in the field (Friedland, 1807) Russian military power was eventually decisive in defeating Napoleon and emerged from the wars dominant in Europe. *Larousse*

EUROPEAN ALLIANCES AGAINST FRANCE, 1797–1812

1797 TREATY OF CAMPO FORMIO—1st COALITION

Ireland (1796)
GREAT BRITAIN
Batavian Republic
RUSSIA
PRUSSIA
FRANCE
AUSTRIA
Savoy
PIEDMONT
Avignon Nice
Venetia
Cisalpine Republic
Ligurian Republic
Papal States
PORTUGAL
SPAIN (allied to France in 1796)
KINGDOM OF NAPLES
SARDINIA
Ionian Isles
Malta

1807 TREATY OF TILSIT—4th COALITION

SWEDEN
GREAT BRITAIN
Kingdom of Holland
Hanover
PRUSSIA
Duchy of Warsaw
RUSSIA
Duchy of Berg
Saxony
Kingdom of Westphalia
FRANCE
Helvetic Republic
Republic of Valais
Kingdom of Italy
Lucca
Ancona
OTTOMAN EMPIRE
PORTUGAL
SPAIN
Kingdom of Naples
Ionian Isles

1802 PEACE OF AMIENS—2nd COALITION

GREAT BRITAIN
Batavian Republic
RUSSIA
FRANCE
AUSTRIA
Helvetic Republic
Italian Republic
Piedmont
Ligurian Republic
Rep of Lucca
Parma
Kingdom of Etruria
OTTOMAN EMPIRE
PORTUGAL
Olivença (1801)
SPAIN
Elba
Roman Republic (1797-99)
Kingdom of Sardinia
Parthenopian Republic
Corfu
Egypt (1798-1800)
Kingdom of Sicily
Malta (to France 1798-1800)

1809 TREATY OF VIENNA—5th COALITION

GREAT BRITAIN
Oldenburg
Kingdom of Holland
Hanover
Mecklenburg
Duchy of Warsaw
RUSSIA
East Galicia
West Galicia
FRANCE
BAVARIA
AUSTRIA
Helvetic Republic
Republic of Valais
Salzburg
Illyrian Provinces
Kingdom of Italy
Lucca
PORTUGAL
SPAIN
Etruria
Papal States
Ragusa
Kingdom of Naples
Corfu

1805 PEACE OF PRESSBURG—3rd COALITION

GREAT BRITAIN
Batavian Republic
RUSSIA
Baden
BAVARIA
Wurtemberg
AUSTRIA
FRANCE
Republic of Valais
Tyrol
Kingdom of Italy
Venetia
Dalmatia
Lucca
PORTUGAL
SPAIN
Kingdom of Naples
Corfu

French territory
Satellite states
Allies
Confederation of the Rhine
Napoleonic influence
Allied powers (at the beginning of the Coalition)
Countries not engaged
League of Neutrality (1800-1801)
0 250 500 Miles

1812 SIXTH COALITION UNTIL THE SUMMER

SWEDEN
GREAT BRITAIN
Oldenburg
PRUSSIA
Duchy of Warsaw
RUSSIA
FRANCE
Helvetic Republic
Republic of Valais
AUSTRIA
Bessarabia
Lucca
Kingdom of Italy
PORTUGAL
SPAIN
Catalonia
Papal States
Kingdom of Naples

Nelson at Portsmouth before his last voyage. His destruction of the combined Franco-Spanish fleet at Trafalgar gave Great Britain a preponderance at sea which lasted until 1914 and was the basis of the *Pax Britannica* of the nineteenth century. *Mansell*

Napoleon on the field of Austerlitz, the battle (2 December 1805) which gave France the military hegemony of Europe. The Russian and Austrian armies were defeated, Austria made peace and Prussia hastily came to an agreement with France. *British Museum*

hours' mastery of the Channel; the operation would, in fact, have needed several days, and was impossible without previously defeating the British fleet. Napoleon tried to lure it away to the West Indies. He directed the Toulon fleet, under Villeneuve, to break out, join the Spanish fleet at Cadiz and then sail for the New World, luring Nelson to follow it. While the British fleet dispersed, Napoleon's own squadrons would concentrate. The plan depended on the supposed stupidity of British admirals, but they were, in fact, as superior at sea as Napoleon himself was on land. On 21 October 1805, when danger of invasion was already past and Napoleon himself was far away in Bavaria, Nelson caught Villeneuve outside Cadiz, and annihilated the combined fleets of France and Spain in the battle of Trafalgar. The victory left colonial Spain and France at the mercy of the British fleet, but it was dearly paid for. Nelson had fallen in action and Britain mourned the loss of her greatest admiral. French naval power was at an end: Napoleon's object now became in his own phrase, ' to conquer the sea by means of the land '; in other words, to vanquish Britain on the continent.

Britain had already made the first moves. In the spring of 1804 the fall of Addington's Cabinet brought William Pitt back to power. Pitt's ambition had been to be a peace minister, but all his years in office after 1793 were spent at war. He now began to forge yet another Coalition, the third of the six in which European resistance to France was organised between 1792 and 1815. Alexander, disgusted by the murder of d'Enghien, had already made a defensive treaty with Austria in anticipation of further French encroachments. On 3 December 1804 Britain and Sweden formed an alliance, on 11 April 1805 Britain and Russia. Britain promised to Alexander and Gustavus IV the financial backing needed for the campaigns they planned ' to restore to Europe the independence and happiness of which the inordinate ambition of the French Government had deprived her ' — in other words, to confine France to its 1792 boundaries and clear Germany, Holland, Belgium, Switzerland and Italy of French troops. Finally, on August 9, the Emperor Francis II decided to join the Coalition because of Napoleon's assumption of the Lombard crown.

Francis, believing that Napoleon was fully occupied at Boulogne with his preparations for the invasion of England, opened hostilities by invading Bavaria on 8 September 1805. Its sovereign, Maximilian Joseph, who belonged to a cadet branch of the House of Wittelsbach, and for twenty years held a colonel's commission from Louis XV and Louis XVI, had entered into a secret alliance with France. If, therefore, Napoleon marched to save Munich, picking up contingents from Baden and Würtemberg en route, he could ' free ' the Bavarian capital as the champion of ' German liberties '. When the French fleet had not appeared at Boulogne as arranged, Napoleon swiftly altered his plans and led the Grand Army with extraordinary rapidity to the Danube. On October 20 General Mack was forced to surrender at Ulm. In November Napoleon entered Vienna without opposition. The Tsar tried to persuade Frederick William to abandon his policy of neutrality, but failed. In spite of his annoyance at a frontier violation of his enclave of Ansbach, the King of Prussia still wavered but finally agreed to impose an armed mediation. When the armies of Russia and Austria finally joined — and on December 2, the anniversary of the

Pauline Bonaparte (1786–1825). In 1803 she married Prince Camillo Borghese and went with him to Rome. She soon returned to Paris however where her conduct caused her brother Napoleon some embarrassment. *Archiv für Kunst und Geschichte*

Joachim Murat, Napoleon's brother-in-law, was given the throne of Naples in 1808. Abandoning Napoleon before his fall, he was allowed to remain until he sacrificed his advantage by joining Napoleon during the Hundred Days.

coronation, decisively crushed by Napoleon at Austerlitz — Frederick William's envoy Haugwitz, instead of offering his services as a mediator and presenting an ultimatum in the event of such services being refused, hastily presented the King of Prussia's compliments to the victor. The Russians left their recent Austrian allies to conclude the Peace of Pressburg (December 26) by which Austria was compelled to yield the last of her Italian possessions — Venetia, Istria and Dalmatia — to the Napoleonic Kingdom of Italy. The Tyrol and Trentino were ceded to Bavaria,' which became a kingdom over which the Austrian Emperor renounced all rights. Würtemberg, also made a kingdom, received Austrian Swabia and Constance, while Baden was given Ortenau and Breisgau. In all, four million Austrian subjects changed their nationality.

Napoleonic Europe: the end of the Holy Roman Empire

William Pitt died on 23 January 1806. The inevitable break-up of the Coalition after Mack's capitulation at Ulm had been a grave blow to him, and the news of the disaster at Austerlitz proved fatal. Napoleon's reply to Trafalgar seemed to be decisive. Not only was Austria

Talleyrand, bishop of Autun, Foreign Minister to the Directory and Napoleon, engineer of the Bourbon restoration, ambassador to Great Britain for Louis-Philippe. He rendered both Europe and his country great services. *Mansell*

Q

257

broken, but the Coalition was in ruins. Napoleon was the uncontested master of Germany and Italy, which he could re-organise as he saw fit. Within six months he so refashioned the political map of Europe that it was unrecognisable. In May-June the Batavian Republic of Holland became a kingdom and Napoleon's brother Louis its king. The Kingdom of Italy was swelled by the acquisition of the Venetian states, while in the south the Kingdom of Naples changed hands. Ferdinand IV and Maria Carolina had been imprudent enough to join the Coalition, and on 27 December 1805 the lightning struck: the proclamation of Schönbrunn stated briefly: 'The dynasty of Naples has ceased to reign', and on March 30 Joseph Bonaparte received the crown. Though the fugitive Bourbons and their court took refuge in Sicily, shielded by the guns of the British fleet, and the dethroned sovereign of Piedmont was similarly secure in Sardinia, southern Italy was overrun and pacified by Masséna, in spite of popular resistance by the peasants and an outburst of banditry in Calabria. Since Pius VII wished to remain neutral, relations between him and Napoleon soon deteriorated. The French occupied the Papal ports. Meanwhile Napoleon's sister Pauline Borghese had become Princess of Guastalla, while Talleyrand and Bernadotte received the two former Neapolitan fiefs of the Papacy, Benevento and Pontecorvo. In Switzerland another of Napoleon's marshals, Berthier, was given the principality of Neuchâtel, which had been ceded by Prussia in the Treaty of Paris in February 1806 in exchange for Hanover.

But it was in Germany itself that the battle of Austerlitz produced the greatest changes. On his return from Austerlitz Napoleon had stopped in Munich for the solemn proclamation of Maximilian's promotion to royal rank. At the same time he had asked Maximilian for the hand of his oldest daughter for Eugène de Beauharnais, Napoleon's stepson and Viceroy of Italy. The Wittelsbachs were the oldest ruling family in Europe. Maximilian hesitated. Napoleon thereupon legally adopted his stepson on January 12, which made him, after Napoleon himself, the first personage in the Empire. Beauharnais was also designated as Napoleon's successor to the throne of Italy, whose separation from that of France in perpetuity at Napoleon's death had been confirmed by the Treaty of Pressburg. Maximilian no longer hesitated, and two days later Eugène married the Wittelsbach princess Augusta. When Napoleon's brother-in-law Murat complained that he was merely showing Europe how highly he valued what they all lacked — namely illustrious birth — Napoleon replied: 'This marriage which so displeases you I regard as a success equal to the victory of Austerlitz.' It was, in fact, his policy to knit together by matrimony a series of vassal states, to form as it were a family confederation of brothers and members by marriage of the Bonaparte clan to act as his vice-regents. Josephine's niece, Stéphanie de Beauharnais, whom Napoleon also adopted, married the heir to the Margrave of Baden; still later Jérôme, whose marriage to Elizabeth Patterson of Baltimore was annulled by Napoleon, married the daughter of the King of Würtemberg. In 1806 Murat, the husband of Caroline Bonaparte, was made Duke, then Grand Duke of Berg, which had previously been Bavarian territory in the Rhineland. The two new Kings — of Bavaria and Würtemberg — the new Grand Dukes of Baden, Berg and Hesse, plus other petty princes of southern and western Germany finally, on 12 July 1806, formed the Confederation of the Rhine with its capital at Frankfurt and Napoleon as its 'Protector', in charge of its foreign policy and of its armed forces. On 1 August 1806 at the Diet of Ratisbon the Confederation of the Rhine formally declared that it 'no longer recognised the existence of the Germanic Constitution', thus withdrawing from the Holy Roman Empire. Napoleon's envoy declared that France no longer recognised its existence. Five days later Francis II laid down his Imperial title and became simply Francis I of Austria. Thus, unregretted, the Holy Roman Empire passed into history, and the long drawn out German Middle Ages came to an end.

The Fourth Coalition

Britain continued the struggle against Bonaparte, under a 'Ministry of All the Talents'. It was led by Grenville and, with Grey at the Admiralty and Erskine as Lord Chancellor, it was predominantly Whig, though Tories like Sidmouth and Ellenborough were also members of it. Fox, who had been in opposition for twenty-three years, took charge of Foreign Affairs. His sympathetic attitude to the French Revolution was well known and his appointment raised hopes for the possibility of peace; but he died in September, and Lord Yarmouth, who was sent to Paris to negotiate, did little to advance the cause of peace. At this time the Turkish Government was fully occupied with a Serbian uprising led by Karageorge — 'Black George' — founder of the Karageorgevic Dynasty which later ruled Yugoslavia. Selim III, who was in the process of building a new regular Turkish army, was also in difficulties with the Janissaries. The Tsar Alexander seized the opportunity to sound the French Government about a possible partition of Turkish territory, but finally signed a treaty agreeing to respect the integrity of the Ottoman Empire. To Haugwitz, the Prussian Minister, Talleyrand suggested that to balance the French-dominated Confederation of the Rhine a similar North German Confederation could be formed under the leadership of Prussia, and hinted at the possibility of an imperial title for the Prussian king. But the French were unpopular at Berlin. Many Prussians felt that the declaration of war on Britain, to which they had been compelled by Napoleon after Austerlitz, and the occupation of Hanover were dishonourable. Around Queen Louisa a war party of patriotic young officers had gathered; under its influence the hesitant Frederick William III refused an alliance with Napoleon. When it was revealed that Napoleon, seeking peace with Britain, had secretly promised to return Hanover to George III, Frederick William reacted by allying himself with the Tsar and declaring war on France.

The Anglo-French peace negotiations were broken off and Alexander tore up his treaty with France. Napoleon replied with a lightning offensive, of which he was a master. One Prussian army was annihilated by Napoleon himself at Jena, while on the same day (14 October 1806) a second Prussian army was overwhelmed by Marshal Davout at Auerstädt. On October 27 Napoleon entered Berlin as a conqueror. Had Frederick William ratified the armistice signed at Charlottenburg the Fourth Coalition would have collapsed then and there, but he refused to do so. Napoleon did not wait for a peace treaty to settle the fate of conquered Germany. From Berlin he issued the decree of November 21 which initiated the

After the battles of Jena and Auerstädt the military prestige of Prussia was in ruins. She entered the war because of Napoleon's re-arrangement of Germany. The occupation of Berlin and a humiliating peace were the results. *British Museum*

French policy kept Turkey at war with Russia from 1806 to 1812. When a British squadron under Duckworth tried to intimidate the Ottoman government it was driven away with the loss of two ships, thanks to French advice and support.

The Corn Exchange, London 1808, by Pugin and Rowlandson. Although British trade suffered slightly, Europe was too disorganised for Napoleon's blockade of Britain to be successful. *Radio Times Hulton Picture Library*

Continental Blockade designed to bring Britain to her knees. He wrenched from Prussia all her provinces west of the Elbe and seized Brunswick, whose Duke had been mortally wounded at Auerstädt, as well as the domains of the Prince of Orange and the Prince of Hesse-Cassel, both generals in the Prussian army. The small state of Weimar, whose Duke had also commanded a division in the service of Frederick William, was spared in deference to the illustrious names of Goethe, Wieland and Schiller, who had died the previous year. Napoleon made an especial effort to conciliate Saxony. On the day after Jena he set free thousands of Saxon prisoners and sent them home, and in the Treaty of Posen of December 11 he created the Elector of Saxony one of the kings in the Confederation of the Rhine. In September the Confederation had also been joined by the Grand Duke of Würzburg, a brother of Francis II and one-time Archduke of Tuscany.

From Berlin Napoleon marched east, where Frederick William still held out behind the Vistula. Russian troops had joined the Prussians and the ensuing Polish campaign was fought in the mud and snow of a northern winter. A bloody and indecisive battle fought at Eylau on 8 February 1807 was a partial setback for Napoleon, although it was followed by the withdrawal of the Russians. During a leisurely winter idyll with Marie Walewska in the Castle of Finkenstein Napoleon found time to re-organise the Paris Opera, the museums, and the establishments of the Legion of Honour, to arrange loans to manufacturing concerns in financial difficulties and to attend to the street-lighting of Paris. He also concluded a Persian alliance with Riza Khan, in which he promised to send to the Shah of Persia military instructors, muskets and cannon. One of his aides-de-camp was ordered to go to Persia. Napoleon's wish was to form a Franco-Turco-Persian pact against the Russians on the one hand and against the British on the other. In Constantinople his new ambassador, General Sebastiani, had been successful in bringing about a rupture between Turkey and Russia. In March 1807 with improvised artillery Sebastiani helped to defend the Sultan and his capital from an attempted bombardment by Admiral Duckworth. Duckworth then withdrew to Egypt and landed an expeditionary force which seized Alexandria. Attacked by Mehemet Ali, the Albanian who had been Pasha since 1805, the force was cut to pieces and the great square of Cairo was hideously decorated with a thousand heads. The remaining British forces re-embarked and sailed away in September, having inadvertently introduced Mehemet Ali into European history.

In April the Tsar with difficulty revived the enthusiasm of Frederick William, whose possessions were by now reduced to little more than Königsberg. In May Danzig fell to the French after a siege directed by Marshal Lefebvre, who had begun his career as an infantry private and was now rewarded by the title Duke of Danzig. On June 3 the Russians, forestalling Napoleon, resumed the offensive. But on June 14 — the anniversary of Marengo — Napoleon overwhelmed Bennigsen at Friedland, a victory which proved as decisive as Austerlitz. At Tilsit Franco-Russian and Franco-Prussian treaties were signed. Alexander found Napoleon more conciliatory than he had expected. No territorial sacrifice was demanded of him and the Tsar bound himself — in the very likely event of Britain's refusing to accept Russian mediation — to join the

Continental Blockade and make war on British commerce. He also formally recognised the kingdoms of Napoleon's brothers and, in a secret article, gave up Cattaro and the Ionian Islands. On Frederick William, however, the victor imposed harsher terms. Prussia was dismembered and reduced to the four provinces of Brandenburg, Pomerania, Silesia and East Prussia; the touching entreaties of the lovely Queen Louisa were unable to save even Magdeburg, the capital of Prussian Saxony. From the spoils Napoleon created two new states: a Kingdom of Westphalia, where in the very heart of Germany he made the error of installing as King his youngest brother Jérôme — who spoke not a word of German; and a Duchy of Warsaw — a resurrection in miniature of Poland — which by another error of judgment, he gave to the King of Saxony.

The Continental Blockade

The battle of Jena had enabled Napoleon to extend his Continental System which, by denying British shipping access to ports, was his sole method of reducing the island to submission. Tilsit seemed to promise more: the unification of the entire continent against his persistent enemy. With Austria and Prussia at his feet, Russia his ally, and a Continental System which could be enforced, Britain could have no alternative but to sue for peace. Blockade had in the past been a British weapon against which neutral powers had periodically protested or struggled in vain. The League of Armed Neutrality of 1800 had been such an effort and more recently, in April 1806, the Americans had passed the Non-Importation Act forbidding certain British products from entering the United States. From a new British Order in Council, declaring that the coast from Brest to the Elbe was in a state of blockade, Napoleon borrowed the phraseology of this decree and declared that the British Isles were themselves in a state of blockade. No French fleet existed to enforce it but France and her allies were forbidden to trade with Great Britain, all European ports from the Vistula to the Adriatic were closed to British ships and neutral ships which had called at a British port were to be confiscated on reaching the continent. Any British subject discovered in territory occupied by France or her allies would be interned and all merchandise belonging to Britain or of British or British colonial origin would be seized and destroyed. On the day the decree was issued Napoleon ordered Talleyrand to make it instantly known to all his allies and to demand its immediate enforcement. Joseph, Louis and Eugène hastened to comply. The occupation of Germany enabled a vast quantity of British goods to be confiscated. Ruthless seizure of similar property in Etruria — Tuscany — and in the Papal domains was a prelude to the replacement of the Queen Regent by Elisa, and to a breach with the Pope, followed by his deportation and imprisonment. In Spain Godoy was acquiescent and in February 1807 consented to give his help in imposing Napoleon's System on neighbouring Portugal. In Constantinople Napoleon had less luck. In May 1807 Selim III was dethroned by the Janissaries and replaced by his cousin Mustafa IV who strangled him a year later, and was himself instantly overthrown by Mahmud II. The success of the Continental System depended on its being universally applied, and Turkey alone on the continent never agreed to co-operate.

Persia had adhered to the System in the treaty of 4 May 1807, and General Gardane had received orders to see that the terms of the treaty were respected while, at the same time, he prepared to invade India. The Shah of Persia, however, disliked Napoleon's new Russian alliance and gave a willing ear to the British Envoy-Extraordinary, who arrived bearing gifts of gold and caskets of pearls. In February 1809 Gardane was unceremoniously dismissed.

In the north of Europe the Tsar had undertaken to bring the Scandinavian countries into line. But in London an important change of Government had taken place. The Ministry of All the Talents had fallen over the question of equal political rights for Catholics, and in 1807 an anti-Catholic Government took office. Its authority was confirmed by elections in which the Whigs were damaged by the cry ' No Popery ' raised against them. The elderly Duke of Portland formed a Cabinet with Spencer Perceval as Chancellor of the Exchequer, Hawkesbury — soon to become Lord Liverpool — at the Home Office, and the ultra-conservative Lord Eldon as Lord Chancellor. The Minister for War was Castlereagh and the Minister for Foreign Affairs was Canning, who regarded himself as Pitt's successor. Canning acted swiftly and, bombarding neutral Copenhagen again, seized the Danish fleet in September 1807 before it could fall into enemy hands. This ruthless measure secured his country undisputed supremacy at sea, although, almost as soon as the British fleet sailed away, the Kingdom of Norway and Denmark joined the Continental System. On November 8 Alexander broke off relations with Great Britain. In February 1808 Austria had joined the System. Prussia followed suit in December. There remained only the King of Sweden, who received subsidies from Britain and was, in 1808, to lose Finland and, in 1809, his crown.

It is debatable whether the Continental Blockade could ever have been made to work. Even had he been wise enough to conciliate the diverse and conflicting interests of so many nations, it is unlikely that Napoleon could have welded Europe into an impregnable bloc. In the event, his System, with its ultra-protectionism of French industry and its one-sided commercial treaties, became a cloak for economic as well as for political imperialism. In spite of — or perhaps more accurately because of — the increasing severity of the decrees he issued, and the increasing violence with which he directly intervened to enforce them, Napoleon never succeeded in making Europe the hermetically sealed unit which alone could have made the experiment successful. Britain suffered, but the peoples of Europe suffered more. And in the meantime smuggling flourished.

Napoleon was very conscious that contraband could destroy his System and he raged against the slackness of his subordinates, threatening his brother Louis, for instance, with the confiscation of prohibited merchandise in his Kingdom of Holland. Not only Holland, but Germany, Italy and Spain were overflowing with smuggled goods. To supply the continent with the products of their manufacture the British established great depots off the mouth of the Elbe on the island of Heligoland and in Oldenburg after the Hanseatic towns became unavailable, in the Swedish port of Gothenburg, in Malta and Sicily. Turkey renewed her British alliance in January 1809 and British merchandise could then make the long detour of the Balkans or the Danube valley, and penetrate Europe from the

Ferdinand VII, briefly king of Spain in 1807, lived contentedly in France in exile until 1814 when he re-entered Spain and assumed the throne again. He succeeded in losing the Spanish American Empire and in identifying the monarchy with unrelenting reaction. *Anderson-Giraudon*

east. Napoleon's Berlin Decree of November 1806 was countered by Great Britain in the following November by the Orders in Council which extended the blockade to every country from which the British flag was excluded, but authorised neutral vessels to trade with such countries provided that they had first called at a British port and cleared the cargo by paying twenty-five per cent of its value. Napoleon replied to this by his Milan Decree in December, which declared that any vessel which had accepted these British conditions was lawful prize — with the exception of ships of ' those nations who were able to make the British respect their flags '. It was an obvious appeal to neutrals to fight back, and was aimed especially at the Americans who, since the Non-Importation Act, had become more and more incensed at the high-handed treatment their ships received from British men-of-war and privateers. In reply to both the Berlin Decree and the Orders in Council President Jefferson signed the Embargo Act of December 22, prohibiting all international trade with American ports and forbidding American ships to sail in the war area. The embargo was not successful. On 1 March 1809 Congress repealed the Act and replaced it with the Non-Intercourse Act, which authorised the resumption of trade with all nations except Great Britain and France. Smuggling nevertheless continued and, as Napoleon's measures to stop it became harsher, tension grew until in 1810 the Continental System needed total reconstruction.

Spain and the Peninsular War

In Spain the Queen's lover Godoy, expecting a Prussian victory, had mobilised the Spanish army before Jena, a foolish gesture which Napoleon was quick to note and which he avenged in his own fashion. Instead of the lightning blow expected, Spain was obliged on 27 October 1807 to undertake to assist Napoleon in Portugal, which was still open to British trade. It was agreed that after conquest by a joint expedition Portugal should be partitioned. A French army under General Junot entered Lisbon on November 30 to find that the Court had embarked for the Portuguese colony of Brazil. Napoleon had already proclaimed the deposition of the House of Braganza. Under the convenient pretext of the Portuguese campaign Napoleon then sent ' reinforcements ' pouring over the Pyrenees which, under Murat, seized the frontier strongholds and marched on Madrid. Indignation against the royal favourite who had opened the gates to the infidel foreigner swept the country. In the riots which broke out the universally loathed Godoy narrowly escaped with his life. The royal family, itself deeply divided, intrigued with the Emperor's lieutenant Murat, and during 1808 a dramatic series of events occurred in swift succession: the Aranjuez riots ended in the abdication of the wretched Charles IV in favour of his treacherous and cowardly son Ferdinand, Murat entered Madrid, refused to recognise the new King and Charles was ordered to withdraw his abdication. The whole royal family was then lured towards Bayonne, deluded by a report that Napoleon himself was coming to meet them. Finally on May 2 the unarmed people of Madrid spontaneously rose against the intruders and were mercilessly mowed down by French gunfire. The blood shed on the *dos de Mayo* immortalised in Goya's picture roused hatred in the Spanish people which would not be

261

satisfied until the last Frenchman had been killed or driven from Spanish soil. Meanwhile, the royal family remained in semi-captivity at Bayonne, Ferdinand being forced to restore the crown to his father Charles, who in turn was forced to present it to Napoleon. The ex-king and ex-queen were then packed off to Compiègne and later transferred to Marseille. Ferdinand passed the time more agreeably as Talleyrand's guest in the sumptuous *château* of Valençay until the wheel of fortune turned and he was restored to the throne of Spain as Ferdinand VII.

The Spanish resistance to Napoleon was unique. France found fewer sympathisers than in any other country. The immense majority knew nothing about the French Revolution or the rights of man, but clung to their Catholic religion and their traditions. A middle class was practically non-existent and the peasants followed a conservative nobility and a fanatical clergy. In the country of the *Reconquista* Catholicism was identified with patriotism. The response to an anti-Papal monarch furnished with a ' liberal constitution ' and backed by French bayonets was fierce. When Napoleon's brother Joseph accepted the Spanish crown (to the fury of Murat, who had to be satisfied with that of Naples resigned by Joseph), his new subjects rose against him. The Asturias, Galicia, Leon, Castile, Andalusia all revolted against the intruder, and everywhere the insurrectional *juntas* made contact with Britain. Eleven days after his solemn entry into his new capital King Joseph was forced to leave it. At the same time a French army under Dupont was encircled at Bailen and on 22 July 1808 surrendered nearly 20,000 prisoners, its guns and its Eagles. A month later on August 30 Arthur Wellesley, who had landed in Portugal with a British expeditionary corps, forced Junot to capitulate at Vimiero. It was the end of the legend that French arms were invincible.

Napoleon knew that it would be fatal to his prestige to leave such reverses unavenged. After his conference with the Tsar at Erfurt he felt that he could rely on Russian support in the event of a German uprising on the Spanish model. He therefore evacuated Prussia and marched to Spain to crush Iberian resistance and hurl the British back into the sea. Madrid was obliged to submit on December 4. There, in a series of imperial decrees, Napoleon at once suppressed two-thirds of the monasteries and convents, abolished the tribunal of the Inquisition and swept away all feudal privileges and internal customs barriers — reforms accomplished in France almost twenty years before. He dissolved the Council of Castile, imprisoned its members and confiscated their property. Then he advanced on the British, who were now commanded by Sir John Moore. Moore, threatened by the imminent concentration of superior French forces under Marshal Soult, retreated through the windswept mountains of Leon amidst glacial torrents of sleet and snow to embark his weary soldiers at Corunna where, on 16 January 1809, he died beating off Soult's final assault.

On the same day Napoleon hastily left Spain, leaving Joseph in nominal command of the French army. A courier from Paris had just revealed to him the gravity of the situation in Austria, and the disquieting intrigues of Talleyrand and Fouché. Saragossa was besieged by Lannes and after the desperate resistance of its starving Spanish garrison finally fell. Joseph, however, faced a British force under Arthur Wellesley at Talavera and was defeated. Wellesley, who had learnt his soldiering in India, became

262

On 2 May 1808 the people of Madrid rose against the occupying French forces and succeeded in expelling them briefly. Goya painted one of his greatest canvases to commemorate the rising, which began the War of Independence. *Mansell*

Administration under the Old Regime. A detail from a picture by Goya of the Junta (or Council) of the Philippines which administered Spain's oriental territories. *Giraudon*

Sir Thomas Lawrence's portrait of the Duke of Wellington, commander of the British forces in Spain and Portugal 1809–14 and of the allied army at Waterloo, his only encounter in battle with Napoleon. *Victoria & Albert Museum*

Lord Wellington after the victory of Talavera. The presence of a British force and the supply of arms and money also helped to keep the guerrilla war of the Spaniards alive. Napoleon had underestimated its importance. The Spaniards' discipline was ragged and their morale uncertain, but they were masters of guerrilla warfare. Wherever the French appeared, ambush and massacre lurked; as often as Spanish forces were dispersed they re-formed, elusive, dangerous and persistent. Neither did Napoleon, giving his orders from afar, reckon on the jealousies between his own commanders. Above all, Napoleon made the mistake of neglecting the effects of the tenacious presence of Wellington's army and the alliance of the Seville-Cadiz *junta* with the Cabinet in London. The danger should at all costs have been met before he embarked on a further and even more fatal adventure.

The Fifth Coalition

The conference at Erfurt in September and October 1808 not only gave Napoleon a chance to dazzle the Tsar, but also offered Talleyrand an opportunity. In August the year before Talleyrand had been replaced as Foreign Minister and had been given the nominal dignity of Vice-Grand-Elector of the Empire—the sole vice, it was feebly remarked, which he had lacked. Napoleon brought him to Erfurt as an expert adviser. There he thwarted Napoleon's plans to secure the Tsar's support in the north by persuading Alexander to become the defender of the old system of European equilibrium. The 'natural frontiers' — the Rhine, the Alps and the Pyrenees — Talleyrand pointed out, were conquests of France. Further conquests were simply those of the Emperor, and France would not insist on them. He confided the upshot of his secret negotiations with Alexander to Metternich, who had been Austrian Ambassador in Paris since August 1806. 'Alexander', he summed up briefly, 'can no longer be inveigled into attacking you .'

Metternich's chief, Count Stadion — who had succeeded Cobenzl in December 1805 — was head of the anti-French party and had already approached Britain with a request for subsidies. In touch with the new German secret society, the *Tugendbund*, or League of Virtue, Stadion negotiated an alliance with Prussia, from which French occupying troops had been withdrawn. Prussia had profited by the terrible lesson of Jena and Frederick William realised that reforms were needed. Hardenberg, who was regarded as being friendly to Great Britain, had been dismissed at Napoleon's command; the task of reform was therefore given to the liberal Baron von Stein. He began the abolition of serfdom and the replacement of a feudal by a modern society, permitting ordinary citizens to hold commissions in the army and the nobles to engage in trade. Stein, though no democrat, hoped to identify the citizen more closely with the State and pointed out the importance of a vigorous public opinion in Britain. Napoleon had Stein banished. But the Austrian Foreign Minister counted on an uprising against the French not only in the north of Germany but in the south, where the sovereigns of the Rhine Confederation had the support of popular sentiment, especially in Saxony, Franconia and Swabia. Above all, the Tyrol, a country of peasant mountaineers, Catholic and pro-Habsburg, which had been annexed by anti-clerical Bavaria and was centrally ruled by Maximilian I

The atrocities of partisan warfare in the age of national struggles was first revealed in the Spanish War of Independence. A widespread guerilla movement preyed on French communications and gave Wellington information. Here Goya depicts the French reaction and the mounting tide of reprisal and counter-reprisal which was the consequence.

Prince Metternich (1773–1859), Chancellor of Austria and opponent of France and the revolutionary danger. He once wrote of himself: 'error has never approached my mind'. 1848 took him by surprise and the Austrian court did not try to support its servant against the demand for his removal. *Mansell*

and his minister, Monteglas, was ripe for revolt. Stadion's negotiations with London, however, were long delayed and it was not until 24 April 1809 that Canning concluded the secret Treaty of London which promised Austria only a part of the aid she had hoped for.

Napoleon had suspected nothing of the double Austro-Russian game Talleyrand was playing. The courier whose arrival had caused Napoleon to leave Spain so hurriedly had opened his eyes. He reached Paris on 28 January 1809 and castigated Talleyrand's diplomatic indiscretion in a flood of invective. On the following day Talleyrand allowed his name to be inscribed on the secret list of those who received funds from Vienna. His first act was to warn the Austrians on February 1 that Marshal Oudinot was about to march. The Emperor Francis I did what he could to hasten negotiations for the British subsidy. But time was wasted in changing plans of operation before the Archduke Charles, instead of driving north to rally the northern German states to the Austrian cause, invaded Bavaria. The Austrian army that entered Bavaria was far better trained and led than the armies Napoleon had defeated at Marengo and Austerlitz, and a new note was sounded when it appealed to 'the German Nation' and declared that it fought to restore 'the independence and national honour of Germany'.

Napoleon had in confidence already warned each of the princes of the Rhine Confederation of the imminent outbreak of hostilities. Since 1806 the Confederation had grown and it now occupied the entire western half of Germany to the right of the Rhine, from Denmark and Holland to Italy. Westphalia had been given a constitution with a piece of advice to Napoleon's brother, its king: 'You must see that your subjects enjoy a liberty, equality and happiness previously unknown to the peoples of Germany.' The experiment of grafting French institutions on this German stock included the suppression of privileges, the introduction of Departments, Prefects, Mayors, the *Code Napoléon*, religious equality — and military conscription. Six months later Bavaria adopted a very similar constitution. Other less important members of the Confederation followed the Bavarian example. The Bavarians received the brunt of the Austrian attack and furnished the French divisions which had been rushed to strike first at the Austrian menace; if this could be met, the rest of Germany presented no danger. A lightning campaign of less than a week swept back the Archduke Charles's army. Napoleon showed that his brilliance as a commander was undiminished in such battles as Thann, Abensberg, Landshut and Eckmühl — of which Marshal Davout was created Prince.

Vienna was promptly taken, but the Battle of Aspen Essling on May 22 stopped the French succession of victories; it was inconclusive and the French failed to cross the Danube. Napoleon made more elaborate preparations and six weeks later successfully transported his immense force to the north bank of the Danube where at Wagram the Austrian army waited. There were other indications that the Spanish infection had spread. In Prussia there were sporadic uprisings, such as that led by the Duke of Brunswick-Oels and his Black Brunswickers or the Prussian Major Schill, which came to nothing. Similarly in July the British landing at Walcheren in an attempt to seize Antwerp and the Scheldt failed, and in December ended with the death of thousands of British soldiers

Napoleon's meeting with Alexander and Frederick William III and Queen Louise of Prussia at Tilsit in 1807. The Tilsit treaties marked his complete domination of the Continent but his enemies rallied once more and he next turned for security to a diplomatic marriage. *Archiv für Kunst und Geschichte*

Political propaganda and psychological warfare in the Napoleonic era. A British cartoonist depicts Napoleon under attack from all sides in 1808. The Emperor maintained his position for another six years. *Mansell*

from fever. The revolt of the Tyrol against Napoleon's Bavarian allies was much more serious, and was prolonged until after the end of the war when its innkeeper hero, Andreas Hofer, was shot because his amnesty arrived too late. By then, on July 6, the hard-fought and decisive battle of Wagram brought victory to the French, though the Austrians retired in good order. Peace was made at Vienna on October 14. By its terms Austria was compelled to pay a large indemnity and reduce the size of her army. Salzburg and the region of the Inn were ceded to Bavaria, western Galicia went to the Grand Duchy of Warsaw, while 400,000 inhabitants of eastern Galicia became subjects of the Tsar. Finally France took the Illyrian provinces — Trieste, Fiume, Carniola and parts of Carinthia and Croatia. Napoleon's Empire — with the Kingdom of Italy — now stretched unbroken to the Turkish borders, and Austria was cut off from the sea.

The Austrian marriage

Napoleon now again gave thought to the vexatious problem of a successor. To have no direct heir was not only disappointing but added to the insecurity of his position. Josephine had borne him no children, but that that was not his fault other women had demonstrated — Marie Walewska, for instance, by whom he had had a son. He decided to divorce Josephine and marry someone who could perpetuate his line. Josephine was persuaded to resign herself to the Emperor's will, and the Senate decreed the divorce. The Pope at the time was Napoleon's prisoner at Savona, and it was the officiating Archbishop of Paris who declared null and void the religious ceremony which had united Josephine and Napoleon the day before the coronation in Notre Dame. The victim of this arrangement retained her rank and title of Empress, received a settlement of three millions and the domain of Malmaison, to which she retired until her death five years later.

The project of a Russian marriage had been in the air since Erfurt, but St Petersburg vetoed the idea, stressing the tender age and Orthodox faith of the Tsar's sister. Napoleon's own advisers, moreover, deliberating this grave question in February 1810 at a special session of the Council, were in favour of the Austrian marriage offered by Metternich, who officially replaced Count Stadion as Foreign Minister in October 1809. The marriage contract was a copy of the contract between Marie Antoinette and Louis XVI nearly forty years before. The moment it was signed Marshal Berthier, Prince of Neuchâtel — who tactfully refrained from employing his new title of Prince of Wagram — departed for Vienna where he officially asked for the hand of the Emperor's daughter. The Archduchess Marie Louise was eighteen; she was all that Francis could offer to gain the security he needed in order to recover from his recent disasters. On March 11 the union was blessed — by proxy — with much pomp and ceremony. Napoleon, who was waiting impatiently at Compiègne, rode leagues to meet his young Viennese bride. On April 1 the Arch-Chancellor performed the civil marriage at St Cloud, and on the following day the religious ceremony took place — as in 1804 — with dazzling splendour. Napoleon's hopes were fulfilled and, on 20 March 1811, Marie Louise bore him a son, who, in his cradle, was proclaimed 'King of Rome'. None the less, Napoleon was later to complain that this marriage was the greatest mistake of his life; it embroiled him irreparably with Russia and he had overestimated the support which his father-in-law could give him. For the German world it constituted a reversal of previous alliances which led inevitably to rancour and irritations that culminated three years later in the defection of members of the Rhine Confederation. Above all, it led to the break with Bavaria, whose friendship had been the keystone of Napoleon's German policy.

The 'Grand Empire'

But in the spring of 1810 the French Empire was at the zenith of its power. Napoleon had reached his forties and, absorbed in conjugal life, was putting on weight. Though his energy was as inexhaustible as ever his imagination had developed to the point of ignoring reality. Since 1806, the Republican calendar had been abandoned; the words 'French Republic' had disappeared from coins in 1808, the year when the Imperial nobility had been inaugurated. Although founded on personal merit or on service to the State and accessible to all, the Imperial nobility was hereditary; the right of the oldest son to inherit his father's title was inalienable. Napoleon's ministers, senators like the regicides Sieyès and Grégoire, prefects, important magistrates, bishops, to say nothing of the soldiers, were made dukes, counts, barons or chevaliers. To accompany these titles, ' fiefs ' — or rather place-names implying no territorial rights — were created on paper from the Italian annexations of 1806. Thus Cambacérès and Lebrun became the Dukes of Parma and Piacenza, Maret of Bassano, Caulaincourt of Vicenza, Savary of Rovigo, and so on. Later, titles were derived from victories, the first of these being Danzig, of which Lefebvre was created Duke. Masséna, already Duke of Rivoli, became Prince of Essling; Ney, Duke of Elchingen, became Prince of the Moskva, while Augereau was made Duke of Castiglione, Kellerman Duke of Valmy, and so forth. All this was accompanied by a revival of court life and the reappearance of some pre-Revolutionary names among the highest functionaries of the Empire.

Other institutions also made their appearance. In 1808 the Imperial University, a non-clerical State monopoly, was organised. In 1810 the State prisons were re-established. A department to control printing and publishing was created and, in order to assure a proper ' public spirit ', assigned to a general. The number of newspapers was reduced — to one for each Department and four for Paris. Finally, after the wholly admirable Civil Code and the Codes of Civil Procedure, of Criminal Procedure and of Commercial Law, a Penal Code was promulgated which revived the savage punishments of branding and the *carcan*, or iron collar. It was enforced by a formidable police, both official and secret.

This social and political development set up two currents of disaffection which broadened as the Emperor's power became more absolute. The aristocracy, again influential, as well as a large part of the popular masses, had been profoundly relieved by the revival of Catholicism which followed the Concordat, and had been further encouraged by the Imperial Catechism of 1806. They were increasingly disturbed, however, by the Emperor's unfortunate Italian policy and the breach with the Vatican which it entailed. In 1809 Napoleon imprisoned the Pope, who thenceforth refused canonical investiture to the bishops he appointed. Rome itself was annexed and proclaimed the ' second city of the Empire '. The bull of excommunication which Pius VII issued in June 1809, though it did not expressly name the ' Usurper ', was spread abroad by priests and by the monks who had reappeared, especially the Jesuits, calling themselves ' Fathers of the Faith '. Their efforts to undermine the Emperor's authority were supported by a curious freemasonry of clerico-Royalists called the Chevaliers of the Faith which was founded by a man whose father, the Intendant of Paris, had been slaughtered by the mob after the storming of the Bastille. This did not come to much. More significant was the fact that the middle classes — when they did not, like a few intellectuals such as Benjamin Constant and Royer-Collard, oppose the Emperor on ideological grounds — were dissatisfied with a war which interfered with business and chafed under the financial and economic upheavals brought about by the Continental System.

Intellectual trends

The enormous scale of public and political events since 1789 long obscured the interesting and vital evolution which was taking place in the intellectual world at the turn of the century. The revolution had brought new circulation to the works of eighteenth-century philosophy. Among those who built on the Enlightenment tradition in France, the most important were the so-called *Idéologues*. They maintained an anti-clerical rationalist link between the revolutionary Assemblies and the *salons* which reappeared under the Directory and the Consulate. This was bound to make them suspect to Napoleon. Prominent among them had been Destutt de Tracy, the disciple of Condillac, and the materialist physician Cabanis. Their influence was important in the Institute, especially in its moral and political sciences section, abolished in 1803. They were carefully excluded from the educational institutions of the Empire. Although mixed up in the opposition of *salons*, they never represented a danger to the regime, but they kept alive in Imperial France the philosophic and liberal traditions of the eighteenth century.

This was important during the religious revival which the Concordat made possible. An intellectual counter-revolutionary offensive was led by the ultra-conservative Vicomte de Bonald, who published his *Primitive Legislation* in 1802 and by the Abbé Lamennais, whose *Reflections on the State of the Church*, expressing horror at the overthrow of religion, was published anonymously in 1808. Joseph de Maistre from St Petersburg denounced the Revolution as the work of Satan in his *Principe Générateur des Constitutions Politiques*. Between these two poles of thought — materialist and idealist — Maine de Biran (1766–1824) was evolving a shallow spiritualism which anticipated Victor Cousin's eclecticism.

There was no one in France of the stature of Kant, who died in 1804 as German philosophy was entering its golden age. Fichte (1762–1814) in the works that he published between 1794 and 1798 (*The System of Moral Philosophy*, etc.) arrived at an idealism so attenuated that it denied all ultimate reality except the Ego. After the disaster of Jena in 1806 Fichte, a loyal Prussian, gave his *Addresses to the German Nation* of 1807–8 which did much to rouse German resistance to Napoleon. His immediate successor was

A mounted cavalry officer, painted by Géricault. This swash-buckling picture is typical of a vigorous yet romantic nine-teenth-century style which was quite different from the realism of Géricault's great contemporary Goya. *Mansell*

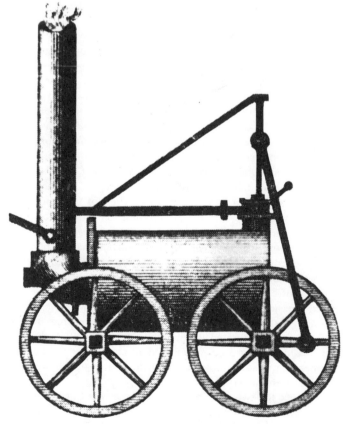

Neither the steam-engine nor the railway were nineteenth-century inventions but they were both brought together for the first time in 1804. Richard Trevithick (1771–1833) then produced the first locomotive. *Mansell*

Schelling (1775–1854) who, though less important as a philosopher, confirmed the predominant trend to subject-ivism. In his *Transcendental Idealism* (1800), his *Philosophy and Religion* (1804) and his *Essence of Human Liberty* (1809) he displayed perhaps more artistic and poetic imagination in his juggling with categories than intellectual rigour; he was important in the history of German romanticism. The greatest figure in the movement in German philosophy, which began with Kant, was Hegel (1770–1831). Hegel taught philosophy at Jena and, in fact, finished his *Phenomenology of Mind* to the sound of cannonfire. Though in later life he became a patriotic Prussian and a loyal servant of the State, he was a fervent admirer of Napoleon at the time of the battle of Jena. From an early interest in mysticism Hegel retained a conviction that separate finite objects were an illusion: the comprehension of ultimate reality could only be sought in the totality. His rare metaphysical insight and broad intellectual interests embraced most branches of human knowledge — logic, law, the philosophy of history, aes-thetics, religion — and the influence of Hegelianism has been immense not only in Germany but universally. His *Philosophy of History* was the basis of Karl Marx's dialectical materialism, while his idealisation of the State was distorted later to serve as an element in the ideology of fascism.

The study of society in non-philosophical terms was still largely a matter of economics. In his *Treatise on Political Economy* of 1803 Jean-Baptiste Say reaffirmed the doctrine of liberalism which Adam Smith had in 1776 laid down in the *Wealth of Nations*. But the optimism of this school of political economy had already been assailed and shaken: in England in 1798 Malthus had anon-ymously published his famous *Essay on the Principle of Population and its Effects on the Future Improvement of Society*. It appeared to indicate that misery inescapably awaited the human race if its population grew unchecked. The influence of David Ricardo, the son of a Dutch Jew, was perhaps greater than that of any economist since Adam Smith. The Ricardian law of rent, the iron law of wages, and the labour theory of value, were his chief contributions to the science, which he made look as dismal as Malthus had made demography. Sismondi, the Swiss historian and economist, also opposed the theory that in order to permit the free play of supply and demand social injustice must be tolerated, and asserted the necessity of State intervention. Count Henri de Saint-Simon (1760–1825), who had served with the French army in America and returned to support the Revolution, taught that the industrial revolution produced profounder effects than mere changes of government. Society should be so organised that even the poorest classes might enjoy its benefits. In the books he published between 1803 and 1814 he expressed ideas which anticipated the 'socialism' of a later generation. The *laissez-faire* economy was in fact giving birth to its own critics. One of them, Robert Owen, made the first efforts to run co-operative industrial enterprises.

Science, literature and the arts

The physical sciences also built on eighteenth-century foundations. In the footsteps of Lavoisier other French chemists like Gay-Lussac and Berthollet, Sir Humphry

Davy in Britain and the Swede Berzelius discovered a series of chemical elements — sodium, potassium, boron, silicon, iodine, etc. — and laid down the fundamental laws of their science. From his researches into the constitution of mixed gases John Dalton (1766–1844) developed the atomic theory in 1803 to explain the facts of chemical combination. An important contribution to the theory was made in 1811 by the Italian physicist Count Amedeo Avogadro in his hypothesis that equal volumes of gases at the same temperature and pressure contain equal numbers of molecules. André-Marie Ampère's great work was in electro-dynamics and he gave his name to the unit by which an electric current is measured. Galvani, who was professor of anatomy at Bologna, studied the relation of animal muscle to electricity and the words galvanism and galvanometer are derived from his name. He died in 1798 and his compatriot, Alessandro Volta, found the true explanation of the 'galvanic' effect when he invented the Voltaic cell — or the electric battery. The volt — or unit of electro-motive force — is named after him. Though Galvani refused in 1797 to take an oath to the new Cisalpine Republic and was deprived of his chair at the university, Volta was honoured by Napoleon, who made him a Count and a Senator. In a similar fashion he rewarded the mathematician and astronomer Laplace, the naturalist Lacépède, the mathematicians Lagrange and Monge, Cuvier, Berthollet and many others. The great naturalist Lamarck in his *Philosophie Zoologique*, published in 1809, in many ways anticipated the theory of evolution. The astronomers Delambre and Méchain succeeded in measuring the arc of the meridian — between Barcelona and Dunkirk — and their work was continued by the young Arago. In Germany at the University of Göttingen the mathematician Karl Friedrich Gauss (1777–1855) propounded the first mathematical theory of electricity and used to say that he 'knew how to calculate before he knew how to talk'. Britain also produced the physician and physicist Thomas Young (the first man to translate the inscription on the Rosetta Stone); Benjamin Rumford, whose remarkable career included becoming a Count of the Holy Roman Empire, founding the Rumford medals of the Royal Society, the Rumford professorship of physics at Harvard, and marrying the widow of Lavoisier; and Sir William Herschel, who as a youth was an oboe-player in the band of the Hanoverian Guards and later did pioneer work in the study of the heavens, among his discoveries being the planet Uranus.

In France the Empire separated two literary eras. Classicism expired in a final burst of activity with certain minor poets who prolonged it in tedious tragedies, interminable poems, or lyrics whose chief recommendation was their brevity. Delille's death in 1813 was mourned as a national loss; he now remains unread. In Germany Wieland, the author of *Oberon*, died in the same year, while Johann Wolfgang von Goethe (1749–1832) continued at the court of Weimar his Olympian existence as the acknowledged literary and intellectual giant of his day, basking in the friendship of the Duke and Duchess. He was at the zenith of his creative power and in 1808 published Part One of his masterpiece *Faust*, which with Part Two occupied him in the intervals of other work — he was Privy Councillor and President of the Chamber of Finance, a botanist, anatomist and mathematician of no mean quality, as well as the author of innumerable literary works — for nearly

fifty years. Napoleon admired Goethe as well as Wieland, and conferred on both the insignia of the Legion of Honour.

Both in Germany and in Britain the romantic movement was already in full swing. In the following generation, disseminated by the wars and the return of the *émigrés*, it would have a decisive influence in France too. Goethe's close friend at Weimar, Schiller, whose dramas *Don Carlos*, *Wallenstein* and *William Tell* were highly admired, died prematurely in 1805. But in 1801 he had already described his *Maid of Orleans* as a 'romantic tragedy'. Two years before this the young Berlin poet Tieck had entitled his first collection *Romantic Poems*. In origin the word 'romantic' merely indicated the historical character of the work, or that the subject matter was drawn from the 'Romances' of a past age. The two Schlegel brothers, August Wilhelm — whose most famous achievement was his translation of Shakespeare — and Friedrich, shared the critical leadership of literary romanticism and might be called the founders of the movement. They attacked the 'three unities' of the classical theatre and its Graeco-Latin inspiration. The theatre, they urged, should recapture the liberty of scene, time and action it had enjoyed with Shakespeare and Calderon. Authors should seek material in the Middle Ages, from the Minnesingers; love, religion, chivalry. The marvellous and even the macabre should be cultivated: fairies, elves, demons. Authors of this school included Novalis, Chamisso and Hoffmann. Ludwig von Arnim and his friend Clemens von Brentano collected old popular legends and songs while travelling through Germany which they published in three volumes entitled *Des Knaben Wunderhorn*. Heinrich von Kleist, perhaps the most talented of the school, wrote the drama *The Prince of Homburg*, patriotic lyrics, the tale *Michael Kohlhaas* and carried 'romanticism' so far that with his fiancée he committed suicide at the age of thirty-five.

The most important single event in the history of English literature in this period was the publication in 1798 of the *Lyrical Ballads* of Wordsworth and Coleridge. In these poems the incident and speech of everyday life were given a new place in poetry; the lives of ordinary people were used as a source of moral insight, and simple countrymen were given a heroic dignity. In Wordsworth's nature poems, too, there also survived something of the eighteenth-century cult of the sublime; in the *Rime of the Ancient Mariner* Coleridge began the poetry of the subconscious. A shallower mysteriousness was exploited by writers of 'Gothic' horror novels, like Ann Radcliffe, whose creaking plots and preposterous settings were guyed in *Northanger Abbey*, one of the novels of Jane Austen. Jane Austen's half-dozen masterpieces (of which *Pride and Prejudice* and *Emma* are the best known) cannot be forced into any conceivable category of 'romantic' literature. She became less celebrated abroad than Scott, later, for his Waverley Novels, and above all Byron, whose *Childe Harold* appeared in 1810. The one celebrated history, the other individualism: both could therefore be assimilated in some way to the continental romantic movement. Their greatest triumphs, however, were to come after 1815.

In France the two chief exponents of the new European literary movement were an *émigré* recently returned from England — the Vicomte de Chateaubriand — and the cosmopolitan daughter of the Genevan banker, Necker, and wife of the Swedish Ambassador, Madame de Staël. Chateaubriand had been an *émigré* in London until 1800,

In 1809 Finland, until then Swedish, passed to Russia by the treaty of Friedrichsham. In this painting Alexander I is shown receiving the homage of the Finnish Estates. Finland obtained its independence only in 1917. *Larousse*

earning a livelihood by giving French lessons. In 1802 his masterpiece *Le Génie du Christianisme* appeared and three years later *René*, the first romantic expression of the *mal du siècle*, disenchanted melancholy. In them he revealed himself to be one of the great masters of French prose. He resigned from the diplomatic corps after the execution of the Duc d'Enghien and further offended Napoleon by refusing in his inaugural address to the French Academy in 1811 to soften the political criticism of his predecessor, Marie-Joseph Chénier. Germaine Necker, Baronne de Staël-Holstein by marriage in 1786, travelled widely in Switzerland, England, Germany and Italy. She quarrelled with Napoleon and was exiled in 1803. In Weimar she visited Schiller and Goethe, and in Berlin August Schlegel. Her most famous book *De l'Allemagne* — a romantic evocation of an ideal Germany — had political implications which led to its being confiscated in France, but it re-appeared in London, where in intellectual circles Madame de Staël was warmly welcomed.

The Emperor was unfortunate in the two outstanding literary figures of his reign; his painters served him better. David, whose fame had been made in 1785 with his rousing canvas *The Oath of the Horatii*, was in 1804 appointed court painter by Napoleon and made a Commander of the Legion of Honour. The choice was justified by the propaganda value of such vast classical canvases as the *Coronation of Napoleon* and the *Distribution of the Eagles*. He also painted powerfully realistic portraits of, for instance, Pius VII and Napoleon himself. David's two best pupils, Gérard and Gros, approached him in excellence: Gérard in his portraits of Madame Récamier and the King of Rome, and in vast compositions like *Austerlitz*; Gros, a master of the dramatic and picturesque, in

Bonaparte at the Bridge of Arcole, *Napoleon visiting the plague-stricken at Jaffa*, *The Battle of Eylau* and so forth. Dramatic though many of these were, more of the vigour of nineteenth-century romantic painting can be seen in the work of such as the young Géricault, in his *Mounted Cavalry Officer*. In Italy the classical tradition continued in the painting of Appiani and the sculpture of Canova. But by far the greatest painter of the day was the unclassifiable Spaniard Goya (1746–1828) whose portraits of the Spanish royal family were unsparing in their profound insight into human frailty. The penetrating satire of his caricatures, the poignancy with which he depicted the uprising and suppression of May 1803, and the bitterness with which he castigated the *Disasters of War* are unforgettable. Great Britain, cut off from the continent, continued to add to its aristocratic portrait gallery with the polished and graceful canvases of Raeburn and Lawrence and saw the first of the great landscapes of the master of that genre, John Constable.

The so-called 'Empire Style' was the final development of a tendency to seek inspiration in antiquity which characterised the end of the eighteenth century. Its effect on painting was marked, but on sculpture and architecture too, from one end of Europe to the other, its influence was supreme. Napoleon particularly admired Canova (1757–1822) — though he disapproved of Canova's nude *Reclining Venus*, for which the model was Napoleon's sister Pauline. Canova's pupil, the Danish sculptor Thorwaldsen, who became Roman by adoption and whose statue of Byron is now in Trinity College, Cambridge, also surpassed the best French sculptors of the day, though the busts of the elderly Houdon, done in the traditions of the past century, were outstanding. In architecture the 269

Empire Style produced its best-known memorial in the two *Arcs de Triomphe* at Paris. The classical revival led to neo-Greek temples such as those which housed the stock exchange and the church of the Madeleine. Above all the Empire Style dominated furniture and interior decoration, making much use of mahogany inset with bronze, and decorative motifs — sphinxes, swans, chimeras — drawn from antiquity.

In music, this was not France's greatest age, and Cherubini is the only Italian composer of the period of real stature. In reality the capital of the musical world was no longer either Paris or Milan but Vienna. In 1791, the year *The Magic Flute* was written, Mozart had died at the age of thirty-five. Haydn died at the age of seventy-seven in 1809; Beethoven, born in Bonn in 1770, died in Vienna in 1827. In the classical forms of the past, he initiated the romantic trends of the future — a giant striding two epochs. His third symphony, the Eroica, completed in 1804, had been inspired by and dedicated to Bonaparte; but Beethoven tore up the dedication in disgust when Bonaparte became the Emperor Napoleon.

The Continental System in 1810

During 1810 the Continental System was in some quarters relaxed, and in others was tightened to the point of absurdity. Relaxation was forced by economics, finance and politics, both French and American. To simplify the disposal of British goods by neutrals the British had invented a method to enable smugglers to outwit, or overcome the scruples of, continental customs officers. Neutral ships were issued with 'licences': a double set of papers, one to show that the cargo had been cleared and paid for in Britain, and the other — presented to the French authorities only — a 'certificate of origin', more or less authentic, to prove that the ship was neutral. 'Neutral' in practice meant American, and those who benefited from this device were chiefly New England shipowners and sea captains who ignored both the U.S. Non-Intercourse Act and Napoleon. The Non-Intercourse Act prohibited American ships from trading with either of the belligerents; and Napoleon, arguing logically that ships which defied the order were flying the American flag illegally, decreed that all French and French-controlled ports were closed to American shipping. But on 1 March 1810 Congress repealed the Non-Intercourse Act and authorised the President to permit trade with the belligerent power — France or Britain — which revoked its decrees against the neutral trade of the United States; and, further, if only one of them did so, to re-impose restrictions on the one that did not.

Now merchandise made in Britain was easily recognisable by its superior quality, while the origin of colonial products was impossible to ascertain. Colonial products, moreover, consisted either of raw materials, like cotton, which were indispensable to continental manufacturers, or of essential foodstuffs and drugs. Napoleon therefore decided to tighten restrictions against British goods while allowing American produce to enter freely. This satisfied the Americans and brought raw materials to French industry, which was on the verge of collapse. High duties imposed on American imports also helped the Treasury. The American Ambassador was told on August 5 that as far as the United States was concerned the Berlin Decree and the Milan Decree would be revoked, as from November 1, if the British would also withdraw their Orders in Council or, alternatively, if America would force Britain to respect American rights. On November 2 President Madison withdrew all restrictions against trade with France and French dependencies. The American rupture with Britain which Napoleon had counted on this manoeuvre to bring about was, however, deferred until 1812 — which was too late to affect the outcome of the Anglo-French struggle.

In Napoleon's efforts to halt the evasion of import duties he had the Tariff of Trianon translated into every language of Europe and he demanded that all his allies should strictly apply it; he even ordered that existing stocks be set apart, inventoried and taxed before release. But Napoleon had as early as January 1810 authorised French privateers to auction off the contraband merchandise they captured, paying for the privilege with forty per cent of the money realised, thus assuring the arrival on the market of some needed British merchandise. To a certain extent the ingenuity of inventors, stimulated by Government encouragement, supplied some of the commodities which were so desperately required. Substitute dyes were developed, the planting of tobacco, which became a State monopoly in 1810, was encouraged, and two new crops were introduced which had enormous future importance: chicory as a substitute for coffee, and beetroot. It had already been demonstrated that the sugar in beets was identical with cane sugar, and in January 1811 the first sugar-loaf was presented to Napoleon, who displayed it in the palace and decorated the chemist responsible with his own cross of the Legion of Honour.

To facilitate the direct importation from the United States of cotton and other goods necessary to industry a decree issued ten days before the Trianon Tariff permitted such produce to enter France in exchange for American importation of French goods of equal value. This condition would prove valuable to the silk industry of Lyon in 1811. The creation of these 'American permits', instead of being kept a secret, was instantly known in all the Chancelleries of Europe. The effect was particularly disastrous in St Petersburg where Alexander — who distrusted his 'friend of Tilsit' as much as Napoleon distrusted him — replied by opening Russian ports to all ships flying a neutral flag and adopting tariffs favourable to colonial and adverse to French imports (31 December 1810). The Continental System, universally unpopular, had in fact been nowhere more disliked than among the merchants and nobles of Russia.

The other measures which were taken during the year 1810 to bolster up the Continental System had consequences no less grave. In the first place the war on British industry was intensified. The Decree of Fontainebleau of October 19 ordered that all goods of British manufacture should be seized, slashed, pulped or burned. The newspapers of every allied or occupied country in Europe were filled — though with slight result — with vivid descriptions of spectacular raids and the subsequent consignment of forbidden merchandise to the 'avenging flames'. Secondly, the 'Coastal System' was extended. In Holland Louis's support for his brother's policy was lukewarm, and his kingdom was therefore annexed. In December Jérôme, King of Westphalia, was deprived of his coastline when the North Sea coast as far as Denmark was annexed, and with it the Duchy of Oldenburg and the Hanseatic towns, including Lübeck on the Baltic. France, now inflated to 130 Departments, stretched from Denmark to the Kingdom of Naples, and French prefects sat in cities like Amsterdam, Münster and Hamburg. But the Duke of Oldenburg was an uncle of the Tsar — and his deposition also contributed to Alexander's dramatic ukase of December 31 which was to be the ostensible cause of the Franco-Russian War.

British naval supremacy and the overseas world

Napoleon had by now jeopardised his chances of success by the inordinate lengths to which he had pushed his Continental System. He had alienated most of Europe and fanned the embers of national resistance; at home his plans were sabotaged by evasion and corruption. Britain, however, was also seriously endangered by economic and financial difficulties which were acute at the times when the Continental System was working effectively. In 1811–12 the distress among the working class produced the Luddite Riots, in which bands of manual labourers smashed the machinery they thought responsible for their unemployment. Bank notes depreciated and the pound tottered. Britain's survival and eventual victory was, notwithstanding the military accomplishment of the Coalition powers, due to the indomitable confidence and adaptability of her industrial and commercial system and, above all, to the overwhelming superiority of her maritime power. Her naval effort was immense. In 1814 the British navy counted 240 ships of the line, 300 frigates and 600 smaller vessels; from 1806 to 1814 France and her allies lost 125 ships of the line, 160 frigates and 290 smaller vessels.

In the West Indies, between 1803 and 1810, the British seized in succession St Lucia and Tobago, Dutch Curacao, the islands of Marie-Galante and Désirade, Martinique and Guadeloupe, as well as French and Dutch Guiana. In Africa they occupied the Cape of Good Hope and took possession of Madeira and other Portuguese colonies, Goré and finally Senegal. In the Indian Ocean, Captain-General Decaen of the Mascarene Islands — Mauritius, Réunion and Rodriguez — held out until 1810, harassing British communications until the British put an end to his forays by capturing the Ile Bonaparte — formerly the Ile Bourbon and later Réunion — Mauritius and the Seychelles. Finally in 1811 they took the French settlement of Tamatave on the coast of Madagascar. In the Dutch East Indies, Louis Bonaparte's Governor-General had already lost Sumatra, Borneo and Amboina in the Moluccas. General Janssens — who since Napoleon's annexation of Holland was officially chief of the 'Empire's Far Eastern Possessions' — capitulated in 1811 and Java thus passed into British hands. After the Peninsular War, Spain was a British ally; this assured her continued possession of the Philippines, but Great Britain was henceforth the sole Western power in India and the China Sea.

In India the aggressive policy of Wellesley had led to his recall in 1805. His successors — Lord Cornwallis, Sir George Barlow and Lord Minto — pursued a policy of conciliation and pacification which corresponded with the wishes of the East India Company itself. It was also a prudent policy, for beyond the North-West Frontier lay the distant twin menace of Russian expansion and the vast

Not only the cotton plantations, but many other industrial and agricultural enterprises in the New World were based on slave-labour. The illustration shows slaves washing for diamonds in Brazil. *Radio Times Hulton Picture Library*

Napoleonic strategic ambitions. At the beginning of the century the lower valley of the Indus, the Sind, was still ruled by independent Moslem emirs, but the power of the Sikhs had been increasing continually in the Panjab. From his capital at Lahore Ranjit Singh (1791–1839) — the 'Lion of the Panjab' — ruled a powerful Hindu state. Driving back the Afghans to the far side of the mountains, he had extended his territory as far as Kashmir and Peshawar. In 1809 Ranjit Singh made an alliance with the British and thenceforth protected them on this front. He re-established friendly relations with Afghanistan, which reoccupied Baluchistan and the Sind. Beyond, in Persia, the Shah Fath Ali, who had torn up the treaty made with Napoleon at Finkenstein, was once again a British ally.

The two decades between 1790 and 1810 which were so decisive in the history of the West were a passing moment in the Afro-Asian world, an insignificant fraction of eternity, marked only by the disturbance caused by the duel between the two European powers. In Africa, apart from the changes in colonial masters already mentioned, Bonaparte had invaded Egypt and failed to retain it, Duckworth had repeated the attempt and also failed. Mehemet Ali's rise to power had begun. Otherwise only the reconnaissance of Algiers and of Morocco made in 1808 by two French officers, Boutin and Burel, is worth recording, not because it roused interest at the time but 271 because of its future significance. In China Kien-lung was succeeded by his seventeenth son, the indolent and drunken Kia-king (1796–1820). Kia-king profited by the Napoleonic Wars to close his Empire even more securely to Western influence, and in 1805 expressly outlawed Christianity. The Emperor was at loggerheads with numerous secret societies, one of which, ' the White Water-lily ', occupied the Imperial Palace in 1813. Meanwhile he disdained European advances with Olympian arrogance. To a formal missive from George III, who entitled himself Hai-lung, ' Dragon of the Sea ', dated the twenty-second day of the Fifth Moon 1804, the Emperor condescended to reply, indulging in a lengthy diatribe against France, land of subversive ideas. Confirming his suzerainty over the south-east peninsula he authorised Gia-long to change the name Annam to Vietnam, when Gia-long during his eighteen years of aggressive reign founded Cochin-China and Tongking. In Siam, which was as hermetically sealed to foreigners as Japan, the Chakkri Dynasty, founded by Rama I in 1782, was consolidated under Rama II (1809–24).

Latin America

If in the opening years of the nineteenth century little of consequence occurred in Asia, the emancipation of Latin America and the emergence of the Spanish and Portuguese colonies as the first ' new nations ' was an event of immense importance in world history. Although this transformation was not fully accomplished until the following period, the initial impetus of the movement for independence was a by-product of the Continental System and of the Anglo-French struggle. The flight of the Portuguese royal house to Brazil before the invading French army had made Rio de Janeiro a capital city and Brazil itself an empire before it became a republic; the substitution ' of the intruder Joseph Bonaparte for the Spanish Bourbons was the signal for the uprisings in Central and South America. Both Brazil and the Spanish colonies at once benefited by opening their ports to Great Britain, with whom trade increased from eight million pounds sterling in 1805 to twenty million in 1808–9. To Britain, this new market provided an alternative to a Europe closed by the Continental System. The insurrectionary movement, at first unorganised and sporadic, was the result of many deep-rooted causes already touched upon: the selfishness with which the descendants of the conquistadores had exploited the continent, the inefficiency of a distant central government, hardship among the Indian populations, the growth of liberal ideas among the Creoles, and finally the rigid system by which trade was exclusively reserved for the home country.

A Creole born in Caracas, the Venezuelan patriot Francisco de Miranda, was the precursor of the Spanish American revolutionary movement. During the North American War of Independence Miranda had fought for the colonists as a Spanish officer. In France he had been a Girondin general under the Legislative Assembly and the Convention and subsequently experienced prison under the Terror and banishment under the Directory. In London Pitt encouraged him to found a South American ' circle ' (1797) of which many protagonists of the future struggle for Latin American independence were members. In Spain, in the absence of a legitimate sovereign, the *juntas* assumed the government and defence of the country

in 1808. The overseas possessions of the Madrid monarchy, the kingdoms, viceroyalties and captaincies-general of the Crown of Castile, were placed juridically on the same footing as the provinces of the Spanish peninsula. Regional and municipal councils throughout the Spanish world, following the example of the *juntas*, refused to receive the emissaries of ' King ' Joseph, and at the cost of much bloodshed seized power, without, however, denying the legitimacy of Ferdinand VII, a prisoner-guest in France. In June 1806 a British expedition seized Buenos Aires. The British were, however, driven out, not by the Spanish Viceroy, who had ignominiously fled, but by the Creole colonists. The discovery that, unaided by Spanish or French arms, citizens could defend themselves inevitably encouraged thoughts of independence. With Pitt's concurrence Miranda had in April 1806 attempted to seize power in Caracas, but without success. In 1808, however, when Joseph was made King, Venezuela at once revolted, and its proclamation of independence in July 1811 was a triumph for Miranda, who was acclaimed dictator. A year later he was defeated in a Royalist counter-offensive and put under arrest by his lieutenant, Bolivar, the future ' Liberator ', who accused him of treason. Miranda was sent to Cadiz, where in 1816 he died in prison.

Joseph Bonaparte's enthronement had similar repercussions in Buenos Aires where on 25 May 1810 a provisional *Junta* was formed which shot the French Viceroy and began the struggle for Argentinian independence. The year after the revolutionary *Junta* lost Upper Peru — later to become Bolivia — and Paraguay, thus limiting the one-time Spanish viceroyalty to the territory of the future Argentine Republic. A triumvirate of dictators, saved by the victory at Tucuman over the Royalists of Upper Peru, was overthrown by the *pronunciamiento* of Alvear and San Martin. In 1813 an assembly was convoked to draw up a constitution and in 1816 the Republic of the United Provinces of the Rio de la Plata was proclaimed. In Mexico the parish priest of Dolores, Miguel Hidalgo (1753–1811), a Creole intellectual deeply influenced by the French Revolution, issued his ' cry of Dolores ' — *el Grito de Dolores* — on 16 September 1810, from which the Mexican War of Independence is dated. The uprising was marked by atrocities and followed by equally ferocious Royalist reprisals. Hidalgo's ill-organised native army was crushed. Hidalgo himself was captured and shot. Morelos, a fellow rebel and also a priest, continued the struggle, and in 1813 a revolutionary assembly proclaimed the independence of Mexico. But two years later Morelos, too, was captured and shot. By the time Ferdinand VII regained his throne Spanish control had been re-established over all his transatlantic dominions except Argentina. All, however, were ripe for independence.

1812 and the Russian campaign

In 1807 peace had been forced on Alexander by the severity of Russian losses, and the uneasy alliance concluded in July 1807 at Tilsit had been at the cost of the Russian economy. The Continental System meant breaking with Britain, Russia's best customer. By 1812 Russia was threatened with bankruptcy in spite of reforms introduced by Speransky, to whom Alexander had entrusted the re-organisation of the financial, constitutional and administrative machinery. The son of a village priest, Speransky

had learned much from the French Revolution, but only a part of his excellent and comprehensive programme of reform was put into effect. Financial collapse was averted mainly by reopening Russian ports to foreign trade — which made a breach in the Continental System that jeopardised the entire scheme. There were other causes for the increasing coldness between the Emperor of France and the Tsar of Russia: the Polish question, Napoleon's Austrian marriage, Russia's war with Turkey, and the Swedish affair. In 1809 the insane Gustavus IV was deposed by the Diet and the throne was offered to his uncle, who became Charles XIII. At the sudden death of his heir, in May 1810, Charles XIII had to adopt another, and at the wish of the army, eager to gain French support after the loss of Finland to Russia, chose a French Marshal, Berna-dotte, brother-in-law of Joseph Bonaparte. Bernadotte, already Prince of Pontecorvo, was able to persuade the Swedish Diet that the choice would be acceptable to Napoleon, and on August 21 was elected Crown Prince under the name Charles John. This seeming French victory was an additional source of irritation to the Tsar. But as the arms race of 1811 was followed in 1812 by diplomatic preparations for war, Alexander hastened to bribe the ambitious new Crown Prince with the offer of Norway, which had been Danish since the fifteenth century. Napoleon, preferring to retain the friendship of Denmark, had refused to make a similar offer to his ex-Marshal. On April 9 the secret pact of Abo — expanded in July by an Anglo-Russo-Swedish treaty — assured Alexander of at least the benevolent neutrality of Sweden. The Russo-Turkish peace, signed in Bucharest on May 28, restored the Roumanian principalities to the Sultan in exchange for Bessarabia, and released the Russian army of Moldavia for action against the French.

On his side Napoleon made military alliances with Prussia in February and with Austria in March. In May he summoned together the German princes of his Confed-eration of the Rhine at Dresden, where he received Francis I and Frederick William III almost as vassals. But neither the Austrians nor the Prussians could be expected to exert themselves against the Russians — except in the event of Napoleon's overwhelming success. On June 24, without a formal declaration of war, Napoleon crossed the Niemen, at the head of 600,000 troops, of whom one-third were French and the remainder Dutch, Westphalian, Bavarian, Saxon, Polish, Prussian, Austrian, Croatian,

This relief depicts Barclay de Tolly, commander of the Russian forces at the start of the French invasion of 1812. He retreated as far as Smolesk without offering battle and was replaced in command by Kutuzov, who fought the battle of Borodino (7 September) with heavy losses before resuming the retreat. *Marburg*

José de San Martin (1778–1850) one of the two outstanding leaders of the South American rebels against Spain during the Wars of Independence. He found it difficult to co-operate with Bolivar, the other liberator. *Radio Times Hulton Picture Library*

The French army leaves a burning Moscow. It took more than six weeks for the French to re-cross the Beresina and by that time (26 November) the Grand Army was in ruins. *Deutsche Fotothek, Dresden*

The losses of the Russian campaign denuded France of troops. For the remainder of the war, Napoleon was outnumbered. Russia became the dominant military power, moving steadily westwards. *Victoria & Albert Museum*

Dalmatian, Swiss, Italian and even Spanish. The Russian army, commanded by the Baltic Baron Barclay de Tolly and the Georgian Prince Bagration, was so inferior in numbers to this vast 'army of twenty nations' that it withdrew towards Moscow. Halfway there an indecisive rearguard action took place at Smolensk. Barclay de Tolly, who had abandoned Smolensk, was replaced by the elderly Kutuzov, and on September 7 a stand was made at Borodino. In the ensuing battle Napoleon's losses amounted to 30,000 troops and forty generals, while Russian casualties numbered some 50,000, including Bagration.

This costly victory — it was known as Moskva — delivered the ancient capital of Muscovy into Napoleon's hands; but when his weary soldiers reached it they found the city deserted and, shortly afterwards, in flames. On the orders of Rostopchin, the Governor, Moscow was burned to prevent the invader from finding quarters for the winter. Napoleon waited five weeks for the Tsar to ask for peace terms. Alexander remained silent. The French withdrawal from Moscow was thus delayed until the third week in October. Then, in early November, the winter set in — six weeks earlier than for the past forty years — and withdrawal became disastrous retreat. Only the heroism of Marshal Ney, in command of the rearguard, prevented the total annihilation of the rapidly dwindling Grand Army. In the ice flows of the River Beresina, under the fire of Russian cannon, the conqueror's star set. On December 5 Napoleon abandoned the remnant of his army and hastened towards Paris, from which news of the 'Malet affair' in October had been a salutary warning. The republican General Malet had escaped from prison and, on the false announcement that the Emperor was dead, attempted a coup d'état in which even Savary, the Minister of Police, had been put under arrest. It was true that Malet and his accomplices were seized and shot, but the incident revealed to Napoleon how precarious his position had become. It came just when he had urgently to raise fresh troops to withstand the new Coalition which the victorious Russian resistance portended.

1813 and the German War of Liberation

Of the 600,000 troops who had marched into Russia hardly 50,000 survived. Germany saw the straggling, typhus-ridden remnants as they emerged like spectres clad in rags, and some felt that the 'hour of deliverance' of which Fichte had spoken was at hand. After Tilsit Prussia had inaugurated her national regeneration with administrative and social reforms which, although they were not pushed so far by Hardenberg as Stein would have wished, began the transformation of feudal into capitalist society. In 1810 the University of Berlin was founded by Karl Wilhelm Humboldt; it became a centre of patriotic propaganda for all the German-speaking world. The army was reformed by Scharnhorst and Gneisenau. Its size was limited by treaty, but was capable of rapid expansion from the reserves accumulated by passing conscripts rapidly through their training in the standing army. The Prussian troops in Napoleon's Grand Army still remained intact on the Russian front, and Yorck, their commander, took the initiative on 30 December 1812 at Tauroggen by suspending hostilities, as a preliminary to changing sides. Stein, who arrived in East Prussia with the Russian army, easily persuaded that province to follow suit. Frederick William, escaping from Berlin, concluded the treaty of Kalisch (28 February 1813) with Alexander, promising Russia the Prussian share of the partitions of Poland. For himself Frederick William insisted only on Saxony, against whose King he bore a grudge. On March 16 he declared war on Napoleon.

To prepare for absence from Paris Napoleon appointed the Empress Regent, which lessened the danger of a coup d'état. To regain the loyalty of the Catholics, he had discussed a new Concordat with the Pope at Fontainebleau in the preceding summer, and this was signed in January 1813. In March, however, Pius VII was persuaded by the scruples of his Cardinals to disavow it. But Napoleon's chief accomplishment had been to raise a new army. It was an army of conscripts, and mere boys had been enrolled in its ranks, but that Napoleon was still dangerous and a strategist of genius was demonstrated by victories over the Russo-Prussians at Lützen and Bautzen in May. But they could not be decisive because of Napoleon's lack of cavalry for pursuit. Though he had cleared Silesia and Saxony, he needed time to bring troops from Italy into Germany. He therefore signed a two months' armistice at Plaswitz. Metternich now offered his mediation and went to Dresden to discuss terms with Napoleon. Metternich persisted in demanding that Napoleon should abandon all his conquests, to which Napoleon had the imprudence to retort: 'And how much has England paid you?' Shortly after this episode Austria made a secret alliance with Prussia and Russia. On August 10 at midnight Metternich announced that his master, Francis I, had entered the war. The Coalition now had 860,000 men against Napoleon's 700,000.

In Britain, after the failure of the Walcheren expedition, Castlereagh and Canning had quarrelled, fought a duel and both resigned from the Cabinet (1809). But in 1812 Castlereagh was again Foreign Secretary under Lord Liverpool. Britain financed the revived Coalition, to which Bernadotte now contributed Swedish troops. He also commanded the Army of the North, Blücher the Army of Silesia, and Schwarzenberg the Army of Bohemia. Napoleon defeated the allies at Dresden, but again failed to destroy their main army. In other engagements during August and September Napoleon's lieutenants — Macdonald, Vandamme, Oudinot, Ney — were beaten. Finally the allies, 320,000 strong, converged on Leipzig, and for three days — 16-19 October 1813 — the bloody slaughter known as the Battle of the Nations raged. Napoleon's 190,000 troops were cut to pieces and the disaster was complete. Napoleon's Saxons had changed sides in the middle of the battle and their King, personally loyal to Napoleon, was made prisoner. The Confederation of the Rhine collapsed. Jérôme's Westphalia came to an end. One after the other, Würtemberg, Baden, Hesse and even Bavaria joined the Coalition. Germany was lost, and at the same time Holland, under Prince William of Orange, rose and threw off the French yoke.

Already in 1811 Masséna had been checked in Portugal before the lines of Torres Vedras and retired into Spain. Wellington, advancing into Spain, had defeated Marmont at Arapiles in July 1812. Finally on 21 June 1813 he overwhelmed Joseph Bonaparte and Marshal Jourdan at Vittoria. It was the prelude to Wellington's invasion of France itself. Soult, who had replaced Jourdan, was driven inland from Bayonne and at Toulouse in April 1814 was

The Orthodox, Lutheran and Catholic monarchs of the east express their piety on the battlefield of Leipzig. This battle was the greatest of the wars, nearly half-a-million men being involved, and was decisive in liberating Germany. *Mansell*

Frederick William III (1797–1840) under whom Prussia re-entered the war against France in 1813. After 1815 it seemed for a little that he would support a liberal ministry, but he was soon won over to reaction by Metternich and abdicated the leadership of Germany to Austria. *Larousse*

defeated in the last battle of the war. In December 1813 Switzerland, invaded by the Austrians, denounced Napoleon's Act of Mediation. In Italy all was confusion. Eugène de Beauharnais held on to Lombardy as long as he could but was compelled to retire, leaving northern Italy in Austrian hands; in Naples Murat and Napoleon's sister Caroline announced their defection by opening their ports to the British. In January 1814, in an effort to retain his crown, Murat signed a formal treaty of alliance with Austria. He later changed sides yet again, was deposed, and shot after attempting to re-enter his former kingdom.

1814 and the allied victory

In November and December 1813 the allies met at Frankfurt to try to agree on their war aims. Britain, apart from retaining her colonial gains, was eager to erect a Dutch-Belgian barrier state under the Prince of Orange which would halt French expansion towards the North Sea, and she still supported a Bourbon restoration. The Tsar wished to revive Poland as a Russian appanage and to extend his sphere of influence in the Balkans. He entertained vaguely liberal plans for setting up Bernadotte as a constitutional King of the French, a project warmly endorsed by the Benjamin Constant-Madame de Staël faction. Austria wanted to recover the territories she had lost and to restore a balance of power which would protect her from Russia and Prussia. In addition Austria wished to assure the heritage of Napoleon's son — who was of course Francis I's grandson — by the regency of Marie Louise over a France reduced to its 1792 frontiers — and this was probably the secret desire of many who directed French policy, beginning with Talleyrand and Caulaincourt himself. It was Caulaincourt, well known to be a partisan of peace, whom Napoleon on his return from Russia had made Minister of Foreign Affairs in place of Maret, an advocate of war to the death.

Napoleon made conciliatory gestures. He sent Ferdinand VII back to Madrid in December, and in January returned the Pope to Rome. Later, he restored the Papal States which had previously been occupied by Murat and the Neapolitans. But he would not accept the terms that the allies offered, by which France would have retained her 'natural boundaries'. Early in 1814 three separate invasions of France began. Schwarzenberg entered by way of Basle and the Belfort gap; Blücher crossed the Rhine and penetrated Lorraine; Bernadotte came through Belgium. Napoleon had scraped together every soldier at his disposal, and fought a campaign which was perhaps the most masterly of his strategic career. In February Brienne, Champaubert and Montmirail were brilliant victories — but fruitless. The allies pressed on. At the Congress of Châtillon — from February 5 to March 19 — Caulaincourt found that allied demands had hardened: the 'pre-Revolutionary limits' of France were now insisted on. Napoleon, who had been persuaded to accept the 'natural frontiers', refused peace at a price which would have wiped out all the gains the Revolution had made. And while he wasted a month in counter-marches between the Aube, the Marne and the Aisne, Castlereagh arranged the pact of Chaumont between the four Great Powers — Britain, Austria, Russia and Prussia — which sealed their union for a period of twenty years.

In a risky manoeuvre Napoleon left Paris uncovered, and the allies decided to march directly on the capital, where the Royalists were already active. On March 31 the allies entered Paris, to the applause of some Royalists, and published a statement declaring that they would no longer treat with Napoleon Bonaparte nor with any member of his family. The Tsar became Talleyrand's guest, and Talleyrand, now an enthusiastic advocate of the Bourbon restoration, persuaded him that such was the will of the enlightened nation. On April 1 something less than half the Senate assembled — 64 out of 140 — and Talleyrand

276

had himself named President of a provisional government of five members. The same Rump-Senate proclaimed that Napoleon was deposed and then drew up a constitution which ' freely called to the throne Louis Stanislas Xavier of France, brother of the last King '.

Augereau had already surrendered Lyon to the Austrians without resistance, and the mayor of Bordeaux had received the British and declared for the Bourbons. At Fontainebleau Napoleon's Marshals, Ney especially, weary of the struggle and convinced that further resistance would be futile, persuaded the Emperor to abdicate. Napoleon's consent was at first conditional and made in favour of his son, the ' King of Rome '. But when his decision was brought to the Tsar, Alexander had just learned that Marmont had agreed to withdraw his corps from the French Imperial army. This treachery revealed how low the morale of the French command had sunk and the Tsar felt able to insist on Napoleon's unconditional abdication. Napoleon signed. He was then allowed to retain his title, and was given sovereignty over the island of Elba, a battalion of the Imperial Guard and an income. Marie Louise, with her son, was entrusted to the care of her father, Francis I. She, too, retained her title and in addition received the Duchies of Parma, Piacenza and Guastalla. On April 20, abandoned by his Marshals and his personal servants, Napoleon bade a moving farewell to his Grenadiers drawn up at Fontainebleau Palace, embraced their flag and took the lonely road to Elba.

The balance sheet

The Napoleonic adventure was not finished: in a few months the exile would return — for ' one hundred days '. But the balance sheet of the Revolutionary and Imperial epic was already drawn up and could be examined. The American Revolution had, indeed, already offered to the world one example of an experiment in emancipation.

But the American Revolution had taken place in a new land and in a spirit which was essentially Anglo-Saxon. Under the impetus and clash of new ideas the French Revolution took place in an ancient country where institutions and a class system had been hardened — and sometimes worm-eaten — by centuries of practice. For this traditional past the Revolution appeared to attempt to substitute a system based on logic and reason — and hence universally applicable. From constitution to constitution, from declarations of the ' rights of man ' to dilatory recollections of the ' duties of man ', under the threefold rallying cry of Liberty, Equality and Fraternity, France had in twenty-five years tried one by one a Constitutional Monarchy, the dictatorship of a single Assembly, an unstable regime based on the separation of powers, a Presidency in the American fashion disguised as a triple Consulate, and an autocratic and aggressive Empire whose conquests spread abroad the progress which the Revolution had achieved and forced other nations to adopt its institutions in self-defence. The idea of the ' Fatherland ' — and soon of the ' Fatherland in danger ' — gave rise to great conscript armies which the abolition of a privileged officer class provided with new leaders. Bonaparte, the most gifted of them, having first restored national unity, held the forces of reactionary Europe in check long enough to sweep away the surviving traces of feudalism, to introduce civil codes based on equality before the law and on religious toleration, and, by quickening the cultural exchange between peoples of different nationalities, to invigorate the intellectual life of Europe. He had been able to do this because he led the most powerful and populous country in the West. The result was a new world. One of its features, unperceived for many years, was that French ascendancy was now over. Population changes, the industrial revolution and the strength gained in the long struggle would transfer leadership to France's old rival. The nineteenth century would be the ' British century '. 277

CHAPTER FIFTEEN

RESTORATIONS AND REVOLUTIONS

THE NINETEENTH CENTURY

FROM THE CONGRESS OF VIENNA TO 1830

The return of the Bourbons and the Hundred Days

Talleyrand's co-operativeness towards the allies and far-sighted realism made certain that the new King would freely pardon his past and also that he himself would have direction of the regime he had chosen. In the event he proved his worth, for he obtained for France the relatively favourable peace terms which Caulaincourt had been refused. By the armistice it was agreed that, with the immediate suspension of hostilities, the occupying armies would simultaneously withdraw beyond the frontiers of France as they had been drawn in 1792. But on May 30 he negotiated the Treaties of Paris, by which France was allowed to retain certain gains made during the Revolution in Belgium, Savoy, Alsace and the Rhineland. The lost overseas colonies were also returned to France with the exception of Tobago, St Lucia and Mauritius.

These six treaties also contained a series of separate and secret clauses which dealt with the special interests of individual nations. One of these recognised the transfer of Norway to Bernadotte, another arranged that Belgium should be given to Holland while Austria and Piedmont would share northern Italy. Finally it was agreed that a congress should be held in Vienna ' to establish a genuine and durable system to preserve the balance of power in Europe ' on the basis of the treaties, open and secret, which had been signed.

Louis XVIII was a gross and gout-ridden old gentleman without prestige, but he was sagacious, witty and not without finesse and a sense of moderation. He was quite aware that an attempt to wipe out all 'the accomplishments of the Revolution and the Empire would indeed be to have ' learned nothing and forgotten nothing ' — as his less uncompromising critics were later to say of him. France was therefore provided with a Charter of constitutional government, but the Charter was granted by the King, which satisfied neither those who believed in Divine Right nor those who believed in the sovereignty of the people. And he committed the psychological error of dating the Charter from the nineteenth year of his reign — as though the intervening years, during which so much had happened to so many, had not existed. It was not long before disillusion set in, stimulated by the imprudence of the Ultras, former *émigrés* who were eager to revive the trappings of a past which was beyond recall, among

Hardship after the war led to demands for Parliamentary reform. In 1819 a reform meeting at St Peter's Fields, Manchester, ended with a yeomanry charge and bloodshed, and passed into history as ' Peterloo '. *Public Record Office*

them the White Flag of the Royalists. Former dignitaries of the Empire, officers on retirement pay who had carried the triumphant Tricolour over half Europe, felt humiliated, while those who had acquired property by buying nationalised lands felt insecure. Less than a year of the new reign was sufficient to provoke deep disappointment.

On the island of Elba the exiled Emperor was kept well informed of events in France. His faith in his own destiny was not yet extinguished. One heroic last fling had more appeal than a derisory sovereignty over tiny Elba. Suddenly, on 1 March 1815, Napoleon landed at Golfe Juan on the French Riviera with a handful of men. Audaciously he took the route through the Alps towards Grenoble where the soldiers posted to bar his progress acclaimed him and joined his growing band of followers. The inhabitants of Grenoble themselves forced open their gates to admit him. Soon he entered Lyon; everywhere regiments sent to oppose him fell in behind his standard. At Auxerre, on March 18, Marshal Ney, who had sworn to bring him back in an iron cage, embraced his old commander with emotion. In three weeks, as Napoleon himself had predicted, the ' Eagle ' had swooped from belfry to belfry, to reach the towers of Notre Dame. On March 20, welcomed by cheering crowds, Napoleon was again installed in the Tuileries, which Louis XVIII had precipitously vacated the night before to take refuge in Ghent.

To placate liberals Napoleon declared he would rule as a constitutional sovereign. He at once instituted a parliamentary system with two chambers, peers and representatives, which during the Hundred Days proved a nuisance, since the moment was not one in which to discuss institutions but to prepare for the re-invasion of the country by the allied armies. The Congress which sat in Vienna had lost no time in pronouncing Napoleon a usurper and an outlaw, and the Anglo-Prussian forces of Wellington and Blücher, deployed in Belgium from Liège to the sea, were ready to march on Paris. In scarcely two months Napoleon had raised an army of some 120,000 veterans, many of them prisoners of war who had been released after his abdication. In June, he threw himself into Belgium, anticipating the Anglo-Prussian invasion. On June 16 he drove Blücher back at Ligny while Ney engaged the British at Quatre Bras. Two days later the long duel which had opened twenty-three years before with the cannonade of Valmy was finally decided on the rain-soaked fields of Waterloo. Napoleon's aim was to destroy Wellington's army before it could regain contact with the Prussians. Wellington's thin line yielded ground but remained unbroken. Even Ney's furious cavalry charges and the onslaught of the Imperial Guard failed to break it. Then towards evening Blücher's Prussians arrived. The British

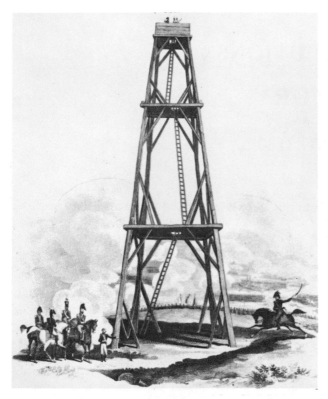

Napoleon's Hundred Days culminated at Waterloo in 1815.
He had thrown his army into Belgium in order to destroy the
nearest allied army before overwhelming odds could be concentrated against him. This tower was built for him as an
observation post. *Mansell*

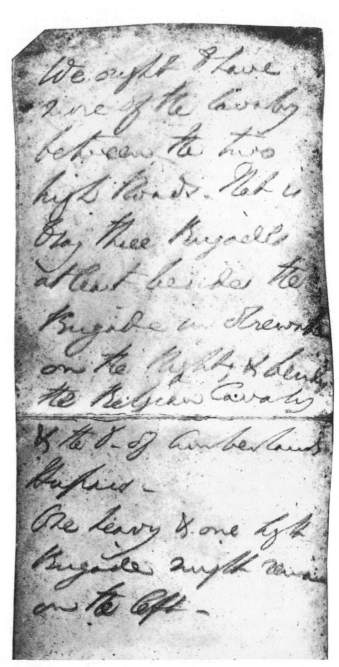

At Vienna assembled in 1814 a Congress of statesmen and
monarchs who settled the map of Europe for fifteen years
(and then the appearance of an independent Belgium was
its only important modification). Talleyrand secured the participation of France in the making of the peace. *Larousse*

Wellington, commanding the allied army at Waterloo, awaited
the French at the best position he could find before Brussels.
These were some of his written orders for the disposition
of his troops. *Victoria & Albert Museum*

advanced, the French army wavered, broke and, pursued by Prussian cavalry, retreated, abandoning guns and equipment. Napoleon himself escaped to Paris. There, apart from the steadfast devotion of the poorer classes, he found indifference and hostility. He had shaken Europe too thoroughly to expect mercy, and on June 22 he abdicated for the second time. The Chamber of Representatives proclaimed Napoleon II and formed a provisional government under the Duke of Otranto, and as Minister of the Interior Carnot, who had rallied to the cause of a liberal Empire. From Malmaison Napoleon reached Rochefort, hoping to embark for America. A British cruiser blockaded the port. He hesitated for a day and then addressed a letter to the Prince Regent of England as ' the most powerful and most generous of his enemies ' and surrendered himself to Captain Maitland of the *Bellerophon*. On the order of the British Government he was transferred to the *Northumberland* and conveyed to distant St Helena in the South Atlantic, 1,200 miles off the African coast. There, as the prisoner of Sir Hudson Lowe, the Governor, he died on 5 May 1821. During those six years he dictated memoirs of extraordinary lucidity and cultivated that aura of political martyrdom from which the ' Napoleonic legend ' arose.

The Congress of Vienna

When Talleyrand had arrived in Vienna in September 1814 he found the plenipotentiaries of the four victorious powers determined to run the Congress in their own way. During the previous five days Metternich, Castlereagh, Hardenberg assisted by Humboldt, and the Russian Nesselrode, had already decided among themselves how to regulate the affairs of Poland, Italy and Germany without even waiting to consult their own respective sovereigns. Talleyrand was a consummate diplomatist and his technique in this case was to announce from the beginning that he alone asked for nothing, and then skilfully to defend the rights of secondary powers against the manifest greed of the big four. The doctrine which he invoked was the ' principle of legitimacy '. The protocol of October 8, which adjourned the Congress until November 1, provided that the deliberations would take place not between the four Great Powers alone but between the eight signatories of the Treaties of Paris — the eighth being Spain, who had signed later. A phrase in the protocol — suggested by Talleyrand — implied that partition violated public rights. Humboldt demanded to know what public rights had to do with it, and Talleyrand smoothly pointed out that it

The battle of Waterloo lasted all day, taking the form of a succession of frontal attacks by the French on the allied line. The last was made in the evening and failed just as the Prussian army under Blücher began to arrive. The rout of the French army followed. *British Museum*

The defeated Emperor. His second abdication and an attempt to escape to America soon followed Waterloo. He finally surrendered to a British ship at Rochefort and was taken across the Channel before sailing to St Helena. *Mansell*

281

After Waterloo the relief was intense. Wellington was the hero of the hour. A banquet greeted his return to England, but the allied sovereigns also showered honours upon him. The shadow of a renewed French domination of Europe was removed forever. *Victoria & Albert Museum*

St Helena, the place of exile of Napoleon, depicted in a seventeenth-century engraving. Here the Emperor lived until his death in 1821, bitterly quarrelling with his captors and assiduously creating the legend of the Napoleonic Prometheus, chained to his rock by the jealousy of smaller men. *Giraudon*

was by such a right that he, Humboldt, was here. Talleyrand was in fact behaving — in Alexander's judgment — as though he were the Minister of Louis XIV.

The Tsar, who since 1812 had been convinced that he was the chief architect of the allied victory, was the dominant figure in this crowded Congress of sovereigns and envoys from all Europe. In all, 216 chiefs of mission had been received and entertained by the Austrian Emperor, Francis I, aided by Prince Metternich and Gentz, Secretary to the Congress and one of Napoleon's most virulent critics. Alexander was in particular agreement with his Berlin ally, the weak Frederick William III. Both were eager to slice up Poland and to tear apart Saxony — which had remained faithful to Napoleon. Britain and Austria, however, opposed these ambitions. Talleyrand did not leave the disagreement unexploited, and on 8 January 1815 he persuaded Britain and Austria to sign a secret pact of alliance with him. His efforts to widen the rift between the victors were simplified by the personal antipathies which arose among the victors themselves. Alexander began to loathe Metternich, whom he referred to as ' that plaster dummy '. Meanwhile Metternich, very much at home in Vienna, not only organised balls and receptions but supervised the police and the censorship. The political intrigues of the Congress were relieved — and sometimes complicated — by amorous intrigues and sentimental adventures.

As Congress danced it suddenly learnt that Napoleon had left Elba and landed in France. Talleyrand saw all the fruits of his patient diplomacy endangered, and the territorial integrity of France again compromised. His personal fear and hatred of Napoleon was expressed in the declaration which the Congress published on March 13: ' Napoleon Bonaparte has placed himself outside the pale of civil and social relations and, as the enemy and disturber of the peace of the world, has exposed himself to public indictment. ' As Talleyrand wrote to an elderly princess of his acquaintance: ' We have expelled him from the human race. ' The four Great Powers renewed their Pact of Chaumont, and Talleyrand in the name of ' His Most Christian Majesty ' added his signature to it. While the Coalition, revitalised by a British subsidy of five million pounds, prepared to execute the anathema, Congress went on with its work. At last, on 9 June 1815, the ' Final Act ' was signed.

The Holy Roman Empire with its 360 states had, in 1803 and 1806, received fatal blows from Napoleon, and nothing could revive it. Instead, on the ruins of Napoleon's Confederation of the Rhine, after endless border adjustments, repartitions, restorations, reparations, sanctions, etc., a loose German Confederation of thirty-nine independent states was erected. Suggestions for a really close union which might have led to a strong empire under Prussian control were quashed by Metternich, and it was Austria which was to preside over the new German Diet, a clumsy and complicated organisation with its seat at Frankfurt.

The Kings of Hanover, Bavaria, Würtemberg and Saxony retained, or resumed, their recently granted royal dignity, while the Dukes of Oldenburg, Mecklenburg and Saxe-Weimar became Grand Dukes. Hamburg, Bremen, Lübeck and Frankfurt again became free cities. On the other hand the new Confederation was enlarged by the inclusion of William I of Orange, the new King of the

Netherlands — which now comprised both Holland and Belgium — in his capacity of Grand Duke of Luxemburg. As Duke of Holstein — which had been joined to Schleswig — the King of Denmark too was a member. Austria, in exchange for the Netherlands and the scattered German possessions she had formerly owned, reoccupied the Tyrol and Salzburg, the Illyrian provinces and, most important, the 'Lombard-Venetian Kingdom' — as the former Napoleonic north Italian kingdom was now renamed. Italy, parcelled out among numerous sovereigns, for the most part restored, was destined to be dominated by Austria. But the Papal States were returned to the Pope, and Piedmont, augmented by Genoa, emerged as the future nucleus of an Italian nation. Prussia left most of her share of Poland to Russia, but retained Thorn, Danzig and Posen, as well as the northern half of Saxony, whose King was thus penalised for his support of Napoleon.

As a bulwark against France Prussia also recovered her Rhenish provinces, together with most of the old Electorates of Cologne and Treves. Increased Prussian power on the Rhine and the inevitable desire of the Hohenzollerns to reunite these scattered territories were of great political significance for the future. The wishes of the inhabitants were equally ignored when Holland and Belgium were fused into a barrier state to prevent French expansion towards the north. Russia received the major part of Poland, which the Tsar made into a kingdom — under his own sovereignty. Its capital was Warsaw and Alexander endowed it with a constitution. Cracow remained a minute independent republic. The Treaty of Kiel of 14 January 1814, by which Norway had been wrested from Denmark and given to Prince Bernadotte of Sweden, was confirmed, thus punishing Denmark for her adherence to the Continental System. In compensation, however, she received Holstein. The Swiss formed a confederation which was augmented by the three Cantons of Geneva, Valais and Neuchâtel, while Swiss neutrality in perpetuity was solemnly recognised. Great Britain retained many of the acquisitions made during the course of the war, including not only Malta but the former French possessions of St Lucia, Mauritius and the Seychelles, and the Dutch colonies of Ceylon and the Cape of Good Hope, for which, however, she paid the King of Holland six million pounds in compensation. With such naval bases British maritime supremacy was beyond challenge by any other nation.

These arrangements seemed to obviate the danger of further French aggression. But the Hundred Days had jolted the powers assembled in Vienna. Waterloo had demonstrated that France was not immune to the 'Usurper's' appeal and a second Treaty of Paris (November 20) rectified the frontiers so as to make France more vulnerable than ever. In addition, Prussia, implacable in her desire to avenge the humiliation inflicted on her by Napoleon, insisted that France should pay a heavy war indemnity, to be guaranteed by the occupation of the country by 150,000 troops for five years. Talleyrand refused to sign the treaty. But Alexander, who had learned with fury of Talleyrand's secret pact with Britain and Austria of January, had forced Louis XVIII to replace Talleyrand with the Duc de Richelieu. Richelieu resigned himself to the inevitable, and with 'patriotic grief' the Chamber ratified the treaty.

The Holy Alliance

In this tremendous redistribution the powers of Europe had been guided by political considerations only. In their anxiety to reverse the effects of French Revolutionary expansion by setting up balanced power groups, an essentially conservative operation, they naturally ignored nationalist sentiment, or regarded it fearfully as a disruptive force. The result was admirable. The map of Europe they had drawn would, with certain minor modifications, remain unchanged for more than forty years, during which there were to be no wars between the Great Powers.

Their work, then, had the practical result of assuring a period of peace which after twenty years of bloodshed Europe sorely needed. The settlement assumed a startling aspect when Alexander suggested that the affairs of Europe should thenceforth be conducted on 'the principle of that holy religion which the Divine Saviour hath imparted to mankind'. In short, the Tsar proposed a Holy Alliance. He had recently developed mystical tendencies, partly under the influence of the Baroness von Krüdener, the authoress of a sensational romantic novel who later became converted to Maravian Pietism. Thus in September 1815, in the name of the Blessed Trinity, Alexander proposed to the rulers of Europe a union of monarchs who would govern their peoples as a father governs his family, following the Christian precepts of justice, love and peace — the 'sole means of consolidating human institutions and remedying their imperfections'. Without great conviction the Catholic Emperor of Austria and the Lutheran King of Prussia responded to the Orthodox Tsar's appeal by signing in person this curious treaty of 'indissoluble fraternity' (Paris, September 26). Louis XVIII and most of the sovereigns of Europe followed their example. Britain, Turkey and the Papacy did not. The vague and mystical phraseology of the Holy Alliance was described by some as 'rigmarole' and by others as 'political nullity'; but Metternich undertook to give it practical meaning. In his hands the Holy Alliance soon became an instrument of reaction.

Metternich, as a student in Strasbourg during the Revolution, had witnessed scenes of disorder which filled him with an unspeakable and ineradicable horror of popular violence. Convinced that liberal ideas could lead only to dangerous subversion, he stamped them out ruthlessly. But many of the ideas and ideals of the Revolution had spread throughout Europe in the wake of the victorious armies of France. For Metternich the welfare of Europe could only be served by combating the fatal alliance of liberalism and nationalism. When, therefore, the older dynasties had been safely restored, he made himself the 'policeman of Europe.' For more than thirty years he remained the guardian of public order as established by the Congress of Vienna, and transformed the Holy Alliance into a union of monarchs against the people. A directory, first of four, then of five powers, in the course of successive Congresses saw that the status quo was respected and firmly opposed those who, under pretext of expressing the will of the people, attempted to disturb any of the frontiers which had been established or any of the sovereigns who had been re-established. Later, the Holy Alliance shrank again to an association of only the three Eastern Powers and in this form was the much condemned target of liberal criticism as late as the Crimean War.

Restoration France

In the eyes of most European statesmen France still presented the worst danger of revolutionary contagion. Louis XVIII's position was difficult. He came back in the baggage-train of an invading army and had to authorise concessions to France's enemies. His own partisans, eager to avenge their long exile, made themselves hated. In the Royalist 'White Terror' old revolutionaries were murdered; Ney and La Bédoyère, who had welcomed Napoleon from Elba, were tried and shot. The Assembly, which was elected by limited suffrage — of nearly 25 million inhabitants only 90,000 could vote — was so reactionary that Louis XVIII found it uncontrollable; it was more Royalist than the King. The courts of Europe, however, felt reassured by it. In 1818 the first post-war Congress met at Aix-la-Chapelle, and it was decided to end the occupation more quickly, to reduce the war indemnity and finally to admit France to the Concert of the Great Powers. The Quadruple was thus joined by the Quintuple Alliance. The adversaries of the Restoration were not, however, inactive — as the murder of the Duc de Berry, the King's nephew, sensationally demonstrated. Secret societies, such as the *Charbonnerie* — connected with the *Carbonari* of Italy — were formed; plots were fomented, one of which cost several lives at La Rochelle. But these were surface disturbances and, under moderate ministers like Decazes and Richelieu, France continued to retain the confidence of the Holy Alliance, indeed to such an extent that she was entrusted with the task of restoring autocracy in Spain by an armed expedition in 1823.

Louis XVIII died in 1824 and was succeeded by his younger brother, the Comte d'Artois, who became Charles X. Charles was in every respect unlike his good-natured predecessor. He remained the embittered *émigré* leader he had been during the war. Ultra-Royalism took over the Government. Liberal middle-class opinion was outraged by laws inflicting stern penalties for sacrilege, the re-introduction of primogeniture and a project to indemnify *émigrés* for their confiscated lands. In such measures the bourgeoisie saw a return to the Old Regime. The growing influence of the clergy was supported by the revived Society of Jesus.

At this time the French connection with Algiers — the centre of Barbary piracy — was established, when the consul there was insulted by the Dey of Algiers, who struck him with his fan. In June 1830, 30,000 men landed at Sidi-Ferruch and the French conquest of North Africa began (on a plan left by the Empire). But French opinion, fully absorbed in the situation at home, remained indifferent and the Government derived no benefit from African successes. Relatively moderate ministers were followed by Polignac, the representative of the extreme Right. Even the Chamber of Deputies demanded his resignation; it was dissolved by the King. In the ensuing elections a still greater number of Charles X's opponents was returned. The crisis of the Restoration was near.

Reaction and insurrection in Germany and Italy

As president of the German Confederation and mistress of Lombardy and Venetia, Austria possessed legal rights in Germany, and *de facto* power in Italy. She could intervene in the affairs of both countries, and Metternich was quite prepared to do so to preserve established order. In Austria itself a mosaic of different peoples — Hungarian, Czech, Croat, Slovene, Polish, Italian, Roumanian — was ruled by a relatively small Germanic bureaucracy.

The German Confederation, even after Napoleonic simplification, still suffered from its complex divisions. The restoration of petty sovereigns, jealous of their traditions and determined to retain their individual courts, made the situation even worse. This confusion could not quite stifle a sentiment of racial community derived from a common past and a common language, but national consciousness was confined to a small class. It was, perhaps, strongest in the universities. Nationalism, however, was suspect because of its 'Jacobin' associations. An association of students founded at Jena, the *Burschenschaft*, with its proud device, 'Honour, Liberty, Fatherland', and its colours, red, black and gold, which became the banner of Pan-Germanism, was suspected by Metternich of liberal tendencies. In 1817 a festival was held at the Wartburg to commemorate the tercentenary of Luther's break with Rome, and representatives from all parts of Germany attended. The liberal movement had already won over certain German princes, eager to win the sympathies of their subjects by granting them constitutions. In 1816 the Grand Duke of Weimar gave the example, and he was followed by the rulers of Bavaria, Baden and Würtemberg. Even the hesitant King of Prussia promised to look into the matter. Then, in March 1819, a student stabbed the writer Kotzebue, who was suspected of being an agent of the Tsar. Metternich saw the spectre of revolution in this. He at once imparted his fears to Frederick William of Prussia. Frederick William revoked his promise and the Prussian era of reform begun by Stein was over. A conference at Carlsbad decided on a series of measures which the German Diet, dominated by Austria, was entrusted to execute: strict inspection of the universities, removal of professors charged with liberalism, dissolution of societies judged to be subversive, re-establishment of the censorship, and an enquiry into revolutionary activities. Patriots were thrown into prison and professors had their courses banned. These measures restored apparent calm.

Italy had been partly unified by Napoleon, but it had reverted to being — in Metternich's phrase — 'a geographical expression'. It consisted of ten very unequal states, among which one clearly predominated. This was Sardinia, which with the annexation of Genoa had added a valuable port to its mainland territory of Savoy and Piedmont. The kingdom took its name from the island of Sardinia — which also belonged to it. In the centre of the peninsula the Pope was again temporal sovereign over the Papal States, which stretched from the Tyrrhenian Sea to the Adriatic. The Bourbons again occupied the throne of Naples, or the Two Sicilies, as the kingdom was called. The Grand Duchy of Tuscany, an appanage of the Lorraine-Habsburg family, was now restored to the Archduke Ferdinand, ex-Grand Duke of Wurzburg. The Duchy of Modena was again ruled by the House of Este, the Duchies of Parma and Guastalla had been given to the ex-Empress Marie Louise, while the ex-Queen of Etruria was now the Duchess of Lucca. This meant, in effect, the domination of the entire peninsula by Austria. Not only did she directly administer Venetia and the rich plains of Lombardy, but she occupied Ferrara and family ties kept Tuscany and Parma in her grasp.

Charles X, brother of Louis XVIII and Louis XVI, succeeded to the French throne in 1824. This medal represents him before his accession as the Comte d'Artois. He was one of the first émigrés of the revolutionary era. *Giraudon*

George IV, king of England 1820–30 and previously Regent during his father's insanity. Proud of his claim to be 'the first gentleman of Europe', George was distinguished also by his fatness, cowardice, self-indulgence and extravagance. One of his monuments, Brighton Pavilion, is in the background of this engraving. *Victoria & Albert Museum*

Some of the restored Italian sovereigns behaved like despots in their haste to re-establish the old pre-Revolutionary order. This encouraged the liberal elements who preserved the ideals of the revolutionary Italian states. In Naples the heavy hand of the Bourbons was so intolerable that in 1820 revolution broke out. The King promised to grant concessions and secretly called on Austria for succour. Metternich was naturally anxious to intervene, but not all the powers shared his impatience. A Congress was summoned to meet at Troppau in October and the Tsar insisted that the right to intervene be recognised.

Britain deplored the assertion of a general right of intervention but did not oppose action by Austria in defence of her interests. ' But ', said Castlereagh, ' if they will be theorists, we must act in separation. ' Louis XVIII hedged, torn between the uncertainty of French public opinion and his own family connection with the King of Naples. In the New Year, at Laibach, Austria, Russia and Prussia pronounced themselves in favour of coercion; Britain protested; France had reservations. Ferdinand of Naples now felt no scruples in repudiating his royal word and, with the help of an Austrian army, repressed the revolution and withdrew the Constitution he had granted. Shortly afterwards it was the turn of Turin to become the theatre of disorder. A group of army officers and members of the *Carbonari* seized power, hoping that Charles Albert, a royal prince, would set up a constitutional regime. Victor Emmanuel I abdicated in favour of his brother Charles Felix, and in the subsequent confusion Metternich — fortified by the Neapolitan precedent — defeated the constitutionalists and established Charles Felix firmly with Austrian arms. Secret societies and *Carbonari* were clearly inadequate instruments for the liberation of Italy in the face of Austrian power, which in Lombardy shattered the conspiratorial organisation and imprisoned its members. One of them, the poet Silvio Pellico, described his ten years' incarceration in the subterranean dungeons of the Spielberg in a book which was widely read throughout Europe. It helped to make Italy's liberation the most popular liberal cause of the age.

Regency Britain and George IV

Britain at this moment should have been enjoying one of the most glorious periods of her history. She was undisputed mistress of the seas, and Wellington's victory at Waterloo had given her immense military prestige on the continent. Her long-established parliamentary institutions seemed able to combine liberty and good government and she was in large measure sheltered from the political currents which disturbed Europe. George III, deranged, continued to occupy the throne, but since 1811 his eldest son had acted as Regent. The Tories seemed secure in office, yet the country faced serious problems. Bad harvests, the difficulty of disposing of stocks of merchandise accumulated during the Blockade and the Anglo-American War of 1812, the appearance of an urban working class born of the rapid development of industry and mechanisation, all fed a sense of unrest. Dissatisfaction took two forms — the increasingly vocal demands of those who actually suffered hardship, and a growing feeling among the better-off that the reform of Parliament was the key to all other solutions. The demand for an extension of the suffrage grew. Here and there riots occurred. The most notorious incident took place in 1819 at Manchester where, in St Peter's Field, a large crowd gathered to demand Parliamentary reform was charged by yeomanry, who killed eleven people. It became known, ironically, as the 'Peterloo Massacre' but it was followed by a lull in agitation when conditions improved in the early 1820s.

The Regent came to the throne as George IV in January 1820 under the cloud of a divorce action which added yet another royal scandal to those of his youth. In 1822 Castlereagh committed suicide and the direction of foreign affairs fell to the brilliant and eloquent Canning, who soon appeared as a more outspoken advocate of a liberal foreign policy than his predecessor, whose policy, nevertheless, he continued. While he disapproved of the Austrian interventions in Italy and the French intervention in Spain, he gave every encouragement to the Greek insurrection and the revolt of the Spanish colonies in South America. At home the 'Liberal Toryism' of men like Huskisson revived Pitt's tradition of cautious economic and fiscal reforms which introduced gradual improvements rather than violent alterations. The penal code became more humane. The lowering of tariffs was a first step on the road to free trade. Finally in 1824 the Combination Laws, which had forbidden any combination of masters or workmen to raise or lower wages, were repealed, and the trade union movement could legally begin.

Catholic emancipation troubled politicians more than economic reform. Catholics would undoubtedly have been excluded from holding public office for many more years had not the demands of the Irish to vote and sit in Parliament become increasingly vociferous. These rights, promised when the Act of Union was passed in 1800, had never been granted. In 1823 an Association was formed in Ireland to promote Catholic emancipation and in Daniel O'Connell it found an advocate of genius. In spite of his ineligibility O'Connell succeeded in winning election to the House of Commons, much to the Government's embarrassment. The question arose: should the doors be barred to him? The King was disposed to say yes. The Duke of Wellington, Prime Minister at the time, reluctantly came to the conclusion that reform was imperative and pointed out the danger of civil war among a poverty-stricken people given to violence. Roman Catholics thenceforth had the right to sit in Parliament as well as to hold most civil offices. This destroyed Tory unity.

Russian autocracy from Alexander to Nicholas I

Like Britain but at the opposite extremity of Europe, Russia formed a world apart. Alexander I, an autocrat troubled by liberal impulses, governed his immense empire by imperial decrees with the co-operation of a Council of State and his confidential adviser, Count Arakcheyev, chief of an inefficient and meddlesome bureaucracy. The aristocracy owned great estates which they administered through stewards with small regard for the wretched condition of their serfs. There were no industries, no popular representative institutions, and the enormous majority of the population was illiterate. Apart from a brilliant élite, Russia remained as backward as she had been in the preceding century. And yet Alexander I provided Finland with a relatively liberal statute, and even accorded an advanced constitutional regime to Poland, which was governed by his brother Constantine. His

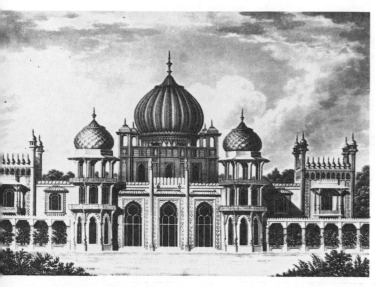

Brighton Pavilion: the west front. This building was not only a pleasurable retreat but one of the last, and perhaps the most outstanding, of the extravaganzas of English romantic architecture. *Mansell*

Fashion after the war reacted violently against the simplicity and elegance of *Directoire* and Empire styles. Trousers, it may be noted in this sketch by Cruickshank, were beginning to replace breeches and boots as acceptable day-wear for gentlemen. *Victoria & Albert Museum*

character was full of such contradictions, and towards the end of his life his melancholy and brooding mysticism were so marked that he became the subject of a strange and persistent legend. In December 1825 he died at Taganrog, a village on the shores of the Sea of Azov, where he had brought the ailing Tsaritsa. According to the legend his solemn funeral rites were a sham and his tomb in the cathedral of St Petersburg a mere cenotaph, while Alexander himself — the ' parricide ' who had consented to the Tsar Paul's death — became a mysterious hermit whose piety was for many years the wonder of the villagers of Siberia.

Alexander left no son and the problem of his successor arose. Should the throne go to Constantine, who on his Polish marriage had renounced his rights to it? Or to the younger brother Nicholas, in virtue of a secret testament? A group of officers in Moscow took advantage of the temporary confusion produced by these questions to engineer an uprising on December 14. Their plan to reform the country had been inspired by contact with Western civilisation during the occupation of France. The interregnum between the death of Alexander and the accession of the new Tsar seemed to furnish an opportune occasion. Knowing the despotic sentiments of Nicholas, the ' Decembrists ' hastened to swear allegiance to Constantine. In the neighbourhood of Kiev a similar uprising led by Colonel Pestell even took on a republican aspect. In both cases, in Moscow and in Kiev, the populace looked on with indifference, and the rebellious officers received the support of only a part of their troops. The repression which followed was pitiless. Nicholas justified his reputation by having the principal insurgents hanged and the rest deported to Siberia. Russia again sank into political lethargy. The new Tsar increased the number and activities of the secret police, though he also showed an interest in the development of the universities and the codification of the laws. Nicholas I's ambitions, however, lay beyond the frontiers of his empire, to the south and east.

Turkey, the Balkans and Greek independence

As the power of the Ottoman Empire declined the burdens it imposed on the subject races increased. The weaker the Sultan became the more the local Moslem authorities oppressed the *rayahs* — their Christian dependents. The Serbs had been the first to achieve a certain degree of autonomy, won during the revolt of Karageorge ' Black George ', the giant peasant who had captured Belgrade in 1806; he was recognised by the Russo-Turkish Treaty of Bucharest in 1812. A year later, when the Russians could no longer aid him, he was forced to flee; and in 1815 his lieutenant and rival, Milos Obrenovic, assumed leadership of a fresh insurrection. The new uprising was successful, and when Karageorge returned Obrenovic had him murdered. The hatred of the two rival families was to darken the history of Serbia for many years to come. In the meantime Obrenovic played his cards so skilfully that, for fear of seeing him become a client of Russia, the Sultan freely acknowledged his hereditary right to rule in Serbia (1830).

Among the Balkan peoples the Greeks were the most advanced and ripe for independence. With a national clergy, a maritime vocation and their rich and teeming

The heading of a list of resolutions drawn up by London hat finishers in 1820. They had an old chartered organisation ante-dating the Trade Union movement which was to form the main expression of working-class demands. *Mansell*

The Greek War of Independence (1821–30) appealed to Western European romanticism, which saw in the struggle a re-living of the legend of Thermopylae. The reality, like most 'nationalist' movements, was less edifying. *Larousse*

communities beyond the borders of Greece itself — such as Phanar, the Greek quarter of Constantinople — they enjoyed advantages unknown to their neighbours when the doctrines of the French Revolution ultimately stirred the Balkans. The retreat of Turkish troops sent to put down the revolt of the Albanian Pasha of Janina was the signal for insurrection in 1821. Germanos, the Bishop of Patras, ' transforming his chasuble into a war banner ' led the uprising. At his appeal, Mavromichalis liberated Morea while Canaris harried the Turks at sea. Thus encouraged, a national Assembly which met in Epidaurus in January 1822 demanded independence. The Turkish reply was grim: the Greeks of Chios were savagely slaughtered and Morea recaptured. Lord Byron met his death at Missolonghi during this episode. Among the Greeks themselves discord arose, but their cause found ardent supporters among those whose memories of classical antiquity were refreshed by romantic sentiment. When the Sultan called upon the Egyptians to crush the rebels, Britain, France and Russia — though the Tsar was seriously disturbed by the democratic complexion of the insurgents — proclaimed their sympathy for the Greeks in the Treaty of London and decided on a naval demonstration. On 20 October 1827 at Navarino a fortuitous incident changed the demonstration into a battle in which the Turco-Egyptian fleet was destroyed. The echo of the cannonfire of Navarino made a deep impression in France, and General Maison was sent to drive the Egyptians out of Morea. The Tsar, too, indirectly contributed to the Greek cause by declaring war on Turkey, though his object was purely to satisfy ambitions of his own. Nevertheless, in 1829, when the Russian armies marched on Constantinople to impose the Treaty of Adrianople on the Sublime Porte, the Sultan was forced to confirm the independence of Greece which a few months previously had been recognised by the Protocol of London. Greece was confined to narrow frontiers — from the Gulf of Arta to the Gulf of Volo — but thus reduced, her independence was solemnly proclaimed on 3 February 1830. Personal quarrels disturbed the early days of the new state. The murder of the head of government, Capo d'Istrias, a native of Corfu, brought in the three protecting powers, who installed a monarchy to be entrusted to a foreign sovereign, a Bavarian prince, who in 1832 became King Otto of Greece.

These events had repercussions in the Danubian principalities of Moldavia and Wallachia. An insurrection had taken place in 1821 led by Alexander Ypsilanti, nephew of a former *hospodar* and an officer in the Russian army; but it found little support. By the Convention of Ackerman, however, Russia obtained considerable advantages in the Danubian principalities. It was the Sultan's refusal to agree to these concessions that brought on the war terminated by the Treaty of Adrianople, by which Turkey was obliged to pay an indemnity guaranteed by Russian occupation of the disputed regions. For six years Russia implanted her influence here; established on the shores of the Black Sea, Nicholas I thenceforth assumed the role of protector of the emergent Balkan nations.

The Iberian peninsula and Latin America

Returning to Spain in 1814 after six years of exile, Ferdinand VII found it hard to recognise his kingdom. The *juntas* which had organised the resistance to Napoleon had given way to the *Cortes* of Cadiz, which drew up the Constitution of 1812 (modelled on the French Constitution of 1791), proclaimed the sovereignty of the nation, and abolished the Old Regime. Ferdinand soon closed the doors of the *Cortes* and imposed the death penalty on anyone who attempted to apply their decrees. Then, surrounding himself with a reactionary clique which presided over the savage reaction which ensued, he reigned as an absolute monarch. The Inquisition was re-established and the prisons were soon overflowing with liberals and *afrancesados* — as those who had co-operated with the Napoleonic Government were called. The harshness of the reprisals roused discontent which led to plots and conspiracies. In the American colonies, on the other hand, the return of the Bourbon King of Spain was at first followed by a successful series of operations. The King's troops set about recapturing positions which had fallen into the hands of the insurgents. Morelos was executed in Mexico and Chile was reconquered. Bolivar, driven from Venezuela, took refuge in the West Indies. At this favourable moment Ferdinand had not the wit to grant a certain measure of autonomy and freedom of trade needed to preserve his colonial sovereignty. He was as intransigent overseas as at home, and insisted in re-imposing his absolute authority by force. A force of 20,000 men was prepared to embark at Cadiz to crush the rebels; but these soldiers then became the backbone of a revolution in Spain itself.

They lent a willing ear to liberal propaganda and in January 1820 enthusiastically followed one of their officers, Riego, who proclaimed the re-establishment of the 1812 Constitution; the entire region joined their cause. The revolt led to cruel reprisals. The Great Powers were disturbed, though they could not agree on what to do about it. The Tsar, Metternich and Frederick William were once more in favour of armed intervention, Canning opposed them, while Louis XVIII and his minister Villèle sat prudently on the fence. In his eagerness to see the Royalist White Flag share the military glory that the Tricolour had once known, Chateaubriand played an important role at the Congress of Verona in 1822. The eloquence with which his convictions were expressed won the King's consent and the mission of restoring order beyond the Pyrenees was given to France. Six months after its departure for Spain the French force reached Cadiz without difficulty, and the capture of the Trocadero, the fortress which commanded the port, brought the campaign to its conclusion in August 1823. The re-establishment of Ferdinand VII brought violently reactionary measures.

Absolutism thus triumphed in Spain. In the Spanish American colonies, however, Royalist reverses occurred which led to the loss of the greater part of the overseas empire. Argentina had in 1816 already proclaimed her independence, and her hero, San Martin, in a bold march across the Andes, liberated Chile. Bolivar — the great *Libertador* — won a brilliant victory at Boyaca that enabled him to occupy New Granada, which was renamed Colombia. Then in a campaign remarkable for its boldness he finally assured the freedom of his native Venezuela, while in 1821 San Martin liberated Peru. In Mexico, where the revolt appeared to have been stifled, an ambitious Spanish general, the Creole Iturbide, passed over to the insurgents and revived their cause. In 1822 he assumed the title of Emperor; within two years he was shot, but Mexico was free. The United States of America decided

Simon Bolivar (1783–1830) liberator of half of South America, died before he could fulfil the work of consolidation and unification. After his death, the states he founded fell into disorder and revolution. *Mansell*

James Monroe, president of the U.S.A., formulated the 'Monroe Doctrine' which warned European powers against any further attempts to colonise or intervene in the western hemisphere. *Radio Times Hulton Picture Library*

in 1822 to recognise the young emancipated republics, with whose efforts to win freedom North Americans had from the beginning been sympathetic; they, too, had fought for their freedom and favoured the new republics as much from sentiment as from commercial considerations. In the following year, President Monroe warned the European powers that the United States would view with disfavour any attempt by them to interfere in the affairs of the New World. The 'Monroe Doctrine', together with British naval superiority, cut short several projects which had been envisaged, notably those of the Tsar, who was the most ardent advocate of restoring Spanish sovereignty, or, in default of that, of making certain that the new states became monarchies. On the other hand, Britain had for some time been secretly helping the rebels by sending them arms, munitions and even volunteers, some of whom, like Admiral Cochrane, were persons of consequence. Canning hesitated no longer to recognise the independence of the rebel states and hastened to sign a commercial treaty with Argentina. From then onwards the rebels won victory after victory. The last Spanish army was destroyed at Ayacucho in 1824 and the last Spanish garrison, that at Callao in Peru, surrendered in 1826; with it disappeared the last relic of Charles V's immense mainland American empire. Whether the young republics would have the wisdom to agree among themselves was still questionable. Bolivar, who had made Upper Peru into Bolivia and become its president, was hopeful; but in 1826 the Congress of Panama tried in vain to weld the new republics into a federation. It failed even to unite Colombia, Peru and Bolivia. The perpetuation of the division of South America into numerous separate states whose borders were roughly those of the former Spanish viceroyalties aroused conspiracies and bitter personal enmities and led to frontier disputes often followed by armed conflict. These tendencies disillusioned the architects of the liberation. Bolivar attempted unsuccessfully to impose his own dictatorship. Discouraged, he resigned from office shortly before his death in 1830.

Although Portugal was going through a period of internal agitation no less distressing than that of Spain, Brazil achieved its freedom more peacefully than the Spanish colonies. In August 1820, imitating the example of Cadiz, Portuguese officers stationed in Oporto led an insurrection which spread as far as Lisbon, the capital. The uprising could in part be attributed to the neglect of his own kingdom by John VI, who since 1808 had been living in Brazil. In the beginning of 1821 he therefore decided to return to Lisbon, where he took an oath to defend the constitution which the army had drawn up. Brazil, not wishing to become an ordinary colony again, took this opportunity to declare its independence. The Regent, Dom Pedro, eldest son of the King, was proclaimed Emperor of Brazil in October 1822, and John VI bowed before the accomplished fact. Meanwhile in Portugal, with the co-operation of the Queen and the support of the army, the King's younger son, Dom Miguel, who was hostile to the constitution, seized power. John VI shortly afterwards succeeded in regaining his throne. Then, in 1826, he died — leaving the Emperor of Brazil, Pedro I, the legitimate successor to the crown of Portugal. Pedro, however, resigned the crown to his daughter Maria, who was seven years old, on condition that she married her uncle Dom Miguel. Miguel was made Regent, but two years later had himself proclaimed King. He at once abolished the constitution while the child Maria took refuge in England. Aggravated by dynastic rivalry, the threat of civil war hung over Portugal, torn between the partisans of the absolutist Miguel and the liberals, supported by Britain. The British fleet commanded the banks of the Tagus and Britain had not ceased to exercise her traditional influence in the affairs of Portugal.

The development of the United States

On 24 December 1814 a peace treaty signed at Ghent put an end to the war which, since June 1812, had existed between the United States and Great Britain — a kind of ' second war of independence '. The conflict had arisen formally over maritime rights, especially the claim of the British navy — then at war with Napoleon — to the right of searching American ships at sea and its habit of pressing American seamen into British service. The growth of the opinion in the American west that from Canada the British were stiffening the resistance of Indians to the further advance of the frontier was, however, just as important in making the war popular. An American attempt to invade Canada failed, but the victory of General Jackson at New Orleans avenged the brief and rapid British seizure of Washington, during which the Capitol was burned to the ground. The young American navy had shown great promise and achieved several brilliant victories in single-ship actions. But the war had been fought without engaging national passions and was wisely terminated by a peace which changed very little.

During the brief period between 1812 and 1821 six new states were added to those which had already enlarged the territory occupied by the original thirteen British colonies. The centre of gravity of the new republic had moved noticeably towards the west, while at the same time a movement southward, down the valley of the Mississippi, was in progress. In 1819 Spain ceded Florida, and the position of the United States on the Gulf of Mexico was further strengthened. This territorial growth was accompanied by a corresponding growth in population, which between 1790 and 1830 rose from four to twelve million inhabitants. Nor had the great flood of transatlantic immigration yet begun to be felt. In the eastern states the war with Britain had encouraged rapid industrial development, since it was necessary to manufacture locally products which had previously been imported. With the introduction of machinery and the exploitation of the nearby iron and coal mines, the textile industries and metallurgy now began to make immense strides. As the working population increased the towns of New England grew rapidly into cities, although in 1830 over ninety per cent of the population was still classified as ' rural '. In the west the plains still awaited the arrival of pioneers to develop their potential riches. In the south, where tobacco, indigo and sugar-cane had long been cultivated, the cotton gin had made cotton the staple crop. Between 1800 and 1830 its production was multiplied ten times. Transportation was made cheaper and distances greatly reduced by such public works as the Erie Canal, which joined Lake Erie to the Hudson River, by the application of steam to navigation and, shortly afterwards, by the construction of railroads. An expanding economy, seemingly limitless space, an absence of the social assumptions of European society and a legacy of British political institu-

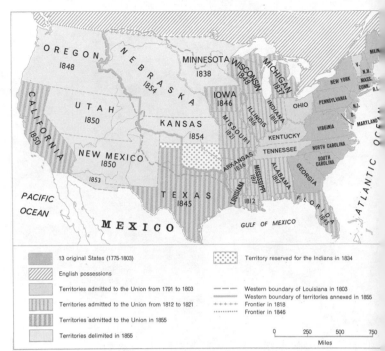

EXPANSION OF THE UNITED STATES 1775-1855

tions and ideas produced a new sort of American, a democrat undiscouraged by the prospect of work and hardship, knowing that there was every chance that one day his labours would be rewarded with affluence.

As the United States grew in wealth and population, so the nation's consciousness of its own identity developed; it became aware of the role it could play in world affairs. While the powers of Europe were debating at Verona the advisability of crushing the Spanish colonial insurgents by armed intervention, the United States had made its appearance on the international scene by addressing a warning to Europeans about their activities in the New World.

A few years later, in 1829, a President was elected whose strong personality and reputation conferred on him exceptional authority. In Andrew Jackson, born in the backwoods, an orphan, self-taught, in turn workman, farmer, lawyer and the general who defeated the British at New Orleans, the passionately egalitarian American people recognised one of themselves. No lover of tradition, the new President broke with the earlier political parties and proclaimed himself a Democrat. He was an opponent of centralisation, and an enemy of monopolies and the Bank of the United States. He befriended both the farmers of the west and the planters of the south. Thus he assumed a position on the two burning questions which were beginning to occupy public opinion. The industrial north clamoured for higher tariffs to protect the products of its new factories; the agricultural south, which exported cotton and purchased manufactured articles, pressed equally for free trade. Needing abundant cheap labour for its cotton fields, the south also was determined to maintain slavery, whose abolition was demanded with increasing force in the north. The slavery controversy had already become so acute by 1820 that when two new states — Maine and Missouri — were admitted to the Union it was necessary to find a compromise. In order to preserve an equilibrium between ' free ' and ' slave ' states it was agreed that south of the parallel 36° 30′ slavery should be tolerated, and north of it abolished. Popularly the line of demarcation became known as the Mason-Dixon line.

The apogee of romanticism

Romanticism was not simply a literary and artistic phenomenon but a new way of thinking, and, more especially, a new way of feeling. It emphasised the sensibilities and the unique importance of the individual. In romanticism feeling took precedence over reason. It delighted not only in the emotions of the human heart but in nature, which was also a source of emotion, and even in inanimate objects to which poetry lent a soul. In reaction against the abstract and artificial, romanticism willingly neglected the constant and universal to concentrate on the individual, the personal and the idiosyncratic. The romantic sympathy was engaged more by the sorrows and disillusions of life than by its joys, and attracted more towards the humble than the powerful. The romantic hero saw himself misunderstood, unappreciated, and suffering from being unable to realise insatiable desires: ' Man is a fallen god who still remembers heaven. ' This attitude resulted in an urge to rebel, to revolt against society, against the established rules and, in general, against all forms of restraint. Romanticism, it was said, ' is insurrection '. In its desire to break with the familiar it showed a lively curiosity in foreign peoples, and this lent it a cosmopolitan air: it was drawn by strange and distant lands and scenes, which led to a taste for the exotic.

In a generation which had come of age during the upheavals of the Revolution and the Napoleonic Wars such tendencies were understandable. Too many who had fought, as they thought, for a new and better world found only frustration or disillusion. The first of the great French romantics, Chateaubriand, in his *René*, had already in 1805 spoken of this ' *mal du siècle* '. His masterly *Mémoires d'Outre-tombe*, a partly fictionalised account of his own life, had immense influence. It was, indeed, in literature that romanticism originated. The classicism of the French seventeenth and eighteenth centuries was a vehicle of thought for a cultured élite, and yearned after universality. Instead, the romantics offered popular and national works. For the measured and logical argument of classicism they substituted passion and lyricism. The author, formerly discreet on the subject of his own personal life, no longer hesitated to write about himself or to display and exaggerate his own private sentiments. Sexual love became the inexhaustible theme, explored again and again. Means of expression also altered, and a torrent of unrestrained verbiage took the place of classical brevity and clarity. Victor Hugo set the example with his exotic vocabulary and his violent distortions of the classical Alexandrine metre.

In Germany the romanticism of the Napoleonic period continued to affect philosophy by its emphasis on the historical. Hegel continued the construction of his system with the publication in 1821 of his *Philosophy of Right*, and with the delivery of lectures on the *Philosophy of History* to which students flocked from all over Germany.

An early American railroad. The first public one was the Baltimore and Ohio in 1828. Railroads played a major part in opening the West and bringing its food products to the Eastern markets. *Association of American Railroads*

The fashionable philosopher, however, was Schopenhauer, whose *The World as Will and Idea* (1819) became the handbook of pessimism. German poetry had two great exponents in the Austrian dramatic poet Grillparzer and Heinrich Heine, born in Düsseldorf of Jewish descent. Heine's delicate and subtle lyricism had an ironic and rather French flavour, and he went to Paris, where he wrote in both German and French. In England, Wordsworth and Coleridge were still writing, and Byron between 1816 and 1824 published *Manfred* and *Don Juan*; Shelley, whose *Prometheus Unbound* appeared in 1820, and Keats, the outstanding English exponent of a new aesthetic of sensation, belonged to the succeeding generation. Britain's best-known romantic literature in Europe, however, was not poetry but prose; the historical novels of Scott — *Kenilworth, Quentin Durward, Ivanhoe* — were read with enthusiasm everywhere. When Lamartine published his *Méditations Poétiques* in 1820, Vigny his *Eloa* four years later, and when in 1827 the young Victor Hugo issued the new romantic school's manifesto in the challenging preface to his unproduced drama *Cromwell* they did not appear as innovators — the movement was already well under way. In Italy the poems of Alessandro Manzoni had met with general admiration in 1810, though his great historical novel *I Promessi Sposi* appeared only seventeen years later. The pessimistic and despairing poems of Leopardi marked the appearance of romantic melancholy in Italy. It spread as far afield as Russia, where *The Prisoner of the Caucasus* by Pushkin appeared in 1822.

The other arts underwent a similar evolution, varying from country to country according to each one's peculiar genius. In France the pictorial arts prevailed. While Ingres — a worthy pupil of David — was still painting according to the canons of classical art in 1827, with his *Apotheosis of Homer*, Géricault's *Raft of the Medusa* (1819) brought a new sense of violent emotion to painting. The fiery Delacroix revolutionised painting with his *Dante* 291 in *Charon's Boat* and his *Massacres of Chios*, while the silvery landscapes of Corot were a poetic evocation of the beauties of nature. Constable, the greatest English artist of his day, was in the next generation to have more influence on the development of European painting than any other English painter. In Spain the elderly Goya painted an equestrian portrait of Ferdinand VII himself and also produced the series of engravings known as the *Disparates*, as enigmatic as the frescoes in his villa on the banks of the Manzanares. In Bordeaux, where he died in 1828 as a refugee octogenarian, he produced astonishing bullfight scenes by means of new lithographic techniques. German romanticism found its highest expression in music. Beethoven's Choral Symphony — his ninth and last — was first played in 1823. Schubert followed him with songs which touched the heart and symphonies of which the 'Unfinished Symphony' became a popular favourite. The music of Weber, Mendelssohn and Schumann would be thought outstanding in any age in which it had not to be set against such gigantic cultural achievements as these.

Romanticism was not limited to art, music and poetry. It also invaded the field of history. The German Schlegel wrote a *Philosophy of History* and Michelet began his presentation of the history of France as a passionate, colourful historical pageant. In 1817 — in the early Restoration days, when 'throne and altar' were united — Lamennais published his *Essay on Indifference* in which he attacked religious tepidity in violent language. Later he turned against the Bourbons, founded a society to encourage Ultramontanism and was soon embroiled with the conservative and Royalist Gallicans. He appealed to the Pope only to be condemned. His greatest work, *Paroles d'un Croyant*, was put on the Index and he died excommunicate.

Even political life could not fail to be infected by romanticism. Sentiment and passion played a part in the philhellenism that sent ardent volunteers to fight for the insurgent Greeks, in the sympathy which the young South American republics aroused, in the benevolence with which the awakening of national consciousness in Italy, Germany and the Balkans was generally regarded.

FROM THE 1830 REVOLUTION TO THE 1848 REVOLUTION

The 1830 Revolution

When the elections in France returned a majority against him, Charles X showed his contempt by dissolving the new Chamber of Deputies and, on 26 July 1830, set about governing by means of decrees, one of which suspended the freedom of the press. Then he went to Rambouillet to hunt. At the news the people of Paris at once rose. During the course of the 'Three Glorious Days' (July 27–29) students and workers raised barricades and made themselves masters of Paris. Charles X, astonished by the unexpected violence, abdicated in favour of his grandson the Duke of Bordeaux. This solution was not practicable. The July Revolution had been the work of liberals and Bonapartists. After his death Napoleon had become a legendary hero who not only embodied the epic glory of

the Empire but had become the symbol of liberty. The insurgents hoped to tear up the ' shameful treaties of 1815 ', to restore their country to its proper rank within its 'natural' frontiers, which would include Belgium and the left bank of the Rhine.

It was exactly these ideas which frightened Europe — as the more intelligent of the liberal leaders were quick to realise. Thiers, a young and active journalist of great talent who had just founded a new paper, *The National*, and Laffitte, an influential banker, attempted with their friends to find a way of ending the crisis. The Duke of Orleans belonged to the cadet branch of the Bourbon family, but he had fought for the Republic at Jemappes and was known for his liberal sentiments. By accepting a throne offered to him by the two Chambers, by publicly adopting the Tricolour and embracing that ' grand old man of the Revolution ' Lafayette, he gave promise of becoming a King of the French rather than the King of France. Thus a revolution which had sprung from the people's discontent resulted in the establishment of a bourgeois monarchy. It was an equivocal situation from which Louis Philippe's entire reign was to suffer. In the meantime Europe, in spite of the new sovereign's display of moderation, remained on its guard. Metternich did not disguise his mistrust. The Tsar haughtily spoke of deposing this ' king of the barricades ', and Frederick William III of Prussia would willingly have helped: both, however, soon had other things to worry about. Revolutionary fervour had spread beyond the borders of France and threatened all Europe.

Belgian independence

The Belgians, united to Holland against their wishes by the treaties of 1815, endured their fate with growing impatience. A number of them were in favour of being annexed to France again, but the majority desired independence. Flemings and Walloons were in agreement to put an end to a union which affronted their national sentiments. A month after the uprising in Paris an insurrection broke out in Brussels, followed on October 4 by a proclamation of Belgian independence. Holland at once appealed to the guarantors of the Treaties of Vienna, who were all the more inclined to take action since the disturbances threatened to spread to the Rhineland, Switzerland and even Italy. But Britain, faithful to her traditions and determined to keep the Great Powers out of the Low Countries, was resolutely opposed to this course, while the new Government of France, still shaky, found itself presented with a dangerous choice. To satisfy the partisans of annexation would be to gain enormous popularity and fulfil the wishes of the majority in France, at the same time pleasing a certain section of Belgian opinion. It would also — and without the least doubt — provoke the anger of Britain. It was a basic axiom of British policy to prevent France above all powers from occupying the mouths of the River Scheldt.

Louis Philippe, who was as pacific as he was reasonable, chose to disappoint his compatriots rather than to risk war. Talleyrand was recalled from his retirement and entrusted with the difficult mission of negotiating with Britain. As ambassador to London Talleyrand, now seventy-six and still in favour of an alliance with Britain such as he had advocated during the Congress of Vienna, was able to assure his British friends that France was disinterested. On 11 November 1830 an armistice put an end to the hostilities between Holland and Belgium, and shortly afterwards Belgium was declared to be independent and neutral. Belgian neutrality, like the neutrality of Switzerland in 1815, was recognised in perpetuity and guaranteed by all the Great Powers. The Tsar, who was the least pleased with this arrangement, was soon busy with trouble nearer home in Poland. Belgium, it was decided, must be a monarchy, but the choice of a monarch presented difficulties. The choice eventually fell on Prince Leopold of Saxe-Coburg, who later married a daughter of Louis Philippe. There remained the question of frontiers. The Belgians claimed Maastricht, Limburg and Luxemburg. Contesting these claims, the Dutch broke the armistice and invaded Belgium, whose King called upon France for help. France sent troops to occupy Brussels. A treaty known as the 'Twenty-four Articles' was signed on 15 October 1831 and appreciably reduced the frontiers originally assigned to the new state. Holland retained Maastricht and a part of Limburg, while the major part of Luxemburg was made into an independent Grand Duchy and allotted to William of Orange. But Holland still refused to sign the treaty, continued to protest and held on to Antwerp until the combined action of a French army and a British fleet dislodged her in December 1832. Only in April 1839 did Holland at last sign the treaty recognising the independence and neutrality of Belgium.

The uprising in Poland

Alexander's efforts to unify Russia and Poland had met irreconcilable differences of culture, religion and tradition. The relative moderation of the Grand Duke Constantine, morganatically married to a Polish woman, had not prevented the Tsarist bureaucracy from reducing as far as possible the constitutional liberties which had been granted, nor from undermining the influence of the universities and exiling to Russia persons judged to be dangerous — such as the poet Mickiewicz. The inevitable response was the formation of secret societies among young Poles, societies with patriotic and even revolutionary leanings. Their activities met with increased severity after the accession of Nicholas I.

Thus the atmosphere was already threatening when it became known that the Polish army would be called upon to join the Russians to stamp out the revolutions in France and in Belgium. It was this news that unleashed the popular insurrection of 29 November 1830 which the army itself immediately joined. But in spite of its courage the Polish army, under the orders of successive leaders, was unable to act as a unit. It was defeated by overwhelmingly superior Russian forces commanded by Paskevich. Similar disunity prevailed at Warsaw, where despite the efforts of Prince Adam Czartoryski, who had been chosen chief of the national government, members of the Diet failed to agree among themselves. In October 1831, after six months of struggle, order — Russian order — reigned in Warsaw. In the harsh reprisals which followed thousands of Poles left their country. Most of them went to France, where the Polish uprising had aroused the liveliest sympathy. Paris became the hearth from which hopes of a 'Free Poland' radiated and the intellectual centre of the Poles. During this time in Poland itself patriots were deported, the

Delacroix painted *Liberty at the Barricades* to commemorate the French revolution of 1830, which was the most important of a series of revolutions which convulsed Europe for nearly two years. *Marburg*

The July Revolution in Paris led to the flight of Charles X and the overthrow of the Bourbon house. Its replacement by a constitutional monarchy narrowly averted the establishment of a radical republic under Lafayette (depicted here fraternising with his supporters). *Mansell*

293

Louis Philippe, former Jacobin, soldier of the Revolution, and King of the French 1830–48, drawn by Daumier. A much-maligned monarch, unpopular because he gave France un-spectacular middle-class government. *Mansell*

universities closed and the Diet suppressed. Endowed with an 'organic statute', the country was savagely Russianised, and this example was imitated by Prussia, who treated Poles within her frontiers equally brutally.

Italian and German insurrections

Austrian satellite rulers and Austrian troops in the Milanese did not prevent Italian responses to the events in France and Belgium. In February 1831 there were revolutionary outbreaks in the Grand Duchy of Modena, which became the leader of the liberal protest. The movement spread to the neighbouring Duchy of Parma, from which the ex-Empress Marie Louise was expelled, and was intensified in the Papal States. The most serious disturbances occurred in the Romagna, especially in Bologna. The Pope lost no time in appealing to Austria, ever ready to stifle attempted revolt, always alert to the call of the Holy See. Louis Philippe, who had been raised to power by liberal opinion, could not, of course, accept such intervention; and his Government, under the guidance of the banker Laffitte, made it known that France did not recognise Austria's right — except in Lombardy and Venetia — to interfere in the affairs of the Italian peninsula. The warning did not prevent Austria from re-establishing Marie Louise in Parma and occupying Bologna in January 1832. Laffitte's successor, Casimir Périer, thereupon acted with firmness: a detachment of French troops was sent by sea to occupy Ancona and stayed there until 1838, as long as the Austrian troops remained in Bologna.

In Germany only minor disturbance occurred but national sentiment grew steadily, especially after the Greek revolt. Encouraged by the revolution in France, the people of Saxony, Hanover and Hesse obliged their sovereign to grant them constitutions, while the subjects of Duke Charles drove him temporarily out of Brunswick. Prussia, however, remained undisturbed. Closely supervised by Metternich, Germany in general was not at this moment endangered by the revolutionary ferment.

The first years of the July Monarchy

The new regime in France began in a troubled atmosphere. A revolt had brought Louis Philippe to the throne and he was always aware that it could be followed by another. When Charles X's ministers were merely imprisoned and not sentenced to death there was tumultuous protest. Supporters of the new regime were split into a progressive wing known as the 'Movement' and a moderate party known as the 'Resistance'. By calling Laffitte to power the King revealed his preference for the Movement; but Laffitte, careworn and financially ruined, resigned and was replaced by one of the leaders of the opposing party, Casimir Périer, who shortly afterwards died of cholera. Périer was succeeded for four years by a ministry of three in which Thiers, quick and supple, Guizot, rigid and doctrinaire, and the moderate Broglie cancelled each other out. They then gave way to Molé, an advocate of conciliation. Certain reforms were, none the less, introduced. The Charter was revised so that the King no longer had the right to govern simply by decree. The franchise was extended, doubling the number of electors. Finally the peers ceased to be hereditary and were named for life. The clericalism of Charles X was disavowed, to the great dissatisfaction of Catholics. But the real enemies of the July Monarchy were the Republicans, the Legitimists and the Bonapartists. The first could not forgive Louis Philippe for having deserted the Revolution; the second for having accepted a crown which legitimately belonged to the elder branch of the Bourbon family; the last because he abjured the glorious traditions of the Empire. All three formed conspiracies and staged demonstrations. The most frequent and dangerous disturbances were the work of the Republicans who, clamouring for social reform, all too often transformed the streets of Paris and Lyon into battlefields where the National Guard, and even the army, was called in to fire on the mob. The plundering of St Germain l'Auxerrois in 1831, the battle in the cloisters of St Merri in 1832, and the rising of the silk workers in Lyon in 1834 were followed by exceptionally stringent measures on the part of the Government — which in turn gave rise to more riots and further bloodshed. Meanwhile the Legitimists attempted to raise a new revolt in the Vendée. The rising failed. Napoleon's son, the Duke of Reichstadt, whom the Bonapartists called Napoleon II, died in July 1832 at the palace of Schönbrunn in Vienna; the new head of the family, Napoleon's young nephew Louis Napoleon Bonaparte, in 1836 attempted to rally the garrison at Strasbourg to his cause. The indulgence with which he was treated encouraged him to try again four years later. This time he was imprisoned, though later he escaped. Attempts on the King's life were also made. In 1835, for instance, an infernal machine exploded as he passed, but failed to achieve its object.

The reign of Louis Philippe was none the less an era of prosperity. The King encouraged the well-to-do middle classes, who thrived and became rich. Money was the ruling passion, and its importance is vividly portrayed in the novels of Balzac. The financiers, industrialists and merchants of the upper bourgeoisie benefited most from the great strides which were being made in agriculture, the rapid development of machinery, the completion of public works and the construction of the first railways. They were the profiteers of the regime and enjoyed the material comforts of the world, blind to the mounting rage of the masses who, awakening to a consciousness of their own strength, felt exploited and frustrated. To this discontent, born of poverty, was added the restiveness of those Frenchmen whose sense of patriotism had been humiliated. To appease Europe, and especially Britain, the Government had pocketed its pride and given way in the Belgian affair. In Algeria it proceeded slowly. It seemed willing to make any concession to preserve a peace which was good for business and much to the King's personal taste. To elevate prudence and economy to the rank of cardinal virtues was a bourgeois ideal; it did not appeal to workers, soldiers or young romantics.

Great Britain and electoral reform

Social and political changes in Britain were accelerated by events which occurred on the continent, though their origins were local. Electoral reform had already long been disputed. William IV, who succeeded to the throne on the death of his brother George IV in 1830, was thought to favour reform. The issue came to a head when in the same year Wellington's Government resigned and the Whigs,

William Wilberforce (1759–1833), the Evangelical leader of the campaign to abolish slavery in the British Empire. A Conservative, he struggled fiercely against the vested interest in the slave trade. *Popper*

The plan of a slave-ship, showing the conditions in which slaves crossed the Atlantic. The slave trade was abolished by Great Britain in 1807, and other countries were persuaded to follow suit in 1815.

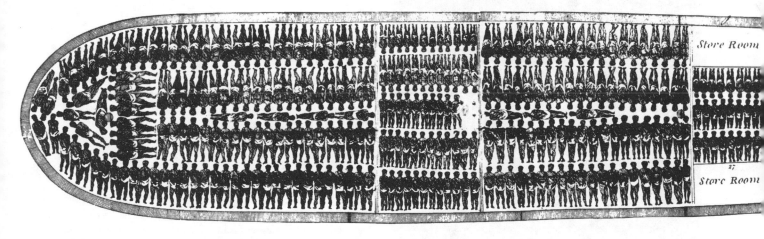

after a long eclipse, took office. The electoral map of the country did not correspond to the distribution of population. Corrupt 'rotten boroughs', sometimes almost unpopulated, continued by virtue of ancient rights to return members to Parliament while new, populous and active cities were scarcely represented. It was widely felt that the landed gentry was favoured to the detriment of the business classes, the true source of wealth of the new industrial Britain. Lord Grey now introduced measures of reform which were supported by so narrow a majority that he dissolved Parliament and appealed to the country. He was successful in the elections, but the House of Lords now refused to pass the Bill. Finally, the King promised to create enough Lords to swamp Tory opposition in that house and Wellington gave way. Parliament finally passed the Reform Bill in June 1832. A great number of the old borough constituencies were abolished and some hundred

Parliamentary seats that they had formerly possessed were distributed among the large cities. The franchise was extended so that everyone occupying a house or shop of an annual value of ten pounds could vote; this at once added about 250,000 voters to the rolls, mainly from the middle class. The Act still did not satisfy popular wishes, but it was a beginning and it succeeded in calming agitation for a few years. The reform also resulted in a new alignment of political parties and a change in party names: a minority of radicals joined the Whigs and were sometimes called Liberals, while the Tories, still under the leadership of Peel, became the Conservatives.

The importance of this electoral reform, a vital step in the evolution of Great Britain towards democracy, overshadowed further reforms, in general of a humanitarian nature, which were adopted in the next decade. The abolition of slavery in the West Indies, for which compensation

The Great Reform Act of 1832 did much to destroy England's 'rotten boroughs'. But the overall change in the nature of the House of Commons was less than had been hoped for. *Radio Times Hulton Picture Library*

Mahmoud II, Sultan of Turkey from 1809 to 1839. He attempted to restore the power of the Sultanate but had to face revolts in Serbia, Wallachia and Greece, and the rise to virtual independence of Mehemet Ali in Egypt. *Hachette*

was paid to West Indian planters, factory laws to limit and regulate child labour, the reform of municipal government — these measures aimed partly at dissipating social unrest due to the emergence of new working-class demands, and partly at satisfying the middle class's wish for cheaper and more efficient government. The aims were bound to conflict, but both seemed reconciled in the growing agitation against import duties on corn which raised the price of bread — and therefore of wages — solely in the interest of the landlord. Richard Cobden founded the Anti-Corn Law League in Manchester in 1838 and made his maiden speech in Parliament on the subject in 1841. Public opinion was roused and five years later both Peel and Russell were converted to Cobden's view and the Corn Laws were repealed. On the Irish question the country was still divided, but the movement for repeal of the Act of Union was growing.

Such was the situation when, on the death of her uncle William IV in 1837, an eighteen-year-old princess came to the throne. Queen Victoria inaugurated a reign which was to last for more than sixty years and was to be one of the most glorious in the history of Great Britain. Despite her youth the Queen was not long in making her firm and resolute character felt. Shortly after her coronation she married her cousin, Albert of Saxe-Coburg, and — in contrast to the disreputable personal behaviour of her predecessors — gave her people an example of respectable and happy family life. Since by the laws of Hanover women could not inherit the throne, the personal union of Hanover and Britain ended with the accession of Victoria.

Dynastic struggles in the Iberian peninsula

In Spain, as in Portugal, lack of a political consensus combined with social and cultural backwardness to hinder development towards constitutional government. The troubles which resulted were similar in both countries and the analogy was underlined by a curious and purely accidental similarity in the dynastic struggles which rent both nations.

Ferdinand VII had scarcely been installed on his throne in Madrid before he began that series of savagely reactionary measures with which the name of his minister Calomarde is associated. Childless and a widower, Ferdinand VII married for the fourth time in 1829. His queen Maria Christina, a princess of Naples, bore him a daughter, Isabella, and persuaded him to repeal the existing Salic law (which prohibited female succession) in order that Isabella could succeed him. In this way he excluded his brother, Don Carlos, from the throne. A second daughter was born shortly before the King's death in 1833. Don Carlos, denying the legality of his brother's action, at once proclaimed himself King; he stood for traditionalism in religion and absolutism in politics, and rallied the clergy and a large section of the country to his cause. Abroad, the autocratic monarchs of Austria, Prussia and Russia gave him moral support by refusing to recognise the regency of Maria Christina, who was encouraged by Britain and France, the 'liberal' powers. For seven years civil war raged intermittently. The 'Carlists' dominated the north: the Basque Provinces, Navarre, Aragon, Catalonia. In Castile they made less headway, but at one time they succeeded in penetrating as far as Andalusia.

While the confused struggle continued and its issue remained uncertain Maria Christina faced grave difficulties.

A 'royal statute' promulgated in July 1834 at the instigation of the minister Martinez de la Rosa made her situation somewhat easier. Just before this, in April, France and Britain had given an earnest of their sympathy when, after a joint request from Madrid and Lisbon, they signed with the two Iberian states a Quadruple Alliance, promising their aid in expelling the two absolutist pretenders, Don Carlos and, in Portugal, Dom Miguel. But in August 1836, while Maria Christina was in residence at her summer palace of La Granja, pressure was brought on her to grant a constitutional government with two elective chambers. When the elections brought a conservative majority the progressive party appealed to General Espartero to deal with their opponents, led by General Narvaez. Espartero was successful and fresh elections gave the upper hand to the progressives. If the 'constitutionals' were thus divided among themselves, the Carlists were in an even worse state of disagreement. Indeed strife in their own camp resulted in the defeat of the Carlist cause. By the peace of Vergara in August 1839 Don Carlos renounced his pretensions to the throne and sought refuge in France. This success won for Espartero the title Duke of the Victory and a popularity which enabled him to become chief of a powerful liberal movement. Maria Christina called upon him to form a Government, but when in 1840 he insisted on her accepting his ministers she chose to resign the regency and go into exile in France.

In Portugal the reactionary measures imposed by Dom Miguel were of such a ruthless character that in July 1831 Louis Philippe's Government sent a naval squadron to the mouth of the Tagus by way of warning. Dom Pedro, moreover, soon returned from Brazil to defend the rights of his daughter Maria. He began by establishing a provisional Portuguese Government in the Azores; then, with the support of Britain and France — in virtue of the Quadruple Alliance — he succeeded in landing at Oporto. His progress, though slow at first, at last brought him to Lisbon, and Dom Miguel fled to Genoa. The *Cortes* met in August 1834 to confirm the regency of Dom Pedro, but he died shortly afterwards. His daughter was then declared to be of age and, taking an oath to defend the Constitution, became Maria II of Portugal. In spite of certain reforms, such as the abolition of tithe and feudal rights, the nation demanded more radical measures and the Queen was obliged to re-establish the more liberal Constitution of 1822.

The Egyptian crisis of 1840

During his long reign Mahmud II had witnessed the steady enfeeblement of the Ottoman Empire and the beginnings of disintegration. In June 1826 a revolt of the Janissaries was suppressed by a massacre and followed by a re-organisation of the army — a task to which the Sultan had given all his energy. But the reforms which were undertaken were as ineffectual as they were unpopular among the faithful of Islam. Greece had gained her independence, Serbia her autonomy, while the Danubian principalities, with the by no means disinterested support of Russia, were on the road to emancipation. Such was the Sultan's record in Europe when in Africa a new threat of secession arose.

The ambitious Viceroy of Egypt, Mehemet Ali, had increased his power and enlarged his domains to such an extent that he had become a rival to the Sultan himself. With French aid and advice Mehemet Ali had revived Egypt. The production of cotton rose; a new canal and other public works were completed with the aid of forced labour. At the same time the Egyptian army and navy, under the direction of French officers, were vastly improved, and had shown their quality in the conquest of the holy cities, the defeat of the Wahabis in Arabia in 1816, and the seizure of Nubia in 1822. Egypt had become mistress of the greater part of the African and Asiatic shores of the Red Sea. The Sultan had therefore appealed to his Egyptian Viceroy to help him stamp out the Greek insurrection. Although the Egyptian army had been driven from Morea after the intervention of the Great Powers, it had rendered aid to the Sultan, and Mehemet Ali demanded his reward. He was offered Crete, but what he wanted was Syria.

Towards the end of 1831 a quarrel with the Pasha of Acre over his harbouring of refugees from Egyptian conscription gave him the pretext he needed, and an army commanded by his son Ibrahim, an excellent strategist, invaded Syria. Rapidly pursuing his victorious advance, Ibrahim reached Cilicia, crossed the Taurus Mountains and defeated the Turkish army at Konya, in the depths of Anatolia. For a moment it appeared that a young and vigorous Moslem power was about to replace the tottering Turkish Empire. The Tsar was the first to be alarmed. Forcing the Sultan to accept Russian protection, he sent a naval squadron to Constantinople, always the goal of Russian ambitions. Britain and Austria, without sharing the sentiments of France — where Mehemet Ali was immensely popular, and where it was hoped to make Egypt a bastion of French influence in the Near East — also brought pressure on the Sultan who, by the Treaty of Kutahya in May 1833, granted to his Egyptian Viceroy a hereditary title and made him Pasha for life. The Egyptian army withdrew and the Russians left the Bosphorus; not, however, before they had concluded at Unkiar-Skelessi an eight-year treaty of alliance with Turkey (July 1833); this made Nicholas I the protector of the Sultan, who also agreed to close the Dardanelles to the Tsar's enemies.

Britain, whose policy was to resist Russian advances towards the Dardanelles and to foster her own trade in the Mediterranean, found little difficulty in prompting Turkey to take her revenge in the spring of 1839. The valiant army of Ibrahim, however, overwhelmed its adversaries at Nezib on 24 June 1839; Mahmud II died, the Turkish fleet surrendered to the Egyptians, and the Great Powers decided to intervene. Britain was resolved to curb the ambitions of Mehemet Ali, while in France, where Mehemet Ali was a hero, this course was repugnant. Relations between the two countries became strained and the tension mounted when, under the pressure of public opinion, Thiers, the hope of the warlike nationalists, was called to power in March 1840. While in London a conference was discussing the terms of the ultimatum to be addressed to Egypt, Thiers attempted on his own account to persuade Turkey and Egypt to come to a direct agreement between themselves. Palmerston, truculent and Francophobe, was outraged. In reply he hastened the ultimatum, which was sent on 15 July 1840 without further consultations with France. France felt this exclusion

297

to be an insult. Feelings, already excited, ran so high that war was actually envisaged, while patriotic ardour was further inflamed by a vote of credit for the return of Napoleon I's ashes from St Helena. Louis Philippe, always reasonable and realistic, was fully aware of the danger of starting a war to which all Europe, beginning with Russia and Prussia, objected. He had the courage to draw back and to dismiss Thiers. Foreign affairs were thereafter directed by Guizot, the ambassador to London. Meanwhile Palmerston sorely tried his allies by his uncompromising attitude. He was resolved to humiliate Mehemet Ali, and had Beirut bombarded by the British fleet. Finally agreement was reached by which Mehemet Ali retained Egypt as a hereditary ruler but returned Syria to the Sultan. France rejoined the concert of Europe on 13 July 1841 when she signed the Straits Convention, which modified the Treaty of Unkiar-Skelessi by closing the Dardanelles and the Bosphorus to warships of all nations. Peace was saved, but Europe had been badly shaken by the first crisis of the nineteenth-century 'Eastern Question'.

The expansion of Victorian Britain

Britain had forced France to give way in Egypt, and had limited the influence of Russia in Turkey. The increased prestige and unpopularity she had thus gained was largely the achievement of Palmerston, who during the course of some twenty years was on many occasions called to direct British foreign policy with the firmness, pride and tenacity which were characteristic of him. He appeared to support liberal movements abroad, and this made him the bugbear of the Holy Alliance powers. But Britain's domestic history evolved more rapidly. Her population was by 1850 increasing faster than ever and though the 'hungry forties' brought hard times to her workers, she was on the brink of her greatest enrichment. A Whig Prime Minister was succeeded in 1841 by the Tory Sir Robert Peel who resumed the Pittite tradition of reasonable, practical reform. He was in sympathy with the views of the business classes, who liked his fiscal measures and administrative policies although they continued to oppose factory regulations. Finally, to the horror of his protectionist followers, he was even converted to the free trade views of Richard Cobden. Defying a large section of his Conservative followers, he reduced by stages the number of articles on which import duty was paid. In 1845, when Ireland was ravaged by famine, he no longer hesitated to propose the abolition of the Corn Laws which maintained the high price of wheat. The boldness of this gesture split his own party. One of its most brilliant and eloquent members, Disraeli, withdrew to lead the protectionists. The 'repeal' of the Corn Laws in 1846 was followed by the political cleavage of the Tory Party into Peelites and Conservatives that was to keep Whigs in office for almost the whole of the next twenty years and the immediate collapse of Peel's Government. Meanwhile, far from damaging commerce, as the Opposition had predicted, increased economic liberty brought increased prosperity, and Free Trade soon became an article of faith in the Victorian creed.

Industrialism, besides creating wealth, was also transforming the face of Britain. The first urban and industrial society of modern times appeared in the smoke of factory chimneys, trains and steamships which burnt the coal

A colliery near Leeds in 1813. Steam is already applied to winding up the cages in which the miners descend to the coal-face, and to transporting coal-trucks on a light surface railway. *Mansell*

on which the energy revolution was built. The export of textiles, and later metal goods and machinery, enormously multiplied Britain's share of world trade. London was the centre of a web of commercial houses, banks and shipping agencies. More and more financial business flowed from the rest of the world into the City. Growing rich in this turbulent activity, the middle classes were content to enjoy their good fortune without seeking more political power. Faithful to the traditions of their class, they still showed marked respect for the aristocracy, the great landed families whose manners and luxury they admired, and who in practice constituted the ruling class. There was little of the republicanism of the continent; under the new Queen and her Consort the court, which so recently had been an object of scandal, set a national example of sobriety and hard work. Austerity seemed not incompatible with prosperity, success the reward of virtue. These precepts were founded in an unbreakable religious faith, the bedrock of Victorian middle-class respectability and the source of its nervous and energetic pursuit of excellence.

Across this bright prospect two shadows fell. In scarcely fifty years the population had grown from sixteen to twenty-seven million, and the increase had taken place in the towns and great cities. In many of them, living conditions were terrible. The 'condition of England' obsessed reformers. Another even more painful problem was the distress of Ireland. On the fall of the Whig Government O'Connell resumed his campaign for Irish independence. In 1844 he was condemned to prison on a charge of sedition; but, set at liberty a few months later, he returned to Dublin in triumph. O'Connell, however, was opposed to violence and preferred exile to open rebellion. It was O'Brien, the leader of the 'Young Ireland' party who attempted an armed revolt, though without success. At this time the potato crop failed twice in succession and in the famine that followed many perished. More than a million Irish, fleeing from their native land, emigrated to the United States; and in 1845–6 the population of Ireland was reduced by almost half. On their return to power the Liberals attempted to improve the situation by better agrarian laws. These measures proved quite ineffective, however, and the martyrdom of Ireland continued.

The British colonial empire was also changing in character. India was still administered by the East India Company, but other small colonies were acquired by the Crown. This was not a popular policy; it was generally assumed that colonies cost the mother country more than they were worth and were bound, in the end, to break away into independence. This attitude was fostered by the facts of emigration. More and more emigrants from the British Isles went abroad and were going to demand their rights as British subjects in their new homes. In this way southern Australia had ceased to be a land to which convicts were deported; in 1834 it was made a self-governing colony. A few years later another and highly prosperous region of the continent, New South Wales, was given the same status. Then, in 1839, New Zealand became a dependency of New South Wales, to be granted a separate constitution a few years later. In Canada the population of French descent still chafed at government by a minority of different race and religion. In 1837 there was a rebellion which was soon quelled. At the same time the Conservative and the Reformist English Canadians fell out. To solve these difficulties a Legislative Act of Union was passed in 1840 which united the two parts of Canada and gave it responsible government. Finally, in 1847, a Ministry was formed in which both French and English Canadians participated. In South Africa the British, recently installed in the Cape of Good Hope, displeased the former Dutch colonists by the protection they gave to the natives. The Boers moved north towards Natal in the Great Trek (1835–7) and in 1842 continued their exodus into the almost unknown territory of the Transvaal when Britain made a colony of Natal. In 1838, to assure her sea route to India, Britain annexed a new naval base, Aden, the southern key to the Red Sea. In India itself, although the Company retained certain privileges, a series of enlightened Governors-General pressed forward with reforms and innovations which began to stir the subcontinent's passivity. A new educated and Westernised class of Indians began to appear. At the same time, new territory was being acquired. Assam was taken in 1826 and a struggle with Russia for influence in Persia, Afghanistan and Turkestan began. After an attempt to reach agreement with Russia, the British conquered Baluchistan, then Afghanistan, and in 1839 entered Kabul. Kabul, however, rose in revolt two years later and the British were massacred. The massacre was avenged by a punitive expedition, but the region was then evacuated and the effort to conquer Afghanistan ended in failure. Shortly afterwards, in 1846, victory over the Sikhs gave Great Britain command of the Panjab. Finally, to the east, the British controlled the coast of Burma and in 1819 had possession of Singapore, from which they were able to dominate the Malay peninsula.

But the gates of China remained obstinately barred to the foreigner. Canton was the sole Chinese port accessible to foreign trade, which was almost exclusively in the hands of the British. In 1839, shortly after the importation of opium had been prohibited, twenty thousand cases of the drug, shipped from India, were seized and destroyed by the Chinese authorities. Palmerston's reaction in defence

British colonial policy was from the start marked by a consciousness of trusteeship for the native population. This proclamation by the first governor of New South Wales makes the point graphically. *British Museum*

The export of European institutions sometimes led to the blending of British and native law. This Indian picture shows a murder trial in the eighteen-forties before an East India Company judge. *Victoria & Albert Museum*

of free trade was swift and brutal: a British squadron bombarded Canton, seized Shanghai, sailed up the Yang-tze to Nanking and there in 1842 forced the Chinese to sign a treaty which ceded the island of Hong Kong to Great Britain and opened five ports to British trade. Thus, to the sound of cannonfire, China entered into a new period of her history.

The zenith and unpopularity of the July Monarchy

Since the Egyptian crisis of 1840 French foreign policy had been less dramatic; some Frenchmen deplored its dullness. Behind the façade of the Guizot Ministry Louis Philippe pursued personal policies which appealed less and less to a country still not resigned to life without glory. Political stagnation, however, found its reward in the steady growth of wealth, and on the whole France remained quiescent. Two movements, as yet faint, had, however, begun. One came from the liberal Catholic tendencies, inspired by Lamennais and Lacordaire; they claimed absolute liberty for the Church within the State and at the same time demanded social reforms, an attitude which drove them farther from the King and closer to the people. The other, more broadly based, called for universal suffrage. In 1847 the cause was publicised by banquets during which speeches were made and toasts were proposed — not always to the health of the King.

Abroad, Guizot tried to end France's diplomatic isolation by a closer understanding with Britain. Though this 'marriage of convenience' could have been profitable to France, Britain saw no advantage in an *entente cordiale* rendered difficult by a series of incidents. Agreement could not even be reached on the question of the search of ships at sea, a corollary of the abolition of the slave trade. Negotiations for a customs union between France and Belgium were broken off because of British objections and whenever the question of colonial expansion arose France at once met British resistance. In Tahiti the expulsion of a British missionary was a grave incident which was settled only when the French Government climbed down. Serious friction finally arose over the subject of the marriage of the young Queen Isabella of Spain. London supported a Saxe-Coburg suitor, cousin of the Prince Consort, while Paris supported the Duke of Montpensier, one of Louis Philippe's sons. In the end the Queen married her Spanish cousin, the Duke of Cadiz, and her sister Luisa married Montpensier. This semi-success for France, involving as it did the possibility of an eventual union of the French and Spanish crowns, roused indignation in Britain and put an end to Guizot's attempts to establish cordiality. In spite of the good will of the British and French sovereigns and a friendly exchange of royal visits, the conflicting interests and popular sentiments of the two nations doomed his efforts to failure.

During these years, nevertheless, France was the only country other than Britain which was adding substantially to her colonial empire. Senegal was occupied again in 1817 and from there in 1828 the first European had gone to Timbuktu. A foothold was gained in Guinea, and a settlement was founded at Gabon in Equatorial Africa. Troops landed on the coast of Madagascar but they did not penetrate into the interior. In Oceania the French navy hoisted the Tricolour over the Marquesas Islands.

Finally in China, by the Treaty of Whampoa in 1844, France obtained pacifically the same advantages which had been accorded to Britain, and in addition guaranteed toleration for Catholics.

The most important developments took place in Algeria. To avoid complications, the French Government had been content to occupy the coastal towns and leave the interior to the Algerian patriot Abd-el-Kader. Though this state of affairs had been confirmed by treaty in 1837, the French position became increasingly insecure. French troops therefore seized Constantine and then marched in pursuit of Abd-el-Kader, whose retinue they captured. After this defeat, Abd-el-Kader took refuge with the Sultan of Morocco, and in 1844 the French fleet bombarded Tangier. The French army was victorious at the River Isly, but British intervention led to a cessation of hostilities. They were, however, renewed with the breakdown of Guizot's efforts to establish cordial relations with Britain; and in the subsequent operations in Algeria Abd-el-Kader surrendered. In 1848 Algeria was organised as three Departments of France. But in spite of these successes, in which the King's sons played a distinguished part, Louis Philippe's unpopularity grew. France was bored. Unmindful of the benefits of peace, the average Frenchman hummed the Bonapartist couplets of Béranger and applauded with fervour the bellicose speeches of Thiers.

Russia in the 1840s

If the Tsar's Empire enjoyed a surface appearance of total calm it was the calm of a deep-freeze. The repressiveness of the autocratic government led to the labelling of Nicholas's reign by the radical Alexander Herzen as 'the plague-zone of Russian history'. Poland after 1830 was intensively Russianised, and Lithuania was submitted to a similar process. Universities were closed or strictly supervised, the number of students limited and the severity of the censorship redoubled. To avoid the contagion of subversive ideas it was made almost as difficult for a Russian to leave his own country as for a foreigner to enter it. The sole creative achievement of government in this period was the codification of the laws under the direction of Speransky.

Abroad, however, Nicholas I pursued a vigorous policy. The enfeeblement of the Ottoman Empire — 'the sick man' in the words of the Tsar, who waited eagerly for his share of the inheritance — furnished him with several occasions for successful intervention. In addition Russia began in 1828–9 to slice into Armenia from both the Turkish and the Persian sides. In the Caucasus Russian settlement met with resistance, and an army had to be stationed in Georgia. Finally the vast stretches of Siberia, formerly reserved for deportation, began towards 1825 to be settled by colonists. From there, fanning southwards, Russian expansion encountered the British thrust northwards from India. In 1839 a Russian expedition to Turkestan against Khiva met with a setback almost as resounding as the British defeat two years later at Kabul. As their forces neutralised each other the British and the Russians agreed in 1843 to establish a kind of joint rule in Persia, and in Turkestan to respect the *status quo*. The Russians, however, soon renewed their activities in these regions.

Italy and the 'Risorgimento'

Among the dismembered states of Italy demands for liberal reforms yielded after the outbreaks of 1830 to aspirations for national unity. This movement, which developed above all among the intelligentsia, was called the *Risorgimento* or 'resurrection'. The Italians who rallied to the cause of national unity were all equally patriots, but they differed in their opinion of how the goal of national unity could be attained. The Radicals were inspired by Mazzini, a kind of revolutionary mystic, whose austerity and passionately held convictions won him followers, especially among the young. Most of his life was spent in exile, and in France he founded the society Young Italy, whose programme was expressed in two words: Unity, Republic. Its aim was to reach the Italian people throughout the peninsula, to stir them, alone and unaided, to expel the Austrian foreigner and create a democratic Italian Republic. Sporadic conspiracies broke out here and there with the sole result that their authors were shot. In view of such failures and because of distrust of radical revolutionaries, the moderates, and the middle class in general, preferred the federalist and monarchist method recommended by Vincenzo Gioberti. In 1843 the publication of his book, *Il Primato*, caused a stir: it argued that Italy could recover her ancient primacy if she organised herself into a confederation under the sovereignty of the Pope. The federalist solution was also advocated by the Piedmontese nobleman Balbo, whose book *Le Speranze d'Italia* appeared in 1844. Balbo saw in the King of Sardinia the potential creator of confederation, and since his accession to the throne in 1831 Charles Albert had become the chief hope of many patriots. But Charles Albert hesitated to challenge Austria. Nevertheless the ferment continued and the idea of national unity stirred not only writers like Manzoni but also practical politicians.

Germany and the 'Zollverein'

In the German Confederation, even more than in Italy, liberal tendencies were repressed by Metternich. Although some people still talked of national unity, the most significant change of these years was the revival of the old Prusso-Austrian rivalry of the previous century. By the pact of Confederation each state was authorised to regulate its own commercial relations, and in 1819 Prussia profited by this to conclude customs agreements with the small sovereign states which formed enclaves in her own scattered territories. Little by little this Customs Union — or *Zollverein* — was enlarged, and by 1834 it extended from the Niemen to the Rhine. It constituted a large economic unit under the aegis of Prussia from which Austria found herself excluded; and economic unity began to prepare the way for political unity. With ten million inhabitants, an economy developed by a budding industry and the construction of the first German railways, and her army, Prussia possessed a force of attraction which only Austria could have balanced. But Austria, with her negative and reactionary attitude, had proved a disappointment.

German national sentiment was strikingly revealed in 1840, when France seemed to be preparing for a war of revenge. Beyond the Rhine feelings at once ran high and the hymn composed on this occasion, *Die Wacht am Rhein* (*The Watch on the Rhine*), became an unofficial national

A German peasant girl painted in 1828 by Ludwig Emil Grimm (1790–1863). The example of Prussia fostered national self-consciousness in Germany and pride in her own customs and institutions. *Marburg*

301

anthem which well expressed the mood of Germany. Philosophers, writers and men of learning contributed to heighten the sentiment of patriotism whose intellectual authority was found in the theories of Hegel and Humboldt. Work of historians and linguists reinforced the ideal of the German Fatherland so that even conferences of learned bodies strove to promote the grandeur of Germany quite as much as the advance of knowledge. In 1840 Frederick William IV had come to the throne of Prussia and with him had come renewed hopes of Prussian leadership. In 1846 at Frankfurt a congress of intellectuals called for a German Parliament to be summoned. In 1847, yielding to popular pressure, Frederick William IV convoked the Prussian Assembly — the *Landtag*, although when he heard its demands he rapidly dissolved it. Germany was revealing its impatience to tread new paths.

Switzerland and the 'Sonderbund' crisis

In Switzerland the antagonism of the Catholic Cantons, who wanted more local autonomy, and the Protestant Cantons, who desired a strongly centralised federation, was a grave threat to the unity of the country. The struggle of the Protestants with the religious orders led in 1845 to a civil war which broke out in Lucerne, where the Catholics formed themselves into an autonomous confederation of seven Cantons, the *Sonderbund*. They appealed to Austria and to France for support. The Protestants then raised an army which in 1847 occupied Lucerne and Fribourg, the two most active Catholic centres. The *Sonderbund* was dissolved and the religious orders were expelled. The defeated Catholic Cantons were obliged to adhere to a new constitution drawn up on liberal and federal principles. The unity of the Swiss Confederation was thus safeguarded.

Persistent disorder in the Iberian peninsula

After the resignation of Maria Christina and her departure from Spain the successful General Espartero was appointed regent by the *Cortes*. But party quarrels continued, and he set up a military dictatorship. In July 1843, a coalition among his opponents forced him to leave Spain. The Princess, who was thirteen, was declared to be of age and became Queen Isabella II; but this scarcely changed the situation until in the following year General Narvaez, chief of the Conservatives, seized power and established a new constitution which strengthened the monarchy. It was at this time that the question of the young Queen's marriage captured the interest of Europe until it was settled in 1846 by her marriage to her cousin, the Duke of Cadiz. The personal relations of the royal couple rapidly deteriorated and soon added to the numerous national dissensions.

In Portugal the period of tranquillity which followed the granting of a liberal constitution by the youthful Queen Maria II did not last long. As early as 1842 disorder resulted in a military insurrection which installed the Conservatives. Like Espartero in Spain, the Portuguese minister Costa Carbal set up a dictatorship. The reforms which he introduced clashed, however, with the interests of the absolutists, who rebelled again at Oporto in 1846; this led to the arrival of a British force to restore the *status quo*.

The growth of the United States

During the fifteen years which followed the election of President Andrew Jackson the United States made remarkable economic progress. The population increased, swelled by the first big wave of immigrants, and expansion into new territory continued. In 1835 the Pacific coast was reached. In the following year American settlers established the Republic of Texas. The optimism engendered by prosperity led to financial speculation which in 1837 caused a panic; the conversion of bank notes was suspended and many banks failed. Jackson in his long and stubborn fight against centralisation had removed Government funds from the Bank of the United States and distributed them among state banks, and his opponents blamed him for the crisis, which was, however, short-lived. Although the Presidency had taken on the aspect of a 'monarchy by plebiscite' and Presidential elections monopolised a large part of political activity, Jackson's successors — Van Buren, Harrison, Tyler — were far from possessing his strong personality.

The problem of slavery was becoming a more obvious threat to internal peace. The number of slaves in the south was growing and northerners condemned the inhumanity of the institution with increasing fervour. In the 1840s a movement was formed to demand not the limitation of slavery but its total abolition. The Texas affair raised the question in an acute form. Texas had been an immense province of Mexico, containing, apart from a few Indians, hardly three thousand inhabitants of Spanish origin. But already by 1830 nearly twenty thousand American immigrants had settled there, together with their slaves, though slavery was prohibited in the province. The Mexican Government's attempt to enforce the law led to revolution and the independence of the Texan Republic. In 1845, the United States Congress voted its annexation. Mexico, refusing to accept this *fait accompli*, declared war. She was rapidly beaten, her capital occupied and, in 1848, obliged, for an indemnity of ten million dollars, to cede the territories of Texas, New Mexico and Northern California. In this way the United States was enlarged by a region which was the size of half Europe. By a further stroke of good fortune gold was found in California and the discovery at once led to the famous gold rush of '49.

The growing-pains of Latin America

The United States and Canada, peopled almost entirely by European immigrants among whom the surviving Indians played no political role, retained the parliamentary traditions of Britain and many European cultural and social assumptions. Latin America, on the contrary, contained a very small minority of Spanish descent who were scattered over vast territories and were swamped by a heterogeneous mass of Indians, half-castes and Negroes. Even the Spanish minority, who had lived under an autocratic monarchy that no longer existed, were totally without political experience. They were divided into two groups: citizens with liberal tendencies and great landed proprietors who wanted strong government. This lack of racial and political unity led to the partition of Latin America among numerous independent states which not only fought each other but were subject to frequent civil wars. These tended to produce military dictatorships. The dictator of Peru was

British public opinion was horrified when illustrations such as this in Government reports showed the working conditions of women and children in the factories. *Radio Times Hulton Picture Library*

Santa Cruz; of Venezuela, Paez; of Argentina, Rosas; of Uruguay, Oribe; of Chile, Portales. In Central America Honduras conquered Guatemala in 1829 and dominated a confederation which disintegrated in 1837. In the south, Argentina attempted to annex Uruguay in 1826 and in the process provoked a war with Brazil which was stopped by British intervention. Dreams of hegemony inspired Peru to attack Chile in 1839 and then, in spite of defeat, to try — again in vain — to subjugate Bolivia in 1845. As for Mexico, she had just lost half her territory to the United States in 1848. Chile, more fortunate than her neighbours, pursued a calmer course which encouraged her material and intellectual development. Finally Brazil — which alone preserved the older monarchical institutions, now constitutional — proved remarkably stable, in spite of the attempted secession of the southern provinces of the country.

Social problems and the birth of Marxism

The introduction of machinery was bringing about a world revolution which was at once industrial, economic and social. Until this time the structure of society had been dominated by the distinction between townsman and peasant. The emergence of the new towns with their massed industrial workers profoundly modified this. The rapidly developing factories required manpower; population was drained from rural areas to swell the city slums, where the new proletariat led an exhausting and wretched existence. Cheap labour encouraged exploitation of the worker by the employer, who demanded intense effort for low wages. Twelve and thirteen hours of work a day were miserably rewarded, especially in the case of women and children. For all workers unemployment meant starvation.

The problems which arose from this situation were universal. In every country the lamentable fate of the worker produced a cry for social justice and demands which knew no frontiers: shorter hours of work, restricted employment of women and children, higher wages and improved working conditions. These were problems of international scope and they suggested to some an international solidarity of interest among the exploited class. Yet by 1848 this process was only beginning. The overwhelming majority of Europeans were still peasants. Only one country already possessed a mature industrial economy and had less than a quarter of her working population dependent on agriculture, and this was Britain.

Britain was both the first industrialised society and the first to face the problems posed by this. Workers' movements quickly appeared. Robert Owen, the philanthropic industrialist, tried to form a general trades union in the 1830s. In 1833 a Factory Act reduced the exploitation of children and appointed a paid inspectorate to enforce the new regulations. Subsequent acts prohibited the employment of women and children underground in mines and the first public health measures became law. This did not satisfy working-class discontent. A programme of political reform called the People's Charter appeared in 1836. Hard times in the 1840s made this the centre and symbol of working-class agitation. But the Chartist movement was ill co-ordinated, faced determined Governments and wilted away when prosperity returned. The trades unions, co-operative organisations and education societies which had been the less spectacular part of the working-class movement survived to play a vital role in the formation of the Labour Party half a century later.

In France, which was industrialised later and more slowly, the situation was different. In 1848 three-quarters

303

The greatest gold rush of the century followed the discovery of gold in California in 1848. The mining towns which sprang up near the first strikes were violent, short-lived communities where much of the legend of the 'Wild' West was created. *Radio Times Hulton Picture Library*

Karl Marx, philosopher and revolutionary agitator (1818–83). Arguably the greatest figure in the history of the socialist movement, he formulated a view of history whose sweep and comprehensiveness provided the intellectual framework for a century of socialist thinking. *Viollet*

of France was still agricultural, and in Paris there were 65,000 employers for only 342,000 workers. Nevertheless the workers who had played such an important part in the July Revolution of 1830 were aware of their strength and knew how to use it in order to get their claims a hearing. They were no longer content with the 'patience and resignation' which Casimir Périer recommended. Hence the frequent riots and strikes which in Paris and Lyon disturbed the opening years of Louis Philippe's reign. Results were obtained: in 1841 a law was passed to regulate child labour; in 1843 a uniform scale of wages replaced the mutual bargaining which had generally been to the advantage of the employer; in 1845 workers' associations, until then camouflaged as mutual assistance societies, were legally recognised. But it was in theoreticians that France was especially rich. Saint-Simon, the precursor of socialism — the word in its present-day sense was first used in 1832 by the militant Pierre Leroux — left disciples who after his death sought to put his theories into practice. Such were Fourier, who proposed to replace the State with working cells or *phalansteries*, and Louis Blanc, whose small book on the *Organisation of Labour* in 1840 advocated 'socialist workshops'. Proudhon went further and condemned private property in the famous epigram 'property is theft'. For capitalism he wished to substitute a State credit system. In spite of these speculations and suggestions, the working day throughout France remained fixed at a very minimum of ten hours, and a

great many children were employed from the age of eight.

In Germany only the first steps towards industrialisation had been taken. Krupp installed his first steam-engine in 1835 and employed sixty workers; ten years later the number of his employees was still only about a hundred. But Germany produced the greatest theorist of industrial society, Karl Marx (1818–83), historian and philosopher, who had gone to London at the invitation of his compatriot and disciple Engels, on the occasion of the first international congress of workers' associations, and there issued in January 1848 the *Communist Manifesto*. Claiming to base his arguments on science alone, he sketched a theory of social evolution which described the historical process as a series of revolutionary social and political changes arising from irresistible changes in the material forces at the base of society. These changes, he warned, expressed themselves concretely in the antagonism of classes. The final stage of the class-struggle was at hand; only one antagonism remained, that between the property-owning bourgeoisie and the industrial proletariat. To the latter, Marx addressed the words of his brilliant pamphlet which opened a new age: 'Workers of the world, unite!'

The Execution of a Witch (c. 1820). Under the Bourbon monarchy the Spanish Inquisition was zealous in denouncing and exterminating heretics. Goya was equally zealous in his denunciation of oppression. *Alte Pinakothek, Munich*

CHAPTER SIXTEEN
REVOLUTIONS AND NATIONAL WARS
LIBERAL UPRISINGS AND NATIONAL UNIFICATIONS

The revolutions of 1848

When in February 1848 revolution broke out in Paris Europe had been seething with unrest for two years. Switzerland's difficulties had begun in 1845; a Galician jacquerie of the peasants against the Polish nobles and the Austrian annexation of the Republic of Cracow (the last vestige of an independent Poland) had taken place in 1846. In the same year Pius IX became Pope. He was reputed to have liberal views and a liberal Pope was something Metternich had not believed possible. Enthusiasm swept Italy. Reforms were undertaken in Tuscany and Piedmont. But Milan was Austrian, and Austria, with the tacit approval of the sovereigns of Parma, Modena and the Two Sicilies, safeguarded her predominance in Italy by occupying Ferrara. Then, in January 1848, a revolt in Sicily followed by a revolt in Naples forced the King, Ferdinand II, to grant a constitution. The Papal States, Piedmont and Tuscany at once demanded and obtained the same concession.

The Paris revolution and the Second Republic

In France, the regime was already unpopular when on February 22 a public banquet which had been organised in the campaign for suffrage reform was forbidden by the police. Paris rioted, and the middle-class National Guard, which until then had supported the regime, joined them. The killing of some rioters had been the signal for barricades to be raised. On the second day of the fighting Louis Philippe, rather than assume responsibility for a civil war, chose to abdicate in favour of his grandson. The mob, invading the Assembly, demanded a Republic and a provisional government of seven members was named, among them the poet Lamartine. More extreme revolutionaries had installed themselves at the Hôtel de Ville and the two groups fused and issued a ' declaration of peace ' to reassure the courts of Europe (which were, as it happened, extremely busy dealing with troubles of their own). Though for a while the workers commanded the streets of Paris, the new Government could rely on the support of the moderates. But bad economic conditions made concessions to Parisian demand inevitable. The working day was reduced to ten hours. Public works were organised to relieve unemployment but only provided the focus for further agitation. The April elections confirmed the Republic and gave a majority to the moderates. The disillusioned workers demanded radical social reform, to

A Union cavalryman. *Cooper Union Museum*

which the new Assembly replied by stopping the public works programme. A savage class-war now broke out in earnest; in the ' June Days ' (June 23–26) a proletarian insurrection was crushed with greater loss of life than any of the insurrections of the Revolution of 1789. Ten thousand workers were killed, six hundred transported and a division appeared between the bourgeoisie and the Paris workers which was to shape the politics of the French Left for fifty years. But the moderates had won. The Constitution which was approved in November declared the Republic to be ' democratic, one and indivisible, and based on the family, work, property and public order '. It established universal suffrage, a single Legislative Assembly to be re-elected every three years and, on the American model, a President of the Republic with executive powers, elected for a term of four years — but ineligible for re-election. Without adopting the extreme solutions advocated by the socialists, the Constitution nevertheless envisaged important reforms: education was to be made more democratic and the condition of the working class improved.

Disillusionment with the generous theories which had inspired many of those who had taken an active part in the revolution led to a reaction towards order. The country expressed this by electing as President Prince Louis

Top: ' The Rocket ', George Stephenson's winning locomotive in the 8-day Liverpool and Manchester Railroad competition in 1829.
Bottom: An early steam carriage. British Museum

T

Napoleon Bonaparte, nephew of Napoleon I, by five and a half million votes. The name Bonaparte was in itself a guarantee of authority, order and prestige. Cavaignac, the Republican candidate, had received less than a million and a half votes, while Ledru-Rollin, the representative of the left wing, received scarcely 400,000. Lamartine, the hero of February, was practically forgotten. The swing towards the Right was even more marked in the elections of May 1849. The Republicans were reduced to a small minority faced by an imposing group of Conservatives and even of Royalists, who lost no time in passing reactionary measures. Three million voters were disfranchised and the press was gagged. Education was remodelled in the interests of the Church. The new Prince-President trimmed his sails to these reactionary winds and relied on his personal popularity, posing as the defender of the people's sovereignty while at the same time he encouraged the army to acclaim him with cries of ' Long live the Emperor '.

The anniversary of the battle of Austerlitz, 2 December 1851, was the date chosen by Louis Napoleon for a coup d'état. The Assembly had recently refused to revise the Constitution, which made the President ineligible for re-election. The Chamber was surrounded by troops and dissolved. At the same time Louis Napoleon proclaimed the re-establishment of universal suffrage, and in his ' appeal to the people ' suggested a constitution on the lines of the Consulate. A plebiscite gave him overwhelming support: more than seven million voted ' yes ' to 600,000 who voted ' no '. Sporadic resistance to the coup d'état was quickly crushed and followed by harsh reprisals: massive arrests, deportations to Algeria or Guiana, banishments or voluntary exiles, such as that of Victor Hugo. On 14 January 1852 the government of the French Republic was entrusted to Prince Louis Napoleon Bonaparte with all the powers which had once been bestowed on the First Consul, his uncle. A Council of State, a Legislative Body and Senate were also provided. The next step was inevitable. Another plebiscite endorsed the restoration of the Empire. The Duke of Reichstadt — in theory Napoleon II — had died in 1815, and the new Emperor assumed the name Napoleon III.

The early success of the revolutions

Towards the end of February 1848 a liberal movement originating in the Grand Duchy of Baden began rapidly to spread through southern Germany where, under the pressure of public opinion, liberal ministers were brought to power who demanded the calling of a preparatory Federal Parliament at Frankfurt. In Vienna riots had broken out on the arrival of news from Paris. On March 13 Metternich fled from the disordered city. He had been the embodiment of repressive absolutism for thirty-three years, and as he left for England he remarked: ' I am that which was. ' The words might have been his epitaph; for his life work, the European order of 1815, was crumbling into ruin. The Emperor Ferdinand gave General Windischgrätz the task of subduing the rioters, but was nevertheless obliged to convoke a constituent assembly. The King of Prussia, Frederick William IV, had already been forced by mob pressure to promise a similar concession and assumed the leadership of the movement for German unification. The preparatory Parliament which met at Frankfurt

in March without Austrian representatives called for German unity and decided to summon an assembly of representatives from all the German states, elected by universal suffrage.

At this moment Bohemia exploded. The Czechs, who since the Thirty Years' War, two hundred years before, had virtually disappeared from the historical scene, now sent delegates to Vienna to demand the fusion of Bohemia with Moravia and Silesia, and the abolition of feudalism. In April Prague claimed complete autonomy and, profiting by the Emperor's difficulties, set up a provisional Czech government with a parliament.

Hungary, under the leadership of Kossuth, had already demanded a national government and, on 23 March 1848, obtained recognition as an independent nation. Shortly afterwards the Emperor sanctioned this by visiting Pressburg, appearing in person at the Hungarian Diet.

In Italy the Austrians had been forced to evacuate insurgent Milan, while Venice drove out the occupying troops and proclaimed a Republic. The Dukes of Parma and Modena had fled, and only the fortified cities of Mantua and Verona remained in Austrian hands. Austria herself, swamped beneath the revolutionary wave, was thus under attack everywhere at once; the people of Vienna now seized the occasion to rise again when constitutional concessions were made which they considered insufficient. The Emperor abandoned his disorderly capital and for the moment democracy triumphed in Austria.

In Italy, the head of the House of Savoy, Charles Albert, was now looked to for leadership in a war of liberation. Under pressure from the Romans Pius IX sent him troops, and the Grand Duke of Tuscany and even Ferdinand II, King of the Two Sicilies — though much against his will — followed the Papal example. Charles Albert crossed the River Ticino and occupied Milan. But Austria was recovering from her first dazed confusion. For the moment leaving the problems of Bohemia and Hungary unsettled, she concentrated her efforts on Italy. The head of the Catholic Church could not long be expected to make war on the chief Catholic power of Europe, and the Pope recalled his troops. Riots in Naples gave Ferdinand II an excuse to follow suit. In spite of these defections Charles Albert defeated the Austrians at Goito at the end of May and Lombardy, Piacenza, Parma and Modena all asked for union with Piedmont. Venice soon followed their example, so that from the beginning of July all northern Italy was gathered under the aegis of the House of Savoy.

In Germany the proposed assembly met in Frankfurt as the Federal Parliament on May 18. Now the new King of Denmark, Frederick VII, had established a constitution which was valid for his entire realm — which included the German-speaking duchies of Schleswig and Holstein, in which separatist sentiments prevailed. As the Frankfurt Parliament was a gathering of all German-speaking states it invited these two Danish duchies to send delegates. It also set up a provisional government under the presidency of the Archduke John of Austria, brother of the preceding emperor, who was made Vicar Imperial. A zealous defender of the German cause, Frederick William IV of Prussia had in the meantime rushed to the aid of the Germans in Schleswig and Holstein without waiting for the Parliament of Frankfurt to take action. With the co-operation of Hanover, he had already, in April, 1848, driven the Danes out of the duchies. At this point Sweden,

REVOLUTIONS AND NATIONAL WARS

Russia and even Britain grew uneasy, and Frederick William IV was obliged to sign a truce at Malmö in August 1848, which installed both Danish and Prussian administrators in the duchies, and left the basic problem unsolved. With this affair at least provisionally settled, the King of Prussia set about the task of providing his country with a liberal constitution. This was granted in December 1848, but soon modified by an electoral law favouring property-owning classes.

Repression and reaction

The high-water mark of revolution had now been reached. Except in France, the aims of revolution had been nationalist or constitutionalist. It was now to be seen that the nationalists could not make common cause with the constitutionalists in resisting the old regimes. The Czech insurrection was the first to be crushed. In June 1848 a Pan-Slav Congress, in which Poles participated, met in Prague. It ended in riots and bloodshed thus giving General Windischgrätz the excuse he had been waiting for. Prague was bombarded and a few days later occupied by Austrian troops. The Czech national movement at once collapsed. During the pause in hostilities which followed, the Constituent Assembly promised by the Emperor met in Vienna on June 22 but, politically and racially divided, it accomplished little except the emancipation of serfs throughout the Austrian Empire.

Austria then concentrated on putting an end to the resistance in Hungary which, despite the diversity of races that inhabited the country, was much more stubborn than in Bohemia. Croats, Slovenes and Serbs clamoured for the creation of an autonomous state of the South Slavs. The Serbs summoned a Congress which met at Carlowitz in May 1848, and the Roumanians of Transylvania, meeting at Blasendorf, rejected any suggestion of union with Hungary. Their demands were refused by Kossuth, who was as insistent on Magyar domination of the Slav races within Hungary as on the freedom of Magyars from Austrian rule. Austria turned this to good account. The Emperor Ferdinand appointed Baron Jellacic, a Croat, as Ban — or Governor — of Croatia; in September 1848 the Croats invaded Hungary. They were driven back and Austrian reinforcements were on the point of being sent to Hungary when, to prevent their departure, the population of Vienna rose for the third time. Ferdinand, fleeing once more, took refuge in Olmütz. Windischgrätz, however, acted with his customary energy: Vienna was besieged and three days later, on October 31, capitulated. The inevitable reprisals and executions followed. Overwhelmed by this succession of events the wretched Emperor abdicated, possibly on the advice of Prince Schwarzenberg, who ruled as virtual dictator until his death three years later. The throne passed to the eighteen-year-old Francis Joseph. On 4 March 1849 Francis Joseph, considering himself free from the engagements of his predecessors, granted the entire Austrian Empire, including Hungary, a new constitution which provided for two Chambers.

Later in the same month the Frankfurt Parliament produced a constitution giving the direction of a confederated Germany to a hereditary emperor. A slight majority voted that this title should be offered to Frederick William IV. Austria and a few southern German states opposed this, and Frederick William declined in order not to accept

Parisians defending the barricades in February 1848. National Guards, middle and working classes were united at this stage, though the collapse of the July Monarchy provoked disagreement about what should come next. *Mansell*

In February 1848 Louis Philippe's government was overthrown; an attempt to save his line by abdication in favour of his grandson failed when a crowd invaded the Chamber of Deputies and demanded a Republic. *Larousse*

1848 was everywhere a year of revolutions. All over Europe, in back rooms and cellars, revolutionary clubs and meetings such as this proliferated and maintained the ferment. *Radio Times Hulton Picture Library*

the Imperial crown from the hands of democrats. This was the end of the Frankfurt Parliament. But political agitation, far from being calmed, again broke out in Prussia as well as in Saxony and the Grand Duchy of Baden. These regions were the scene of troubles provoked by the democrats with whom, for the first time, communists mingled. Communists had appeared in Saxony under the leadership of the Russian Bakunin, but by May 1849 the democratic movement in Germany had been stamped out by the Prussian army.

In Hungary, on the other hand, the struggle continued. The insurgents recaptured Buda and Pest and on 14 April 1849 Kossuth proclaimed the fall of the Habsburgs. The Tsar, Nicholas I, then offered Russian troops to put down the revolt. Overwhelmed by the combined efforts of the Imperial troops, the Serbo-Croats under Jellacic and the Russian army, the Hungarians evacuated their capital and finally capitulated at Vilagos in August. Kossuth abandoned the struggle and went into exile, and Hungary underwent a severe repression.

Austria had also recovered in Italy. Charles Albert was too weak to exploit his victory at Goito; he made things worse by his indecision. After defeat at Custozza he was forced to accept an armistice which re-established the *status quo* by restoring Lombardy and Venetia to Austria. This damaged the prestige of the monarchy and the direction of the national movement passed into the hands of the Republicans. Manin lost no time in restoring the Republic in Venice on August 13, and the Radicals seized power in Tuscany. In Rome, the Pope had entrusted the government to a liberal minister. The murder of this minister and an insurrection in November 1848 at last severed Pius IX from the revolution. He fled to Gaeta and an assembly was elected by universal suffrage in Rome which pronounced the Pope's deposition as a temporal sovereign, and inaugurated a Roman Republic. In Tuscany the Grand Duke fled to join the Pope after having to accept a democratic government. Charles Albert, under pressure from the radicals and hoping that the Austrians were too deeply entangled in Hungary to resist, now broke the armistice and attacked the Austrian army. A five-day campaign ended at Novara with his defeat on 24 March 1849. He abdicated and his son Victor Emmanuel II opened his reign by signing a new armistice. These events encouraged Ferdinand II to re-establish absolutism in Naples and to reconquer Sicily. The Grand Duke of Tuscany returned to Florence with an escort of Austrian troops. Finally, after a heroic resistance which lasted for months, Venice succumbed to bombardment and famine. Throughout the peninsula 'Austrian order' again prevailed — except in Rome. Rome was still in the hands of a triumvirate which included Mazzini. But the Roman question was of passionate interest to all the Catholic powers and not only to Austria. Louis Napoleon, the new President of France, wished both to conciliate the Catholics and to retain his liberal supporters. He compromised by sending a fairly weak French contingent to Rome. The Emperor of Austria and the King of the Two Sicilies meanwhile occupied the Papal States, but the Republic in Rome held out. The first French attacks were repelled by the republican soldier Garibaldi, and a stronger French army had to be sent out. On 1 July 1848 the French entered Rome and re-established the temporal power of the Pope. Pius IX had been cured of his former liberalism; his police now

The photographic van of Robert Fenton. He sailed to the Crimea to make the first photographic record of warfare. Mathew Brady later followed him as photographer of the American Civil War. *Pictorial Press*

filled the prisons and drove thousands of his subjects into exile. In all the peninsula there remained only one constitutional sovereign: Victor Emmanuel II, who in the eyes of Italians became the sole hope of achieving national unity.

Calm and authority had everywhere been restored — at least in appearance. Czechs, Hungarians, Serbs and Roumanians were again obedient to Austria, whose grip on Italy was recovered. In Germany she had obliged Prussia to draw back, though a long and complex duel for German hegemony would shortly ensue. But liberal and nationalist aspirations had not been eradicated and were to reappear even more dangerously within a few decades.

The Eastern Question and the Crimean War

Incapacity to reform her government, the beginnings of nationalist risings and the anxious patronage of Britain, France and Russia were the factors which made the collapse of the Ottoman Empire seem more and more likely as the nineteenth century went on. If this collapse were to occur, it was important that Britain and Russia should agree about what should be put in the Empire's place and in 1844 an informal agreement was made that the two powers should consult together in this eventuality. Neither wanted Turkey to disappear; nor did France, which had long been influential at Constantinople, and had everything to lose by the dismemberment of an Empire with which she had long been on friendly terms. Thus shortly after the failure of Guizot's laborious attempts to promote an *entente cordiale*, France and Britain found themselves able to agree in opposing the undue extension of Russian influence at Constantinople.

Towards the end of the 1840s the Tsar of Russia became more and more convinced that the Turkish Empire could not last and that he should abandon the policy so far pursued of trying to shore up the tottering structure. The Balkan principalities, despite their remoteness from the West, had not escaped the nationalist fever of 1848. In Greece, where the despotism of King Otto had caused discontent, a military revolt had occurred as early as 1843 and the King had been obliged to grant a constitution. To the Greeks the British attitude had proved even more disappointing than their new sovereign. Palmerston in 1850 blockaded their coast in support of the dubious claims of a British subject. In the Ionian Islands all propaganda in favour of Greater Hellas was sternly repressed by the British. Thus it was towards Russia that Greece began to turn in the hope of realising her ambitions.

In Serbia the return of the Karageorgevic Dynasty, which supplanted its Obrenovic rival in 1842, had brought Prince Alexander to the throne. Alexander, in his eagerness to deal tactfully with Austria, received a sharp warning from Russia. Montenegro, on the other hand, remained faithful to her traditional protector. When, in 1852, power in Montenegro was secularised — to the great annoyance of the Sultan — the country had relied on the Tsar's aid in putting an end to the patriarchal regime of its Prince-Bishops. But it was in Bucharest that nationalist aspirations had echoed most ardently. To deal with the popular excitement which swept Moldavia and Wallachia in 1848 Nicholas I once more had the two principalities invaded by Russian troops, who were soon joined by Turkish troops. Russia was still primarily concerned to preserve the Turkish Empire from decay and in 1849 a Convention maintained the separation of the Danubian principalities against their will, and imposed upon them a government supported by Russian occupation.

In spite of these tensions and of a growing awareness in Britain of the danger of Russian influence in Central Asia and Persia, the Crimean War should never have occurred. The final crisis began with a ridiculous quarrel between Napoleon III and Nicholas as the champions, respectively, of Catholic and Greek Orthodox claimants to the custody of the Holy Places in Palestine. The Sultan's acquiescence in Napoleon's claims threatened the long-standing Russian claims to special status as patron of the Christian subjects of the Porte. In February 1853 a special mission was sent to Constantinople to impose a Russian alliance on Turkey, obtain concessions in the matter of the Holy Places and secure formal recognition of the Tsar's pretension to protect the fifteen million Orthodox subjects of the Sultan. Although Nicholas knew that the British were not prepared to consider an immediate partition of Turkey, he had no reason to believe that they would object to this. When his emissary Menshikov (whose arrogance did nothing to help his case) presented his requests, they were in fact rejected on the urging of the British Ambassador, Stratford de Redcliffe, who acted vigorously and independently as the agent of a divided Government in London. Menshikov left without achieving his ends. His threats led to the appearance of an Anglo-French fleet outside the Dardanelles. This surprised the Russians who, however, still found it incredible that Britain should seriously intend to support Turkey with force, and occupied the Danubian principalities to force Turkey to come to terms. The signatory powers of the Straits Convention of 1841 met in July at Vienna and proposed mediation. The Sultan wrecked this initiative,

Florence Nightingale's military hospital at Scutari. Revelations of the inadequacy of the British Army's administrative and medical services led to a new wave of inquiry and reform by Parliament. *Pictorial Press*

sure that Britain would support him. Disorder at Constantinople gave him an excuse to ask for the backing of the fleets; in passing the Dardanelles, the fleets broke the Straits Convention. Turkey then declared war on October 5. The annihilation of a Turkish squadron at Sinope brought the Anglo-French fleet into the Black Sea in January 1854. War was now inevitable, and was declared by Britain and France on March 28.

It was easier to do this than to begin operations in the first war between the Great Powers for forty years. Diplomacy went on while war aims were defined, and threatened Austrian intervention led Russia to evacuate the principalities in August. Nicholas never forgave this blow from his former partner of the Holy Alliance. Militarily, its effect was to sterilise one possible theatre of operations. The Allies still had to find a way to strike at Russia. A British raid in the Baltic led to nothing and it was decided to concentrate on the capture of Sevastopol, the great naval fortress in the Crimea. French and British forces landed there in September and after some early success settled down to a long siege conducted in terrible conditions. These were made worse for the British — and, to a lesser extent, the French — by their administrative incompetence. The British troops fought at the end of 2,500 miles of sea-borne communications. They were unprovided with stores and equipment needed to resist the winter. The only redeeming feature of the war was the heroic administrative achievement of Florence Nightingale in organising the nursing of the wounded.

In January 1855 Sardinia entered the war and sent an army to the Crimea. Nicholas died in March. It still took until September to force the abandonment of Sevastopol, and by this time Russia and France both wanted peace. The new Tsar, Alexander II, was further encouraged in this wish by Austrian threats to enter the war against him

The rulers of the states which made the peace of Paris in 1856. It preserved the Ottoman Empire for another twenty years and marked the summit of Anglo-French co-operation during the Second Empire. *Larousse*

A satirical drawing by Cruickshank of the effects of female emancipation. Agitation for various women's rights grew in strength and effectiveness during the nineteenth century. *Mansell*

After the Great Famine, Irish emigration to America and Canada rose sharply. Steamships made cheap, but often appalling, crossings and many hopeful emigrants died before arrival. *Radio Times Hulton Picture Library*

if he did not accept terms rejected by Nicholas the previous year. Under this pressure, preliminaries of peace were agreed at Vienna, on 1 February 1856. A peace congress opened the same month at Paris. Its location marked the resurgence of French prestige and influence. The presence at it of Cavour, Prime Minister of Sardinia, announced the beginning of a new era of national questions. Cavour used the Congress to advertise Italy's subjection to Austria. Napoleon drew closer to Sardinia. Austria distrusted him, by now well aware of his willingness to overturn the whole 1815 settlement. Russia accordingly drew closer to France, in reaction against Austria.

This dislocation of the Holy Alliance and the initiation of the long Austro-Russian conflict in the Balkans was the most important consequence of the Crimean War. The peace neutralised the Black Sea and attempted to guard against a new explosion by placing the principalities under a collective guarantee of the powers. Kars, captured by Russia, was returned to Turkey. An international commission was set up to secure the safe and free navigation of the Danube. A number of questions of maritime law were also settled. Finally, the powers applauded a decree of the Sultan which gave his Christian and Moslem subjects the same rights, and undertook to respect his independence and the territorial integrity of his domain. In fact, Turkey went on much as before, incapable of reforming itself. Sooner or later a new crisis would mean that the 'Sick Man of Europe' would again need attention. All that had happened was that the first phase of the nineteenth-century 'Eastern Question' was over. The period of Austro-Russian antagonism was about to begin.

The Second French Empire

Few individuals have aroused more conflicting opinions than Napoleon III who, even in his lifetime, was extravagantly praised by his own partisans and dismissed with contempt by Republicans and Royalists. Nurtured on the Napoleonic legend by his mother, Hortense Beauharnais, Napoleon's step-daughter and sometime Queen of Holland, the young Louis had been a State prisoner in Ham, a fugitive in the United States and a *carbonaro* in Italy; long experience as a conspirator had taught him to dissimulate. Ambitious and unscrupulous, humanitarian and idealistic, he was a strange combination of visionary and cynic. A simple appraisal of him is impossible. He became Emperor in 1852 at the age of forty-four. Short in stature, his head and shoulders were impressive; dreamy eyes softened a facial expression trained to impassivity. In January 1853 he married a young Spanish countess of remarkable beauty, Eugénie de Montijo, whose political influence was to prove unfortunate. In 1856, during the Congress of Paris, she bore him a son and this, like the birth of the 'King of Rome', seemed to assure the dynasty.

The regime benefited not only from the name of Bonaparte and the lustre gained from the Congress of Paris but also from a few prosperous years. A year before a world exhibition, inspired by the Great Exhibition of London in 1851, had revealed the great strides made by French industry. Though the peasants regarded Napoleon III as the defender of property against socialist depredations, the 'Authoritarian Empire' relied more on this new national prosperity than on the decrees which controlled the press, the system of 'official candidates' in elections, or constant supervision of opponents by the police. Economic growth was striking. Between 1848 and 1869, 1,125 miles of railway grew to 10,500 and the production of coal rose from four to more than thirteen million tons.

In January 1858 an attempt made on the Emperor's life outside the Opera House led to even stricter measures of police control. But a year later an amnesty was announced which inaugurated the ' Liberal Empire ', and for the next ten years there was a progressive return to parliamentary government. In November 1860 a decree was issued which gave the Legislature fuller, though still limited, powers; a year later still it was allowed to examine the budget. Such concessions merely encouraged the opposition. The five Republican Deputies who had sat in the Chamber in 1858 had by 1863 become thirty-two. In 1864 workers were granted the right to strike and protection was abandoned when in January 1860 Napoleon concluded a commercial treaty with Britain which considerably lowered tariffs between the two countries. Industrialists, threatened by British competition and forced to lower their prices, turned against the Second Empire as the bourgeoisie had turned against the First after the crisis of 1810. However, two successful wars — the Crimean War and, shortly afterwards, the victorious Italian campaign — added to the nation's prestige and to its area. In April 1860 the inhabitants of Nice and Savoy approved of their union with France by a vote which was almost unanimous.

In Paris all was gaiety. It was the epoch of *La Vie Parisienne* and everyone enjoyed Offenbach's light-hearted operettas. The Court continued to set the tone of elegance for Europe, but the Emperor was obliged to handle the opposition with care. Further concessions were made to Deputies and Senators, press restrictions were gradually relaxed, and public meetings were again permitted. In 1869 the pugnacious lawyer Gambetta was elected to the Legislature and with him forty other Republicans. On 2 January 1870 Napoleon III took a decisive step, proclaimed an entirely new Constitution and inaugurated the ' Parliamentary Empire ' with cabinet ministers responsible to the Legislature. The nation accepted it by a vote of 7,500,000 to 1,600,000. The Empire appeared to be consolidated.

The zenith of Victorian Britain

The middle decades of the century brought an unprecedented prosperity to Great Britain. On this prosperity rested the imposing stability of Victorian civilisation. Popular discontent was allayed by increasing wages. The middle class confidently moved forward to assume privileges previously reserved for the aristocracy. Politicians, roughly grouped in two loose coalitions, were divided by no violent lines of principle after the abandonment of Protection. Finally, society was presided over by the stabilising influence of a Queen who was a model of rectitude and conscientiousness.

The temper of the whole country was, by any contemporary standard, liberal; the assumptions of *laissez-faire* economics, equality before the law and religious toleration were unquestioned. Constitutional monarchy was a faith to Conservatives and Liberals alike. Very little divided them from one another except personal loyalties. Governments of both groups passed important reforms and sometimes took up those proposed by their opponents.

Alexander II (1855–81). His reforms (of which the greatest was the emancipation of the serfs) won him the title of 'Tsar Liberator' but his rule became more reactionary with time and he was eventually assassinated. *Marburg*

The second Polish Revolution, in 1863 (the first had been in 1830), spread into Lithuania and White Russia. Here Russian peasants are disarming Polish fugitives near Dünaburg. *British Museum*

311

Their leaders were still aristocratic in the 1850s. The outstanding Liberal leaders were Russell and Palmerston. Only when Palmerston died in 1865 did Gladstone, for many years his collaborator, become leader of the Liberals. Among the Conservatives, Lord Aberdeen and Lord Derby long stood in the way of the brilliant Jew Disraeli. Only one great constitutional change was made during these years and it opened a new phase of British industry: this was the passing in 1867, by Derby and Disraeli, of a new electoral reform act which almost doubled the size of the electorate and gave the vote to nearly two million in all. Most of the new voters were townsmen of the skilled working class, which naturally inclined towards Liberalism. Disraeli had hoped to win their support but in the elections of the following year the majority none the less voted Liberal, and Gladstone formed his first Cabinet.

In the domain of economics Liberalism stimulated the rapid development of industry, trade and shipping. The first world exhibition — the Great Exhibition of 1851 — vividly illustrated the amazing prosperity which economic freedom had produced. The merchant marine covered the seven seas, while in London great banks multiplied, making the City the financial capital of the world. At the same time colonial expansion continued so vigorously that Britannia, who already ruled the waves, now dominated much of the earth's land surface. Colonies which had been peopled by immigration organised themselves on lines closely modelled on the mother country, so that London was beginning to become the centre of a world-wide federation of British dominions. In spite of the Irish exodus, the population of the United Kingdom had risen by some two and a half million inhabitants. Trade unions had already become a power in the land. They now commanded sufficient financial resources to enable them to assist members who were unemployed or on strike. In 1859 a strike broke out among workers in the building trade which resulted in a reduction of the working day to nine hours.

Only one grave problem seemed to remain. Ireland was more bitter than ever. The massive emigration of the Irish to the United States led to the foundation in New York of the United Irish Brotherhood in 1858. Its members, the Fenians, promoted and financed riots and outrages, sending agents for that purpose to Ireland and to the Irish communities in England. In 1865 their leaders were arrested in England, but Gladstone realised that the problem could not be solved by repression alone. In 1869 he disestablished the Anglican Church in Ireland and passed an Irish Land Act in the following year to improve the condition of the peasants by giving them greater security of tenure. It was a striking interference with the hitherto unchallenged assumption of the absolute right of ownership.

Reforms in Russia and Poland

Russia, in spite of the courage and endurance of her army, was defeated in the Crimea because of her economic and social backwardness. The country had a single railway, almost no other transport or heavy industry, and a population of which eighty per cent were illiterate, half-starved peasants, whose methods of cultivating the land were archaic and who were kept in a state of serfdom. Alexander began to modernise his Empire by lowering the barriers which shut off Russia from the rest of the world, by relaxing the censorship, reducing protective tariffs, reopening universities and granting amnesty to political exiles. But the most intractable problem was that of the serfs. The nobles, indifferent to a social evil from which most of them derived profit, remained hostile to the abolition of serfdom. Alexander II began in 1858 by emancipating all the serfs of the Crown domains, of whom there were some twenty million. They became tenants for life of the land they cultivated and were given the right to purchase it. General emancipation followed in 1881. The former lord of the domain was forced to grant leases to his peasants, who could acquire their land by paying for it. Payment was facilitated by the creation of a ' Peasants' Bank '. The *Mirs*, or former rural communes which had been dependent on the local lord, were made into self-governing communities and attached to the State. Unfortunately, this great reform was unpopular even with the peasants, who found themselves saddled with redemption dues. Many of them had holdings too small to support them and had lost some of their previous security. And as the population was rising, their standard of living did not improve.

In Poland the peasant was not interested in politics, but members of the nobility and clergy, students and army officers all demanded independence. This was refused, although important concessions were made by the Tsar. But when an attempt was made to conscript Poles for military service an insurrection broke out in January 1863 which the Russian General Muraviev drowned in blood — in spite of British and French protests. Among his methods was the arming of peasants against their noble masters. The Polish serfs were in fact rewarded by emancipation in 1864, but thousands of patriots were deported and the Russification of Poland was intensified.

In Russia itself reforms continued in local and judicial affairs but the rising in Poland led Alexander into making more and more concessions to reaction. The result was the appearance of terrorism and, significantly, in 1866 the first attempt by a Russian to assassinate the Tsar.

The Ottoman Empire, Greece and the Balkans

In the Ottoman Empire the Sultan had promised to improve the lot of his Christian subjects, but the promise remained more or less a dead letter. The Moslems showed little enthusiasm to put the reforms into practice, and the Christians equally little to take advantage of them. Their distrust of the Turkish authorities remained unshaken and certainly few Christians desired the privilege of a career in the Turkish army. Actually only the Orthodox Church found its status modified. Henceforth its powers were strictly limited to religious questions; this encouraged the creation of national Churches such as the Bulgarian Church which in 1860 attempted to break away from the Greek Patriarch of Phanar and, thanks to Russian support, succeeded in 1870 in becoming an independent exarchate.

In Greece King Otto had become increasingly unpopular and abdicated in 1862. After a plebiscite the Greeks, forgetting their recent anti-British sentiments, hoped to flatter Britain — and in the process persuade her to cede the Ionian Islands — by offering the vacant throne to Queen Victoria's second son, Prince Alfred. Other powers opposed this and in the end the Greek crown was given to Prince George, son of the King of Denmark. In appreciation of the gesture that had been made Britain evacuated the Ionian Islands in 1863, on the condition that Corfu should be neutralised. In the following year a new Greek Constitution established parliamentary government and universal suffrage. Party strife at once broke out; ministry followed ministry. Crete, which was peopled largely by Greeks, demanded reforms in its turn, rebelled against Turkey and asked for union with Greece. The Sultan, profiting by dissension among the Great Powers, stamped out the revolt.

In Serbia Prince Alexander Karageorgević had also become so unpopular that towards the end of 1858 the Serbian assembly demanded his abdication. The elderly Milos Obrenović, who had been forced to abdicate twenty years previously, was recalled to power, but reigned for only a few months. His pro-Russian son Michael, the first Serbian prince to be educated in the West, undertook the re-organisation of the country. By a series of astute diplomatic manoeuvres, he obtained the withdrawal of the last Turkish garrison from Belgrade and by 1867 Serbia was completely liberated. Michael followed this by secret arrangements with Montenegro, Roumania and Greece which envisaged an eventual Balkan federation. Unfortunately, he was assassinated in 1868, to be succeeded by his nephew Milan. Meanwhile the small mountainous country of Montenegro, though invaded and forced to recognise Turkish supremacy, began to modernise its structure during the long reign of Nicholas I (1860–1918).

The two principalities of Moldavia and Wallachia, which had been separated by the obstinacy of the European powers, presented the world with a *fait accompli* in 1859, when both elected the same ruler — or *hospodar* — Prince Alexander Cuza. He at once proclaimed the union of the two countries and shortly afterwards assumed the title of Prince of Roumania. His reforms — among them the emancipation of the serfs — were introduced too hastily. A conspiracy against him was formed, and in February 1866 he was forced to abdicate. He was succeeded on the throne of Roumania by a Prussian prince, Charles of Hohenzollern, who became Carol I, thanks largely to the support of Napoleon III, still pursing his policy of encouraging nationalism.

Italian unification

Of all the peoples who aspired to independence and unity the Italians were among the most favoured by circumstances. Although much of the peasant population probably did not care at all about unification, most of the political élite who favoured unification at all had come to believe after 1848 that the future lay with Piedmont and its young king Victor Emmanuel II. The House of Savoy had loyal subjects, the only good army in the peninsula, the sympathies of Britain, and the services of an outstanding statesman, Count Camillo Cavour. Cavour had travelled widely in Europe and his knowledge of politics and economics was profound. His great experience was equalled only by his diplomatic skill. He was determined that a united Italy should not be made by revolutionary radicals like Mazzini. In 1852 Victor Emmanuel II made him Prime Minister. At home he pursued liberal, anti-clerical, anti-republican policies. Abroad, he was quick to see and quick to seize every opportunity which could bring Piedmont and Italy to the notice of Europe. He soon showed his firmness towards Austria when he gave refugees from

Giuseppe Garibaldi (1807–82), the hero of the Italian national movement both to his countrymen and to foreigners. A military leader of genius, his political rashness made him an embarrassment to Cavour. *Deutsche Fotothek, Dresden*

At Solferino, the second big battle of the Italian war of 1859, Napoleon III was shaken by heavy casualties. Alarmed, too, by the progress of revolution in Italy, he abandoned his ally, the King of Sardinia, and began to negotiate independently with the Austrians.

Lombardy haven in Piedmont, a policy which led to a rupture in 1853. At the beginning of the Crimean War he played his cards with skill. While the Austrians pursued their devious and equivocal course Cavour showed no hesitation in committing Piedmont: well-disciplined troops were dispatched to the east to reinforce the Anglo-French armies, and Cavour had no need to emphasise the contrast in the Austrian and the Piedmontese attitudes. At the Congress of Paris participation in the Crimean War was rewarded by a seat at the conference table — in spite of Austrian objections. The presence of Piedmont at the Congress was in itself a recognition of her new international status. The Italian question was not officially debated at the Congress, though Napoleon III had wished it to be. None the less Walewski, the President of the Congress, alluded to it and Cavour, representing Piedmont, supplied the delegates with a written report on the subject. Finally, conversations with Cavour reaffirmed Napoleon's interest in the cause of Italian national unity.

Much had already been done, therefore, when in January 1858 Napoleon III narrowly escaped an attempt on his life. The would-be assassin was an Italian patriot, Orsini, who declared that he had wanted to punish Napoleon's failure to liberate Italy. A letter from Orsini, imploring the Emperor to come to the aid of Italy, was published in the official *Moniteur*. Napoleon invited Cavour to confer with him and in July a secret meeting took place at Plombières. An agreement for a defensive alliance in case of attack by Austria was quickly reached. After victory the King of Piedmont-Sardinia was to receive Lombardy and Venetia, so that his kingdom would extend from the Alps to the Adriatic. France's reward was to be the annexation of Savoy and Nice. For the rest of Italy, a Kingdom of Central Italy was envisaged, which together with Rome and Naples was to make up a federation of four states. Cavour, having gained the assurance of French support, then went to Prussia to make sure that there were no difficulties in that quarter. Bismarck told him that Prussia would not object, providing that the first blow was not struck by Piedmont.

Tension mounted until on 1 January 1859 Napoleon III publicly expressed to the Austrian Ambassador his regret that relations between their two countries were not as happy as he could have desired. A few days later the Franco-Sardinian alliance was signed. Soon troops concentrated on both sides of the border, Italians in Piedmont, Austrians in Lombardy. At this threat to peace Britain offered her mediation while Russia proposed a congress of the Powers. The Russian suggestion was on the point of being accepted when, on 23 April 1859, Austria committed the blunder of sending Piedmont an ultimatum demanding demobilisation within three days. Cavour, who had seen the long awaited opportunity slipping through his fingers, rejoiced: Austria would be responsible for the first attack. And, in fact, Austria at once opened hostilities, hoping that Prussia would join her. For the moment Prussia did nothing. It was the French army that moved, with the Emperor in command.

A series of victories opened the gates of Milan to him. It was then that Prussia, disquieted by the rapid success of the French, began to mobilise while, to the astonishment of Napoleon III, a number of the states in the centre of Italy made known their intention of fusion with Piedmont. The bloody French victory at Solferino on June 24 decided the Emperor to end the fighting. He was alarmed both by the Prussian attitude and by the spontaneous unification movement in central Italy. Napoleon and Francis Joseph agreed to an armistice at Villafranca (July 8) without consulting Victor Emmanuel, and arranged the preliminaries for peace. Austria would cede Lombardy not to Piedmont, but to Napoleon III, from whom Victor Emmanuel would then receive it. On the other hand, Austria refused to give up Venetia. The sovereigns of Tuscany, Parma and Modena, who had been driven out of their states, were to be restored, while the Pope was to be invited once again to introduce reforms in the Papal States.

When these conditions became known bitter disappointment was felt throughout Italy by nationalists suddenly deprived of the vision of a promised land extending from the Alps to the Adriatic. Cavour resigned in protest, though he continued privately to agitate the country. Victor Emmanuel II, with sound political sense, accepted the situation, aware that the forces which had been unleashed would remain active. Meanwhile Napoleon III, the champion of nationalism, wondered in embarrassment how he could close the floodgates he had himself opened. For the nationalist movement still gained in momentum, pushed on by careful Piedmontese encouragement. Victor Emmanuel II, assured of the moral support of Britain, disregarded the terms of the final treaty and occupied all central Italy, pleading popular invitation, while Napoleon III had neither the desire nor the ability to stop him. Arguing that the annexation of Tuscany, which had not been envisaged at Plombières, was equivalent in value to the annexation of Venetia, Napoleon now insisted that the promise of Nice and Savoy made by Cavour — who had returned to power — should be fulfilled. In March 1860 two plebiscites were held in which the results were equally overwhelming. Tuscany, Parma, Modena and the Papal 'Legations' of Bologna, Ferrara, Ravenna and Forli — voted in favour of joining Piedmont, while Savoy and Nice — the birthplace of Garibaldi — chose to be attached to France. Cavour could now say to Napoleon III: 'We are accomplices.'

The Italian nationalists regretted what they had not obtained, however, even more than they appreciated what they had acquired. Rome — the natural capital of Italy — remained the supreme objective. Again Napoleon found himself on the horns of a dilemma: if he abandoned the Pope he would incur the enmity of the French Catholics, if he protected the Pope he would thwart Italian patriotism. He chose the latter course, and for the moment Garibaldi abandoned his plans to attack the Papal States. Instead he embarked at Genoa in May 1860 at the head of his Thousand Volunteers to land in Sicily where, with the aid of local insurrectionists, he seized Palermo. Further volunteers swarmed to his colours and he soon threatened Naples. Napoleon III proposed an Anglo-French intervention to stop him but Britain refused. Garibaldi was able to enter Naples in September. By now, Cavour was alarmed at the progress of a popular revolutionary leader who might march on Rome, coming into conflict with France and Austria. He also feared the capture of the cause of unification by democracy and resolved to halt the advance on Rome of Garibaldi's 'Red Shirts'. But in order to do so Piedmont troops had to march through Papal territory. On 18 September 1860 they clashed at Castelfidardo, where the Papal army, under a French general, was beaten. On October 15 Victor Emmanuel's troops entered the Kingdom of Naples, which a week later elected almost unanimously to join Piedmont. Garibaldi, from a sense of patriotic duty, retired from the political scene. At Gaeta Francis II, the former King of Naples, soon capitulated.

Except for Rome and Venice the Italian peninsula was now united. The first National Parliament met in February 1861 at Turin. On March 14 it passed a law creating the Kingdom of Italy, with Rome as its capital. Being for the moment unable to install itself in Rome, the Government had to be satisfied with a symbolic transfer in that direction — from Turin to Florence. Shortly afterwards, Cavour died on the eve of his victory.

From now on the Italian problem became the Roman question and it interested the entire Catholic world. Another Garibaldian attempt to seize Rome in August 1862 was stopped at Aspromonte. The Roman question remained unsolved. In France it aroused bitter controversy between Liberals and Clericals. Pius IX, disillusioned by the repeated failure of his policy, became very reactionary. Ignoring appeals by liberal Catholics to come to terms with the principles of the age, the Pope, in his *Syllabus* of 1864, condemned rationalism and almost every facet of modern thought — including universal suffrage.

Napoleon's chimerical dreams of playing the role of protector to the emergent young nations had in Italy earned him nothing but ingratitude. His prestige had not gained by the annexation of Nice and Savoy, nor by the Italian victories. On the contrary, since the Congress of Paris, the international situation had so changed that the year 1860 already marked the beginning of the Emperor's decline. Russia had not forgotten Sevastopol after all and Austria had now Solferino to remember. Prussia, to which Napoleon had a curious attachment, had adopted a disquieting attitude as champion of Germany. Britain remained the sole possible ally, and since this was obvious to her too, it was hardly a basis for forming an alliance on a footing of equality. Nevertheless Napoleon III made the attempt, and it was then that he inaugurated his policy of freer trade, signed the commercial treaty of 1860 with Britain, and, at home, began to liberalise his Empire.

Meanwhile German affairs had become more complicated and gave Italy the opportunity to advance one step further towards her unification. She became an ally of Prussia in 1866 and when the Prussians were victorious in a war with Austria, Italy benefited. On October 3, by the Peace of Vienna, Venetia, which had been formally ceded to Napoleon III by Austria, was given to Victor Emmanuel II, in much the same way as Lombardy had been transferred.

The more grateful Italians felt towards Prussia the more bitter they grew towards France and her defence of Rome. Garibaldi again tried an attack on what remained of the Papal domains, and his ' Red Shirts ' were defeated at Mentana in November 1867 by Papal forces supported by French troops from the garrison in Rome, using the newly invented breech-loading Chassepot rifle. Finally, three years later, when French reverses in the Franco-Prussian War entailed the recall of this garrison, Italian troops entered Rome on 20 September 1870 and Italian unification was thus completed.

The Holy See continued to refuse to enter into any relation with the Kingdom of Italy. The Pope became a voluntary prisoner in the Vatican and, henceforth deprived of all temporal power, would remain a sovereign whose dominions were purely spiritual. The new emphasis on his spiritual leadership had, in a sense, already been prepared before the occupation of Rome. In 1869, Pius IX had convoked an Oecumenical Council at the Vatican, the first since the Council of Trent. In April 1870 the Council proclaimed the infallibility of the Pope when speaking *ex cathedra* on matters of faith and morals.

Towards German unification. Bismarck

The reaction which followed 1848 crushed the liberal movement in Germany and Austria, but left national aspirations as alive as ever. It became increasingly evident that they could be satisfied only by the unification of the German peoples. Archaeology, history, philology, were all mobilised to demonstrate the antiquity, the unity, and the superiority of the German race, while the swift rise of German industry and commerce was a new source of pride.

Austria and Prussia each sought to canalise this movement to its own advantage, and it was obvious that the century-old rivalry between the two for hegemony in Germany could be settled only on the battlefield. As early as May 1849 Prussia convoked delegates from the German states to meet at Erfurt with the object of revising the Federal Constitution. In this way, under Prussian leadership, a ' Restricted Union ' was formed which gathered together some twenty-eight minor German states, but not Austria, Bavaria, Württemberg and a few other states of lesser importance. Austria took offence at this Prussian move and in response to her threats Frederick William IV accepted at Pillnitz in September 1849 an ' Interim Regime ' which established a joint Austro-Prussian direction of German affairs. Then, in February 1850, under pressure from Vienna, Hanover and Saxony withdrew from the Restricted Union and allied themselves with Bavaria and Württemberg, forming the anti-Prussian ' League of the Four Kings '. In March 1850 the delegates of the Restricted Union — now reduced in number — again met at Erfurt and adopted a Federal Constitution drawn up by Prussia. To this Schwarzenberg replied in April by inviting the sovereigns of Germany to send representatives to Frankfurt, with the object of re-establishing the former Diet. Germany was on the point of being split into two camps: partisans of ' Little Germany ' led by Prussia and partisans of ' Greater Germany ' led by Austria.

In September 1850 the sovereign of Hesse was driven from his Grand Duchy by an insurrection. Schwarzenberg was planning to restore him with the aid of Federal troops when Prussia forestalled him and occupied Hesse. The audacity of this move angered Austria and an ultimatum was addressed to Prussia, demanding the withdrawal of Prussian troops from Hesse and the dissolution of the Restricted Union. Prussia, not yet feeling in a position to resist, bowed to these demands at Olmütz. The climb down humiliated Prussian pride. Austria meanwhile exploited her success and summoned the German states to meet at Dresden, where they were obliged to approve a Constitution which resuscitated the Diet and reaffirmed Austrian hegemony. In August 1851 the Diet met at Frankfurt where it hastened to abolish the liberal measures which had been adopted in some member states. Freedom of the press was suspended and the police were reinforced; in short, absolutism was everywhere triumphant. In the Austrian Empire itself the work of Germanisation was intensified and the great landowners formed a privileged class. In Prussia the upper legislative chamber became a House of Lords in the hands of the squirearchy.

Politically Prussia had been defeated, but she took her revenge in the economic field. The Customs Union — the *Zollverein* — which was a Prussian creation, was enlarged in September 1851 by the inclusion of the North German states. Austria replied by attempting to form her own customs union, an attempt which Frederick William did his best to frustrate. The rulers of South Germany were nevertheless drawn into the Austrian orbit by the ' Coalition of Darmstadt ' in April 1852. In reply Prussia dissolved the *Zollverein*. This move brought such disaster to the general economy that at the request of the German states themselves the *Zollverein* was renewed a year later — but it still excluded Austria.

During the decade which followed Austro-Prussian relations appeared to have become more peaceful. In reality the balance of power had been reversed. The energetic Schwarzenberg died in 1852 and for the next seven years Austrian affairs were guided by Bach, leader of the Conservative party, who persecuted the non-Germanic peoples within the Empire. The Hungarians, inspired by Ferencz Deak, were impatient to efface the memory of their defeat, while the Czechs were equally bent on resistance. Abroad the situation was also unsatisfactory. The ambiguous attitude of Austria during the Crimean War had offended the Western Powers, while the defeat of her armies in the Italian war lowered her prestige.

On the other hand, in Germany itself remarkable developments were taking place. The country was rich in iron and coal, the railway system was extending, and the tonnage handled by the port of Hamburg had trebled. The creation of joint-stock companies and great banks stimulated the circulation of money and a prosperous business class had come into being. This affluence was a further prop to German patriotism, which found its political expression in the 1859 Constitution, the constitution of *Nationalverein* — National Union. Prussia had played a preponderant part in these developments: it was in the Prussian Rhineland that the mines and the blast furnaces which Krupp had built in the Ruhr were situated. Between Berlin and Frankfurt the electrical engineer Siemens installed an underground telegraphic cable, and in Berlin the *Diskonto Gesellschaft* was founded. The Prussian thaler would soon become the monetary unit of Germany.

Prussia owed her growing diplomatic influence above all to the energy and skill of Otto von Bismarck, the son of an impoverished but ancient Junker family from Pomerania, who had distinguished himself as a Conservative Deputy and been made Prussian delegate to the Diet of Frankfurt. He was at once a mystic and a realist who venerated power and put his considerable talents at the service of his King and of Prussia. In 1859 he left the Federal Diet, having taken the measure of Austria, to become Frederick William's Ambassador in Russia, where he strengthened the ties which already existed between the two oppressors of Poland. He then became Minister to France, where his plain-spokenness won him popularity. Bismarck was well versed in European politics when in 1862 he was recalled to Berlin to be made Prime Minister by

the new King, William I — who, since 1858, on the deterioration of his brother Frederick William IV's mental health, had acted as Regent. Prussian to the bone, Bismarck put through the military reforms over which at that moment the King and the *Landtag* were quarrelling. Bismarck's policy with regard to this constitutional crisis was simple: he ignored it. He had already come to the conclusion that Austria must be expelled from the German Confederation, ' not by speeches and majority votes, but by blood and iron '. Only then would Prussia be able safely to allow German unity to be achieved under conditions which guaranteed the survival of her political and social system. Roon, the Minister of War, and Moltke, Chief of the General Staff, were to forge the instrument necessary for the realisation of Bismarck's vast design. As for the King, his confidence in his Prime Minister's advice was complete, though at times he argued with him. In this way the most formidable engine of war in Europe was built, to achieve not the absorption of Prussia by Germany — as Piedmont had been absorbed by Italy — but German unity under Prussian domination. In other ways Bismarck's hand was soon felt: the *Landtag* was dissolved, the press gagged, and recalcitrant officials replaced. His policy was applauded in Russia, to which he lent aid during the Polish insurrection. He signed a commercial treaty with France, but remained so firm with Austria that on his advice William I declined the Austrian invitation to attend a congress of German sovereigns in Frankfurt.

The Austro-Prussian duel

The opportunity to humble Austria arose from the question of the duchies of Schleswig, Holstein and Lauenburg. It had been a source of difficulty ever since 1849. In November 1863 the King of Denmark, Frederick VII, died without an heir, and his throne devolved on his nephew, who became Christian IX. The German-speaking inhabitants of the duchies, however, preferred a German candidate, the Duke of Augustenburg, who was supported by the Diet of Frankfurt. Thereupon William I, determined ' not to allow brothers of his race to be oppressed ', came to an agreement with Francis Joseph, and in 1864 Prussian and Austrian armies invaded the duchies. In October Denmark was forced to cede them to the two sovereigns. Later, by the Convention of Gastein, Austria was awarded the administration of Holstein and Prussia that of Schleswig and Lauenburg with Kiel, an important strategic point between the Baltic and the North Sea.

The administration of the duchies, as Bismarck had foreseen, proved to be the bone of Austro-Prussian contention he required. In October 1865 he met Napoleon III at Biarritz to obtain France's approval of his plans. Napoleon, seduced by vague promises of compensation, gave his acquiescence. The grant of Venetia to Italy as the price of Italian participation in the forthcoming struggle was also a tempting prospect. Assured of the neutrality, and even of the good wishes of France, Bismarck turned to Italy, and in April 1866 signed a secret alliance with Victor Emmanuel valid for three months. Bismarck now only required a pretext for war with Austria. He lost no time. Complaining of Austrian mal-administration in Holstein, he invaded the duchy in the beginning of June. In face of this aggression, Austria proposed that Federal troops should he sent against Prussia. The Diet carried the motion on June 14, and two days later Prussia declared the German Confederation dissolved. On June 18 Prussia went to war with Austria, whose forces were joined by those of the majority of the South German states. The Italians, invading Venetia, helped to divide Francis Joseph's forces.

The superiority of Prussia, manoeuvring from a central position, was overwhelming. Manteuffel defeated the Hanoverians, while Moltke drove back the Bavarians and the Saxons. Their two armies then converged on König-grätz in Bohemia, where on July 3 the decisive battle of Sadowa took place and the Austrians were crushed. In a month the campaign had been finished; the Italian reverses at Custozza and Lissa had done little to alter the situation, and Prussia now had Austria at her mercy. Would the Prussians advance on defenceless Vienna and annihilate an enemy already in the throes of Hungarian and Czech separatist agitations? That was the advice of the King and of a good many on the General Staff. But Bismarck opposed this course. He was aware that the collapse of Austria would upset the balance of Europe; then, too, by treating Austria with moderation he might retain her friendship, or at least neutrality, when afterwards it was most needed. After heated discussion in which the Crown Prince supported Bismarck's arguments, this view prevailed. William I resigned himself to signing a peace treaty which he considered humiliating. Preliminary agreements were confirmed by the Peace of Prague in August. The German Confederation was dissolved and Austria thus excluded from Germany. Prussia made no claim to any territory belonging to the Austrian Empire, but she annexed the duchies of Schleswig and Holstein, Hanover, Hesse and Frankfurt — in other words, some four million inhabitants whose wishes had not been consulted. Finally Venetia was transferred indirectly to the Kingdom of Italy.

After the Prussian annexations there remained in North Germany a few states like Mecklenburg, Oldenburg and certain free cities, in all containing about six million inhabitants. Among them Bismarck set about organising a North German Confederation under his leadership. The command of its army and the direction of diplomacy and finance was given to Prussia. To the Federal Council — or *Bundesrat* — which was modelled on the former Diet of Frankfurt and represented the local interests of its members, Bismarck added a *Reichstag*, elected by universal suffrage, which represented the nation as a whole. It was a solution which was more democratic and at the same time led to greater centralisation. The states of South Germany — Bavaria, Baden, Würtemberg, Saxony — in their turn formed a Confederation which signed military pacts with Prussia. From all this Austria was excluded. The Germany of Vienna had made way for the Germany of Berlin.

In the rest of Europe these events produced profound reactions, above all in Austria itself, whose defeat incited the non-German peoples of the Empire to renew their demands. In the case of the Hungarians, the moderation of their leader Deak led to negotiations between his representative Andrássy and the Austrian Minister Beust, which concluded with the independence of Hungary, of which the Emperor Francis Joseph — advised by a Hungarian Minister — was recognised as King. A Minister of the Empire was created to regulate affairs of common interest — the army, diplomacy and finance. Such was the result of the *Ausgleich*, or Compromise, of 1867 which established the Dual Monarchy — 'the Austro-Hungarian monarchy' united by the House of Habsburg. Its essential core was the recognition that one of the races of the Empire — the Magyars — should be given special privileges in order to join the Germans in oppressing the rest.

The war of 1870

In spite of Napoleon III's early sympathy for Prussian ambitions, the victory of 1866 suddenly gave rise to misgivings in France. Matters were made worse by the fact that the French Emperor's position had already been weakened by the muddled Roman situation and the deplorable tragedy in which a Mexican adventure had ended. Napoleon III attempted to recover his waning prestige by reminding Bismarck of their interview at Biarritz. Prussia, he argued, had benefited greatly from French neutrality during the Austro-Prussian War, and France now required her reward, the Emperor first suggesting the cession of the left bank of the Rhine. Bismarck, who had no intention of yielding an inch of German territory, merely revealed Napoleon's ambitions to the South German states, whose natural reaction was increased distrust of France. Napoleon then reverted to his project of annexing Belgium, with no result — except to present Bismarck with the opportunity of revealing French designs to Britain, always sensitive on the subject of Belgian independence. In despair Napoleon III insisted that France should obtain at least Luxemburg. Bismarck gave him plainly to understand that Luxemburg was German territory which would never be ceded, and spread the word about that the French Emperor's policy was that of begging for 'tips'. Meanwhile Napoleon III's difficulties gave the growing opposition in the Popular Chamber in France its opportunity to make him re-establish a liberal parliamentary regime, and in January 1870 Emile Ollivier formed a Ministry.

The storm broke from an unexpected quarter of the European horizon: Spain. Isabella, the Queen, had been dethroned and the kingdom was in search of a candidate

The German Emperor surveys Paris after the capitulation in January 1871. Ten days earlier the German Empire had been founded and the greatest of the wars of nationality of the mid-nineteenth century had achieved its goal. *Ullstein*

for a crown which, in the circumstances, few coveted. It had been twice refused, but on 2 July 1870 it was accepted by the young Prince Leopold, of the Catholic branch of the Hohenzollern-Sigmaringen family, a brother to the king whom Napoleon had himself installed in Roumania. At the news indignation swept France. A German on the throne of Spain would be like reconstructing the Empire of Charles V! Napoleon requested the withdrawal of Prince Leopold's candidature and the King of Prussia informed him that Prince Anthony Hohenzollern — Leopold's father — had in his son's name renounced the Spanish throne. The affair would have ended there had not Napoleon foolishly allowed himself to be persuaded that this diplomatic victory was not enough. William I, then on holiday at Ems, was required by the French Ambassador to give his pledge that the Hohenzollern candidature would never be renewed. To this the Prussian King courteously replied that he had nothing to add to his previous declaration. A report of the interview was telegraphed to Bismarck. Bismarck at once edited it in a manner which falsely suggested that the exchange had been uncivil and abrupt. In this abbreviated form he released the famous ' Ems telegram ' to the press. It achieved the object Bismarck intended. France read with fury that ' the King of Prussia had refused to receive ' her ambassador. Feelings, already high, boiled over at the imaginary insult and the war party, supported by the Empress, won over the Emperor, who was ill at the time. On July 19 Ollivier, with ' a light heart ' announced the French declaration of war on Prussia. In spite of the assertions of the Minister of War, the country was not prepared, while Prussia, with a modern and well-trained army at her disposal could, when attacked, at once rally behind her all the states of Germany. Napoleon III had presented Bismarck with the war he had been waiting for, and under the conditions that Bismarck desired.

Not only was France in the midst of political and military re-organisation, but Bismarck had made certain that she was diplomatically isolated. Russia sympathised with Prussia; Britain, forewarned of French ambitions in Belgium, would remain neutral. As for Austria and Italy, on whose support Napoleon had counted, the former had reason to entertain more respect for the power of William I than of Napoleon III, while the latter's sole ambition was to occupy Rome. French defeats followed in quick succession. From the beginning of August French armies were defeated in Lorraine and in Alsace, at Wissembourg, Froeschwiller and Forbach. Strasbourg was besieged and the main French army under Marshal Bazaine was encircled in the fortress of Metz, while the army under MacMahon and the Emperor himself, which marched to the relief of Metz, was surrounded at Sedan. There, on 2 September 1870, it surrendered and Napoleon III, at the head of 80,000 men, was made prisoner. At the news of Sedan the people of Paris invaded the Assembly on September 4, declared the Empire at an end and formed a Government of National Defence at the Hôtel de Ville containing Republicans like Jules Favre and the fiery radical Gambetta. Favre met Bismarck at Ferrières, but to Bismarck's instantly expressed demand for Alsace Favre replied that France would never cede an inch of her soil. Shortly afterwards the siege of Paris began. Some of the Government had already left for Tours, others remained in the beleaguered capital. Gambetta escaped by balloon and,

resolved on resistance to the death, set about raising fresh forces in the south and west. Meanwhile Thiers, despite his seventy-three years, undertook the painful mission of seeking help in the capitals of Europe, only to return with empty hands. In October Metz capitulated with 180,000 troops. Gambetta had succeeded in organising three new armies which moved to the relief of Paris, whose garrison made fruitless efforts to break out. After a few local successes all three were defeated; but France's continued resistance surprised Europe and inspired respect. Finally Paris itself, after four months of siege, starvation, bombardment and bitter cold, capitulated. On 28 January 1871 an armistice was signed and arrangements made for an election to provide France with a legal Government with authority to treat with the conqueror. Peace was dearly purchased by preliminary agreements later ratified at Frankfurt in May 1871. France had to pay an indemnity of five thousand million gold francs and — despite the pathetic protest of the Deputies of the two provinces — had to surrender Alsace and a part of Lorraine: that in which there were mines.

Bismarck's triumph was more than the defeat of an army: it also forged the German Empire. Shortly after Sedan he had begun negotiations with the South German states with a view to drawing them into Prussia's North German Confederation. One by one they agreed to join, all except Bavaria who, isolated, was obliged at last to give way. By December 1870 the principle of a unified German Empire had been accepted. Its formal consecration took place a month later, on January 18, the anniversary of the foundation of the Kingdom of Prussia. In the Hall of Mirrors in the palace that Louis XIV had built at Versailles, William I was crowned Emperor of Germany by the King of Bavaria, who was more easily persuaded to accept the new order of things by being awarded this honour. The new German Empire — the Second Reich — was as Prussian as the Holy Roman Empire had been — at least in theory — universal: and it was by this Empire that Alsace-Lorraine, described in the Treaty of Frankfurt as *Reichsland* — Imperial territory — was annexed.

While Europe's attention was occupied by the Franco-Prussian War, Russia seized the occasion to denounce the clauses of the 1856 Treaty of Paris by which the Black Sea had been neutralised. A conference in London resulted in a treaty which gave back to Russia the right to maintain warships and arsenals in the Black Sea, which would no longer be closed except in the event of war. Alexander II thus effaced the consequences of the Russian defeat in the Crimea, and his country was free to resume its expansion towards the Balkans.

OTHER PARTS OF THE WORLD
The smaller states of Western Europe 1848-70

While Napoleon III, Cavour and Bismarck were giving the third quarter of the nineteenth century a radically different aspect from the twenty-five preceding years, replacing local agitation and internal strife with an era of great wars fought in the cause of national unification, the smaller nations of Western Europe, avoiding recourse to war, tended to stabilise themselves. A general current can be distinguished despite the inevitable differences of circumstances, dates and national temperaments; this trend can be partly traced to the example set by Great Britain, but it was also determined by the unrivalled preponderance of British trade and industry. Throughout the West, and especially in the Netherlands, growing economic resources and the extension of railways, giving lower prices and quicker transport, stimulated urban development. With the distribution of wealth came the birth of intellectual movements which were both critical and constructive, and stimulated political and social evolution modelled on parliamentary monarchy as practised in London.

Parliamentarianism in Belgium and Holland

Political parties had been unknown in Belgium until 1839, the year in which her independence was finally recognised. Public opinion was then divided between Catholics and Liberals, who were separated by different views on the relationship between the Church and society, especially in the field of education. As in Britain progressive parliamentary government functioned smoothly. The Liberals won the elections in 1847, and during the Ministry of Charles Rogier extended the franchise, improved the conditions of the working class and increased the number of State schools. In 1852 Rogier made way for Brouckère, who was more careful to appease the Catholics, for they had gained many more votes in the elections. Two years later the Catholics' success in the polls was so clearly marked that they were able to form a Government. After a short term in office, however, the bitter controversies which arose on the subject of monasteries, convents and clerical property brought about the dissolution of the Chamber. The new elections brought back Rogier and the Liberals; they remained in power until 1870 despite a split in the party caused by the formation of a radical wing, the Progressives, who advocated major reforms in electoral methods and in public education. Again following the British example, Belgium adopted free trade and this increased her prosperity. The country was rich in coalmines, and spinning mills and factory chimneys multiplied. Holland had retained the right to levy tolls on ships using the mouth of the Scheldt, but Belgium repurchased it. After this the port of Antwerp grew again in importance. In 1865 Leopold I died and was succeeded by his son Leopold II, then thirty years of age, who was to preside over his country's destiny and prosperity for nearly half a century, to the benefit of his countrymen and the misfortune of the inhabitants of the Congo.

Holland followed a similar path. Parliamentary government functioned smoothly with the alternation of two parties, divided, as in Belgium, by the religious and the educational problem. In 1868 compensation was paid to owners and slaves were freed throughout the Dutch West Indies and Guiana; two years later forced labour was abolished in Indonesia.

The progress of federalism in Switzerland

The Congress of Vienna had re-established Prussian suzerainty over the Swiss Canton of Neuchâtel, recently a principality carved out for the benefit of Napoleon I's Marshal Berthier. In 1848, however, Neuchâtel decided to throw off Prussian rule and provide itself with a democratic constitution. The long Helvetic-Prussian struggle which followed assumed dangerous proportions when in 1856 a reactionary coup d'état took place. This led to the diplomatic intervention of Napoleon III. In the course of a conference held in Paris in 1857 Frederick William IV agreed to renounce his claims to the Canton, though he retained his title of Prince of Neuchâtel. A year later it was Napoleon III who had occasion to complain of the activities of French and Italian refugees in the Canton and to demand their expulsion from Swiss territory. Apart from these incidents, Switzerland pursued its peaceful and prosperous existence. Internally the only conflict which took place was that between partisans of Swiss unification and partisans of federalism, which had been established in 1848. The Federalists, encouraging individual initiative and popular control within the Cantons, had the better of the argument, while at the same time democratic institutions spread from the great industrial centre of Zürich throughout the country. Finally, the neutrality of Switzerland made possible the creation at Geneva in 1864 of the International Red Cross, inspired by the Swiss Henri Dunant, who, with the co-operation of General Dufour, worked for the adoption of international agreements on the humanitarian treatment of wounded soldiers.

The growth of democracy in Scandinavia

Norway, still reluctantly attached to Sweden, had possessed a Parliament since 1814. Denmark, on the other hand, did not achieve the benefits of a constitutional regime until 1849, a postponement in part due to the Schleswig-Holstein difficulties. In 1866 the Danish Constitution was revised and two Chambers were created — the *Landting* and the *Folketing*. The two Chambers began a long struggle over funds for national defence. As for Sweden, it was not until 1866 that she abandoned her old system of four Colleges or Estates — representing the peasantry, the bourgeoisie, the nobility and the clergy — and replaced it with a newly created, genuine bi-cameral Parliament. In spite of this delay in the political field, social and educational reforms had already been achieved in Sweden, as in the other Scandinavian countries.

Portugal and Spain

Thanks to Queen Maria, who had been won over to liberalism and had the support of Britain, the Portuguese Constitution was more or less respected until the seizure of power in May 1851 by a group of radicals led by General Saldanha, who imposed an extension of the franchise. Portugal then settled down to two or three decades of sham parliamentary life under Peter V (1853–61) and Louis I (1861–89).

Spain was again in disorder. Since the strengthening of the monarchy, the absolutist tendencies of the young Queen Isabella II had been encouraged by the clergy. By 1851 she was governing the country personally, supported by the Church. This despotic policy led to revolt. In 1854 O'Donnell forced the Queen to convoke the *Cortes*, which drew up a new constitution and passed a measure authorising the sale of ecclesiastical property held in mortmain. A few years of calm ensued during which Spain attempted to renew her colonial expansion, notably by an expedition to Morocco in 1859 and participation in Napoleon III's Mexican adventure. The Queen got rid of O'Donnell in 1863 and reassumed power herself. Two years later a fresh uprising obliged her to recall him — only to dismiss him again and replace him by Narvaez, who until his death in 1868 maintained a reign of terror. General Prim then led a final revolt which drove Isabella II to France. In the civil war which followed Spain was so torn that Prim sought to restore the monarchy by offering the throne to a foreign prince. It was then that he proposed the candidature of Prince Leopold of Hohenzollern, which precipitated the Franco-Prussian War.

The federalisation of Canada

The growth of national sentiment and the fear of being absorbed by the United States led both English and French Canadians to wish to change their country into a confederation built on solid foundations. By 1864 preparatory conferences had worked out an arrangement which received the sanction of Parliament in London. Thus in 1867 the British North America Act was passed which established a confederation under the name of the Dominion of Canada, consisting of four provinces: Quebec, Ontario, Nova Scotia and New Brunswick. Expansion towards the west, and the rapid exploitation of the rich prairie wheat fields, soon justified the creation of new provinces, Manitoba and British Columbia (1870 and 1871), which marked the beginning of an era of prosperity. The railway which was to become the transcontinental Canadian Pacific Railway was authorised in 1871.

The American Civil War

The question of slavery and of the issue (which was inextricably tangled with it) of states' rights overshadowed the United States at a time when the country was rapidly expanding, when its economic growth had accelerated, and when its population was swelled by newly arrived English, Irish and German immigrants, eager to make their fortunes by exploiting the untapped resources of vast empty territories. From 1850 to 1860 the population rose from twenty-three to nearly thirty-two million. Expansion into fresh territory inevitably brought with it the question whether slavery should be allowed to follow the settlers. Without this, the South, more and more conscious of its individuality as a community, felt that it would soon have no protection in a Senate increasingly dominated by non-slave states. In 1850 a fresh compromise was attempted: slavery was prohibited in states of recent creation, but fugitive slaves were to be returned to their owners in those where slavery was still legal. This situation gave rise to many tragic and pathetic incidents emphasised by Harriet Beecher Stowe in her novel *Uncle Tom's Cabin*, which appeared in 1852 and was read throughout the world. Presidential elections and the creation of new states or territories in Kansas, Nebraska, Utah and New Mexico all sharpened the conflict so that public opinion was more and more divided on geographical lines. The democratic and industrial North was abolitionist, and stood for union and protective tariffs; the agrarian North-West supported it. Besides its ' peculiar institution ', therefore, and its aristocratic traditions the South was also conscious of its economic interest in the preservation of the free trade which kept down the price of foreign goods bought with its cotton exports. In 1860 the Presidency was contested by four candidates. Abraham Lincoln was elected and his election was a purely sectional triumph of the North and North-West. Lincoln, born in a log-cabin of humble parentage, self-taught, tall and awkward, was destined to become one of America's greatest Presidents. But his election was the final provocation to the Southern states. In December 1860 South Carolina seceded from the Union and declared its independence. In January 1861 this example was followed by Mississippi, Alabama, Florida, Georgia and Louisiana, and a month later by Texas. On 12 April 1861 the war began with a Southern attack on Fort Sumter, which commanded the port of Charleston. The outbreak of hostilities at once brought Virginia, Arkansas, North Carolina and Tennessee into the Southern Confederacy.

In strength the two opposing camps were very unequal: the Union contained twenty-three states with a total population of twenty-one million; in the Confederacy of Southern States there were eleven states with some twelve million inhabitants, of whom nearly four million were Negro slaves. The Union also had great financial, industrial and naval superiority. The President called for 75,000 volunteers, an insufficient number, who were at first indifferently commanded, while the Confederate states, struggling for their very existence, had far better generals, among whom Robert E. Lee was outstanding both as a soldier and as a man of noble character. For two years, the Confederate armies won victories, while the North, a prey to military rivalries, suffered heavy losses and strove in vain to march on Richmond, which under the presidency of Jefferson Davis had become the capital of the South. Finally in 1863 Lincoln made military service obligatory (a year after the Confederacy had done so) and gave command of the Union armies to General U. S. Grant, whose talents had until then been unappreciated. Grant, brilliantly seconded by General Sherman, reversed the situation. The Confederates lost New Orleans and on 3

A slave auction in Virginia, 1861. For many Americans, in North and South, the Civil War was a war about slavery. But for both governments it was a war about the Union and its authority over the component states. *Mansell*

A group of pearl fishers. Japanese print by Kuniyoshi. 1833. British Museum. *Holford*

July 1863 were defeated in the decisive battle of the war at Gettysburg. After this, the North was never again in danger. The next day Vicksburg fell and Virginia was cut off from the west. Then, in 1864, Sherman, spreading devastation, reached the sea at Savannah. The circle closed round the Confederate armies: the Confederacy's sea-coast was blockaded and its land frontiers closed. Supplies were no longer obtainable. At last the capitulation of Richmond itself was followed by an armistice, signed on 9 April 1865 in the Court House at Appomattox. The Civil War was over. The North was victorious and the Union had been saved; Lincoln had achieved his object. He had been re-elected President in 1864 and had already made clear his wish to deal generously with the defeated opponent when, five days after the armistice, he was assassinated in his box at Ford's Theatre in Washington. His death deprived the Republic of one of the greatest leaders democracy has yet produced and made immeasurably more difficult the arduous task of reconstruction after the war.

The South was in ruins. The war had taken a dreadful toll and the economy was shattered. Hatred still smouldered and the Negroes, freed since 1 January 1863 by Lincoln, were far from being able to profit from their unfamiliar liberty. In 1866 they received civil rights and two years later the franchise. These rights could not, however, of themselves achieve the integration of former slaves with a society which kept them at arm's length and found their presence a constant source of disturbance. But the country as a whole, though its recovery was marred by certain scandals caused by adventurers and speculators, and though the South remained a backward region until the next century, soon resumed its forward march, while the construction of transcontinental railroads further stimulated prosperity.

The Mexican intervention

In Mexico Juarez, an Indian leader of the Liberals, had attempted to free his country from the domination of the Church and the influence of foreign financiers. His methods were ruthless and Britain, Spain and France decided that their interests were endangered. In July 1861 the three countries signed an agreement and prepared for a joint expedition to collect the debts owed to them by Mexico. The British and Spanish soon thought better of the enterprise and withdrew. Napoleon III had larger ideas of establishing a Catholic Empire in Mexico. Napoleon III believed this would regain the allegiance of those French Catholics who had quarrelled with his policy on Rome. By offering the imperial crown of Mexico to the Archduke Maximilian, brother of Francis Joseph, he hoped also to please the Austrian court. After a long siege the French expeditionary force occupied Puebla in May 1863, and entered Mexico City. There an Assembly was convoked which offered the throne to the Archduke Maximilian, a man of admirable intentions, handsome and benevolent — whom, unfortunately, the Mexicans did not want. Meanwhile the American Civil War ended with the victory of the North, which supported the liberal faction in Mexico. In October 1865 the Government at Washington peremptorily ordered the French to depart. Though the melancholy failure of the expedition was already apparent, Napoleon did not withdraw his troops until February 1867, when events in Europe obliged him to do so. Maximilian was abandoned to his fate. His wife, the 'Empress' Carlotta, returned to France where she pleaded in vain for the help Napoleon was unable to supply. She went on to Rome where she threw herself at the feet of the Pope, and in the end went out of her mind. In June 1867 the unhappy Emperor of Mexico, seized by Juarez, was executed by a firing squad at Queretaro.

Convulsions in South America

The states of South America continued their troubled existence of wars, civil wars, military coups, and constantly changing political structures. Thus in 1864 Venezuela, of which Monagas for long remained dictator, broke up into a confederation of twenty autonomous provinces, only to become a united nation again as a result of a fresh revolution. Colombia, after a civil war which ended with the dictatorship of Mosquera, adopted a federal constitution in 1862. In Ecuador, Moreno had seized power in

Abraham Lincoln (1809–65) became President of the United States by a small majority in 1860. His authority and popularity grew throughout the war years until his assassination one week after General Lee's surrender. *Popper*

Australian bark drawing of a kangaroo and mythological animals. Arnhem Land. British Museum

U

The first industrial war produced the first attempts at submarine warfare. This rough sketch shows the Confederate submarine *Hunley* which sank with the loss of its crew after sinking a Union ship. *Submarine Library*

A highly imaginative portrayal of a group of Yankee Doodles marching south. Many odd uniforms appeared during the early months of the war when the amateur element still predominated. *Collection of Mrs John Nicholas Brown*

Ulysses S. Grant (1822–85), commander of the Union forces in the West, and from 1864 commander-in-chief, was the general Lincoln needed. His fame as a soldier made him President in 1869. *U.S. National Archives*

By the end of the war, both sides were using Negro troops (this is a Union soldier). Grave fears were expressed about the dangers of racial war and Negro troops were chiefly used for non-combatant duties. *Mansell*

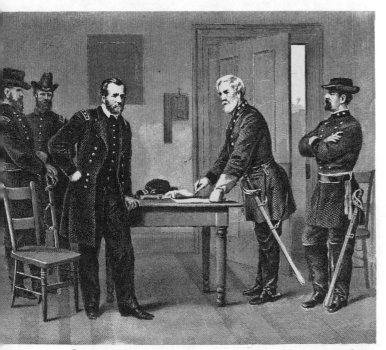

General Robert E. Lee surrendering with his army to Grant at Appomattox Court House. Lee had fought with outstanding brilliance and courage and left a reputation of great chivalry and nobility of character. *Mansell*

322

Europeans forced their way into China as missionaries and merchants in the nineteenth century supported by their governments in the hope of winning a share of such trades as the Chinese silk industry. *Giraudon*

The Indian Mutiny (1857–58) shattered British confidence in the Indian population and in the wisdom of allowing India self-government for decades. This print shows British soldiers on the march to Umballa. *Mansell*

1861 and instituted a regime with theocratic tendencies, while Bolivia was in the grip of anarchy. In 1864 Peru was attacked by Spain, which attempted to seize the Chincha Islands. Peru's neighbours, Bolivia and Chile, for once settled their quarrels and came to her aid, whereupon the Spanish fleet bombarded Valparaiso, thus disturbing the calm of a country which under representative government had made progress. After its dictator Rosas had fled in 1852, Uruguay enjoyed a surge of prosperity based on its exports. Argentina, provided with a liberal constitution, turned into a Confederation; the capital, Buenos Aires, at first seceded, but in 1859 decided to join. The stability of Argentina attracted immigrants, above all Italians, who developed its agriculture. Brazil's stability was even more marked. The Emperor of Brazil, Pedro II, a moderate and cultured man, presided over smoothly working parliamentary institutions. The exceptional tranquillity of his vast empire was disturbed only in 1864 by the aggression of Paraguay, under its dictator Lopez. An alliance with Argentina and Uruguay — and five years of savage warfare — finally brought the defeat of the aggressor. From this disastrous adventure Paraguay emerged ruined and depopulated.

French intervention in the Lebanon

In 1860 the massacre of the Maronite Christians by their neighbours, the Druses, was a pretext for Napoleon III to send an expedition to restore order. The Sultan was obliged to grant the Lebanon a special statute which was guaranteed by the European powers.

British difficulties in India

British domination of India, which had seemed solidly established after the repression of the Sikh rebellion in 1849, was badly shaken eight years later by a mutiny among its native troops, the Sepoys. The Indian Mutiny broke out in May 1857 and turned into an insurrection which quickly spread through the whole Ganges basin and reached Delhi. The Indians, led by the Rajah Nana Sahib, were joined by Moslem partisans of a descendant of the Grand Mogul. British officers were massacred and their families were taken prisoner; but the British, at first surprised, soon rallied. With the co-operation of the Sikhs, who were hostile to the Sepoys, British forces entered Delhi, where in July 1858 the revolt was ruthlessly stamped out.

The East India Company was held responsible for the troubles and its privileges were abolished. The subcontinent passed to the Crown and in 1876 Queen Victoria was proclaimed Empress of India. From 1861 onwards the Royal Government began the introduction of reforms designed to give Indians a share in government. A beginning was made with the appointment of Indian magistrates and the creation of legislative and executive councils containing Indian representatives. At the same time, the shock given to British confidence by the Mutiny only served to accentuate the very sharp social division between the two races which had begun to establish itself from the moment when English women first began to settle in India in the early years of the nineteenth century.

Indochina and Burma

The Indochinese peninsula was divided into two zones of influence: in the west British, in the east French, separated by independent Siam. In Burma British merchants had been molested, and in 1852 the Governor-General of India had Pegu and Rangoon occupied. Britain thus commanded the estuary of the Irrawaddy, isolating north Burma in the interior. Shortly afterwards the accession of a new Emperor of Annam, Tu Duc, was followed by the massacre of missionaries, and in 1858 France made a naval demonstration in the Bay of Tourane. On the return of an expeditionary force sent to China in 1860 the French seized Saigon, and by a treaty signed on 5 June 1862 Annam ceded to France the three provinces which formed Cochin-China. Possession of the Mekong delta allowed the French to sail up the river and in 1863 to establish a protectorate over Cambodia. They reached Tongking and, by the valley of the Red River, penetrated as far as the Chinese province of Yunnan.

The end of Chinese isolation

The treaties by which foreign powers forced China to open her frontiers revealed how weak the vast Chinese Empire had become. Towards 1846 the wretched and half-starved population of the Yangtze basin revolted against the hated Manchu Dynasty at the call of a visionary named Hung Hsiu Chuan, who preached a religion inspired by doctrines borrowed from Confucianism and the Bible. By 1851 the insurgents — the *Taiping*, i.e. ' The Great Peace ' — had seized Hankow and then Nanking, which became the capital of the Taiping Empire. The revolt continued to spread and the Imperial generals who were given the task of suppressing it could not even recapture Nanking. The Western Powers, who had toyed with the thought of encouraging this presumably reformist movement, saw that the civil disorder was harmful to trade and decided to support the Court at Peking instead. Foreign officers, above all British, led the Chinese Imperial armies to victory. Nanking was retaken and the Manchu Dynasty saved, but the rich provinces of central China had been devastated.

In the meantime the treaties signed with Britain and France had at best been unwillingly complied with by the Chinese authorities. The seizure of a British ship and the murder of a missionary were the pretext for an Anglo-French expedition which, after bombarding Canton and capturing the forts of Taku, in 1858 imposed the Treaty of Tien-Tsin. Armed resistance to the Anglo-French plenipotentiaries sent to ratify the treaty was followed by a new joint expedition. A French victory at Palikao opened the road to Peking while the British burned the Imperial Summer Palace, as a reprisal for the ill-treatment of British prisoners. New treaties, signed in Peking in 1860, opened eleven ports to foreign trade, ports in which foreigners could reside without being subject to Chinese jurisdiction. China agreed to receive diplomatic missions and confirmed the freedom of Western missionaries to teach Christianity. Symbolically, a ministry of foreign affairs was set up for the first time. With her ports no longer under her own control and foreign inspectors in charge of her customs service, China was bound to continue to undergo the revolutionary effects of contact with the West.

The interior of a nineteenth-century Japanese theatre by Toyokuni. The highly stylised heroic theatre was one of the great popular arts of Japan. *Giraudon*

The Emperor Theodore (1855–68), ruler of Ethiopia, holds court. A harsh ruler, he also fell foul of Great Britain and committed suicide after defeat by a British expedition supported by his rebellious subjects. *Camera Press*

A popular Russian illustration showing the mortal frame of man and his struggle between good and evil. The strong mystical element in Russian thought was a barrier between her and Western Europe. Bibliothèque Nationale. *Giraudon*

Russian expansion in Siberia

When Russia's expansion towards the Balkans was stopped by the Crimean War she turned to the east. Siberia was colonised by free pioneers, many of whom had formerly been serfs. The Tsar's troops occupied Khiva and Merv, on the borders of Persia and of Afghanistan, as well as Tashkent and Khokand on the way to the Pamirs. As the long frontier between Russia and China took form, contacts between the two countries became more frequent. Muraviev, the Governor of Siberia, had the Amur valley explored, and by the Treaty of Aigun in 1859, the river was ceded to Russia. The way to Manchuria and towards the warm-water Pacific ports beyond was now open.

The awakening of Japan

In Japan the Emperor's power was shadowy and the country was ruled by the shoguns. Still feudal, Japan had remained closed to all foreigners, except for a few Dutch. Forestalling Russian intentions, the United States, which had already reached the Pacific coast, dispatched Commodore Perry to Yedo Bay. There, in July 1853, he delivered papers from the American President requesting a treaty of trade and friendship. When he returned to Yedo a year later the partisans of conciliation had prevailed and on 31 March 1854 Japan signed the treaty which opened two small Japanese ports to American trade. Shortly afterwards further ports, including Nagasaki and Yokohama, were opened. In them Americans could reside with extraterritorial privileges and the Japanese authorities agreed to receive a diplomatic mission. Between 1854 and 1859 Britain, Russia, Holland, France and Portugal obtained the same advantages. Japan had opened her gates to the foreigner without resistance — but not without internal reaction. Already an important section of the community clamoured for the restoration of the Emperor's power and the modernisation of the country. In the resulting disorders political assassinations occurred in which the victims were sometimes foreigners. Reprisals inevitably followed: in November 1864 an international squadron forced the straits of Shimonoseki and obliged the Emperor to ratify treaties which had remained in abeyance. In January 1867 the accession to the throne of the young Emperor Mutsuhito hastened the growth and solidarity of the Imperial party. Breaking with the xenophobes, the Imperialists abolished the shogunate in January 1868 and, defeating their adversaries, established a single ruling power. A new era in Japanese history began with the Meiji period.

Oceania

In 1851 Australia was convulsed by the discovery of gold in New South Wales. During the gold rush of the following two years nearly a quarter of a million immigrants made for Bathurst and then for Ballarat, near Melbourne. This influx of population was in itself sufficient to cause trouble, while the feverish search for gold, leading to the neglect of every other activity in a country whose real wealth was derived from agriculture and grazing, unbalanced the economy. Under an Act of 1850 the continent was divided into five separate colonies with largely independent governments. Other colonies were later constituted as separate entities. Australia became the first British dominion to introduce universal suffrage and the payment of Members of Parliament. The main problems of the colonies — the ending of the convict deportations, the regulation of land settlement and the restriction of Asian immigrants — could at first be handled by the individual local administrations, but in 1885 the first loose federation was created. New Zealand, administered until 1852 by a private company, received a federal constitution in that year.

Africa

The unorganised and backward state of Africa attracted the European powers, who exploited those regions of the continent which were easily accessible. The only African state of importance was Egypt, which had been modernised by Mehemet Ali. Mehemet Ali's work was continued by his fourth son Said, whose approval of Ferdinand de Lesseps's great project enabled the Suez Canal to be constructed. The Canal was opened in 1869 by Said's lavish successor Ismail, in the presence of the Empress Eugenie.

Under the long and successful proconsulate of General Randon the pacification of Algeria proceeded with vigour and efficiency. The French penetrated the Sahara, pacified the Moroccan border and in 1817 crushed the Kabyles in the high plateaus which sheltered them. After the revolution of 1848 in France political prisoners and unemployed workers were deported to Algeria; the immediate results were not entirely satisfactory, though in the long run the new colonists added to the material progress of the country and increased its European population. A Ministry for Algerian Affairs was created in 1850, and ten years later the first railways were built. The country then had 200,000 European inhabitants.

In Senegal the long and energetic administration of General Faidherbe, who arrived in 1852, did much to develop the region. Dakar was founded, and the Senegal River became a French waterway.

With the growth of the white population in South Africa, Cape Colony was granted its own legislative assembly in 1853. The independence of the Boer Republics in the Transvaal and Orange Free State was recognised; Natal, however, was annexed in 1843. The stability of these arrangements was to be threatened later by the discovery of diamonds in the Orange River in 1867.

Finally, during the period of her revived colonial ambitions, Spain conquered the Moroccan region of Tetuan in 1859. British objections, however, prevented the enterprise from being further pursued.

Intellectual movements

The year 1850 marks a very rough division between two manners of thinking and two modes of expression. Romanticism, an escape from reality by way of the imagination, yielded by reaction to realism. Contributory to this change in attitude was the sense of failure and disillusion which followed the revolutions of 1848. Europeans had witnessed the futility and defeat of all their generous and humanitarian dreams, of their ideals of liberty, of their national aspirations. It was a hard lesson. Refusing to nurse vain illusions any longer, Europe became pessimistic. Only science, which had made enormous progress, inspired unbounded confidence. For many science had become the new religion. In all realms of thought experimental methods,

Industrialism begins to provide subject-matter for art. This is one of several paintings and drawings of scenes in railway-carriages by Daumier (1808–79) a major figure in the development of realist painting. *Mansell*

In the middle of the century a great boom in railway-building began in England and on the continent. Freight trains such as these began to replace pack-horses for the transport of heavy goods. *Science Museum, London*

The Clipper ships, designed for the New York to China trade, marked the peak of sailing-ship design. One of them set a sailing record from Boston to Liverpool — twelve and a quarter days — which is still unbeaten. *Mansell*

so successful in the physical world, were applied. Henceforth all facts were minutely scrutinised and subjected to rigorous analysis without fear that ancient idols might, in the process, be upset.

France led the way; the frivolity of the Second Empire misleadingly conceals intellectual activity of great importance. In 1852 Auguste Comte published his *Catéchisme Positiviste* in which he formulated the doctrine of a new philosophy, one which attempted to restrict itself to the examination only of facts verified by experience, employing only data supplied by science. The positivist school of thought found in Hippolyte Taine a disciple of talent who applied its principles not only to psychology but to history and to art. In his book *De l'Intelligence*, which appeared in 1870, Taine held that the senses were the basis of all knowledge. By affirming that the evolution of the human being was conditioned by his race, environment and epoch, he took up a resolutely determinist attitude. Ernest Renan, on the contrary, arrived by similar methods of thought at scepticism. He had been a seminarist, and his work in Biblical exegesis led him to deny the supernatural and, in his celebrated *Vie de Jésus* (1863) to present a portrait of Christ which was tragically human. In the domain of historical studies the positivist approach tended to make history a science which retraced events by means of abundant documentation submitted to critical examination. Tocqueville and Fustel de Coulanges produced works of originality and value on these lines, but the philosopher Taine, in *Les Origines de la France contemporaine*, was still inclined to allow facts to be distorted by preconceived ideas.

In the literary world, though the mighty romantic voice of Victor Hugo could still be heard, it was heard from afar — from the Channel Islands where he had gone into voluntary exile. From there in 1853 he stigmatised 'Napoleon the Little' in the burning and passionate verses of *Les Châtiments*. There, too, he continued his work as a romantic novelist, publishing *Les Misérables* in 1862. But with Baudelaire, the forerunner of symbolism, poetry had already taken another course. In *Les Fleurs du Mal*, which appeared in 1857, human suffering was no longer the object of sentimental effusions, but an analysis no less painful for its brutal sincerity. Poetry, repudiating lyricism, strove to achieve technical perfection. In 1852 Theophile Gautier had given the example of delicately wrought verse in his *Emaux et Camées*. But it was with Leconte de Lisle and his Parnassian School that this form of 'art for art's sake' attained its full development. His *Poèmes antiques* and *Poèmes barbares* represented a type of poetry which, attempting impassivity and achieving elegant concision, tended to coldness and formality. As for the novel, the imaginative aspect still marked in the works of Balzac yielded to the demands of strict reality. The success of Flaubert's *Madame Bovary* in 1856 set novelists on a path which was followed by the Goncourt brothers, Alphonse Daudet and others. Finally, with Zola, realism became naturalism, and the emphasis was on a description of life which concealed nothing. In this way the novel became more 'democratic' and its subject matter tended to be drawn from the lives of ordinary people. The writer collected 'human documents' and his notebook replaced his inspiration. Criticism as a literary form assumed an importance it had not previously known, and in this field Sainte-Beuve was the undisputed master.

The same tendencies were apparent in the arts, especially in France, the chosen land of painters. Painting became both realist and popular when in 1850 Courbet, chief of the school which succeeded Delacroix, exhibited his masterpiece the *Burial at Ornans*, Millet painted his *Angelus* exalting the life of the humble and Corot added a new dimension of light to nature, a quality which was accentuated in the work of Manet, whose *Olympia* in 1865 announced the arrival of impressionism. Meanwhile Daumier satirised and caricatured aspects of bourgeois and working-class life with a skill amounting to genius. In the domain of music Berlioz, underrated by his contemporaries, presented his *Damnation of Faust* in 1846, which in 1859 was eclipsed in popularity, if not in value, by Gounod's *Faust*, with its ballets and sumptuous scenic effects.

In Germany the philosophy of Hegel and the pessimism of Schopenhauer had prepared the ground for the reception of positivist doctrines. Hegel's greatest disciple, Marx, living in London in these years, published the first volume of *Das Kapital* in 1867. Positivism was reaffirmed in the works of David Strauss, for whom science and religion were irreconcilible. The Germans, with their patient research and methodical application, excelled in the fields of history, ethnology and philology. Outstanding were Grote, Curtius and above all Mommsen, whose *Roman History* inaugurated a new school of historical studies. Their work tended to glorify the German race. Germany at this time lacked great painters; on the other hand, with Wagner and Brahms, it dominated the musical world. After the success of Richard Wagner's *Tannhäuser* in 1845, other operas — the *Ring, Tristan and Isolde*, etc. — confirmed the originality and power of a master whose emotional intensity has been rarely equalled. Compared with the fiery genius of Wagner, celebrating the legends of ancient Germany, the talent of his compatriot Brahms seemed restrained and classical. In Italy Rossini and Verdi remained faithful to the melodic genius of their race.

In England Herbert Spencer (1820–1903) was, like Comte, universal in his spirit of inquiry and, again like Comte, a philosopher whose tendencies were positivist. Charles Darwin (1808–98) published his epoch-making *On the Origin of Species by Means of Natural Selection* in 1859, and revolutionised biology and man's conception of his own place in nature. Turner, who died in 1851, was a landscape painter whose gift for capturing the transitory effects of light proved an inspiration to the impressionists. The English novel followed the broad trend towards realism, but with discretion. Dickens made his work acceptable to Victorian society by tempering realism with humour and sentimentality. Thackeray, whose success was assured on the appearance of *Vanity Fair*, was a severe critic of his age, but careful not to offend its prudery. Carlyle, though of questionable authority as a historian, had an incomparable gift of expression and exercised a strong influence on the intellectual élite of his day, especially marked in the case of the distinguished art critic, Ruskin. The ideas of English liberalism were essentially pragmatic but, in so far as they could receive abstract exposition, they did so in the works of John Stuart Mill.

But the intellectual world had suddenly widened in area: newcomers had appeared on the horizon who for various reasons had until now played a secondary part in the thought and art of Europe. The Russians made an impressive entrance on the scene with writers like Gogol, whose *Government Inspector* in 1836 satirised the vices of provincial officials, and Dostoyevsky, an agitator turned mystic, whose novel *Crime and Punishment* made 1866 a date in literary history. At this time Turgenev, with *A Sportsman's Sketches* (1852), and the great Tolstoy, with *War and Peace* (1864–9) were at the beginning of their careers. The literary talent of such authors was matched by their musical compatriots, the group known as the 'Five', of whom Borodin, Rimsky-Korsakov and Mussorgsky — who composed the popular opera *Boris Godunov* — were best known. To express and exalt the Slav soul these composers strove to free Russian music from Western influences. The Scandinavians also made their appearance, the first social dramas of the Norwegian Ibsen dating from 1863. The Czechs contributed the poet Jan Kollar and the composer Smetana.

On the other side of the North Atlantic the New World was emancipating itself from purely European inspiration. By producing thinkers like Emerson, poets like Walt Whitman, story-tellers like Edgar Allen Poe and novelists like Mark Twain the United States began to play its part in the cultural life of the world, which henceforth grew steadily richer by the new contributions from all lands.

Industrial, economic and social evolution

The discoveries of science and the exploitation of previously unknown sources of energy intensified and spread the mechanisation of industry until it reached even Russia. In the middle of the century an unprecedented surge of industrial activity began. Metallurgy made great strides after the invention of the Englishman Bessemer's process for the manufacture of steel in 1855. Great Britain, until now unrivalled in the richness of its coal measures, began to feel the competition of the United States, where in Pittsburgh the Carnegie brothers created an important centre of the iron industry. The German factories based on the coal basins of the Ruhr and Silesia also began to offer competition. Similarly in the textile industries British manufacturers were obliged to compete with American cotton goods and French textiles, for France still excelled in the manufacture of silk. From 1861 the United States began to experiment with a new and exceptionally powerful source of energy, petroleum; Rockefeller founded the Standard Oil Company in 1870. At about the same time the electric machines of the Belgian engineer Gramme foreshadowed the day of the dynamo. Advances in chemistry contributed to material prosperity, notably in the manufacture of fertilizers, which increased agricultural production.

In the realm of transportation the power and rapidity of the new engines upset all previous notions of distance. The network of European railways increased at the rate of some 3,000 miles annually. Britain still led the way, but France and Germany had by 1860 already laid about 6,000 miles of track, and Russia, lagging far behind, had made a beginning. Tunnels were bored — like the Mont Cenis tunnel in 1857 — to overcome obstacles erected by nature. At sea the sailing ship was still used for heavy cargoes, but steam navigation had developed to such an extent that great shipping companies had been created: in Britain the Cunard and White Star Lines, in France the *Messageries Maritimes* and the *Transatlantique*, in Germany the *Norddeutscher* and *Hapag*.

Doré's engraving of mid-nineteenth-century London conveys vividly the over-crowding and squalor which made revolutionary changes in urban administration necessary. *Mansell*

In 1859 the *Great Eastern*, a British liner of 23,000 tons, crossed the Atlantic in fifteen days. In 1850 England and France were joined by submarine cable, while a transatlantic cable connecting Europe and America was laid in 1866. The acceleration of communications brought peoples closer together, encouraged the exploitation of new territories, and stimulated the exchange of products.

In all countries where civilisation was advanced the result was a continued growth of a prosperity unbroken by economic crises. The climate of confidence encouraged the organisation of credit, and financial establishments multiplied. These accumulated capital to invest in the commercial enterprises of companies whose shares, negotiable on the stock exchange, were sometimes the objects of speculation. One of the products of this development was the creation of the multiple department store.

Population everywhere increased. Two tendencies were noticeable: the abandonment of rural areas for the industrial cities, and the prolongation of human life due to improved living conditions and the advance of hygiene. But the distribution of wealth remained very unequal. Those who owned vast domains — the landed nobility — could still be found in Russia, Hungary, East Prussia

and also in Great Britain. But the great fortunes were henceforth usually made by industrialists, shipping magnates, merchants. Such fortunes were numerous in Great Britain, while in the United States multi-millionaires flourished; as well as the Carnegies and the Rockefellers there were now the Vanderbilts, Morgans and Goulds, compared to whose fortunes those of the Péreires and Foulds in France or of the Bleichröders in Germany paled into insignificance — though the Rothschilds, originally from Frankfurt but now international, competed with the richest across the Atlantic. By the side of such millionaires the prosperous middle classes cut a modest figure. But with their investments and savings, they, too, venerated the power of money, which was a guarantee of security and independence, and a foundation from which their families might rise in the world.

Confronting this new, essentially capitalist society, was the working class. Although wages had risen and competition had lowered the prices of manufactured articles, food and lodging remained expensive, and the condition of the workers was far from satisfactory. Sympathy for the sufferings of the poor was reflected in the literature of the day and in philanthropic work. Sometimes factory owners set up canteens and built houses for their workers. But though their material situation continued to improve — with the introduction of an eight-hour day, the prohibition of child labour, etc. — the proletariat was insistent on attaining certain rights: the right of association and the right to free schooling, which was especially demanded by 'popular education' groups like those organised by Bebel, leader of the Social Democrat Party in Germany. The workers' movement tended towards the formation of occupational unions which in Britain became national federations, solidly organised to defend their own interests. Impressed by their example when they visited the International Exhibition in London in 1862, French workers obtained on their return to France the right to form trade unions.

Working-class agitation spread throughout Europe. In Britain it had assumed a reformist character, but in France its tendency was revolutionary and in Germany authoritarian: in Germany, under the leadership of Lassalle and Liebknecht, the workers formed a political party. In Russia the anarchist Bakunin advocated the complete overthrow of the social order. Despite these differences the solidarity of the proletariat was affirmed when in London in September 1864 fifty delegates from various countries formed the first International Workers' Union, of which Karl Marx was the virtual founder, inspiration and theoretician. He proposed to replace the State in which the individual was free to make his fortune but the majority could not by one based on the principle 'From each according to his abilities, to each according to his needs'. The first congress of the International was held in Geneva in 1866 and its outlook was already political, a character which was accentuated in the congress which met at Brussels two years later and declared 'war on war'. In the following year at Basle it demanded the abolition of private property, and State ownership — 'collectivisation' — of land, mines and railways. In 1870 a new delegation joined the International from the United States but the congress which had been arranged to take place in Paris that September was cancelled because of the war.

CHAPTER SEVENTEEN

TOWARDS WORLD WAR

From 1871 to 1914 the world enjoyed a period of peace between the Great Powers during which material wealth increased prodigiously. Though the dominant sense of well-being concealed the fact from the great majority, it was, however, a precarious peace, a constant vigil of arms. The armaments contest ravaged national budgets, and the outbreak of limited conflicts revealed the strains and stresses which could at any moment convulse the world. Russia fought Turkey in 1877–8, Serbia fought Bulgaria in 1885, Greece fought Turkey in 1897 — preliminary rounds of the Balkan Wars of 1912–13. There were struggles beyond the confines of Europe: Chile against Bolivia and Peru in 1879–83, Japan against China in 1894–5. There was the Boer War of 1899–1902 and the Spanish-American War of 1898. In 1904–5 the war between Russia and Japan offered a foretaste of the future conflict on a world scale which, with the First World War in 1914, would brutally mark the true terminating date of the tumultuous, seething — but in the main fruitful — nineteenth century.

THIRTY YEARS OF EUROPEAN AND AMERICAN EXPANSION

The French Republic

Vanquished, France had yielded her position as the first power on the continent of Europe to Germany. When the first peacetime elections were held, in February 1871, an Assembly was chosen containing an overwhelming majority of Deputies who were in favour of peace, i.e. of Monarchists, since the Republicans were suspect for having talked too much of war to the death. The National Assembly, with more than four hundred Monarchists to two hundred Republicans, met at Bordeaux and appointed Thiers as head of the executive power. He had been elected by twenty-six Departments because in July 1870 he had entreated the Imperial Government to refrain from breaking with Prussia. The peace preliminaries which he signed on February 26 were ratified in the Assembly by a vote of 546 to 107.

Almost as soon as the war with Germany was over a violent and fearful civil war broke out: the Commune. Paris, humiliated, Republican in sentiment and in great economic hardship, was handled maladroitly by the Assembly. When, on the morning of March 18, riots broke out in Montmartre and two generals were murdered, Thiers and his ministers left Paris to join the National Assembly at Versailles. From Versailles Thiers applied himself to the task of reconquering Paris, where the Commune issued a series of revolutionary proclamations. He gathered an army and on May 21 penetrated the Paris defences at the beginning of a week of savage fighting. The murder of hostages and the burning of the Tuileries

by the Communards were remorselessly and excessively avenged and they were pitilessly crushed. The insurrection in Paris had spread to other cities, notably Marseilles, and — except in certain advanced Republican circles — shocked and horrified the world.

The Germans still occupied forty-three Departments of France, and in order to liberate the country the heavy reparations imposed by the peace treaty had to be met. This was done. Government loans were floated with immense success and as each instalment was paid the Germans evacuated part of the country, until in September 1873 the last German soldier left French soil. The speed with which the debt had been paid and the vitality of a country so recently laid low amazed the world. The question was whether France would now restore the monarchy. The Monarchists had begun to suspect that Thiers, Chief of State and Leader of the Government, had given up the idea of a Monarchist restoration for reasons of his own. Thiers had realised that it was the Republic which divided France least and the Assembly which in March 1873 decreed that Thiers deserved the gratitude of France, now forced him to resign. On the same day, Marshal MacMahon, well known as a Monarchist, was elected President of the Republic. From this moment the functions of Chief of State and Leader of the Government were, in fact, separated. The President appointed the Monarchist Duc de Broglie Prime Minister. Unfortunately, although Monarchist sympathisers were in office, the pretender, the Count of Chambord, made his own restoration impossible by stubbornly renewing his refusal to accept the Tricolour. ' I do not,' he declared, ' wish to become the legitimate king of the revolution.' In November 1873 the powers of the President of the Republic were confirmed for a period of seven years by a majority of sixty-eight votes, thanks to the support of the ' defenders of moral order '. The seven-year period would offer a delay during which ' the door remained open for the restoration of the monarchy '.

No one, except a few Bonapartists, wanted a return of ' personal power ', and the Assembly realised that it must install either a constitutional monarchy on the British model or, if that was impossible, a Conservative Republic. Most of the Republicans, led by Gambetta, showed willingness to compromise. They agreed to a Legislature consisting of a Chamber of Deputies and a Senate, and further conceded that the Senate need not be elected by universal suffrage. The principle of republicanism itself slipped in almost undebated among these concessions.

The National Assembly of 1871 was dissolved on 31 December 1875 after having designated seventy-five Senators appointed for life. These, thanks to a cunningly devised alliance of the Republicans with the extreme Right, were chiefly Republicans, so that in the Senate which was elected in January 1876 there was only a slight Conservative majority. In the Chamber of Deputies, elected in February and March, the Republicans began to display their strength: of the 533 Deputies only 150 were Monarchists. President MacMahon had to call upon moderate Republicans like Jules Simon to take office. The direction of affairs thus passed from the Right Centre to the Left Centre. The tone of the Republican press became more violently anti-clerical.

MacMahon, blaming Jules Simon for yielding to pressure from the Left, dismissed him on 16 May 1877. The Duc de Broglie again became Premier, and when on June 5 the Deputies refused by 363 votes to 158 to give him their confidence he dissolved the Chamber, with the acquiescence of a narrow majority of the Senate. MacMahon appealed to ' men of order ' throughout the country. But in spite of every effort of Monarchists, clergy and Government pressure, the new Chamber proved to contain a Republican majority of over a hundred. MacMahon briefly considered resistance but was wise enough to recognise at length that he had to reinstate a Republican Government. The President of the Republic had, in the end, submitted to the electoral verdict of October 1877. In January 1879, refusing to sign a decree which relieved five generals of their command, he resigned. The Republic was firmly established. The President of the Chamber of Deputies, Jules Grévy, became President of the Republic. After having been a republic without Republicans, then a ' Conservative Republic ', the Third Republic had finally become a republic of the Republicans.

Bismarck's diplomacy

The annexation of Alsace-Lorraine against the will of its inhabitants created an abyss between France and Germany. It was generally believed that French desire for revenge constituted the chief danger to the peace of Europe, but

the case was less simple. France also feared further German aggression; she felt at the mercy of the new German Empire. In April 1875 the French Minister of Foreign Affairs frankly told the German Ambassador that, if the German armies again invaded France, French forces would retire without fighting to the south of the Loire. In September 1876 Gambetta stated: ' Unfortunately we have no forces which are comparable with the German troops. ' In reality Bismarck, far from planning further aggression, aimed only at preserving what he had gained. Peace was required by the new Empire. If, however, Bismarck was determined to maintain such peace he was quite willing, by intimidation, to make certain that France did not rearm and to threaten preventive war in 1875. Decazes, fearing a preventive war, was successful in persuading Britain and Russia to advise Bismarck to pursue a moderate policy.

With his habitual brutal frankness Bismarck in fact declared that he encouraged the Republic in France because, in his estimation, a Monarchist France could more easily form alliances than a ' disintegrating republic '. Moreover, since the ' May laws ' of 1873, Bismarck had been engaged in a violent struggle with the Catholic Church in Germany. Numerous ecclesiastics had been imprisoned and religious orders outlawed. The *Kulturkampf*, as the conflict was called, had excited passions and Bismarck was irritated by the clerical agitation in France. His nightmare was the remote possibility of a coalition. France, however, was isolated, and furthermore the German Empire was on terms of cordiality with two other European empires: Austria and Russia.

Austria had abandoned all hope of regaining hegemony in Germany and in the opinion of the Austrian Chancellor, the Hungarian Andrássy, her only course was to become

Bismarck, Minister-President of Prussia and Chancellor of the German Empire. He built a united Germany and then worked to avert conflicts which might shake his creation. *Archiv für Kunst und Geschichte*

reconciled with Berlin. In September 1872 Francis Joseph visited Berlin, to which Alexander II had also been invited. This meeting sealed the alliance of the three Emperors, the *Dreikaiserbund*, of which the object was to maintain the *status quo*, though France mistakenly feared secret clauses aimed at herself. Yet the Austro-Russo-Prussian alliance was at first far from stable. Andrássy was aware that the Tsar's Empire represented a threat to Austria-Hungary and believed that in the long run war between them was inevitable. Russia shared this belief. Bismarck, in the last resort, could not tolerate the enfeeblement of Austria, which had become his principal ally. In view of all this Thiers and Gambetta could hope that a Russo-German rupture was at least a possibility, while Prince Gorchakov, the Russian Foreign Minister, was in the habit of saying that Europe had need of a strong France.

The Eastern crisis

Rivalry between Great Powers served Bismarck's designs. For Great Britain the preservation of the Ottoman Empire's integrity remained a basic principle of policy. In the Eastern crisis which began in 1875 Anglo-Russian antagonism was again the crucial factor. Then, at the end of June, the Christians of Bosnia and Herzegovina rose against the Turks. The Pan-Slavs of Russia did much to encourage these risings, and Pan-Slavic sentiment was outraged at the thought of Christian Slavs being crushed by Moslem Turks. But in the Balkans the interests of Austria and Russia were opposed. Austria was passionately interested in the ' road to Salonika ' and strove to extend her influence throughout the Balkans. A Note from Andrássy, which had the approval of Russia and Germany, urged the Sultan to introduce reforms. The Note was accepted by all the powers of Europe and, indeed, by the Sultan himself. But the Bosnian and Herzegovinian insurgents, encouraged by the Pan-Slavs, refused to submit and the rebellion spread to the east of the Balkans. The Bulgarian uprising was crushed by Turkish irregular troops, the Bashi-Bazouks, who massacred some twelve thousand Christians. These ' Bulgarian atrocities ' aroused the indignation of Europe, above all of Great Britain, where the pro-Turkish policy of Disraeli, reluctant to intervene, was eloquently attacked by Gladstone, who advocated expelling the ' unspeakable Turk, bag and baggage ' from the rebellious provinces. Disraeli firmly supported the Sultan's right to put down the revolt. The Turks, convinced that they would not be abandoned by Great Britain, made no concessions. Serbia and Montenegro aided the insurgents and themselves prepared to enter the war against the Sultan, nominally their sovereign.

When in May 1876 the French and German consuls at Salonika were murdered, the Russian, German and Austrian Chancellors met in Berlin and drew up a programme of reforms. Great Britain, believing the Turkish troops to be on the point of victory, refused to adhere. The British fleet sailed into Besika Bay at the entrance to the Dardanelles, under pretext of protecting British subjects. This act was interpreted as support for the Sultan, who had no serious intentions of putting into effect reforms which would ' impair his dignity '. Alexander II and Gorchakov hoped to avoid war, but weary of the Sublime Porte's eternal temporising they were over-ridden by Pan-Slavs like Ignatyev, the ambitious Russian Ambassador at Constantinople.

On 30 May 1876 the Sultan Abdul Aziz was dethroned and replaced by Murad V, of whom the British approved. Three months later he was deposed by his brother Abdul Hamid II, who promised reforms, a constitution and a parliament. Disraeli chose to believe that the troubles in the Balkans were the result not of Turkish oppression but of Pan-Slav agitation, and he had, in fact, prevented serious collective action on the part of the other Great Powers. A certain amount of blood-letting was in order, he felt, when the Serbs and the Montenegrins — who were quickly beaten by the Turks — entered the war on 1 July 1876. Tension between Britain and Russia mounted. In November 1876 both Alexander II and Disraeli made warlike speeches. As for Bismarck, he was convinced that ' Pan-Slav dynamism ' required the safety-valve of war, and rather than have Austria bear the brunt he was resigned to a localised Russian attack on Turkey. Considering the Ottoman Empire to be in any case bound for inevitable decomposition, he believed that reforms were useless and was prepared to satisfy everyone by a partition at the expense of the Turks.

The Tsar first concluded a pact with the Austrians to insure against danger from that quarter, offering them the right to occupy Bosnia and Herzegovina in return for benevolent neutrality. In April 1877 Russia declared war on Turkey, proclaiming that her object was to improve the sorry condition of the Sultan's Christian subjects. Roumania, proclaiming her full independence, allowed the Russian army to pass freely across her territory. But until December 1877 the Russian advance was held back before the Turkish fortress of Plevna, and Russian financial and even military weakness became evident. At last, however, the fall of Plevna opened the way to Constantinople. The Sultan suggested mediation by the Great Powers. Russia refused to consider the proposal, and Austria, indignant at the Russian refusal to accept mediation and unwilling to be presented with a *fait accompli*, spoke of mobilisation and proposed a European conference. The Russian troops halted their advance about ten miles from Constantinople. The British squadron stationed in Besika Bay sailed through the Dardanelles in February 1878 and anchored off Constantinople. But on March 3 a peace treaty was signed by Russia and Turkey at San Stefano which provided for the creation of a ' Big Bulgaria ' extending from the Danube to the Aegean Sea, autonomous, but tributary to the Sultan. Furthermore, Kars, Batum and Dobruja were to be ceded to Russia. These stipulations were considered unacceptable in London and in Vienna. Disraeli prepared for war with Russia. Lord Derby, Secretary of State for Foreign Affairs, who inclined to a more moderate policy, resigned from office and was replaced by Lord Salisbury. Britain was resolved at all cost to prevent Russia from seizing Constantinople and the Straits.

At this moment Bismarck offered the Powers his services as ' an honest broker '. Bismarck had no wish for armed conflict between the Great Powers, and he worked for a peaceful solution of the problem which would not upset the Prusso-Austro-Russian alliance — though, from fear of Pan-Slavism, he was inclined to favour Austria at the expense of Russia. But the Balkan Question, he was later to say, was not worth the bones of a Pomeranian grenadier to Prussia. Britain began discussions with Austria designed to curb Russia, and there was talk of an Anglo-Austrian treaty. Negotiating in secret, Austria reached an agreement with Great Britain on May 31, by which the project for a Big Bulgaria was abandoned and Russian annexations in Turkey-in-Asia were reduced. A similar agreement followed between Russia and Austria.

The Congress of Berlin

A European Congress, which had been agreed upon in principle on 6 March 1878, met in Berlin in June. That it was held there affirmed and increased the pre-eminence of Germany. Russia, though the victor, lost many of the advantages she had gained by the Treaty of San Stefano. Bulgaria was divided into an autonomous principality in the north tributary to the Sultan and a southern part — known as Eastern Rumelia — provided with administrative autonomy and a Christian Governor appointed by the Sultan, who retained suzerainty. The Congress authorised Austria-Hungary 'provisionally' to occupy and administer Bosnia and Herzegovina which nominally remained Turkish provinces. Austria was also granted the right to maintain garrisons in the district of Novibazar, on the road to Salonika. Turkey resigned herself to these provisions under heavy pressure not only from Vienna but from London. Thus the Austrian Habsburgs, who had lost so many provinces since 1848 and been obliged to yield their supremacy in both Italy and Germany, achieved a conquest which was to cost great sacrifice and much bloodshed to retain.

Great Britain — in 'compensation' for Russian acquisitions — demanded a naval base in the Aegean and took Cyprus. A secret Anglo-Turkish pact guaranteed the Asiatic possessions of the Ottoman Empire in the event of further Russian aggression. When, a month later, the terms of the Cyprus agreement were revealed, the news was received with surprise and indignation — which, however, was quickly dissipated. To smooth over the Cyprus incident Lord Salisbury, on Bismarck's advice, encouraged Waddington, the French delegate to the Congress of Berlin, to occupy Tunisia.

Russia, protector of the Ottoman Empire's Christian subjects, was for many years to lose the friendship of Serbia, which was far from being satisfied and transferred her allegiance to Austria. The same reorientation of policy occurred in Roumania, which was obliged to abandon Bessarabia to the Russians and felt ill-compensated with the award of Dobruja. The Roumanian King, Carol I, was a Hohenzollern and very German in his personal sentiments: in October 1883 he adhered to the anti-Russian Triple Alliance. In spite of the resistance of the Albanians, Montenegro received in 1881 the district of Dulcigno. Also in 1881 Greece, after lengthy negotiations and threats of war, obtained Thessaly and a part of Epirus — which amounted to slightly more than half the territory she was promised at the Berlin Congress three years earlier.

Russia was extremely dissatisfied with the results of the Congress of Berlin. The Tsar complained bitterly and old Prince Gorchakov spoke of the 'darkest page' of his long diplomatic career. Bismarck, accused of having betrayed a traditional friend, was disquieted by Russian rearmament and by the belligerent manifestations of Pan-Slavism. In August 1879 he decided to form an alliance with Austria which appeared to be directed against Russia.

Certainly if the Russians now attacked Austria they would have Germany against them. In Alexander II's immense Empire the grip of the absolutist bureaucracy was lax and inefficient. Among the young a yearning for liberty had been stimulated by the Turkish war and revolutionary activities had increased. After the Congress of Berlin criminal outrages became frequent and on 1 March 1881 they culminated in the assassination of the Tsar himself. Alexander II had in fact granted a constitution and done much to modernise Russia. His son, Alexander III, swore to safeguard 'autocratic order' and a crushing despotism imposed the appearance of tranquillity on an Empire no longer a prey to the nihilist nightmare. The new Tsar loathed Austria, nor had he the veneration of the Hohenzollerns that his father had felt. Nevertheless he sought in Germany the support he needed against the dangers which threatened him from within Russia. On 18 June 1881 Bismarck renewed for three years the former Three Emperors' Alliance between Germany, Austria and Russia. In 1884 it was again renewed. Thus, in spite of the Austro-German alliance, Bismarck succeeded in maintaining the traditional Russo-German connection.

In the meantime Bulgaria had created an awkward situation for Russia. The crown of Bulgaria had been given to the young Prince Alexander of Battenberg, who had served in the Tsar's army but quarrelled with the Russians over their authoritarian methods. In September 1885 Eastern Rumelia rebelled against the Sultan and proclaimed its union with Bulgaria. The Tsar disapproved of Bulgarians taking possession of Eastern Rumelia without his assistance, while in November the Serbs, alleging that the act had upset the balance of power in the Balkans, attacked the Bulgars. The Serbs were beaten. A group of some hundred Bulgarian officers who wished to retain the friendship of Russia forced Alexander of Battenberg to abdicate in August 1886. He was soon recalled to Sofia by an insurrection which brought Stambulov, a sworn enemy of Russian influence, to power. In view of the Tsar's fury Alexander of Battenberg, however, decided to abdicate again. Stambulov, who desired a 'Bulgaria for the Bulgarians', governed tyrannically. In July 1887 he presented the crown of Bulgaria to Ferdinand of Saxe-Coburg. In July 1895 Stambulov was assassinated at Sofia. The powder magazine of Europe, the Balkans were indeed the theatre of complications which led to endless conflicts. The Bulgarian affair had so strained Austro-Russian relations that at the expiration of the Three Emperors' Alliance in 1887 it was not again renewed. The Tsar insisted on 'having a few words with Germany to make sure that no harm was intended'. Bismarck hastened to satisfy him and signed an agreement of mutual reassurance, valid for three years. Since Austria was Russia's adversary and at the same time Germany's ally, the Russo-German agreement was highly secret. Bismarck's aim was to make sure that an unattached Russia was not available as an ally to France.

Colonial expansion

After 1880 overseas problems, until then secondary, assumed major importance. Colonial rivalry, frequently spurred by financial interests, occupied the centre of the international stage. The new imperialism is not easy to understand and no single explanation suits all the specific

Benjamin Disraeli, Lord Beaconsfield, the Jew who rose to be leader of the Conservative party and Prime Minister of Great Britain (1868 and 1874–80). He popularised the Imperial idea in England, initiated welfare legislation and was Gladstone's most able opponent. *National Portrait Gallery*

cases of a movement in which most of the European powers and even the United States took part. The ' scramble for Africa ', where much of the new colonial territory lay, had in it large elements of imitativeness and a simple desire not to be left out. What is clear is that few of the new colonies were economically advantageous, that their acquisition made European quarrels world-wide, and that imperialism was popular because it responded to some of the ideals and psychological needs of the age. Explorers had never been more popular, nor had so many of them ever roamed unknown parts of the globe. Africa had already been partially opened up by the travels of the great missionary pioneer David Livingstone, while Richard Burton — who had described his pilgrimage to Mecca disguised as an Indian Pathan in a bestselling book — had with Speke discovered the sources of the Nile in 1858. *Wanderlust*, scientific curiosity, Christian evangelisation alike served the colonial cause. Finally, whatever the economic realities, some people believed that colonies would offer new markets and cheap raw materials.

Tunisia

In France public opinion was lukewarm and even hostile to the policy of conquest. To most Frenchmen it seemed to imply costly adventures which could lead to all kinds of unpleasant complications. Paris hesitated before Lord Salisbury's offer of a free hand in Tunisia. Italy, however, with a large Italian colony already established in Tunis, did not disguise her ambitions — which were encouraged by Austria, glad to recompense her for the loss of the Trentino. Roustan, the French Consul, a man of great energy and much experience of the East, where he had made his career, arrived in 1875 in Tunis where he was able to forestall Italian action. Jules Ferry — then French Premier — made an incident on the Algerian-Tunisian frontier the pretext for bringing pressure on the Bey in Tunis who, on 12 May 1881, signed the Treaty of Bardo which authorised France to protect and reform Tunisia. The expedition had cost little effort and the risings which followed it were quickly repressed; but in the Chamber of Deputies both the Right and the extreme Left, whose spokesman was Clemenceau, accused the Government of ' disloyalty ' by engaging the country in war in spite of its promises not to do so. Italy, enraged by the French occupation of Tunisia, adhered in May 1882 to the Austro-German alliance. This meant that French isolation in Europe was now complete, for in the meantime relations with Britain were ruined as the result of events in Egypt.

Egypt

Disraeli's return to power in 1874 had marked the beginning of the new era in British imperialism. Disraeli, unlike Gladstone, dreamed of reviving the glories of Palmerston's day. In 1876 he had Queen Victoria proclaimed Empress of India. He had a flair for the theatrical and sumptuous, and during his premiership the imperial idea was triumphant. Yet most of his new acquisitions were made only in order to defend older imperial interests, above all the routes to India. Afghanistan was the scene of a long and bitter struggle in which Britain strove to offset Russian influence at Kabul. In February 1877 Great Britain proclaimed the annexation of the Orange Free State and the

Transvaal Republic. The Boers rose, and at Majuba Hill in February 1881 defeated the British troops. In 1879 Sir Garnet Wolseley made war on the Zulus. Public opinion repudiated these adventures, and in the elections of April 1880 the Liberals overwhelmed the Conservatives. Gladstone replaced Disraeli and reversed his policy in Afghanistan and in South Africa, where the independence of the Orange Free State and the Transvaal was again recognised.

Wishing to avoid embroilment with France, Disraeli had refused to discuss a British occupation of Egypt which Salisbury had already considered in September 1876. The situation there was very unstable. Ismail, the Khedive of Egypt, always short of money, in 1875 sold his foundation shares in the Suez Company to Great Britain, which thus acquired for four and a half million pounds sterling rights in the Suez Canal more or less equal to those of France. Ismail needed the money to pay for disastrous failures in the Sudan. In view of his rash spending it seemed advisable to safeguard loans to Egypt by setting up some form of control. The states to which Egypt was principally indebted were Britain and France; and an Anglo-French condominium was instituted in 1876 for managing Egyptian finances.

Foreign control, which entailed the abdication of Ismail, not unnaturally irritated the Egyptians, and a national movement under Arabi Pasha appeared. Gambetta, while Prime Minister of France, prepared for a joint Anglo-French military intervention; but on 18 January 1882 he was forced to resign. Freycinet, his successor, considered it too dangerous to send troops to Egypt, and a British and a French squadron went to Alexandria instead. During rioting there some sixty Europeans were killed. When Arabi Pasha garrisoned the forts of Alexandria, the British admiral thereupon summoned them to surrender, while the French squadron, to avoid participation in military action, sailed away. The British fleet then bombarded the forts. The British Government reluctantly agreed that armed intervention was necessary and suggested to France a joint action to protect the Suez Canal. When Freycinet proposed this compromise solution — namely an occupation limited to the Suez Canal — he was supported by only seventy-five votes in the Chamber and resigned.

When the French withdrew, British troops landed not only at Suez but at Alexandria to 'restore order and protect the Europeans'. In September 1882 they routed Arabi Pasha's troops at Tel-el-Kebir, and Egypt at once submitted. The French were excluded from the valley of the Nile and the Anglo-French condominium was ended. It was believed that the British occupation of Egypt would be temporary; it lasted for seventy-four years because of the difficulty of assuring the safety of the Canal in Egyptian hands. The Egyptian army was placed under the command of a British general while Alexandria, like Malta, became a naval base. British advisers, in theory aiding Egyptian ministers, in practice wielded almost complete authority. Without being legally incorporated into the British Empire Egypt was, in reality, a British colony under Lord Cromer, proconsul from 1883 to 1907.

At the same time, there was anxiety in London to confine the occupation to the minimum consonant with security. Unfortunately, the recently conquered Sudan was in full revolt against Egypt. In 1881 the Mahdi, a religious leader, rallied the discontented to his cause and two years later destroyed an Egyptian army under a British general. In spite of Gordon's death at Khartoum, however, the British Government persisted in the abandonment of the Sudan. It was reconquered only in 1898, when the headwaters of the Nile seemed to be menaced by France. Kitchener at the head of a re-organised Egyptian army marched up the Nile, destroying the Mahdi's army before Omdurman, and reassuming control of the Sudan as a condition of Egyptian security.

The French regarded with sullen eyes the exclusion from government in Egypt for which their own lack of initiative was responsible. Until the agreements of 1904 they did their best to make Britain's position in Egypt as difficult as possible. Feeling reached its height during the 'Fashoda Incident' when Kitchener, pushing on after his victory at Omdurman, found at Fashoda a certain French Captain Marchand who had left the French Congo twenty-five months previously with the mission of forestalling the British on the Upper Nile. Kitchener protested at the presence of the French flag on territory belonging to the Khedive. A peremptory British ultimatum was issued, and on November 3 Marchand received orders from Paris to evacuate Fashoda.

From 1882 to Fashoda Anglo-French discord, arising from colonial rivalry and above all from the disagreement in Egypt, was a vital factor in international politics. It was now to wane rapidly, thus permitting a new alignment among the Great Powers.

French expansion

France pursued her colonial expansion elsewhere than in Egypt. Hanoi was taken in 1873, and in 1874 Annam was forced to acknowledge a French protectorate. As China refused to recognise it, Annam appealed to Peking for aid against France. In April 1882 Hanoi was again seized, this time by Rivière, whose mission was to police the pirate-infested Red River. In May 1883 Rivière suffered the same fate as Garnier ten years earlier; he was killed and beheaded. Jules Ferry, who had just formed his second Ministry, determined to exploit the territory 'acquired by Rivière', and Admiral Courbet forced the Government of Annam to capitulate in August 1883. A French expeditionary force of 25,000 men then advanced up the Red River valley. In May 1884 China, which had in theory remained at peace with France, signed the treaty of Tien-Tsin which recognised the French protectorate of Annam and undertook to withdraw the Chinese troops which had been sent to Tongking. Hostilities were renewed when the French attempted to occupy Langson, which the Chinese troops had not yet received the order to evacuate. France then attacked China itself. Courbet bombarded the arsenal of Foochow, sank a number of Chinese warships, landed in Formosa and occupied the nearby Pescadores Islands. In the Chamber of Deputies the opposition, led by Clemenceau, accused the Government of waging a war against the will of the country. Ferry was driven from power in March 1885 when it was learned that the Chinese had defeated the French at Langson. China, however, now declared that she was prepared to accept the conquest of Tongking by France, and hostilities were suspended.

Between 1875 and 1882, without using force, the explorer

Savorgnan de Brazza, a naturalised Frenchman of Italian birth, created at the derisory cost of 300,000 francs a French colony in the Congo which was greater in area than France itself. In 1882 Borgnis-Desbordes left Senegal, reached the Niger and founded Bamako. In 1894 Timbuktu was occupied. The old trading posts on the Atlantic coast became colonies. In Guinea Futa Jalon was occupied in 1896. Three years previously a colony had been formed in the Ivory Coast, and a year before that Dahomey was conquered. These territories were connected with the French possessions of Senegal and Niger to the north. In Niger the chief of the Mandingos was made prisoner by Gouraud in 1898. French authority was also extended over the Lake Chad region where the ruler, Rabah, was killed in 1900.

The territory of Obok on the Gulf of Aden, which had been purchased in 1862 from a local chieftain in view of the opening of the Suez Canal, also became a colony and a railway was begun in 1909 to connect Djibouti with Addis Ababa in Ethiopia, where French and Italian interests conflicted. By 1885 in Madagascar French possession of the Bay of Diego-Suarez and the islands of Nossi-Bé and Sainte-Marie was uncontested, and over Madagascar itself a protectorate, vague and difficult to enforce, was set up. Paris decided to reduce the island's resistance by force. An expeditionary force took Tananarive, the capital, in 1895. A new treaty establishing a French protectorate at once met with stubborn local resistance, and in the following year the protectorate became an outright annexation under the governorship of Colonel Gallieni. In 1897 the Queen of Madagascar was deposed and deported. In the Pacific France had occupied some of the New Hebrides islands in 1885. Australia protested and by an Anglo-French convention the archipelago was put under the joint control of Great Britain and France. In October 1893, after a naval demonstration before Bangkok and an ultimatum which outraged British opinion, France forced Siam to yield Luang-Prabang and certain territory situated on the left bank of the Mekong, which became part of French Indochina.

British expansion

In many parts of the globe France and Great Britain clashed. In 1885, when France was taking Tongking, Great Britain occupied Burma. In 1890 Sikkim, between India and Tibet, became a British protectorate and Chitral was occupied in 1895. In India itself the spinning and weaving of textiles — cotton and jute — was a thriving industry, while more and more native Indians took part in the administration of their country. Nationalist feeling was beginning to develop and from 1885 an Indian National Congress held meetings. It demanded Home Rule and the dignity of dominion status. An ' India for the Indians ' movement slowly began to take shape. But the Moslems, who formed more than a third of the population, kept alive their ancient quarrel with the Hindus.

In Africa Bechuanaland, to the west and the north-west of the Boer Republics, became a Crown colony in 1885. In 1886 companies with British charters were actively engaged on the lower and the middle Niger, penetrating eastern Africa two years later and southern Africa in 1889. British suzerainty was proclaimed over the rich Zambezi territory as far north as Lake Tanganyika and Lake Nyasa.

General Cronje, a legendary Boer War figure. At first under-rated by the British, he led the Transvaal forces at the sieges of Mafeking and Kimberley and inflicted heavy losses before surrendering in 1900. *Rex Features*

In 1890 the Sultan of Zanzibar was placed under British protection. Germany ceded Uganda to Great Britain and in exchange received the island of Heligoland. It was, as the explorer Stanley pointed out, like trading a new pair of trousers for an old button. Great Britain had occupied Somaliland in 1884. Nyasaland was occupied in 1891 and Uganda in 1894.

Much of British expansion in Central Africa was the work of Cecil Rhodes, the ' diamond king ', who dreamed of a railway through the continent from ' the Cape to Cairo '. A chartered company of which he was virtual dictator developed the territory to which, in 1895, he gave his name: Rhodesia. He clashed with Kruger, who since 1883 had been President of the Transvaal Republic, where the discovery of important gold deposits caused a rush which upset normal conditions. In December 1895 Jameson led the disastrous and unsuccessful raid into the Transvaal from which so many troubles stemmed. Jameson, a friend of Rhodes, was captured and the German Kaiser, William II, telegraphed his congratulations to Kruger. British opinion was not to forget this ' slap in the face ' from Queen Victoria's grandson. Relations between the Boer Republics and Great Britain continued to be embittered by the treatment of foreign miners and prospectors who had flooded into the Transvaal. War broke out in October 1899. The skill and tenacity of the Boer farmers had been underrated and serious defeats were inflicted on the British forces. The arrival early in 1900 of Lord Roberts, the conqueror of Afghanistan, and of Kitchener, conqueror of the Sudan, improved the situation of the British, but the war did not end until May 1902. Though the Boers were granted the same civil liberties as those enjoyed throughout the British Empire, the two small farmer republics of the Transvaal and the Orange Free State disappeared, and British domination now extended throughout all South Africa. Unfortunately, generous treatment of the Boer was bound to clash, in the long run, with protection of the Black African.

The Fiji Islands were annexed in 1874 and in the same year British authority was established over the Malay peninsula. In 1884 the south-east of New Guinea was annexed, and in 1888 North Borneo became a protectorate. In 1889 the Samoan Islands were submitted to the common sovereignty of Great Britain, the United States and Germany, while in November of the same year, following a partition, a British protectorate was proclaimed over the Tonga Islands. The British Empire now stretched all round the globe.

Following the precedent of the Canadian federation, established by the Act of 1867, Australia ceased in 1901 to be a collection of colonies often in disagreement among themselves and became a self-governing dominion attached to the British Crown. The independent Boer Republics had been the last obstacle to the unification of South Africa, and seven years after the Boer War, in 1909, the Union of South Africa was established on the Canadian and Australian models.

Expansion of other European powers

With the exception of Austria, all the great Western powers were engaged in colonial expansion, above all in Africa. Germany, which produced great explorers like Rohlfs, Nachtigal and Carl Peters, caught the colonial fever, and Bismarck, although he was himself without overseas ambitions, had to yield to popular sentiment. In 1884 South West Africa was placed under German protection as well as the Cameroons and Togo. A year later the colony of German East Africa was formed. At the same time in the Pacific Germany seized a part of New Guinea and the Marshall Islands, the point of departure for the annexation of the Solomon Islands and the Bismarck Archipelago. In July 1899 Germany bought the Caroline, the Marianas and the Pelew Islands from Spain. In the same year she shared with Britain and the United States a protectorate over the Samoan Islands, receiving in November 1899 the two chief islands of this archipelago. The German colonies were installed in good strategic positions near territories of doubtful stability: the Transvaal, the Portuguese colonies, the Congo Free State and, in Oceania, near the magnificent colonial empire of the Dutch East Indies.

William II also spoke often of the 'yellow peril' which threatened the world and was eager to obtain a firm base in China. In November 1897 two missionaries were murdered, and the Germans seized the excuse to land at Kiaochow, which with the neighbouring territory China was forced to lease for ninety-nine years. Finally in the Near East, though without aiming at territorial acquisition, Germany pursued her economic expansion. In Turkey she was able to obtain the privileged position that Great Britain had lost by occupying Egypt and France had forfeited by her alliance with Russia. William II made much of his friendship with the Sultan and proclaimed his enthusiasm for the Moslems. A Berlin to Baghdad railway was part of his plan to exploit Asia Minor.

Italy, too, wanted colonies. In 1881 the future colony of Eritrea was founded. It spread along the coast and in 1885 Massawa was occupied. Pushing towards the interior this Italian enterprise led to conflict with Ethiopia. Menilek, Ras of Shoa, who was an ally of the Italians, became Negus of Ethiopia in 1889, and at Ucciali signed a pact of friendship with Italy. Menilek, however, had no desire for an effective protectorate and in 1893 he denounced the pact. The Italian Premier Crispi dreamed of having King Humbert crowned Emperor of Ethiopia. In July 1894 General Baratieri invaded Ethiopia. Menilek, who by now was the implacable enemy of Rome, called upon his people to expel the invader. In December 1895 and in January 1896 the Italians suffered serious reverses. On March 1 their army, 25,000 strong, was annihilated at Adowa. In a wave of indignation Crispi was swept from power and Rome made peace with Ethiopia.

Leopold II, King of the Belgians, also wanted colonies. As honorary President of the 'International African Association' — which was created in Brussels in 1876 to encourage African exploration and protect the natives from the slave trade — Leopold II acquired an empire in spite of the resistance of Europe, and indeed of Belgium itself. The celebrated explorer Stanley was engaged by the International African Association which became the International Association of the Congo. From 1878 expeditions, probing in all directions, resulted in treaties with hundreds of native chieftains. In 1882 Leopoldville was founded. King Leopold's ambitions were served by the greed and rivalry of the Great Powers; furthermore the international suggestion of his title and the neutrality of his country offered him advantages in Central Africa.

An international conference took place in Berlin in 1884 and 1885 on Africa. It established the principle of 'spheres of influence': every civilised nation installed on the coast of Africa was granted rights to the hinterland and could push back the frontiers of its possessions until it encountered either another nation's sphere of influence or an organised state. The Berlin Conference sanctioned the constitution of an independent Congo state, the government of which was delegated to the King of the Belgians. Leopold's attempt to make the Congo a paying proposition by means of brutality and forced labour was soon criticised with extreme violence, even in Belgium. In 1889 Leopold II announced that he would bequeath the Congo to his own country and in October 1908 the Congo Free State became a Belgian colony.

The Portuguese had a glorious colonial past to defend but not much of a future. Their ambition was to connect Angola on the west coast with Mozambique on the east; and when in 1890 they occupied territory claimed by Cecil Rhodes's chartered company their troops were defeated. In 1891 the frontiers of Angola and Mozambique were defined by treaty. In 1898 and again just before 1914 agreements were made between Great Britain and Germany for a partition of the Portuguese Empire in the event of its collapse.

Spain, less fortunate than Portugal, lost almost all that remained of her once great Empire. In the Spanish-American War the United States deprived her of Cuba, Puerto Rico, the Philippines and Guam. In the distress of defeat Spain, in June 1899, sold the Caroline, Marianas and

Leopold II, King of Belgium (1865–1909), was devoted to colonial expansion. In 1885 he assumed sovereignty over much of the Congo where his rule was disfigured by terrible atrocities. *Belgian State Tourist Office*

Pelew Islands to Germany. Of the immense conquests of the past Spain retained only a few scattered fragments: the Canaries, the island and coastal territories of the Gulf of Guinea, the sands of the Rio de Oro and a few garrison towns in Morocco.

American expansion

The American imperialism of this period was unprecedented. The economic expansion of the United States was in full swing. The population, which was thirty-nine million in 1870, had by 1900 reached seventy-six million. In the single year 1905 more than a million immigrants landed. The frontier of unsettled land in the West at last disappeared from the map.

Republicans dominated national politics for twenty years after the Civil War. Among them U.S. Grant, the successful Northern general in the Civil War, was President from 1869 to 1877; President Garfield was assassinated in 1881, and in September 1901 McKinley, also assassinated, was automatically succeeded by the Vice-President Theodore Roosevelt, who remained President until 1909. Among the Democrats Grover Cleveland was President from 1884 to 1888 and served a second term between 1892 and 1896; Woodrow Wilson was elected in 1912.

Cuba, which rebelled against Spain in 1895, aroused the active sympathy of the United States. American intervention in the Cuban insurrection followed when, in February 1898, the U.S. battleship *Maine* mysteriously blew up in the port of Havana with the loss of two hundred and fifty lives. Spain was sent an ultimatum and even when she complied with it diplomatic relations were broken off. War, declared on April 25, led to the annihilation of the Spanish fleets in the harbour of Manila and in Santiago Bay. American troops landed in Cuba and in the Philippines and also took possession of Puerto Rico. Thus, by the Treaty of Paris in December, Spain was obliged to recognise the independence of Cuba and cede to the United States Puerto Rico, the Philippines and Guam, one of the Marianas Islands. The Filippinos, forming a republic, fought a guerrilla war against American troops for three years. Cuba, after three years of American administration, was given independence — which, however, was limited by the Platt Amendment, permitting American interference in Cuban affairs under certain conditions.

In the Pacific the United States annexed the Hawaiian Islands in June 1897, and then Wake Island. In 1889 the sovereignty of the United States, Great Britain and Germany had been established in the Samoan archipelago. By the partition of November 1899 America received the island of Tutuila. In the West Indies Denmark sold the Virgin Islands to the United States in 1917.

The first Pan-American Conference had met in 1889. Theodore Roosevelt's policy, reinforcing the Monroe Doctrine with pretensions to hegemony in Central America, did not, however, advance Pan-American understanding. The United States had decided to construct a canal in Panama to connect the Atlantic and Pacific Oceans — a canal which would be opened in 1914. Panama was Colombian territory and the Colombian Legislature refused to ratify an agreement which had just been concluded with Washington. Thereupon — on 3 November 1903 — a 'revolution' broke out in Panama — under the protection of the United States. The United States hastened to recognise the new Republic of Panama, which was thus created at the expense of Colombia. Latin America was the scene of much internal disorder, and insurrectionary turbulence was frequently accompanied by bloodshed. But the revolution which changed the Brazilian Empire into a Republic in 1889 was accomplished without violence. In Mexico the long dictatorship of Porfirio Diaz (1877–1911) was followed by ten years of revolutions. Wars between South American nations were now rare: from April 1879 to January 1883 Chile was at war with Peru and Bolivia, who were defeated and obliged to yield certain territories.

Russian expansion

Russia colonised without crossing the seas. Checked in her advance towards Constantinople, she turned towards Asia. Bismarck encouraged the Russians to advance in Asia where they represented ' progress and civilisation ', while in Europe they merely ' caught nihilism and other diseases '. The British, on the other hand, were alarmed. Piece by piece Turkestan fell into the hands of the Muscovites. In January 1881 General Skobolev took Geok-Tepe by assault. In 1884 Merv was occupied; in March 1895 the oasis of Penjdeh. The danger to the frontiers of India seemed grave. From 1890 to 1892 the Russians gained a foothold in the Pamirs. After the Trans-Caspian

Railway, connecting Europe and Central Asia, had reached the gateway to China, the Russians then constructed the Trans-Siberian Railway, work on which had begun in 1891. This 'peaceful penetration' had done much to establish their influence and their credit in Peking, where they protected the decrepit old China of the dowager Empress Tz'u Hsi — 'the old Buddha' — from the ambitions of Japan. In March 1898 they obtained from China a ninety-nine year lease of the Liaotung peninsula and the ice-free Port Arthur.

The Far East

In Liaotung the Russians encountered Japan. Since 1868, Japan had undergone an astonishing transformation. Learning rapidly from the foreigner the means to keep the foreigner himself at bay, Japan had become the youngest of the Great Powers. The era of *Meiji* — or 'enlightenment' — had opened with the Emperor Mutsuhito. Feudal Japan was reformed to become a modern state and soon challenged China for the possession of Korea. China declared war in July 1894 and was crushed on land and sea. After a vain appeal for aid to the Western Powers China signed the Treaty of Shimonoseki on 17 April 1895; under the terms of this she renounced her claims to Korea, promised to pay a war indemnity and yielded Formosa, the Pescadores and the Liaotung peninsula to Japan. By collective action, firm but friendly in tone, Germany, Russia and Russia's ally France invited Japan to renounce Liaotung. Japan could only yield. In this way Great Britain, traditionally opposed to the Russians in the Far East, found in Japan new anti-Russian support. Great Britain had not been associated with the surrender. In 1898 Japan saw with fury her own conquest of Liaotung ceded to the Russians by China. The dismemberment of China now seemed inevitable. After Germany had seized Kiao-chow and Russia had acquired Liaotung, Great Britain took possession of Weihaiwei and France obtained Kwangchowan. It was in vain that the Emperor Kuang Hsü attempted to introduce reforms in June 1898. His liberal empire lasted only a hundred days before the dowager Empress resumed power. Her desire was to close China to the rest of the world as in the old days. The Boxer Rebellion, born of a fanatical hatred of foreigners, broke out in the spring of 1900. That June, in Peking, the German Minister was killed and the foreign legations besieged. An international column arrived in July to relieve them. From August 1900 to September 1901 Peking was occupied by international troops under the command of the German General von Waldersee. The Boxer Rebellion had in fact postponed the dismemberment of China, but the Manchu Dynasty was drawing near its end.

German policy

Although imperialism played a considerable role in the last two decades of the nineteenth century it did not in itself explain the course of diplomacy after the Congress of Berlin: other activities had engaged the Western Powers.

In Germany Bismarck dominated the Government until 1890. He had not given Germany a strongly centralised regime: Bismarck's Germany remained a federation. Only in certain limited domains were the administration

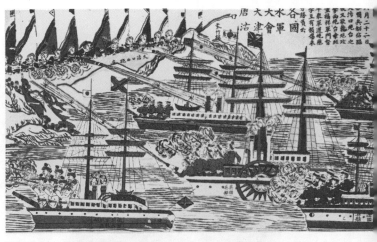

The Boxer rebellion. European and Japanese landing parties on their way to the relief of the European legations. A humiliating treaty was later imposed on the Chinese government. *British Museum*

and law of the Empire applied. The states which composed it were allowed to subsist and the Empire was obliged to respect their judiciary, legislative and administrative autonomy. The numerous and continual sacrifices which the states made for the Empire were counterbalanced by the concessions which the Empire made to their needs. These sacrifices and these concessions were the object of incessant negotiations which made the *Bundesrat* important. The *Bundesrat* was an assembly of delegates who were entirely responsible to the federated governments that appointed them, revoked their appointment and gave them firm instructions how to vote. The powers of the *Bundesrat* were equal to those of the *Reichstag*, which could do nothing without its concurrence. The *Reichstag* was elected by universal suffrage and in it Bismarck had seen an instrument by which particularism could be broken down. In practice he found his Parliament difficult to manage, and he gained the majorities he required by negotiating with various groups, as and when circumstances dictated.

He abandoned the *Kulturkampf*, a struggle between State and Church which had proved to be a grave error. By making peace with Rome he gained the support of the Centre Party which, under the direction of Windhorst, united Catholics of all classes and became the largest single party, whose vote was decisive. In Social Democracy Bismarck recognised his chief enemy. After two attempts on the Emperor's life in 1878 he dissolved the *Reichstag* and in the new Legislature had a law passed prohibiting Socialist associations, meetings and newspapers. But the Socialist movement, far from being stifled, continued to grow.

William I died at the age of ninety-one on 9 March 1888. His son Frederick III reigned for only ninety-nine days. He was repaced by a young man of twenty-nine, William II, whom the world was to know as Kaiser Wilhelm. William II very soon disagreed with his 'Iron Chancellor', who for twenty-eight years had been accustomed to run things his own way. In March 1890 Bismarck was dismissed and German affairs took a new course. The Emperor decided to be his own Chancellor. In place of Bismarck he called upon General Caprivi, a soldier broken in to discipline who, four years later, was replaced by a contemporary of Bismarck's, formerly Ambassador to Paris and Governor of Alsace-Lorraine, the elderly Prince Clovis von Hohenlohe. Hohenlohe was assisted by a Secretary of State for Foreign Affairs, Bernhard von Bülow, a diplomat of beguiling plausibility, who in 1900 himself became Chancellor.

Germany, with the prestige of its universities and its technical skills, was at its economic zenith. Pan-Germanism was intensified by the foundation of the Pan-Germanic League in 1890. German policy, instead of maintaining its pre-eminently European character as in the days of Bismarck, who had striven above all to preserve the Reich's continental predominance, now launched on a policy of world aggrandisement which inevitably brought friction with Britain.

British isolation and the Irish crisis

Although Germany was the first power on the continent of Europe, the predominant world power was still Great Britain. British trade and industry had long been in advance of the rest of the world and the country was strong in accumulated wealth. Bismarck had always hoped for an understanding with Britain and in his time no conflict of interests had existed between the two nations. Great Britain, faithful to its centuries-old policy of the balance of power, desired only to remain detached from European quarrels: no ally was required. British isolation was voluntary. In case of necessity, dissension among the continental powers would make it simple to find allies.

During the last third of the nineteenth century the Irish problem had become increasingly vexatious. Ireland, in perpetual revolt, wished to achieve nationhood: she demanded Home Rule. Parnell, a king without a crown, was a constant embarrassment to the Government; and in Parliament he used the Irish vote without concern against both Liberals and Conservatives. Behind him stood a powerful agrarian movement based on the discontented peasantry. A Land League organised their efforts. Gladstone's Irish Land Act for the relief of the embittered Irish peasants had proved insufficient because of an agricultural depression. In 1882 the Secretary of State for Ireland, Lord Cavendish, was assassinated in Phoenix Park, Dublin.

In 1885 Gladstone suddenly championed the cause of Irish Home Rule; but his party, the Liberals, split over the question. The Unionists, led by Joseph Chamberlain, refused to follow the ' grand old man ' in his newest adventure. Gladstone foresaw in Dublin a Parliament which, in all that concerned the internal affairs of Ireland, would have complete autonomy. The elections of July 1886, however, sealed the defeat of the Home Rulers and the success of the Conservatives. Parnell, compromised in a divorce scandal, vanished from the political scene in 1890. In the elections of July 1892 Gladstone, with the support of the Irish Nationalists, obtained a narrow majority, and returned to power at the age of eighty-four. The Home Rule Bill which he presented was rejected by the House of Lords in September 1893. Gladstone then considered an appeal to the country to reform or abolish — ' to mend or end ' — the House of Lords. Public opinion was not, however, with him, and he took the chance of resigning in March 1894. The elections of July 1895 were a great victory for the cause of unionism.

Mr Gladstone (1809–98) the greatest parliamentarian of the century, with his wife. More than the leader of the Liberal Party he was the moral embodiment of liberalism itself for a quarter of a century. *The London Museum*

The British electorate had ratified the verdict of the House of Lords against Home Rule.

French parliamentary difficulties

The President of the French Republic, Jules Grévy, detested adventures. He was thus in harmony with the mood of a country which had tired of revolutions and civil disturbance. The return of the Senate and Chamber of Deputies to Paris in November 1879 was a return to normal political life. In 1880 a general amnesty effaced the traces of the tragic disorders of the Commune. Grévy distrusted Gambetta, who had been the soul of the national defence in 1870–71, the founder of the parliamentary republic in 1874–75, and finally the hero of 1877 when MacMahon was forced to yield to popular opinion. Only in November 1881 did Grévy ask Gambetta to form a Government. Gambetta's Ministry lasted only seventy-three days; a few months later he died at the age of forty-three and the most able radical leader was removed from the stage.

Divided between a Left and a Right which rarely agreed, French ministerial instability was such that it was denounced as the deep-rooted evil of the Republican system: the average life of French Governments was a bare seven months. Among the Republicans themselves the Moderates were accused by the Radicals of insincerity. A religious struggle was at its height and somewhat obscured this.

Jules Ferry, Minister of Education since February 1879, had become a person of great influence. He tackled two burning and closely connected problems: education

339

and religion. Violent battle was engaged over teaching by members of religious orders and in March 1880 decrees reaffirmed existing laws relative to the dissolution and banishment of the Jesuits, and summoned the other non-authorised congregations to apply for authorisation in the normal legal way, under penalty of being suppressed in their turn. An attempt to enforce the decrees in October unleashed passionate emotions: convents were closed and schools outlawed; barred doors were forced and barricades broken down. The *Kulturkampf*, abandoned in Germany, now raged in France. Jules Ferry, in the teeth of resistance, continued his educational programme, establishing free and non-clerical primary schooling, which in 1881 became by law universal and obligatory.

Bismarck had helped the French Republic to create a colonial empire; he had not, however, been able to lessen the bitterness caused by the loss of Alsace-Lorraine. After the fall of Jules Ferry in March 1885 Franco-German relations deteriorated again. The elections of 1885 had seemed for a moment to endanger the survival of the Republic itself and the country entered an era of confused politics of which General Boulanger was the centre. In the military review which took place during the July 14 celebrations in 1886 the handsome Boulanger on his black charger was the idol of Paris. As War Minister he did the army's morale good. As ' General Revenge ' he reawakened French confidence. Bismarck, disliking these belligerent manifestations, tried to get the *Reichstag* to increase the size of the German army. When the *Reichstag* refused to grant military credits for the seven years demanded he dissolved it in January 1887 and used his charm to win the elections. The new *Reichstag* hastened to vote the military credits Bismarck wanted.

Italy, where the elderly Crispi, an ardent partisan of the Triple Alliance (which was renewed in 1887), had assumed power in July 1887, was violently hostile to France. Commercial relations between the two countries were broken off in 1887; Italy also concluded an agreement with Britain on Mediterranean affairs which was obviously aimed at isolating France. Austria-Hungary, too, adhered to this agreement. Without actually joining the Triple Alliance Spain bound herself to Italy in a pact signed in May 1887 to maintain the *status quo*.

There was more and more talk of war. In Alsace-Lorraine, a French customs-officer was arrested on German territory and accused of espionage. Public opinion in France was outraged and Boulanger displayed his flair for bluster and publicity. The incident was closed when Schnaebelé, who had been arrested on the occasion of a professional conference with a German colleague, was set free. But people believed that it was Boulanger's threats which made Bismarck give way. The Republicans grew uneasy at Boulanger's boastful imprudence, and dropped him from the Cabinet. Then came a scandal which led to Grévy's resignation from the Presidency. The opposition made much of it. The partisans of Boulanger rallied the discontented and clamoured for the dictatorship of a soldier, dissolution of the Chamber of Deputies, revision of the Constitution, and the election of a new ' constituent ' assembly, to alter the system of government. Boulanger, who had been relieved of his command and put on the retired list in March 1888, ran as a candidate in the constituencies which were vacant and received enthusiastic support. In January 1889 he was triumphantly elected

Deputy for Paris. He might at that moment have succeeded in overthrowing the Republic and proclaiming a dictatorship, but lost his nerve and in April, fearing arrest, fled to Brussels. His party dispersed. Boulanger was condemned *in absentia* to deportation and imprisonment, and shortly afterwards committed suicide. The general elections of September 1889 were a triumph for the Republicans. Many Conservatives had rallied to the Republic, and so did many Catholics, on instructions from Pope Leo XIII.

Unfortunately French parliamentary life was now discredited by another scandal in which ministers and members of the Chamber of Deputies were accused of having received bribes from the Panama Canal Company. Ministers and Deputies resigned and the Government was seriously weakened. Carnot had succeeded Grévy as President of the Republic but in June 1894 he was stabbed to death in Lyon by Caserio, an Italian. The next President was Casimir-Périer, a grandson of Louis Philippe's Minister, a man of wealth who seemed to symbolise a return to power of the upper bourgeoisie. Casimir-Périer soon tired of being the butt of scurrilous pamphleteers and resigned the Presidency. He was succeeded by Félix Faure, the candidate of the Moderates and the Right.

In view of German might, Italian threats and British hostility, the French Government sought support abroad in the only quarter available: Russia. An effort was made to create an atmosphere of understanding between the two countries. But the Tsar, Alexander III, entertained a profound contempt for the godless Republic with its ' ignoble government '. French investors, eager to lend Russia money, were, however, to overcome the hesitations which the Russian autocrat felt at the idea of an alliance with the Republic. In 1890 French and Russian military chiefs held repeated discussions to decide exactly what simultaneous action the armed forces of the two nations should take in the event of war. The Tsar expressed the desire to see the French flag flying in Russian waters, and in July 1891 he listened, bareheaded, to the *Marseillaise* as he received the French fleet at Kronstad. Two months later Ribot, the Minister of Foreign Affairs, could speak of ' a new situation '. The courtship which had lasted so long culminated towards the end of 1893 in a formal alliance. Two great systems of alliances now existed: the Dual Alliance of France and Russia, and the Triple Alliance of Germany, Austria and Italy. Europe was henceforth divided into two mutually suspicious camps.

A third scandal now burst on French public life. Dreyfus, a Jewish captain of artillery, had been accused of treason, court-martialled and sentenced to life imprisonment on Devil's Island. By 1899 half France was convinced that the charge was trumped up, the evidence forged, and that Dreyfus was innocent — which indeed later proved to be the case. France divided into two camps which, broadly speaking, represented Republicanism and Reaction. When Félix Faure died suddenly in February 1899 and was succeeded by Emile Loubet, Waldeck-Rousseau was called to form a Government of ' Republican Defence ' which lasted for three years — a record for the Third Republic. When he retired for reasons of health Combes, supported by the ' Bloc ', pursued with vigour the Republican struggle against clericalism which had been revived by the Dreyfus Affair. Leo XIII's successor, Pius X, was less friendly towards the French Government, and differences of opinion with the Vatican led to the recall in May 1904 of the French Ambassador to the Holy See. In 1905 the French Government denounced the Napoleonic Concordat and the separation of Church and State followed.

Other European states

Spain's instability persisted during the last third of the nineteenth century. The second son of Victor Emmanuel II, Prince Amadeo, accepted the throne in 1870, found the country impossible to rule and abdicated in 1873. A republic was proclaimed. Moderates like Figueras and Castelar in the main prevailed over the extreme Left, led by Pi y Margall. But the anarchists gained control in several ports, such as Cartagena, while certain sections of the north were in the hands of the Carlists. In 1873 a grandson of the Old Pretender, Don Carlos, assumed the leadership of a Carlist force in Navarre. In January 1874 a coup d'état brought General Serrano to power and an unpopular dictatorship followed. The Vatican denied the claims of Don Carlos to the throne, and supported those of Queen Isabella's son, Alfonso, Prince of Asturias. Bismarck also feared the 'Ultramontane' tendencies of the Carlists and was in favour of Alfonso. In December 1874, following an uprising by the partisans of Alfonso in Madrid, the Bourbon Dynasty, which had been expelled six years earlier, was restored. Civil war continued until 1876.

Alfonso XII reigned until 1885, when he died. His son was born six months after his death and became Alfonso XIII. Governments were formed alternately by Liberals and Conservatives, and it seemed that the era of coups d'état and *pronunciamientos* was gradually receding. But the anarchists, who were particularly numerous in Barcelona, frequently threatened the life of the sovereign and his ministers. The Conservative Canovas del Castillo was assassinated in 1897, the Liberal Canalejas in 1912. In July 1909 the trial and execution of the anti-clerical Ferrer provoked storms of protest in Spain as well as in liberal circles throughout Europe.

The political life of Portugal was even more troubled. King Charles had reigned since 1889, but in 1908 he and his oldest son were assassinated. His second son, the young King Manuel, was driven from the throne in October 1910 by the Republicans, and it looked as though anarchy must ensue.

In Belgium the Liberals had attempted to introduce a more neutral attitude towards religious matters in State education, and in the process unleashed a 'school war'. The laws they passed in 1884 resulted in an electoral triumph for the opposing Catholic party, which for thirty years was to hold uninterrupted power. Meanwhile the Flemings were insistent in their claims for linguistic equality, and the Flemish language gained ground both in the field of education and in the administration.

In the Netherlands William III died in 1890 and his crown was inherited by Wilhelmina, a child of ten.

Christian IX, who reigned in Denmark from 1862 to 1906, was the 'grandfather' of Europe: one of his sons had become King George of Greece, while the Queen of England and the Tsaritsa of Russia were his daughters. In northern Schleswig the Danes were by no means happy with the arrangement that had made them Prussians,

but Danish Governments had long since realised the futility of belligerent action. The Swedes and the Norwegians, united by the Congress of Vienna, had continued to live in disagreement. The Norwegians longed for independence, and when it was attained no one was surprised. On 7 June 1905 Norway simply declared that Oscar II, King of Sweden, was no longer King of Norway, and the unsatisfactory union was dissolved.

FROM THE TURN OF THE CENTURY TO THE FIRST WORLD WAR

Europe in 1900

For decades the people of Europe had seen their fumbling efforts to create a better world frustrated by periodic outbreaks of war. But at the turn of the century hopes were high that means to end this evil were available. At the Hague in May-July 1899, representatives of nearly every nation in Europe had met representatives from the United States, Japan and China, at what was optimistically hailed as 'The Peace Conference'. The conference had attempted to limit armaments and, at the least, to 'humanise war' by prohibiting the military use of poison gas, expanding bullets and missiles dropped from balloons. More encouraging was acceptance of the principle that disagreements between states should be settled by arbitration and a permanent court was created to sit at the Hague for this purpose. The conference had been initiated by Tsar Nicholas II, and though it achieved little in the field of limiting armaments it met again in 1907 when an amended convention for the settlement of international disputes was passed. Optimism still prevailed. Fried, the Austrian pacifist who in 1911 was awarded the Nobel Peace Prize, announced that as the nineteenth century had been the century of nationalism so the twentieth would be the century of internationalism.

The whole world appeared to be improving. Europe was at peace and seemed secure; her anxieties were apparently slight. It was true that in 1908 revolutions broke out in Turkey and in Persia, and in 1911 in China. But they were simply warnings, something to be expected in the case of corrupt states. Nor did they take place in Europe. Foreign policy was in large measure regulated by a kind of international family of European monarchs, and in the larger affairs of the world national parliaments played a relatively subordinate part. To be sure sovereigns no longer had the absolute authority in foreign policy they had once enjoyed: they were forced to take into account public opinion, parliamentary opposition, financial pressure and economic interests. But, with the assistance of a few counsellors, they generally retained the initiative in foreign affairs. In May 1913 guests at the marriage of Victoria Louisa, the only daughter of William II, included Tsar Nicholas II, William II's cousin, the Tsaritsa, his first cousin, and the King of Great Britain, George V, also his cousin. George V, the Tsaritsa and the Kaiser were all grandchildren of Queen Victoria. Members of the reigning families knew each other intimately, often saw each other, could converse without interpreters, and continually wrote to each other. It seemed relatively simple

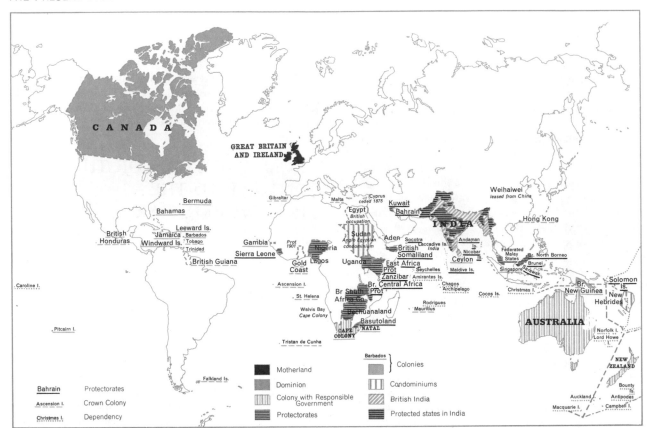

THE BRITISH EMPIRE IN 1900

to anticipate the psychological reactions of a small set of people whose characters, tendencies and weaknesses had long been well known to each other. It was only at the beginning of a new reign that a critical period of uncertainty ensued. But in 1914 the Emperor of Austria had already occupied his throne for sixty-six years, the Kaiser of Germany for twenty-six years, the Tsar for nineteen years and Victor Emmanuel III of Italy for fourteen years. When, after two world wars and their manifold consequences, those who knew Europe before 1914 recalled those days to memory they did so with something of the melancholy Talleyrand expressed after the upheavals of the French Revolution and the Empire when he spoke nostalgically of the 'sweetness of life' during the Old Regime. During the peace of the nineteenth century, uncertain and unstable as it was, wealth had accumulated prodigiously, machinery had vastly improved and activity of every kind had been stimulated. In the world as it then was the economic preponderance of Europe was uncontested, and above all that of Great Britain; for the nineteenth century — which may be said to have ended in 1914 — was pre-eminently the 'British Century'.

In spite of the 'European Concert', the seeds of world conflict were maturing. The struggle for power appealed to the imagination of the masses more strongly than to the somewhat weary scepticism of the old ruling classes. There is no doubt that nationalism and democracy have frequently gone hand in hand, and it is certain that the popular press has frequently fanned imperial ambitions. The will to dominate has often seized countries which see in themselves the ordained instrument of providence.

Great Britain, with interests in every corner of the globe, found that the 'splendid isolation' which Lord

Victoria, Queen of Great Britain and Ireland, and Empress of India 1837–1901. Her reign saw the zenith of British Imperial power, supported by British wealth and the supremacy of the fleet. *Victoria & Albert Museum*

342

Salisbury had advocated could not be maintained. During the South African war there had been nothing splendid about it, but it had been impressive: the British were at that moment almost universally unpopular but no one could do anything about it. In January 1901, before the Boers were finally overcome, Queen Victoria died at the age of eighty-two, in the sixty-fourth year of a reign majestic both in its length and its brilliance. The new King, her son Edward VII, was already sixty and had until his accession prolonged a tumultuous youth during which his knowledge of the world and foreigners had widened.

British policy was at this moment ready to consider an alliance with Germany. German diplomats were convinced that Anglo-Russian antagonism was insurmountable and that nothing more was required than to let this antagonism persist while keeping an attentive eye on development; they therefore let the opportunity go. Worse still, irked by Britain's supremacy at sea, Germany began to strengthen her fleet. Britain felt herself seriously threatened by German commercial competition and began to be convinced that Germany, in her restless desire for hegemony, had ambitions of world-wide conquest. German armaments of all kinds, but above all her naval preparations, aroused growing British distrust. British diplomacy was also unsuccessful in reaching an understanding with Russia to check her advance in Asia. It was felt that Russian expansion must be stopped, and with this object in view Great Britain concluded an alliance in January 1902 with Japan. This surprising alliance was followed, in April 1904, by an Anglo-French understanding, inspired by a common fear of Pan-Germanism which threatened the peace of the world not only by its desire for territorial expansion but by challenging Great Britain at sea. This was the end of British isolation.

From 1904, however, the German preponderance that had lasted since 1870 was challenged by a policy that the British and the French called 'the balance of power' and that the Germans called 'encirclement'. The new era was inaugurated by the agreements which France made with Great Britain, with Italy and with Spain. In exchange for French recognition of Great Britain's position in Egypt, the British granted France complete liberty of action in Morocco. On this basis, the removal of old colonial dissensions, the Anglo-French convention of 8 April 1904 was concluded: it prepared the way for the *Entente Cordiale*. France had already, in secret arrangements concluded in 1900 and 1902, re-established satisfactory relations with Italy: Italy, by recognising French rights in Morocco, was given a free hand to pursue her own expansion in Tripolitania. Not without difficulty, an understanding was also reached with Spain over Morocco. Although all these agreements were confined to colonial questions, their import was of wider European significance. The French Foreign Minister Delcassé, a disciple of Gambetta, had always dreamed of a British alliance to reinforce the existing Franco-Russian alliance, a triple entente of France, Russia and Britain. But it appeared that Britain and Russia, opposed to each other in so many parts of Asia, could never reach agreement.

The Russo-Japanese War

Then, in February 1904, Japan, in a wild burst of patriotism, flung herself on Russia. Neither the Tsar nor

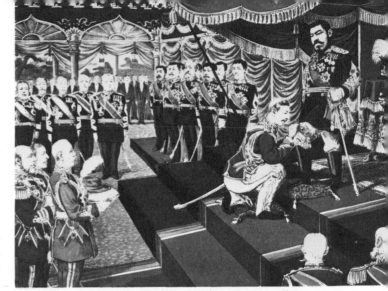

Japan emerged from her isolation to become a great power with unprecedented speed. An alliance with Great Britain recognised the fact. The Emperor was admitted to the Order of the Garter. *British Museum*

his ministers had any desire to embark on warlike adventures. The Russians were fully occupied in consolidating their influence in Korea and installing themselves permanently in Manchuria. Furthermore they had been sure that little Japan would not dare to affront the Russian colossus. Through administrative confusion and governmental incompetence Russia stumbled blindly into a war which was absurd, which could have been avoided, and which the Russians believed would prove little more than a simple punitive expedition.

The first blow was struck by the Japanese, who during the night of 8 – 9 February 1904 put three Russian battleships out of action at Port Arthur; later they destroyed the Russian Vladivostok fleet north of the Korean Straits. In May Russian troops were beaten on the Yalu River, and in August General Kuropatkin was forced to withdraw towards Mukden. For three months the two armies faced each other in their trenches. In January 1905, after seven months of siege, Port Arthur fell to the Japanese. The battle before Mukden raged for two weeks until the Japanese entered the city. On May 27, off Tsushima, in the Korean Straits, Admiral Togo annihilated a Russian fleet which had sailed from the Baltic in October under Admiral Rozhdestvenski.

The repercussions were immense inside Russia. In July 1904 Plehve, the Minister of the Interior, was killed by a bomb. Major strikes broke out in December 1904 and in January 1905. On Sunday January 22, a mob, marching to the Winter Palace in St Petersburg under the leadership of a priest, attempted to present a petition for reforms to the Tsar. The multitude, preceded by portraits of Nicholas II, was greeted with volleys of gunfire. On that 'Red Sunday' nearly a thousand were slaughtered and five thousand wounded. The situation worsened. Universities were closed. The Grand Duke Sergei, Governor of Moscow — the Tsar's uncle, who was married to a sister of the Tsaritsa — was blown to pieces by a bomb. And then in June 1905 the seamen of the battleship *Potemkin* mutinied and murdered their officers.

In that same month President Roosevelt offered his mediation. On 5 September 1905 a treaty was signed at Portsmouth in New Hampshire by which Russia yielded to Japan Port Arthur, the southern part of the island of Sakhalin, and the South Manchurian Railway. Japan also received authority to make Korea a protectorate. For the first time since the beginning of European expansion in the nineteenth century Asians had gained a victory over Europeans.

The 'Entente Cordiale'

Since Great Britain was an ally of Japan and France was an ally of Russia, German diplomats had hoped that the Russo-Japanese struggle would not remain localised. British and French diplomats were, however, equally determined to avoid becoming involved. Great Britain now desired closer agreement with France, especially in view of the very rapid build-up of the German fleet and the possibility, however remote, of the French fleet fighting at its side. The Anglo-Japanese alliance was therefore supplemented by the Anglo-French *Entente Cordiale*. Germany's might was evident and German intentions seemed more and more disquieting: while Great Britain and France thus drew closer in order to meet the danger which appeared to threaten them both, it became the policy of Germany to break up the *Entente Cordiale*. In March 1905 the Kaiser visited Tangier, and provocatively declared that Germany recognised no authority in Morocco other than that of the Sultan. In other words, the Anglo-French Moroccan agreement gave France no particular rights in Morocco. Hoping to profit by the enfeeblement of France's ally Russia, the Kaiser demanded a conference to settle the Moroccan question which was, he insisted, of international concern. Delcassé refused to comply, arguing that to give way after the 'Tangier incident' would be further to encourage German ambitions.

Far from breaking up the *Entente*, as Germany had hoped, the Tangier affair was followed by Great Britain drawing closer to France. Delcassé, however, was forced to resign in June — a resignation which was soon felt in France to be a national humiliation. He was succeeded by Rouvier, a financier inclined to think in terms of business, who decided that France, deprived of Russian support, was in no condition to fight Germany, even if the military co-operation of Great Britain was assured. At that moment the German High Command was, in fact, eagerly hoping for war. To avoid the danger Rouvier came round to the suggestion of an International Conference which was held in Algeciras from January to April 1906 and, as it happened, recognised French *de facto* preponderance in Morocco. During the conference the French had been backed not only by Britain but by Theodore Roosevelt, and the United States thus for the first time intervened directly in the affairs of Europe. Even Italy, although allied to Germany, supported France. Thus the Moroccan crisis had not achieved what Germany hoped. In January 1906 the British General Staff had already been authorised to discuss with the French General Staff plans for 'common military action'.

It was not long before Great Britain settled her differences with Russia, still weak from the war with Japan. Despite the splendours of its court the Tsarist regime was an anachronism in the twentieth century, though in all realms of cultural life Russia's prestige had never stood higher. Russian ballet was the admiration of the world, and lent life and colour to the other arts, Russian musicians were universally applauded, while the Russian novelists had added much to the profounder knowledge of man. But cracks in the façade of Tsarism had long been visible and were widening. Tsar Alexander III's sole quality as a ruler had been his energy. His son, Nicholas II, who succeeded him in 1894 at the age of twenty-six, was not the man to wield an autocratic sceptre. He was incapable of making up his mind and he refused to see that the regime was heading for the abyss. In the most critical moments he maintained 'terrifying serenity'. His Tsaritsa was a woman of haughty and mystical temperament, whose influence over her husband was disastrous. An ex-Lutheran, she plunged into Orthodoxy with extravagant devotion.

Having previously borne four daughters, she gave birth in 1904, during the Russo-Japanese War, to a son, Alexis, who was sickly and suffered from haemophilia. Doctors were first summoned to treat him and when they failed she resorted to holy men — and finally to the monk Rasputin. Rasputin, a Siberian peasant who was incapable of writing correctly, was a rascal with a mysterious air which made women responsive to him. He was introduced to the imperial family who, falling under his hypnotic influence, let themselves be persuaded that he could cure the Tsarevich. Soon the Tsaritsa had confidence only in the advice and prayers of Rasputin.

In 1905 Nicholas II was saved by Count Witte. Witte, having concluded peace with Japan, prepared the manifesto of October 17 in which the country was promised a national parliament (*duma*). Witte remained Prime Minister only until April 1906. A few months later Stolypin, a minister of energy and intelligence, came to power. Stolypin was the last great figure of Tsarist Russia. He governed the country with a tyrannical hand and deported thousands to Siberia. But at the same time he undertook wise agrarian reforms. In July 1906 he dissolved the *Duma*. The new *Duma* which met in March 1907 was even more radical than the first, and was in its turn dissolved three months later. A third *Duma* lasted until 1912, and a fourth until 1917. Three parties of roughly equal strength disputed political power in these legislative bodies. In 1911 Stolypin was assassinated in the theatre at Kiev in the presence of the Tsar and the Tsaritsa.

A friend of Stolypin, Count Isvolsky, had become Minister of Foreign Affairs in May 1906, and it was he who managed the *rapprochement* with Britain. In August 1907 differences between the two were settled by defining each country's respective spheres of influence in Asia. The Triple Entente, Anglo-Franco-Russian, thus came into existence — much to the disappointment of William II, who had himself tenaciously sought an alliance with Nicholas II. Copious correspondence on the subject had been exchanged between 'Nicky, Admiral of the Pacific' and 'Willy, Admiral of the Atlantic' and in July 1905, at Björkö, near the Finnish coast, Nicholas II had signed a paper which seemed to give eminent satisfaction and joy to the Kaiser. But the German Chancellor Bülow violently criticised his master's initiative, while the Russian ministers pointed out to the Tsar that the French alliance made it impossible to carry out such an agreement. William II, finding that Britain had been successful in making an alliance with Russia where he had failed, bitterly denounced his 'Uncle Edward's efforts to encircle him', and the German press represented Edward VII as a satanic monster.

The collapse of the Ottoman Empire

The disintegration of the Ottoman Empire continued. The Congress of Berlin had urged the Sublime Porte to introduce reforms in the Turkish provinces inhabited by the Armenians. The despotic Abdul Hamid, 'Abdul the Damned', decided to solve the Armenian problem in his own way. Between 1893 and 1895 Europe learned with horror that more than 200,000 Armenians had been slaughtered like sheep.

In February 1897 the Greeks attempted to take possession of Crete, whose inhabitants had risen in revolt against the Turks and expressed a desire to be annexed by Greece. The Powers intervened and the island was blockaded. But Hellenistic enthusiasm was undampened and bands of Greeks attacked the Turks in Macedonia, while in Athens mobilisation was decreed. Turkey declared war on April 18, crushed the Greeks in Thessaly, and the Greeks entrusted their fate to the Concert of Europe. An armistice in June was followed by a peace treaty in December. The Greeks were compelled to yield a small portion of Thessaly, to pay a war indemnity and to withdraw from Crete which, while it continued to fly the Turkish flag, became virtually independent, with Prince George of Greece as High Commissioner.

After the Armenian and Cretan revolts the Macedonians rose: the *komitadjis* demanded 'liberty or death'. But Russia, fully engaged in the Far East, desired to maintain the *status quo* in the Near East, even if that happened to be anarchy. In Austria Count Goluchowski, who had directed the Dual Monarchy's diplomacy since 1895, pursued a cautious policy and also desired peace in the Balkans. Macedonia, ravaged by inter-racial strife, became a permanent European sore spot. In July 1903 a general insurrection broke out and European officers were sent by the Powers to do what they could to improve the situation. Thanks to Austro-Russian agreement at this moment the upheavals in the Near East did not upset the general equilibrium in Europe itself. But Austro-Russian understanding was exceptional and provisional, and it would not be long before the old problem of Eastern Europe cropped up again and — as the diplomats foresaw — set all Europe on fire. Meanwhile the former antagonism of Austria to Russia in the Balkans had been inherited by Germany; and Russo-German rivalry in the Near East became one of the causes of the First World War.

Many thousands of Turks had fled abroad in order to escape the tyranny of Abdul Hamid. They had been influenced by Western liberal ideas, and now demanded a constitutional form of government for their own country. Known as the 'Young Turks' they succeeded in organising a Committee of Union and Progress which engaged in active propaganda among Turkish officials in European Turkey. In July 1908 revolution broke out in Salonika and in Monastir. The Sultan promised to restore the Constitution of 1876 and a Parliament was summoned to meet in December. In April 1909 Abdul Hamid attempted to disperse the Parliament by force, and was himself obliged to abdicate. He was replaced by his brother Mehmet V and a parliamentary system was in theory established. In practice it was scrapped, for external complications were soon to make the government of the Young Turks a dictatorship. The chief source of these complications was Austria.

Gregory Rasputin, the dissolute and vicious 'Holy Man' whose ascendancy over the Tsaritsa helped to paralyse the Russian Empire in its last years. He was murdered by officers in 1916, but his removal came too late. *Popper*

Agitation in Austria-Hungary

That singular 'league of nations', the Empire of the Habsburgs, already tottered slightly: the many races which composed it were in constant ferment and their agitations were an ever-increasing threat to the monarchy's survival. As in the Ottoman Empire, nationalist passions dangerously shook the state's foundations. The 'Young Czechs' were indignant with the 'Old Czechs' who humbly sacrificed their rights in order 'to crawl under the table and pick up the crumbs'. They extolled the solidarity of the Slavs, and to the Germans Pan-Slavism became a bogy. Strossmayer, Bishop of Zagreb, assumed the leadership of a national movement the aim of which was to free Croatia from the Hungarians and make it the centre of attraction for all Southern Slavs — 'Yugoslavs'.

In October 1908 Austria-Hungary annexed Bosnia and Herzegovina, which she had administered since the Berlin Congress. Bosnians and Herzegovinians already did their military service in the Imperial or Royal armies, which showed that so-called Turkish suzerainty was a fiction. The annexation was undertaken largely to curb the subversive influence of Serbia. Little Serbia had burning ambitions to unite all the South Slavs of the Habsburg Empire and play a role similar to that played by Piedmont in the unification of Italy. During the reign of King Milan Obrenovic, who drew a pension from Vienna, Serbia had remained a client of Austria. But a conspiracy of officers was formed in Belgrade and in June 1903 Milan's son and successor, Alexander, was assassinated, while his brothers, Queen Draga and several ministers were brutally killed. It was the end of the Obrenovic dynasty. A national assembly proclaimed Peter Karageorgevic King. King

345

Peter received a pension from Russia and the Russophile radicals seized power. Karageorgevic Serbia was considered a satellite of St Petersburg.

Given these circumstances, the Austrian annexations of 1908 strained Austro-Russian relations almost to breaking point. Russia supported Serbia against Austria, while William II ostentatiously supported Austria, whom he referred to in an unfortunately worded dispatch as his Viennese ' brilliant second '. Russians and Serbs were obliged to yield in March 1909, and Isvolsky, the Russian Foreign Minister, was not to forgive Austria for having made him swallow this ' bitter pill '. Russian and Austrian policies continued increasingly to conflict, even after 1910, when Isvolsky left the Ministry of Foreign Affairs to become Ambassador in Paris. Sazonov, a relative of Stolypin, succeeded Isvolsky and remained Foreign Minister until his disgrace in 1916.

Moroccan complications

In the Balkans war had been near. Scarcely had the peril been averted when peace was again endangered by trouble in Morocco. In August 1907 French troops had landed in Casablanca, where Europeans had been massacred; the French had remained and penetrated the interior until under Clemenceau, an old opponent of colonial adventures, who was Prime Minister for thirty-three months, they were installed in Morocco. In February 1909 an agreement was concluded between Germany and France by which nationals of both countries associated in the affairs of Morocco. The agreement, however, settled little, and in July 1911 the German gunboat *Panther* suddenly dropped anchor in the port of Agadir. Again, as in 1905, the Moroccan question came to the forefront. Great Britain bluntly asserted that she would not tolerate German occupation of Agadir, which would have provided a naval base. The Germans yielded, but conceded France's protectorate of Morocco only in exchange for compensation in the French Congo. A Franco-German treaty to this effect was laboriously negotiated by the French Premier, Joseph Caillaux. France's gains in Morocco patently outweighed her losses in the Congo, and the German nationalists, including the Crown Prince, greeted the treaty with unconcealed dissatisfaction. In 1912 the Franco-German treaty was, after hard bargaining, supplemented by a Franco-Spanish agreement. Thus the French protectorate of Morocco was established and General Lyautey was appointed Resident-General.

After the Agadir incident the general feeling in France was that war was inevitable and could not long be delayed. To replace Caillaux, whom Clemenceau had overthrown, Poincaré was called upon in January 1912 to form a strong Government which would be able to act in complete accord with Russia. In 1909, during the Bosnian-Herzegovinian crisis, Clemenceau's Minister of Foreign Affairs had refused to go as far as war over a Balkan affair which did not affect the ' vital interests of Russia '. On the contrary, Poincaré, who was both President of the Council and his own Foreign Minister, stated firmly that France, rather than ruin the alliance with Russia, would support her ally even if war resulted from a conflict in the Balkans — which, in view of Balkan unrest, was not unlikely. Relations between the two great power-groups grew tenser, though their approximate equality of

strength still safeguarded the peace, at least for a period.

The Balkan War

The events in Morocco had had their repercussions in Italy. Inspired by the success France had achieved there, Italy decided in September 1911 to appropriate Tripolitania and Cyrenaica. The decision led to a war between Italy and Turkey which did not end until October 1912 and, enfeebling Turkey, unleashed the Balkan War — from which the First World War would arise. In March 1912 a secret alliance was concluded between Serbia and Bulgaria under the auspices of Russia, still filled with bitterness over her diplomatic defeat in 1909, when forced to recognise Austrian annexation of Bosnia and Herzegovina. Once more the Balkans occupied the centre of the stage. The Russian Minister at Belgrade encouraged Serbia's most ambitious dreams. Bulgaria and Greece also concluded an alliance. Both these Balkan pacts were made with a view to war against Turkey. At the end of September Bulgaria and Serbia mobilised, and Greece followed their example. Then Montenegro declared war on Turkey. To the general astonishment of Europe the armies of these small Balkan states easily defeated the Turks. For Germany their victory was both a political and a military reverse, for Turkey was Germany's vassal and pupil. The threat of war with Russia, whose interests in the Balkans increasingly conflicted with those of Austria-Hungary, loomed larger.

In France the sense of imminent danger was expressed by the election of Poincaré as President of the Republic in January 1913. In Germany armaments piled up. To counter German preparations, Briand, an enthusiastic supporter of Poincaré for the Presidency and, in 1913, his successor as Premier, introduced a bill for three years' compulsory military service. He was defeated by Clemenceau on a question of electoral reform and replaced by Barthou, who carried on the fight for the three-year bill which in spite of the Left became law in August 1913. Britain continued to construct dreadnoughts with the intention of enabling the British navy to equal in strength the combined navies of any possible coalition.

After the defeat of the Turks in the Balkans the victors quarrelled over the spoils. On 24 June 1913 the Bulgarians attacked the Serbs without warning. The Greeks then joined the Serbs and the Roumanians also invaded Bulgaria. Meanwhile the Turks advanced on Adrianople. The Treaty of Bucharest, which was signed by Bulgaria on one side and on the other by Roumania, Serbia, Greece and Montenegro, did not relax the international tension. Peace seemed daily to become more precarious. In May 1913 Deputies from France and from Germany held an interparliamentary conference at Berne to seek closer understanding between their two countries. They met again in May 1914 at Basle, and again their efforts were fruitless. Since 1911 war had appeared inevitable: only the internal disunity of the opposing nations seemed to offer hope that it might still be avoided.

In Germany the elections of January 1912 had been a triumph for the Social Democrats who, with 110 seats, became the largest party in the *Reichstag*. France was plunged ' into the cesspool ' — as Maurice Barrès called it in the title of an embittered book — a cesspool of personal quarrels, polemics and mud-slinging in which reputations were tarnished. Barthou's Government was brought down on 2 December 1913 by Caillaux, and Poincaré called on the radical Doumergue to form a Cabinet which included several adversaries of the three-year conscription law, notably Caillaux himself. The elections of April-May 1914, in which the Left, especially the Socialists, gained ground, were a serious setback for Poincaré. Doumergue retired and Poincaré called upon Ribot, leader of the moderates, to form a Government which favoured three-year military service. Ribot was defeated on 12 June 1914, the first day he addressed the Chamber of Deputies.

Britain, too, seemed to be lost in domestic strife. In the elections of January 1906 the Liberals, who had spent ten years out of power, had been triumphant. The Liberal Cabinets of Campbell-Bannerman (1906–8) and of Asquith were engaged in a bitter political struggle. When the Budget of 1909, the work of Lloyd George, was rejected by the House of Lords Asquith determined to go to the country and ask for a mandate to curb the anomalous powers of the Upper House. In the 1910 elections the Liberal coalition retained a working, though reduced, majority. Asquith threatened to create four hundred new peers, which would give the Government a majority in the Upper House; the Lords resisted vehemently. In the midst of this constitutional crisis Edward VII died and was succeeded by his second and only surviving son George V. Parliament was again dissolved and the elections of December 1910 confirmed those of January. In August 1911 the House of Lords capitulated. It was deprived of the right of rejecting or amending any Finance Bill. All other public Bills passed three times by the Commons in the course of two successive sessions would become law, even if rejected by the Lords. The life of the House of Commons was reduced from seven to five years. The reforms of the Lords allowed the Irish question to crop up again with greater immediacy, for it was in the Lords that the Irish demands had last been rejected.

Since the elections of 1910 the Liberals had needed the support of Irish members to attain a majority in the House of Commons. In April 1912 the Liberal Government presented a Bill for Irish Home Rule which was passed in November. The Lords could, of course, reject it for two parliamentary sessions — which meant that it could not receive the royal sanction until 1914. Ulster, however, protested violently against the Home Rule Bill. Arms were smuggled into Ulster, and Ireland was on the verge of civil war. Armed volunteers gathered on both sides. In March 1914 officers in the British Army resigned their commissions rather than execute the orders of the Government. Lloyd George declared that it was the gravest problem that England had faced since the Stuarts. In 1914, then, the chief preoccupation of Great Britain was not the Balkans, but Ireland.

Origins of the First World War

The First World War sprang directly from Balkan complications themselves tragically complicated by national pride. As Lloyd George put it, the diplomats were tripped up by imperialism, and at the time diplomats were particularly clumsy in Russia, in Germany and especially in Austria-Hungary, where the Minister of Foreign Affairs, Count von Berchtold, successor to the skilful Count von Aehrenthal who had died in 1912, approached virtual nullity. The war arose above all from Austro-Russian

This picture was taken an hour before Princip fired the shot which made the World War. The Archduke Francis Ferdinand and his wife were about to drive through the streets of Sarajevo. An hour later they were dead. *Larousse*

antagonism in the Near East, and was a conflict less of peoples than of rival Chancelleries, disputing priority in the Balkans. The explosive potential of their conflict was immensely increased by the profound mistrust which existed between the Germans and the French.

On 28 June 1914 the Archduke Francis Ferdinand, heir to the Austrian throne, was shot in Sarajevo by Gavrilo Princip, a young Bosnian fanatic. The outrage had been planned and prepared in Belgrade, and the Serbian press indiscreetly boasted of the fact. Indignation swept through Austria-Hungary, an impossible ultimatum was issued to Belgrade and Count Berchtold persuaded the Emperor to embark on a ' punitive expedition ' against Serbia. He was encouraged by Germany, who wished to revive a flagging ally threatened by nationalist agitations with disintegration, even at the price of European conflict, if there was no other way of doing it. If the Austro-Serbian operations could not be kept localised, then in Berlin's judgment the moment was favourable for a war against Russia and against France. It seemed to be the 1909 situation repeated five years later. But Russia was stronger in 1914 than she had been in 1909 and refused to submit to a new humiliation. She would not see Serbia swallowed up, as Bosnia and Herzegovina had been, by Austria.

The Austro-Serbian conflict thus grew into an Austro-Russian conflict — and that brought the alliances, Dual and Triple, into play. Poincaré, President of the French Republic, had arrived in St Petersburg on 21 July 1914, a visit which had been long before decided on. He declared that France was firmly resolved to fulfil the ' obligations imposed by the alliance ' in the event of Germany's intervening against Russia. Great Britain, on the other hand, refused to become involved in a Balkan conflict and would not commit herself. From July 27 Austria-Hungary had been at war with Serbia. The same day London proposed a conference to settle the conflict to be attended by Britain and France, Germany and Italy. Berlin rejected the proposal, sure that the moment for a decision had come. On July 29 London negotiated directly with the Austrians, who had bombarded Belgrade. The British Government was divided and still hesitated. On July 31 Poincaré begged George V for a categorical declaration so that the Central Powers should not 'speculate on the abstention of England'. The royal response of August 2 was limited to the statement that His Majesty's Government would continue to examine freely and loyally with the French Ambassador all aspects of the matter which could concern the interests of the two nations. Even then, when war appeared imminent, Great Britain refused to commit herself.

Bethmann-Hollweg, the German Chancellor, hoped for British neutrality in the event of war between Germany and France. On July 29 he promised the British Ambassador that a victorious Germany would not seek any territorial compensation in Europe at the expense of France. Although Sir Edward Grey informed the German Ambassador on July 31 that Britain would be unable to remain neutral in a general conflict, he refused, on the following day, to promise the French Ambassador actual military support. In the end, the invasion of Luxemburg and the ultimatum to Belgium changed the British attitude. On August 3 Sir Edward Grey promised the intervention of the British fleet if a German squadron attacked either the French coast or the French navy. William II had on August 1 declared war on Russia. On August 3 he declared war on France. Belgium was invaded: 'necessity knows no law', cried Bethmann-Hollweg. On August 4 Great Britain, having summoned the Germans to halt the advance of their troops in Belgium, declared war, three members of the Cabinet resigning. During the days that followed Great Britain and France also declared war on Austria-Hungary, while Serbia declared war on Germany. Italy had renewed the Triple Alliance in 1912. She was, however, bound to France by a secret pact which, under certain conditions, provided for her neutrality in case of a Franco-German rupture. Italy declared her neutrality on August 3, which enabled France to leave the Alps as lightly defended as the Pyrenees. Like Italy, Roumania, although she had renewed her treaty of alliance with Austria in 1913, refused on August 3 to fight on the side of the Central Powers — in spite of the efforts of Carol, the pro-German King of Roumania.

The war which had begun would later be called the 'Great War'. At that moment the experts prophesied that it would last a few months. It was to last for four years.

Science, literature and the arts from 1871 to 1914

Towards the end of the nineteenth century many ideas which since the days of Newton and Descartes had been accepted by thoughtful men as axiomatic were questioned and reappraised, with results that altered all previous conceptions of the physical world and made the period between 1871 and 1914 the prologue to an entirely new era. The very principles on which knowledge of the physical world had been based were overthrown by two theories of capital importance: the Theory of Relativity elaborated by Albert Einstein and the Quantum Theory, propounded by Max Planck. Classical theories of space and matter, attached to the old concept of the ether, had been rudely shaken as early as 1881 by Michelson's experiments, and shortly afterwards by Lorentz's work with electrons. One of the major results was to demonstrate that matter is only condensed energy, that matter and energy are two aspects of a single reality and can be changed one into the other. This concept would guide future work in nuclear science and lead to atomic fission.

The consequences of this revolution — still far from being exhausted — were not immediately apparent, and this in part explains the impression of disorder and extreme confusion in the intellectual and artistic life of the period. The picture is one of contradictions as violent as they were basic. If Nietzsche founded morals on the vital energy of the individual and his will to power, Einstein sought to avoid the subjective as far as possible, and first to examine the arguments of pure mathematics in order afterwards to compare the results thus obtained with the facts of observation and experiment. If Tarde examined social phenomena with the strict eye of a logician, Bergson, resolutely irrationalist, demanded an intuitive approach to a reality deeper than that accessible to the intelligence alone. For scientific materialists religion and science were irreconcilable. For others science could not be pursued to its limits without becoming tinged with mysticism and charged with faith. Einstein himself considered that science without religion was lame and religion without science blind.

The domain of literature was no less filled with contrast. Zola, an 'experimental' novelist, based his vast novel-cycle, *Les Rougon-Macquart* — significantly sub-titled 'The Natural and Social History of a Family under the Second Empire' — on the laws of heredity. If mathematical calculations had enabled Leverrier to predict the discovery of the planet Neptune, then there was no reason why an exact analysis of the parents should not enable the novelist to predict the behaviour of the children. On this superficial analogy with scientific certainty Zola constructed a work of imagination which exerted considerable influence throughout Europe and in America. The growth of popular education had greatly increased the number of readers. Never had so many people read, or read so many novels. Literature became a social phenomenon, supported by the press, which was an insatiable consumer of serial fiction. The great artist Tolstoy was above all a social reformer and dealt with the problems of human nature. He was followed by Gorky, a man of the people who wrote for the people. In France, Huysmans passed from naturalism to Christian mysticism, while Anatole France expressed his scepticism in learned and witty prose. Kipling was widely travelled and his brilliant short stories of India inspired the pride of his compatriots in the British Empire. George Meredith was a skilled portrayer of human motives with a studied and affected style, while Thomas Hardy's Wessex novels were written with powerful realism and psychological insight. The science fiction of H. G. Wells gained a wide circle of readers for an author whose interests were sociological. The American expatriate Henry James was distinguished for subtle character analysis, while in Spain Ibañez's novels of peasant life in Valencia were so outspokenly critical that he spent much time in prison. In poetry Verlaine broke with tradition and took pleasure in a half-sensuous, half-mystical impressionism. With Arthur Rimbaud he prepared the way for symbolism, an attempt to transcend reason which dissolved into anarchy. The same sensuousness, at times degenerating into sensuality, was found in the poetry of Swinburne. A. E. Housman's *Shropshire Lad*, apart from its pessimism, caught something of the spirit of the Greek Anthology. Rilke, born in Prague, enriched German literature by his lyric poetry.

In the world of entertainment similar contrasts were in evidence. In Paris the vaudeville, with its 'Boulevard' high spirits, had survived the Second Empire. On the

The Wright brothers made the first successful flight in a powered heavier-than-air machine in North Carolina in 1903. The longest of the first aeroplane's flights lasted 59 seconds. *Radio Times Hulton Picture Library*

German-born Albert Einstein (1879–1955). In 1905 he published his first formulation of his theory of relativity, described as 'the most important intellectual fact that the present time can show'. *Fitzwilliam Museum, Cambridge*

Thomas Edison (1847–1931) invented the moving picture (as he did the gramophone, incandescent lamp and power station). The cinema became a major medium of entertainment and this poster advertises a French film of 1903.

other hand, great interpretive artists like Sarah Bernhardt and Lucien Guitry appeared in serious plays, in tragedy and historical dramas. The comedy of manners found a supreme exponent in Oscar Wilde, while Bernard Shaw's humour veiled social criticism. Drama dealing with crises of conscience, grim or pathetic, by Scandinavian playwrights like Björnson, Ibsen and Strindberg, were successfully presented. Social drama was staged with realism and an attention to life-like properties and scenery. The art theatre, on the contrary, re-established the rights of fantasy and with creative imagination staged works like Maeterlinck's *Pelléas et Mélisande*. Gordon Craig, Max Reinhardt and Stanislavsky each rebelled in his own manner against the demands of tradition or of fashion, above all employing the new resources of arti-

ficial light. The new stage-lighting did marvels for the music hall, in which a taste for the sumptuous and the fabulous was curiously allied to light and erotic suggestion. Isadora Duncan and Serge Diaghilev freed the dance and the ballet from both classical and romantic traditions. In 1895 in Paris the Lumière brothers presented the first cinematograph performance: the motion pictures would for many years remain animated photographic reproductions of scenes from life or the theatre, rather than creations of a new art form. In 1899 Marconi established wireless communications between France and Britain, and wireless telephony — or radio — began its development with the vacuum tube, invented by Fleming in 1904. But even in 1914 people were far from grasping the importance of these events and their future repercussions in the realms of art, politics and education.

In music, too, the taste of the Second Empire continued for a while to retain the loyalty of the French public. Offenbach could still triumph with his *Tales of Hoffmann*. In Vienna Johann Strauss II, son of the ' Waltz King ' continued his famous family's contribution to the gaiety of nations with his operetta *Fledermaus*, while in London the Savoy operas of Gilbert and Sullivan delighted even those who were the butt of their urbane satire. The taste in opera was sentimental, Bizet's *Carmen* and Massenet's *Manon* being especially popular. Though Gounod's most successful work, *Faust*, continued to be presented time and time again in the opera houses of the entire world, Richard Wagner was the composer who aroused most controversy and finally conquered Europe. Wagner brought new life to romanticism with his massive sonorities and daring chromaticism. In Vienna his influence was felt by the great classical-romantic symphonists, Bruckner and Mahler, and even in the strange and moving songs of Hugo Wolf. His musical heir was Richard Strauss, whose opera *Der Rosenkavalier* was produced in 1911. But already the revolt against Wagnerian domination had begun, and Stravinsky's *The Rite of Spring* shocked the musical public of 1913. In France Claude Debussy founded what might be called the impressionist school of music, a refinement rather than a revolt against romanticism, while the Belgian César Franck, much influenced by Bach and Beethoven, remained loyal to an older tradition. Edward Elgar, deeply imbued with mysticism, added to the repertory of English choral music and produced major symphonic works. The Russians, with Tchaikovsky, Borodin, Mussorgsky and Rimsky-Korsakov, captivated the ear of audiences throughout Europe and America with their brilliant orchestral colour and melodic vein. Italy continued her tradition of *bel canto* and the operas of Verdi, Mascagni, Leoncavallo and Puccini, known by heart throughout the peninsula, soon achieved universal popularity. Symphony orchestras giving regular concerts sprang up in most great cities and enabled the average music lover to develop his taste. The gramophone was also slowly bringing music to a wider public.

In architecture and the decorative arts the beginning of the period under consideration was still dominated by a taste for the neo-classical, the neo-Romanesque and the neo-Gothic. Nevertheless, a revolt against these revivals of bygone styles was in the air. Structural ironwork, which had been employed in the Crystal Palace as early as the Great Exhibition of 1851, had come into general use — though invariably concealed by ' period ' façades — and bolder spirits were beginning to demand new architectural forms which would exploit the possibilities of the new materials and building processes — in fact, a ' functional ' architecture. In 1889 the use of structural ironwork had enabled the first skyscraper to be built in New York, while in Paris in the same year the Eiffel Tower was erected. For the construction of a church in Paris in 1894 Contancin and Baudot hit upon a system of hollow bricks, strengthened with steel, into which cement was poured. The process only required perfecting to become reinforced concrete. By pouring concrete into shuttering lined with steel bars and removing the shuttering after the concrete was dry Hennebique built an entire house in 1903, and thus inaugurated a revolution in building construction.

Towards the end of the century there was a kind of renaissance in the decorative arts, but the so-called ' Modern Style ' — which was applied less to the structure and manner of building than to decoration — was of brief duration. The contemporary movement was to be consolidated only in Berlin, Vienna and above all in Munich. Although the word *urbanism* is recent, being first used in 1910, town-planning of sorts had of course always existed. Urbanism as an art and a science became a necessity only during the nineteenth century as the result of a modern phenomenon: the great city. Between 1810 and 1910 the population of London rose from 800,000 to 7,200,000, while that of Paris rose from 647,000 to 3,000,000. In the face of this enormous growth and its attendant problems of traffic, transport, sanitation, etc., legal measures were finally taken and plans drawn up, but by the outbreak of war in 1914 little in the nature of true town-planning had been achieved.

Between 1871 and 1914 painting, the graphic arts and sculpture underwent a revolution which was as complete as that which had taken place in science. Academic art, still relying on the authority of Ingres, held that a painting existed in an ideal light which had no relation to the light of day. For the Impressionists, light, atmosphere and colour were everything and the subject hardly mattered. In 1874 Claude Monet exhibited his picture called ' Impression, Sunrise ', which gave its name to a movement that caused unprecedented scandal. The neo-Impressionists, among whom Seurat was outstanding, handled colour and the systematic division of tone in a scientific spirit, analysing light, and studying the work in optics of physicists like Helmholtz. In this their methods were related to those of the literary naturalists like Zola. Cézanne, and then Gauguin and the Symbolists were the first to react against this cult of direct sensation considered as the sole source of truth. The Symbolists demanded not a faithful representation of the outer world, but a suggestion of the inner world through symbolic allusion and luxuriant decorative form. Van Gogh exalted the colours of nature to such a paroxysm of lyrical intensity that Baudelaire, had he known Van Gogh's works, would doubtless have called it supernaturalist. He had no direct descendants, but his influence was felt by the *Fauves*, like Matisse, Vlaminck and Derain, who rioted in colour and whose explosive exhibition in the *Salon d'automne* in 1905 provoked an uproar. Cubism, more austere in its use of colour, went still further and substituted for the object as the eye sees it the object as the spirit knows it — the world in its essence, not in its appearance. The Orphists — a term coined by the poet Apollinaire — considered painting as an art capable, like music, of expressing all emotions without recourse to the technique of pictorial representation. It was in France and particularly in Paris that the new schools of painting, from Impressionism to Cubism, arose and developed. They affected the evolution of art throughout the world. Even the Japanese, whose prints had contributed to the formation of Impressionism, rallied to the school of Paris, which was itself influenced by Negro sculpture, by the primitive art of Oceania, by children's designs, by the work of the simple-minded and indeed by that of the mentally unbalanced and insane. German Expressionism would derive from the schools of Paris, as would the many adventurous experiments and triumphs of Picasso.

THE TWENTIETH CENTURY

CHAPTER EIGHTEEN

THE FIRST WORLD WAR AND THE FAILURE OF PEACE

1914

The first French military operations in 1914 were inspired by the disastrous doctrine of the offensive at all costs. The best defence was attack: imprudence was felt to be the soundest form of insurance. Heavy artillery and superior armaments were as nothing against the faith which beat in human hearts. In this spirit French troops were thrown against the east and north-east in the ' battle of the frontiers '. They liberated Mulhouse, but were almost at once forced to retreat. Nevertheless, what Poincare called the ' mad offensive ' was continued. Including the German counter-attack, the battle of Lorraine lasted from August 9 to August 21, until the French armies fell back to re-form. Losses had been staggering; France had lost the flower of her army before the main struggle began, yet Lorraine had already become a secondary theatre of operations.

The main weight of the German offensive had been thrown against Belgium, in pursuance of the long-matured Schlieffen plan. The plan was to guard the Russian frontier in the east with a few divisions only while sweeping into France through Belgium and Luxemburg to win the war in the west in a few weeks. Unexpected Belgian resistance delayed the German timetable, though not seriously. The last forts of Liège fell after heroic resistance on August 17. French attacks were made against the flank of the German armies as they marched westwards across Belgian Luxemburg, but failed to halt the advance. The French left wing risked encirclement. The British expeditionary force under Sir John French, which had gone into action in the region of Mons, was driven out of Belgium. General Joffre, Commander-in-Chief of the French, ordered the armies of the north to retreat. Under the impression that disaster was imminent Viviani's Ministry fled from the capital on August 26. For the first time the Socialists now joined a coalition ministry. Delcassé became Minister of Foreign Affairs, Millerand Minister of War, and Briand of Justice. But the rapid advance of the Germans continued and the communiqué of August 29 startled France with the news that battles were raging ' from the Somme to the Vosges '.

French morale was sustained by hopes of help from Russia, where the war had been greeted with joyful enthusiasm. St Petersburg, the Germanic form of the word, was patriotically changed to the Slavic Petrograd. Though the huge Russian army, popularly known as the ' steamroller ', might suffer an occasional setback, its advance must be irresistible. At the end of August 1914 Poincaré himself was certain that the Russians would reach Berlin by November. To relieve the pressure on their French

The experience of a major land-war in Europe was a hundred years away from Britain in 1914. The Crimea had been far away, the Napoleonic wars were history. Perhaps this was why Englishmen went cheerfully to fight. *Imperial War Museum*

Tanks were first used by the British, in the battle of the Somme in 1916. The First World War revolutionised tactics and destructive techniques. Men were slaughtered on a scale hitherto unknown. *Imperial War Museum*

allies two Russian armies had driven into East Prussia, spreading terror through Germany. The German commander gave orders for a retreat to the Vistula. The German High Command then took a decision which was heavy with consequences: to stem the Russian advance they withdrew two vital army corps from the west. Von Prittwitz was replaced by an old Hanoverian general who, knowing the terrain, emerged from retirement: Hindenburg. Actual command was exercised by his young chief-of-staff, a Colonel Ludendorff, who had distinguished himself at Liège. Hindenburg's imperturbable calm and Ludendorff's harsh and abrupt character were to form a harmonious combination which made for success. From August 27 to 30 at Tannenberg Samsonov's army was annihilated and Samsonov shot himself. Rennenkampf's army, until then unengaged, was heavily defeated at the Masurian Lakes in September and forced to retreat in haste. The Russians had been completely swept from East Prussia.

The Western Allies did not count on Russia alone, for the conflict had already extended beyond the borders of Europe. In the Far East Japan had summoned Germany to evacuate Kiao-chow and, declaring war on August 23, lost little time in seizing it herself. But French diplomats tried in vain to persuade the Japanese to lend military support.

On September 1 the Government left Paris for Bordeaux; German cavalry was at the time ten miles from the capital. But, leaving the forces which screened Paris unengaged, von Kluck, who commanded the German right wing, swung towards the south-east with the object of destroying the main body of the French armies. Kluck's force had been depleted by the withdrawal of the two army corps sent to the Russian front and also by the siege of Maubeuge which took three German divisions. Gallieni, the Governor of Paris, urged an immediate offensive to take advantage of the situation which momentarily presented itself. On September 4 Joffre ordered a general offensive to begin at six o'clock that morning from the Meuse to the Ourcq. Thus the decisive battle of the Marne began. It continued until September 12. Kluck had left a breach of some twenty-five miles between his army and Bülow's. Into this breach Sir John French slowly advanced. When the German armies failed to resume contact, General von Moltke, Chief of the German General Staff and nephew of the victorious Moltke of 1866 and 1870, delegated a staff officer, Lieutenant-Colonel Hentsch, to advise Bülow and Kluck. On September 9 Hentsch, with Bülow's concurrence, gave the order for retreat to the Aisne. The German plan of achieving a rapid decision in France had thus failed. The Germans abandoned Château-Thierry, Châlons-sur-Marne and Rheims, entrenching themselves behind the Aisne. There, reinforced by the divisions until then engaged at Maubeuge and others drawn from Lorraine, they halted the French forces, exhausted by their all-out effort.

The Germans, considerably reinforcing their right wing, now attempted to turn the Allied positions from the north-west, and on October 11 seized Lille. The French command in its turn withdrew forces from Lorraine. The long Western Front was beginning to take shape. A ' race to the sea ' began. In early October furious fighting took place in the region of Arras, and later near Lille before the front was stabilised. The Germans tried desperately to take Calais, the base of the British army, which held the Allied left wing. The battle of the Yser

Air warfare began with primitive, unarmed machines. This painting depicts the first air reconnaissance over enemy territory in 1914, carried out by Captain Philip Joubert in a Blériot II monoplane. The biplane is a B.E.2a. *Flight*

was fought from late October to the end of November and behind this little river the Belgian army retained a narrow strip of Belgian territory, while French marines held out at Dixmude. Few actions were more tenaciously contested than the first Battle of Ypres, which raged from October 30 to November 24. But on the blood-stained ' fields of Flanders ' the Germans were held.

By winter it was obvious that the war of movement was no longer possible. It had given way to a war of attrition which would last for nearly four years. The machine gun had immensely increased the power of the defensive. Both sides dug themselves into trenches behind barbed-wire entanglements which formed a continuous front extending from the North Sea to the Swiss border. In this new sort of warfare, industrial strength was a vital element. Munitions had been expended on an unprecedented scale and there was the risk of shortages. The seas were open to the Allied Powers, who could communicate freely with America. The Central Powers were, on the contrary, blockaded.

The weight of Russia's effort had fallen on Austria-Hungary and the Russian Commander-in-Chief, the Grand Duke Nicholas Nicholayevich, had advanced into Galicia and occupied Lemberg. The Austrians were retreating towards Cracow. At the end of September they were thrown back into Upper Silesia and western Galicia. In the battle of Lodz, from November 16 to December 15, the Germans attempted to encircle the Russians, and were themselves threatened with encirclement. They succeeded, however, in disengaging themselves and took Lodz on December 6.

Events in the Near East were more complicated. As early as 2 August 1914 the Germans had concluded a secret treaty of alliance with Turkey. Two German cruisers, the *Goeben* and the *Breslau*, escaping the British, sailed through the Dardanelles on August 7 and were fictitiously sold to the Turkish Government. The *Goeben* and the *Breslau*, flying the Turkish flag and rebaptised with Turkish names, proceeded to bombard the great Russian

Field Marshal von Hindenburg, Commander-in-Chief of the German armies from 1916, and, with Ludendorff, effectively ruler of Germany until 1918. His reputation, like that of Ludendorff, was made on the eastern front. *P.A.Reuter*

Poison-gas, one of the new horrors of war, blinded these men and many more. First used by the Germans in April 1915, it never achieved a decisive success, but was a powerful weapon against morale. *Imperial War Museum*

A wood near Ypres. Incessant shellfire in low-lying, slow-draining land often produced conditions worse than this and made the life of the defender a misery and the task of the attacker suicidal. *Imperial War Museum*

A British ammunition factory. Both material and men were needed in greater quantities than ever before. One answer was an unprecedented entry of women into the factories and into many other male occupations. *Imperial War Museum*

port of Odessa, and from November 2 the Ottoman Empire found itself at war with Russia and the *Entente*. The Caliph launched an appeal for a Holy War and the Russians found themselves faced with a new campaign against the Turks in the Caucasus. Turkey's entry into the war also obliged the British to send reinforcements to Egypt and to Mesopotamia. In the meanwhile the Serbs had recovered and in December 1914 triumphantly reoccupied their capital, Belgrade.

1915

On the Western Front 1915 was the first year of gruelling and interminable trench warfare. The French Government had returned to Paris. As the generals of the day considered inaction a reflection on their honour, and no one had begun to think of ways of avoiding head-on attacks on prepared positions, fierce and costly efforts were made to gain a few yards of mud; these bloody engagements left the general situation unchanged. In February and March in Champagne, and in May and June in Artois, more important offensives were undertaken: they were quickly checked by the Germans.

The entry of Italy into the war in 1915 did not lead to the decisive improvement that the Allies had hoped for. Gabriele d'Annunzio's fiery oratory was aided by Italian appetite for *Italia Irredenta* — Trentino and Trieste — which the Allies promised in return for Italian co-operation. On May 24 Italy declared war on her ally Austria-Hungary, but not on Germany. Her intervention coincided with the defeat of the Russian armies in Galicia. A month earlier the Russians had seized the fortress of Przemysl and taken more than 100,000 prisoners. Then, in the first days of May, Mackensen, at the head of German and Austro-Hungarian armies, broke through the Russian centre in Galicia, reoccupying Przemysl and on June 22 recapturing Lemberg. The Russians were running short of ammunition. In the beginning of July a new Austro-German offensive, in co-ordination with Hindenburg in the north, made the situation of the Russians critical. The field armies of the Tsar were defeated again and again, until in August Nicholas II himself assumed supreme command. The fall of fortresses like those of Ivangorod, Kovno and Brest-Litovsk entailed enormous losses in prisoners. In five months the Russians lost Galicia, Poland and Lithuania, but managed to save their armies from annihilation.

Both in Britain and in France a diversion in the Near East had long been considered. On the advice of Winston Churchill, First Lord of the Admiralty, an expedition to the Dardanelles was decided on. Prepared on February 19 by a bombardment, the naval enterprise failed on March 18; in spite of heavy sacrifices the fleet was unable to force the mine-strewn passage. On April 25, under the command of Sir Ian Hamilton, an Anglo-French expeditionary force, which included Australian and New Zealand divisions, landed on the peninsula of Gallipoli, but was held by the Turks. As towards the beginning of 1916 its situation became increasingly untenable, the force was evacuated —without the loss of a man. But the enterprise had already cost heavy Allied casualties. Its failure meant that the Allies could not establish easy sea-communication with Russia and had repercussions throughout the Balkans, where the Allies were attempting to gain the support of Greece and Roumania, while maintaining Bulgaria,

which inclined towards the side of the Central Powers, in a state of neutrality. Greece was allied to Serbia, but the King of Greece, Constantine, was the brother-in-law of the Kaiser and disapproved of the policy of intervention advocated by Venizelos, who in March 1915 was forced to retire. On September 6 Bulgaria concluded an agreement which bound her secretly to the Central Powers.

To the increasingly effective British blockade Germany retorted by submarine warfare. This troubled German relations with the United States, especially when in May 1915 the Cunard liner *Lusitania* was sunk by a U-boat with the loss of 1,200 lives, more than a hundred of whom were Americans. Indignation swept the United States, where Germany and Austria were already fomenting strikes in munition factories working for the Allies. Following the seizure of certain documents revealing underground activities in the United States, Austria-Hungary was obliged to recall her ambassador. The sinking of another liner with the loss of twenty-six more American lives was blamed by the German Government on the U-boat commander, and the German Foreign Secretary announced that no further passenger ships would be sunk without previous warning and without ensuring the safety of non-combatants. But it was urged in Germany that six weeks of unrestrained submarine effort would be sufficient to force Britain to sue for peace at any price.

During 1915 the British expeditionary force had become a great army of a million men. Kitchener, whose calm was imperturbable, was opposed to costly offensives which resulted only in the loss of lives. In France, too, many military chiefs, among whom Pétain was prominent, urged a less reckless expenditure of troops and demanded the procurement of more heavy artillery. Italy and Russia, however, insisted on an immediate offensive. In September, accordingly, Joffre attempted a breakthrough in Champagne. Only the forward German lines were broken and some 25,000 prisoners taken. Simultaneous attacks had been launched at Loos by the British. Meanwhile, Serbia was crushed by an Austro-German attack which followed a Bulgarian declaration of war. The King of Serbia with his troops then crossed the mountains of Albania and reached the Adriatic coast, where an Allied fleet transported them to Corfu. The Central Powers were thus able to effect a junction with their Bulgarian and Turkish allies. This rally deprived of value an attempted Allied diversion at Salonika, where 15,000 British troops joined 65,000 French troops who landed at the end of October. This army, commanded by General Sarrail, was threatened by a concentration of Greek forces. King Constantine, in spite of the British offer of Cyprus, insisted on maintaining strict neutrality with regard to the Central Powers. The Franco-British army of Salonika was the subject of incessant bickering, for French and British general staffs considered that resources had been deflected from the main theatre of war, the Western Front.

1916

At the beginning of 1916 the German High Command decided to throw its weight back on to the Western Front and to annihilate the French armies once and for all. Joffre was at the time preparing for a summer offensive on the grand scale. He was anticipated by a massive German onslaught on the fortress town of Verdun in February which was at first irresistible. Pétain was put in command at the Verdun front and, at the cost of tragic losses, the German advance was gradually checked. The fortress of Vaux, which had been under attack since March, fell only in June. Meanwhile, in May, the Austro-Hungarians had attacked the Italians on the Adige front. Salandra, the Italian Premier, was accused of not having pursued the war with sufficient vigour and in June was replaced by the elderly Boselli, who formed a Cabinet of ' national concentration' which even included former neutralists.

By the end of June the violence of the German offensive had abated. In Germany, and even more in Austria, the war had taken its toll; starvation threatened and a desire for peace was spreading. In August 1914 even the Social Democrats had been entirely behind the Government in the Germans' ' defensive war '. It was not long, however, before an opposition group began to form among the Socialists. In December 1914 Karl Liebknecht voted against further military credits. By March 1916 the Social Democrats had split into two parties, the ' independents ' who refused to grant military credits, and the ' majority ' group who voted the credits in the name of the majority of the party.

In Britain the Irish question had again reached a crisis. Irish extremists had not been slow to take advantage of Britain's difficulties and, with the aid not only of Irishmen in America but of Germans, armed themselves. An uprising occurred at Easter 1916, and for a few days the rebels were masters of Dublin. The insurrection was quickly crushed and Sir Roger Casement, one of its chief instigators, was hanged.

On 31 May 1916 the only great naval battle of the war was fought at Jutland. Although Vice-Admiral Beatty suffered serious losses, which gave rise to a rumour of defeat, the battle reaffirmed Great Britain's mastery of the seas, and the German High Seas fleet never again ventured to challenge it.

During the summer the Allies began to press the Central Powers harder. From June to November General Brusilov directed an offensive in the southern sector of the Russian front which resulted in important victories over the Austrians. On July 1 an Anglo-French offensive over a twenty-five-mile front in the Somme began a tragic epic of heroism and butchery which lasted until the end of September. It cost enormous casualties, but it relieved the pressure on Verdun and inflicted terrible blows on the Germans, who suffered casualties of nearly half a million on the Somme. In September tanks were first employed on the battlefield, although early experiences with them were not encouraging and the battle petered out in the autumn rains. In August the Italians captured Gorizia, Roumania declared war on the Central Powers, and Italy declared war on Germany. But the Roumanian army in Transylvania was annihilated, Wallachia and the Dobruja were occupied, and on December 6 the Central Powers entered Bucharest. The remnant of the Roumanian army held a line on the Sereth, while the Allied force in Salonika was unable to push farther forward than Monastir.

In face of these reverses the conduct of the war was increasingly criticised in both Britain and France. On December 6 Lloyd George replaced Asquith as Prime Minister. Briand, accused of insufficient firmness, re-formed

French soldiers fighting in the Vosges in 1916. In this hilly country, fighting was at closer quarters than in the plains of Flanders. *P. A. Reuter*

his Cabinet, reduced the number of ministers and appointed General Lyautey Minister of War. Joffre was replaced as Commander-in-Chief of the Western Front by General Nivelle, who had distinguished himself at Verdun.

Amid these events, a historical event of another kind occurred, as though to evoke memories of a past epoch. On 22 November 1916 the Emperor Francis Joseph died at the age of eighty-six. His grand-nephew, who was twenty-nine, succeeded him as Emperor Charles I of Austria and King Charles IV of Hungary. He called upon Count Czernin, formerly an intimate collaborator of the Archduke Francis Ferdinand, to direct Foreign Affairs. Charles was very unwilling that the ancient Habsburg monarchy should remain a vassal of Germany and, in his desire to end hostilities, took the initiative in promoting discussions which could lead to a restoration of general peace. On December 12, after their Roumanian victory, the Central Powers proposed negotiations to establish such a peace. The Allies denounced the proposal as a ' trap '.

In the United States the Democratic candidate, Woodrow Wilson, was re-elected President in October 1916, after a hard-fought campaign. Wilson's success owed much to the fact that to many of his compatriots he was the man who had kept America out of the war. When for a few hours it seemed that he had lost the election, there was public rejoicing in Britain and France. On 20 December 1916 Wilson invited all the belligerents to state exactly what their ' war aims ' were. There was, he felt, a possibility that the various claims were not incompatible.

1917

In a Presidential address on 22 January 1917 Woodrow Wilson still spoke of ' peace without victory '. It was his last effort to bring the war to an end by mediation. Ten days later he broke off diplomatic relations with Germany. Pressure from Ludendorff had made the Government of 355

Germany resume the unrestricted U-boat campaign. The German Admiralty affirmed that from the point of view of the war the importance of the United States 'was equal to zero', and on January 31 the Germans notified the United States that certain zones off the coasts of Great Britain and France were in a state of blockade and that all ships found in these waters would be sunk without warning. On February 3 Wilson handed the German Ambassador his passports and the American Ambassador in Berlin was recalled.

In Russia, revolution was in the air. There were whispered accusations against the 'German' Tsaritsa and against 'hidden powers'. The elderly and apathetic Prime Minister Goremykin, who was inclined to collaborate with the *Duma*, was in February 1916 replaced by Stürmer, who had the confidence of Rasputin and was capable of keeping the Liberals in check. Sazonov, the Foreign Minister, resigned in July, and Stürmer, already Chief Minister, assumed responsibility for Foreign Affairs, although he was very suspect to the Allies because of informal contacts with the Germans. In the *Duma* opposition to 'traitors' became so outspoken that the Tsar felt obliged to remove Stürmer. In December 1916 the monk Rasputin was assassinated by a group of young noble officers. In February 1917 an inter-Allied conference was held at Petrograd. General dissatisfaction was felt not only in the army but in all classes of Russian society. Even the Grand Dukes spoke freely of the necessity of removing the Tsar and the Tsaritsa. The rise in prices and shortages of food had caused disturbances in Petrograd since January 1917: disorder became much more serious in March as coal and bread steadily disappeared. The garrison at Petrograd revolted and fraternised with workers on strike. The Government resigned. Nicholas II, at General Headquarters, had not been informed of the gravity of events. His generals advised him to abdicate in order to save the dynasty. Quite unmoved, Nicholas II abdicated in favour of his brother Michael, since the Tsarevich Alexis was too delicate to reign. But Michael, after consultation with those who at the moment directed affairs, handed over the supreme power to the provisional government which had been set up.

Thus the weak government of Nicholas II, so badly in need of reform, had vanished without bloodshed, and Russia seemed at last to have become an integral part of Europe, moving towards a liberal regime which would take the form of a constitutional monarchy or of a republic, dominated in either case by 'bourgeois parliamentarianism'. The will of the country would be expressed by a constituent assembly, and Russia, no longer shackled by Tsarism and its attendant abuses and inefficiency, would become a democracy like its Western allies. Hence the Allies in no way deplored the revolution which had taken place. They had done nothing to produce it, but they welcomed it with hope, believing that an enlightened Russian democracy would pursue the struggle against the Central Powers with greater effect.

The revolution of March 1917 brought to power men attached to the ideals and traditions of democracy, but who were without political experience. At their head Prince Lvov, a representative of the oldest aristocracy, had struggled against absolutism and bureaucracy. Miliukov, the Minister of Foreign Affairs, was a distinguished historian but lacking in political acumen. He

In March 1917 the first Russian revolution set up a liberal regime which wished to continue the war on the Allied side. Troops like these took the oath to the new government but were tired of fighting a war they could not believe in. *Radio Times Hulton Picture Library*

embarked on a programme which would still have been valid in 1916, but corresponded in no way to the situation in 1917. The aim of his policy was to acquire Constantinople and the Straits. Incapable of conforming to the demands of the masses, he resigned from the Government in May. Guchkov, the Minister of War, was a Moscow merchant of generous spirit. He had fought by the side of the Boers in the Transvaal against the British and struggled energetically against the 'forces of darkness' — in other words, against Rasputin. He revolutionised Tsarist army regulations. But the crucial fact was that the people wanted peace. The sympathy with which almost the entire population had welcomed the provisional government soon faded, and many of its leaders who at the beginning of the revolution had passed for revolutionaries were very shortly to be denounced as reactionaries. For, at the same time as the provisional government was formed, workers' and soldiers' councils — or *soviets* — which were dominated by the Socialists sprang up as though of their own accord, first in Petrograd and then in Moscow. These *soviets* quickly obtained effective administrative powers, and the provisional government could do little but assent to their demands. It soon became apparent to the Western Powers that the events of March 1917 had considerably weakened the military potential of Russia.

In France Briand's Cabinet was tottering. French marines, landing at Athens in December 1916, had been greeted by rifle fire and French public opinion was enraged by the ' ambush '. Briand was blamed, resigned and was succeeded by his Minister of Finance, Ribot, a veteran of parliamentary strife, who formed a hybrid Government in which he himself was Minister of Foreign Affairs and the distinguished mathematician Painlevé was Minister of War. Painlevé was extremely uneasy about the great offensive which Nivelle was preparing. The United States was on the point of entering the war and it seemed to Painlevé an error to expend further troops before the American reinforcements arrived. In February the Germans had anticipated the French attack by withdrawing to the ' Hindenburg line '. When in April Nivelle attempted to smash the German defences over a fifty-mile front in the Aisne, his troops were everywhere stopped after an advance of a few miles and everywhere suffered withering losses. The offensive on which France had pinned such hopes had disastrously failed. The situation was more than disquieting. No more diversions could be expected from Russia, the morale of the army was collapsing and in May mutinies occurred. Pétain was made Commander-in-Chief, took the army in hand and went over to the defensive while waiting for American help.

On 2 April 1917 the United States declared war on Germany and threw the weight of the New World into redressing the balance of the Old. It was the end of the age of European world supremacy. American public opinion had been enraged not only by the resumption of unrestricted U-boat warfare but by the ' Zimmermann telegram '. Zimmermann, a German Foreign Office official, had telegraphed Carranza, the President of Mexico, promising him, in case of war with the United States, generous financial backing and the return of the territories lost in 1848. The Zimmermann telegram was deciphered by the British Secret Service and released to the Americans — with explosive results. The intervention of the United States was accompanied by declarations of war against Germany by other American states: Cuba, Panama, Guatemala, Honduras, Costa Rica and Bolivia, followed in the autumn by Brazil, Peru and Ecuador. But the United States did not join the *Entente* powers as an ally and did not accept the *Entente's* war aims. This mattered less in 1917 than the participation of American manpower and industrial strength. By the end of 1917 American troops were already landing in France.

On the other hand Russia collapsed. In May 1917 the Socialist Kerensky became Minister of War. He was later to become Prime Minister and even Commander-in-Chief. He delivered a series of eloquent speeches to encourage the army to go on fighting. The army, however, now elected its own officers and was no longer reliable. After one offensive in July, the troops decided that they would not fight and completely evacuated Galicia.

There was, however, a reasonable hope that Austria-Hungary might be induced to make peace. In March 1917 Prince Sixtus of Bourbon-Parma, who served as a captain in the Belgian army, brought to President Poincaré a confidential letter from his brother-in-law, the Austrian Emperor. It offered support for ' France's just claims to Alsace-Lorraine ', the re-establishment of an independent Belgium ' without prejudice to the indemnity which she may receive for the losses she has suffered ', and independence and access to the Adriatic for Serbia as well as important economic concessions.

In May the Emperor Charles dismissed Tisza, who had been the virtual dictator of Hungary since June 1913. Tisza was replaced by Count Maurice Esterhazy who, unsuccessful in establishing the electoral system on a democratic basis, retired in August 1917. While Wekerle, an old political leader of the Liberal Party — Tisza's party — remained chief Hungarian minister until October 1918, Count Michael Karolyi, a member of one of the great families of the Magyar aristocracy, broke the ' holy union ' of the Dual Monarchy by forming a ' peace party ', whose efforts were encouraged by the Russian Revolution of March 1917. Karolyi made contact with the Allied Powers in Switzerland.

In Austria itself Count Stürgkh had been Prime Minister since 1911 and, since the war, had thrown off all parliamentary control: his dictatorship came to an end with his assassination a few weeks before the death of Francis Joseph. The Czech national independence movement was becoming organised: Professor Masaryk, one of its chief proponents, had escaped to appeal to the Allies for help for the suppressed nationalities of the Dual Monarchy. Numerous Czech detachments had deserted to the Allies, and Wilson's entry to the war encouraged hopes of Allied support for self-determination.

Everywhere pacifist propaganda was on the increase. Pacifist elements in France waged a fierce campaign against Poincaré and the war. Many Germans, too, were becoming doubtful of ultimate victory. Erzberger, an active Swabian Deputy of the Catholic Centre Party, who had been an ardent war-propagandist, ceased to believe in victory when he realised that Austria was on the verge of collapse. He was received by the Emperor Charles and the Empress Zita, who explained their desire for peace. A note, dated 12 April 1917, was handed to him by Count Czernin, the Austrian Chancellor: peace, it stated, must be concluded that same year. In July, to a committee of the *Reichstag* meeting in secret session, Erzberger declared that in view of the gravity of the situation the *Reichstag* must extricate Germany from the war. His speech produced an enormous effect. Ludendorff, who since August 1916 had been practically a dictator, remained a firm Pan-Germanist. He was as opposed to universal suffrage in Prussia as he was to a peace which did not entail extensive annexation. He used this opportunity to get rid of Bethmann-Hollweg, convinced that the war would be lost if Bethmann-Hollweg remained Chancellor. At the instigation of Erzberger the Centre Party declared that the retention of Bethmann-Hollweg in power made the conclusion of peace more difficult.

The Kaiser than named as Chancellor Dr Georg Michaelis, an almost unknown functionary. On July 19 the *Reichstag* adopted a ' peace resolution ' in favour of ' a peaceful understanding and a durable reconciliation between all peoples' without annexations and without indemnities. Thanks to Erzberger's efforts the *Reichstag's* ' peace resolution ' was followed by a note from the Holy See indicating the basis on which a just and lasting peace might be established. But the German reply proved a grave disappointment to the Pope. Germany, as Erzberger later said, only discussed the question of Belgium when she was in no position to speak. Meanwhile the general impression was that Germany intended to annex Belgium and was already preparing its dismemberment. The deportation of more than 100,000 Belgian workers who were sent in October 1916 to work in Germany had aroused universal indignation. In February 1917 Flemish nationalists, the ' activists ', set up a ' Council of Flanders ' and attempted to form a Government.

During the summer the German sailors at Kiel, condemned to inactivity, grew restive under the rigours of shore discipline and wretched food. Ten sailors were condemned to death for mutiny and two were executed in September. The German Admiralty's relations with the *Reichstag* were stormy, the independent Socialists arousing its especial opprobrium. Politicians of importance, such as the Socialist majority leader Ebert, firmly opposed the Chancellorship of Michaelis who, indeed, proved his inadequacy and disappeared in consequence of the Kiel disturbances. He was succeeded by the ageing Count Hertlin, a man of the Catholic Centre.

In France politics had become more and more confused. In July Ribot refused passports to Socialists who wished to go to an international socialist congress on peace conditions in Stockholm. The Cabinet seemed nevertheless to be tottering under the pressure of those who demanded peace at any price. In the Senate in July Clemenceau pronounced a passionate indictment against Malvy, Minister of the Interior since 1914. In August Malvy resigned, and his resignation brought about the fall of Ribot's Government. A weak Government under Painleve, in which Ribot remained as Minister of Foreign Affairs, followed. The Socialists, more and more divided among themselves, refused to take part. The ' sacred union ' no longer existed. The minority of 1914–15, who were disposed to resume relations with the German Social Democrats, had now become the majority in the party.

The military horizon was sombre for the Allies. The Greek affair had, it is true, been satisfactorily settled. With the agreement of Great Britain, Constantine had been forced to abdicate and Venizelos, taking over the government, broke with the Central Powers. In addition, the British campaign in the Near East and the Arab rising against the Turks were going well. In the summer of 1915 Britain had signed an agreement with Hussein, the Emir of the Hejaz, which provided for the establishment of a vast Arab kingdom. In November 1916 Hussein was recognised by the Allies as King of the Hejaz. By the end of 1916 the ' Revolt in the Desert ' which Colonel Lawrence had inspired, led to the total loss by Turkey of Arabia. On 11 March 1917 British troops marched into Baghdad. In Africa all the German colonies had been conquered by the Allies: only German East Africa, under the command of General von Lettow-Vorbeck, was to hold out until the armistice. Most important of all, the British had at last mastered the U-boats: the submarine blockade on which the German High Command had relied to starve Britain had failed. But neither in Italy

nor the Balkans had Allied efforts achieved success of any consequence. On the Western Front, the third Battle of Ypres, undertaken by the British in order to distract German attention from the demoralised French army, achieved its aim at a cost of 400,000 casualties. The offensive finally petered out in the muddy horror of Passchendaele after five miles had been gained in four months. Just as much ground was won in a few hours at a cost of few casualties when the first massed tank assault in history was made at the end of November at Cambrai.

As the fighting in Flanders was coming to a close, the Allies' hopes were gravely compromised by events in Russia. Entangled with the radicals of the Petrograd Soviet, the provisional government struggled to keep Russia in the war. The failure of the summer offensive was followed by an unsuccessful Bolshevik attempt to seize power. Reactionaries hoped for a return to strong government after this and supported General Kornilov, the new Commander-in-Chief, when he attempted to seize power in September. His attempt failed, but from this time Kerensky was unable to resist the Bolsheviks who had helped to thwart it. The masses had by now lost faith in the provisional government, which could supply neither peace nor bread, and when on 6 November 1917 the Bolsheviks seized Government buildings and arrested the Ministers, the regime collapsed without defenders. Kerensky fled disguised as a sailor. A council of the Peoples' Commissars under the presidency of Lenin seized power. It immediately declared the dictatorship of the proletariat, put all land at the disposition of agrarian committees, and turned over the control of factories to the workers. It repudiated all agreements which Nicholas II had made with the Allies, who were lumped together with the Germans as ' imperialist and capitalist brigands '. It proposed to all the belligerent powers a ' fair and democratic peace '. On December 15 an armistice was concluded with the Central Powers and negotiations for peace were begun on December 20 at Brest-Litovsk. In elections for a new Constituent Assembly, however, only 225 Bolsheviks were returned against more than 400 of their opponents. This embarrassment was dealt with by dispersing the Assembly by military force as soon as it convened in January 1918.

Forty German divisions could now be sent to the Western Front. Already in Italy war-weariness and demoralisation had resulted in the disastrous defeat of Caporetto (October 24–27). Driven back from the Isonzo, the Italian army broke in helpless confusion and withdrew to the Piave, leaving 300,000 prisoners in the enemy's hands. The army was stiffened by French and British divisions, but its future value remained uncertain. In France, political squabbles and pacifism eventually led the President to call upon Clemenceau, the destroyer of so many Governments, to become Prime Minister again at seventy-six. It was a brilliantly successful choice. Clemenceau's patriotism was unassailable; in him the ruthless spirit of 1793 lived again. For the war he was ready to make any sacrifice and to use his popularity and authority unsparingly. Although opposed by the Socialists and a section of the Radicals, he soon dealt with defeatism. He arrested and shot certain pacifist conspirators, and finally, in January 1918, brought Caillaux to trial before a court-martial on a charge of endangering the safety of France.

1918

The Bolsheviks had asked for a 'fair and democratic peace'; the Central Powers offered nothing of the sort. Bukharin refused to accept terms which would befoul the very name of the Bolshevik Party. Trotsky, then the Commissar of Foreign Affairs, who wished to avoid both 'revolutionary war' and a humiliating peace, said: 'We will not sign the peace and we will not resist — nor will the enemy dare to advance.' On 18 February 1918, however, the enemy did advance. There was no resistance, for Lenin rejected romantic ideas of pursuing the war. War was not a thing to be laughed at. 'The peace which has been offered to us', he agreed, 'is a shameful peace. But the army no longer wishes to fight, and our revolution must at all costs be safeguarded.' Accordingly on March 3 the Treaty of Brest-Litovsk was signed. Russia surrendered vast tracts of territory — including Finland, Esthonia, Livonia, Courland, Lithuania and Russian Poland. Then Roumania, to avoid being totally crushed, capitulated to the Central Powers, and in May accepted the harsh terms of the Treaty of Bucharest.

In June 1917 Albert Ballin, the great Hamburg shipbuilder, had written to Stresemann with remarkable farsightedness: 'We were waiting for a miracle and it has occurred: I mean the Russian Revolution. But the miracle is two-edged: though it enormously facilitates our military operations it also stimulates the movement of the masses against the war.' Most Germans, however, saw in the events in Russia only an assurance that Germany would now win the war. The 'peace resolution' of July 1917 for peace without annexations and indemnities was no longer taken seriously. The Treaty of Brest-Litovsk was accepted by all the bourgeois parties, and the Social Democrats were content to refrain from voting. Imperialist plans for further annexation flourished. Ludwig III of Bavaria claimed Alsace. Saxony demanded Upper Alsace. Prince Frederick Charles of Hesse, the Kaiser's brother-in-law, was actually to wear the crown of Finland for a few weeks. But the great mass of the German people suffered atrocious privations. In January 1918 strikes stopped steel production, first in Berlin and then in most other great German cities. Ludendorff decreed stern measures to deal with the situation: a state of siege was declared, factories were placed under military command, workers were incorporated into the army and arrests were numerous.

Since November 1917 Ludendorff had been preparing for a series of offensives along the entire Western Front. On 21 March 1918 the last great German effort of the war was launched at the British line between the Somme and the Oise, at the point of junction between the British and the French armies. Under an intense barrage of shells from four thousand guns the British Fifth Army fell back. Field Marshal Haig gave orders that the Channel ports should at all cost be covered. But nine days later, on March 30, the offensive was held before Amiens. The Germans had advanced forty miles over a forty-five mile front. A long-range cannon — known as 'Big Bertha' — bombarded Paris from a distance of seventy-five miles.

The success of the German offensive had demonstrated the danger inherent in separate Allied commands. General Foch, who sat on the Supreme Inter-Allied War Council which had been set up after Caporetto, was first given the task of co-ordinating the action of the Allied armies on the Western Front, then received the 'strategic direction of military operations', and finally became Commander-in-Chief of the Allied armies in France.

In Flanders the British, still weakened by the March offensive, were now supported by the inexperienced Portuguese expeditionary corps on whom the next wave of Ludendorff's offensive fell on April 9. The Germans gained ground near Ypres that had been conquered at the cost of formidable British sacrifices: Armentières and Kemmel Hill were lost. By the end of April, however, this second advance had been halted and had proved less dangerous than the March offensive. Moreover, the German army had suffered heavier casualties than the British since March 21.

In 1914 the Germans struck a medal showing a charging cavalry officer with the words 'nach Paris' (to Paris). This bitter French parody was issued during the German retreat in 1918. *British Museum*

During this onslaught, Clemenceau somewhat impetuously refused any conversations with Austria-Hungary. On 2 April 1918 Count Czernin, the Dual Monarchy's Minister of Foreign Affairs, had alluded imprudently to secret negotiations taking place with France. Clemenceau angrily stated that 'Count Czernin had lied' and, disclosing the confidential letter from the Austrian Emperor, added, in effect, that it was the work of a diseased imagination. Needless to say the Emperor Charles was thenceforth discredited in the eyes of his German allies. The Habsburg Monarchy, already undermined by its nationalist minorities, was further shaken by the resignation of Czernin.

The weight of Ludendorff's third offensive now fell on the French front at the Chemin-des-Dames, which dominated the Aisne. Surprise was complete and he was able to achieve the most rapid advance of the war on the Western Front. The French soon lost all the ground they had won since October 1914. The Germans swept forward across the Aisne and across the Marne, to occupy Soissons and Château-Thierry, an advance of some forty miles in fifteen days, during which 50,000 prisoners were taken. But the German offensives had lengthened the front and casualties had been serious. United States divisions were now beginning to arrive. In June the German Secretary of State for Foreign Affairs said to the *Reichstag*: ' We can hardly expect that an absolute solution of the problem can be obtained by military means alone without a certain amount of diplomatic negotiation. ' This confession so enraged Hindenburg and Ludendorff that Kühlmann was obliged to resign. He was replaced by Admiral von Hintze, who had the confidence of the Pan-Germanists. But Hintze, when he had examined the realities of the situation, was at once filled with total pessimism.

The end of the war

In mid-June the Italians repulsed a major Austro-German attack on the Piave. In July Ludendorff's fourth offensive, launched in Champagne, was a complete failure. Thanks to American reinforcements, the Allies had built up powerful reserves and now began to attack. On July 18 the French attacked successfully between the Marne and the Aisne; the tide had turned. Château-Thierry was re-occupied. Foch, promoted to the rank of Marshal of France, began to hammer the front with a series of blows. On August 8 the British and the French attacked between Amiens and St Quentin. For Ludendorff this was the ' black day ' of the German army. Having offered his resignation to William II, he withdrew to the positions which he had held before his March offensive. From then on symptoms of disorganisation spread, but the German troops still resisted with energy. They occupied part of France and almost all of Belgium. They were in Finland, in the Baltic provinces, in the Ukraine, and in the Caucasus. By a series of murderous engagements the Allies pushed forward with difficulty. The situation in Austria-Hungary appeared to be desperate; Turkey was lost. In the Imperial Council which met at Spa on August 14 William II concurred with Ludendorff's declaration that to continue the war would be an irresponsible act, to play a game of chance. It was imperative that peace feelers be put out.

On September 15 the Americans under General Pershing attacked the salient of St Mihiel with complete success. On the same day the Allies took the offensive in Salonika, where the Bulgarians collapsed before French and Serbian troops. In the Balkans the Central Powers had by now lost the war. On September 14 an Austro-Hungarian Note, immediately rejected by the Allies, proposed that negotiations should take place in some neutral country. The Bulgarians asked for an armistice, which was granted on September 29. King Ferdinand of Bulgaria abdicated in favour of his son Boris. Turkey was no longer capable of resistance. Lord Allenby advanced into Palestine and entered Damascus. On September 26 the Americans attacked again in the Argonne, and the French in Champagne. The next day, the British and the French attacked in the region of St Quentin and La Fère. On September 28, Belgian, French and British armies moved from Dixmude towards Bruges.

On that same day, Ludendorff at last lost heart. He invited the astounded Chancellor Hertling to address President Wilson and ask for an immediate cessation of the war. ' The army ', he stated, ' cannot hold out for another forty-eight hours. ' Hintze, the Secretary of State, put forward a policy which was hastily adopted: to prevent an upheaval from the masses below, a revolution from above was essential. In other words, some democratic institutions must be introduced, to preserve the internal unity of Germany and to facilitate negotiations with the American President. Ludendorff suddenly demanded a parliamentary system with a cabinet dependent on the confidence of the *Reichstag*. Since the war was lost Ludendorff wanted to unload the army's political responsibilities. The Kaiser called on Hertling's cousin, Prince Max of Baden, to be Chancellor. He was reputed to be in favour of peace by conciliation, and formed a parliamentary Government supported by the Social Democrats, who were also represented in his Cabinet. He hesitated to ask for an armistice so soon after the establishment of the parliamentary system, but the High Command insisted with vehemence, reporting that the military situation grew daily worse. During the night of October 3–4 a Note was sent to President Wilson asking for an armistice based on his Fourteen Points.

The exchange of Notes between Wilson and the German Government prolonged the war for a month. Wilson was insistent that Germany should get rid of the German ruling caste: William II, discredited by defeat, remained an obstacle to peace. His abdication was publicly discussed, though the Kaiser himself did not seriously consider the question, deeming himself indispensable. Even Ludendorff now found Wilson's demands unacceptable, and on October 26 asked to be put on the retired list. In Austria-Hungary the Emperor issued a manifesto on October 17 which delivered the death blow to the Dual Monarchy of 1867. He announced the transformation of Austria into a Federal State which the ' National Councils ' of the minorities could — if they wished — establish. This was not their wish: the Czechs and the Yugoslavs refused to enter into discussion with Vienna. In Budapest the parliament decided to recall Hungarian troops to Hungary. A national Hungarian Council was formed by Count Karolyi and his friends.

On October 27 the German Government sent its last Note to Wilson. It stated that the Government awaited ' armistice proposals which would open the way to a just peace ', of the kind suggested by the President in his declarations on the subject. On the same day Count Andrássy, the Dual Monarchy's last Minister of Foreign Affairs, denounced the German alliance which his father had negotiated some forty years previously and Austria-Hungary accepted the conditions for an armistice laid down by President Wilson. The Italian armies occupied Vittorio Veneto on October 30. There was no longer an Austrian front. Revolution had broken out in Hungary. On October 31 Karolyi was named Prime Minister, while Tisza was shot by soldiers. The Ottoman Empire signed an armistice on board a British cruiser in the Aegean Sea on October 30. On November 3 a delegation from the Austro-Hungarian army signed an armistice near Padua.

In Wilhelmshaven, at the announcement that the German navy intended to challenge the British navy in a supreme effort, mutiny broke out among the German crews. Three times the squadron which proposed to confront the British fleet was thus prevented from putting to sea. The German admiral sailed to Kiel in the hope that when the crews landed they would recover their calm, but instead the sailors merely discussed the situation with the men who worked in the naval yards. Having closed the workers' trade union headquarters, the military authorities attempted to imprison two hundred sailors. The dockers thereupon

THE FIRST WORLD WAR

rose and in a clash with the troops eight were killed.
The Socialist Deputy Noske arrived as commissioner from
the Government and order was finally restored. These
events, however, were considered even in Berlin to be
of merely local importance: news of them only vaguely
reached the Allies. The German army continued, foot by
foot, to give ground — as ordered on November 5 — until
it had fallen back to the line of Antwerp-Brussels-Char-
leroi-Mézières. An American Note had informed the German
Government that the Allies were disposed to conclude
peace on the ' basis of the Fourteen Points ', but that it
must ask Marshal Foch for armistice conditions. Although
the Germans accepted these conditions they did not admit
that they were vanquished, and the feeling persisted in the
German army that they had been defeated not by arms,
but by revolution behind the lines.

From Kiel the revolution first spread to the other
great ports. In Munich, which was directly threatened
with invasion after the military collapse of Austria, revolution broke out on November 7, led by the journalist
Kurt Eisner, an Independent Socialist. The soldiers left
their barracks and the Bavarian King, Ludwig III, fled.
The Republic of Bavaria was proclaimed. Kurt Eisner
had set the republican example for all Germany. The
Secretary of State, Scheidemann, argued that if the monarchy was retained in Prussia after Bavaria had become
a republic the unity of Germany would be endangered.
Everywhere seamen, messengers of the revolution, instigated
uprisings and demanded peace. Attempts to resist the
revolutionaries were at once smashed. The established
forces of law and order seemed to be paralysed. On November 7 the Minister Erzberger departed at the head of a
delegation to negotiate, as he thought, with Marshal
Foch. During the evening the Majority Socialists who
participated in the Government issued an ultimatum to
the Chancellor: the workers of Berlin, they said, would
take over the capital if the Kaiser, a refugee in his headquarters at Spa, did not abdicate before the following
midday. There still ensued three days of confusion before
the Kaiser finally crossed the Dutch frontier. On receiving
the news that workers and soldiers had seized power,
Prince Max resigned the Chancellorship, and Scheidemann proclaimed the republic from a window of the
Reichstag, a revolutionary gesture designed to prevent
the outbreak of real revolution. Ebert formed a Council
of People's Commissars with Majority Socialists and left-
wing Independents. Erzberger, who had arrived at his
destination, asked Berlin if he was to sign the armistice.
He was instructed to ask for milder terms; but in case
of refusal, he was ' to sign all the same '. The Allied conditions remained unaltered, and in Foch's railway coach
in the forest of Compiègne the armistice was signed on
November 11. By its terms Alsace and Lorraine would
be restored to France, the Rhineland occupied by the
Allies, the German fleet and all military material turned
over to the victors, and all Russian territory evacuated.
It was the end of the greatest war in history, in which
ten million men died.

The Soviets

The Great War — as it was to be called until 1940 —
generated a series of revolutions. In Russia, even after
the Bolshevik success, nationalist revolutions took place

After a last colossal effort the German armies were halted
again in 1918 and forced to retreat. Under repeated allied
attacks, their defences at last cracked and prisoners such
as these were taken in their thousands. *Imperial War Museum*

Lenin, leader of the Russian Bolsheviks, addressing a meeting in Moscow. He seized power from Kerensky's government
in 1917 and founded the first socialist state to become a great
power. The figure on the right in semi-uniform is Trotsky.
Popper

Abortive allied interventions for various purposes turned the
new Russian regime violently against the West. The British
evacuation of Archangel in 1919 was accompanied by the
destruction of quantities of stores. *Mirrorpic*

among the non-Russian peoples of the old Tsarist Empire. Germany was ravaged by internal conflicts in which Communists, Socialists, Liberals and partisans of the old regime fought for power. The collapse of the Habsburgs gave rise to a series of revolutions, some nationalist in character, others social protests against the remnants of feudalism which still persisted in Hungary. Finally the Ottoman Empire had been destroyed and disorder reigned in large tracts of Asia.

The Bolshevik revolution was, nevertheless, far more important than the others. Over one-sixth of the globe a communist and totalitarian regime was organised — and, to the stupefaction of the world, was to endure. This gigantic event helped, by reaction, the later formation of equally totalitarian anti-communist regimes copying, directly or indirectly, the methods of the Russian revolution and its millennial hopes. Ideological struggles were again to dominate not only internal politics but the foreign policy of nations as they had not done since the French Revolution. Unrestrained propaganda, the suppression of freedom of speech and action, and the threat to freedom of thought were to endanger the very basis of existing civilisation. The old autocratic and unitary Russia of the Tsar gave way to a Russia of Soviets composed of workers, peasants and soldiers, under the new autocracy of the Communist Party. The Soviets became simple organisms which transmitted the decisions of the central power. The former 'exploiting' class was deprived of all political rights. Terrorism was the order of the day and a new secret police succeeded the Tsarist organisation. Lenin himself proclaimed that 'the great problems of the life of nations are resolved by force alone'. The press was gagged and personal liberty eliminated. 'Today the basis of socialism', Lenin said, 'is to find bread.' Rich peasants were accused of starving the people and treated accordingly. Arrests and executions provoked, in reply, assassination. Peasant uprisings broke out in the Ukraine.

In May 1918 martial law was proclaimed, and during that summer the Terror was officially organised. The Tsar, his wife and his children were slaughtered; other members of the Romanoff family were also executed. In August Lenin, who had previously escaped an attempt on his life, was seriously wounded. Civil war had already begun in May. There were about 35,000 Czechs in Russia, prisoners of war taken between 1914 and 1917, or deserters from the Austro-Hungarian armies. After the treaty of Brest-Litovsk, Masaryk wished to bring these prisoners to France, via Vladivostok, in order to fight against Germany. In exchange for part of their arms, the Czechs were authorised to travel to Vladivostok on the Trans-Siberian Railway. But fighting occurred between Czechs and local Soviets in May in central Russia. At that time, when no organised Red Army existed, the 'Czech Legion' represented a formidable force, which was soon supported by anti-Bolshevik groups within Russia. By August the fate of the Soviets seemed to hang by a very slender thread.

With the armistice of November 1918 the civil war in Russia became more intense. The *Entente* powers became involved. The region of Odessa and a part of the Crimea were occupied by some forty thousand men, largely troops from France and the French colonies, Greeks, Serbs and Poles. In the extreme north of Russia there were twenty thousand British and Americans sent there to safeguard Allied stores. In the east and in western Siberia were the Czechs, while Japanese and American troops entered eastern Siberia. In January 1919 President Wilson invited representatives of the White Russians and of the Soviets to confer on Princes Island, near Constantinople. The Soviets made haste to accept the invitation, but the Whites, supported by France, declined to 'compound with crime'. From then on the civil war and limited intervention became more and more tangled up in what was afterwards depicted as a deliberate capitalist attempt to crush the new socialist society. At the beginning of 1919 the Soviets were cut off from contact with the outside world. From all sides they were threatened by White Russian armies which received arms, munitions and money from the Allies. But it was soon decided to leave the 'Russian experiment' to develop in its own way, roped off from the outside world by a *cordon sanitaire*. The Allied troops were withdrawn. Wilson thought it best 'to leave the Bolsheviks to stew in their own juice'. In October 1919 a new and dangerous crisis threatened to wipe out the Soviets. The White Russian General Denikin drove to within one hundred and eighty miles of Moscow while Yudenich threatened Petrograd. Earlier, in March, Admiral Kolchak had approached the Volga. His reverses began in May in the Urals. Abandoned by the Czechs, who refused to interfere any longer in the internal affairs of Russia, Kolchak was taken prisoner at Irkutsk and shot in February 1920. Denikin, attacked from the rear, was replaced by General Wrangel, who vainly attempted to hold the Crimea. His troops were hastily evacuated by the French navy. Meanwhile Yudenich's army was driven back into Esthonia.

Behind the shield of the Russian civil war, Finland, the Baltic states and Poland had succeeded in establishing themselves as separate nations. The Allied intervention, sporadic and unorganised as it was, had helped to push back the western frontiers of Russia for two decades; 35,000,000 people lived on the territory which Russia had lost since 1914. At the beginning of the World War no one had dreamed of the emergence of the Baltic states: they were now reasonably well governed with the support of peasant co-operatives. To the north, a free and autonomous Finland was a necessity which even the Russians acknowledged. On the other hand, they had never recognised the annexation of Bessarabia by Roumania. While they agreed to the creation of a Poland which numbered some twenty million inhabitants of actual Polish blood, they were indignant at being deprived of a large stretch of territory which was undeniably Russian.

Armed conflicts also broke out in November 1918 in Germany, in Hungary, in Albania and in most of Asia. Though no longer at war, the world was still far from being at peace. In this chaos the Bolsheviks believed they saw the beginnings of world revolution. Lenin said: 'We were only the spark; the flames are spreading.' Russia launched the Third International, which was opened in Moscow in March 1919. The Soviet state thus assumed the leadership of a world-wide revolutionary movement. While the Allies were negotiating the Treaty of Versailles which aspired to endow the world with a new order, Moscow strove to unite all the revolutionaries, all the oppressed, all the defeated. The serious strikes which in November 1918 broke out even in Switzerland and Holland were attributed to Soviet agents.

Leon Trotsky (Lev Bronstein), Commissar for Foreign Affairs and later Commissar for War. He had to accept the Peace of Brest-Litovsk. Subsequently he fell foul of Stalin and went into exile, living abroad until his assassination. *Radio Times Hulton Picture Library.*

In Germany the Council of People's Commissars was a purely Socialist Government. The Majority Socialists, such as Ebert and Scheidemann, co-operated with Independents. But Ebert had a secret understanding with Ludendorff's successor, General Groener, designed to 'combat the revolutionary movement', which showed signs of following the Russian example. Blood was spilled when riots broke out in Berlin during December. The Majority Socialists alone retained power and Noske, rallying the elements that remained of the old German army, crushed the Spartacists — the radical Marxist group which Karl Liebknecht and Rosa Luxemburg had founded in 1917 — during the 'bloody week' of 6–11 January 1919. Lenin had believed that the German revolution of November 1918 was the first step towards world revolution. But when in January 1919 Karl Liebknecht and Rosa Luxemburg were put to death it was evident that no proletarian revolution would take place in Germany. In the ensuing elections the left-wing Independent Socialists were disastrously defeated. As for the Majority Socialists, their victory had been indecisive and they were obliged to collaborate with two bourgeois parties: the Catholic Centre and the Democrats. It was agreed to set up a parliamentary republic. The National Assembly met at Weimar and elected Friedrich Ebert President of the Reich. Scheidemann formed a Government which included the Socialist Noske and the Catholic Erzberger. In March 1919 a serious insurrection was suppressed. In Bavaria the head of the Government, the Independent Socialist Kurt Eisner, had been murdered in February. A republic governed by communist workers' councils was proclaimed on April 7 but collapsed three weeks later.

But it still seemed that the Russian Revolution might set all Europe alight. Germany made good use of this terrifying possibility, especially in dealing with Great Britain and America. Colonel House, who was President Wilson's personal representative in Europe, wrote: 'We are sitting on a powder keg.' In March 1919 the proletarian revolution triumphed in Hungary but it retained power for only four months. Bela Kun, chief of the Hungarian Soviets, was at war with the Roumanians, the Czechs and the Serbs — which gave the counter-revolution its opportunity. Admiral Horthy seized power and reimposed a reactionary regime. Communist attempts to gain power completely failed in Austria. The revolutionary faith of the masses was shaken by these setbacks, but revolutionary propaganda had some success. Above all, it helped to prepare the way for the triumph of dictatorship by frightening the middle class. The victory of democracy at the time of the armistice, when so many thrones collapsed, was not to last. Social tumult produced reaction. The forces of order stiffened. Noske, crushing the Spartacist rebellion, had foreshadowed the coming of Hitler.

The Treaty of Versailles

The Soviets took no part in the Treaty of Versailles, which was made without them and in a certain sense against them. Russia's very absence affected the terms of the peace. The many difficulties created or revealed by the World War had been enormously complicated and increased by the war itself. The negotiations were, in practice, directed by three great and conflicting personalities: Wilson, Lloyd George and Clemenceau. Wilson, like a twentieth-century Gladstone, enjoyed immense prestige. The triumphal welcome with which Europe had received him revealed his hold on the imagination of the public. The cheers with which he was greeted were cheers for eternal peace. The noble enterprise he had in mind was the perpetual alliance of democratic peoples in a League of Nations dedicated to the maintenance of peace. This lofty idealism had to contend with the French Premier: Clemenceau, a witty and realistic octogenarian, was devoid of illusions, and since the armistice the idol of France. The third member of the Big Three was a formidable antagonist: Lloyd George, a Welsh liberal, or rather radical, of extraordinary inventiveness and able to hit upon a solution to every problem. Shrewdly sensing British public opinion, he won every point which it was possible to win for the British Empire. Beside these three outstanding figures was the Italian Premier Orlando, an amiable jurist with a flowery turn of speech. He was assisted by Sonnino, his Minister of Foreign Affairs, who never ceased referring to the 1915 Treaty of London, which was his own work. As Italy wanted Fiume, which was not mentioned in the 1915 treaty, there were to be violent controversies later. The Italians held that the rewards offered to them in the negotiations did not do justice to their victory, and had withdrawn from the conference by the time the Germans were summoned to receive the conditions for peace. (They returned, however.)

The Europe which emerged from Versailles was intended to be founded on the more or less strict application of the principle of nationality. But demographic realities made this principle hard to maintain in practice, and the new nations which were created did not always form viable units. The new state of Czechoslovakia contained not only Czechs but three million Germans, as well as Poles, Ukrainians and Slovaks who for ten centuries had lived under Hungarian rule. In Yugoslavia there were Slovenes, Serbs, Croats, Bosnians and Montenegrins, peoples who had formerly belonged to four distinct kingdoms and who practised differing religions. Poland, though more homogeneous, had to accommodate the millions of Germans, Ukrainians and Russians who lived on Polish soil.

Article 231 of the treaty — which declared that Germany was responsible for the war — was an error which diplomats of an earlier age would never have committed. German publicists would later find an eager response in German hearts when they denied that their country alone bore the burden of guilt. Other defects in the treaty arose from geographical or historical circumstance. Although the Polish corridor was undoubtedly peopled by Poles, the physical separation of East Prussia from the rest of Germany was an inevitable source of friction. The sudden disappearance of the Dual Monarchy left a power vacuum in a large area of Eastern Europe. While Austria and Hungary were treated as vanquished states and subjected to heavy penalties, the young nations carved from the old Empire at once insisted on making full use of their newly acquired sovereignty. Later it would seem that the Big Three of Versailles had made a bad mistake in not having imposed economic federation on the states which had inherited the ruins of Austria-Hungary. Finally, though the treaty had been negotiated by the American President, the United States repudiated it. In view of this, Great Britain dropped the guarantees against Germany

Lloyd George, a radical reformer and Prime Minister of Great Britain 1916–22. His dynamism carried his country to victory in the war, but he then spent his popularity trying to remain in office. *National Portrait Gallery*

which she had given, conjointly with the United States, to France — guarantees which had persuaded Clemenceau to renounce any thought of French hegemony on the left bank of the Rhine.

In 1919 it was sincerely and naïvely believed that the final curtain of the tragedy which had begun in 1914 had fallen. It was thought that after the war the world would resume its old peaceful course. But the ruins which world-wide conflict had left in its wake were unprecedented. The world economy had been built on European preponderance: its very foundations had been shaken. The great industrial nations of Europe, victors and vanquished alike, had been devastated and impoverished. Meanwhile the other continents had greatly increased their share of the world's production and trade. The economic expansion of the United States had been particularly striking; a debtor nation before the war, she had emerged at the end of it as a formidable creditor. Europe, it is true, would soon regain her 1913 level of production, but never again would she recover the dominant position she had once held in the economic life of the world.

The future co-operation of the Allies — at least in so far as the collection of war indemnities was concerned — seemed assured by the creation of a ' Reparations Commission '. During the conference the Allies had been unable to agree on how much they could demand from Germany. Astronomical sums were suggested beyond all reason. The instrument by which new wars were to be prevented and peace maintained was the League of Nations, which formed the subject matter of the last of Wilson's Fourteen Points. In many parts of Europe belief in the League of Nations amounted to religious faith. But the League's effectiveness was immeasurably reduced by America's refusal to join it.

THE FAILURE OF PEACE

The aftermath of the Treaty of Versailles

Woodrow Wilson attempted in vain to engage his country in a policy of collective security. In September 1919 a stroke left him incapable of defending his work at Versailles. In the Presidential elections of November 1920 he was defeated by a Republican candidate, Harding, who polled more than sixteen million votes against Wilson's nine million. The reaction against Wilsonian policies led to the enactment of neutrality laws designed to prevent the United States from becoming involved in any future world conflict.

Clemenceau, after his victory in' the elections of 1919, became a candidate for the presidency of France in 1920. He was defeated by the President of the Chamber of Deputies, the academic Paul Deschanel. The majority in the Chamber was made up of the extreme Left, a section of the more moderate Left, numerous Catholics, and Deputies who were dissatisfied with the Treaty of Versailles. Millerand, a former Socialist, succeeded Clemenceau as Premier and after the retirement of Deschanel became President of the Republic.

Lloyd George strove primarily to maintain the balance of power in Europe. His calculations were, however, upset by the fact that Great Britain rapidly disarmed while France did not. Soon after the Treaty of Versailles Lloyd George was forced to the conclusion that France was lacking in moderation and a sense of justice. In his speeches he described his late ally as typically militarist, though he alternated his attacks on France with efforts to improve Anglo-French relations. But in October 1922 the Lloyd George Ministry fell and he never regained power.

Two weeks later Mussolini ' marched ' on Rome — in a railway carriage. The Italian Socialists had rallied to the Third International in September 1919; their extremism had set in motion a sharp reaction in Italy which paved the way for fascism. Mussolini, a former Socialist of thirty-eight, seized power in a country terrified by the threat of anarchy. The Duce's easy victory inspired the

ambitions of other potential dictators; the influence of fascism was great and its example contagious. Rome came to be looked on as ' the necessary antidote to Moscow '.

When the terms of the Treaty of Versailles were made known in Germany they were denounced as ' insupportable and unacceptable '. Scheidemann's Ministry was divided on the subject. His Minister of Foreign Affairs was against signing the treaty, while Erzberger wanted to accept it ' to prevent chaos '. General Groener declared that military resistance was impossible. To sign the treaty the Socialist Gustav Bauer in June 1919 formed, without the Democrats, a ' red and black ' Government of Socialists under Noske and of Catholics under Erzberger. The Republican regime, thus obliged to shoulder responsibility for a treaty which the immense majority of Germans considered infamous and brutal, then promulgated the Weimar Constitution, with a black, red and gold flag instead of the black, white and red flag of Imperial Germany. It was first challenged in March 1920 by an attempted right-wing coup d'état. Six thousand soldiers occupied Berlin, and the Government was obliged to go first to Dresden and then to Stuttgart. A general strike was thereupon called by the trade unions — and after four days the Kapp *Putsch* fizzled out.

The situation in June 1919, when Germany first learned the terms of the Peace Treaty, was repeated in May 1921 when the Allied Powers informed Germany that her bill for war reparations amounted to one hundred and thirty-two thousand million gold marks. The Government of the Catholic Fehrenbach resigned. Another member of the Centre Party, Wirth, the Minister of Finance, formed a new Government which bowed to the Allied demands. Rather than risk a renewal of the war, the occupation of the Ruhr, and financial, economic and monetary catastrophe, Wirth accepted the cost of defeat. Inflation of the mark now began to make things even worse. French opinion was firmly set against any ' nibbling ' at, any softening of, the harsh terms of the Versailles Treaty. In January 1922 Poincaré, exactly ten years after his first premiership, again became Prime Minister and Minister of Foreign Affairs. He opposed any reduction of German reparations and spoke of seizing German means of production to guarantee their payment. Wirth when Chancellor had tried to meet reparation payments, but in November 1922 Wilhelm Cuno replaced him and a violent conflict with France ensued. Germany fell behind with her deliveries in kind — deliveries of coal and coke and telegraph poles — and the Reparations Committee noted the fact. Poincaré thereupon decided to occupy the Ruhr. In January 1923 a French army, reinforced with Belgian units, accompanied the mission of French engineers — and their Belgian and Italian colleagues — who entered the Ruhr to collect the materials which had not been delivered. This occupation of the Rhineland aroused a wave of anger against France and Germans replied with their only weapon: passive resistance. The French found themselves obliged to expel or imprison thousands of German industrialists, civil servants and workers. Schlageter, who was shot for sabotage, became a national hero. Monetary distress became so acute that the country seemed to be on the verge of dissolution. Stresemann, who became Chancellor in August 1923, realised that Germany, defeated a second time, ran the risk of disappearing altogether. He was Chancellor only until November

1923, and, at the head of a coalition ministry, which the Opposition named ' the ministry of the great capitulation ' he put an end to the movement of passive resistance. He hoped to improve relations with France so as to secure the evacuation of the Rhineland and remained Foreign Minister until his death in October 1929.

For several years Poland, threatened by her two redoubtable neighbours, Russia and Germany, caused tension. Poland had revived, thanks to the fortunate circumstances which had destroyed the three states among whom she had been partitioned — Russia, Austria and Germany. Pilsudski, a passionate enemy of Russia, had fought the Russians during 1914 and 1915 at the head of a Polish legion, and then in July 1917 broken with the Central Powers. In November 1918 he was freed from internment at Magdeburg, and proceeded to Warsaw where he assumed supreme civil and military power and proclaimed the Polish Republic. The Allies, however, recognised only the Polish National Committee as legal Poland. The Committee had been installed in Paris in July 1917 and gave orders to a Polish army which had been formed in France. Ignacy Paderewski, the great pianist, who had represented the Polish National Committee in the United States, succeeded in forming a national coalition government with Pilsudski, whom a Constituent Assembly, elected in February 1919, confirmed in his position as Chief of State.

The Treaty of Versailles delimited the German frontier, established the Polish corridor and made Danzig a free city. Plebiscites were planned for Marienwerder and Allenstein where, in 1920, an enormous majority chose to remain part of Germany. The plebiscite which took place in Upper Silesia in March 1921 resulted in over 700,000 votes for Germany against 484,000 for joining Poland. In October 1921 the League of Nations arranged a partition which gave Poland the major part of the coalfields.

The eastern frontiers of Poland were not fixed but as uncertain as the future of Russia itself. The Russians had reoccupied part of the territory which the Germans had evacuated after November 1918: Vilna, Pinsk, Brest-Litovsk, which were retaken by the Poles during the spring of 1919. The ' Curzon Line ' was drawn in December 1919 as representing the fairest ethnographical frontier. It guaranteed, as a minimum, Polish possession of territory which was incontestably Polish. Pilsudski contemplated the liberation of the Ukraine, but an expedition he undertook against Kiev in 1920, hoping to profit by Soviet confusion, was a total failure. The Russo-Polish war was brought to an end by the battle of Warsaw in August 1920 when the Poles drove back the Russians. The Treaty of Riga, signed in March 1921, fixed the eastern frontiers of Poland on lines which remained unaltered until 1939. After this communism seemed to have been banished from European territory and confined to Russia.

The Near East

Among the ' treaties of the Parisian suburbs ', as Hitler contemptuously called them — namely, the Treaty of Versailles with Germany, the Treaty of Saint-Germain-en-Laye with Austria, of Neuilly with Bulgaria, of Trianon with Hungary, of Sèvres with Turkey — that with Turkey disappeared first: in fact almost before the ink with which it was signed on 10 August 1920 had dried. The Ottoman

Empire was suddenly replaced by a nationalist Turkish state. In Constantinople the old regime had lingered on into 1919 while the vigorous forces of Turkey, withdrawing to Anatolia in Asia, came to life. An assembly at Ankara proclaimed the fall of the Sultan. In May 1919 the Greeks, encouraged by Lloyd George, disembarked at Smyrna with the blessing of the Allied Supreme Council and advanced inland. A Turkish officer, Mustafa Kemal, an ardent ' Young Turk ' who in 1915 had been a hero in the resistance to the Allied landing in the Dardanelles, organised resistance. In September 1921 he halted the Greeks and then drove them back to the Afyon-Karahissar line, which they held for nearly a year. In the following August Kemal routed them. The Turks occupied Smyrna. Great Britain, France and Italy then intervened and forced the opponents to sign the armistice of Mudanya on 11 October 1922. The Government at Ankara returned in triumph to Constantinople. In November 1920 on the death of his son and heir Alexander, King Constantine had been recalled to the Greek throne as a result of a plebiscite which had gone against Venizelos. He now abdicated in favour of his son George II, who was to lose the crown in 1924 and regain it in 1935. The Graeco-Turkish peace treaty, negotiated in Lausanne, entailed the loss to Greece of Asia Minor and eastern Thrace. The Turkish inhabitants of Greece were transported to Asia Minor, while the Greeks left Asia Minor. Mustafa Kemal was proclaimed President of the Turkish Republic on 29 October 1923 and at once began to introduce Western reforms. Resolved that Turkey should remain genuinely independent, he renounced all claims to non-Turkish territory and refused to consider plans for Turkish domination over the Arabs.

The ambitious dreams of Arab nationalists were only partially realised. Though the Allied victory in 1918 had delivered the Arabs from Turkish rule, the fragmented nations of Islam were baulked by British interests, French interests and the aspirations of the Jews. At the San Remo Conference in April 1920 France obtained a mandate over Syria and the Lebanon which, with the support of Britain, was disputed by the Emir Faisal, one of the sons of Hussein, sherif and Emir of Mecca. Driven from Syria in August 1921, Faisal became King of Iraq, over which Great Britain had received a mandate. His brother Abdullah became Emir of Transjordan, another British mandate. The father of Faisal and Abdullah, the Emir Hussein, whom Britain had put on the throne of the Hejaz, was defeated between 1919 and 1925 by the Sheik Ibn Sa'ud, who had become chief of the Wahabis, the ' Calvinists of Islam '. Hussein died in exile. Ibn Sa'ud seized all of Arabia with the exception of the Yemen.

In 1922 Great Britain had received a mandate over Palestine. Lord Balfour's Declaration, made in November 1917, had contained the solemn undertaking to the Jews that Great Britain would regard with favour the establishment in Palestine of a national home for them. The declaration had roused great hope among the Jewish people that the Promised Land was in sight; immigration to Palestine began and continued in the teeth of Arab hostility.

British imperial troubles

In December 1914 nominal Ottoman suzerainty of Egypt had come to an end and a British protectorate was set up.

In February 1922, after nationalist riots and strikes, Egypt obtained independence, although Great Britain continued to control her foreign and much of her internal policy. Fourteen years later complete Egyptian freedom was achieved by the treaty of August 1936, signed three months after the death of King Fuad and the accession of his young son Farouk. The treaty provided for the eventual withdrawal of British troops, which was, however, postponed by the Second World War.

Britain also resigned itself to Irish independence. The Irish elections of December 1918 gave an enormous majority to the revolutionary Sinn Fein party. In January 1919 De Valera, a rebel of 1916, was proclaimed President of the Irish Republic. A bitter interval of terrorism followed. Civil disorder was countered by British reprisals and a state of siege. Lloyd George, desperately eager to restore peace, forced a new Home Rule Bill through Parliament in December 1920 which provided for two Irish parliaments and two governments, one for the south in Dublin, and one in Belfast for Ulster, with a Federal Council to be elected by both parliaments. De Valera refused to recognise the secession of Ulster; but in December 1921 Lloyd George succeeded in persuading Collins, chief of the Irish Republican Army, and Griffith, founder of the Sinn Fein, to sign a treaty which established the 'Irish Free State'. The elections of June 1922 ratified this solution by an overwhelming majority. British troops were withdrawn, but Ireland remained a prey to civil war for another year and Collins was assassinated.

In India Gandhi was the spokesman of the national movement. In spite of his advocacy of non-violence, riots broke out and in April 1919 at Amritsar in the Panjab British troops fired on the crowd and killed four hundred people. The India Act of December 1919 was designed to bring about a progressive approach to responsible self-government but the campaigns of non-co-operation and civil disobedience continued.

The Far East

At the end of the First World War, China had for years been in a state of anarchy. In the last years of the Manchu Dynasty, the revolutionary and republican movement called the Kuomintang was led by Sun Yat-sen, who committed it to the regeneration of China by the adoption of the three Western principles of nationalism, democracy and socialism. His struggles from exile were crowned when he became first President of the Chinese Republic after the revolution of 1911. Almost at once he was replaced by Yuan Shih-kai, who had delivered the death blow to the Manchu Dynasty. Sun fled to Japan after a second unsuccessful revolution in 1913 and Yuan governed until his death in June 1916. China, at the mercy of its generals, was then split into fragments. Sun Yat-sen was elected President of the southern republic in May 1921, but was soon forced to flee. In 1923, he turned to Russia for help and, finally victorious, arrived at Peking, where he died in March 1925. Chaos and anarchy continued and Chinese nationalists protested violently against the injustice of treaties imposed on China by foreign powers and demanded a China for the Chinese. When in 1919 the Peace Conference awarded Shantung to Japan, China had refused to sign the Treaty of Versailles. The population, notably in Shanghai, rose against the concessions by which foreigners enjoyed

Mahatma Gandhi returned from Africa to India in 1914, and from then until his death in 1948 he was the leader and inspiration of Indian nationalism and its expression, the National Congress Party. *Popper*

special privileges. Soviet Russia had given aid to the Kuomintang and had, in the process, urged that Chinese Communists should co-operate with the national movement. The coalition produced great success. Chiang Kai-shek, a brother-in-law of Sun Yat-sen, who had become the chief figure in the Kuomintang, or Nationalist Party, seized Hankow, Nanking and Shanghai during 1926 and 1927. Then he turned on the Communists, beginning with a bloody purge of the Shanghai Communists. Nationalists and Communists, formerly allies, were from now on bitter enemies.

Japan had made good use of the war in Europe to pursue her political and economic expansion in China, to whom, in January 1919, she presented her 'Twenty-one Demands', by which she obtained numerous privileges. But Japan soon found herself without support. Under pressure from the United States and from the British Dominions, Great Britain did not in 1922 renew the old Anglo-Japanese alliance of 1902. Japanese efforts to penetrate China were momentarily checked. Japan restored Kiao-chow to China, withdrew her troops from Shantung and renounced many of the privileges she had obtained. In the name of Asian equilibrium the Nine-Power Agreement — the United States, Great Britain, France, Italy, Holland, Belgium, Portugal, Japan and China being the signatories — put a brake on Japanese expansion.

Europe after inflation

Europe, ruined by the war, now underwent a monetary inflation which brought about immense alterations in the structure of society. The currency of Central and Eastern Europe lost all value. The German mark fell to a one hundred thousandth part of its pre-war value: at the moment when inflation was at its worst — at the end of

1923 — an ordinary bus ticket cost one hundred and fifty thousand million marks. Such runaway inflation led to chaos and suffering which in many countries seemed almost more unbearable than the war itself had been.

Then between 1924 and 1929 Europe enjoyed a few years of hope — or at least of illusion — in a more relaxed atmosphere. In France the elections of May 1924 resulted in the victory of the Radical and Socialist coalition over the National Bloc, whose leader Millerand was obliged to give up the Presidency to Gaston Doumergue. Herriot's Ministry strove for better relations with London. But in April 1925 the financial crisis resulted in its fall; ephemeral governments followed until in June 1926 Poincaré formed a government of National Union. During this shifting of ministerial teams Briand remained in charge of Foreign Affairs from April 1925 almost to his death in 1932 and tried unremittingly to soften the terms of the Treaty of Versailles.

An improvement in Franco-German relations was made possible by the supple diplomacy of Stresemann who, like Briand, directed Foreign Affairs during the seven years between 1923 and 1929. When in February 1925 the President of the Reich, Friedrich Ebert, died at the age of fifty-four, four months before the term of his office expired, Field Marshal von Hindenburg, the victor of Tannenberg, was elected President of Germany by plebiscite. For several years he seemed to be the rock on which the republican regime rested — a regime accepted as the best in the circumstances and capable of raising Germany from the ruins of defeat. In Great Britain the Labour Party won the elections of December 1923 and Baldwin's Government was succeeded for a few months by that of Ramsay MacDonald before the Conservatives returned to power in October 1924. Baldwin's Secretary of State for Foreign Affairs was Austen Chamberlain, who worked amicably with Briand and Stresemann to further the cause of peace.

In 1924 the American Dawes plan, designed to ease the burden of reparations, came into effect. The Locarno agreements, concluded in 1925, seemed to offer great hope for the peace of Europe. In 1926 Germany became a member of the League of Nations. Europe was recovering, wounds were healing, currency was becoming stabilised and there was a brief period of prosperity. The spectre of international upheaval receded and so did that of world revolution of the proletariat. In 1921 Russia found it necessary to replace belligerent communism by a new economic policy — the NEP — which marked a seven-year retreat during which essential transition measures were adopted: the suppression of requisitions, the restoration of some commercial freedom and a temporary reversion towards a market economy. Lenin's health broke down in the summer of 1922 and in January 1924 he died at the early age of fifty-three. A period of uncertainty followed. Trotsky, the Commissar for War, considered himself as Lenin's heir, the natural leader of the Party and of the State, chief not only of Soviet Russia but of international communism. It was, however, the general secretary of the central committee of the Communist Party, Joseph Stalin, who by cunningly concentrating power in his own hands little by little took over the supreme position which Lenin had occupied. Stalin took several years to achieve this position, but finally his success was total and the Soviet State revolved about him.

While the Soviet regime was taking root it limited its efforts to expand; it was at first essential to concentrate on establishing the system in Russia itself. Trotsky insisted on demanding ' a permanent revolution in the name of communist principles' but Stalin, calculating what was and what was not possible, proposed first of all to make Russia a great industrial and military power. His policy was to give the Soviet Union the internal economic self-sufficiency required to face danger from abroad. Trotsky was relieved of his official functions in January 1925, expelled from the Communist Party in December 1927, and in January 1929 exiled. The official party line became Stalinism, which struggled to suppress all ' deviations' and, in its shifts of policy, liquidated many old Bolsheviks who claimed to return to the line formerly followed by Lenin. From 1934 purges of extreme violence became common and did much to convince foreign observers that the regime was fundamentally unsound.

Trotsky accused Stalin of a narrow, nationalist attitude to communism. Stalin, however, was of the opinion that even in the midst of a capitalist world it was possible to erect a single socialist state, providing that that state was a great nation — ' not a Montenegro but a Russia '. To make the Soviet Republic impregnable he therefore inaugurated in 1928 the enormous effort known as the ' Five-Year Plan ' which was to be followed by further five-year plans. By these plans Russian industrialisation proceeded at a furious pace. From 1929, the key year, Stalin resumed the orthodox line in respect of the collectivisation of farms. Industrial progress demanded a corresponding improvement in agricultural production — factory workers had to be fed. This was only possible by growing crops on a large scale and employing modern methods such as the use of tractors and agricultural machinery. The peasants were grouped on collective farms and agrarian collectivisation proceeded at an increasingly rapid rate. Large peasant proprietors — the *kulaks* — were liquidated, as other capitalist elements had been disposed of ten years earlier.

The world economic crisis

While within Russia these great changes were taking place the rest of the world was stricken by a new economic crisis. The slump began in the autumn of 1929, with the crash of the New York Stock Exchange, when the financial structure of the whole world was shaken to its foundations. No continent escaped the catastrophe, but in Europe its consequences were tragic. The slump swept Germany like a hurricane, leaving wreckage and despair in its wake. Without this disaster it is possible that the Nazis might never have risen to power. Fate itself seemed to have pronounced against the maintenance of peace. Stresemann, perhaps the sole man who was capable of altering the course of events which led to the Second World War, died in October, a few days before the Wall Street crash.

The slump struck the United States with full force and put an end to the reign of the Republicans. There

Bushman painting of South Africa. A Grinqua (*top*) in the employ of the posse of white farmers (*below*) on the track of cattle rustlers. *H. C. Woodhouse*

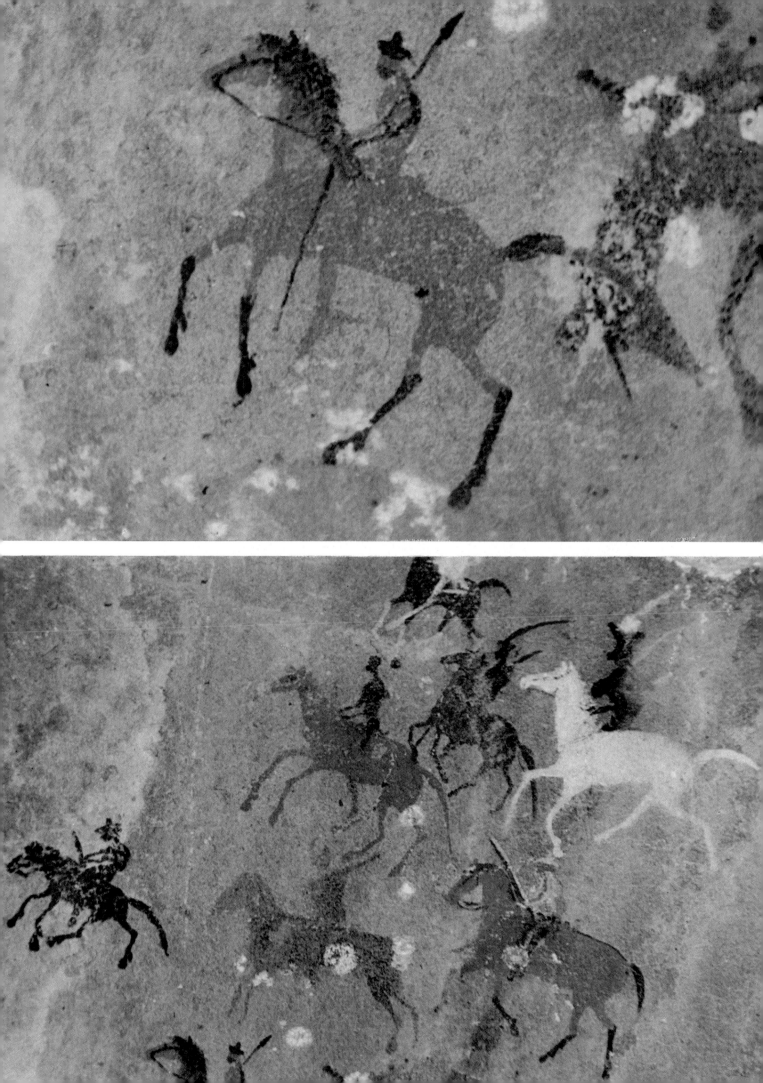

had been three Republican Presidents since the war: Harding, Coolidge and Hoover. Franklin Delano Roosevelt, a Democrat, was elected in November 1932 and introduced economic and social reforms of such scope and novelty that they might be said to constitute a revolution — the New Deal.

In Great Britain the elections of May 1929 resulted in the defeat of Stanley Baldwin and the formation of a Labour Government under Ramsay MacDonald. But the economic crisis was so grave that in August 1931 MacDonald was obliged to form a coalition, the National Government, which included Conservatives, Liberals and a splinter group of the Labour Party. The coalition was effectively a Conservative Government, though under Baldwin, who succeeded MacDonald in June 1935, and Neville Chamberlain, who became Prime Minister in May 1937, it continued to be called a 'National' Government. On the death of George V in January 1936 the Prince of Wales became King as Edward VIII but abdicated before he was crowned In December 1936 his brother George VI succeeded to the throne.

Since 1910 Portugal had lived through some twenty revolutions. This era of perpetual political convulsion ended in 1926 with a conservative dictatorship. In that year the republic collapsed and a military dictatorship was soon followed by the birth of a 'New State' under Dr Salazar, who was at first Minister of Finance and then in 1932 Chief of the Government.

In the Far East momentous events were taking place. In April 1927 Baron Tanaka became Prime Minister and Minister of Foreign Affairs of Japan. During the two years he was in power Tanaka substituted for Japan's previous 'policy of friendship towards China' a 'positive policy' which was based on military ambitions. The 'Manchu Incident' in September 1931 provided Tokyo with an excuse to resort to force against China. An explosion had taken place near Mukden, in the neighbourhood of the South Manchurian Railway, which was guarded by Japanese troops. The Japanese at once occupied numerous towns under pretext of preventing acts of sabotage. It was in vain that the League of Nations — after inviting the United States to participate in its sessions — demanded the evacuation of the areas which the Japanese had occupied. The Japanese had undertaken the conquest of Manchuria and of Jehol, a former province of China in Inner Mongolia. In January 1932 they landed at Shanghai, where they encountered energetic Chinese resistance. Under the Emperor of the old Manchu Dynasty they set up a puppet state called Manchukuo. Following an agreement with the League of Nations Japan formally withdrew from Manchukuo in March 1933.

Nazism

In April 1930 the Chancellorship of Brüning, a Catholic who, in order to have a free hand to deal with the economic crisis, wished to govern Germany without the collaboration of the Socialists, marked the beginning of the end of

Carved wooden figure believed to represent the fishermen's god Tarianui (great ears). Hervey Islands. British Museum

In its symbolism and myths the Nazi movement expressed the primitivism that lay at the roots of its practice and ideology. The swastika became its most famous distinguishing totem. *Bavaria Verlag*

A Nazi artist's interpretation of the *Putsch* preparations in 1923, when a Nazi attempt to seize power in Munich was easily put down and Hitler was imprisoned for five years. *Radio Times Hulton Picture Library*

the Weimar Republic. Brüning dissolved the *Reichstag* and the elections of September 1930 resulted in Hitler's first success. The deflationary measures for which Brüning was responsible were extremely unpopular in a country which counted some six million unemployed. The two years of his rule by emergency decree swelled the ranks of Hitler's followers and those of the German Communists. At this date Hitler himself, an Austrian by birth, was not even a German citizen. It was not until 1932 that he acquired German nationality as a result of his appointment by a National Socialist Minister to a position in the small state of Brunswick. In April 1932 he had the audacity 369

x

The Imperial General Staff tradition succumbs to the power of the Vienna gutter. Hindenburg, President of the German Republic, accepts the leader of the Nazi Party as Chancellor of Germany, 30 January 1933. *Keystone Press*

to present himself in the elections as a presidential candidate. His opponent was none other than Field Marshal von Hindenburg, whose seven-year term of office had expired and who, despite his advanced age (eighty-five), had decided to stand for re-election. Hitler was beaten, but obtained nearly fourteen million votes. Hindenburg, eight weeks after his arduous presidential campaign, dismissed Brüning and asked Franz von Papen to form a Government. Von Papen was a new man of the Catholic Centre Party whose political role had been obscure. He formed an authoritarian Government, a ' cabinet of Junkers '.

The Nazis enjoyed great advantages in money, organised forces for street-brawls and the fear of communism. The elections of July 1932 were a triumph for Hitler. As he was leader of the majority party it seemed obvious that he must now be asked by the President of the Reich to form a Government. But Hitler insisted on imposing his own programme, and was uncompromising in his demands. Hindenburg intimated that he would refuse to tolerate Hitler as Chancellor. The *Reichstag*, having elected Goering as President, was again dissolved. In the subsequent elections — those of November 1932 — the Nazis did less well, polling two million fewer votes than in July. But von Papen, in spite of this relative success, was still unsure of a parliamentary majority, while the army admitted that it was incapable of permanently maintaining public order if it had to deal with the National Socialists and at the same time with the Communists.

General von Schleicher, who had backed von Papen for the Chancellorship, was made War Minister and in December 1932 became Chancellor himself. He formed a Government from which he excluded members of the Nazi Party, despite the efforts of Gregor Strasser, one of the chief theo-

reticians of National Socialism, who hoped for the position of Vice-Chancellor. Schleicher's Government lasted only two months, having incurred the hostility not only of Hitler but of von Papen himself, who held Schleicher responsible for his own downfall. To repel the Nazi danger Schleicher was prepared for a restoration of the monarchy, though he was also accused of Bolshevik tendencies.

President Hindenburg dismissed Schleicher, and on 30 January 1933 called to power the candidate whom he had defeated in the presidential elections nine months earlier: Adolf Hitler. It was a plunge into the unknown.

Europe in 1933-4

The Europe which Hitler found on his accession to the Chancellorship was in a state of chaos which gave his wild ambitions full scope. In most countries domestic policy was inextricably entangled with foreign policy. The attitude towards communism and fascism within various countries directly affected their external policy towards the Soviet Union on the one hand and towards Nazi Germany on the other. Politics and ideology were linked as they had not been for three centuries. Fascism had spread in all directions: dictatorships had already been set up — although in various and dissimilar forms — in Russia, in Turkey, and since 1920 in Hungary; since 1922 in Italy, since 1926 in Poland and since 1929 in Portugal; finally in Yugoslavia a dictatorship was established by Alexander, the Yugoslav king who in October 1934 would be assassinated in Marseilles. Dictatorship was now established in Germany, in Austria, in Bulgaria, in the Baltic states and in Greece.

Meanwhile France was passing through an extremely difficult period. The financial situation had since 1932 again become critical. Feeble Governments followed each other at an accelerated rhythm. In January 1934 the Stavisky affair shocked the world as an unprecedented example of financial corruption. The savings of thousands of innocent people had been pocketed by swindlers, and the scandal was quickly exploited by enemies of the parliamentary majority. On February 6 Parliament strongly supported Daladier's Government and a mob gathered in the Place de la Concorde with the intention of assaulting the Chamber of Deputies. It left behind it some twenty dead and several hundred wounded. A Government of appeasement, a new ' National Union ', was formed by the former President of the Republic, Doumergue; but the country remained divided and seething with resentment. Fascist leagues appeared and clashed with the Communists. Even in Britain a handful of fascists appealed for a while to some of the frustrated and unbalanced victims of economic depression and fear of communism.

The Spanish Civil War

Spain was even more agitated. In December 1923 Primo de Rivera, Captain-General of Catalonia, had encountered no resistance when he seized power, after having accused the parliamentary government of leading the country to ruin. It was a return to the old Spanish tradition of the *pronunciamiento*: once more the army had pronounced its will. Alfonso XIII entrusted the government to Primo de Rivera who, though arbitrary, was a dictator of some mildness and charm and restored outward order. A brief

Guernica, by Picasso. The heavy bombing of this Spanish town in 1937 horrified world opinion, but both sides in the Second World War killed more civilians. *Giraudon*

'golden age' began. The calm was superficial, however, and discontent increased. In January 1930 the King abruptly withdrew his support from Primo de Rivera. Alfonso's intention was to return to the system of alternate Liberal and Conservative Governments — the ' rotative system ' — which had been the pattern in Spain since the nineteenth century. But the last monarchical Governments found themselves unable to control the upsurge of republicanism. In the municipal elections of April 1931 the Republicans won an overwhelming majority. Alfonso XIII bowed to this electoral decision and left Spain.

Alcalá Zamora, an Andalusian, became head of a weak provisional government which was incapable of maintaining order: riots broke out in various parts of Spain, during which convents and churches were pillaged and burned. In June 1931 a constituent *Cortes* was elected and the success of the Republican coalition was confirmed by the voters. Alcalá Zamora was elected President of the Spanish Republic in December 1931. Torn between the Right and the Left, he attempted in vain to steer a central course.

For two years the country was governed by the Socialist majority led by Manuel Azaña. In August 1932 there had been a military insurrection which was put down without difficulty. Then the elections of November 1933 resulted in the victory of the CEDA, or *Confederación Española de Derechas Autónomas* — in other words of the Catholic Party. Directed by Gil Robles, it relied on the support of various right-wing groups. One result was the revolution of October 1934 when Catalan Nationalists, Socialists and Asturian miners rose, giving Spain a foretaste of the tragic events in store. There were strikes throughout Spain. Azaña was imprisoned and the insurrection harshly suppressed. In the beginning of 1936 Alcalá Zamora, hoping that a Centre Party would at last emerge between the violent extremes of the Right and the Left, dissolved the *Cortes*. But in the elections of 18 February 1936 the

Popular Front emerged victorious. Azaña again became Prime Minister and in May President of the Republic.

The situation now rapidly deteriorated. The State was powerless to deal with the violence of antagonistic elements, and had proved incapable of carrying out necessary reforms. Calvo Sotelo, a former Conservative minister and moral chief of the Opposition, was murdered two days after a Communist Deputy was alleged to have openly threatened his life. Four days later, on July 17, a military uprising began with the aim of restoring ' order '. The Generals' plot had been long matured and Franco was not at first its sole leader, although circumstances were to make him so. This time the *pronunciamiento* was not immediately successful, as it had been in 1923. Instead it was the signal for a pitiless civil war which did not end until March 1939, when nearly a million had died, Madrid had capitulated and General Franco had achieved total victory. While the Western Powers were engaged in interminable conferences designed to maintain ' the farce of neutrality ', the international forces of communism and fascism employed the bloodstained soil of Spain as a convenient field for experiment and manoeuvre, testing weapons and preparing for the approach of the Second World War.

Science, literature and the arts from 1914 to 1938

By 1914, the accepted fundamentals of the various branches of science had been found to be less secure than the materialists at the end of the preceding century had supposed. Scientists began to feel the necessity of re-examining problems, and sometimes in the process they hit upon unsuspected discoveries. But the striking feature of the new approach was its implications for philosophical questions — the different solutions obtained were often less significant than the way in which problems were examined in a heretofore unfamiliar intellectual context. 371

The validity of mathematical axioms, the assumptions of logic, determinism in physics, the reality of Euclidean space, the continuity of evolution in living creatures, and so forth, were all called in question. In order to find one's way from day to day in a world of reality which was always unexpected and always changing, new ways of thought were required, and old principles had to be jettisoned. The existentialist philosophers renounced the objectivity of the scientist, to whom man was primarily an object of physical and biological interest, or of historical and ethnological study. They sought instead to consider the individual as the product of his destiny, which could be shaped by the exercise of his will in face of the potentialities which are his existence. Predetermination was denied and no dogmatic solutions of eternal questions were possible. This new humanism — a new attempt to make man the self-sufficient centre of the universe — strongly influenced novelists, playwrights and poets all over the world, and led some eventually to Marxist materialism while to others it supplied arguments for remaining loyal to their traditions or religious beliefs. Psycho-analysis, on the other hand, offered a methodical exploration of the world of dreams, of neuroses, of the unconscious and of the roots of mundane human reality. It inspired writers and artists to produce works in which the problems of sex were considered without reference to a system of morality founded on the concept of original sin. Sigmund Freud expressed in scientific terms many phenomena which before him few had dared to consider, and none had been able to explain. Finally it may be noted that the spirit of free enquiry often clashed dramatically with the official totalitarian philosophy of certain nations, fascist and communist alike.

Never had so much interest been taken in literature. Not only did magazines of huge circulation reach millions of readers, but the success of weeklies of more purely literary interest bore witness to the desire and social need for specialised critical, intellectual and artistic information. In spite of the development of expression by means of images — posters, motion pictures, illuminated signs, the comic strip, the many new applications of photography — the written word maintained its prestige as the world grew more literate with the spread of education. The new hunger for information was, not unexpectedly, exploited by certain governments and political parties. Between the literature of propaganda and 'engaged' literature the free and disinterested writer often found it hard to make a living. Such authors took refuge in individualism or, like André Gide, went so far as to accord value only to acts devoid of all human significance other than the pursuit of pleasure. The novel was the most widely practised literary form, and its popularity was fanned by powerful publicity campaigns, book clubs, cheap editions and, on the continent, by literary prizes such as the Prix Goncourt which helped to make famous the work of Marcel Proust, the greatest twentieth-century writer to exploit and enlarge the traditional novel form. It was the age of the bestseller, of *Grand Hotel*, of *Gone with the Wind*. The First World War inspired a series of vivid works, of which Erich Maria Remarque's *All Quiet on the Western Front* was the most famous. More influential in literary history was James Joyce's experimental novel *Ulysses*, which created a new school of English prose. In France the tradition of Balzac's *Comédie Humaine*,

dealing in a series of novels with a vast canvas of inter-related characters, was revived by Romain Rolland, Duhamel and Jules Romains. Similarly in England Galsworthy wrote the saga of the Forsytes, and in Germany Thomas Mann that of the Buddenbrooks. In the United States, social preoccupations of a different sort appeared in the works of Dreiser, Dos Passos, Steinbeck and Sinclair Lewis. All these writers, and many others, were read mainly by the middle-class cultural élite which had been one of the finest achievements of nineteenth-century capitalism. But even this comparatively restricted class was not able to assimilate all the literary experiment which was going forward. Culture was being more and more fragmented not only by the philosophical and scientific questions which eroded its foundations, but by impatience with traditional forms which led many artists to reject the the idioms familiar to their audience. An epoch was marked in English poetry by the work of T. S. Eliot, which seemed obscure and difficult to the traditional reader of poetry. In the 1930s political and social influences also came into play to restrict the audience to which the poet could appeal.

At the same time, mass culture was being influenced by quite different forces. Apart from the sensational cheap press the vast popularity of the detective-story, especially in the English-speaking world, was the only literary manifestation of this. Much more important was the radio, which from 1920 onwards devoted more and more time to literary, artistic and especially to musical activities. For the great public, however, athletics — or rather watching athletic spectacles — became the rage. Crowds were attracted to international football matches, Olympic games, Wimbledon tennis, the Tour de France, motor races. Motion pictures had not only invaded village halls and taken over theatres which had once housed live drama, but huge new buildings had been erected for the purpose of accommodating large audiences. What the theatre lost financially as the purveyor of cheap entertainment it gained in artistic and intellectual quality. Its role as a social commentator, initiated by Ibsen, led it to experiment and attempt more ambitious themes, tackle philosophical and psychological subjects, analyse the political and social problems of the day. The theatre attracted serious authors. Motion pictures followed a different course. Usurping the theatre's functions as entertainer of the masses, they rapidly gave rise to a vast industry which, centred at first in Hollywood, enjoyed great prosperity and attracted actors and directors from Europe as well as from America. Early productions were not unexpectedly naïve, and while they imitated the theatre the evolution of an individual art form was faltering. Action, spectacle and comedy were the fields in which they surpassed. Charlie Chaplin, an English actor in Hollywood, created a universal type of little man, half-funny, half-pathetic, which endeared him to the world. Spectacular films like *Ben Hur* and *The Four Horsemen of the Apocalypse* thrilled millions, while 'Western' and 'Gangster' films drew immense audiences. In 1927 the silent pictures gave way to the 'Talkies'. The motion picture soon discovered those techniques which are peculiarly its own, and, drawing inspiration from continental developments — German expressionism, Russian dramatic power, French wit and charm, British documentary skill — was well on the way to achieving its right to be called the 'seventh art'. It continued, however, to remain a fundamentally commercial creative form, while its direct appeal to the unselective multitude made it a powerful means of propaganda which totalitarian governments did not fail to make use of. Towards the end of the period television made its appearance, the first practical demonstration having been given in 1926 by J. L. Baird. The first high-definition television service in the world began in November 1936 with the opening of the British Broadcasting Corporation's transmitting station at Alexandra Palace in London. The new means of communication and expression would rapidly sweep the world.

In music it was a period of experiment and of revolt, not only against the classical forms and traditions of Brahms, but against Wagnerian chromaticism and the impressionism of Debussy. The old distinction between discord and concord had broken down, and the key system itself was largely abandoned. But though romanticism was abjured, emotional content was by no means missing. Four composers dominate the era, though all were born in the last decades of the nineteenth century: the Austrian Schönberg, the Hungarian Bartok, the German Hindemith and the expatriate Russian Stravinsky. Jazz had invaded Europe from America, where it had emerged from ragtime, brought from Africa by Negro slaves and matured in New Orleans, St Louis and Harlem with the co-operation, often enthusiastic, sometimes commercial, of white musicians, notably Irving Berlin. It conquered war-weary Europe and its influence was felt in the works of 'serious' composers and in the so-called classical orchestra, which was enriched by surprising new sounds and instrumental techniques; these trends were strikingly illustrated by Stravinsky's work of the early twenties. Many European composers were influenced by jazz and even the stately Viennese Opera presented a jazz opera, *Jonny spielt auf*, by Krenek.

The reconstruction of towns and villages devastated by the war produced disappointingly few results of architectural or aesthetic interest, and opportunities for town-planning were neglected. Both in detail and in over-all planning the chief effort was to restore pre-war appearances, to modify streets, parks and buildings as little as possible. Gothic churches were even reconstructed in reinforced concrete. In Britain, however, garden cities were built. In France the housing problem was solved by the construction of huge blocks of flats at modest rentals. In the U.S.S.R. the abolition of private property facilitated the task of urban planners. Russian architecture, at first functional, reverted to neo-classicism as soon as the Soviet authorities decided that the proletarian masses, too, were entitled to columns, capitals and pediments. The idea of planning in the building industry and its future industrialisation was, however, advocated both by the teaching and practice of Walter Gropius, founder of the *Bauhaus* in Weimar, and by Le Corbusier, a Frenchman of Swiss origin, who put forward the doctrine that 'a house is a machine for living in'.

In painting most of the French Cubists and *Fauves* had by 1910 abandoned their wilder extravagances. Matisse returned to a decorative flowing line and the use of fresh, harmonious colours. Friesz, in the footsteps of Cézanne, rediscovered the virtues of logical composition and simple tones. Derain was also reconverted to the old classical spirit. Braque, once so obscure, seemed to be on the way to joining the traditionalists. The champion of the great and irreversible revolution which had taken place in

painting remained the Spanish genius Picasso. He experimented ceaselessly with every form of painting, and his influence was world-wide. He worked in Paris, which for artists had become the world capital of modernism. Indeed the school which then existed in Paris was comparable to the school of Rome in the seventeenth century. Russians like Soutine and Chagall, Italians like Modigliani and Chirico, Japanese like Foujita, Bulgarians like Pascin, all worked in Paris and made disciples. Surrealism, basing its theories on Freud and the poets, revived careful craftsmanship and precision in drawing in its depiction of the irrational, the delirious and the hallucinatory. In a reaction against the excesses of intellectualism passionate interest was taken in the art of simple peoples, those who painted by instinct, like Utrillo, and in modern primitives, heirs of the 'Douanier' Rousseau, such as Bauchant. Thanks to the experience of the great collectors of the nineteenth century who, by acquiring the work of painters praised by competent critics, had finally realised handsome financial profits, paintings had now become objects of speculation, and a lively market for them existed. Sculpture, more awkward to handle, was less in demand. After 1918 the proliferation of war memorials almost always resulted, from the artistic point of view, in deplorable productions. French classicism was represented by Maillol, whose nudes were in the tradition of Rodin, and other outstanding sculptors were the Roumanian Brancusi, the Russian Zadkine, the Croat Mestrovic and the New York-born Epstein.

The industrial revolution continued; mass production had improved manufacturing efficiency and scientific research had yielded fruitful discoveries. Synthetic products had begun to make their appearance: artificial rubber, plastic materials, fibro-cement. The pharmaceutical range was enriched by new medicines: insulin, vitamins, sulfa drugs, which in a matter of days cured diseases once fatal. Radio and television services were based on important new technical achievements. New elementary particles were discovered — the neutron and the positron in 1932 — and a rapid development of the understanding of nuclear structure followed. Wave mechanism and quantum theory revolutionised the physicist's approach to the properties of matter; experiments with heavy water, the transmutation of elements, artificial radio-activity and the fission of uranium foretold the imminent liberation of atomic energy.

The bathysphere explored the sea to a depth of 2,975 feet, while the old-fashioned balloon reached a height of 72,000 feet, unknown at the time to aircraft. A transatlantic passenger service by air was still provided only by dirigible, but in 1919 Alcock and Brown had flown the Atlantic for the first time in an aircraft. By 1939 such long-range flights were common, the world speed record stood at over 400 m.p.h. and the first jet aircraft were being conceived.

Origins of the Second World War

Unlike the events of August 1914 the war which began in September 1939 took few by surprise except, perhaps, the aggressor. Adolf Hitler had made no secret of his aims or the means by which he proposed to achieve them; he did not expect the invasion of Poland to provoke a world war. His previous successes had given him more and more confidence and he easily overrode the objections of German diplomats and generals.

The Western Powers, faced with the fearful threat of

war, chose the path which in fact led to war by adopting the 'policy of appeasement'. The assumption that Hitler's aims, if grandiose, were none the less not without limit allowed Hitler to annul one by one the points in the Versailles Treaty to which Germany objected. Almost no attempt was made to prevent his doing so, and the zeal which the recent victors displayed to satisfy him only increased his appetite. Self-determination, the principle upheld by Woodrow Wilson at Versailles, was now invoked to justify the re-incorporation of German communities abroad into the new Reich. Astutely Hitler absorbed his victims one after the other, proclaiming each to be his last, and the comprehensive benevolence of his adversaries did little to discourage further excesses. Germany, which within a few years had spent ninety thousand million marks on rearming, had again become a formidable military power. Sooner or later war was inevitable. It could have been avoided only if Hitler had been convinced that it would certainly result in his own downfall and the defeat of his people. There was nothing to convince him of this.

The last occasion when he might have been persuaded was in March 1936 when Germany reoccupied the Rhineland, which had been demilitarised not only at Versailles but by the Locarno agreements. France felt too weak to take action without the support of Great Britain and Belgium. According to the judgment of Winston Churchill in his memoirs — the decision to do so might nevertheless have been taken had France had a Clemenceau to guide her. It was on the eve of a general election and Albert Sarraut, the Premier, declared that he would not leave Strasbourg at the mercy of German artillery. His military advisers, however, replied that general mobilisation would be required to meet the German threat and that general mobilisation would lead to war in earnest. It was decided to do nothing. From the reoccupation of the Rhineland the course of events, hastened by Hitler's fits of impatience, ran more swiftly to their tragic outcome. The League of Nations had been reduced to impotence and there remained nothing to restrain Germany from waging war except Italy and the Soviet Union.

The formation of the Axis

Great Britain and France still nursed the illusion that their combined force was sufficient to contain the threat of German expansion — the 'need', as the Nazis put it, for *Lebensraum*. It was confidently believed that Hitler would draw back at the last moment unless he was convinced — as the German leaders in 1914 had been — that Great Britain would remain neutral. The British in fact continued to repeat that they would intervene. But Hitler had made a careful study, as he thought, of the strength of each European power. He grossly overestimated the military importance of Fascist Italy, so proud of its air force and fleet. Italy, like France, desired to maintain the independence of Austria. When in July 1934 the Austrian Chancellor Dollfuss was assassinated, Mussolini reacted with energy and dispatched Italian troops to the Brenner Pass on the frontier. Franco-Italian relations had become excellent: agreements between the general staffs of the two countries provided that an Italian army corps would be sent to the Belfort region in case of war with Germany. Italy then attacked Ethiopia and the ensuing war led to

a diplomatic rupture between Italy and Great Britain. This was followed in November 1936 by the Rome-Berlin Axis and a military pact between Germany and Italy. Nevertheless, even at the last moment and after Italy had in April 1939 absorbed Albania in compensation for German gains in Austria and Czechoslovakia, Italian diplomacy strove to prevent the outbreak of war.

The policy of the Soviet Union

Hitler had overestimated the power of Fascist Italy; he underestimated that of the U.S.S.R., for whose army he had little respect. The military experts of all countries affirmed that sixty per cent of Russia's senior officers had been liquidated in Stalin's purges, and agreed that the Russian army could only be used defensively. With a Germany growing stronger and stronger as her neighbour, Russia desired peace. For this reason in 1934 Russia joined the League of Nations, from which until then the Soviets had turned in derision. Meanwhile Nazi Germany had proclaimed its mission as the champion of Europe in the struggle against Bolshevism and this deceived some people. In November 1936 the Nazis concluded an Anti-Comintern pact with Japan, and a year later with Italy, and invited other nations to join. The fighting forces of the rival ideologies confronted each other in Spain during the Civil War. Soviet Russia was at the time going through a crisis which, in the event, proved to be nothing more serious than growing-pains.

The policy of France

France, deeply pacifist in feeling and bound to a Great Britain which was even more pacifist, had from 1935 been allied to the Soviet Union by a pact of mutual assistance, the terms of which were vague in the extreme and contained little of positive value. France was also the victim of social unrest that in May 1936 became acute after the electoral success of the 'Popular Front' which, for the first time, led to a Socialist Government. Leon Blum formed a Cabinet. When in the autumn of 1937 the French Minister of Foreign Affairs — Yvon Delbos — made a tour of those countries friendly with France, he visited Warsaw, Prague, Bucharest and Belgrade — but not Moscow. It appeared that the diplomatic edifice erected in 1921 was crumbling. Poland, allied to France, had since 1934 also been allied to Germany by a pact of friendship. The 'Little *Entente*' which united the states which succeeded the Habsburg Monarchy — Czechoslovakia, Yugoslavia and Roumania — also broke up. In Yugoslavia the underhand dealings of the Prime Minister, Stoyadinovich, gave cause for alarm, while Roumania, infected by Nazi propaganda and anti-semitism, was allied to Poland, which daily became more anti-Czech.

The 'Anschluss' and Munich

Meanwhile the military power of Germany continued to grow rapidly. In the early spring of 1938 the Western democracies looked on helplessly while Austria was annexed by Hitler. The swastika waved over Vienna on 13 March 1938. Kurt von Schuschnigg, the Austrian Chancellor, made desperate efforts after his interview with Hitler at Berchtesgaden to ward off the arrival of the Nazis. But he only precipitated matters by altering Hitler's timetable. The *Anschluss* — or attachment of Austria — suddenly decided Hitler to hasten the course of operations originally planned to take place at a much slower pace. The ease with which Austria had fallen into his hands made him sure that his personal instincts were superior to the pedestrian arguments of his advisers. After Austria, it was soon the turn of Czechoslovakia. Czechoslovakia was a Slav nation, a Russian ally, and possibly the only country which could have made the Soviet Union stir from the isolation in which she was entrenched. The Czechoslovakian crisis of 1938 was not, in fact, resolved by war, since on September 29 at Munich it was patched up by an arrangement which preserved peace at the price of Czechoslovakia — an arrangement by which that unfortunate country was abandoned by the Western Powers and left, as Mussolini cynically remarked, like a sausage to be sliced up by all who cared to help themselves. As far as Poland was concerned, the defection of Colonel Beck, the Polish Minister of Foreign Affairs, led to tragic vacillation among those who had presented a defensive front to Germany. Already in 1934 Poland had concluded a pact of friendship with the Reich; Polish greed and blindness now led Beck to claim some of the spoils of Czechoslovakia and he seized the Silesian town of Teschen.

The Soviet Union was gravely disturbed at the betrayal of Czechoslovakia by the Western Powers, and also by the Munich Conference itself, to which Russia had not been invited. Proceeding as always by devious and underground methods, Soviet diplomacy was to decide upon a total reversal of previous policy with regard to Nazi Germany. Only a few days after Munich a Russian diplomat told the French Ambassador that Russia had been left with no alternative but a fourth partition of Poland.

At Munich the Treaty of Versailles was at last torn up, and with it all the pacts which had been signed to reinforce it. But Munich was not sufficient to satisfy Hitler's insatiable appetite, and in the middle of March 1939 all Slovakia was placed under the 'tutelage' of Berlin; Bohemia and Moravia were integrated in the Third Reich under a 'protector', in whose estimation 'one or two generations would be sufficient to transform the Czech people into a historical curiosity'.

By this time, in Great Britain especially, it was felt that the appeasement of Hitler had gone far enough and no further compromise was possible. The British, who had never wished to become involved in the complications of Central and Eastern Europe, and who had obstinately preferred a dubious compromise to a straightforward settlement, if settlement implied the necessity of assuming responsibility of any kind, suddenly began to offer guarantees to states threatened by Hitler's ambitions. Above all, Great Britain guaranteed the integrity of Poland, for whom she had never shown the slightest concern hitherto.

The German invasion of Poland

Hitler at first believed he could come to a satisfactory arrangement with Colonel Beck. He had very carefully made no claim on the Polish 'corridor' which, since 1919, had separated East Prussia from the remainder of Germany. He limited his demands — made, however, only three weeks after Munich — to the right to construct an extra-territorial passage — i.e. a military road — through the

Neville Chamberlain, Prime Minister of Great Britain 1937–40, meeting Benito Mussolini, *Duce* of Italy, at Munich, 1938, where the chance of effective Czech resistance to Germany was undermined by her friends. *Keystone Press*

corridor, and the political return to the Reich of Danzig, Polish economic privileges in Danzig to be respected. Danzig was in reality a German city, and since no one could pretend it was Polish it had been made a free city by the Treaty of Versailles. The free city of Danzig, with its three hundred thousand inhabitants, might seem to be of little significance when compared to the three and a half million inhabitants of the Sudetenland who had just been detached from Czechoslovakia at Munich; but national sentiment in Warsaw was outraged at the suggestion of losing Danzig.

The events of March 1939, when Prague was occupied by the Germans and Memel re-annexed by the Reich, revealed to the Poles the extent of their peril. They would, however, cede nothing and, if necessary, fight the Germans single-handed. The Poles believed in their army, which had thrown back the Russians in 1929; Polish courage would now face German numerical superiority.

The reversal of Soviet policy

The Poles were reluctant to accept Russian help, distrusting Soviet troops who could so easily enter Poland on the pretext of confronting the Germans and, instead of fighting them, simply occupy eastern Poland themselves. It was on this point that the never very enthusiastic Western attempts to obtain a guarantee from the Soviet Union against German encroachments broke down.

The Kremlin calculated that war between Germany and Poland was inevitable and that the defeat of Poland was certain. It therefore seemed wise to avoid the conflict for the moment in order to intervene later when the adversaries had been exhausted by war and the cause of world revolution could be better served. In the meantime, it would be possible to restore the territorial frontiers of 1914, at least in part, to recover not only a large part of Poland itself, but to reoccupy the former Baltic provinces — those 'windows' on the West and seaports which Peter the Great had conquered for his country, provinces which in Peter's day had numbered some thirteen million inhabitants and now contained two hundred million. A Nazi-Bolshevik alliance had seemed the last possibility in the world. Stalin none the less concluded the pact of friendship which enabled Hitler to start the Second World War. 375

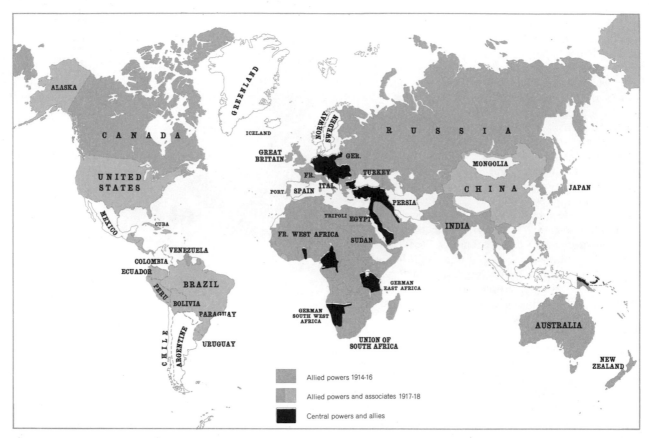

THE WORLD IN WORLD WAR I

Allied powers 1914-16

Allied powers and associates 1917-18

Central powers and allies

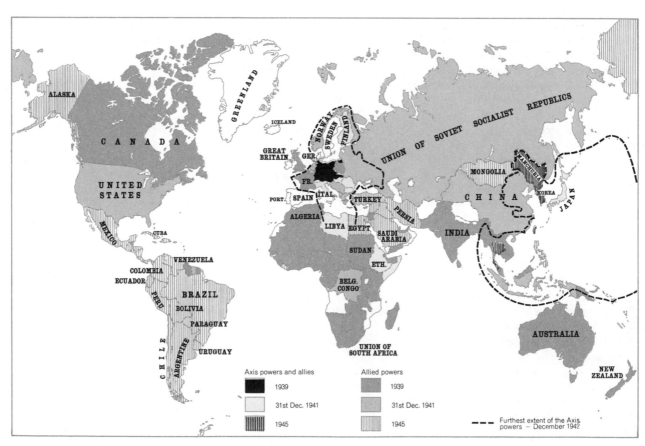

THE WORLD IN WORLD WAR II

Axis powers and allies

1939

31st Dec. 1941

1945

Allied powers

1939

31st Dec. 1941

1945

Furthest extent of the Axis powers – December 1942

CHAPTER NINETEEN

THE SECOND WORLD WAR

Before it finished, the Second World War had led to
fighting over a far larger area of the globe than had the
First. It was fought, moreover, with more powerful
weapons and in a more unrestricted way; civilian populations might, in certain localities, have suffered as much
in the past, but they had never been so completely involved
in the processes of warfare in such great numbers. This
led to an enormous extension of the powers of the State;
in all the great combatant nations, labour was controlled,
economic life re-directed and personal liberties suspended
on an unprecedented scale. In part, this explains the
treatment of civilian populations as legitimate strategic
targets for blockade, bombing and propaganda offensives.
Yet, oddly enough, the decisive battles were still those
of the armed forces. These were given enormously increased
range and mobility by the mechanisation of armies and
the addition of air power and, as a result, land warfare
emerged from the bloody stagnation which seemed to have
been imposed on it in the First World War. At sea,
aircraft took over more and more of the duties of surface
vessels and engagements between capital ships were rare;
instead, in the great Pacific battles, fleets of aircraft-
carriers fought one another at ranges of two or three
hundred miles. In such fighting, the technician and scientist
became more and more important. By 1945, it was already
clear that pilotless aircraft and rocket missiles were about
to change the nature of warfare yet again and would,
in the foreseeable future, make the aircraft itself obsolete
as a means of delivering firepower. The explosion of two
atomic bombs was the final demonstration of the dangerous
power now made available for the pursuit of political
aims: happily, these terrible weapons were in the hands
of a pacific nation, uninterested in imposing its will on
another's and anxious to construct a viable world order
on the basis of co-operation.

The Polish, Finnish and Norwegian Wars

The Second World War began almost by mistake, because
Hitler, a prey to megalomania and his 'intuition', was
determined to break the resistance of Poland, a country
whose strategic significance to Britain and France was
small. Mussolini attempted to persuade him to delay
before embarking on a war. Behind Britain and France
there loomed the danger of the United States. In three
years, as Mussolini pointed out, Germany would be much
stronger. This had no effect. Hitler's determination was
unshakable, because he did not really believe the British
and French would fight.

Poland was attacked on 1 September 1939 and 'liquidated' in a fortnight. The Polish armies were unable to
resist the lightning advance of the German motorised
and armoured divisions with their massive air support.
Poland's Western allies, who declared war on September 3,
were incapable of furnishing any practical aid. Between
the supposedly impregnable fortifications of the Maginot
Line and the German Siegfried Line the 'phoney' war
would continue until May 1940. In Poland the U.S.S.R.

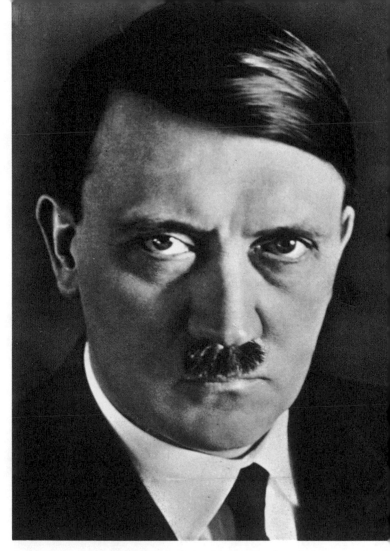

As the war proceeded, Hitler exercised more direct control,
especially after a plot against his life in 1944. He maintained
his ascendancy until the end, when he committed suicide in
the ruins of Berlin. *Popper*

profited handsomely from the German victory. Soviet
troops, advancing to 'restore order', established a new
frontier which was agreed upon by Ribbentrop and
Molotov in Moscow on September 28. By the agreement
the Soviets obtained military, naval and air bases in
Esthonia, Latvia and Lithuania. Since Finland refused to
concur in these arrangements, Russia attacked her on
November 30. Finland, however, resisted courageously.
The U.S.S.R. was expelled from the League of Nations
and it was not until 12 March 1940 that Finland was
forced to sign in Moscow a treaty by which she ceded
to Russia the isthmus of Karelia, and a thirty-year 'lease'
of the port of Hanko and the neighbouring mainland.
During the Russo-Finnish War Great Britain and France
had seriously considered intervening, though nothing
definite had been done. Daladier's Ministry, accused of
pursuing the war half-heartedly, resigned in March, and
Reynaud, the Minister of Finance, formed a Government
dedicated to waging 'total war'. In London on March 28
Reynaud signed a declaration by which Britain and France
engaged not to negotiate a separate armistice or peace.

Norway, in spite of her traditional neutrality, was
dragged into the war when Hitler decided to occupy
Norway as a convenient base for an attack on Britain.
April 9 was fixed as the date for invasion and, in order
to 'protect the operation', Denmark was occupied. But

Norway resisted and from April 14 British and French contingents landed in an effort to help. In these operations the Germans were so superior to the Allies that Mussolini no longer entertained doubts about Germany's success.

The Battle of France

After these two unforeseen diversions — Finland and Norway — the war which had begun in September 1939 was resumed in the west. Hitler now threw the weight of his entire force against the West. The 'lightning war' — the *Blitzkrieg* — began at dawn on 10 May 1940. The Germans flowed into Holland, Belgium and Luxemburg, under pretext of 'safeguarding their neutrality', while French air bases were bombed. The British and French armies in Belgium took up a line passing through Breda, Antwerp and Namur. Meanwhile the Dutch army collapsed: the Netherlands capitulated on May 15 and the Dutch Queen Wilhelmina escaped to England. The Belgian army, commanded by King Leopold III, was crushed and beat a hasty retreat. The Meuse was crossed north of Dinant. Sedan fell on May 14. These two breaches were rapidly enlarged and yielded a passage to German armour which was supported by an enormous number of aircraft. Abbeville, the Germans' immediate objective, was reached within ten days. With the object of encircling the Allied armies of the north, the Germans then drove towards the sea. In Britain Chamberlain fell and Winston Churchill became Prime Minister. In France Reynaud took over the Ministry of National Defence and recalled Pétain, who was Ambassador to Spain, to become Minister of State. General Weygand replaced General Gamelin. The Belgian army surrendered on May 27. The major part of the British Army, together with many Allied units, withdrew to the Dunkirk beachhead and, abandoning their equipment, were evacuated to England by the British navy. Weygand attempted in vain to hold the Germans on the Somme and the Aisne. On June 10 the French Government left Paris for Tours and on the same day Italy declared war on France and Britain. France was finished, and the German army encountered almost no further resistance. On June 14 Paris was occupied. Weygand, supported by Pétain, declared that there was no alternative but to sue for an armistice. The French Government, by now at Bordeaux, was divided. On June 16 Pétain succeeded Reynaud and asked for an armistice. Two days later General de Gaulle, who had been Under-Secretary of State in Reynaud's Cabinet, spoke from London on the B.B.C., calling on France to resist: France had lost a battle, not the war. On June 22 French plenipotentiaries accepted the terms which Germany had offered. The ceremony of surrender took place in the railway carriage used after the defeat of Germany on 11 November 1918. On June 24 an armistice was signed in Rome with Italy. Mussolini, whom Hitler had authorised to occupy the left bank of the Rhône, Corsica, Tunisia and Djibouti, in French Somaliland, agreed to be satisfied with a demilitarised zone thirty miles broad along the French frontier. The armistice terms had not included the delivery to the Germans of the French fleet, which the French Government had unanimously refused. The whole of France was to remain under the direct administration of French authorities, even the 'occupied zone' which comprised the entire Atlantic seaboard.

Pétain's Government

Pétain's Cabinet moved to Vichy in the so-called 'Free Zone', where a National Assembly was convoked which on July 10 voted full powers to the octogenarian Marshal Pétain. Constitutional decrees published the following day made Marshal Pétain Head of the French State. The Presidency of the Republic was suppressed and the parliamentary body prorogued indefinitely. Soon the effigy of Pétain appeared on banknotes and his profile was substituted for that of Marianne, while the formula 'Work, Family and Fatherland' took the place of the device 'Liberty, Equality and Fraternity'. Freemasonry was forbidden, trade unions were dissolved, civil servants dismissed and several politicians interned. From December 1940 Jews were expelled from administrative posts and and deprived of many civil rights. The Dreyfusards had a belated triumph.

After the fall of France Hitler had hoped to reach an agreement with Great Britain, but the British remained deaf to the appeal. A series of air attacks was therefore begun to prepare the way for invasion, but by the end of September the *Luftwaffe* had suffered such losses that daylight raids had to be suspended and the invasion postponed. The 'Battle of Britain' had been won. By October Hitler had abandoned his plans for a landing in England, though preparations for an invasion were ostentatiously pursued.

Left alone, the British, obsessed with the danger which an intact French fleet represented, not unnaturally wished to avoid the risk of its falling into the hands of the Germans. The French squadron, at anchor at Oran, was on July 3 accordingly given an ultimatum; when the conditions of this ultimatum were rejected the French fleet was attacked; 1,400 French were killed. Hitler made much of this tragic incident and ordered the German press to deal sympathetically with France, which was to be offered the prospect of compensation at the expense of Great Britain. The battle which took place in September, in which Free French forces under de Gaulle attempted unsuccessfully to seize Dakar, made an even greater impression and had important consequences for Spain. Franco had already occupied Tangier and it was widely supposed that he would now enter the war. Even before the armistice he had officially claimed all of Morocco, the territory of Oran and the enlargement of Spanish possessions in the Rio de Oro and Guinea. In order to avoid antagonising Vichy, Hitler adjourned discussion of these claims until after the war. The possibility of a *rapprochement* between Germany and France filled Italy with distrust. Italy had no wish to see her position in the Axis weakened by French participation.

The U.S.A. and the U.S.S.R. - the Balkans and Italy

A three-power pact signed in Berlin on 26 September 1940 by Germany, Italy and Japan had disturbed American opinion, already sympathetic to the cause of Great Britain. Britain placed great hopes in American support, but there was no prospect of the United States actually taking part in the war. Roosevelt did what he could to lend at least material and financial aid to Great Britain. In September 1940 he turned over fifty destroyers in exchange for the use of British islands in the Atlantic as American naval

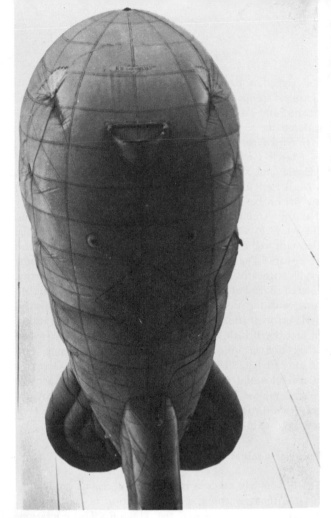

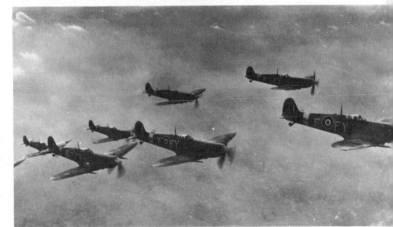

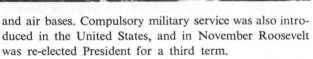

Above: Sir Winston Churchill, Prime Minister of Great Britain 1940–45 and again after the war. *Above left:* A familiar sight during the Battle of Britain, barrage balloons over strategic targets. *Below left:* Commonwealth troops in the Western Desert, the main theatre of war in 1942. *Below:* Spitfires, with Hurricane fighters, the backbone of Britain's Fighter Command in the early war years. *Bottom:* The bombing of civilians became a commonplace in Europe. During the bombing of London, many made a practice of withdrawing every night to the deep shelter provided by underground railway stations.

and air bases. Compulsory military service was also introduced in the United States, and in November Roosevelt was re-elected President for a third term.

The Russians had also been extremely worried by the extent of German successes in May and June 1940, and while Germany was still fully engaged strove to obtain the maximum advantage possible. In the name of Russian ' security' they incorporated Lithuania, Esthonia and Latvia into the U.S.S.R. as federated republics. Massing troops on the Roumanian frontier in June, the Russians had demanded that Roumania ' restore ' the provinces of Bessarabia and northern Bukovina. The Hungarians also demanded the return of former Hungarian provinces ceded to Roumania, and a Balkan war seemed imminent. The Roumanian and Hungarian Ministers of Foreign Affairs were summoned on August 29 to Vienna, where Ribbentrop and Ciano, acting as arbitrators, traced a new frontier by which Roumania lost two-fifths of what she had gained in 1919. King Carol, obliged to abdicate on September 6, was replaced by his son Michael I, under the dictatorship of General Antonesco, who enjoyed the confidence of the Germans. In the beginning of October German troops occupied Roumania under pretext of protecting the oil wells from British sabotage.

The Russians, who had not been informed of German intentions, at once complained. Mussolini, also not informed, decided to pay Hitler back in his own coin. Late in October Hitler learned of 'an imminent action against Greece', whereupon he expressed a desire to meet Mussolini in northern Italy. The result of their interview was apparent on October 27, when an ultimatum was sent to Athens announcing that Italy proposed to occupy various key positions in Greece in order to prevent Great Britain from using them as naval and air bases. Greece was given just six hours to reply to the Italian ultimatum and, not unnaturally, considered it equivalent to a declaration of war. When, on the following day, Hitler arrived in Florence to ask that the operation against Greece should be postponed, Mussolini informed him that the attack had already begun: Greece, he said, would collapse in a few hours. Almost at once things went wrong: the campaign went badly for the Italians, who were forced to beat a hasty retreat into Albania. Italy was already proving to be the Achilles' heel of the Axis. The Italian army was also badly mauled in Africa. After occupying British Somaliland, the Italians had attacked Egypt in September. Their offensive was soon halted and at Sidi Barrani in December Graziani was disastrously defeated by General Wavell. Alarmed, Germany sent help, at first air support, but by the end of February 1941 ground forces. The British and German armies met again near Benghazi after 400,000 Italian prisoners had been taken by Wavell and Cyrenaica cleared of Axis forces.

In order to appease the Russians Ribbentrop invited Molotov to Berlin. The object of German policy was to encourage Russian ambitions in zones harmless to the Axis. It was proposed to Molotov that Russia should expand southwards, towards the Persian Gulf. But Molotov insisted on an exact delimitation of the two countries' spheres of influence. He was determined that Bulgaria should form part of the Soviets' zone of security and demanded a firm guarantee that only Russian warships should have free use of the Straits. Hitler, however, refused to 'abandon Constantinople and Bulgaria'. A month later, on December 18, he had plans drawn up for an attack on Russia. On 1 March 1941 the Germans entered Bulgaria, and Bulgaria's adhesion to the Tripartite Pact was proclaimed. This followed the pattern already established in Hungary, Slovakia and Roumania.

On March 3 British troops landed in Greece, whereupon Hitler decided on the 'total occupation' of Greece. German military action was, however, retarded by dramatic events in Yugoslavia. Public opinion there favoured the Allies, although the Government of Prince Paul, the Regent, was benevolently inclined towards the Reich, especially in economic matters. The Axis Powers did their best to persuade Yugoslavia to join the Tripartite Pact. Prince Paul agreed, but on March 26 there was a pro-Allied coup d'état in Belgrade: power was seized by the young King, Peter I. Hitler, enraged, decided to 'annihilate' Yugoslavia. On April 6 — the day after Belgrade

had signed a pact of friendship with the U.S.S.R. — German troops invaded the country. Yugoslavia was crushed and occupied, and very quickly afterwards Greece suffered the same fate.

In Africa, too, the Germans recovered their ally's losses. In March General Rommel defeated the British at El Agheila and soon arrived at the Egyptian frontier. On 4 April 1941 Rashid Ali seized power in Iraq and attacked the British base at Habbaniya; there seemed a possibility that the Arab world would turn against Great Britain. On May 20 Crete was attacked and occupied by the Germans eight days later, after the first airborne assault in history. The Mediterranean seemed to have become the chief theatre of war. The British, reacting with energy, entered Baghdad and suppressed the revolt in Iraq. In June, with the aid of 'Free French Forces', they invaded Syria before it could become a base for German operations. In fact the British had already won what Mussolini called 'their first genuine victory' over the Nazi regime. For, on May 10, Rudolf Hess, the chief figure in Nazi Germany after Hitler and Goering, arrived in Scotland in a plane he had piloted himself with an offer of peace, provided only that Britain got rid of the 'Churchill gang'. Hess was held as a prisoner of war.

The war against the U.S.S.R.

The Führer had taken a momentous decision: on 22 June 1941, without warning, and in violation of the treaty of August 1939, he attacked the U.S.S.R. The operations which had been planned had already been delayed for more than five weeks by the campaign in the Balkans. Convinced that the U.S.S.R. would be liquidated in three months, Hitler felt able to guarantee the defeat of Russia before winter set in. Supported by Finland and by Roumania, the German onslaught had spectacular success. By July 29 Smolensk had been taken and huge numbers of Russian prisoners had surrendered. But Hitler had underestimated the power of recuperation of so huge a country. The Russians recovered their nerve and withdrew, fighting heroically, buying time with space. As they withdrew, they destroyed all that they could not take with them. The civilian population, many of whom had at first welcomed the Germans, soon reacted against the savage brutality of the 'master race', and turned to partisan activity; the atrocities which marked the German invasion were countered by ferocity equally desperate. On August 22, when the German armies were only one hundred and eighty miles from Moscow, Hitler threw the main weight of his strength against the Ukraine, whose crops were a tempting prize. Kiev capitulated on September 26 and the Germans took nearly 700,000 prisoners. But by the time the drive on Moscow was renewed it was October and the bad weather had already set in. The Germans at first appeared unconquerable, but from November 12 the cold became intense, and as in 1812 'General Winter' took a hand in the operations. Hitler ordered that the offensive should continue. By December 5, when the Germans were in sight of the Kremlin, however, it was impossible to proceed; they were obliged to retreat some ninety miles, while the Russians counter-attacked. Victory had eluded the Germans. On December 21 Hitler announced that he himself had taken personal command of the German army.

Above: Joseph Stalin, dictator of the Soviet Union during World War II. Distrustful of his allies, he showed great acumen in securing her interests in the war's closing stages. *Radio Times Hulton Picture Library*

Left: Field Marshal Rommel, grudgingly admired by the British as commander of the apparently invincible Afrika Korps, but eventually responsible for the dispositions which led to defeat at El Alamein. *Keystone Press*

Japan and the United States enter the war

1941 had, in fact, been the crucial year of the war. Not only had Hitler committed himself to the colossal expenditures of the Russian campaign, but the United States entered the war. The Germans had ceaselessly urged Japan to seize British possessions in the Far East. It seemed of little importance whether this provoked the United States to enter the war, since America was already lending Britain all possible aid. Roosevelt, in fact, had turned the United States into the 'arsenal of democracy'. By the Lease-Lend Act of March 1941 masses of war material were delivered to Great Britain. In April the United States occupied Greenland and in July Iceland. In May the United States Navy received orders to fire on ships or aircraft which attempted to interfere with its movements. The Atlantic Charter, in which on 14 August 1941 Roosevelt and Churchill proclaimed their joint peace aims, specifically mentioned 'the final destruction of Nazi tyranny'. In Japan, Prince Konoye wished to avoid war. His replacement by General Tojo in October could only mean a reversal of Japanese policy. According to the Tripartite Pact, Germany and Italy were not obliged to help Japan unless Japan was the object of direct aggression.

But when Tojo made it plain that Japan proposed to attack not only Great Britain but also the United States, Berlin and Rome promised him their complete support. On 7 December 1941, while a Japanese mission was in Washington discussing problems between the two nations, a Japanese fleet launched a surprise attack on the United States fleet in Pearl Harbor. It repeated, on an even greater scale, the success of Port Arthur in 1904. The American carriers escaped, but the battlefleet was, for the moment, immobilised. But the attack was a political blunder, for it united America behind its President as nothing else could have done.

Japanese success followed. Singapore capitulated on 15 February 1942, the worst disaster in the history of British arms. In March the Japanese wrested Batavia from the Dutch. They also advanced into Burma, threatened Australia and India, seized Hong Kong, and invaded the Philippines, where General MacArthur resisted them tenaciously. Hitler felt that his instincts had been sound and that he had acted wisely in allying himself to Japan, even though this entailed war with the United States. But Roosevelt decided to launch American effort first against Germany. For, as Churchill observed, the defeat of Japan would not necessarily entail the defeat of Hitler. 381

The British, having lost Singapore, seemed to be on the point of losing Egypt. Renewing the offensive in Cyrenaica in November 1941 they reached Benghazi. But again Rommel counter-attacked and by January 1942 the British had been driven back. The Germans opened a fresh offensive on May 27. At Bir Hacheim the Free French held out valiantly against continual attacks, but on June 20 Rommel, wheeling sharply westward, fell on Tobruk. The defeat at Tobruk was avenged at the end of October 1942 at El Alamein, when Rommel's Afrika Korps was routed by the British Army under General Montgomery. In the West the strategic initiative at last passed to the Allies.

In Vichy the spirit of 'collaboration' had slowly given way to a sense of expectancy, and the forces of resistance had rallied. The underground movement extended its activities. Sabotage and the mysterious assassination of German soldiers increased. Reprisals followed which further roused French indignation. Jews were rounded up in thousands, deported to concentration camps and tracked down not only in the occupied zone but in the so-called Free Zone. In April 1942 Laval, to all intents and purposes now Hitler's agent, assumed dictatorial powers. To escape forced labour for the Germans many young French vanished and joined the *Maquis*.

Since May 1942 the German people, who had acquired the agreeable habit of always dealing blows and never receiving them, had begun to feel the might of the British air force: that May and June one thousand R.A.F. bombers took part in massive raids on Cologne, Essen and Bremen. The tide was turning. The United States was beginning to assert its superiority in the production of armaments. In early May, in the Battle of the Coral Sea, an American naval force inflicted serious losses on the Japanese. A month later a combined air and sea encounter took place near Midway Island, in which American superiority was again demonstrated. These battles gave the Americans naval supremacy. In the Pacific, too, the initiative had now changed hands and in August the Americans landed in the Solomon Islands. In Russia the German spring offensive which had begun in May 1942 penetrated to the banks of the Don, which was crossed at the end of July. On July 1 General von Manstein conquered Sevastopol after a siege of two hundred and fifty days. The campaign of 1942 thus resulted in vast gains for the German armies, which had pushed forward as far as the Volga. Their front had, however, been over-extended and their lines of communication strained to the utmost. Ahead of them lay Stalingrad — and disaster.

The Allied landings in North Africa and Italy

On 8 November 1942 American and British forces under General Eisenhower landed in North Africa in the greatest amphibious operation which had yet been undertaken. The landings had been timed to coincide with the British Eighth Army's new thrust towards the Tunis-Tripoli frontier. A message from Pétain in Vichy France ordered resistance to the invaders, who were, in fact, greeted as liberators. Admiral Darlan happened by chance to be visiting Algiers at the time of the landings and he was persuaded, three days later, to countermand Pétain's order. Declaring that he had himself assumed authority in North Africa in 'the name of the Marshal', Darlan

then ordered further resistance to cease. General Giraud, who had escaped from Germany, took over the command of the French forces in North Africa. The Resident-General of Morocco, the Governor of Algeria, and the Governor of French West Africa rallied to Darlan who, with the approval of the American authorities, became High Commissioner and, on December 4, Head of the French State in North Africa.

Following the Allied landings in North Africa the Germans occupied the whole of France. As they approached Toulon with the intention of seizing the remainder of the French fleet it was scuttled by its crews. On Christmas Eve Darlan was assassinated in Algiers. Meanwhile in Tunisia violent fighting was taking place. Hitler had sent German and Italian forces under General von Arnim to hold the country as a bridgehead for further operations in Africa. The result was that von Arnim's forces, together with Rommel's famous Afrika Korps, were caught between Eisenhower's troops from the west and Montgomery's army from the east, and on 13 May 1943 were forced to surrender. In January 1943 Roosevelt and Churchill had met at Casablanca, where they agreed that the ultimate surrender of the Axis Powers must be unconditional. Also present were General Giraud from Algiers and from London General de Gaulle, who had there organised the Free French Movement. In July 1942 de Gaulle had created the Fighting French Forces and already controlled much of the French colonial empire. On 3 June 1943 the French Committee for National Liberation was formed in Algiers, which became the capital of Free France, under the joint presidency of the two generals. From November, however, Charles de Gaulle assumed sole authority of the Committee.

The War in Africa had been won, and the attack on Europe began on 10 July 1943 when British and American forces invaded Sicily. A fortnight later the King of Italy, Victor Emmanuel, ordered the arrest of Mussolini, who was replaced by Marshal Badoglio. This announced the coming defection of Italy; after secret negotiations, Badoglio signed an armistice with the Allies on September 3. The German reaction was swift and violent. They occupied Rome, rescued Mussolini, shot his adversaries, including his son-in-law Ciano, and put him at the head of a puppet Fascist Republic. Meanwhile, on October 13, Italy officially declared war on her recent Axis partner. Sardinia was easily occupied and Corsica liberated; but the conquest of the Italian peninsula was long, arduous and costly. An advance landing was made at Anzio and the beachhead held for four months before the main Allied forces arrived from the south. On June 4, under the command of General Alexander, the Allies entered Rome and continued their dogged advance. By the end of August Florence was liberated. The German front was finally broken and the Allies entered Rimini in September.

Stalingrad and the landing in Normandy

In Russia Hitler had suffered a series of disasters. On 26 August 1942 a battle had begun thirty miles from the city of Stalingrad (today renamed Volgograd). Stalingrad, reached by September 12, then defended itself against the besiegers: street by street, and house by house. Six months later, in February 1943, General von Paulus, with the tragic remnant of the German army, capitulated. The

Germans were forced to evacuate the Caucasus and Rostov-on-Don. The Russians, forcing the Dnieper, re-entered Kiev on November 6. Stalin, who complained that the Allied campaign in Italy in no way helped Russia, was ceaseless in his demands for ' an immediate second front '. Agreement on the second front was reached at the end of 1943 when Stalin, Roosevelt and Churchill met at the conference of Teheran in Iran, which the British and the Russians had occupied in August 1941. In May 1943, as an earnest of his good intentions, Stalin had suppressed the Comintern.

In France the prospect of Allied victory seemed ever nearer and brighter, and the French population had become almost unanimously hostile to the German occupiers, in spite of repeated bombing by the R.A.F. and afterwards by the American Air Force. The Vichy Government had lost all moral influence. Most of the Pétainists had been removed from the Cabinet formed by Laval and replaced by ' collaborators ' like Darnand, chief of the militia, and Déat, later executed for treason.

On 6 June 1944, the Allied armies, under the supreme command of General Eisenhower, landed in Normandy. The Channel crossing had not been smooth and hard fighting took place. But in spite of tremendous preliminary bombardment and air attacks the Germans were taken by surprise and the vast operation was an immense success. The much vaunted ' Atlantic Wall ' had not held. Allied superiority in the air was overwhelming, while guerrillas of the *Maquis* — or French Forces of the Interior — cut German communications and hampered the arrival of provisions, ammunition and reinforcements. Nazi savagery, and fear of partisan warfare, was as brutally shown in France as it had been in Russia and Yugoslavia. At Oradour-sur-Glane, four days after the Allied landings, seven hundred men, women and children were brutally butchered. While the British held strong German forces engaged between the lower Seine and the Normandy forest, the Americans broke into the Cotentin peninsula and captured Cherbourg. The British captured most of Caen. The breakthrough then began and soon General Patton's American Third Army swept south to the Loire before turning north to march on Paris. The German situation appeared to be desperate. A conspiracy of high-ranking German officers was formed to get rid of Hitler. The attempt on his life was made in his headquarters on 20 July 1944, but failed. It led to a purge in the High Command and the appointment of Himmler as chief of all security forces.

Meanwhile in France the German defeat had become a disaster. Caught between the American thrust towards Argentan and the British and Canadian advance towards Falaise, the German Seventh and Fifth Panzer Armies were in August systematically annihilated in the Falaise gap. Churchill, in spite of Russian objections, had urged a further landing in the Balkans to support the increasingly important operations directed by Tito. The Americans, however, decided to invade the south of France instead, and liberated the south and centre of France within a few weeks. Meanwhile, General Patton exploited the Normandy breakthrough with such audacity that his tanks crossed the Seine at Troyes on August 25. On the previous evening General Leclerc — who had led his troops from Lake Chad in Equatorial Africa — entered the capital of France at the head of the French Second Armoured

6 June 1944, D-Day. The greatest amphibious operation in history on that day seized the bridgeheads on Normandy beaches. Within a hundred days Paris and Brussels were liberated and Germany was faced with invasion. *Popper*

Division. General de Gaulle was installed in the liberated capital. The Allied advance continued and the British and the Canadian armies entered Belgium, freeing Brussels on September 5. But the Allied advance was now halted, largely by supply difficulties. German resistance was also stiffening. Before their line of defence could be consolidated Montgomery made a bold attempt to capture the Arnhem bridges. On September 10 airborne and parachute troops were dropped at Arnhem and Nymegen. The expedition was ill-fated and by September 28 had failed heroically with the loss of seven thousand men. In the Vosges, however, the German lines were pierced by American and French forces and in November Strasbourg was liberated.

The advance of the Russians was no less spectacular. By March 1944 they had reached the Bug, then the Dniester. Odessa and the Crimea were liberated in April, Sevastopol in May. By June the Russians were in Poland, and nearing Warsaw. Within the city the Polish Resistance movement had organised a massive insurrection to support the advancing Soviet armies. The Poles were tragically disillusioned: no Russian aid was forthcoming, and after desperate fighting they were ruthlessly crushed by the Germans. The Russians then resumed the offensive, and during the course of the summer captured the greater part of the Baltic lands. Finland signed an armistice with Russia in September and Roumania surrendered in the same month. Bulgaria, on whom Russia had just declared war, was rapidly overrun. In Yugoslavia the Russians joined forces with Tito, and Belgrade was liberated on 21 October 1944. They crossed the Carpathians, penetrated Slovakia, and fought in the neighbourhood of Budapest, which fell in February 1945. Greece and Crete rose, and were liberated by the British.

The end of the war

1945 brought the collapse of Germany and the capitulation of Japan. Roosevelt, re-elected for a fourth term, met Churchill and Stalin at the end of January at Yalta in the Crimea to allocate administrative zones in Germany among the Allies after victory. But the Rhine was still uncrossed. In December General von Rundstedt had launched a desperate counter-offensive in the Ardennes: 383

Churchill and Stalin with Roosevelt at the Yalta conference (7–12 February 1945). The decisions taken at this conference were afterwards bitterly criticised for being too favourable to Russian imperialism. *P.A. Reuter*

the attack was held and the Germans thrown back three weeks later; but in the meantime their V-2 rockets were falling on London, while a feverish search for even more lethal secret weapons continued.

Japan had begun to fall back in Burma, where Lord Louis Mountbatten was in supreme command, while General MacArthur was recovering the Philippines. But the Japanese still held Hong Kong, Singapore and Indochina. Their defeat was only a question of time, but how much time? They might resist for years. At Yalta Stalin promised to declare war on Japan two or three months after the capitulation of Germany. Roosevelt, in order to obtain this assurance, made certain important concessions, notably the right of veto in the proposed United Nations Organisation. Since the U.S.S.R. participated in the war against an already defeated Japan for only a few days, these concessions later appeared excessive. On his return from Yalta Roosevelt died suddenly on April 12; he left a heavy responsibility on the shoulders of Vice-President Truman, his successor.

In February the Germans were forced to abandon the Alsatian bank of the Rhine. In March the Americans crossed the Rhine at Remagen, to the south of Bonn. After that the collapse was swift. Frankfurt was occupied on March 27. German troops who attempted to hold the Ruhr were encircled, although they still held out in the Netherlands. The Americans went on to the Elbe, captured Magdeburg and drove towards Saxony and Bavaria. Leipzig fell on April 14 and Augsburg a fortnight later. Meanwhile the British had captured Hamburg and Bremen. In the north of Italy Mussolini was scarcely more than the shadowy chief of a phantom government, and the Allied victory was completed in April. Italian partisans captured Mussolini and shot him.

The Germans, stubbornly resisting the Russian onslaught in the east, still held out in Poland and in Hungary at the beginning of 1945. The Red Armies took Posen in February and on April 9 Königsberg. The next day they were in Vienna; by April 25 they had reached the outskirts

of Berlin. The American and Russian troops met on the Elbe. On April 30 Hitler committed suicide, leaving Admiral Dönitz as his successor. The Germans surrendered in Denmark, in the Netherlands and in Norway. The Americans, who had captured Munich on May 2, linked up two days later by way of the Brenner Pass with the British arriving from Italy. Over Berchtesgaden floated the French Tricolour. In Rheims on May 7 a German delegation signed the ' unconditional surrender ' which the Allies demanded. Their war aims were not only achieved, but surpassed: Germany had disappeared.

For the Japanese, too, the war was lost. But it could be murderously prolonged should they decide to struggle to the end. Immediately after the death of Roosevelt, Truman had been informed that a new explosive of unprecedented destructive power was on the point of perfection. To prevent further loss of American lives he decided to employ this terrible weapon. On 6 August 1945 the first atomic bomb exploded over Hiroshima, destroying four square miles of the city and killing some 80,000 people. It demonstrated how needless had been the concessions made to Stalin during the Yalta Conference. As sole possessor of the atomic bomb, the United States was suddenly, and incontestably, the world's first power. The Russians, declaring war on Japan two days later, entered Manchuria. On August 9 a second atomic bomb left Nagasaki in ruins, and on August 14 Japan accepted the Allied demand for unconditional surrender.

The United Nations Organisation and the peace treaties

The Atlantic Charter had spoken of ' a system of general security '. The old League of Nations had failed; something new was required. The American State Department had prepared a project for a ' United Nations declaration ' which was signed on 1 January 1942 by the nations then at war with Germany and Japan. The declaration also envisaged a system of post-war peace and security. In October 1943 in Moscow the American Secretary of State, Cordell Hull, won round the U.S.S.R. to the idea of an international organisation which would assure the continuance of collaboration when the war was finished. At the Teheran Conference a month later Stalin, Roosevelt and Churchill agreed that such an organisation should be established.

Two conferences which were held in September and October 1944 at Dumbarton Oaks in the United States, the first with the Russians and the second with the Chinese, agreed on tentative proposals for the establishment of the future international organisation. France, whose provisional government had not yet been legally recognised by the Allied Powers, did not participate. At the Yalta Conference in February 1945 it was decided that a conference should take place at San Francisco to prepare the United Nations Charter. Every nation which had declared war on Germany before 1 March 1945 was to be invited to attend the assembly at San Francisco, the inviting powers to be the United States, Great Britain and the U.S.S.R.,

384

The Praying Jew (Rabbi of Vitebsk). Painting in oil on canvas by Marc Chagall, 1914. *Art Institute of Chicago*

together with China and France. France, not having taken part in the Yalta Conference, declined the honour.

The San Francisco Conference opened on 25 April 1945, and by June had drawn up the United Nations Charter. At Yalta the Russians had insisted that the Ukraine and Belorussia — or White Russia — should be admitted to the United Nations as individual members since several of the British Dominions were thus accepted. The Charter of the United Nations recognised the sovereign equality of all member states and expressly declared that the organisation had no right to interfere in the purely internal affairs of such states. It provided that all member states should be represented in a General Assembly holding annual or, when necessary, special sessions. The principal organ of the United Nations was a Security Council, composed of eleven members of whom six were elected for two-year terms by the Assembly; the other five — the United States, Great Britain, the U.S.S.R., France and China — were permanent members and had the right of veto. The Russians had demanded this right for the permanent members of the Security Council, hoping by its exercise to prevent the General Assembly from debating matters on which Russia had her own inflexible views. Finally the Soviets conceded that the General Assembly should have the right to discuss all questions connected with international peace and security, and to make recommendations on the subject to members of the United Nations. They did not, however, give way on their right to veto any action proposed by the Assembly.

The fact that America, which had never joined the League of Nations, gave the United Nations enthusiastic backing augured well. The new organisation would have financial and technical resources far superior to those of the League of Nations. Nevertheless, the United Nations did not inspire the almost religious fervour which had greeted the League of Nations. In 1945, after a second and even more savage world war, it was impossible to revive the high hopes of 1919. It soon appeared that the better world which had been eloquently heralded by the Atlantic Charter was hard to realise. Since the unanimous agreement of the Great Powers was rarely attained, the smooth working of the Security Council was immediately compromised. Fundamental disagreement between the Soviet Union and the United States soon appeared. It is true that the United Nations' subsidiary bodies were able to do valuable work in economic, social and intellectual fields; but for the essential task of preserving peace the United Nations did not seem adequate. Victory had been total, but it was followed by neither the stability nor the relaxation which the optimistic had expected. If there was no more war, neither was there peace.

There were at least peace treaties — signed some eighteen months after the armistice, and arrived at with great difficulty. Treaties were signed in Paris during the spring and summer of 1947 with Italy and the German satellites: Finland, Bulgaria, Roumania and Hungary. The peace with Italy imposed certain minute readjustments of the French-Italian frontier and the loss of part of Istria. Italy

On 9 August 1945 an atomic bomb was dropped on the Japanese city of Nagasaki, three days after one destroyed Hiroshima. On 2 September the Japanese formally surrendered and the war ended. *Deutsche Fotothek, Dresden*

was allowed to retain Treviso, Gorizia and Monfalcone, but obliged to give international status to Trieste and the surrounding region. The treaty provided that the United Nations Security Council should ensure the independence and integrity of the ' Free Territory of Trieste '. Finland got worse terms than she had done in 1940; the U.S.S.R. annexed the region of Petsamo (Pechenga) which meant that Norway and Soviet Russia now had a common frontier. The frontiers between Roumania and Russia remained those which had been drawn in June 1940: Russia retained Bessarabia and northern Bukovina. Greece and Yugoslavia gained territory lost in 1941 to Bulgaria. Roumania recovered Transylvania and her frontiers of January 1938 with Hungary. Hungary was once again confined to the frontiers drawn after the First World War, boundaries which she had long and indignantly complained of. Certain small rectifications were made on her Czechoslovakian border, and in February 1946 Budapest signed an agreement with Prague on an exchange of populations: Hungarian-speaking inhabitants of Slovakia were transferred to Hungary, while Germans resident in Hungary were expelled.

Top: Launching the Atlas rocket carrying Gordon Cooper's spacecraft (*Faith* 7) on its successful flight in May 1963. *Associated Press*
Bottom: The United Nations Assembly, New York.

385

Coventry, shattered by the war, built a new cathedral as a symbol of resurgence. Epstein's statue of St Michael stands near its entrance. *Camera Press*

Europe faced a huge task of reconstruction in 1945. Towns like Caen (*below*) were not too badly damaged. Others were almost levelled by bombing and street fighting. *Popper*

CHAPTER TWENTY

THE POST-WAR WORLD

Europe

Within fifteen years, the material damage done by the war had been more than made good. Yet in 1945 this damage appeared almost irreparable, at least in Europe. Two of the pre-war European Great Powers, Italy and Germany, were in ruins after serving as battlefields. France, less dependent on industrial wealth than Germany, had also suffered severely both from fighting on her soil and the exploitation she had suffered at the hands of the Germans. Thousands of her workers had still to be brought back from forced labour across the Rhine. Even Great Britain had been strained to exhaustion by the effort required to defeat Germany and Japan and faced problems comparable to those of 1918 with less resources than ever before. Of the two super-powers, Russia, too, had suffered great material losses and had already set to work to recoup them at the expense of the territories occupied by her armies.

Morally, Europe had suffered even more. As the Allied armies had advanced, more and more evidence — at first incredible — came to light about the nature of the Nazi domination of Europe. Above all, the sufferings of the Jewish people, millions of whom had been deliberately slaughtered by the Nazis, with the knowledge and connivance of thousands of German soldiers and civil servants, horrified a Europe which had, until 1939, believed that it had left the Dark Ages behind. The bitterness of the victors was understandable; one expression of it was the trial of war criminals, many of whom, unfortunately, seemed to their compatriots to be paying not the price of crime but only that of defeat. It was in an atmosphere of hatred and fear, and amid harsh physical deprivation that the reconstruction of Europe had to take place. In the end, it may seem amazing that so much was successfully achieved. By 1950 Europe was, economically at least, again on its feet. Paradoxically, it owed much to the rivalry of the U.S.A. and the U.S.S.R.

In 1945, Great Britain elected a Labour Government under Clement Attlee which had at once to embark upon readjustment to peacetime conditions, the reassertion of British diplomatic and commercial interests all over the world and the re-shaping of British life on socialist principles. France, under General de Gaulle, whose provisional government was sanctioned by elections in October 1945, gave itself a new constitution in November and

On 20 November 1945 the trial of German war leaders and prominent Nazis on charges of war crimes began at Nuremberg. The attempt to enforce international law by the victors left many people sceptical. *Radio Times Hulton Picture Library* inaugurated the Fourth Republic. Trouble arose almost at once over the claims of the large French Communist Party which entered a Government together with the Socialists, and the Popular Republican Movement (M.R.P.). General de Gaulle resigned from the premiership shortly afterwards but the coalition was maintained. The constitution which the Assembly had drawn up was submitted to the electorate and narrowly rejected by some ten million to nine million votes. Coalition government continued while another constitution was prepared; this was accepted in October 1946, but only by some nine million to eight million abstentions. General de Gaulle condemned it.

In May 1947 the Communists, who represented slightly more than a quarter of the electorate, were excluded from the Government and replaced by the Radicals. Holding himself aloof from party politics, Charles de Gaulle appealed to the country in 1947 to ' close its ranks ' for a ' *Rassemblement du peuple français* ' to regenerate the State whose institutions, instead of representing the overall interests of France, were merely ' a juxtaposition of individual interests '. It was obvious that France could not play the part of a major power while so much doubt was felt about her fundamental institutions and while so many of her citizens felt greater loyalty to the Communist Party than to the nation.

The rivalry between the U.S.A. and the U.S.S.R.

It was against this background of French and British weakness that the rivalry of the United States and of Soviet Russia soon divided the world into two camps: the ' Free World ' and the ' Communist World '. Until 1950 Europe was the chief arena in which they faced each other. During the Second World War the Soviet Union had, in Churchill's opinion, been a cantankerous and pig-headed ally; and from 1944 it was a partner extremely difficult to deal with. Nevertheless President Roosevelt and his most intimate advisers, such as Harry Hopkins, had been convinced that the West could live on good terms with the Russians, who had ' proved that they could be reasonable and clear-sighted '. The Americans believed that they could rely on Stalin, who appeared to be a ' sensible and understanding ' conciliator.

The American army was, therefore, demobilised as soon as the war was over and servicemen returned to civilian life as quickly as possible. The United States alone possessed the atomic bomb and felt no sense of insecurity. The American example of rapid demobilisation was not followed by Soviet Russia. Stalin suspected that the British and the Americans had joint designs against Russia.

The Russian position, thanks to the misconceptions of American political and military strategy, was very strong. Russia had not only made huge territorial gains but the eclipse of Germany had left her the predominant military power in Europe. Red Armies occupied Berlin, Warsaw, Vienna, Budapest, Prague, and completely dominated the Balkans. The provisional rights of a conqueror were exploited by setting up satellite regimes.

The satellite states

Even before the end of the war problems arising from Poland had caused tension and difficulty. At the news — revealed by the Germans — that they had discovered near Katyn the bodies of more than ten thousand Polish officers taken prisoner in 1939 by the Soviet army, the chief of the Polish Government in London, General Sikorski, demanded an enquiry by the International Red Cross at Geneva. The U.S.S.R., which had renewed diplomatic relations with the Polish Government in 1941, thereupon accused Sikorski of complicity with Hitler and broke off diplomatic relations with him in 1943. Sikorski was killed a few weeks later in an air crash and replaced by Stanislas Mikolajczyk, leader of the Polish Peasant Party. A clandestine Government had also been formed in Poland itself. At the end of 1943 it moved to Lublin and in 1944 proclaimed itself the Provisional Government of the Polish Republic. In 1945 it was installed in Warsaw. Thus there existed two Polish Governments: one in London which was supported by the British and the Americans, and one in Warsaw which was recognised by the Russians.

At Yalta Churchill had made it clear to Stalin that Great Britain, having declared war on Germany in the first place in order that Poland might remain a free and sovereign state, could never accept a solution of the problem which did not in fact restore Poland's freedom and sovereignty. For his part Stalin was determined to close the gateway by which Russia had always been invaded from the west, and he demanded that the Government at Warsaw should be ' a friend of the U.S.S.R. '. The Yalta communiqué announced the re-organisation of the Polish Provisional Government on broad democratic lines: free elections, with universal suffrage and the secret ballot, were to take place at the earliest possible moment. Roosevelt confided to his entourage that it was the best that could be done for Poland for the moment. In Yalta the three statesmen also agreed that the Curzon Line should mark the eastern frontier of Poland. It was understood that Poland should be compensated for this loss in the east with territory in the west to be defined during the peace negotiations after the war. Immediately after Yalta a serious incident occurred. Sixteen leaders of the Polish Resistance movement who had gone from London to Moscow to take part in the re-organisation of their country were arrested, and were to be tried as ' traitors '. Churchill and Truman complained bitterly that the Soviets, in defiance of their given word, were attempting to impose a puppet government of their own choice. Mikolajczyk, whom Stalin refused to accept as Polish Prime Minister, was forced to negotiate with the Communists under impossible conditions. On 28 June 1945, however, a provisional government ' of national unity ' was finally formed. It consisted of the Communist group from Lublin and a sprinkling of Poles from London including Mikolajczyk who, agreeing to step down, became Vice-President. In August 1943 at Potsdam the U.S.S.R. announced the partition of East Prussia with Poland, Poland to receive territories situated to the east of the Oder and Neisse Rivers. Great Britain and the United States chose to view these annexations as an interim measure to be re-examined when the peace treaties were concluded. Poland, however, considered the annexation final. For the land lost to Russia in the east, she had received at the expense of Germany 44,000 square miles which contained nearly ten million inhabitants. A large part of the German population was expelled.

Unlike Poland, Czechoslovakia was not a source of immediate contention. Since the Prague insurrection in

May 1945, there had been Communists in the Czech Government and its head, Gottwald, was a Communist. Benes, after seven years of absence, returned as President of the Republic. Czechoslovakia expelled the Germans from the Sudetenland and in June ceded Subcarpathian Ruthenia to the U.S.S.R.

In Yugoslavia the Communist Tito, having organised the resistance to the Nazis during the war, took over the country after its end. At Yalta Churchill had hoped to broaden Tito's Government in order to prevent the establishment of a Communist dictatorship. His hopes had been disappointed. General Mihailovich, recognised by the exiled Yugoslav Government of King Peter as War Minister, was executed. In Croatia the Catholics were ruthlessly subdued and Stepinak, Cardinal-Archbishop of Zagreb, thrown into prison. In defiance of an agreement signed in February 1945 with Field Marshal Alexander, the Allied commander in Italy, Yugoslav troops seized Trieste in April, and evacuated it only under Anglo-American pressure. The Trieste region was then divided into two zones, one administered by an Anglo-American military government, and one controlled by the Yugoslavs.

In Roumania, in Hungary, in Bulgaria and in Albania, where Communist Parties were not strong, Communist regimes entitled ' Peoples' Democracies ' were installed with the aid, direct or indirect, of the Red Army. From January 1945 a ' patriotic front ' held power in Bulgaria: it was dominated by the Communists and the head of the government was George Dimitrov. A few days later it was the turn of Roumania. Vyshinsky, the Vice-Minister of Foreign Affairs, arrived at Bucharest on 27 February 1945 to present an ultimatum to King Michael, demanding the instant replacement of the Roumanian Prime Minister, Radesco, an energetic cavalry officer. With the ' democratic bloc ' Groza, a Transylvanian, formed a ' Popular ' Government on March 2, and thenceforth the Communists laid down the law. In all this Russia's allies had not been consulted.

Germany and the Occupation Zones

German problems also widened the gap between the Anglo-Americans and the Russians. In February 1945 at Yalta it had been decided that the three Great Powers should occupy separate zones of the conquered country, while a central Allied authority controlled and co-ordinated the activities of the occupying powers. In spite of Stalin's opposition, the Yalta Conference had invited France to participate in the central control commission and to occupy a zone which would be supplied from sectors held by the British and the Americans. This was done in June 1945. The Big Three also agreed to dismember Germany and to take steps to make it impossible for Germany to begin the war again: demilitarisation, denazification, democratisation, the trial and punishment of war criminals.

After the unconditional surrender of Germany had been accepted on 8 May 1945 the Yalta system, which Churchill described as a very exclusive club with an entrance fee of at least five million soldiers or their equivalent, was reaffirmed at Potsdam. The Potsdam Conference in July and August 1945 was attended by Truman, Stalin and Churchill (who was replaced after the British general elections by Attlee). But it was very soon apparent that the Allies would not succeed in dealing with dismembered Germany as a political and economic whole. Each occupying power administered its zone in its own manner and set up *Länder*, or states. The Four-Power control system was supposed to be directed from Berlin — itself, though in the Russian zone, divided into four sectors — but failed to function, owing to the divergent views of the four governments. The Russians treated their zone like conquered territory. The Americans, while practising centralisation, aspired to federal government, looser than that developed by the British, but more closely knit than that advocated by the French, who feared a powerful central government.

While this was going on, a starved and often homeless population had to be fed, sheltered and medically tended. The first serious rupture between the Russians and the Americans took place as early as the end of 1945 over reparations. At Yalta the Soviet Union had demanded reparations to the value of ten thousand million dollars to be paid not only by the seizure of industrial equipment but out of current production. In their own zone the Russians dismantled factories without payment. General Clay, the Military Governor of the American zone, banned the export of material destined for the payment of reparations from the American to the Russian zone. Meanwhile refugees flooded westwards from the provinces of eastern Germany and from Czechoslovakia; their number, rising to twelve million, added greatly to the existing distress in the west. In October 1946 Great Britain and the United States decided on the economic fusion of their zones.

Since the end of 1945 pessimism had been growing. Doubts were more and more frequently expressed about Russian intentions. In their public speeches the Communist leaders exalted the overwhelming part which the Soviet armies had played in the war, and correspondingly belittled what was done by the other Allies. Stalin declared that lasting peace was an impossibility so long as capitalist economy existed and, ' as a guarantee against Western treachery ', he announced the development of Soviet heavy industry. People began to speak of the ' Third World War '. Debates in the United Nations became more and more acrimonious, and international conferences were the scenes of angry dissension. In the popular press Molotov, with his habit of disagreeing with every Western proposal, was called ' Mr *Niet* '. A battle of Notes, uncompromising, caustic and accusatory, denounced Soviet imperialism on the one hand and, on the other, capitalist imperialism. There were two Europes between which open struggle had been engaged. On 5 March 1946, at Fulton, Missouri, Winston Churchill warned the world of the mounting Soviet peril as, not many years before, he had predicted the growing menace of Nazism. He spoke of ' the Iron Curtain ' which had descended across Europe from the Baltic to the Adriatic. Confronted by a Soviet Russia which sought to extend its power and doctrines ' the English-speaking peoples ' had need to demonstrate their firmness. Stalin denounced Churchill as a ' warmonger '.

Iran, Turkey and Greece

It was not only in Europe that peace appeared to be imperilled by Russian activities. Iran caused grave uneasiness. Supported by the Russians, who still occupied a large part of the country, the local Communists in December 1945 proclaimed the ' Autonomous Republic of

Azerbaijan', and seemed to threaten the Iranian capital, Teheran. The United States, convinced that Russia had an eye on the Iranian oilfields, protested so effectively that the U.S.S.R. finally decided to withdraw her troops — whereupon the Republic of Azerbaijan at once collapsed.

The Soviet danger had been provisionally warded off as far as Iran was concerned, but it remained acute in Turkey, the traditional object of Muscovite ambitions. On 20 March 1945 the U.S.S.R. denounced her treaty of friendship with Turkey. She demanded a 'more friendly orientation' of Turkish policy and even claimed certain territorial concessions in districts lost in 1921. In July 1946 Moscow proposed to the Turks an agreement which would exclude from the Straits every nation except those which bordered the Black Sea — which were all Communist. The two contracting powers — Russia and Turkey — would jointly safeguard the Straits. Turkey, encouraged by the United States and by Great Britain, firmly rejected these demands. But Turkish resources were sorely taxed to maintain the large number of men under arms which she believed to be necessary.

Greece, which had suffered cruelly from famine and German occupation, was in an even more perilous situation. Many of the Greek partisans were Communists. They decided that the King, George II, who was in exile in Cairo, should not return to Greece before the elections. The British, who had occupied Athens in October 1944, repressed a violent revolt led by the Communists, and set up Archbishop Damaskinos as Regent. The Monarchists won the elections of March 1946 and, following a plebiscite in September 1946, George II returned to Athens. But civil war, sustained by the neighbouring Bulgarians, Albanians and Yugoslavs, continued, while some forty thousand British soldiers prevented the country from being dragged into the Soviet orbit.

The Truman Doctrine and the Marshall Plan

Byrnes, the American Secretary of State, strove to meet Russian pressure with firmness. In January 1947 General George Marshall, who during the war had been Chief of the United States Army General Staff, returned from China, where for the last year he had been on a diplomatic mission, and replaced Byrnes. Firm and unharassed, Marshall was not only a great soldier but a great administrator. It was obvious in Washington that without the aid of the United States no nation was capable of standing up to Russia, and that Russia would not require great effort to bring a weakened and divided country like Greece into the Communist camp. Once Greece had fallen, Turkey, as Truman observed, would become an indefensible outpost in a sea of communism. The success of the U.S.S.R. in such regions and America's openly expressed indifference would, he stated, lead to the expansion of Communist Parties in countries like France and Italy, where their menace was already far from negligible. In brief, the moment had come when the United States had deliberately to make a stand — at the head of the free world.

On 24 February 1947 Great Britain informed the American State Department that her financial situation was such that she could no longer furnish aid to Greece and to Turkey in their struggle against communism. An official request for aid came from Athens. In his address to Congress on 12 March 1947 President Truman promised

Marshal Tito, darling of the Communist bloc until the expulsion of Yugoslavia from the Cominform in 1948. A skilled guerrilla leader during the war, Tito showed skill in continuing in power during the Cold War. *Camera Press*

The Berlin wall. The 'Iron Curtain' which came down in Europe at the end of the war seemed to be wearing thin by the end of the next decade — except here, where the wall provided its most dismal embodiment. *Camera Press*

The Berlin airlift. Coal being unloaded from American aircraft. The airlift was not only a convincing demonstration of the West's determination but a technical achievement of an astonishing kind. *Keystone Press*

American support to 'free peoples' in order that they might 'preserve their liberty' in spite of Communist methods of 'coercion and political infiltration'. The United States would oppose further extension of Soviet domination whether it was effected by negotiation or the deployment of force. Truman asked, to begin with, that aid amounting to two hundred and fifty million dollars should be immediately granted to Greece, and one hundred and fifty million dollars to Turkey. Totalitarian regimes had already been imposed on a series of countries: what had happened in those countries must be prevented from happening elsewhere.

This — the Truman Doctrine — marked a decisive turning-point in the history of American foreign policy, affirming as it did that wherever direct or indirect aggression endangered peace America's own security was involved. Since 1946 Communist pressure had increased in Bulgaria, in Roumania and in Poland — by means of so-called elections, cynically rigged. The U.S.S.R., seeking to enlarge its sphere of influence, had been quick to snap up weak nations, but careful to avoid threatening the United States directly. America now found that she had shouldered heavy responsibilities in Europe as well as in Asia.

American aid was not limited to Greece and Turkey. During the two years which followed the Second World War the United States spent more than fifteen thousand million dollars for the relief of war victims. But to revive the economy of Europe an even vaster programme was required. On 5 June 1947, at Harvard University, Marshall, the Secretary of State, made a staggering offer of aid to Europe by promising American financial support for the efforts which Europe should make for her own economic recovery. It was, he declared, essential to re-establish a healthy situation in world economy, without which there could be neither political stability nor peace. To restore European prosperity and prevent political and social dislocation, the United States was prepared to lend very considerable aid — which would be free. It was up to the European nations themselves — not to the United States — to draw up a programme for recovery.

In July 1947 a conference was held in Paris to examine this astonishing American proposal. Great Britain, France, Italy, Portugal, Iceland, Greece, the Netherlands, Ireland, Belgium, Luxemburg, Switzerland, Turkey, Austria, Denmark, Sweden and Norway attended. This conference of the 'Sixteen' reported on their deliberations to Washington. Communist countries had refused to take part in the European Conference. Finland expressed her regrets; Czechoslovakia at first accepted but was constrained to decline the invitation. Molotov accused the United States of wishing to create a Western bloc against the U.S.S.R. by interfering in the internal affairs of European nations and of using its economic resources as a means to exert political pressure.

The Cold War

Molotov's declaration was a declaration of 'cold war'. In November 1947 Congress in Washington, before voting interim aid, was presented with the European Recovery Programme to assure the maintenance of the independence and integrity of European nations. In September 1947 the sixteen beneficiaries of Marshall Aid recommended that Western Germany should be admitted to the European Recovery Programme. The Soviet reply to the Marshall Plan was not long delayed. At the end of September 1947 a conference of delegates from the Communist world met at Warsaw and decided to create a Communist information bureau, the Cominform, which, with its headquarters in Belgrade, would replace the Comintern that had been dissolved by Stalin as a gesture to his allies in May 1943. American imperialism was accused of desiring to 'impose its hegemony on the world' and of 'destroying democracy'. Tension mounted dangerously. In Germany General Clay had the impression that war could break out with dramatic suddenness. The peace of the world seemed to hang by a thread at the line of demarcation where American and Russian troops faced each other.

The march of events quickened. In Bulgaria, Nicolas Petkov, chief of the non-Communist Agrarian Party, was arrested in June 1947 and in September hanged. In Roumania, Manin, the old leader of the Agrarians, who enjoyed considerable prestige, was condemned to solitary confinement for life; at the end of the year King Michael was forced to abdicate. In Hungary, where the Communist regime had been well established in the spring of 1947, the elections of September confirmed its power. Mindszenty, the Cardinal-Archbishop of Budapest, was given a travesty of a trial and sentenced to life imprisonment. In Poland, after the elections of January 1947 had given an overwhelming majority to the Communists, Mikolajczyk was in February eliminated from the Government. He fled to England in October, in order to escape arrest. Two years later, in November 1949, the Russian Marshal Rokossovsky, Polish by origin, would be appointed Commander-in-Chief of the Polish army and Minister of National Defence.

The U.S.S.R. continued to refuse a peace treaty to Austria, which in September 1945 had been placed under the authority of an Allied Commission and governed by a coalition of Socialists and Christian-Socialists. The Russians demanded from Vienna an indemnity for 'German property' in Austria which the Russians claimed, having already in fact seized a great part of it. Though they no longer supported Yugoslav claims to Villach and Klagenfurt, they continued to obstruct all efforts to negotiate a treaty with Austria.

In Italy on 31 May 1947 the Italian Premier de Gasperi dismissed the Italian Communist ministers (thus following the French example). Four-Power conferences took place in Moscow during March and April 1947 and in London during November and December, attended by the Foreign Ministers of the United States, Great Britain, France and Russia: Marshall, Bevin, Bidault and Molotov. They succeeded only in revealing the impossibility of reaching agreement on Germany. The Russians hastened to create an economic commission for their zone and the American and British Military Governors set actively about the total fusion of their two zones. France gradually fell in step and in March 1948 all three zones were united. Western Germany was about to emerge.

Communist pressure in Czechoslovakia continued to increase and on 24 February 1948 the Communists seized complete power in Prague. Jan Masaryk, the Minister of Foreign Affairs, took his own life. Gottwald replaced Benes, who resigned in June only to die in September. Czechoslovakia had passed completely over to communism.

Finland, which had twice been at war with the Soviet

Union, had succeeded in not becoming a Russian satellite. Although Russia occupied bases in Finland, the country was not governed by Communists. In 1948 the Kremlin ' invited ' Finland to sign a treaty of co-operation and mutual assistance.

The Russians naturally hoped to include Yugoslavia in their economic system and, indeed, to dominate the country totally. In the latter respect they suffered an unexpected reverse, and in June 1948 the quarrel between the Kremlin and Tito became publicly known. In September 1949 the U.S.S.R. denounced its pact of friendship with Belgrade, and Yugoslavia drew nearer to the United States and Great Britain. In 1949 and 1950 it looked as though war might break out between Tito and the U.S.S.R., and it seemed more than likely that such a war would spread. The defection of Yugoslavia was followed by a second Soviet reverse. From January to October 1949 the Greek civil war had gone against the Communists and Albania now found herself isolated from the other satellites.

The Communist coup d'état in Prague had been quickly followed by a succession of serious events in Germany. On 20 March 1948 the Russian Marshal Sokolovsky suddenly ended the administration of Germany by the Inter-Allied Control Council. Almost all the quadripartite institutions ceased to function. The two conflicting forms of government now faced each other in Berlin. The Iron Curtain had fallen and Germany was cut in two.

The year 1948 marked a change in the system of alliances, which were no longer directed against Germany as the Franco-Soviet treaty of 1944 had been. Little by little France abandoned her intransigent attitude towards Germany. In the end she limited her demands to the economic detachment of the Saar, which had been part of the French occupation zone. Great Britain and the United States had declared that they had no objections to this. In December 1946 France, on her own initiative, isolated the Saar from the remainder of her occupation zone by a customs barrier. The U.S.S.R. rejected the French claims. In October 1947 a plebiscite was held and an enormous majority voted for ' an autonomous and democratic ' Saar; the inhabitants had no wish to remain part of a ruined Germany and turned towards France which, recognising Saar autonomy, replaced the Military Governor by a High Commissioner.

In June 1948 a successful monetary reform took place in West Germany. Production rose, hidden stocks made their appearance and the shop windows filled with goods. The stabilisation of the West German mark not only encouraged economic consolidation but revealed the weakness of East German currency. The Russians replied by a total blockade of the three Western sectors of Berlin. American, British, French, and Russian troops occupied separate parts of Berlin, though the city itself was in the Russian zone of occupation.

Berlin had, however, been granted special status; the three Western Powers had access to Berlin by means of a corridor which was controlled by the Russians. Since April the Russians, on pretext of ' technical difficulties ', had often suspended communications by road, rail and water between Berlin and the West. After the stabilisation of the mark they entirely cut off communications between West Berlin and East Berlin, and also those between Berlin and West Germany. As a result more than two million Berliners were threatened with starvation. The situation quickly became tragic. It was the first big attack by the East against the Western positions, and on June 26 the West replied with an ' airlift '. Food supplies and even coal were brought in by aircraft.

The Communists had undoubtedly hoped to force the Western Powers to abandon Berlin, but they had no desire to spread the conflict any farther. In September 1948 they announced Red Air Force manoeuvres in the area that bounded the air corridor which the Western Powers were using to supply Berlin. When informed that the airlift would continue just the same, the Russians did not press the point. Defeated in this test of nerves, the Russians called off the blockade on 12 May 1949.

The North Atlantic Treaty

The Communist coup d'état in Prague had been a rude lesson which resulted in the signing of two treaties, the Brussels Treaty and the North Atlantic Treaty. Great Britain, encouraged by the United States, had at the beginning of 1948 proposed bilateral defensive pacts with France, with Belgium, the Netherlands and Luxemburg. From these arose a regional arrangement, the ' Brussels Treaty ' of March 1948. The Five Powers — Great Britain, France and the three ' Benelux ' countries — engaged to strengthen their ' economic, social and cultural ' ties and to organise themselves for common defence. A consultative council of foreign ministers was created as well as a permanent body, a military committee, and committees of experts.

The United States wished to enlarge the Brussels Treaty which, as the ' Western Union ', still bore the aspect of an alliance directed against possible attack by Germany. It was the American policy to encourage the nations of Europe to unite in regional agreements founded on individual effort and mutual aid. Senator Arthur Vandenberg, a Republican of forceful character, persuaded the Senate to vote a big majority in favour of these agreements. The Vandenberg resolution, adopted on 11 June 1948, authorised the President to conclude alliances with non-American nations in times of peace. It marked a revolution in United States foreign policy, and a prologue to the North Atlantic Treaty of 1949. Harry Truman, who had been President of the United States for three and half years, was in November 1948 unexpectedly re-elected.

On the suggestion of Great Britain the United States Government held secret discussions with Canada — a northern neighbour of the U.S.S.R. — during the summer of 1948. Other negotiations also took place with members of the Brussels Treaty over plans for the defence of the North Atlantic. Finally, in Washington on 4 April 1949, twelve powers — the United States, Canada, Great Britain, France, the Netherlands, Belgium, Luxemburg, Denmark, Norway, Iceland, Portugal and Italy — signed the North Atlantic Treaty, according to which an armed attack against one or against several of the contracting parties, occurring in Europe or in North America, would be considered as an attack against them all. As Truman pointed out, it was the first military alliance concluded in time of peace by the United States since the adoption of the Constitution. As a shield against the fear of aggression, the treaty was manifestly directed against a possible attack by the U.S.S.R., and was calculated to lessen the threat of further Communist attempts to expand.

When in August 1949 a sufficient number of signatures had been collected, the treaty came into effect and N.A.T.O. — the North Atlantic Treaty Organisation — was set up to group into a single unit the free nations of Western Europe, incapable singly of defending themselves against a powerful armed attack.

The year 1948 — the year of the Brussels Treaty and revolution in American foreign policy — was decisive in a further sense: it was the year when Germany regained her sovereignty, and began to reappear as a European power. Western Germany would soon become the Federal German Republic, with an area of over 95,000 square miles and fifty million inhabitants. At a conference in London from April to June 1948 the United States, Great Britain, France and the Benelux countries agreed on a federal constitution for Germany, the plan to be ratified by the German states — or *Länder* — themselves. On 8 April 1949 the Allies recognised the Federal Republic. Military Governors were replaced by civilian High Commissioners.

The first elections for the German *Bundestag* took place in August 1949 and resulted in the return of two principal groups: the Socialists, led by Kurt Schumacher, who had survived eleven years in Nazi concentration camps, and the Catholics, led by Konrad Adenauer, the anti-Nazi Mayor of Cologne. The Catholic Party, with one hundred and thirty-nine seats, was slightly the larger of the two and could find backing among some of the Liberal delegates. There were one hundred and thirty-one Socialists, and a negligible number of Communists. On 7 September 1949 the opening session of the first Parliament of the Federal German Republic took place in Bonn. Professor Theodor Heuss was elected President of the Republic. The *Bundestag* elected Adenauer as Chancellor, and on November 3 Bonn was designated provisional capital.

While the Western Powers were organising the state of West Germany, the Soviet Union was at the same time engaged in setting up a rival East Germany; and in May 1949 a 'German Democratic Republic' was proclaimed, with an area of 41,000 square miles and seventeen million inhabitants. In October the provisional People's Chamber of East Germany met in Berlin. Otto Grotewohl was entrusted with forming a Government. Wilhelm Pieck was elected President of the new state, which was similar to the other satellite 'People's Democracies' in assuming that the will of the State was identical with the will of the Communist Party. More than two million people soon fled from the German Democratic Republic, escaping from the East to the West more or less clandestinely.

The U.S.S.R. had cause for uneasiness, which recent setbacks had increased: the Communist defeat in Greece, the break with Tito, the success of the Berlin airlift. But on 23 September 1949 President Truman announced that the Soviet Union now possessed the secret of the atomic bomb. For the Americans the atomic bomb had, since the end of the war, represented what the Maginot Line had been to the French before 1940. Truman's sobering news meant that the arms race had begun again. The aggressive policy of the Russians aroused an instinct to organise a common defence.

The Americans especially were eager that West Germany should form part of the defensive organisation of Europe; but before doing so the Germans demanded the restoration of their full sovereignty, while the French continued to insist that controls be maintained. The decision to proceed with German rearmament was taken by the United States in the summer of 1950 under the impetus of the Korean War: the 'military vacuum' of Western Europe had to be filled. In August 1950 the Council of Europe at Strasbourg recommended the creation of a unified European Army, controlled by, and responsible to, democratic Europe, but acting in full co-operation with the United States of America and Canada. On 26 September 1950 the Council of the North Atlantic Treaty Powers agreed on the establishment of an autonomous German armed force.

The French Premier and Minister of National Defence, René Pleven, proposed a plan, adopted by the National Assembly, by which the Germans should form part of a 'European Army' with contingents commanded by Allied officers at battalion level and used only to reinforce combat groups which already existed. In December 1950 President Truman appointed General Eisenhower, former chief of the Inter-Allied forces, as Supreme Commander of a unified West European defence force — composed of members of N.A.T.O.

Towards a united Europe

The European idea was in the air and had even made faltering progress. But, in spite of the attempts made to organise unity, Europe remained little more than a geographical term. Great powers had arisen in other continents and Europe had slipped to a position of secondary importance. Would the decline continue? In April 1948 sixteen European nations had created the O.E.E.C. — the Organisation for European Economic Co-operation — which set itself the task of liberalising trade and achieving closer commercial relations. The European Payments Union — E.P.U. — was formed in 1950. The European Coal and Steel Community was created on the initiative of the French Foreign Minister, Robert Schuman, who in May 1950 published a memorandum which proposed to pool all Franco-German steel and coal production under a single high authority, a communal authority possessing supra-national powers, which other European nations were invited to join. Since August 1949 Strasbourg had been the capital of the European organisation. The Council of Europe remained very limited in its powers and was little more than a consultative assembly where the statesmen of fifteen countries could meet and discuss their common problems.

The Pan-American movement

In much the same way the Pan-American Union, which should have reinforced the position of the United States, was richer in promise than in achievement. In March 1945 an Act had been signed at Chapultepec, a castle in the centre of Mexico City, affirming Pan-American solidarity against aggression. In August 1947 the Treaty of Rio de Janeiro provided for reciprocal inter-American assistance. Then in April 1948 the Bogotà Charter created the Organisation of American States. It was signed by twenty-one American nations and replaced the previous Pan-American Union.

The reason Pan-Americanism was scarcely more than window-dressing was obvious: mistrust was inevitably

Pandit Jawaharlal Nehru, first Prime Minister of independent India (1947). When India became a Republic in 1950 Nehru worked to keep her uncommitted in the struggle between Communist and non-Communist worlds. *Camera Press*

Over much of South-East Asia, poverty and the collapse of colonial rule allowed Communists to mount subversive movements. This is a government notice from Vietnam, warning · peasants against Communist atrocities. *Camera Press*

Vyacheslav Molotov, Foreign Minister of the U.S.S.R. but later disgraced together with many others as an upholder of the mistaken policies of the Stalinist era. *Camera Press*

fostered by the crushing disproportion between the strength of the United States — the Big Partner — and the twenty republics scattered from Mexico to Tierra del Fuego, from the Atlantic to the Pacific, as diverse in size and resources as they were variegated in race — one hundred and fifty million people who shared little more than a common Iberian colonial background. Theoretically equal, some of the Spanish-American states were ' democratic ', others were dictatorships, while the majority were subject to intense social and political agitation in which communist, nationalist and socialist influences conflicted or, more curiously, mingled. Almost all suffered from grave poverty. In all of them the leadership of the United States irritated Latin American susceptibilities. Relations among themselves were often strained, and certain republics were ardent in their struggle against ' colonialism '. Such was the minute Central American state of Guatemala and, above all, Argentina, where the programme of the dictator Juan Peron included attacks on those ' who defended the interests of foreign capitalistic trusts '.

The Far East

The antagonism between Russia and America was also apparent in the Far East, where no other Great Power survived in a condition to assert its will. The Soviet contribution to the defeat of Japan had been insignificant but had meant that there were no occupation zones in Japan. General MacArthur, Commander-in-Chief of the Allied forces there, was a proconsul whose power was unlimited. His hands were therefore free to give the empire of the Mikado Hirohito a democratic facade and a constitution, which was promulgated in May 1947.

On the mainland, communism was advancing rapidly in China. During the war the Soviet Union had supported Chiang Kai-shek and concluded an agreement of friendship and alliance with him when Japan surrendered. The Russian campaign in Manchuria in August 1945 had very rapidly produced more than half a million prisoners and considerable booty in the form of dismantled factories. The Russians undertook to evacuate the Manchu provinces — which had been promised to China — before February 1946, but they gave up Manchuria to the Chinese Communists. The Chinese Communists were thus able to seize enormous quantities of Japanese arms and by the autumn of 1945 were already in a strong position to negotiate with the Chinese Nationalists. In December 1945 General Marshall had just resigned his position as Chief of the United States Army General Staff to General Eisenhower, and he arrived in China, where he strove tenaciously to bring about closer co-operation between Communist and non-Communist Chinese. Chiang Kai-shek, ignoring Marshall's wise advice, believed that he could get the better of his adversaries by refusing a compromise. When hostilities broke out the Americans offered Chiang Kai-shek military assistance, which the Russians at once claimed to be an intrusion in the internal affairs of China.

At the beginning of 1946 the Russians denounced only the ' reactionary elements ' in the Kuomintang, but they soon condemned the entire Chinese Nationalist Party. In the name of non-intervention they attacked the Marshall mission and the presence of American troops in China. By 1947 the Chinese civil war had become general. Chiang Kai-shek's Government, incompetent and corrupt, broke

393

down. Arms which were delivered to the Kuomintang passed into the hands of the Communists. Many of Chiang Kai-shek's generals went over to the enemy camp, together with their troops, equipped at the expense of the United States. From April 1947 Chiang Kai-shek's position grew steadily worse. In October 1948 the Communists occupied Mukden. In January 1949 they captured Peking, then in April Nanking, and in May Shanghai. On September 21 the 'People's Republic of China' was proclaimed. Canton was occupied in October. Chiang Kai-shek took refuge in the large island of Formosa, where he concentrated his troops and received extensive aid from the United States.

The Communist victory in China was a serious setback for the United States. In December 1949 the Communist chief, Mao Tse-tung, visited Moscow, where he remained for nearly two months. A treaty of friendship, alliance and mutual assistance was signed between Communist China and Soviet Russia in February 1950. These circumstances were to lead the United States to restore the independence of Japan in order to counterbalance the weight of Communist China.

Anti-colonialism

The vast changes which had taken place in China were accompanied by upheavals elsewhere, notably in South-East Asia and the Middle East. To a large extent these disturbances were inspired by the wave of sentiment against 'colonialism', which was attacked in the name of the right of peoples to govern themselves. This principle, revolutionary in its consequences, was proclaimed by the Americans, themselves descendants of colonists who had rebelled against Great Britain. The anti-colonial movement not only had the approval of the United States but was greatly encouraged by the Russians, who took full advantage of the confusion caused by American anti-colonialism to advance the cause of the 'anti-imperialist and anti-capitalist' camp. Lenin had said that in the bourgeois nationalism of every oppressed country there existed a democratic element of potential value directed against oppression. This element, he said, must be supported without reserve. Raising anti-colonialism to the dignity of a sacred principle, the Soviet Union posed as the champion and defender of the independence of the formerly colonised nations, and loudly proclaimed the right of their peoples to make full and independent use of their resources.

The Americans who, confronting the U.S.S.R. in Europe, demanded that the inhabitants of the Soviet satellite nations should have the right to choose their own form of government, found it highly embarrassing to refuse the same right to the colonial peoples of their own allies. American anti-colonialism thus hampered American anti-communism, and the United States was alarmed at seeing the upsurge of Eastern nationalism culminate in further successes for communism. President Truman, in his message of 20 January 1949, advocated economic aid to under-developed countries to improve and develop backward regions so that they, too, should 'benefit from the advantages of our scientific and industrial progress'. Truman's 'Point Four' presented a programme of continuing aid, on a world-wide scale, which would put at the disposition of under-developed countries the technical skills of the United States.

The application of 'Point Four' was handicapped by nationalist sensibilities and by the fund of hatred which racial discrimination had long been storing up. Coloured peoples considered any foreign presence as a form of colonialism and large areas of the colonial empires of Great Britain, of France and of the Netherlands demanded independence.

India and South-East Asia

Almost all of South-East Asia changed its political appearance. India was not satisfied with the degree of self-government which the British Labour Party proposed. In July 1946 Indian elections took place for a constituent assembly. The Indian National Congress Party, led by Nehru, won a resounding majority. The Moslem League demanded an independent Pakistan. There were riots and bloodshed, and the Moslems refused to take part in the constituent assembly. On 20 February 1947 Attlee's Government announced that the British would leave India by June 1948 at the latest; the King would thereupon cease to be the Emperor of India.

In April 1947 the Congress Party resigned itself to the division of India into two independent states, Pakistan and India. Both were to be members of the Commonwealth, though India would not acknowledge the sovereignty of the British monarchy. Lord Mountbatten, the Viceroy, played the role of arbitrator between the two states, which on 15 August 1947 entered the Commonwealth. The division of the subcontinent between India and Pakistan was not accomplished without fighting, and large exchanges of population were made. Calm eventually returned, but the problem of Kashmir was unresolved. Although it included a majority of Moslems, most of it was incorporated into the Indian Union. At the same time Afghanistan confronted Pakistan with claims on territory which had become Pakistani. Finally 'linguistic riots', sometimes bloody, broke out in India over the nature of the official language to be used in various states of the Union.

Gandhi, the liberator of his country, was assassinated on 30 January 1948. Ali Jinnah, President of the Moslem League and Governor-General of Pakistan, died on 11 September 1948. The Prime Minister of India, Nehru, the spiritual heir to Gandhi, strove to be neutral between the rival American and Soviet blocs — a policy which in American opinion was advantageous to communism.

In Burma the patriots also refused the offer of self-government, and in December 1946 Attlee granted them complete independence. The Labour Party was more inclined than the Conservatives to reduce Great Britain's overseas commitments. A constituent assembly, elected in April 1947, in June proclaimed the Republic of Burma and decided to leave the Commonwealth. Burma, which gained its formal independence on 4 January 1948, was · shaken by Communist insurrections and by rebellion among the Karens, who formed an ethnic minority. Serious disorders occurred and zones of the country attempted to secede: in July 1947 six ministers were simultaneously assassinated.

Ceylon, which had been a Crown Colony, was granted its independence in January 1948 and became a Dominion; the change of rule took place peacefully. The Malay States formed a federation which was violently disturbed by Communist guerrillas, and rivalry between the Malays, the Indians and, above all, the Chinese.

The industrialised nations continually need more oil, but the oil-producing countries are more fiercely independent than ever before. Oil companies can no longer rely on the support of their governments. *Camera Press*

The Dutch colonies had been stirred to revolt during the Japanese occupation, which had been scarcely resisted, and after the war the return of the Dutch was resented. Indonesians like Sukarno, who had so recently collaborated with the Japanese, demanded power for themselves and for their people. Following negotiations which took place in the Hague and in London, agreements were concluded in November 1946 on the subject of an Indonesian Republic which would embrace Java, Madura and Sumatra in the framework of a ' Dutch-Indonesian Union '. But the agreements signed in Batavia in March 1947 were swept away by the tide of events. The Dutch attempted ' police operations ' in vain. Anti-colonialist India and Australia appealed to the United Nations Security Council, which ordered a ceasefire. Military operations continued in spite of the intervention of the United Nations. U.N. pressure did, however, finally persuade the Netherlands to yield. The Republicans were set at liberty and Dutch troops were withdrawn. A conference was held at the Hague from August to November 1949. On November 2 the Netherlands recognised the independence, under the Dutch crown, of the ' Republic of the United States of Indonesia ', while New Guinea remained a Dutch colony. The newly created republic was a heterogeneous collection of some six million Christians, Brahmins and Buddhists, who were confronted by a Moslem majority — a racial and linguistic medley which led to continual disorder. To cope with the situation Sukarno, the President of the Republic, centralised the government in 1950 and soon set about breaking off all connection with the Netherlands.

Similarly France was to lose Indochina in an exhausting struggle which began as a colonial war and ended as a war with communism. During the Second World War Indochina had been occupied by Japan. Nevertheless, until 9 March 1945, French sovereignty had been maintained. On that date Japan took over the country completely. Tongking and Cochin-China were placed under the authority of Bao Dai, Emperor of Annam: Annam, Tongking and Cochin-China were amalgamated to form Vietnam. After the Japanese defeat Ho Chi Minh, organiser and chief of the Viet Minh — a Communist-led nationalist party — installed himself in the government palace at Hanoi and proclaimed the independence of Vietnam. Bao Dai abdicated. The revolutionary movement spread. In August 1945 the' French sent a large expeditionary force, commanded by General Leclerc. In March 1946 the French recognised the Republic of Vietnam as an independent state and part of the French Union. But Admiral Thierry d'Argenlieu, the High Commissioner, proposed to make Cochin-China an autonomous republic independent of Vietnam. During a conference held at Fontainebleau in the summer of 1946 attempts to reach an arrangement with Ho Chi Minh were made. Incidents nevertheless continued. French convoys were attacked. At Hanoi, in December 1946, the mob fell on the French residents and massacred them. Hanoi was relieved by French troops and Ho Chi Minh fled. The real war in Indochina had begun. France tried to come to an understanding with the Emperor Bao Dai, and an agreement made in March-April 1949 promised the independence of a Vietnam which would include Cochin-China and adhere to the French Union. Similarly Cambodia and Laos were transformed into ' associate states '. The Government of Ho Chi Minh was recognised by Moscow and Peking, that of Bao Dai by Washington and London. United States aid was insufficient to save Bao Dai, who was quickly discredited.

The Philippines became independent in July 1946, the United States retaining a lease on air and naval bases in the islands.

The Middle East

Unrest in the Middle East was due not only to the presence of immensely valuable oilfields but also to the resurgence of Arab nationalism. Great Britain had long striven to cultivate the friendship of the Arab states in order to safeguard the security of the vital line of communication with her Empire which passed through the Suez Canal and, moreover, gave her access to the rich oil deposits of those regions. British companies competed with American companies in the exploitation of Middle Eastern oilfields; but both feared the possibility of their falling into Soviet hands. Soviet policy was to encourage Arab nationalism, to which Islam lent a fanatical character.

Iraq and Saudi Arabia had, before the Second World War, concluded a treaty of ' fraternity and Arab alliance ' and other Arab states had followed their example. When in May 1941 a revolt in Iraq threatened the security of Great Britain Anthony Eden had promised British aid for all efforts tending to strengthen the ties between Arab countries. Egypt had taken up the idea of Arab unity after the Germans had been driven from North Africa. In March 1945 Egypt had — with Syria, Lebanon, Transjordan, Iraq and, a little' later, with the Yemen — formed a ' League of Arab States ', designed to further co-operation and defend their common interests.

The Arab League soon proved its value to the Arabs. Syria and the Lebanon, which had been under French mandate since 1920, had been, in effect, granted virtual independence in September 1941 by General Catroux. In December 1943 France had handed over control of the economic and administrative services. Syria and the Lebanon later became members of the United Nations. General de Gaulle, however, refused to relinquish certain political and military rights. A small number of French reinforcements were therefore landed — which gave Syria and the Lebanon an excuse to break off the negotiations which were taking place with Paris for a general settlement. Anti-French riots soon broke out. Strikes were called as a protest against the threat to Syrian and Lebanese independence. Egypt protested and the Arab League stirred. On May 29 fighting occurred between Syrian and French troops. Two days later the French were issued with an ultimatum from the British to cease fire and confine their troops to barracks. The war with Japan was still in progress and Great Britain did not wish to risk imperilling her lines of communication with the Far East. France, though an ally, had momentarily to be dealt with as a potential danger. With the approval of Washington and of Moscow the British intervened to ' guarantee the Syrian and Lebanon Governments against further pressure on the part of France '.

De Gaulle, who learned of the ultimatum only after its publication, indignantly demanded — though in vain — a conference of the five Great Powers to consider the Arab problem in its entirety. After his offer to bring the question before the Assembly of the United Nations had also been declined he was obliged to resign himself to direct negotiations with Syria and the Lebanon; soon afterwards the French forces were withdrawn. In view of the community of religion, customs and sentiments which existed throughout the Islamic world, these events were to have important repercussions in French North Africa, where nationalist propaganda, actively supported by the Arab League, was already in full swing.

The Arab League, however, was far from achieving unity in the Middle East, whose states — notably Syria and Egypt — were shaken by internal crises.

A new and explosive element in the Middle Eastern situation was the violent hostility with which the Arab states regarded their growing neighbour Israel. Great Britain, hoping to avoid a direct breach with the Arabs, had reversed the policy inaugurated by the Balfour Declaration of 1917. In 1918 Palestine contained only sixty thousand Jews. After the Balfour Declaration more than six hundred thousand other Jews arrived, largely from Central and Eastern Europe. As the Arab states protested vehemently at this wave of immigration, a British White Paper of May 1939 drastically restricted the flow of Jews to Palestine. As mandatory power, Great Britain declared that when she had allowed a further seventy-five thousand immigrants to enter the country her engagements to create a national home for the Jews must be considered finally and completely fulfilled.

The horrors of Jewish experiences during the war led to a flood of requests for visas to enter Palestine as soon as it was over. Jews who tried to land without visas were remorselessly turned away. This led to violence. In June 1946 the chief hotel in Jerusalem, the King David, was blown up, bridges were sabotaged, and riots broke out in Haifa. Meanwhile various plans continued to be proposed and studied by the experts, plans which were approved neither by the Jews nor by the Arabs, who were both equally uncompromising. Harassed by post-war difficulties throughout the Empire, the British Government in April 1947 submitted the problem to the United Nations, with the firm intention of washing its hands of the whole business. In November 1947 the United Nations recommended the partition of Palestine into a Jewish state and an Arab state, Jerusalem to be internationalised. Prospects for an amicable arrangement were non-existent. The Arabs at once declared that they would contest the partition of a country which they considered their own.

In December 1947 Great Britain announced that she would terminate her mandate on 15 May 1948. On May 16 Israel, after some two thousand years, again became a nation and, with Weizmann as President, proclaimed herself an independent state. The Arab reaction was violent. Arab troops attacked, but were defeated by the Israelis. Count Bernadotte, sent by the United Nations to mediate, succeeded at least in arranging brief truces, which were then prolonged. But when he proposed a new partition which would leave the Negev to the Arabs he was assassinated by Jewish terrorists. The United States of America expressed the hope that as many Jews as it was possible to accomodate would be permitted to enter Palestine, and recognised the state of Israel immediately after its independence. The Arab states refused to admit the existence of the intruder. A bloody underground war continued. More than seven hundred thousand Arab refugees were driven out to camp on the frontiers of Israel.

In January 1948 Britain granted Transjordan total independence and a treaty of alliance for twenty-five years. The Emir Abdullah, who was known as a zealous partisan of British policy, took the title of King. His forces were equipped by the British and commanded by a British officer, Glubb Pasha. In December 1949 Abdullah annexed Arab Palestine to Transjordan and renamed the new state thus formed Jordan.

In Syria a succession of coups d'état took place in a struggle between those who advocated and those who opposed a union of Syria, the Lebanon, Iraq and Jordan. Meanwhile the ambitions of Egypt had grown immeasurably. On 26 February 1945 Egypt had declared war on Germany and Japan; on August 6 she felt able to demand complete independence, the withdrawal of British troops and the ' unity of the Nile valley ' — in other words, the annexation of the Sudan. Britain agreed to a friendly revision of the Anglo-Egyptian treaty of 1936. Negotiations dragged on, however, and were interrupted by student demonstrations and a series of strikes aimed at ' Imperialist Britain '. Egyptian premiers were assassinated by fanatics: Ahmed Maher in 1945, Nokrashy in 1948. Nahas Pasha escaped two attempts on his life, one in 1945 and another in 1948. The burning question was whether the Sudan would, or would not, be part of Egypt. In the autumn of 1946 the British had decided that the Sudanese should have the right themselves to determine the future government of their country. In January 1947 Anglo-Egyptian negotiations were broken off by the Egyptians.

Relations between Great Britain and Iran had deteriorated even more violently. The British Government was among the chief shareholders in the Anglo-Iranian Oil Company, which had been founded in 1909. The Iranians, who received few advantages from the exploitation of their oil, demanded, and soon obtained, revisions in the original contract; but these were insufficient to calm nationalists who clamoured for Iran for the Iranians.

CHAPTER TWENTY-ONE

THE GREAT CHANGES OF 1950-60

The next decade produced rapid and important changes in world history, but few of them were unpredictable or revolutionary. For the most part, they continued existing trends. This was especially true of the most fundamental change of all, the rise in world population, which had begun as long before as the seventeenth and eighteenth centuries. After 1945, the human race grew by more than forty million a year. An average annual growth rate of 0.7 per cent in the nineteenth century became 1 per cent between 1900 and 1950, and 1.7 per cent thereafter. This meant that in the second half of the twentieth century the world's population was likely to double in size. A change of these dimensions is in itself startling enough to make all earlier history seem static or trivial.

It was also clear that technology and science were likely to produce changes just as sweeping in the organisation of human life within the foreseeable future. Medical science, of course, itself contributed to the growth of population, and nuclear energy, which had begun by being used for destruction, became more and more harnessed for productive and peaceful ends. In 1956, the first nuclear power-station in the world opened at Calder Hall in Britain and two years later the first nuclear-powered submarine went from the Atlantic to the Pacific under the North Pole. The most dramatic scientific achievements, moreover, implied even greater changes in man's environment. During the International Geophysical Year (which began on 1 July 1957) the first earth satellites were launched into outer space, the second of them, *Sputnik II*, weighing about half a ton and containing an Eskimo dog. Two years later four successful moonflights were made, one of which, that of *Lunik II*, produced the first landing of an object from earth on the surface of the moon. In 1960, an attempt to retrieve a satellite vehicle carrying dogs was successful after it had made seventeen circuits of the earth, and it was clear that it would be only a little time before men could safely make voyages in space. Man was in fact within sight of the greatest expansion of his environment in his history.

It is paradoxical that this astonishing scientific progress was taking place while the physical condition of many inhabitants of the earth was worsening. The division between the have and have-not nations widened as the advanced nations reaped the benefit of an industrialisation which was still, even in 1960, largely concentrated in the northern hemisphere. In the advanced states of the non-Communist world, the acceptance more and more generally of the assumptions of the welfare state meant a wider diffusion of wealth. In the Communist world, the investment achieved by the sacrifices of earlier generations at last established a basis sufficiently solid to permit the production of more consumer goods. Meanwhile, in other parts of the world population expanded faster than food production and in those areas, in spite of help from advanced countries, standards of living declined. Population grew fastest in South-East Asia and South America

The exploration of space was enormously extended by the development of rockets capable of boosting big loads. The picture shows the launching of a 3-stage American Delta rocket, carrying a weather-satellite.

The Soviet spaceship *Lunik III* sent back the first photographs taken of the other side of the moon. By 1960 it was clear that soon men would reach the nearest planets. *Camera Press*

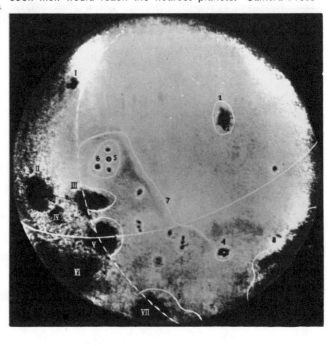

and this set up a vicious circle: because it meant that accumulation of capital for investment was harder, it delayed industrialisation, and so long as industrialisation was delayed, so was the achievement of the relative stability of population which seems to go with it.

This was not unconnected with the major political development of the decade, the continuing emergence of new nations as the old empires broke up. This had begun when Japan occupied large areas during the war; it had been encouraged subsequently by the United States and the Soviet Union. United Nations membership rose from 55 to 99 and many of the new nations did not consider themselves committed to either side in the Cold War. This in part reflected the increasing obsolescence of Cold War conceptions in a changing world. Although there were periods of great tension between the two protagonists, some change in the temperature of the Cold War had appeared by 1960. There was always the possibility of a revival of bitterness, but by 1960 the Communist world was looking less monolithic.

It is, nevertheless, the Cold War which provides the main diplomatic themes of the decade.

The Cold War in Asia

Until 1950 the Russian Government had been more deeply engaged in Europe than in Asia. Although active in the establishment of Communist supremacy in China, the Russians took part only indirectly in Asian affairs, relying on anti-colonialism to embarrass their opponents sufficiently. When North Korea attacked South Korea in June 1950 a new phase opened: the armed forces of the Communist and non-Communist worlds were soon in direct conflict for the first time.

In 1945, when the Japanese surrendered, the Russian and American Governments had agreed that Japanese troops stationed north of the 38th parallel in Korea should surrender to the Soviets, while those south of the parallel should surrender to the United States. It was also agreed that a democratic government should be set up for the whole of Korea, while both American and Russian troops were evacuated. In spite of protests against the country being divided by an artificial frontier, two Koreas evolved, one each side of the 38th parallel. As in Germany, two politically opposed states had formed, though American forces were withdrawn. North Korea was in the hands of the 'People's Party' — the revolutionary government of Kim Il-sung, which had come to power with the elections of November 1946. South Korea, on the other hand, was conservative, governed by the elderly Dr Syngman Rhee, who had been elected in May 1948. South Korea was recognised by Washington in August 1948 as an independent state. The U.S.S.R. and Communist China continued to demand the unification of the two Koreas.

On 25 June 1950 the North invaded the South, which was unable to resist the onslaught. Profiting by the Soviet boycott of the Security Council at that time, the United Nations declared that the North Korean action constituted a violation of the peace and demanded that the aggressors withdraw their troops and suspend hostilities immediately. It recommended help for South Korea, which was the victim of aggression. President Truman thereupon ordered American forces to support South Korea without, however, proceeding beyond the 38th parallel. The Communist

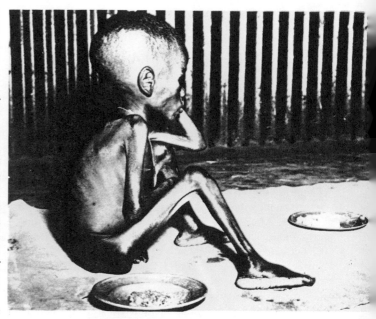

Pressure on food supply by a growing population still means famine, sickness and death in many parts of the world. *F.A.O.*

A Russian mortar-bomb from Korea. The fighting there almost led to war between China and America, while Russia gave indirect support to the Communist forces. *Keystone Press*

Industrialisation may offer the only hope of a higher standard of living in many parts of the world. Often power is hard to obtain and hydro-electric schemes such as this Indian one may combine power-supply with irrigation. *Suschitsky*

challenge in Korea had been accepted. The United Nations Organisation was the formal protagonist, but the bulk of the forces and equipment employed in its name was American or South Korean.

By October 1950 these had pushed the North Korean forces back and United Nations forces were approaching the Manchurian border. This caused Communist China to enter the struggle by providing 'volunteers' and equipment to the North Koreans. The balance of forces was thus entirely changed; by the end of January 1951 Seoul, the South Korean capital, had again been lost, only to be won back in March, when a United Nations offensive pushed across the 38th parallel which had marked the division of the two Koreas. There now seemed to be a chance that the war would spread and President Truman recalled and dismissed General MacArthur for insubordinate statements which suggested that the war would spread if the Communists did not accept a negotiated peace. In fact, in spite of bitter fighting, the Korean front remained fairly stable after this and the Korean people on both sides of it endured the usual dismal privations, destructions and brutalities, which are the lot of non-combatants in modern wars. In July 1951 armistice talks began which went on slowly for two years until July 1953, when an armistice was agreed. By then it was clear that the two Koreas had hardened into units incapable of peaceful amalgamation in the foreseeable future and another Cold War frontier had been established.

Elsewhere in Asia, the Cold War had been continuing in a less obvious manner. In October 1951 Chinese troops occupied Lhasa as part of a process by which Tibet was digested with the acquiescence of its rulers. In Malaya, Communist terrorism had begun in 1948, but did not delay the steady introduction of representative institutions which came to a climax in 1957, when Malaya became a sovereign independent country and the tenth member of the British Commonwealth. In the territory which formerly constituted French Indochina, the Communists were more successful. Anti-colonial movements on the spot were reinforced by a flow of Chinese arms after the Korean armistice. In October 1953 the French gave up Cambodia and Laos and, at the same, time Viet Minh forces began to bring pressure to bear on Thailand. In order to attack Communist communications, a French airborne force seized the base of Dien Bien Phu in November 1953 and it was the target of a major Communist offensive in the following spring. It became the symbol of the French presence in South-East Asia, and its fall on May 7 meant the end of French attempts to maintain forces in the Red River Delta. At the Geneva Conference (April-July) it was agreed that Vietnam should be partitioned between Viet Minh and French forces. The dissolution of the French command in Vietnam was not completed until 1956, but from 1954 onwards French influence in this area tended more and more to be replaced by that of the United States.

Increasingly, indeed, the Cold War in the Far East involved the United States rather than the former colonial powers. America assumed the burden of military and economic aid, gave increased support to Chiang Kai-shek and elaborated a system of alliances in the Pacific which linked her with Japan, Australia, New Zealand and the Philippines. Although the withdrawal of American soldiers from Korea began in 1953, it was in the same year that

President Eisenhower rescinded orders for the United States Navy to prevent seaborne attacks on the Chinese mainland by Nationalist Chinese forces. In the following year, the treaty establishing the South-East Asia Treaty Organisation (S.E.A.T.O.) was signed. It was less important than it seemed, because among Asian countries only Pakistan, Thailand and the Philippines joined the new organisation. Indonesia and, much more important, India remained aloof.

Meanwhile, Communist China's domestic development was going forward, the first five-year plan beginning in 1953. It remains difficult to obtain reliable information about the progress of industrialisation in China, but it is clear that difficulties were encountered — almost equalling those met in food production — which led to less being achieved than had been hoped.

Europe

Elsewhere, the shape of the Cold War was changed by the discovery that Russian nuclear technology was more advanced than had been expected. In October 1952 the first British atomic bomb was detonated, but almost immediately the United States made it known that it possessed a far more powerful weapon in the hydrogen bomb. In the following August it was revealed that the Russians could also make this weapon and it was clear that the nuclear gap between the two World Powers was appreciably narrower. It was at about the same time, however, that Dulles, President Eisenhower's Secretary of State, began to speak of 'liberating' Eastern Europe.

The first years of the decade had seen, if anything, an intensification of the division in Europe between East and West. Although the British meat ration was lowered to eightpence a week in 1951, from that year Western European countries began to grow economically stronger and in France and Italy internal weaknesses caused by the existence of strong Communist Parties had been mastered. Broadly speaking, the continuation of these tendencies under governments which were more and more drawn from the Right, combined with an increasing acceptance of welfare state principles, makes up the internal history of the United Kingdom, France, Western Germany and Italy during the remainder of the decade. In the context of the Cold War, it was equally important that their links with one another were more and more closely developed; by the end of the decade, the outline of a new World Power was dimly discernible in a Europe crystallising around functional institutions. This process began with the creation of the Organisation for European Economic Co-operation (O.E.E.C.) and the Council of Europe. The next great step was the re-admission of West Germany to diplomatic respectability when in 1951 the United States, France and the United Kingdom ended their state of war with her and she joined the Council of Europe. In the same year, a treaty was signed which provided a common market for the coal and steel industries of France, Italy, Germany and the Benelux countries; this great achievement provided for the setting up in 1952 of the European Coal and Steel Community.

In the same year the preliminary arrangements for a European Army were concluded — although this was to prove an abortive project — and the military security of Europe was improved by the establishment of American bomber bases in Spain. In 1954 agreement was reached that Germany should join N.A.T.O. Greece and Turkey had joined it in 1952 and in 1953 they concluded agreements with Yugoslavia for joint staff discussions. The settlement of the Trieste problem in 1953, after a period of extreme strain, also removed a possible weakness for the West.

This consolidation was not matched in Communist Europe. Although Comecon had been set up in 1949 as a reply to O.E.E.C., there was already trouble between Yugoslavia and Russia. In 1948 a Cominform resolution had accused Tito of unfriendliness to the U.S.S.R. By 1951 the Western Powers were giving Yugoslavia assurances of support and the United States had agreed to supply arms to this Communist country. Tito's unruliness undoubtedly contributed to the ferocity with which other sources of heresy were eradicated during Stalin's last years. Between 1948 and 1952 purges of native Communist leaders took place in Albania, Hungary, Roumania and Czechoslovakia. A renewed harshness in Russia itself also seemed to be shown by the announcement of the ' Doctors' Plot' which was made public in January 1953. Then, in March, Stalin died.

In what followed it was not easy for foreign observers at once to detect a pattern. That some decisive change of direction was likely was clear from an announcement of generous amnesties (though not for ' counter-revolutionary ' crimes) and the revelation that the doctors involved in the January plot had been guiltless. It seemed even more significant when it was officially stated that their ' confessions ' had been extorted by illegal methods. Malenkov was appointed Prime Minister, but there was much talk of collective leadership and denunciation of the ' personality cult '. In July it was announced that the head of the secret police, Beria, had been expelled from the Party. In December he was tried in camera, and executed. The usual ritual denunciations followed but in the following year no further important changes occurred in the collective leadership, which seemed to be shared between Molotov, Malenkov and Krushchev. A drive to increase the supply of consumer goods, especially food, was pressed forward. Then, in February 1955, Malenkov was replaced as Chairman of the Council of Ministers by Bulganin and a little later it became clear that Molotov, too, had been demoted. The climax of this series of dramatic changes came at a closed session of the 20th Communist Party Congress in February 1956, when Krushchev denounced Stalin as a tyrant consumed with vanity, who had built a personal despotism by ruthlessly destroying his opponents. At the same time the essential correctness of the Party's attitude was emphasised. It was by now clear that Krushchev had emerged at last as the outstanding leader of post-Stalinist Russia.

These changes had been accompanied by a long period of uncertainty and confusion in other East European countries. In 1953 conditions in East Germany had reached breaking-point when Stalin's death occurred. In the first four months of the year more than 180,000 refugees had fled to the West. An attempt to get higher production for the same wage at last produced a strike in Eastern Berlin. This quickly grew into a full, but tragic, rising in which Berliners fought Russian tanks with stones and bare fists. It was crushed, with considerable bloodshed. By the end of the year 340,000 refugees had defected. Relations between Yugoslavia and Russia began to

improve after Stalin's death. In June 1953 the U.S.S.R. and Yugoslavia agreed to exchange ambassadors once again. In 1954 Soviet propaganda against Tito was stopped and trade negotiations began between the two countries. The new strength which this gave to Yugoslavia's international position was shown when in 1955 she became a member of the Security Council as a candidate acceptable to both the Western and the Communist blocs.

In Poland the principle of ' collective leadership ' was gradually asserted after Stalin's death and in 1954 pronouncements by Party leaders made it clear that more emphasis was to be given to the production of consumer goods. So long as Bierut remained Prime Minister, however, the Stalinists were still in the saddle. His death in March 1956, shortly after Krushchev's attack on Stalin at the 20th Congress, ended an epoch. The release of Gomulka, expelled from the Party in 1949 for 'nationalist deviation' was a sign of change. So was a more generous amnesty than any previous one. To the demands for increased freedom which were now heard was added industrial unrest. At the end of June a wage-riot took place in Poznan which ended with scores of dead — but also secured wage concessions. Party spokesmen did not merely adopt the usual technique of blaming foreign agents but admitted that popular grievances had been mishandled; Russian reactions reflected concern at the independence being shown by the Polish Communists, a concern which deepened as more of those expelled with Gomulka in 1949 reassumed office and membership of the Party. The trials of the Poznan rioters and the September re-assembly of the Polish Parliament gave opportunities for outspoken criticism of mistakes of the regime. In October Gomulka was re-admitted to the Central Committee of the Polish Communist Party and for a while it seemed that Russian troops might be employed at last against the new trend in Polish Communism. Soon afterwards came the Russian intervention in Hungary, which occasioned anti-Russian demonstrations in Poland. By the end of the year, although the Polish-Soviet alliance had been renewed, it was clear that Poland had decisively established its independence in its domestic affairs. Perhaps the most striking evidence of the change was the release of Cardinal Wyszynski, Primate of Poland, in October and the ending of the domestic cold war with the Roman Catholic Church; by the end of 1956 all of its bishops had been released. It was clear that the ' different roads to socialism ' were now a reality within the Eastern bloc.

The 1956 crisis

These developments in Europe had been accompanied by a period of improvement in international affairs which began almost at once after the fall of Dien Bien Phu. In July 1956 the Indochina agreement had been reached at Geneva. It achieved nothing but the generation of an amiable atmosphere, but this was, after all, something new. Although Germany was one of the most enduring sources of disagreement between the two blocs, before the end of the year Russia opened normal diplomatic relations with Western Germany.

An atmosphere of reasonable hopefulness ushered in 1956, which was, if anything, intensified by news of Krushchev's speech to the 20th Party Congress. Then came a series of events which did much to restore the old bitterness to the Cold War.

During the year growing dissatisfaction was shown in Hungary over economic conditions in much the same way as in other Communist states. There was increased criticism of the maintenance of exports to Russia while there were such grave shortages at home. Many Hungarians looked to Yugoslavia for support because earlier in the year Tito had supported the process of de-Stalinisation of the Hungarian Party. As a result of this, Nagy had been re-admitted to the Party.

On October 23 there took place a great demonstration of sympathy for Poland, apparently threatened by Russian armed intervention, and a student programme was presented which demanded not only further de-Stalinisation but free elections, the withdrawal of Russian forces and the neutralisation of Hungary on the same basis as Austria. The enthusiasm with which this was received had disastrous results. Security police fired on the crowd; soldiers called to disperse it joined it and distributed arms. When more shooting took place on the following day and Russian tanks opened fire, a full-blown rising took place in Budapest and was copied in almost every town and village. Overnight the apparatus of Communist rule was dissolved and replaced by Revolutionary Committees.

Nagy, the symbol of patriotic hopes, now negotiated the withdrawal of Russian troops and formed a coalition government. Cardinal Mindszenty was released. Nagy sent a cable to the United Nations announcing Hungary's withdrawal from the Warsaw Pact and asking for recognition as a neutral state.

This was more than the Russian Government could permit. Nagy's coalition had been formed on November 1 but for two days already Russian reinforcements had been entering Hungary. On November 4 these attacked the main industrial towns at dawn and Kadar revealed himself as their instrument by announcing the formation of an all-Communist Government after Nagy had taken refuge in the Yugoslav Legation. Kadar's appeal for support was ignored and a bitter popular struggle against the Russian army began which lasted for a week. Inevitably, the superior forces won and before the end of the year more than 150,000 Hungarians fled to the West. Kadar's Government, though it repudiated the Stalinist era, rested only on Soviet tanks, and endeavoured to gain some internal support by economic reforms. These did not meet the real demands of the Hungarians: that the Russian soldiers should leave. It suddenly seemed to become clear that no real change in the Cold War had occurred after all; the Russians appeared determined not to lose control of the position won by Russian armies in 1944 and 1945. But although the Western Powers reacted with shocked disapproval, it had abruptly become clear that Dulles's talk of 'liberation' meant nothing after all. The United Nations Organisation, too, was helpless, paralysed at the crucial moment by another crisis, that arising from the Suez operation. All that the Assembly managed to do by mid-December was to pass ten resolutions deploring the Russian action.

The Afro-Arab world to 1956

The 1956 crisis in the Middle East was only an episode in the story of emerging nations. This was not always a matter of dissolving colonial empires but also sometimes

The brief Hungarian rising of 1956 produced, among other things, a temporarily unmuzzled press. This news-sheet was issued by the rebels during the fighting. *Camera Press*

Old scores were paid off in the Hungarian revolution. This prisoner under escort was probably an official of the overthrown regime. *Radio Times Hulton Picture Library*

arose over the informal influence or predominance of European nations in the past.

The story in the Far East has already been outlined. In the Middle East and Eastern Mediterranean area another set of problems was a potential threat to peace. In this area three crucial facts meant continuous agitation: the local combination of oil production and communications which made it a strategically sensitive area for the Great Powers (especially the United Kingdom); the quickening vigour of Arab nationalism; and the danger of Communist exploitation presented by economically backward populations.

The creation of the state of Israel in 1948 had been a blow to Arab nationalists. After this, the Western Powers were everywhere distrusted. Attempts to reach agreements over individual problems such as those between the oil companies and Iraq in 1951 were almost all rapidly overtaken by events. Strongly nationalist regimes arose everywhere. In 1951 Mossadeq took power in Iran. In the same year, Jordan, unstable ever since the incorporation

401

of Palestinian Arabs within its borders, began a period of uncertainty. King Abdullah was assassinated. His successor felt obliged to sever the special tie with Great Britain in deference to Arab opinion, although this was not completed until the dismissal of Glubb Pasha in 1956.

At the other end of the Mediterranean the French had to recognise the independence of Morocco and Tunisia. Then, in 1954, the Algerian revolt began. The presence in Algeria of over a million French settlers and the discovery of the oil deposits of the Sahara determined the French Government to resist and by 1956 a full-scale war was in progress between the French army and the National Liberation Front (F.L.N.). The provisional government of the Algerian nationalists in exile received encouragement and support from Arab leaders in other countries, notably Egypt. The period of revolutionary change there had begun in 1951, with the denunciation of the Anglo-Egyptian treaty. In the following year King Farouk was deposed. After confusing changes an Egyptian Republic appeared under an army officer, Colonel Nasser, and his regime proclaimed its aims of nationalism and social reform. The withdrawal of British troops from the Suez Canal Zone in 1955 was subsequently carried out without further marked deterioration in Anglo-Egyptian relations.

Agitation had also begun in Cyprus for *Enosis*, or union with Greece. The resistance of the British Government to such a concession was closely connected with the events of the next year in Egypt.

Rising tension marked 1956. Egypt had already begun to alarm the United Kingdom and United States by buying arms from Czechoslovakia and increasing her trade with Russia. Egypt was also blamed for the decline of British influence in Jordan. Then Nasser recognised Communist China and soon afterwards the United States and United Kingdom withdrew their offer of financial aid for a long-cherished project for a High Dam on the Nile. As a riposte, Nasser seized the assets of the Suez Canal Company, announcing that the Canal's profits could be used to finance the dam (July 24). Britain and France protested violently and it was soon feared that military action was envisaged by them. Interested nations, under the leadership of. the United States, attempted to find a solution which would ensure international control of the canal; this was unacceptable to Egypt. In September, French troops began to arrive in Cyprus.

While the United Nations debated, the Israelis suddenly invaded Egypt, giving as their objective the destruction of bases from which Arab guerrillas had harassed frontier settlements during the whole of 1956 (October 29). The British and French Governments now called on both Egypt and Israel to cease fire and withdraw from the Canal in order to safeguard it. When Nasser rejected this demand the bombing of Egyptian airfields began and on November 5 Anglo-French forces landed at Port Said. On the following day a ceasefire was negotiated by the Secretary-General, Hammarskjöld, on behalf of the United Nations and in December the last Anglo-French forces were withdrawn.

Disastrous as it was in the short run, in a longer perspective Suez had little importance. It did nothing to check the steady appearance of new nations developed from old colonial territories. The Gold Coast and Nigeria were given new constitutions in 1956; and in 1957 the Gold

By 1960, Kwame Nkrumah (below) had been President of Ghana for three years. Jomo Kenyatta (above) widely believed to be the instigator of the Mau Mau rebellion, had not yet assumed the leadership of an independent Kenya where white settlers formed an obstacle to independence not found in West Africa. But in 1960 the independence of Kenya was announced as the aim of the British Government. *Camera Press*

Coast and Togoland together formed the new state of Ghana. Nigeria acquired regional self-government, and full independence was granted in 1960. The Central African Federation set up with high hopes in 1953 only accentuated the demand for independence in Nyasaland. Kenya survived the bitterness of the Mau Mau rising from 1952 to 1956 and, like Algeria, presented the colonial power with conflicting obligations because of the existence of a large white settler population. In 1960, nevertheless, the British Government affirmed unambiguously that full independence was the aim which was being pursued. In the same year, Madagascar and the eleven African states of the French Community all received independence. An enormous amount had, therefore, been achieved in British and French Africa. With the exception of Algeria — the unprecedented spectacle occurred of the major part of a great continent making the transition to self-government in comparative peacefulness.

The Union of South Africa more and more emerged as the major opponent of this trend. Since a Nationalist Government representing Boer traditions had taken power in 1948, South African internal affairs were increasingly dominated by the assertion of white supremacy and the principle of *apartheid* or separation of races (with inferior status for Negroes). Besides leading inside South Africa to a growing adoption of institutions like those of totalitarian states, this policy necessarily strained more and more the ties of sentiment which held South Africa in the Commonwealth. In 1961 they broke. The Nationalists achieved at last an aim cherished since the Boer War. The dream of reconciliation shared for just as long by so many Englishmen evaporated. South Africa from this time followed an independent but lonely path, sharing with Portugal, the last survivor of the first great oceanic empires of modern times, the animosity of the new African states.

In Asia, Indonesia survived the turbulence of the first years of independence but could not solve the problem of creating an economy which could raise the living standards of her enormous population, or even guarantee their maintenance. Under the Presidency of Sukarno, Indonesia moved away from the liberal forms under which it had been founded towards a ' guided democracy '. It was soon obvious that the Indonesian Government might distract attention from domestic problems by gestures of chauvinism abroad. The first example was the setting up of a government-in-exile for ' West Irian ', the new name for Western New Guinea. In 1957 economic relations with the Netherlands were ended. Disturbances soon made it clear, none the less, that chauvinism was not enough to check protest at home. In 1958 a rebellion took place which was stigmatised as receiving aid from the Western Powers. The cost of this was a grave new strain on the economy. ' Guided democracy ' was pressed even further, and in 1960 the Legislature was dismissed.

Elsewhere, India absorbed the last French enclaves in 1954 and the first elected Prime Minister of Singapore took office in 1959. Although such events emphasised the continuing movement towards the removal of the last elements of colonialism, the condition of many of the new Asian nations was not happy. All of them suffered from some of the same problems: growing populations, economic weakness because of dependence on primary products whose prices were falling, internal divisions and

the threat of a powerful China. To lean too obviously on the Western Powers was impossible because of suspicions of colonialism. These states therefore clung uneasily to their neutrality, tending increasingly to evolve more right-wing, sometimes military governments (Thailand, 1957; Burma, 1958). Vietnam's internal security remained as bad as ever and in 1960 criticism of its Government by Ngo Dinh Diem and his family grew louder. Only in South Korea did constitutionalism appear to make an advance, when in 1960 Synghman Rhee was overthrown with military help and American approval.

The tendency of American policy, in spite of its anti-colonial bias, was to draw criticism because in many cases it involved support of corrupt and conservative regimes. Only Chinese intransigence and such dramatic and tragic occurrences as the 1959 flight of the Dalai Lama to India after a rising in Lhasa against the Chinese garrison did something to correct the balance.

Soon after Suez, too, the Americans were becoming unpopular with Arab nations. Convinced that the Anglo-French action had dangerously exposed the Middle East to Communist subversion, Dulles replied with the ' Eisenhower Doctrine ' of January 1957. It promised military and economic aid to countries threatened by Communism and was quickly put into practice when an American fleet was sent to the eastern Mediterranean in April to support the Jordanian Government. In fact, Communism possessed far less dynamism in the area than Arab nationalism. Suez had not changed this but raised Nasser's prestige among Arabs to new heights. In 1958 a year-old economic union between Egypt and Syria was transformed into a political union, the United Arab Republic. Pressure from the new state exacerbated the problems of the Lebanon, which experienced something like a civil war against its pro-Western Government in early 1958. In July a revolution in Iraq overthrew the monarchy (murdering the royal family and Prime Minister) and set up a cabinet under a soldier, Kassem, which at once enjoyed cordial greetings from the United Arab Republic and Communist countries. Following this, the Lebanese Government asked for help from the United States, and American troops were landed and stayed in the Lebanon until October; at the same time, British troops were invited to Jordan, whose King feared that his state, too, was threatened by the new pan-Arabism of its neighbours. In 1959, however, it became clear that pan-Arabism was not enough to guarantee good relations between the United Arab Republic and Iraq, which ceased to participate in Arab League meetings. There was no sign in 1960 of an end to the instability in the eastern Mediterranean and Middle East which had followed the dissolution of the Ottoman Empire. The only problem in the area which at last seemed settled was that of Cyprus, which became an independent republic in 1960.

Central and South America

In 1958 the British West Indies Federation came into existence. Another Caribbean event which attracted less attention was the beginning in the same year of Castro's revolt in Cuba. In 1959 his forces entered Havana and he became Prime Minister of Cuba. Sentimental patronage from the United States quickly gave way to dismay when he undertook the confiscation of American businesses.

Fidel Castro's early popularity in the U.S.A. rapidly gave way to dislike as the Cuban revolution took an anti-capitalist and anti-American turn. By 1960 he was, consequently, enjoying the ostentatious patronage of Russia. *Camera Press*

Konrad Adenauer, Chancellor of the Federal German Republic, who presided over its appearance as a full and respected member of the Western Alliance. *Camera Press*

In 1960 the Castro regime had already established its character as a double threat to the stability and peacefulness of Latin America, first because Castro's more and more obvious sympathy for Russia and dependence on Russian patronage alarmed the United States and spread the Cold War to the western hemisphere, secondly because the revolutionary acts of Castro's regime inspired popular discontent everywhere in the poverty-stricken continent of South America.

The Cold War in Europe after 1956

Suez and Hungary had done something to strengthen the notion of a neutralist bloc uncommitted to Russia or America which had first found expression in the Bandung Conference of 1955. Although Communist countries including China were represented at this conference, its conclusion did not fall into an unambiguously pro-Communist pattern. In the following year, a neutralist ' Summit ' meeting was held at Brioni. From the start, the role of Nehru and India in formulating the ' neutralist ' attitude had been outstandingly important.

In Europe the awareness of the Communist threat still provided impetus for the consolidation of the Western part of the continent in closer ties. The two most important steps in this direction were taken in 1958, when the ' Common Market ' (E.E.C.) and the European Atomic Energy Community (Euratom) were set up, and in the following year when the European Free Trade Association (E.F.T.A.) was created. In 1960 a further step was the reconstitution of the Organisation for European Economic Co-operation. In the following year the United States and Canada became full members and the hitherto purely European body changed its name to Organisation for Economic Co-operation and Development (O.E.C.D.).

Western consolidation stimulated Russian fears. Even more alarming to Russia was the prospect of a rearmed Western Germany with nuclear weapons. In the absence of agreement on a nuclear-free zone in Europe, Russian policy relied upon reinforcing its satellite states. The role of Eastern Germany was crucial here, but Eastern Germany was fatally weakened by the existence in its territory of West Berlin, an example of prosperity and freedom and a temptation to the ablest and most ambitious East Germans. At the end of 1958 the Russians denounced the existing status of the city and announced that they would hand over their authority in Berlin to the East Germans if an acceptable new set of arrangements could not be found. The terms of this ultimatum, it soon became clear, involved the recognition of a permanently divided Germany and the withdrawal of West Germany from N.A.T.O. Under the threat of unilateral action by Russia, the early months of 1959 were spent in preparing for a conference of Foreign Ministers. This conference only revealed that the Russian and Western aims in Germany were diametrically opposed. The deadlock continued, but a visit by Krushchev to the United States seemed to promise at least a better atmosphere for a meeting of Heads of State in 1960 in Paris. Unhappily, that year was bound to be the end of President Eisenhower's term of office; uncertainty about the identity of his successor therefore inhibited diplomatic intercourse from the start. On the eve of the meeting in Paris, an American reconnaissance aircraft was shot down over Russian territory;

the 'U-2 incident' served as a pretext for Krushchev to make unacceptable demands which enabled him to leave Paris before the conference had begun. But it was soon clear that Russian policy was for the moment, at least, not going to be provocative over Berlin. The one achievement of the Cold War, in fact, was the stabilisation of a Europe divided almost along the same lines as in 1945 but with some of the uncertainties of that time removed. The crucial problem remained that of reconciling Russian security with a settlement of Germany and it was unsolved. Yet *de facto* arrangements worked. It was a recognition of this that led to such projects as the Rapacki Plan for a 'disengaged', nuclear-free central Europe.

As the decade ended, it remained true that the prestige of the Western nations was not high in the eyes of the uncommitted nations. As Russian aims still seemed to be served best by turbulence outside Europe, Western observers sometimes saw communism where only nationalism existed (in Europe, of course, Russians had suspected 'capitalist' and 'neo-fascist' elements behind the national movements in the satellite states). The U-2 incident made things worse — notably in Japan — by seeming to show that the United States was at least needlessly provocative, if not the caricature warmonger of Communist propaganda. The French had let off their first atomic bomb in 1959, thus provoking protests from African nations already hostile to France because of her actions in Algeria. Besides practising colonialism abroad, the West seemed tainted with racialism at home, as the troubles at Little Rock in 1957 and 1958 broadcast to the world. Under these conditions it was at least some consolation that Krushchev's violence at the United Nations General Assembly in New York in October offended some of the neutralist powers, who were shocked by his cavalier treatment of the institution in which they put their trust. The year ended with speculation about the possible results of the coming American Presidential election, but feeling was stronger than ever in many countries that the neutralists were right, and the great majority of nations had no interest in either side of the Russo-American quarrel.

At the end of the decade, indeed, it was at first sight hard to be more sanguine about the Cold War than at the beginning. Nothing had been achieved in the weary discussions on disarmament. Berlin's status remained in question. Yet in the 1960 Kremlin Conference there was to be discerned a sign of future change, the beginnings of an open divergence of Communist policy in Russia and China. What was certainly clear, however, was that the problems arising from the ending of the European world hegemony had not been solved since they had begun to appear in 1917. If the new nations had emerged politically, they had still to create viable economies. And it was significant and ironical that, as the dusk fell on the great empires, their successors turned almost unthinkingly to the institutions and ideas of Europe as they sought to equip themselves for independence. Revolution and the struggle against colonialism were conducted in the name of nationalism and the Rights of Man, both of them artefacts of European culture. Poverty and backwardness turned men's eyes to the possibilities latent in the technology and industrialisation drawn from the Western scientific tradition. The physical apparatus and appliances of the West spread rapidly as every new nation demanded its airline or dam; it completed the process of cultural diffusion begun by early European capitalists four centuries before. It was ironical that at a moment when its political influence seemed all but extinguished, Europe's cultural empire should be stronger than ever.

The meeting at Vienna between Krushchev and Kennedy in 1961 was considered disappointing. But it opened a period of closer contact between Washington and Moscow and led to the setting up of a 'hot line' between them. *Camera Press*

Major Yuri Gagarin, the first man to travel in space, orbited the world in ninety minutes in 1961. This exploit touched off ten years of achievements, both Russian and American, and led to an enormous expenditure of resources in a race between the two super-powers.

Opposite: the 'space race' was finally won by the Americans, who landed two men safely on the moon in July 1969, while the third astronaut orbited the planet. *Popperfoto*

Lieutenant-Colonel John Glenn, America's first astronaut. *Camera Press*

CHAPTER TWENTY-TWO

WORLD HISTORY 1961–70

The Space Race

In 1961 the Russians launched and safely retrieved a man-carrying space vehicle, in which the first 'cosmonaut' had just orbited the world in ninety minutes. This began ten years of spectacular achievements, both Russian and American. Two and three-men vehicles were sent up. An American satellite transmitted excellent photographs of the moon before crashing on to it in 1964. Two years later, a successful soft landing of American instruments on the moon began to provide detailed information about the surface on which a landing by men would certainly soon be attempted. Meanwhile, other experiments were going forward to perfect techniques enabling men to leave their spacecraft during their missions and move and work outside them, or to rendezvous with other vehicles in orbit around the earth.

This fantastically expensive activity soaked up huge resources which might have been employed in work yielding more immediate material returns to mankind. There were, of course, some fairly everyday consequences which helped to make this acceptable. Communications satellites, for example, made direct intercontinental television possible, and the whole electronics industry benefited from the ingenuity deployed in devising and 'miniaturising' the intricate machines which went off into space. In the United States, at least, the space industry was soon the major determining factor of the employment of scientific man-power and a huge source of academic patronage. When this was added to the essential glamour of the basic idea of space travel, it is not surprising that public attention was monopolised by the space race in a way that tended to obscure other, possibly more important, scientific work going on in less glamorous fields. A new understanding of heredity, for example, came from research on substances lying at the basis of genetic structure. Other biologists produced for the first time outside the body enzyme systems from a living cell. Such work might eventually transform food supply and end successfully the race between population and food resources. But few could see this at the time. For most people, the purest expression of science in the 1960s was the advance into space, and its cost was hardly questioned: its acceptance registered the dominance of Science in twentieth-century culture, as great temples and cathedrals had marked the dominance of Religion in the past.

The advance into space had all the more excitement since it was seen as a race between two super-powers: the Western European efforts were not in the same league as Russia and the United States. Yet in so far as it was a race for one specific objective–the moon–the Russians retired from it in the second half of the decade. The Americans were left to win it, as they did in July 1969, when the first men (two of them) stepped out of the machine in which they had safely landed on the moon's surface while a third companion orbited around the planet in the vehicle in which they were to return to earth. They moved about, planted an American flag and several scientific instruments, got back into their machine and went back home again. The world was right to be impressed. It was not merely the culmination of an intellectual and technical effort so vast as to be almost unimaginable. It was also the

To the East German government West Berlin was an intolerable, ever-flourishing advertisement for the non-Communist
way of life. The wall built in 1961 to divide the town seemed
brutal, but in stopping the constant flow of refugees from the
east, it did to some extent relieve the international tension.
Planet News

greatest single step towards the enlargement of his environment taken by Man in his whole recorded history. If ever a
date marks an epoch, 1969 does, because of this.

East and West

The space programmes had of course not been stimulated
only by the disinterested thirst for knowledge, far less by
international sporting rivalry. Military concern over the use
that might be made of space and a sense that political prestige
was at stake played the largest part. In this way, the pre-
existing political antagonism between the United States and
Russia found a new expression. Undoubtedly this both
shaped specific policies and, together with suspicion, led to
wasteful duplication of effort. Yet in the same decade came
signs that, however slightly, some of the antagonism of the
Cold War might be on the ebb.

Two trends already discernible before 1961 helped this. One
was the appearance of signs of strain and new foci of loyalty
and interest in the blocs which had clustered about the
two giants. This process was sometimes called 'polycentrism'.
Linked to this was another continuing trend, a shift of
emphasis away from Europe. After 1961, threats of general
war arose less in Europe than overseas, and it began to appear
that although the dangerous potential of extra-European
quarrels might be great, there was also more tolerance of them
on both sides and more caution in handling them.

These changes produced an adjustment of the positions of
Russia and the United States which, although slight, led some
optimistic observers to talk of a 'thaw' in the Cold War.
Tension was very high in 1961, when Kruschev announced
that the Russians would hand over West Berlin to the East
German Republic. The East German government found
West Berlin intolerable because of its visibility and accessi-
bility; it was a huge and successful advertisement for non-
Communist society, and by August 1961, 3,500,000 Germans
had fled to the west through it. In that month the flow was
abruptly cut off. A wall, topped by barbed wire and heavily
policed, was built to divide Berlin. This was brutal, but seemed
to liquidate some of the international tension. The occupying
powers in West Berlin had made it clear that they would accept
no interference with their rights there and the Russians tacitly
allowed their threats to lapse, once emigration from the east
had been ended.

This crisis was not the only active irritant as the decade
opened. There were already other strains, over Africa (where
the Americans suspected the Russians of making trouble in
the Congo) and over Russian disregard for the United
Nations. In such an atmosphere it was not easy to see com-
pensating factors, but in retrospect it now seems that one had
already appeared. This was the election of John F. Kennedy
as President of the United States in 1960. He was a young man
and a Democrat, who took office with a style which seemed to
promise a break with the harsh, moralising associations of the
Dulles era of American foreign policy. Although a meeting
he had with Kruschev at Vienna in June 1961 was cold, both
men were aware of the dangers of a collision; the rapid
progress in missile technology demonstrated by space
exploration was warning enough. Both recognised, too, the
dangers of allowing other states to acquire nuclear weapons,
and both had troublesome allies. There were, therefore, some
grounds for hope of a relaxation, even by 1962. In fact, that
year brought the most dangerous and the last Russo-
American confrontation of the decade to threaten a general
war.

The Cuba crisis

It arose out of the affairs of Cuba, with which the United
States broke off diplomatic relations in January 1961.
Encouragement and, it seems, arms and help were given to
anti-Castro Cubans by American agents; this led to a
miserable disaster when 1,500 of these exiles landed in Cuba in
April 1961 at the Bay of Pigs and were almost at once rounded
up. American prestige suffered a heavy setback from what was
later admitted by Kennedy himself to have been a grievous
error. The United States made a partial recovery in the
following January by obtaining Cuba's expulsion from the
Organisation of American States and, by this time, seemed to
have learnt its lesson; Cuba was no longer regarded as a
problem demanding direct intervention. Unfortunately, a
Russian decision to try to exploit Castro's dependence by
installing on the island missiles which could strike at any part
of the United States changed this. Cuba once more appeared a
grave threat to the Americans.

Photographic evidence of missile sites was available in
Washington early in October. The President waited for it to
be incontrovertible and then on 22 October announced that a
'quarantine' would be imposed by the American navy to
prevent Russian missiles from being delivered to Cuba by sea
and that those already on the spot would have to be withdrawn. One Russian ship was boarded and searched in the
tense days that followed; the American nuclear striking force
was ready to go into action and it seemed that Kruschev
might accept the challenge. In the end, the worst international
crisis since 1948 was resolved in an exchange of personal
letters which, for all Kennedy's careful moderation of tone,
represented a big diplomatic setback for Russia. The missiles

Lyndon B. Johnson takes the oath on the plane carrying him back to Washington after Kennedy's assassination. Also present is Mrs Jacqueline Kennedy. Johnson has been much criticised for continuing with the increasingly unpopular war in Vietnam, but it is undeniable that he showed remarkable courage in pursuing the domestic policies of his predecessor, particularly in the field of civil rights. *Central Press*

Robert ('Bobby') Kennedy, who was an able Attorney-General during his brother's presidency, was generally considered a likely future president. He was assassinated in 1968 during a lavish election campaign. *Camera Press*

were soon removed; in return the Americans promised not to invade Cuba. In a few weeks the Russian bombers left, and in February 1963 it was agreed to remove Russian personnel, too.

Worldwide relief followed this settlement. It seemed that movement towards a better atmosphere could be resumed, as the factors working for improved relationships between the two world powers continued their operation. In 1963 there were two important consequences. One was the conclusion of a treaty between Russia, America and Great Britain (the three states possessing nuclear weapons) which agreed to avoid any tests in the atmosphere and above ground until further notice. Eventually, more than 100 states adhered to this (though, significantly, France and China did not). The second sign of improvement was the establishment of a 'hot line' between Moscow and Washington for direct telephonic communication between the leaders of the two world powers. It was almost everywhere recognised to be a tragedy when Kennedy was murdered in November 1963 (his brother Robert, whom many saw as a future president, was also to be assassinated four and a half years later). The British House of Commons paid the President the unique tribute of adjourning its business for the day–this had never before been done for a foreigner. The former Vice-President, Lyndon Johnson, at once affirmed his decision to continue the policies of his predecessor. Only a few months later it seemed that there would continue to be progress in the thaw of Russo-American relations (even if it was almost glacially slow) when both nations announced cuts in their production of fissile material. Even when Kruschev was removed from office in October 1964, the new Russian leaders were at pains to point out that this meant no change in Russian policy.

409

The Communist countries

There were by now many signs, therefore, to suggest that Russo-American antagonism was no longer the dominating fact of international relations. A possible contributory factor was more and more apparent: the two power blocs were beginning to show cracks. In Communist Europe, Albania quarrelled openly with Russia, and by 1965 Rumania was beginning to show an independence which expressed itself in voting differently from other Soviet satellites in the United Nations. In the background was a far more dangerous split in the Communist camp (which the Rumanians exploited). This was a growing hostility between Russian and China.

There had been signs of difficulty as early as 1958, when the Russians disappointed the Chinese by not making nuclear weapons available to them. In 1961, a sudden withdrawal of Russian economic aid had left China deeply embarrassed. There were also quarrels about territories taken from China by the Russian tsars – and the two states shared 4,500 miles of frontier. By 1969 all these practical and material disputes were given much greater significance by the simultaneous growth of a great ideological conflict.

The Chinese Communist Party had always ostentatiously preserved its revolutionary *élan*. It had accepted de-Stalinisation less enthusiastically than other Communist parties, and had been quick to scent and condemn 'revisionism' or weakening of doctrine in them. To begin with, such condemnations had only touched Russia indirectly, first by attacks on Yugoslavia, after that country's reconciliation with Russia, and then by support for Albania. At Moscow in 1961 it became clear that what was really at stake was a claim to the leadership of international Communism, although the clash between Kruschev and Mao Tse-tung was at first only expressed publicly through disagreement over Yugoslavia and Albania. In 1963 the rift became explicit. Kruschev's removal the following year made no difference to this in the

eyes of the Chinese, who continued to condemn Russia's leaders for betraying the revolution. Although Kosygin went to Peking in 1965, his visit only led to further dispute. The importance of this quarrel was that it not only embarrassed the Russians in their dealings with the West, but strengthened China's claim to lead world revolution, a claim which did much to aggravate the instabilities of Asia and breed more troubles there.

Difficulties with China may have helped to intensify Russian sensitivity about the dangers of divisions in Communist Europe. The Rumanians did not step too far out of line and were, in any case, too far east and too isolated to present a danger. It was Czechoslovakia, the most advanced of Communist states in her social structure and one with a common frontier with the West, which provided once more after thirty years evidence of the powerlessness of a landlocked small state which has inflamed a great neighbour. The provocation which the Czechs presented was nothing like so great as that offered by Poles and East Germans (far less Hungarians) in the 1950s. What was at issue was a series of internal reforms of a liberal tendency; they had their roots in the dismal failures of official economic policy, and the Czech Communists who supported these from their initiation early in 1968 made it absolutely clear that this would lead to no changes in foreign policy or the structure of defence set up by the Warsaw Pact. It may have been new trading ties with West Germany or the prospects of a reconsideration of purges in the past (which might have led to condemnation of the Soviet role in them) which was the decisive factor, or it may have been the support which the Czech reformers received from Rumania and Yugoslavia; whatever the detonator, on 21 August Soviet, Bulgarian, Hungarian and East German forces invaded Czechoslovakia and the liberal interlude was over. It was clear that the Russian attitude had in no way softened since 1956. Then, the Hungarians had threatened the Warsaw Pact itself; in the Czech case, domestic reform by itself had been

The Soviet government offered various justifications for the 1968 invasion of Czechoslovakia, the most firmly held being the need to suppress counter-revolution. The provocation, however, seemed mild: the issue was a series of liberal internal reforms put forward by the Dubček government. Below: buses used for barricades in Vinohradska St, Prague. *Camera Press*

In spite of right-wing bitterness, General de Gaulle's prestige was at its height when he granted independence to Algeria in 1961, and until 1967 his power seemed unshakeable. He resigned two years later when he lost support over a referendum on proposals for constitutional changes. *Camera Press*

The sudden explosion of student rebellion in Paris in 1968 almost paralysed France, and sparked off further student demonstrations and anti-authoritarian behaviour in other European countries. *Central Press*

seen as a sufficient threat. Nonetheless, though Russia lost face throughout the whole non-Communist world (and perhaps within the Communist camp, too) it was clear that no active international opposition was conceivable. Whatever the strains within it, Russia remained master of its own house.

The European stage

Non-Communist Europe had no upheavals like the Czech affair, but it, too, underwent some dislocation and distraction. A Greek-Turkish conflict over community strife in Cyprus in 1964 more than once threatened war between two members of NATO. Nor was the image of NATO much improved by a military *coup d'etat* in Greece in 1967 which attempted to solve the long-enduring problem of building a strong Greek state. This aim was soon forgotten by the world. So were the political weaknesses of Greece before the colonels' *coup* to be forgotten as evidence of their regime's repression and brutality accumulated.

The most important disruptive force in the west was France. General de Gaulle's prestige and authority reached its peak when he ended France's Algerian involvement. An announcement of the acceptance of the principle of self-determination in 1961 was followed by the ending of the war the following year. In spite of right-wing bitterness, an attempted military *coup d'etat*, assassination attempts and signs of a waning of his popularity in the presidential election of 1965, his authority after this long seemed unshakable. It gave French policy a quite new independence and vigour. He threw grave strains on the European Common Market by opposition to its agricultural proposals. In 1963 and 1967, he in effect twice vetoed the entry of the United Kingdom to it. At the same time he rejected American offers of nuclear submarines, announcing his determination that France should go ahead independently to make her own nuclear weapons. NATO, a structure already troubled by attempts to find a role for western Germany which would not give her control of nuclear weapons, was thrown into disarray by de Gaulle's hostility, and was visibly weakened as a military force even before France formally withdrew from it.

Gradually, it became clear that de Gaulle envisaged a Europe of distinct, national communities, free of 'Anglo-Saxon' patronage, and capable of standing between the two world powers as a third; independent and perhaps an arbitrator between them under French leadership. To some extent this was a realistic assessment of the transformation brought about by Europe's revival since 1945; from other points of view it looked like self-deception. It took on much greater significance, too, because of events in Asia, when de Gaulle in 1964 further displeased the United States by exchanging diplomatic representatives with Communist China. But he annoyed others needlessly; notably the Canadians by a tactless endorsement of Quebec separatism.

Nonetheless, even the greatest Frenchman of this century was not able to retain for long the support of his countrymen. Setbacks in elections in 1967 were an early sign that the achievements of French economic planning were not enough for all Frenchmen. In 1968 a sudden explosion of student rebellion seemed for a moment to have paralysed the state and left even de Gaulle staggering, but he did not resign and emerged from the crisis apparently strengthened. This was soon shown to be an illusion. When in 1969 he asked for support in a referendum on proposals for constitutional change he lost and immediately resigned. With him the most considerable individual force making for uncertainty in Western Europe disappeared.

411

China, a potential super-power

Nothing else mattered much in European history in this decade. It was in Asia that the greatest changes occurred, and China was their focus. Almost the whole continent still offered great potential for disorder, for over most of it outside Japan and China, social and economic backwardness tempted political exploitation. The withdrawal of European rule had left behind shaky governmental structures and illiterate populations susceptible to nationalist and racial demagogy. Decolonisation had created territorial disputes among the new states. These facts had been dangerous enough against the background of the Russo-American Cold War, but they now seemed worse, for China's support of subversive movements appeared to imply an alarming willingness to discount the risks of a general war. Suspiciously isolated not only from the West but from Russia too there was little chance that her attitudes would change quickly once she possessed an adequate armoury of nuclear weapons. Finally, she herself advanced certain territorial claims on her neighbours. Her impact on Asian politics, too, was all the greater because one of the nations likely to balance her influence, Japan, remained almost inactive politically. Japan's astonishing economic growth was not matched by a corresponding political influence, although there were signs by 1970 that this state of affairs might not last much longer.

With no correspondingly powerful counterweight on the mainland of Asia, it was therefore China which seemed to hold the key to Asian events and increasingly drew world attention. There was still little precise information to reveal what was really going on there. It was certain that 1959–60 had been marked by grave economic setbacks due, in some measure, to faulty direction and planning. Nevertheless, there was not any faltering in the confident tone of Chinese pro-

nouncements about the future, nor in their intransigence towards the outside world. Tremendous efforts were obviously being made to strengthen China; some of them bore fruit in October 1964 in the detonation of the first Chinese atomic bomb. It had been predicted for some time by the Americans and was of comparatively small size and elementary design; nonetheless, it announced an important change in power relationships in the future, and caused great dismay in other Asian countries. The Chinese said they owed it to the withdrawal of Soviet help, which had forced them to fend for themselves. In 1967 came the detonation of the first Chinese hydrogen bomb.

That China was now potentially a super-power could not be gainsaid. What was not clear was the extent to which she was free from internal troubles. The most obvious sign that something unexpected was occurring was the complicated phenomenon known as the Cultural Revolution. It emerged from the economic failures of the early 1960s and it was also connected with what the Chinese regarded as the renegade role of Russian Communism, which had given up the aims of world revolution. The answer to the first was education of the peasant and party member, and the answer to the second was the same. 'Education' here means political education–the need to keep the idea of the revolution alive. Once again, China was to be the centre of a world civilisation, the centre from which revolutionaries could learn throughout the world because it would be (unlike Russia) a centre in which the ideal of revolution had not grown cold. Enormous purges of the Chinese administrative cadres were the price, but it must be remembered that, so far as can be ascertained, this was not accompanied by anything like the bloodshed of the Stalin terror of the 1930s. What was far less easy to discern was how much of the old China still survived into the old age of Chairman Mao.

Mao Tse-tung watching the celebrations for fourteen years of Communist rule. The ideological conflict between China and Russia was a long-standing one: China had accepted de-Stalinisation with less readiness than other Communist countries. In 1963 the rift became wider, and the Chinese condemned Russia's leaders for betraying the revolution.

Camera Press

The recapture of Hue by American and South Vietnamese troops. American operations in Vietnam, at first directed against the Viet-Cong, were gradually extended to North Vietnam; the first bombing raids began in 1965. By 1966, with North Vietnamese regular troops and some 200,000 American soldiers in action in the South, the war had become the bloodiest since 1945, and the focus for world-wide attention and criticism. *Central Press*

Vietnam

Nor did internal upheaval prevent China from exercising great influence in Asia during these years. South East Asia in particular appeared a danger-spot. Throughout the area, there were dangerously feeble regimes. Laos, where civil strife had long been in progress, was neutralised by international agreement in 1962; this did not end trouble, and 1965 brought a revival of Communist insurgent activity there. But by then, Vietnam was again attracting most attention. Since the *de facto* partition, South Vietnam had not thrown up a stable, widely-supported domestic government. One hindrance was religious rivalry between Buddhists and Roman Catholics; another was the failure to carry out land reform which would unite the peasant population in support of the regime. A pervasive and continuing factor was the apparent corruption of a ruling class which seemed able to survive regime after regime. The Diem regime collapsed in 1963, with the connivance of the Americans, as only appeared some years later. In 1964 and 1965 there were military *coups*. Meanwhile, the activities of the Communist Viet-Cong, supported by North Vietnam, at first with supplies and services and later with regular troops, grew more and more dangerous and wrested large areas from the control of the government in Saigon.

This led to increasing American intervention, beginning under Kennedy, who first committed American forces to Vietnam. In 1962, he had 4,000 'advisers' there to help the South Vietnamese against internal subversion. American operations were gradually extended, at first against the Viet-Cong and then to North Vietnam in order to break its will to support the Viet-Cong. Training of South Vietnamese forces was by early 1964 already supplemented by covert operations and reconnaissance over North Vietnam mounted by the Americans. Then, later that year, attacks by North Vietnamese torpedo-boats provided an excuse for the bombing

of their bases by American aircraft; the first raids on other targets in North Vietnam began in February 1965 and continued with growing intensity, only once interrupted in the hope of permitting negotiation. North Vietnamese regular troops were by this time in action in South Vietnam and 200,000 American soldiers were committed there by early 1966. The number was to go much higher still, to over half a million, engaged in the bloodiest war since 1945, which soon outran Korea in cost and suffering.

The repercussions of such a conflict were only marginally less than its direct impact on the unhappy inhabitants of South East Asia who were its victims. It threatened at times, it seemed, to lead to a direct American clash with China. It again chilled Russo-American relations. Some of America's allies wavered in supporting her and almost all felt uneasy. Characteristically, General de Gaulle went furthest in dissociating himself from American policy, suggesting, in August 1966, the neutralisation of South East Asia in agreement with China, whose existence the United States still refused to recognise formally. By 1967, the American Secretary of Defense, McNamara, felt disillusioned enough with the expensive and distorting cost of the war to his country to commission a special study of what had gone wrong in American policy-making.

The existence of this study and the nature of some of its conclusions did not become public knowledge until 1971. When it did, it confirmed that, among other determinants of American policy had been the fear that failure to preserve South Vietnam would lead to the communisation of other allied or neutral countries in the area. No doubt this was operative, too, in another bitter, though less serious, conflict in this area, in which China was much less obviously involved. This was the so-called 'confrontation' of Indonesia with the Federation of Malaysia which came into existence in 1963, uniting many former British territories in the area.

413

Indonesia and Malaysia

The ruler of Indonesia, Soekarno, had long enjoyed a special tenderness at the hands of the Americans, who had been afraid that he might turn to China for support. Their policy reflected also the old anti-colonialist idealism of the Roosevelt and post-war years, which had always had the great merit of being paid for by friends who could not complain strongly or openly. In 1962, for example, the withdrawal of American support for the Dutch in West Irian led to its absorption by Indonesia in the following year. The exploitation of Indonesian nationalism had always been one of Soekarno's main domestic tactics and he turned now to claim Sarawak and Borneo, which were parts of Malaysia. Attacks by Indonesian troops began and British forces were sent to help the Federation; the United States still gave little support against Soekarno, and Robert Kennedy, the brother of the former president, made his appearance in London as the advocate of a settlement favourable to Indonesia. In 1964 Indonesian landings from sea and air began on the Malayan mainland. These operations, however, like those in Sarawak and Borneo, were mastered by the Commonwealth forces; their failure seems to have played a big part in bringing to a head a crisis in Indonesia itself.

In a way, this showed the logic of Soekarno's earlier moves; only the distraction of foreign adventure enabled him to ride the storm at home, where the economy was beset by food shortages and a huge inflation. The details of the opposition roused by the failure of confrontation are still obscure, but an attempt by Soekarno to forestall his opponents in September 1965 led to the deaths of several officers. This antagonised the armed forces, who then stood by and connived at a popular massacre of Indonesian Communists which effectively destroyed a force on which Soekarno might have fallen back. He had then to accept the progressive limitation and diminution of his power, although the soldiers did not dispense with him altogether because of the residual popularity he still enjoyed. But this enabled the confrontation with Malaysia to be ended, a clear setback for Chinese ambitions. It was unfortunate that Malaysia's success was marred by the secession of Singapore from the Federation in 1965; some said this was convincing evidence of the insolubility of the problems posed in the area by the existence of racial divisions.

India and Pakistan

The other main area of Asian disturbance was the Indian sub-continent. The tension between India and Pakistan, whose roots lay in the Kashmir question, was another problem complicated by China. In October 1962, on the eve of the Cuba crisis, Chinese troops suddenly attacked Indian posts in the Himalayas. This followed a year of Chinese pressure to obtain a revision of the frontier line, a revision for which at least a *prima facie* case could be made out. A month's fighting went badly for India, and although a cease-fire was then arranged sporadic clashes went on. The Chinese aggression severely shook the 'neutralist' concept to which India, and many other Asian countries, had adhered during the Cold War. It also produced further disarray in the non-Communist world by improving relations between China and Pakistan, a member of SEATO. Pakistan, afraid of the use India might make of arms supplied to her for use against China, began to look to Peking for help.

The death of Nehru in 1964 added to India's difficulties that of finding a successor acceptable in a country with so many divisions. Shastri, preferred by Nehru himself, took up office. He had soon to face another crisis. After a period during which tension over Kashmir seemed to be declining, fighting began there in August 1965. Alleging that infiltration from Pakistan was at the root of the trouble, the Indian government launched an attack on West Pakistan in September. Fighting went on for over two weeks with heavy losses of equipment on both sides. It was the gravest crisis of the Commonwealth to date, led to quarrels between India and Great Britain, and to new affirmations of support for Pakistan from China. A reconciliation of sorts was achieved by Russian mediation the following year, shortly before the death of Shastri. He was succeeded by Mrs Gandhi, the daughter of Nehru, who was soon to show herself as accomplished a politician as her father.

Shifting power

Half-way through the decade it was clear that the greatest world problems for the immediate future were those of Asia. Behind all the quarrels of the politicians lay the deeply recalcitrant and seemingly intractable questions of population, nutrition and economic growth. It was against this background that there loomed the spectre of a general war between the United States and China as, increasingly, policy in Vietnam seemed to rely upon direct intervention. Even Japan began to show signs of taking account of the new power of China and had its first diplomatic exchanges with Peking in 1965. This did not prevent subsequent deterioration of Sino-Japanese relations, but Japan's growing independence combined with signs of unreliability among America's other allies to make the United States more than ever anxious to keep friends she could trust. The Australian government showed its support of American policy by sending troops to Vietnam, but the British refused to do so.

Worse still, from the American point of view, the Labour government announced in 1968 its intention to wind up British naval and military commitments east of Suez. Although there

Mrs Indira Gandhi, the daughter of Nehru, who soon proved herself as able a politician as her father, took up office in 1966 on the death of the previous Prime Minister, Lal Bahudur Shastri. *Popperfoto*

were still forces in Singapore at the end of the decade they were being run down rapidly. Looking back on this phase of the British imperial aftermath, it is possible to discern one great success in the area: the preservation of Malaysia. But operations on this scale were expensive and police action would become more and more difficult to sustain because of the erosion of the power on which it was based.

Great Britain and the Commonwealth

The domestic history of the United Kingdom in the 1960s continued to be less dramatic and mercifully less violent than that of many countries but showed few positive achievements. It also lacks the clear theme provided in her foreign relations by the determined liquidation of the relics of world power and two attempts to enter the Common Market. In other ways British governments seemed unable to do more than tinker or utter banalities in confronting their problems.

The core of these problems was economic and psychological. Although still in world terms a rich nation, it was becoming obvious that the United Kingdom depended on a foreign trade which could less and less sustain both a powerful world role and a rising standard of living at home which was more and more taken for granted by the electorate. Neither the Conservative government of 1961 nor the Labour governments elected in 1964 and 1965 showed any capacity to produce in Great Britain the sort of firm government which de Gaulle had given France. Nor was there any sign that the British electorate would tolerate them if they did. There was one important sign of a possible change in the future: both parties committed themselves to trying to enter the European Common Market. The failure to gain entry in 1963 was a serious psychological blow, and the economic measures later necessary to keep sterling afloat annoyed Great Britain's partners in EFTA. The second failure, in 1968, was accepted less bitterly; it was clear by then that French opposition might not always be effective, given changes inside the Market itself, and that another attempt would be made before long. Before this happened, however, the general election of 1970 returned to power a Conservative government which, for good or ill, seemed for the first time since 1951 to hold out a prospect of a radical change of direction and style in British Government.

It immediately inherited a grave problem in Northern Ireland where, it appeared, the political clock had stood still for fifty years. In 1968 the political primitivism of Protestant and Catholic Irish fanaticism broke out anew in communal riots. Social and political grievances with a real content were soon displaced by simple atavistic hatred and fear, a situation which the barbaric thugs of the IRA did their best to inflame. Once more, in 1970, a British government at Westminster was confronted with its maddening responsibility for Irish affairs.

Other parts of the Commonwealth also had troubled British domestic politics during the decade. As a structure, the Commonwealth steadily deteriorated. At the same time, its tenuous hold on the British imagination, which had never responded to it with enthusiasm, slipped further. Commonwealth protests and misgivings about negotiations with the Common Market irritated Englishmen, and Africans, Indians, Pakistanis and West Indians all felt aggrieved by British restrictions on coloured immigration. The creation of a permanent Commonwealth secretariat in 1964 only seemed another step in its assimilation to the mass of other formal and meaningless international institutions. An attempt at Commonwealth mediation in Vietnam in 1965 ended in humiliating failure.

Above: Dr Verwoerd. Below: Ian Smith. The history of the Commonwealth in the nineteen-sixties was a troubled one. In 1961 Dr Verwoerd, Prime Minister from 1958 until his assassination in 1966, withdrew South Africa from the Commonwealth, having offended the whole of Black Africa by his *aparthied* policies. *Popperfoto*. This example was followed later in the decade by Southern Rhodesia: in 1962 Ian Smith's extreme right-wing Rhodesian Front Party won a victory at the elections by promising to attain independence from Britain and to retain white minority rule. His final declaration of independence was made in 1966 after the failure of talks with the British Prime Minister. *Camera Press*

Another sign of impotence appeared to be an increasing anarchy within the Commonwealth as common assumptions faded in a multi-racial structure. Armed conflict took place between the two biggest member states, India and Pakistan. Such structure as had once seemed promising showed every sign of breaking down. Federation had been a favourite answer to many past imperial problems, but Jamaica's defection in 1961 wrecked the Federation of the West Indies, which had to be wound up in 1962. Soon after this the Central African Federation broke up and this was a part of a chain of events which dealt the Commonwealth its heaviest blow of the decade and brought it to the very edge of dissolution.

The origins of this crisis went back to 1961 when South Africa at last withdrew from a Commonwealth whose members increasingly consisted of states offended by her policies of racial discrimination. Boer South Africans did not regret this; independence was an aim their most extreme leaders had cherished since the end of the Boer War. From this time, South Africa followed a prosperous but lonely path, marked by increasing internal tension, towards a practical separation of white and black in their daily lives. South Africans of British stock were dragged in the wake of the Afrikaaners. Portugal seemed the new republic's only friend. What idealism there might be about the policies of *apartheid* all but disappeared when an extremist Prime Minister, Vorster, took office after the assassination of his predecessor, Dr Verwoerd, in 1966. Nevertheless, South Africa's example was to be noticed and followed by other whites in Africa.

Until 1965, South Africa and Portugal, the last survivor of the great oceanic empires, shared the animosity of black African states. Then they were suddenly joined by Southern Rhodesia, which declared its independence of London under a white minority government. The feeble British response convinced many Commonwealth countries that white rebels would never be treated by London as bluntly as blacks would have been. This launched a crisis in the Commonwealth which threatened to break it up, though, in the event, it survived with less life in it even than before. Another conference of Commonwealth Prime Ministers was held in 1970 in Singapore at which yet further acrimony about British attitudes to Africa was expressed for the benefit of progressive world opinion.

Africa

The racial question in Africa was now brought into sharp focus. Those who feared majority rule by the black population pointed to the actual condition of many of the new African nations. (The Commonwealth had added to them Sierra Leone and Tanganyika in 1961, Uganda in 1962, Kenya and Zanzibar in 1963. Then came the dissolution of the Central African Federation, from which there emerged Malawi and Zambia in 1964 and the claim of Southern Rhodesia. The same year, Tanganyika and Zanzibar combined to form the new state of Tanzania. In 1965 Gambia became independent). Although the claims of the nationalists were in some degree satisfied and an Organisation of African Unity appeared in 1963, the continent showed no signs of settling down. Indeed, rather the reverse was true. One example often cited by whites as evidence of the dangers of black rule was provided by the Congo, where a breakdown of government and the secession of Katanga after Belgian withdrawal produced a crisis in 1960. American fears of Russian intervention were not justified, but the Congo was a prey to massacre and destruction which the intervention of a United Nations force only partly contained. The situation was complicated by the support given to Katanga by Southern Rhodesia. There was much denunciation of the forces of 'neo-colonialism', a convenient bogey, since it could mean almost anything. Although the re-integration of Katanga with the Congo was gradually achieved, a withdrawal of the United Nations force because of shortage of funds in 1964 was followed by further bloodshed and a military *coup*.

In the Congo, white residents had often been the victims, but there was also plenty of killing of black by black. Nor did other new African states have settled histories. Dahomey and Togo both had military *coups* in 1963, when an attempt was also made to assassinate President Nkrumah of Ghana. In 1964 there was another attempt to kill him, the military regime in the Sudan collapsed, and Uganda, Kenya and Tanganyika all had to ask for British military help because of internal troubles and mutinies in their armed forces. In 1965 an attempt was made to kill the President of Niger (it was believed to be inspired by Ghana), and Dahomey had two more military *coups*. Others followed in Upper Volta and the Central African Republic, and something of a climax seemed to have been reached when, in 1966, Nkrumah's regime was overthrown during his absence from Ghana on a visit to China.

The most tragic passage of African history of the decade occurred, ironically, in Nigeria, the biggest of the new Commonwealth states and one long regarded as particularly stable and politically mature. It began in 1966 when a military revolution was followed by the murder of the Prime Minister. The background to this had been a rapid deterioration of the economic situation and growing corruption in the first half of the decade. Almost at once, the new rulers proved unable

Patrice Lumumba, deposed Prime Minister of the Congo, who was later murdered by his captors, guarded by soldiers at Leopoldville airport. The breakdown of government in the Congo led to a crisis with the secession of Katanga in 1960. The following wave of violence and destruction was only partly contained by the intervention of a United Nations force.

Planet News

In 1966 a military revolution took place in Nigeria, and the country's new rulers were unable to prevent an explosion of tribal and religious feeling. The eastern region seceded under the name of Biafra in 1967, and the war dragged on until 1970, when the Biafrans, starved and desperately outnumbered, surrendered. Above: Biafran troops, ready for battle after only three weeks of training. *Camera Press*. Below: one of the many victims of a terrible war. *Popperfoto*

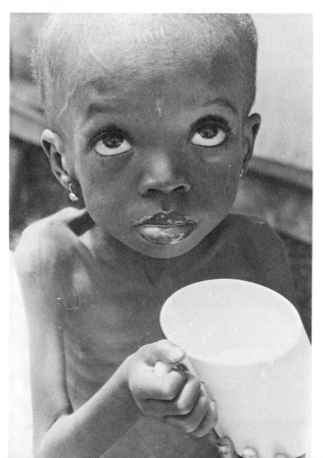

to prevent an eruption of tribal and regional feeling whose most serious expression was a demand for secession by the Muslim north of the country. A new administration began to work out schemes for a federal solution, but before these came to fruition the eastern region seceded under the name of Biafra. There followed more than two years of bitter fighting (prolonged by clandestine French and Portugese support for the Biafrans while the British and Russians backed the central government). Biafra only succumbed in the first days of 1970. The Nigerian state was preserved but at a terrible cost: at one time in 1968 100,000 deaths from starvation occurred in Biafra in a week.

Nothing else in Africa was quite as bad as this. In the first half of the decade, too, Arab Africa seemed to be settling down, though still troubled. Its great achievement of these years was the independence of Algeria in 1962. The lack of confidence felt in the future by European residents was registered by the departure of 800,000 of them, and some violence was indeed shown to them in the days immediately after the end of the fighting. But even in Algeria, civilian rule was replaced by military in 1965. The Moslem states of the Middle East meanwhile showed no great coherence or sense of unity in spite of the ambitions of Colonel Nasser to co-ordinate Arab efforts. In 1961 the United Arab Republic was undone by a Syrian revolt. In 1962 the Arab League was showing signs of a split, and in 1963 Saudi Arabia and Egypt quarrelled over a revolt which had broken out against the monarchist government of the Yemen. The Yemen entanglement, to which Nasser soon committed large armed forces, showed his desire to keep the pot of revolution boiling in the Arab world. So did the pro-Nasser revolution in Iraq which overthrew Kassim in 1963. The only sign of some reconsolidation of Arab unity came in 1965 over opposition to Israel's plans for the future use of the Jordan waters.

417

The Wailing Wall, Jerusalem. The Israelis at last won the city of Jerusalem after three days of gunfire during the Six Days War in 1967. This brilliant campaign, in which the forces of Egypt, Syria and Jordan were completely routed, strengthened Israel's boundaries, but by no means brought peace to the Middle East. *U.P.I.*

Gamal Abdel Nasser, President of the United Arab Republic, whose first step towards the modernisation of Egypt was the building of the Aswan dam. Despite the reverence in which he was held and the efforts he made to co-ordinate Arab efforts, the early years of his rule were marked by internal disputes; a consolidation of Arab unity only became apparent in 1965 with the necessity for strong opposition to Israel. *Popperfoto*

The Arab-Israeli conflict

Out of this grew a new Arab-Israeli conflict. In the background, factors which encouraged the Arab states to take undue risks were encouragement (and practical help) from the Russians and the growing pressure of the *fedayeen*, the groups of Arab refugees from the Gaza strip who kept alive guerilla war against Israel from Jordanian and Egyptian territory. A Palestine Liberation organisation had been set up by the Arab states in 1964 to encourage and help the *fedayeen*. Israel's forces struck back at the guerillas, but inevitably then came into conflict with the forces of their neighbours, as happened on Jordanian territory in 1966 and in an air battle over Syria in 1967. When in that summer Israeli forces were reported to be preparing to attack Syria, Nasser moved his own forces back into Sinai and announced the closure of the Straits of Tiran, Israel's only outlet to the Red Sea.

In spite of American and Russian efforts to cool down the situation the signs of coming conflict rapidly multiplied, notably when a defence agreement was signed by Jordan, Iraq and Egypt. The Israeli decision to anticipate an Arab onslaught was probably made as a result. On 5 June they attacked. Within three hours the Egyptian air force had ceased to exist as a fighting force; in six days the land forces of Egypt, Syria and Jordan had all been routed in one of the most brilliant campaigns in history. The Six Days War gave Israel defensible boundaries at last, but also a new Arab population of over a million to deal with; it had, furthermore not tamed but embittered her neighbours. By 1970 a new war had not come to the Middle East, but neither had peace. The King of Jordan reminded his allies that it had taken seventy years to clear the Middle East of the crusaders, and sporadic fighting continued to flare up along Israel's new boundaries as along the old.

The *fedayeen* meanwhile continued to embarrass their hosts. *Coups* in 1968 and 1969 in Iraq, the Sudan and Libya reminded the surviving traditional Arab rulers that a great potential for disorder still existed in their countries. One faction, the Popular Front for the Liberation of Palestine, finally provoked conflict between Arabs. In September 1970 it hi-jacked three aircraft successfully in mid-air and forced them to fly to the Middle East, where they were then blown up. This certainly won public attention for the PFLP, but was pretty generally condemned in the Arab world. The King of Jordan felt that the moment had come to uproot the nettle and demanded that the *fedayeen* organisation called the Palestine Liberation Movement which had almost taken control of his capital should disband its militia. Several days of fighting left the royal army in possession of the field, but King Hussein's victory looked likely to prove an expensive one, given the damage done to his prestige in the eyes of the rest of the Arab world.

Latin America

With so much of the world in uproar, it might have been expected that the Cold War would have made things much worse. In fact, as the decade wore on, the rivalry of the world powers seemed less important than their shared awareness of a nuclear conflict's dangers. Others saw the dangers of taking sides and this made the great powers cautious of acting in a way which might antagonise 'neutralist' states. Some African states even began to show disillusion with Russia and an African visit by the Chinese Prime Minister in 1965 was generally accounted to have been a failure. Nor, in spite of

British troops clash with Arab demonstrators in Aden. When in 1966 the British government announced its intention to abandon its military base – South Arabia was due to become independent in 1968 – Aden became the centre of a struggle between two nationalist organisations, FLOSY (the Front for the Liberation of Occupied South Yemen) and the NLF (National Liberation Front), backed by the UAR. After continued fighting and terrorist activities Aden achieved independence as part of the Southern Yemen in 1968. *Keystone*

the dangerous potential which existed there, did the Cold War much disturb Latin America. Castro continued to exercise a great appeal to the discontented in other states, but on his own he did not have much power to help them. Indigenous factors were causing more trouble there by 1970 than was interference from the outside. Over much of the continent poverty and brutal government in the interests of small elites alienated workers and the huge peasant masses. They were often Indian, and because of this alienated from the latinised elites of the cities, where power lay. The result was an intensification of struggle both in the field against would-be guerilla movements, by soldiers (often with American support) of the Latin American states, and by the police of the cities, whose brutality was well-publicised. Cubans attempted to exploit these trends. In 1965 Che Guevara left the island to preach revolution elsewhere in Latin America but two years later he was cornered and killed in Bolivia. Latin America was still disturbed in 1970, but there was not much sign that revolution was anywhere likely to succeed there.

Distrust and dislike of the United States remained a potent force south of the Rio Grande. Kennedy made attempts to do something about this by launching in 1961 an 'Alliance for Progress' with the aim of economic and social improvement. But the effects of American policy were more strongly felt in ways unlikely to increase its popularity. Even friendly governments looked with misgiving upon the fiasco of the Bay of Pigs and in 1965 there seemed to be fresh evidence

of the old bullying spirit of American Caribbean policy when American marines were sent to the Dominican Republic in violation of the OAS charter to stop the emergence of a new regime there under Communist guidance and thus nip in the bud any new Cuba. Eventually, these forces were withdrawn, being replaced by men from other OAS states, but it had been found difficult to drum up much support for this apparent endorsement of the American aims.

The United States

In their dealings with smaller states both the United States and Russia were beginning to experience the difficulties of providing world police power and of keeping in line allies some of whom were faltering and some of whom were disreputable. The United Nations, though larger than ever – in 1966 its membership rose from 117 to 122 – was almost paralysed by shortage of funds, internal antagonisms and poor leadership. Such difficulties re-awoke a never very somnolent isolationist sentiment in the United States which became more vociferous as the cost of the Vietnam war rose and disgust grew with the methods employed there. In the second half of the 1960s it became clearer and clearer that though a majority might still be willing to continue the war in Vietnam, American society was more and more bitterly divided over it and that it exacerbated and envenomed still other divisions.

419

To a President as politically conscious as Lyndon Johnson it must have been tempting to respond to this. He began with immense electoral support in 1964 when he won the biggest majority in the whole history of the United States. He later justified his re-election by his unswerving courage in pursuing domestic policies only adumbrated by his predecessor; when it becomes possible to see things in a larger perspective, it seems likely that the major achievement of Johnson's presidency will be judged to have been its reform legislation on welfare and civil rights. Mounting agitation for the ending of school segregation had been the first phase of securing full rights to coloured Americans. Under Johnson there followed Federal intervention to guarantee the full exercise of negroes' political rights, above all the free use of the vote. By 1966 there were clear signs of the passing of the old order in the South. The virtual solution of the southern problem revealed that the deepest and most tenacious forces holding the negro back from his place in 'the Great Society' which Mr Johnson discerned as his goal were poverty, bad conditions and cultural backwardness.

Paradoxically, it was in northern and mid-western cities and, most shocking of all, in Los Angeles, the heart of the 'promised land' of the new West, that violent riots took place in each year from 1964 onwards. Suddenly, it seemed, Civil Rights in the South was not enough. Northern liberals were at last having to face the problems they had ignored in their own backyards while priggishly condemning their Southern neighbours. Such disturbances showed that legal repression of the negro was not all that worried him. Increasingly, leaders were to be heard who advocated violent remedies and claimed that no real benefits could be expected from white and capitalist society. They seemed to unnerve Americans all the more because the violence, verbal and physical, of the blacks coincided with other signs of almost unbearable strain in American society. A new youth culture had grown up almost unnoticed and suddenly erupted in a tantrum of scorn and rage for the work of earlier generations.

The violent race riots which took place in Los Angeles from 1964 came, ironically, after the enactment of the Civil Rights Act. It became increasingly clear to American liberals that Civil Rights in the south were not enough; the negro population was not to be appeased by legal and political representation alone.
Keystone

Richard Nixon, the Republican candidate, was elected in 1968 after a campaign which revealed the bitterness and disillusionment felt by the liberals towards the Democrats, whom they would normally have supported. *Central Press*

Middle-class liberals began to feel excited by what had been done in the name of economic growth to the environment. Standards were suddenly challenged as never before. Even material progress itself was questioned.

This was the background of Johnson's decision in 1968 that he would not again run as a candidate for the presidency, but it is not likely that these facts would have prompted that decision had they not been cut across and enormously inflamed by the Vietnam war. This wrecked every other side of the administration's efforts. The expense of the war was colossal, even for the American economy, but this was not all that was wrong. Growing numbers of Americans believed that their government was pursuing a wicked or an impracticable goal. Some doubted its sincerity in the negotiations which began in 1967 with the North Vietnamese (with good reason, it later appeared). This deeply embarrassed the American government. There was every sign that the North Vietnamese were happy to play for time and wait for American withdrawal to deliver them the winnings they would not need to bargain for. The only American reply seemed to be to intensify the war yet more – and this further weakened the government's position at home.

The 1968 election was won by the Republican candidate, Mr Nixon, after a campaign which revealed all the bitter distrust of the American establishment felt by liberals, blacks and the young. They did not vote for Republicans, but against the Democrats, while middle-class America voted against them. The new president's problem was to find a way of running down American forces in Vietnam without abandoning the South Vietnamese to a collapse which would show that all America's efforts had been futile. The withdrawals began in 1969 and continued more rapidly in 1970. Not surprisingly, the army's morale soon showed signs of deterioration; soldiers who saw no reason to get killed in a dying cause began to murder officers and NCOs who showed an offensive spirit. Others simply took to drugs.

Meanwhile, things did not much improve at home. Economic recession was soon added to the administration's problems. American civilisation seemed even to many of its admirers tired, perhaps corrupt. One symptom was mounting violence and crime: in 1968 Kennedy's brother Robert was murdered as the president had been. The revelation that civilians were deliberately and wantonly massacred by American soldiers in Vietnam acting under their officers' orders seemed to fit the pattern. It was not a happy time for liberals in an America whose new inward-looking mood was reflected in a resurgence of isolationist sentiment reflected in the admiration for the vice-president, Mr Agnew, whose stature, even by the unexacting standards traditional in holders of that office, appeared to be high.

Yet there was a sense in which it was easy to take too sombre a view. The United States still remained in 1970 what it had been since 1948, the greatest concentration of economic power in the world. Her space programme was a huge feat of human ingenuity and skill, by any standard. Her relations with Russia seemed marginally better than ever as the slow but evident progress of Strategic Arms Limitations Talks showed. Until Vietnam, there was no crisis in which she had not shown her capacity to maintain her interests: it might be that withdrawal from the Asian mainland would remove the exception and that she would be as successful as before, once her interests were redefined and clearly discerned. There still was much to build hope on and America's world power was still the most important international fact of 1970 as it had been ten years before.

Summary

Other criteria than political, of course, could lead to other assessments of the decade. In population history, the onward rush of world population growth might well seem the most significant fact of these years. From other standpoints, the cumulative expansion of science, the revolt of youth, the coming of the computer culture or the breeding of doubts about material progress itself might all seem the crucial landmarks. The United States was touched by all these but was not alone in experiencing the problems which they brought. The internationalising of some issues, indeed, was a noteworthy feature of the decade. Some people went so far as to discern a general crisis of authority throughout the world of which such diverse phenomena as the hi-jacking of airlines, unrest in universities and the elevation of the consumption of narcotics into a cult activity were all examples. Racial feeling united coloured men everywhere against cultures and institutions seen as oppressive; on the other hand, non-white peoples showed their capacity to exploit or torment one another in a way which prevented this feeling from resulting in much more than the hot air of many speeches in the United Nations General Assembly. The trans-cultural and international solidarity of youth was more impressive, but as its effective power rests in the end on a dwindling asset – youth itself – it was hard to assess its true importance, or whether it was an autonomous force or just the natural expression by the maturing generations of forces implicit in the changing nature of society as a whole. All such changes are very hard to assess in the short term. And it might be pondered that, from one important, though increasingly disregarded, standpoint, the religious, the pontificate of John XXIII was undoubtedly the great fact of the decade. Such assessments as these require longer perspectives than those of politics, nor can they be measured in the brief compass of a decade.

Pope John XXIII, perhaps the most universally respected man of his time. His wisdom and humanity might have transformed the Catholic Church and exerted considerable influence on world affairs. But he attained the tiara late in life and the promise of his short pontificate was not honoured by his successor. He was deeply mourned. *Camera Press*

CHAPTER TWENTY-THREE

WORLD HISTORY 1971–80

World economic crisis

Overshadowing almost everything else in the 1970s was the world economic crisis which developed from 1974 onwards into the most serious and prolonged recession since the 1930s. Although its effects on the most advanced industrial nations were not as severe as those experienced in the 1930s, the crisis was more widespread, affecting not only the leading capitalist states but also the less developed countries and the Communist world. Moreover the crisis threatened to produce major structural changes in the patterns of economic power and by the end of the decade it was apparent that it carried grave dangers for the internal stability of several states and for the international order as a whole.

There was no single cause of the crisis. An extraordinary boom in production and trade in the early years of the decade produced an overheating of the international economy and spiralling rises in the prices of key commodities whose supply was restricted by natural and political factors. Most notable was the increase in the price of petroleum which multiplied by more than ten in the course of the decade. The result in many countries was an apparently new economic phenomenon — 'stagflation', stagnating production and runaway price inflation. Stagnating production led to increased unemployment and declining world trade. Inflation led to severe currency instabilities, unprecedentedly high interest rates, and a flight from money into gold. The dominant economic philosophy of the West in the post-war period, that associated with the British economist, John Maynard Keynes, now seemed to many to be discredited as being inherently inflationary, and in its place there grew up the new economic orthodoxy of 'monetarism', particularly that version propounded by Milton Friedman and others at the University of Chicago.

A major source of instability was the increasing relative weakness of the American economy. In 1950 the USA produced more than all the rest of the world put together, and

Throughout the 1970s, Sheikh Ahmed Zaki Yamani was the Saudi Arabian oil minister. In general Saudi Arabia, one of the most conservative OPEC states and its largest oil-producer, acted to moderate increases in the price of oil. *Popperfoto*

American dominance of world markets seemed almost absolute. But by 1980 the USA produced barely a fifth of world output, and faced strong competition particularly from Japan and the European Economic Community (EEC). The dollar, linchpin of capitalism since the Second World War, was devalued in 1971 and for the remainder of the decade it declined against such currencies as the Japanese yen and the West German mark. In 1970 the USA imported less than 10% of her petroleum requirements, but by 1980, despite the rapid development of huge oil reserves in Alaska, the depletion of this crucial resource was such that over half of the USA's oil requirements were imported (at more than ten times the 1970 price). Yet the average American continued to consume as much commercial energy as two Germans, three Japanese, or sixteen Chinese. Nor was there much appreciable development of alternative energy resources such as coal or nuclear power. 1974 and 1975 saw a severe recession in the USA with the Dow Jones industrial share average on the Wall Street stock exchange in New York tumbling by almost half, and with unemployment rising in 1975 to a peak of 9·2% (the highest level since 1941). After an uncertain and partial recovery, the end of the decade brought a deepening depression, illustrated by the troubles of the traditional bellwether of the US economy, the automobile industry. One of the largest motor car producers, Chrysler, narrowly averted bankruptcy. Imports of foreign cars rose. And by 1980, Japan for the first time overtook the USA to become the world's largest manufacturer of automobiles.

Other industrial economies were affected no less deeply, although in varying ways. By 1980 it was estimated that there were eighteen million unemployed in advanced capitalist countries. Japan, dependent on imports for 99% of her oil, 92% of her iron ore, and 73% of her copper, experienced a slow down in her dramatic economic spurt. West Germany, which had imported a million 'guest workers' from Turkey and southern Europe in the previous decade, found that she was faced for the first time in a generation with significant unemployment. In 1979 she confronted her largest-ever balance-of-payments deficit. Britain and Italy were afflicted by rapid inflation, labour disputes, low investment, and low productivity, rendering their products uncompetitive in world markets. However, by 1980 Britain's extraction of North Sea oil made the nation self-sufficient in energy, and likely to remain so until the end of the century — the only major Western state in this happy position. As a result, the pound sterling recovered swiftly, although this merely helped to expose the more cruelly the country's remaining weaknesses in economic structure by raising the exchange rate to an uncompetitively high level.

Efforts by the major industrialised countries of the West to achieve international cooperation were often mere hot air, but there were some limited achievements. An International Energy Agency of major consumers was formed in order to meet the challenge posed by the oil-producers' cartel, the Organisation of Petroleum Exporting Countries (OPEC). Although some countries edged towards protectionism in 1977-78, there was no repetition of the trade wars of the 1930s in spite of strong internal pressures for protective tariffs in many countries. The decade saw unprecedented massive rescue efforts by the International Monetary Fund (IMF) and by central banks of major states to help prop up ailing currencies, particularly the US dollar, the pound sterling, and the Italian and Turkish liras. However, such expedients were temporary palliatives rather than cures.

It was in the less developed countries that many of the effects of the crisis were most marked. The so-called 'third world' now split into a relatively affluent group of producers of vitally-needed raw materials, above all oil, and the larger number of impoverished states of the so-called 'fourth world'. Oil-producing countries such as Saudi Arabia, Iran, Iraq, Libya, Algeria, Nigeria, Mexico, and Venezuela received massive inflows of foreign currency and goods which, while they brought great wealth to some, distorted economic structures, accelerated runaway inflation, unsettled traditional social patterns, and rocked governments. The revolution in Iran, which unseated the Shah in early 1979 and inaugurated a chaotic period of religious, social, and ethnic struggle, was the most vivid illustration of the destabilising effects of sudden oil wealth. The problem of 'recycling' the surplus revenues of oil-producers (many of which had small populations and little scope for internal investment) was a major disturbing element in world markets. The Eurocurrency market (money circulating outside the country of issue) as a result grew in volume from about $110 billion in 1970 to an estimated $112 trillion by 1979.

While some states of the 'fourth world' also exported valuable raw materials, the rapid oscillations in price of commodities such as copper and coffee often prevented coherent economic planning. Thanks in large part to the 'green revolution' (a worldwide increase in agricultural productivity), the 1970s saw rather fewer major famines than previous decades. The chief exceptions were a man-made famine in Cambodia in the late 1970s and the famine in the Sahel region of Africa arising from climatic changes and advancing 'desertification'. During the decade there were signs in some areas that population growth might be decelerating slightly, but this was unlikely for long to remove the spectre of mass poverty and hunger, particularly given the continued opposition of the Roman Catholic church to artificial birth control. In the poorest countries such as Ethiopia, Niger, Mali, and Chad, average life expectancy in the 1970s remained under forty (compared with over seventy in Western Europe and North America).

As for the Communist economies, it became clear that they could not boast, as had the USSR in the 1930s, that they were immune to infection from the diseased capitalist economies. The USSR in 1980 was the world's largest oil producer as well as the owner of vast reserves of coal and natural gas. But the Soviet growth rate in the 1970s was the lowest since the Second World War, and the USSR continued to look to the West for the high technology and wheat which she was unable to produce adequately at home. China, too, exploited her substantial oil reserves off shore (expanding oil production five-fold between 1970 and 1977) and sought trade links with the USA, Europe, South America, and Japan. But all Communist economies were affected by the depression, and for the first time were compelled to admit to the existence of inflation. By the end of the decade there were signs, especially in Eastern Europe, that the prosperity of 'goulash Communism' was giving way to a partial return to austerity.

Détente and after

Economic pressures dominated international relations in the 1970s. 'Resource diplomacy' impinged on the relations of the super-powers with the third world, with their partners and clients, and with each other. The intensified competition for finite natural resources underlay both the period of super-power relaxation or 'détente' in the early 1970s and the retreat towards the end of the decade into more hostile attitudes reminiscent of the 1950s.

The interest of the USSR in détente with the USA arose for three main reasons. First, there was the desperate need of the Soviet economy for sophisticated technology and wheat, both of which could, it seemed, most easily be supplied by the USA and Canada. Second, there was the steady worsening of relations between Russia and China and the alarm felt in Moscow at the rapprochement between China and the USA. The visit of American President Richard Nixon to Peking in 1972 in a 'journey of peace' led to the re-establishment of contacts (by 1979 full diplomatic relations) between these erstwhile enemies. As the 'bi-polar' structure of international relations, frozen since 1945, disappeared, the two Communist giants seemed almost to be competing for American favour in the mid-1970s.

A third object of the USSR in moving towards détente was the desire to curb the escalating cost of the east-west arms race. The 1960s had seen striking advances by the Soviet Union in narrowing the quantitative (and in some spheres the qualitative) gap in military equipment between the Warsaw Pact and NATO forces. By the early 1970s the Soviet Union could negotiate on this subject from a position of strength. In May 1972, shortly after his visit to Peking, President Nixon visited Moscow and concluded the first Strategic Arms Limitation Treaty (known as SALT I) with the USSR. This set a ceiling for both the USA and the USSR of 200 anti-ballistic missiles. The number of land-based intercontinental ballistic missiles (ICBMs) which could be deployed by each side was frozen at 1,618 for the USSR and 1,054 for the USA. A formula was agreed for submarine-based missiles which allowed the USSR more missiles but permitted the USA to balance this by deploying several warheads on each missile (multiple, independently targetable, re-entry vehicles, known as MIRVs). In 1974 Nixon's successor, President Gerald Ford, visited Vladivostok with his Secretary of State, Dr Henry Kissinger, and concluded a further agreement with the Russian leader, Leonid Brezhnev. This set a ceiling of 2,400 ICBMs each, of which no more than 1,320 could have MIRVs. Although hailed as making progress towards disarmament, the agreements were criticised on the ground that they still left the super-powers with a multiple capacity for 'mutual assured destruction' (MAD).

Probably the most important achievement of détente was the settlement of the German problem, which had been a festering sore in east-west relations since 1945. This development was greatly assisted by the conciliatory 'Ostpolitik' pursued by the Social Democratic West German Federal Chancellor, Willy Brandt. This imaginative and courageous attempt to heal the bitter wounds of history led to visits by Brandt to Moscow and Warsaw and the conclusion of treaties between West Germany and the USSR and Poland. In 1972 an agreement was reached recognising the status quo in Berlin. In 1975 thirty-five states participated in a Conference on Security and Cooperation in Europe which convened in Helsinki and committed all participants to respect the territorial status quo in Europe. West Germany

In December 1970, West German Federal Chancellor Willy Brandt (2nd left) and the Polish Prime Minister (2nd right) signed the historic treaty between the two nations. *Camera Press*

now recognized the Oder-Neisse line as the border between East Germany and Poland. The commitment of the West to the reunification of the two Germanies was renounced. Other aspects of the agreement proved in the following years to have been little more than the enunciation of high-minded principles, but the political basis of the cold war in Europe seemed for a while to have diminished.

Symbolising the new era of harmony was the meeting in space of an American Apollo spacecraft and a Soviet Soyuz spacecraft. The link-up took place in July 1975 when the crews visited each other's spacecraft and shared meals. After the frenzied rivalry of the space race in the 1960s this event seemed to betoken a new stage in east-west relations. Indeed, in the 1970s both superpowers invested far less money and effort in space research which returned to a more strictly scientific and commercial level, as distinct from the competition for prestige of the 1960s.

The second half of the decade, however, dashed many of the over-sanguine hopes of proponents of détente in both east and west. The USSR objected to the insistence of the American Senate that expansion of Soviet-American trade should be linked to the granting of the right to emigrate to Soviet Jews. Soviet Premier Kosygin complained in 1977 that trade with the USA still constituted only 2% of the USSR's foreign trade. Moreover, the USSR discovered that it could often import many vitally required products from countries such as West Germany and Japan (which together supplied 11% of Soviet imports by 1977) without the attachment of irksome political conditions. The USA, for its part, objected to Russian involvement (sometimes using Cuban troops as proxies) in wars in Angola, the Horn of Africa, and elsewhere.

Although a second SALT agreement was signed in Vienna by Presidents Carter and Brezhnev in June 1979, its ratification by the American Senate was delayed. There was wide-spread suspicion in the West that the Russians were using the SALT negotiations as camouflage for their continued arms build-up. Whereas American defence spending had fallen from a peak of 9·6% of gross national product (GNP) in 1968 (at the height of the Vietnam war) to 5% by 1979, the USSR was still spending between 11 and 15% of its (smaller) GNP on defence in 1979. Moreover, in the late

1970s the USSR could maintain forces simultaneously in Asia and Europe which were superior to both China and NATO. The Warsaw Pact could muster 21,000 main battle tanks in service as against only 7,000 for NATO. On the European central front, Warsaw Pact forces outnumbered NATO by 943,000 to 626,000. Such figures alarmed both official and public opinion and diminished the limited stock of enthusiasm for détente. In December 1979 the USSR, conscious of its burgeoning military strength, and perhaps responding to apparent encirclement by hostile forces as the American-Chinese friendship blossomed, seized the opportunity afforded by the collapse of the Shah's pro-western regime in Iran and invaded the neighbouring neutral state of Afghanistan. A shaky but subservient pro-Moscow government was installed in Kabul, dependent for survival on continued Soviet occupation of the country. President Carter responded by announcing in January 1980 that further American consideration of the SALT II treaty would be deferred and instituting economic sanctions. In July 1980 the USA and many of its allies (also some Muslim states and others, but not the United Kingdom or France) boycotted the Olympic Games which were held in Moscow. Further prospects for détente now seemed slim.

East Asia

It was the termination of American military involvement in the Indo-Chinese war which had been the necessary condition of improved American relations with Russia and China. But American withdrawal did not end the war which continued in different forms, causing the most appalling bloodshed.

The American disengagement from Vietnam during President Nixon's first administration (1969-73) was, in any case, a slow and painful process. Far from reducing the scale of the conflict, the Americans seemed bent on extending it. In March 1970 a military coup in Cambodia ousted the neutralist government of the mercurial Prince Sihanouk (while he was abroad). Six weeks later American and South Vietnamese forces crossed into Cambodia in order to bolster the precarious hold on power of the pro-American General Lon Nol. In February 1971 American forces aided a forty-four day incursion by South Vietnamese troops into Laos. In December 1971, in a last desperate throw, Nixon ordered the resumption of the bombing of North Vietnam. But these attempts to win the war by a knock-out blow

A Chinook helicopter takes off after re-supplying American Marines in Vietnam. *Keystone Press*

A wounded Cambodian Government soldier is helped from an unsuccessful battle to halt the Khmer Rouge advance on Phnom Penh. *Camera Press*

before American troop withdrawals were complete proved a disastrous and costly failure. There was a massive protest in the USA against the continuation of the war. Faced with swelling congressional demands for an end to American involvement and confronting a strongly anti-war Democratic candidate in the November 1972 Presidential elections, Nixon ordered the last American combat troops to leave Vietnam in August 1972. He thus fulfilled his pledge to withdraw American forces before his first term expired, although many questioned his claim that the USA left Vietnam undefeated and with its honour intact.

In January 1973 the lengthy peace talks in Paris finally resulted in an agreement, but this marked merely the start of a new phase in the war. The Americans pinned their hopes on the so-called 'Vietnamization' of the war, in the belief that the South Vietnamese government, headed by General Thieu, would now be able to resist the Viet Cong and North Vietnamese forces unaided. But the Thieu regime proved a weak reed, as corrupt, self-serving, and unpopular as its predecessors. In April 1975, as Communist forces closed in on Saigon, Thieu resigned and fled (with 200,000 other South Vietnamese). With the collapse of the pro-American Saigon regime, the city was renamed Ho Chi Minh City (in honour of the North Vietnamese leader who had died in 1969), and in November 1975 the unification of north and south was proclaimed.

At the same time Communist forces secured victories in the rest of Indo-China. In April 1975 the Communist Pathet Lao took over effective power in Laos, and in November the king abdicated and a republic was declared. Also in April 1975 the capital of Cambodia, Phnom Penh, fell to guerrillas known as the Khmer Rouge who were in an uneasy alliance with Prince Sihanouk. Although restored as head of state Sihanouk remained abroad (save for a brief visit in September 1975). In April 1976 he resigned as head of state and was replaced by Khieu Samphan. Effective power resided with the Prime Minister, Pol Pot, who, it was revealed, was secretary of Angka, the Communist party of Kampuchea (as the country was re-named). The Pol Pot regime almost destroyed the country as an effective social unit. At least one million (perhaps as many as three million) people died in mass executions and famine. The capital city was entirely

evacuated and its population ordered out to the countryside to work the soil as political re-education.

In December 1978 the Pot Pol regime was attacked by Vietnamese forces (who enjoyed the support of the USSR), and in early 1979 it succumbed to the Vietnamese-sponsored regime of Heng Samrin. China, which backed the ousted Pol Pot, reacted in February 1979 by launching a punitive attack on North Vietnam. Although Chinese forces withdrew a few weeks later, having inflicted severe blows on the Vietnamese, border incidents continued. Moreover, inside Cambodia fierce fighting continued between partisans of Pol Pot and Heng Samrin. There were vast refugee movements in the late 1970s as a result of the war: hundreds of thousands of Vietnamese of Chinese descent were forced out of Vietnam, many perishing in small boats on the South China Sea. Refugees from Cambodia fled to neighbouring Thailand, leading to tension and border incidents between those two countries. As the USA rushed a massive arms airlift to Thailand in mid-1980 there seemed little prospect that the devastating series of conflicts in south-east Asia would soon end.

The 1970s were a decade of startling changes in political leadership, diplomatic alignment, and social policy in China. In September 1971 a major political crisis occurred: in a massive purge eleven of the twenty-one members of the politbureau were dismissed, and the minister of defence, Lin Piao, perished. Factional conflict resumed in 1976 following the death of the prime minister, Chou En-Lai. His successor was the obscure Hua Kuo-Feng. Radical elements seemed to have triumphed when Teng Hsiao-Ping was dismissed from all offices and denounced as a 'capitalist roader', an event which provoked protest demonstrations in Peking. The death of Mao Tse-Tung in September 1976 reopened the struggle. The following month the radical leaders, a so-called 'gang-of-four' headed by Mao's widow, Chiang Ching, were arrested. Hua was appointed party chairman in succession to Mao, but real power increasingly seemed to rest with Teng who was restored to office in 1977.

The one constant in Chinese diplomacy in this decade was unremitting hostility to the USSR. Otherwise all was flux. In 1971 the People's Republic finally secured recognition of its right to the Chinese seat at the United Nations, 425

Hua Kuo-Feng, who in 1976 became firstly Prime Minister of China on the death of Chou En-Lai, and then Chairman of the Communist Party on the death of Mao Tse-Tsung. *Camera Press*

ousting the nationalist Chinese regime based in Taiwan. A series of western statesmen, beginning with Dr Kissinger and President Nixon, visited China, and the fierce xenophobia of the late 1960s gave way to a much more open attitude to the USA, Europe, Japan, and South America. Even the attitude to Taiwan changed after the death of Chiang Kai-Shek in 1975, leading to an offer by Peking (angrily rejected) of autonomy for Taiwan within the People's Republic.

Internally, the late 1970s were a period of stabilisation after the chaos of the 'cultural revolution', and of limited liberalisation. Universities were once again permitted to hold exams; French novels, German composers, Italian opera were once again part of the country's cultural life. Wall posters (*dazibao*) afforded a measure of free speech in Peking. But the changes were in many cases more of style than of substance; there could be no questioning of the fundamentals of the Communist system, and by 1980 the unofficial wall posters in Peking had been banned.

By comparison with Indo-China and China, the remainder of East Asia seemed relatively stable in the 1970s. For much of the decade, Japan anxiously sought to balance relations with both the USSR and China. However, by 1978 Japan reached a decision. In a reconciliation as historic in its way as that between West Germany and her eastern neighbours,

Japan signed a treaty of peace and friendship with China. The treaty contained an 'anti-hegemony' clause which affronted the USSR. Internally, Japan's long-ruling Liberal Democratic Party (LDP) was severely shaken by a scandal in 1976 which implicated senior politicians, including a former prime minister, Kakuei Tanaka, in alleged bribery by the American aircraft company, Lockheed. Nevertheless, in subsequent elections in 1976 and 1980 the LDP maintained its hold on power. In South Korea, too, a scandal broke out which involved the bribery of American congressmen by the Korean Central Intelligence Agency (KCIA). In October 1979, President Park Chung-hi, autocratic ruler of the country since 1962, was shot dead at a dinner party in Seoul by the Director of the KCIA. The period of unrest which ensued placed a question mark against the continuation of the remarkable economic growth achieved under the Park regime.

The Indian sub-continent

From December 1970 to January 1971 a general election, the first ever in the country on the basis of 'one man one vote', took place in Pakistan. In West Pakistan the Pakistan People's Party (PPP), led by the flamboyant former foreign minister, Zulfiquar Ali Bhutto, won an overwhelming victory. However, in East Pakistan victory went to the autonomist Awami League, led by Sheikh Mujib ur-Rahman. Talks between the two parties failed, and in March 1971 Sheikh Mujib declared the secession of East Pakistan and its establishment as the independent republic of Bangladesh. Civil war broke out in East Pakistan in which terrible atrocities were committed, and millions of refugees fled to India. In December Indian forces intervened in support of the secessionists and in a twelve-day war decisively defeated the Pakistan army. Bangladesh thus emerged, under Indian protection, as an independent country, but independence did not cure the deep-seated problems of over-population, disease, hunger, and murderous floods which afflicted this, one of the poorest regions on earth. Sheikh Mujib's fragile constitutional regime survived until 1975, when he was overthrown and murdered in a military coup.

With statesmanship Bhutto chose not irredentism but realism in his future relations with his neighbours. In 1972 India and Pakistan reached agreement on a *modus vivendi* over the long-simmering Kashmir dispute: while the

Refugees were tragically commonplace during the 1970s. Here, in 1971, exhausted peasants flee from East Pakistan (Bangladesh) to escape the civil war. *Popperfoto*

Zulfiqar Ali Bhutto, Pakistan's Prime Minister from 1971 to 1977, accompanied by his wife and daughter. *Keystone Press*

426

problem was not solved, it now seemed less likely to lead to a renewed outbreak of war. By 1976 relations between the two countries were re-established.

In elections in 1977 Bhutto's PPP won 155 out of 200 seats. However, accusations of ballot-rigging led to widespread demonstrations. Taking advantage of the unrest the armed forces decided to end Pakistan's brief experiment with civilian rule, and in July a military coup deposed Bhutto. General Mohammed Zia ul-Haq seized effective power. Bhutto was arrested and charged with the murder of the father of a political opponent (as well as with abduction, contempt of court, treason, misappropriation of government funds, and corruption). He was sentenced to death in March 1978, and, in spite of pleas from world leaders for his life, hanged in April 1979. General Zia's regime pursued a policy of ruthless repression based on a supposed return to traditional Islamic values. But tremendous economic difficulties remained unsolved, tribal dissension increased, and as opposition coalesced around the Bhutto family it became evident that the military regime had little basis of popular consent.

The political history of India in the 1970s also revolved around the dramatic vicissitudes of a charismatic leader. In general elections in February-March 1971 Indira Gandhi's Congress Party gained an overall majority in the Lok Sabha (the lower house of parliament). Her slogan was *'Garibi Hatao!'* (Eliminate poverty!). However, the hopes aroused by the ambitious five-year economic plan announced in 1974 were soon dashed. The world economic crisis brought rapid inflation and knocked out the calculations of the planners. There was widespread unrest among peasants and industrial workers. Matters came to a head in the summer of 1975 when Mrs Gandhi was found guilty of electoral malpractice and was barred by the courts from holding elective office for a period of six years. The opposition, headed by the former defence minister, Morarji Desai, and by the Gandhian figure of Jayaprakash Narayan ('J. P.') demanded Mrs Gandhi's resignation.

She responded with a declaration by the President of a state of national emergency. All opposition leaders (except the pro-Moscow communists) were gaoled, *habeas corpus* was suspended, censorship imposed on the press, and Mrs Gandhi's conviction annulled by retroactive legislation pushed through what had become a rubber-stamp parliament. The emergency had some striking successes: inflation

suddenly decelerated (thanks in part to the providential 1975 monsoon), industrial production rose by 10% in 1976-77, and capital investment rose to 30% in the first year of the emergency. But the authoritarian atmosphere accorded ill with the rich diversity hitherto characteristic of the Indian political culture, and there was bitter resentment of the programme of forced sterilisation (in the interest of population control) which was identified with Mrs Gandhi's son, Sanjay.

As one of her emergency measures Mrs Gandhi had postponed the election due in December 1975. When it was finally held in March 1977 Mrs Gandhi suffered a shattering reversal. She lost her own seat in parliament, was repudiated by her party, and arrested; her political career seemed at an end. The electoral victors were the Janata Morcha (People's Front), headed by Desai who became Prime Minister. But the Janata was riven by personal, regional, and ideological rivalries. It soon degenerated into bitter factional squabbling while the high expectations it had aroused remained unfulfilled. Almost its only achievement was the elimination of the emergency. Meanwhile the ousted leader built a new party known as Congress (Indira). Torn by its internal contradictions, the Janata government collapsed in 1979. In elections in January 1980, Janata was smashed, and Congress (I) won a landslide majority. Restored to power Mrs Gandhi was unchastened, but she prudently avoided any repetition of the unpopular excesses of the emergency regime.

The Middle East

During the 1970s the Middle East assumed an unprecedented importance in world affairs. First, because of the rise in oil prices which was pioneered by the revolutionary Libyan regime in 1970, and was greatly accelerated by decision of OPEC in 1973-74. Second, because of the complex ramifications of the 1973 Arab-Israeli war.

In September 1970 Egypt and Israel had agreed upon a truce in the 'war of attrition' which was waged along the Suez Canal. However, the following month President Nasser died suddenly, and his successor, Anwar al-Sadat, appeared at first a much less forceful leader. Sadat, however, soon demonstrated that he was capable of decisive leadership. In 1972 he expelled most of the Russian 'advisers' (including military personnel) from Egypt, and began to steer the country in a pro-American direction. Finding that Israel

Indira Gandhi receives garlands from well-wishers in New Delhi. The 1970s saw remarkable vicissitudes in her fortunes, but at the end of the decade she was firmly in control. *Camera Press*

Golda Meir, Israel's Prime Minister from 1969 to 1974, addressing the Israel parliament during the *Yom Kippur* War. *Topix*

427

A wounded Israeli soldier is escorted from the battle on the Golan Heights during the 1973 Arab-Israeli War. Although driven back initially, Israel had more than regained the lost ground by the ceasefire. *Camera Press*

Prime Minister Menahem Begin of Israel (left) and President Anwar Sadat (right) of Egypt at the 1977 Christmas peace negotiations at Ismailia, Egypt, which marked a further stage in the process of détente between the two nations. *Camera Press*

rejected American peace proposals (which involved the return to Arab sovereignty of virtually all the territories occupied in the 1967 war), and that the Israeli government headed by Mrs Golda Meir dismissed contemptuously Sadat's hints of readiness for an accommodation, Sadat decided to launch a fourth full-scale Arab-Israeli war.

On 6 October 1973, *Yom Kippur* (the Jewish Day of Atonement), Egypt and Syria attacked Israeli forces in Sinai and the Golan Heights. In the initial stages of the war the Arabs, who had caught the Israelis by surprise, won important tactical victories. The Egyptians managed to transport several armoured divisions across the Suez Canal and to engage the Israelis in Sinai. In the north the Syrians pushed deep into the Golan Heights. The armoured battles which developed once the Israelis had hastily mobilised were the largest such confrontations since the Second World War. The Arabs enjoyed massive armaments supplies from the USSR, while Israel received similar support from the USA. After its initial setbacks the Israelis gradually turned the tide: the Golan was recaptured and a further slice of Syrian territory was occupied. In the south an Israeli army under General Ariel Sharon crossed the canal into Egypt and an entire Egyptian army was surrounded. On 25 October the conflict seemed for a moment in danger of escalating into a super-power conflict when President Nixon, reacting to signs of possible Russian military intervention, ordered a world-wide American nuclear alert. However, a cease-fire was established on both fronts with Israel in possession of more territory than when the war had begun.

Nevertheless, as subsequent events were to prove, Israel's political position had been greatly weakened both by her proven vulnerability in the early days of the war and by the mobilisation of the so-called 'oil weapon'—the four-fold oil price increase, and the threat (not successfully effected) of a ban on the supply of oil to countries which supported Israel (notably the USA and the Netherlands). Israel now came under increasing pressure to yield occupied territories. In December 1973 a peace conference, attended by Israel, Jordan, Egypt, the USSR, and the USA, opened at Geneva, but it adjourned after a single day's deliberations and was not reconvened. However, in January 1974 an agreement was signed between the Israeli and Egyptian army commanders providing for the 'disengagement' of their forces in Sinai. As a result of the agreement Israeli forces were withdrawn to a line east of the Suez Canal and a UN buffer zone was formed between the two sides. Thanks to the so-called 'shuttle

diplomacy' of Dr Kissinger, a further disengagement agreement was reached between Israel and Syria in May 1974: this, too, provided for Israeli withdrawal to a line just within the area occupied in 1967. Further lengthy negotiations under Kissinger's auspices produced a second disengagement agreement (providing for further Israeli withdrawals) between Israel and Egypt in 1975.

In May 1977 the Israeli Labour Party, which had headed all government coalitions since independence, lost power in national elections to a right-wing party headed by Menahem Begin. This seemed to have destroyed prospects for further negotiations, but in November, in a remarkable act of political courage (which was also a supreme theatrical display), President Sadat paid a visit to Jerusalem, the first Arab statesman ever to make an official trip to the Jewish state. In a moving speech in the Knesset Sadat pronounced his readiness for a peaceful settlement with Israel and declared to the Israelis: 'We welcome you among us.' Tense months of negotiation followed under American auspices and in September 1978, after twelve days of talks with President Carter at Camp David in Maryland, Begin and Sadat agreed on an outline 'framework' for a settlement. A peace treaty was signed in Washington in March 1979—a revolutionary breakthrough by Israel in her thirty-year quest for acceptance by her neighbours. In return Israel promised to make phased withdrawals from the whole of the Sinai peninsula.

However, the agreement between Israel and Egypt was roundly condemned by most other Arab states on the grounds that it failed to resolve satisfactorily the national demands of the Palestinian Arabs. In the course of the 1970s the Palestine Liberation Organization (PLO), a grouping of factions of Palestinians in exile, had attained general acceptance both among the Palestinian Arabs and in much of the world (save the Western allies) as the legitimate representative of the Palestinians. The Palestine National Charter, approved by the PLO, called for the elimination of Israel and its replacement by a secular, democratic, non-sectarian state. In pursuit of this goal Palestinian terror gangs carried out numerous attacks on civilian targets both inside and outside Israel throughout the decade.

Although expelled from Jordan by King Hussein in 1970, the PLO had established itself in Lebanon whence it carried out attacks into Israel. The result was to provoke Israeli counterattacks in the form of aerial bombardment of Lebanon. By 1975 this expansion of the conflict into

Lebanon (which had not participated in any of the wars against Israel since 1948) upset the delicate communal balance of Christians and Muslims there. Lebanon erupted into a bloody civil war which lasted for much of the rest of the decade and drew in Syrian occupation forces, ostensibly sent in to keep the peace. Israel also intervened, occupying a large swathe of southern Lebanon in 1978 (though Israel withdrew soon after), and supplying arms to some of the Christian militias.

The PLO refused, in spite of American blandishments, to moderate its Charter in order to provide for the possibility of recognizing the existence of Israel. Amply financed by Arab oil-producing states, and enjoying the political support of the USSR and its allies (resentful of what appeared to be a 'pax Americana' in the Middle East), the PLO's position was endorsed by the 'rejection front' of Arab states. Nevertheless, by 1980 there were signs that other Arab countries, notably Jordan and Saudi Arabia, might eventually follow Egypt's lead and come to terms with Israel on condition that Israel withdrew from the remaining territories occupied in the 1967 war.

Africa

The 1970s saw the virtual eclipse of European colonialism (or at any rate of formal European rule) throughout Africa except for the white bastion in the south.

The most important remaining colonies at the start of the decade were the Portuguese territories of Angola, Mozambique and Guinea, where years of warfare between nationalist guerrillas and the Portuguese army had debilitated the military, financial, and political strength of Portugal's autocratic system of government. In 1974 a 'revolution of flowers' restored democracy in Portugal and opened the way for the independence of Portugal's empire in Africa in the following year. In Angola independence was followed by the flight of hundreds of thousands of European residents, and by a bitter civil war between rival nationalist factions. The MPLA, a Marxist faction headed by Agostinho Neto, captured Luanda, but their grip on power was challenged by the intervention of South African troops. However, the MPLA was strengthened by Cuban armoured forces, and by early 1976 they had defeated their opponents, although residual guerrilla activity was still being reported in 1980.

The independence of the Portuguese colonies decisively affected the politics of southern Africa. The white minority regime in Rhodesia, whose successful defiance of UN economic sanctions for the previous decade had been due in large measure to their access to the Mozambique port of Beira, now faced their day of reckoning. Confronted by an increasingly fierce war against guerrilla nationalists, and warned by the South African government that in the last resort South Africa would not fight to uphold his regime, the white Rhodesian leader, Ian Smith, reluctantly gave ground. In 1976, at a meeting with the persuasive Dr Kissinger, Mr Smith (who had once said that Rhodesia would never enjoy universal suffrage in his lifetime) acquiesced in a statement that majority rule would be granted within two years. But a peace conference with the black nationalists held at Geneva later in 1976 broke up without agreement on a new constitution. Capitalising on divisions among the nationalist leaders, Smith concluded an 'internal settlement' in March 1978 with the more compliant black leaders, but the settlement did not secure international acceptance and did not stop the guerrilla war which flared with a renewed

intensity. Finally, in 1979, a further conference took place in London, under British auspices, at which agreement was reached on a return to legality as a British colony, on new elections to be supervised by the British, and on subsequent independence. In the elections, in 1980, the party headed by Robert Mugabe, a reputed Marxist, scored a smashing victory over that of Joshua Nkomo, the other main nationalist leader and that of Bishop Abel Muzorewa. Under Mugabe's leadership, independent Zimbabwe (as the country was now known) sought to conciliate the white minority, the majority of whom remained in the country for the time being.

The events to her north in the 1970s sent shock waves through the South African political system. In 1976 there were severe riots in Soweto, a black township near Johannesburg, in which several hundred blacks (including many children) were killed by security forces. In 1977 Steve Biko, a leader of the 'Black Consciousness' movement, died from brain injuries while in police custody (one of a large number to die in police hands). An inquest held nobody responsible for his death. In 1980 there were further severe riots with many deaths. These events galvanised world opinion against the *apartheid* regime and induced a new mood of self-doubt even among Afrikaner South Africans. In 1976 the first 'Bantustan', or black homeland, the Transkei, was declared independent followed in 1977 by a second, Bophuthatswana, but neither secured international recognition. Nevertheless, the black homeland policy produced in Chief Gatsha Buthelezi, a Zulu, at least one leader of major stature who sought to challenge the system from within. White South Africa was profoundly shaken in 1979 by the so-called 'Muldergate' scandal which led to the retirement from politics of Mr Vorster. By 1980, although riding a wave of prosperity as a result of the massive world demand for gold, the *apartheid* system looked much less durable than a decade earlier.

The 1970s also saw the death of the oldest empire in Africa and the birth of a new one, both of them indigenous rather than European. In 1974, after drought and famine had caused 100,000 deaths in Ethiopia, there were riots in the capital which led in September to the peaceful deposition of

Bishop Abel Muzorewa (left) leaves the table after signing the Zimbabwe/Rhodesia ceasefire agreement, 1979, with the leaders of the Patriotic Front: Robert Mugabe (2nd right) and Joshua Nkomo (right). In the subsequent democratic elections, Robert Mugabe's party gained a clear majority of the votes. *Popperfoto*

Emperor Haile Selassie of Ethiopia (1892-1975). *Camera Press*

countries on earth) one quarter of its entire annual foreign exchange earnings. Two similarly idiosyncratic tyrants emerged in Africa in the 1970s. In Uganda the egregious President Idi Amin Dada held murderous sway thanks to the reign of terror of the thugs of his 'State Research Bureau'. In Equatorial Guinea President Macias Nguema Byogo Negue Ndong massacred a large proportion of the population and reduced what had once been one of the most prosperous countries in Africa to total ruin. All three despots were overthrown in 1979.

Latin America

The difficulties in maintaining constitutional rule in post-colonial states, which caused such anguish in Africa, were only too familiar in Latin America. The 1970s saw the collapse of democratically elected governments in two of the most important states of the sub-continent.

In Chile, in September 1970, Salvador Allende Gossens was elected President with 36·3% of the poll in a three-way contest. He was the first avowed Marxist to win free elections to the presidency of a non-communist state, and his success aroused profound anxiety and hostility among the possessing classes throughout Latin America and in the US administration. Allende tried to implement a socialist programme, which included nationalisations, while maintaining the parliamentary constitution which Chile, almost alone in the sub-continent, had preserved inviolate for more than four decades. But Allende's government was undermined by inflation which reached more than 100% in 1972. Moreover, the US Central Intelligence Agency (it was later revealed) undertook covert activity designed to 'destabilise' Allende's regime. In 1973 a 'middle-class strike' (which included a lock-out by lorry-owners) ended in a military coup in September. Allende was killed in the presidential palace. The army chief of staff, General Augusto Pinochen Ugarte, seized power. His declared goal was to 'extirpate Marxism'. There followed a period of repression, torture, and violation of human rights which aroused world-wide indignation—but these years also saw a perceptible improvement in the country's economy.

In Argentina in 1973 the military establishment permitted the holding of the first free elections for many years. The victor was the Peronist presidential candidate who, it soon

the Emperor Haile Selassie. The 'Lion of Judah' was aged eighty-two and had ruled for all but five of the previous sixty years. An Armed Forces Committee, the Dergue, assumed power and declared a socialist one-party state. Feudalism was abolished and rural land nationalised. But the Dergue was afflicted by internal dissension and by the revolt of autonomists in Eritrea. In 1977 full-scale war developed in the Horn of Africa when Somali troops thrust deep into the Ogaden province of Ethiopia. It required large-scale Russian and Cuban military assistance for the Ethiopians to defeat Somalia (a former ally of the USSR) in early 1978.

Meanwhile, in 1976, a new empire was born when the military ruler of the Central African Republic, Jean-Bedel Bokassa, pronounced himself Emperor Bokassa I and founded the Central African Empire on a supposedly Napoleonic model. In December 1977, 3,500 guests attended a lavish coronation which cost the Empire (one of the poorest

In 1977 the dictator Jean-Bedel Bokassa was crowned Emperor Bokassa I of the Central African Empire in a lavish ceremony costing approximately $20 million. *Camera Press*

President Idi Amin (right) came to power in Uganda in a military coup in 1971 and in turn was ousted by Tanzanian troops in 1979. *Keystone Press*

turned out, was a mere stalking-horse for the return of the former dictator. After seven weeks he handed over power to Perón who returned in triumph from eighteen years of exile, accompanied by his third wife, Maria Estela (Isabel). In September Perón swept to victory with 61% of the popular vote in a further presidential election (in which his wife stood as vice-presidential candidate). Even more than in its earlier incarnations, however, Peronism seemed an ideologically amorphous movement which had strong fissiparous tendencies. These soon materialised when Perón died suddenly, aged seventy-eight, in July 1974, and was succeeded as President by his wife (who thus became the first woman head of state in Latin America). By 1975, with inflation up from 40% in 1974 to an estimated 335%, with the Peronist movement split into rival factions, and with increasing urban terrorism from left-wing guerrillas, it was clear that the civilian government had lost its grip. In March 1976 a junta headed by General Jorge Rafaél Videla carried out a putsch. Under military government Argentina's balance of trade improved, unemployment decreased, and the national football team won the world cup. But inflation in 1978 stood at 169%, and terrorism worsened. The regime resorted to indiscriminate counter-terrorism and ruthless repression. Thousands of political opponents were gaoled, and large numbers of 'desaparecidos' simply vanished.

Throughout the rest of the sub-continent, with few exceptions, military rulers held on to power (or succumbed to further military coups). Perhaps the most significant development of the decade was the increasing involvement of the Roman Catholic clergy in the struggle for social justice and political freedom. Several priests, including Archbishop Romero in San Salvador, were murdered in consequence. A visit to Brazil in mid-1980 by Pope John Paul II accentuated the Church's new commitment to the cause of the poor.

In the Caribbean the decade saw the death of one of the most odious of modern dictators, Dr François Duvalier, 'Papa Doc', who was succeeded in 1971 by his son, Jean-Claude, 'Baby Doc'. In Cuba the Communist regime of Fidel Castro subsisted on a huge annual subvention from the USSR. In the early 1970s there were some indications of a thaw in US-Cuban relations, but after 1975 these worsened again, mainly as a consequence of the Cuban military adventures in Africa. At the end of the decade a deluge of refugees from both Haiti and Cuba descended upon the south-east coast of the USA further poisoning American relations with both countries.

North America

Three traumatic episodes in the course of the decade profoundly affected American society and the American political psyche. The first was the squalid final stages of the disengagement of US forces from Indo-China and the ugly aftermath in south-east Asia. These contributed to a period of introspection and neo-isolationism in the USA. The military draft, which had been one of the most contentious issues of the war in the USA, was abolished in January 1973 (although it was not until 1977 that a partial amnesty was granted to the large numbers of 'draft dodgers' of the Vietnam era). The fact that the USA had been committed to war in south-east Asia by a series of (often secret) presidential decisions, without the formal declaration of war by Congress required by the constitution, led to widespread questioning of the limits of power and prerogative of what was termed (in an influential book by the historian, Arthur Schlesinger Jr.) 'the imperial presidency'.

Such questioning provided part of the groundwork for the second national trauma: the Watergate scandal. In the presidential elections of 1972 the incumbent, Richard Nixon, trounced his Democrat opponent, Senator George McGovern, by an almost unprecedented margin of 61% of the popular vote to 38%. However, after the election, evidence gradually accumulated showing that members of the presidential staff had been involved in 'dirty tricks' directed against the president's political opponents. In particular, agents of the Republican Party were proved to have installed electronic listening devices in the Democrat Party campaign headquarters at the Watergate Hotel in Washington DC.

In April 1973 three of the President's closest advisers were compelled to resign when it was revealed that they were implicated in an attempted 'cover-up' of the Watergate burglary and of White House involvement in the original conspiracy. A few days later Nixon's former Attorney-General, John Mitchell, was indicted by a grand jury. Public concern was fanned by continued publicity particularly in the *Washington Post*, and by the televising, from 17 May, of the hearings of the Senate Watergate Committee presided over by the venerable and shrewd Senator Sam Ervin.

The President's hope that the affair would die down was destroyed in July 1973 when it was disclosed that Nixon had ordered the clandestine tape-recording of all conversations in his office. There were demands that the tapes be made available to the courts to determine whether the President himself had been implicated in the Watergate conspiracy or the attempted cover-up, but the President refused to release the tapes. In October 1973 his position was further weakened when Vice-President Spiro Agnew resigned, admitting to charges of corruption, and was replaced by Congressman Gerald Ford. Matters came to a head on 20 October 1973 when the Watergate Special Prosecutor, Archibald Cox, a respected lawyer, demanded that the President hand over the tapes. Nixon ordered his Attorney-General, Elliot Richardson, to dismiss Cox; however, both Richardson and his deputy refused to do so and resigned. In the so-called 'Saturday Night Massacre', Nixon replaced Richardson with a nonentity who dismissed Cox. In a press conference on 17 November a rattled Nixon declared: 'I am not a crook.' But large sections of American opinion were by now sceptical on this point.

Juan Péron waves to his ecstatic followers on his triumphant return to Argentina as President. His wife, Maria Estela (Isabel) is on his left. *Camera Press*

President Richard Nixon, with his son-in-law David Eisenhower, says goodbye to White House staff after resigning the Presidency to avoid impeachment. *Keystone Press*

President Jimmy Carter (right) and Vice-President Walter 'Fritz' Mondale (left) were the Democrat candidates who narrowly defeated President Gerald Ford in the 1976 Presidential election. *Camera Press*

In February 1974 the House of Representatives authorised its Judiciary Committee to consider the possible impeachment of the President. Under mounting legal and public pressure Nixon agreed on 30 April to release edited versions of the tapes, but these, far from reassuring public opinion, disconcerted and shocked many of the President's former supporters who were particularly upset by the frequency in the transcripts of the phrase 'expletive deleted', which was to pass into American folklore. The climax came on 24 July 1974 when the Supreme Court (consisting in large part of Nixon appointees) rejected Nixon's pleas of 'executive privilege', and by eight votes to none ordered him to hand over the tapes. Impeachment procedures now quickened in

In 1979, popular opposition to the Shah of Iran culminated in his departure into exile in January and the creations of a deeply religious Islamic republic under the leadership of the Ayatollah Khomeini (below). *Camera Press*

Congress. Deserted by leading figures in his own party, Nixon finally admitted that he had been involved in the cover-up and, in a broadcast on 8 August, announced his intention to resign. The following day he took a lugubrious farewell of the White House, the first American President ever to resign. A month later his successor, Gerald Ford, granted Nixon an unconditional pardon for all crimes he 'committed or may have committed'.

The third traumatic event was of a very different nature. In the presidential election of 1976 Ford was defeated (by a margin of 51% to 48%) by the former governor of Georgia, Jimmy Carter, who thus became the first President from a southern state since 1850. The Ford and Carter presidencies were marked by mounting economic anxieties which focused above all on the USA's increasing dependence on foreign imports of oil. Although the domestic retail price of gasoline rose sharply it still remained among the cheapest in the world. Periodic shortages led to acute public dissatisfaction in this, the most automobile-centred society on earth, and in California men were killed in quarrels in petrol-station queues. The deposition of the Shah in 1979 increased fears of an oil shortage.

In the autumn of 1979 the American embassy in Teheran was taken over by anti-American militants encouraged by the Islamic leader, the Ayatollah Khomeini. American diplomats and others in the embassy at the time were seized and held as hostages. Vast mobs gathered daily outside the embassy to hear anti-American harangues. The Iranians refused to release the hostages unless the Shah (undergoing medical treatment in the USA) were returned to Iran to stand trial for his alleged crimes, but the US administration refused to extradite the Shah and facilitated his departure for Panama and thence for Egypt where President Sadat accorded him asylum. Although the Carter administration garnered much public support for its firm stance in the initial stages of the crisis, this was eroded later, especially in the wake of a botched rescue attempt by American forces in the spring of 1980. The episode touched a peculiarly raw nerve in the national consciousness and, in its apparent display of American impotence, seemed to many to symbolise the beginning of the end of the American era in world affairs.

Europe

In Eastern Europe the political status quo founded on Russian military power was not fundamentally challenged in

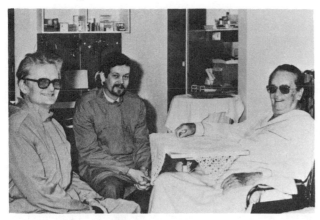

President Tito (right) with his two sons after the amputation of his right leg. The President's eventual death from his illness aroused anxieties that the complex constitution of Yugoslavia would now collapse. *Camera Press*

the 1970s. In 1970, after severe food riots, the Polish Communist leader, Gomulka, was replaced by Edward Gierek. In East Germany, the Stalinist, Walter Ulbricht, was replaced in 1971 by Erich Honecker. Neither of these changes in personnel led to real political reforms. Hungary, under the deft leadership of János Kádár, gradually earned for itself limited freedom of manoeuvre within the narrow bounds set by the Soviet occupiers. In Czechoslovakia the Husák regime, installed by the USSR in 1968, failed to win significant popular support. The reformist leader of the 1968 'Prague spring', Alexander Dubcek, published a letter denouncing the regime's repression of its opponents. But Dubcek remained politically impotent, employed in a menial

The strikes in Poland in 1970 were repeated in 1980 with apparently more far-reaching results including the creation of independent trade unions and concessions to the Roman Catholic Church. Here, people outside the Lenin Shipyard in Gdansk catch leaflets thrown by the strikers. *Camera Press*

job as a forester. In 1977 there was a brave challenge to the regime by a group of 240 intellectuals who signed 'Charter 77' denouncing government repression. The charter aroused great sympathy in the west and gained thousands of signatures inside Czechoslovakia. But at the end of the decade there was no sign of any relaxation of the political atmosphere in the country.

Rumania, Yugoslavia, and Albania, however, all continued throughout the 1970s to maintain their independence of Moscow. The Ceauçescu regime in Rumania preserved diplomatic independence while remaining within the Warsaw Pact. Internally the regime was highly illiberal, particularly in its attitude to national minorities. The death of President Tito of Yugoslavia after a long illness in 1980 awakened fears of the break-up of this far-from-cohesive multi-national state. But the USA and the USSR, it was reported, had reached a prior agreement not to intervene in the internal affairs of post-Tito Yugoslavia, and a collective leadership was installed which undertook to continue Tito's policies. The last of the Stalinist leaders, Enver Hoxha, held Albania fast to the Stalinist road, even to the extent, after 1978, of denouncing his erstwhile allies, the Chinese, without, however, veering back to a pro-Moscow line.

The Soviet empire in eastern Europe thus remained fundamentally secure throughout the decade despite the subterranean nationalist resentment which it evoked almost everywhere (Bulgaria was a notable exception). In the USSR itself there was a freezing into neo-Stalinist attitudes, particularly towards dissident intellectuals. The novelist Aleksandr Solzhenitsyn was seized and exiled abroad; the human rights activist Andrei Sakharov was sentenced to internal exile. Although tens of thousands of Russian Jews were for the first time free to emigrate, some were forbidden to do so and were persecuted for seeking to leave. Significantly, the historical image of Stalin himself gradually improved, and there were celebrations in Georgia on the hundredth anniversary of his birth in 1979. The Russian

Alexsandr Solzhenitsyn (left) was banished from the USSR in 1974. His first refuge was the home of his friend and fellow Nobel laureate, the West German novelist Heinrich Böll (right). *Popperfoto*

leadership by 1980 presented the aspect of a gerontocracy in which the military exercised almost unprecedented influence; as economic difficulties intensified and détente faltered the Brezhnev administration seemed to be near the end of the road.

In western Europe the decade saw the expansion of the European Economic Community (EEC) from its original six members to nine with the entry of Denmark, Eire and the United Kingdom on 1 January 1973. Norway, which had applied for membership, withdrew the application after a

Soviet General Secretary Leonid Brezhnev (centre) and Premier Aleksei Kosygin (right). *Keystone Press*

referendum in the country recorded a majority vote against joining the Community. In the United Kingdom, where there was opposition to membership, particularly on the left, the incoming Labour government in 1974 sought to renegotiate the terms of British entry. The revised terms were placed before the electorate in a referendum (the first ever held in Britain) in 1975, in which two thirds of those voting favoured remaining within the EEC. An important step towards political integration in Western Europe was taken in June 1979 when the first direct elections to the European Parliament were held. The elections returned a broad centre-right majority (although socialists became the largest single group with 112 out of 410 members). The parliament soon demonstrated its determination to expand its effective powers in its threat to reject the proposed EEC budget in early 1980.

The most significant political changes in Europe in the 1970s occurred in the southernmost countries. In Greece, Portugal, and Spain dictatorships gave way to democracy. The regime of the colonels in Greece fell in 1974 as a result of events in Cyprus. A coup on the island against the government of Archbishop Makarios tried to effect the old nationalist aim of *enosis* or union with Greece. The coup led to the swift intervention of Turkish military forces, ordered to Cyprus by the government of Bulent Ecevit. The result was the partition of Cyprus into a Turkish-occupied north (where the Turks established a 'Turkish Federated State' which failed to secure international recognition) and an independent south. The involvement of the colonels in the coup in Cyprus led to their replacement by a parliamentary government headed by the conservative politician, Constantine Karamanlis. In 1974 a military junta headed by General

Spinola restored constitutional rule to Portugal after a peaceful coup. Most remarkably, Spain, following the death of Generalissimo Franco in 1975, rapidly transformed itself into a parliamentary democracy under the able guidance of the constitutional monarch, Juan Carlos. All three restored democracies were by the end of the decade seeking admission to the EEC, and Greece was scheduled to become a full member in January 1981.

The major West European countries weathered the economic down-turn without major threats to their political stability. The chief exception was Italy where the corruption of the ruling Christian-Democrat-dominated coalitions, and the gathering strength of the Italian Communist Party (PCI) seemed likely to endanger the Christian Democrats' long hold on power. The Italian Communists, under the leadership of Enrico Berlinguer, renounced allegiance to Moscow, committed themselves to the parliamentary system, and called for a 'historic compromise' with the Christian Democrats. For a while the Communists gave tacit parliamentary support to weak Christian Democrat governments. This ended in March 1979 when the Communists demanded cabinet seats as the price of continued support. But in the elections of June 1979, the Communist vote dropped for the first time since the birth of the republic, and in subsequent local elections the PCI suffered further reverses. In spite of the terrorist attacks by extreme leftists (who in 1978 kidnapped and murdered the former Christian Democrat Prime Minister, Aldo Moro), the challenge to the republic seemed by 1980 unlikely to effect major changes in the way Italy had been governed since 1946. As for France and Germany, in spite of leadership changes in 1974 (with Helmut Schmidt succeeding Brandt as Federal German

King Juan Carlos of Spain with his wife, Queen Sophia. Juan Carlos acceded to the throne on General Franco's death in November 1975, and has gradually worked to transform the nation into a parliamentary democracy. *Keystone Press*

Scottish Highlanders guard a barbed wire barricade thrown across a street in the Catholic Falls Road district of Belfast. *Camera Press*

Chancellor in 1974, and Valery Giscard d'Estaing securing election as French President after the death of Pompidou in 1974) the political landscapes remained little altered.

Britain, during much of the decade, presented a picture of weak government assailed by rapid inflation and endemic labour disputes. The most tragic problem confronting successive British governments was the continuing crisis in Northern Ireland. British troops had been sent into the province to act as a peace-keeping force in 1969, and direct rule had been imposed in 1972. However, by the end of the decade no resolution to the conflict was in sight, and the death toll of people killed by sectarian violence had risen to over 2,000. In February 1974 the Conservative Prime Minister, Edward Heath, called an unexpected election in an effort to deal with a national strike by coal miners. The result was a narrow Labour victory. For the following five years Labour governments, headed by Harold Wilson and (from 1976) James Callaghan, clung to office with the support of the Liberals and other minor parties. Although Labour reduced inflation to under 10% and brought about a measure of industrial peace in its first three years in office, Britain's apparently inexorable economic decline continued, masked rather than arrested by the attainment in 1980 of energy self-sufficiency. The election in May 1979 of a majority Conservative government headed by Mrs Margaret Thatcher promised a drastic change in direction from the Keynesian economic policies and welfare-state social aims of all previous British governments since 1945.

Above: Margaret Thatcher became the United Kingdom's first female Prime Minister by leading the Conservative Party to a decisive victory in the General Election of May 1979. *Camera Press*

Below: A North Sea oil production platform is towed out to the Thistle oilfield off the Shetland Isles. This platform weighs 35,000 tons and is 606 feet high. *Keystone Press*

The world in 1980

Several of the general characteristics of the 1970s appeared likely to endure into the following decade. In 1980 the world recession was deepening, the competition for energy resources intensifying, and the tendency in most capitalist countries towards 'monetarist' solutions, even at the expense of mass unemployment, gathered force. The characteristic human figure of the 1970s was perhaps that of the refugee—in the Horn of Africa, in Indo-China, in the Indian sub-continent, in the Caribbean. As religious and nationalist xenophobia mounted almost everywhere, the refugee seemed likely to continue to haunt the conscience of the world in the 1980s. The most striking new political ideology of the 1970s was certainly that of international terrorism. The links between such organisations as the Baader-Meinhof anarchist gang in West Germany, the Irish Republican Army (IRA) in the British Isles, the Japanese Red Army, and South American, Palestinian, and Italian revolutionaries posed a serious threat to international order which few governments felt able to meet. One of the exceptions was the Israeli government which in 1976 mounted the successful rescue from Entebbe in Uganda of hostages held there by terrorists enjoying the support of President Amin. But at the end of the decade there was no end in sight to this international scourge.

Certain new trends which became apparent in the 1970s seemed likely to effect radical changes in the 1980s. At the beginning of the 1970s it had seemed probable that the major

Pope John Paul II, formerly Cardinal Karol Wojtyla, in prayer at the Tomb of the Unknown Soldier in Warsaw. *Keystone Press*

technological development of the decade would be the inauguration of commercial supersonic aviation. But the American SST project was scrapped; the Russian Tu 144 was flown only within the USSR; and the Anglo-French Concorde, although introduced into limited service on the British and French national airlines, failed to find a single foreign buyer, and became the most expensive white elephant in modern history. Instead the 1970s saw a major technological breakthrough in the development of micro-processors which held forth the prospect for the next decade of a 'micro-chip revolution' which would change the face of developed societies. A more ominous portent was the increasing danger of nuclear weapons proliferation. In 1974 India exploded a 'peaceful nuclear device', thus becoming the sixth member of the nuclear 'club'. By 1980 several other countries, among them Brazil, Iraq, Israel, and Pakistan were close to possessing the capability to build nuclear weapons.

But perhaps the 'great fact' of the 1970s, like that noted of the 1960s, was not political but religious. The election in 1978 of a Pole as the first non-Italian Pope for four centuries, and the tremendous enthusiasm with which John Paul II was greeted on his tours of Poland, the USA, Ireland, Africa, and Brazil infused a new energy into the Roman Catholic church. Yet it is a sign of the end of the Eurocentric focus of world history that this should seem overshadowed as the most important religious development of the decade by the 'return of Islam'. By 1980 the fervent Islamic resurgence, sweeping across the Muslim world, seemed to pose the most serious challenge to the dominance of the international system of the northern states, capitalist and Communist alike.

INDEX

Index to selected illustrations